The Individual, Marriage, and the Family

Second Edition

Lloyd Saxton:

College of San Mateo

The Individual, Marriage, and the Family

Second Edition

Wadsworth Publishing Company, Inc.
Belmont, California

Acknowledgments

Cover—Sculpture by Gustav
Vigeland. Reproduced
by permission of the
Municipality of Oslo and
the Vigeland Museum.

*Chapter Ten Opening
Quotation*—From "The
Death of the Hired Man"
from THE POETRY OF
ROBERT FROST edited
by Edward Connery Lathem
Copyright 1930, 1939, ©
1969 by Holt, Rinehart and
Winston, Inc. Copyright ©
1958 by Robert Frost.
Copyright © 1967 by Lesley
Frost Ballantine. Reprinted
by permission of Holt,
Rinehart and Winston, Inc.

*Chapter Eleven Opening
Quotation*—From *The
Prophet* by Kahlil Gibran
with permission of the
publisher, Alfred A. Knopf,
Inc. Copyright 1923 by
Kahlil Gibran; renewal
copyright 1951 by
Administrators C.T.A. of
Kahlil Gibran Estate and
Mary G. Gibran.

Preface

after more than a decade of experience in teaching a marriage-and-family course at the College of San Mateo and in counseling troubled couples in San Francisco, I began to see a pattern to the marital problems in our mass society. The "before" and "after" pictures were not following the traditional sequence of beauty-salon advertisements: The students looked upon marriage with breathless romantic idealism; the couples who came to my counseling office were beaten and bitter. I determined that despite the obsession in our society with examining (and then idealizing) love, sex, and all male-female relations, young people are not being adequately prepared for the intelligence, the altruism, the sensitivity, and the *labor* that must be ever present if marital and familial interaction is to be fulfilling and successful. Furthermore, young people (and even persons who have been married for many years) are woefully ignorant about the dimensions and dynamics of love; about the physiological, psychological, and sociological patterns of their sexuality; about the autonomous homogamous and heterogamous factors that predict marital success; about the foundations of personality development and the structure (and structuring) of personality conflict; and about the relational needs that are peculiar to our mass society.

This book was conceived as an answer to these informational gaps and as a theoretical and practical guide to the role interaction, power structure, conflict adjustment, and need fulfillments of dating, mating, and familial relations. In examining the relational needs and behavior of the individual in our society, I have tried to avoid the misleading pulp-magazine prose of some texts in this field, the prissy subjectiveness of others, and the meaningless sociological and psychological jargon of still others. I have attempted to treat sex and the biology of the family objectively; role adjustment and personality theory practically; and social-class data and sociological theory and research informationally. If I have been successful, students should complete this book with new insight into themselves and with new and workable approaches to their relations with others. Moreover, instructors should find this book a useful tool in meeting the challenge of moving their students along the path of self-actualization—toward an emotionally mature, competent, and creative life.

There have been many developments in the marriage and family field since the first edition of this book was published in 1968, and the second edition reflects these developments. The sexual revolution that was not yet detected by sociological research in 1968 emerged full blown by 1970, effecting sweeping socio-sexual changes; VD, a neglected topic and problem in our society, had become a raging epidemic by 1970. New divorce laws and abortion laws were passed in many states. Masters and Johnson published their important research findings on sexual dysfunction. A new decennial census provided an entirely new picture of marriage, divorce, and family life. Every chapter in this book has been revised and updated to include these materials with nearly three hundred new references, and in addition an entirely new chapter on the economics of marriage has been written.

I must acknowledge a profound debt of gratitude to Professor Alfred C. Clarke of Ohio State University and Professor Henry L. Manheim of Arizona State University, who acted as editorial consultants throughout the development of the first edition; to Professor Carl C. Rogers of the La Jolla Institute for the Study of the Person, to whom many of the key concepts may be traced; to my many colleagues and students, who provided a rich source of both inspiration and ideas; to James Arntz, whose help extended far beyond his usual editorial function; and, finally, to my wife, Nancy, whose contribution was one of active collaboration.

One final word: As a matter of grammatical usage (and to avoid the awkward "he or she"), the masculine gender is employed throughout, except in situations where both the male and female point of view are explored. In all other situations feminists and female readers are encouraged to read "she" for "he."

Larkspur, California   L. S.

For Alice, Nancy, and Barbara   Three generations of females.

Contents

Contents

Tables and Figures

Part One

Introduction

Chapter One

The Paired Relation in a Mass Society

*The unexamined life is
not worth living.*

Plato (*Apology*)

very human being has certain basic needs that he seeks to fulfill throughout his existence. He seeks, first, his basic physical needs for such things as nourishment, shelter, safety, and comfort. When these needs are partially satisfied, he seeks to satisfy his basic social needs[1]: (1) direct, intrinsically satisfying interactions, or *primary relations,* with *significant others*[2] who will receive and return the essential satisfactions of companionship, support, love, and, in some relations, sex; (2) a place in his society where he is granted acceptance, recognition, and respect—in short, *status;* and (3) the achievement of meaning or purpose in his life.

In seeking to fulfill these basic physical and social needs, a person will select from among those with whom he has formed a paired relation one whom he will court and marry. He will then attempt to earn a living for himself and his family, rear his children, and find some satisfactions and meaning in the personal interactions of his marriage and family and the group interactions of his vocational and leisure-time affiliations and activities.

How he does all of these things depends upon (1) his genetic makeup, the individual anatomical, physiological, and psychological factors that are unique to him, and (2) his *socialization,* the way he has learned through interaction with his society to view his environment, himself, and his expectations and the way he has learned to interact with others to satisfy his needs. Together, these two factors (genetic and learned) form his *individuation,* his own unique *personality.*

---

[1]In some situations, of course, the social needs will take precedence over the physical needs—for example, the mother who sacrifices herself for her children because of her love for them.
[2]This other person in a primary relation—and particularly in the paired relation—is called the *significant other* because he is chiefly responsible for the fulfillment of many of the social needs of the person with whom he relates.

In other words, although each man is uniquely himself, an individual differentiated in many ways from every other person, he discovers and experiences his existence and individuality within the group—the society and culture into which he is born. He will *introject*[3] the societal norms and experiences to form his own unique personality; yet he inevitably and irrevocably comes to be indistinguishable in many respects from the other persons who are products of his society and culture. He is a socialized individual.

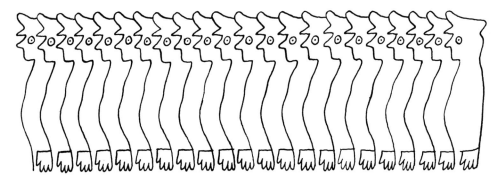

It is the societal aspect of man's behavior—the sameness of persons in a society and culture—that makes a book such as this possible; for we may examine the society and its culture and determine with reasonable accuracy the general behavioral patterns of persons in that society and its sub-societies (or social classes) as they seek to fulfill their individual needs within a paired relation. It is the individuated aspect of man's behavior that makes a book such as this practicable; for we will find that the quality and success of a paired relation depends not so much on the cultural similarities of the two people but rather on their individual differences and their awareness and appreciation of one another's unique qualities, needs, and responses. Such awareness and appreciation are the chief purposes of this book; the dynamics, the success, and the failure of a paired relation in our contemporary mass society are the subjects.

The Nature of a Paired Relation

Accumulating evidence from the rather new science of *ethology*, the study of the biology of behavior, is providing a rather impressive case for the possibility that the need to form a relatively permanent paired relation, either like-sexed or other-sexed, may be one of the most basic of all needs, which comes to us through our evolution from lower forms. Very persistent paired relations have been observed as characteristic of many animals which have social organization. These relations are usually, though not always, heterosexual; they form a mating pair and—with offspring—the nucleus of the family. The herring gull, for in-

---

[3]The values, attitudes, and expectations of the culture that become a part of a person's own unconscious code of behavior are said to be *introjected*.

stance, usually mates for life and recognizes his mate among dozens of gulls flying at a distance of 50 yards (Ardrey, 1966). Geese demonstrate all the paired-relation behavior of human beings (Lorenz, 1966). Beavers, tigers, wolves, whales, foxes, and porpoises all form persistent paired relations, with an obvious loyalty that often apparently endures for the lifetime of the couple. A whale or porpoise will swim into a narrow harbor after its captured mate, making desperate and dangerous attempts at rescue.

Although the paired relation is usually heterosexual, the bond that holds the mates together is not simply sex—in fact, sexual loyalty is not usually observed. The Calicebus monkey, for example, which lives in the forests of Bolivia, forms such a devoted paired relation that the couple often sit, and even sleep, with their tails intertwined (Ardrey, 1966). Yet when the female comes into estrus,

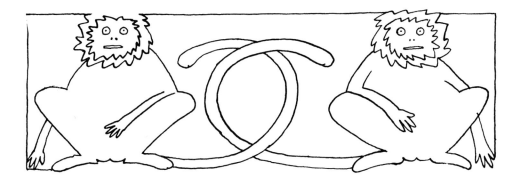

the male becomes very sexually adventurous; and she becomes quite receptive to strange males. Thus, although the Calicebus epitomizes virtually the ultimate in close, paired-relation affiliation, no sexual loyalty occurs.

The need to form a close paired relation often extends across species. The relation between a man and a dog is a familiar example. A dog may be so utterly devoted to a human being that he will actually refuse to eat if they are separated. In 1971, a newspaper report noted that a horse in Morocco stood for days outside his owner's tent when the man fell ill; and when the owner finally died, the horse climbed to the top of a cliff and leaped to his death. A race horse will form such a significant paired relation with a rooster that he will refuse to perform in the rooster's absence. An elephant and a hippopotamus formed such a close friendship in the Oakland zoo (in 1967) that when the hippopotamus escaped he was easily enticed back into his cage by using the elephant as an attraction.

These paired relations are frequently formed very suddenly between pairs who evidently recognize and respond to some unique aspect of each other not readily apparent to another observer. For example, geese may be together for years without forming paired relations with one another. Then a particular goose, whom a gander has apparently not noticed before, will suddenly seem attractive; and the gander will perform a courtship dance before the goose. If she does not respond, no relation is formed. If she does reciprocate, a paired relation is immediately established. The gander may occasionally have a sexual adventure with another goose; but he does so at some distant pond, and the relation is always strictly limited to sex. He will not take walks with the goose he is having a sexual affair with, for example, and will ignore her if she approaches him in his home flock. He will spend much time, on the other hand, with the goose he has formed a paired relation with, remaining near her and demonstrating hostile behavior if she is approached by another. In San Francisco, in 1966, a gander flying with his flock spotted a goose in the San Francisco zoo. Something about her satisfied him in a way no goose in the large flock could. He dropped to her side and initiated the courtship dance, which was reciprocated. He was then torn between his instinct to migrate and the bond with the goose. Although it meant abandoning the rest of the flock and his entire life pattern, he remained with the goose (who could not fly with her clipped wings) as part of the zoo.

Despite the protestations of sociologists that the love at first sight that seems to occur among other animals does not occur among man, it is certainly part of our literary heritage (*Romeo and Juliet* is a notable example) and of our folklore. Whether such a significant paired relation ever occurs at first sight among human beings (or only after a gradual accumulation of loyalties and identification) is somewhat controversial. But there is no question that the need to form a significant paired relation — with deep emotional involvement, reciprocation of need fulfillments, confirmation of the self-image, and relative permanence — is one of the strongest of all needs, although the depth of the need and the degree of involvement, or emotional participation, varies greatly from individual to individual.

What makes one person significant to another in this sense — the sense of the gull recognizing and singling out his mate as different from all other gulls — remains chiefly speculative in light of present psychological knowledge. It is quite obvious, however, that among the thousands of persons at a railway station, for example, one will stand out as a friend and bring a response of exuberant affection, although this one person, objectively viewed, may be as indistinguishable from the others as is a seagull in a flock.

It is simply a matter of common observation that certain people appeal to one another and form paired relations. These significant attractions are relatively rare, occurring only rarely out of thousands of exposures. How many potential paired-relation associations has the individual in our society been exposed to from childhood — with nursery school, kindergarten, grammar school, high school, college, and neighborhood, church, and recreational associations? How many friendships has he formed out of these potential thousands? Why does he form — often spontaneously — the particular one that he does; and why does one person affect him with indifference or even resentment, while that same person would become part of a significant paired relation with someone else?

The ingredients that distinguish a paired relation from other primary relations are the deep emotional involvements of the two persons, the permanence of their emotional involvement and the relation, and the significance to the self of the other in the relation. The paired relation may exist in many forms other than dating and marriage. For example, a mother usually serves as a significant other for a substantial portion of the offspring's life; and during a person's childhood and adolescence, a like-sexed friend will often function as a significant other.[4]

It seems quite clear, however, that for most people the paired relation is a prime prerequisite for a fulfilled and gratifying life. Certainly the need to feel another's deep affection and concern, as well as to feel a deep affection and concern for another person, is essential to self-fulfillment.

Society, Culture, and Socialization

The relatively large and relatively permanent associational aggregate of persons called a society exists essentially to provide collectively for the fundamental needs of its members.[5] A society finds the means for its continued existence by easing the production and distribution of goods, protecting itself from enemies, reproducing, nurturing, and socializing its children, and regulating its internecine quarrels.

Culture is the way that persons in a society behave — as well as the implements, institutions, concepts, and values that they characteristically utilize in their behavior. Thus, culture mediates between the individual and his physical environment, between the individual and all other individuals, between those who are alive and those who are dead or yet to live. In short, the culture of a society provides a body of ready-made solutions to the problems that both the individual and the group typically encounter, enabling him and the group to live through each day without inventing a new method for dealing with every interaction, whether with physical things or with other people.

Acquiring the culture of a society is called *cultural conditioning,* or *socialization.* This process is the chief basis for the formulation of the personality structure of the individual. Since in man all significant behavior is learned — that is,

---

[4] The continuance into adulthood of a paired relation with a like-sexed friend is unusual in our society — especially in the middle class, since the middle-class husband and wife tend to engage in all of their activities together and consequently drop their premarital like-sexed friends or alter the relations to less intimate ones. In the upper and lower class, the continuance of paired relations with like-sexed friends after marriage is more common, although it is still somewhat unusual in our society. Of course, unmarried people in our society may continue such a paired relation all of their lives, and a homosexual marriage is another form of this kind of relation.

[5] Actually, the term *society* may be defined in so many ways and has so many meanings that it is a very loose concept. Brown (1963) defines society as an "aggregate of people who live and work together, and who share a common body of meanings and a common sense of values." Wynne-Edwards (1964) defines society as "a group of individuals competing for conventional prizes by conventional means."

culturally conditioned, or socialized—each person is almost completely the product of the society and culture into which he is born.[6] He is immersed in the culture of the group from birth to death and becomes the person he is through his continuing participation in that culture and through his introjection of cultural norms.

One of the very important aspects of culture and cultural conditioning is that all societies are stratified. That is, in all societies, different persons are granted different degrees of recognition and prestige, or *status*, in the society. This ranking occurs according to the individual's possession of "things actively wanted" by the society, which are always unequally distributed. In our own society these include power, wealth, knowledge, admired skills, and various attributes of "the good life" (Berelson and Steiner, 1964). The opposite characteristics of weakness, poverty, ignorance, inadequacy, and a miserable existence are, by contrast, "actively avoided" and represent low status for the person characterized by them.

The more the person has of such "things actively wanted" by his society, the higher his status; for we respond to the possession of these determinants of status with fear and esteem. Some determinants—for example, power and authority—yield chiefly fear; others, like ownership and family position, yield both fear and esteem; and still other determinants—for example, service or skills—yield chiefly esteem (see Figure 1–1).

The status of a person inevitably affects the way that he perceives his environment and his experience in that environment and will therefore significantly affect his behavior and attitudes.[7] In fact, cultural (behavioral and attitudinal) differences vary so greatly from one status level to another—especially in such sensitive areas as sex, dating, marital interaction, and child rearing—that it is misleading to speak of national norms without acknowledging the variables related to stratification.

Stratification in our society is commonly described in terms of *social class—upper, middle,* and *lower.*

The concept of social class provides a rough but useful index to the individual's position in the social strata. Social class is a hypothetical construct which, despite its generalizations, provides a convenient reference for the correlation of significant behavioral differences among individuals in a society. Not all be-

---

[6] Of course, simple reflexive behavior (the biological functions) and certain needs are unlearned, occurring as characteristic of built-in genetic capacities. For example, breathing, sweating, blinking, and flinching and the *needs* for sleep, food, and love are unlearned. Eating, walking, talking, and the means of loving are all learned, however, and are manifestations of culture.

[7] The difference between the perception and experience of the high status and low status person is intensified by what is called *status congruence*—the tendency of an individual to have either a cluster of things actively wanted or of things actively avoided. For example, the actuarial expectation in our society is that the rich will also be healthy, respected, skilled, and well-informed, whereas the poor tend to be sickly, scorned, unskilled, and ignorant (Lasswell and Kaplan, 1950).

havior, of course, can be ascribed to social-class position; further, many or even most kinds of behavior cross social-class lines. But such important aspects of behavior as language, values, humor, referents, diet, and specific patterns of dating, mating, child rearing, and sexuality—in short, the whole spectrum of culturally conditioned behavior—are markedly different, depending on an individual's position in the societal hierarchy.

Parental income, occupation, and education; location of residence; membership in schools, clubs, and churches; and family traditions, expectations, and attitudes—all are fundamental determinants of social class and contribute to fixing, with a surprising degree of permanence, the person's life-long attitudes and behavior patterns.

DETERMINANTS OF STATUS

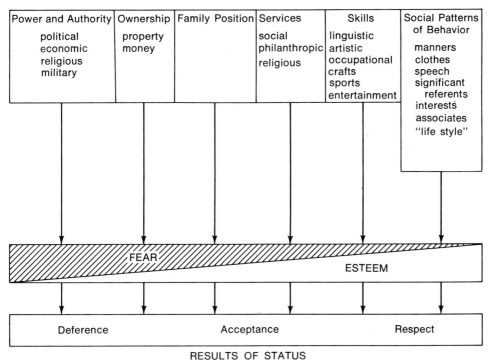

Power and Authority	Ownership	Family Position	Services	Skills	Social Patterns of Behavior
political economic religious military	property money		social philanthropic religious	linguistic artistic occupational crafts sports entertainment	manners clothes speech significant referents interests associates "life style"

FEAR   ESTEEM

Deference	Acceptance	Respect

RESULTS OF STATUS

Figure 1–1. The Dynamics of Societal Stratification

The child typically learns quite early in life, usually by his first years in school, what class he belongs to—not what name to give it but how his beliefs and actions distinguish him from others, who is above and below him, whom to be friends with, and so on (Berelson and Steiner, 1964, p. 468).

Very briefly, the characteristics of the social classes in our society are as follows:[8]

The *upper class* comprises approximately 3 percent of the national population. The upper class is chiefly oriented around leadership (that is, financial or decision-making power), the consumption of wanted goods in our society, and the attainment of a graceful and aesthetically fulfilling life.

The *middle class,* which constitutes roughly 38 percent of the population, is usually divided into *upper middle* (10 percent) and *lower middle* (28 percent). The upper-middle class includes active civic leaders, members of the professions, outstandingly successful artists, and big businessmen. The major characteristics of the upper-middle class are, like those of the upper class, community leadership and consumption. The lower-middle class are clerks, salesmen, white-collar workers, small businessmen, and some skilled laborers. Members of this class tend toward propriety and conservatism; their major characteristic is their concern with respectability. They "approach the ideal typical of the Protestant ethic, being careful about their money, saving, far-sighted, forever anxious about what their neighbors think" (Warner, 1962, p. 76).

Approximately 59 percent of the national population belongs to the *lower class.* Like the middle class, the lower is usually divided into two groups, *upper-lower* (34 percent) and *lower-lower* (25 percent). Warner describes upper-lower-class orientation as being, like that of the lower-middle class, centered around "respectability," although the persons who compose this class have a more limited outlook on the world about them than do the members of the middle class. Blue-collar workers, semiskilled workmen, small tradesmen, and service personnel belong to the upper-lower class. The lower-lower class, whose members live below the poverty line, forms one fourth of the national population. Too poor to afford adequate housing, proper nutrition, and medical and dental care, their primary concern is day-to-day survival.[9]

---

[8] It is important to emphasize, of course, that this division of our society into classes is necessarily arbitrary; actually, each class merges into the one above it and the one below it. Furthermore, there are great individual differences within these arbitrary class lines; all individuals are not necessarily alike in any particular class. Finally, any given person may make the move from one class into another. But although social-class mobility occurs over a wider segment of United States population than it does in, say, the economically poorer areas of southern Europe or in rural India, even in the United States the actuarial expectation is that a person will remain within the subculture of social class into which he is born and will conform to his social-class characteristics.

[9] The *very* low-status person, especially. will find it difficult to be upwardly mobile, because he has neither the skills and training nor the education to form an economic base upon which he can begin to pursue "things actively wanted." Nutrition is poor and health standards are low. Lack of education and training sharply limits the person's perspective and his ability to acquire marketable skills with which to form the economic base necessary to provide more education or training. And so the cycle is self-perpetuating, unless help—in the forms of perspective, economic assistance, and practical training and education—can be infused from outside the cycle.

The Nature of Individuation

Although each person in a society is socialized, and his behavior in dating, mating, marriage, and the family is largely determined by the culture of the substrata (social class) of his society, he is still an *individual*—anatomically, physiologically, and psychologically. It is easy to lose sight of this important point by focusing too closely on the details of socialization. Individuation is in part a result of the fact that the same experience will be perceived differently and responded to differently by each individual, who will form his own cluster of assumptions about the nature of reality and his relation to it. This cluster of assumptions, his *frame of reference*,[10] will then lead to a further differentiation of his perception and responses in all subsequent experiences. Because cultural factors thus fall with different meaning upon each individual, each person has his own unique basis for how he perceives, thinks, and acts. The things he values and strives for, his desires and aspirations, the way he relates to others and the types of relations he establishes, his view of dating, marriage, sex, love, and children—all are based upon his own unique and differentiated, individualistic frame of reference.

Individuation is also a result of the basic differences in the genetic and hormonal characteristics of each individual. Each person is unique at birth, with his own particular anatomy, physiology, and psychology. For example:

Anatomical variations may be quite pronounced and have significant behavioral consequences in normal persons.[11] The branch arteries which rise from the heart's aortic arch may number two in one person and six in another, and both the size and the branch pattern of these arteries may vary considerably, so that the blood supply to tissues is furnished unequally in the two bodies. The behaviorally important thyroid gland may weigh six times as much in one person as in another, and the cerebral cortex, a brain component of great behavioral significance, may be ten times thicker in one brain than in another. The islets of Langerhans (responsible for insulin production) vary over a ten-fold range; stomachs may be six times as large in one person as in another. In short, each person has a morphologically distinctive brain, a unique gastro-intestinal system, and a neuro-muscular system different from that of any other person on earth.

Of even greater behavioral significance are physiological differences in normal persons. For example, some hearts have three times the blood-pumping capacities of others;

---

[10] Essentially, the frame of reference is a cluster of assumptions about *fact* (frigidity is usually the result of socialization or frigidity is usually the result of an organic anomaly), *value* (sex is beautiful or sex is dirty), and *possibility* (children are usually a delight or children are usually a nuisance).

[11] The material on anatomical and physiological differentiation presented here is drawn from Williams, "The Biological Approach to the Study of Personality," in *Readings in Psychology: Understanding Human Behavior*, ed. James A. Dyal (1962), pp. 375–385.

protein-bound iodine in the blood, which measures hormonal output, varies over a six-fold range; and enzyme levels in the blood, which reflect fundamental hormonal differences, vary over a range of fully thirty to one.

Inborn, or genetic, psychological differences among normal individuals are perhaps the most pronounced of all, but they are also the most difficult to measure and so we know the least about them. Psychological capacities that have been measured have proven to be enormously differentiated. For example, intellectual capacity as measured by the Stanford-Binet test ranges from a score of 15 to a score of 185 in the adult — the difference between an idiot and a genius.[12] A difference of 10 or 15 points in the Stanford-Binet scale has immensely significant behavioral consequences.

These two factors of (1) differentiated socialization and (2) genetic uniqueness combine to yield a variation among individuals which is quite formidable and which cannot be ignored in a study of dating and marital interaction. In any social relation, particularly in the paired relation, these individual differences can produce conflict and frustration or mutual support and fulfillment, depending on the differences involved and on how they are manifested and then met. In short, the dynamics, the success, or the failure of all relations are chiefly dependent upon the individuation of the persons involved — the changing needs of the two unique personalities that make up the relation, and the inclination and the ability of these two individuals to fulfill these needs in one another.

The Nature of Our Mass Society

A *mass society* is not simply a large society. It is differentiated from a pre-industrial society in several important ways — chiefly in (1) its mass production of commodities, (2) its mass manipulation of taste (advertising, promotion, "public relations") for the marketing of the mass-produced items, (3) its urbanized community structure, and (4) its specialized roles and functions for individual members of the society (Martindale, 1960). A mass society is further differentiated from a pre-industrial society by its relative reliance upon *secondary institutions* and *secondary relations* for its operation and for the fulfillment of the day-to-day needs of its population. This reliance has led to a dilemma for most individuals in our society. They face a conflict of values between their own needs and the functions they perform in the society. This dilemma has brought an increased emphasis and reliance upon those *primary institutions and relations* that remain for the individual in our society.

Primary and Secondary Institutions

An institution is a collective solution to the needs of the society and the individual and may be either primary or secondary. Secondary institutions are chiefly

---

[12] Other psychological tendencies that are apparently inborn are *"activity level, sensitivity, emotional disposition, adaptability,* and *coping style"* (Coleman, 1969, p. 49).

systems for social organization and order, for provision of goods and services, and for societal conditioning—for example, schools, banks, supermarkets, governmental organizations, and most other service and production facilities. The secondary institution generally provides a symbolic rather than intrinsic reward for the person involved with it. He must then exchange this symbolic reward for the gratification of a real need. Primary institutions, in contrast, are chiefly socially prescribed *procedures* for the relating of individuals—for example, hunting or fishing parties, sand-lot ball games, and, of course, dating and marriage. The primary institution provides an immediate and intrinsic reward, with the person utilizing that reward directly to serve his needs.

Primary and Secondary Relations

A *relation*, as we have noted, is a socially prescribed and learned interaction between two persons and may be either primary or secondary. A *secondary relation* is impersonal, formal, official, and perfunctory, with the individual subordinate to the function he is performing. In other words, each person in a secondary interaction will function chiefly as the embodiment of *role*[13] in that relation, and most of his personal characteristics—his individuality—will be obscured by this role. Thus, we go to a barber or hairdresser because of his function; and in performing that function, the barber or hairdresser acts as the embodiment of his role while we act in the role of customer. The personal characteristics of each person in this secondary relation are relatively unimportant, and emotional satisfaction or recognition and appreciation of the human qualities of each person in the interaction is neither expected nor received.

A *primary relation*, on the other hand, is personal, informal, spontaneous, and intimate, with the emphasis upon the human values of affection, understanding, acceptance, companionship, and a recognition of each other's personal characteristics and individual value and worth. Role behavior is still important to a primary relation of course; indeed, a primary interaction cannot proceed without appropriate and reciprocal role response from each person involved.[14]

---

[13] In very general terms, *role* is the behavior expected of a person who is engaged in any socially defined relation with another person (or persons). The function the person is fulfilling in this relation is known as his *position*. Thus "friend," "lover," "husband," "wife," "parent," "child," "bus-driver," "passenger," "teacher," "student," "clerk," "customer" are all examples of position, and each of these positions carries with it the expectation for specific, prescribed, and appropriate role behavior. If this role behavior is not performed as expected (within certain limits, of course), the relation must break down. Virtually every possible relation that one can imagine is socially defined and carries a culturally prescribed position, with attendant role behavior. A precise definition of role, then, would be *the behavior appropriate to a position in a socially defined relation.* (See Chapter Six for a discussion of role interaction in marriage.)

[14] A person who finds himself attempting or confronted with a relation which, to him, is not socially defined or which suggests no appropriate learned role behavior finds it nearly impossible to relate satisfactorily. For example, the middle-class boy attempting a pickup for the first time in a lower-class neighborhood will have to base his role behavior on learned responses which he has absorbed from movies, his peers, or some other source—which then makes it socially defined—or he will probably flounder and fail in his attempt (unless the girl is unusually cooperative). In short, he must know the expected role behavior that will bring the appropriate response from the girl, as well as how to respond appropriately to any response which she might make, or the interaction will end after a brief series of ineffectual and awkward attempts to establish communication.

However, in a primary relation, the personal characteristics of the *individual occupying* the position are of equivalent or greater importance than the *utilitarian function* of the position. In short, in a primary relation, the important element is the encounter between the two persons rather than the function that is being performed.[15] The persons involved in a primary relation are not interchangeable as they are in a secondary relation. It does not matter very much, for example, who waits upon you in a store—this is a secondary relation—but it does matter, and matters very much, whom you relate with as a friend and whom you date or marry.

The Dilemma of the Individual

With the rise of industrialization in the Western World, the community structure began to change rapidly to meet the requirements of the new social order
and to assume the functions that previously could be performed either in small
primary institutions or by individuals. Most of the needs of the individual in our
contemporary mass society are now fulfilled through the mediation of secondary
institutions, which provide for the needs of the individual only in a formal,
utilitarian way, making the necessary material goods and services available, and
providing physical security, but failing to fulfill the humanistic needs for affection, for emotional support and security, and for individual meaning beyond
the purely functional one of being an interchangeable unit in the production
and consumption of goods.

It is possible (even likely) for a person, if he is living away from his family, to
go through an entire day—housed, fed, transported, taught, nursed, disciplined,
directed, and related to casually or formally by classmates, fellow diners, fellow
passengers and patients—without ever engaging in a primary relation or utilizing a primary institution. If he is related to impersonally in this way for too long,
some essential element of his humanity is eroded away, and he is rendered less a
person. The loneliness that stems from a lack of meaningful personal relations
with significant others is one of the key problems of our time—especially in the
large urban and suburban areas where most of our population now resides.

Secondary relations and institutions have become our society's culturally
accepted mode for most interaction among individuals. The primary relation is
often inconvenient in our impersonal and high-pressure society, except in such
paired relations as dating and marriage. Very little of the person's time is spent
in intimate, affectionate, or informal behavior; instead, much of his life is, for
the most part, passed in formalized, limited, procedural, and impersonal behavior.

Bell and Sirjamaki (1965) describe the life in a mass society as a "fragmentation of the individual . . . his activities tend to be compartmentalized rather than

---

[15] Of course, the concept of primary and secondary relations are absolute terms, representing the
two polar ends of a continuum of possible relations. Any given relation will fall somewhere between
these two extremes, and any secondary relation is potentially primary to some extent. For example,
while the waitress essentially exists to provide the customer with food, the customer may come to
regard her as a person as well.

integrated." In contrast to the intimacy of the persons, roles, and gratifications in a pre-industrial society, the participant in a mass society must often take highly specialized and fractional community roles, which are far removed from, and sometimes inconsistent with, his needs for relating, for love, for caring and being cared for, as well as for achievement, respect, and appreciation. The satisfaction that he receives for his work is seldom intrinsic.[16] The factory worker who tightens one nut after another or fits the same two parts of a shoe together or solders the same connection hour after hour, day after day, for months and then years must be resigned to obtain "real" satisfactions — the things that fulfill his basic physical and psychological needs and make him feel significant as a person — only by exchanging his paycheck (a symbol of "real" value) for these needs through a multitude of secondary institutions (supermarkets, banks, restaurants, and theaters) that mainly involve secondary relations. Thus, he is constantly once-removed from the source of his satisfactions. In addition, the few intrinsically satisfying occupations that do exist require years of preparation

in a mass society. For example, a profession demands years of training, which must start way back in high school; success in high school is, in turn, based upon early experience in the first and second grades; and the second grader is already a potential drop-out or success, depending upon the type of home he comes from.

Thus, the lower-level jobs bring little gratification, either in terms of intrinsic satisfaction or in terms of money; the higher-level jobs often seem completely unattainable — indeed, they *are* unattainable unless preparation starts years before. It is no wonder that the boy or girl in high school, or in the first year or two of college, is often almost hopelessly bewildered: Should he continue school

---

[16] By contrast, the person in a pre-industrial society is closely in touch with the end products of his labor, and the training for his occupation is clearly related to what he will be doing. For example, a person growing up in nineteenth-century America knew that the survival, comfort, and pleasure of his family depended almost entirely upon his father's skills in plowing, planting, harvesting, caring for his livestock, building a barn, and trading part of his harvest for seed, for tools, and for needed goods. Moreover, he learned these skills relatively easily from his father; they were consistent with the rural values of his society; and they provided the immediate satisfactions of food, shelter, comfort, and pride in accomplishment.

or drop out? Get a job or get married? His relation to the total structure of society seems to bear little relation to the reality of his everyday existence as he dates, studies, takes examinations, talks with friends, and views the generation represented by his parents. Many young people attempt to answer this dilemma by renouncing the values of our society and by "dropping out"—either into a rather aimless existence or into a rural nineteenth-century style of life in a commune. They regard their unconventional life styles as more purposive and meaningful in terms of "real" values than the "empty, hypocritical, and self-serving" values of the establishment.

THE PRE-INDUSTRIAL SOCIETY

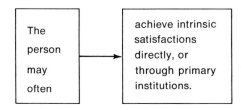

THE MASS SOCIETY

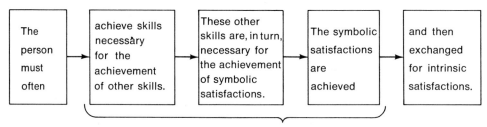

Utilizing secondary institutions

Figure 1–2. The Achievement of Intrinsic Satisfaction in Pre-industrial and Mass Societies

The culture of our contemporary mass society relentlessly emphasizes the urban industrial values of *doing, achieving, producing, efficiency,* and *success* as opposed to the intrinsic humanistic values of *knowing, caring, loving,* and *being known, cared for,* and *loved.* These two sets of values are not necessarily incompatible; but if the "production values" are pursued to the virtual exclusion of the "humanistic values," the person tends to become dehumanized and alienated—not only from others, but, even more importantly, from himself.[17]

To escape the anxiety that is caused by his inability to express and be recognized for his essential humanity, the mass-society man is often driven to identify

---

[17] Even a "successful" person in a higher-level job may be so highly trained and so specialized in the demanding roles of his important but narrow function in the society (for example, business, law, medicine, teaching, research, or politics), that he may lose sight of the profile his life is taking. If this profile involves a serious lack of humanistic values and satisfactions, even this admired and respected person may be bitterly lonely and unhappy, feeling that "life has passed him by."

with the system, trying to do what he thinks is demanded of him rather than trying to fulfill his own intrinsic needs. He becomes, then, "other directed" rather than self directed (Reisman, 1956), a "cheerful robot" (Mills, 1959), a commodity or "personality package" to be sold for success, or what the culture defines as "success" (Fromm, 1970).

The inability of such a person to fulfill his humanistic needs results in a pervasive conflict—of intrinsic or humanistic values versus symbolic or bureaucratic and production values. This conflict may become virtually incapacitating at some points in his life. The person is torn between the need for personal involvement, on the one hand, and socially efficient achievement, on the other, and is unable to do either. Often, the conflict is resolved in favor of the symbolic manifestations of "success" simply because they are more visible and better defined by the mass society, and because they are safer (with secondary relations and institutions, we venture very little personal involvement—very little of "ourselves"— and thereby avoid the emotional demands and attendant vulnerability characteristic of a primary interaction). Instead of *loving people and using things*, this other-directed "personality package" will *use people and love things*.

The Need for Paired Relations

With so much of the average person's time, energy, and attention being occupied with dehumanized and dehumanizing secondary institutions and relations and with the pursuit of symbolic satisfactions and production values, it is not surprising that he places a high value on the relatively few primary institutions and relations available to him. The physical and emotional gratifications available for the individual in the primary institutions of dating and marriage, which are sustained by intimacy, humanistic values, and direct and intrinsic rewards, become increasingly important as a counterbalance to the formalized, limited, procedural, and impersonal behavior with which he must chiefly be involved. This makes marriage in our society both unusually valuable and highly demanding, which may explain the high incidence of failed marriages. So much more is now expected from marriage than in prior generations. The mass-society man becomes highly motivated to form a primary relation with a significant other and to find in that relation the emotional satisfactions that are lacking in the depersonalized warren of power and production, of saturation advertising and anonymous cultural conditioning, which characterizes the modern mass society. The adolescent will seek in dating, and the adult in marriage (or its equivalent[18]), the intimacy, the meaning, the personal fulfillment that are lacking in the depersonalized, formal, exchangeable-commodity world that makes up his existence.

---

[18] Of course, this type of paired relation need not necessarily involve marriage, and it need not necessarily be heterosexual. It would be fatuous not to recognize that many heterosexual couples now choose to live together with mutual love and commitment without entering into a formal marriage. This type of liaison, or paired relation, may be motivated by many reasons (not necessarily mutually exclusive): (1) Convenience (for example, the couple in college who share an apartment, feeling that they derive much more satisfaction—both emotional and physical—as "heterosexual

The great hunger that the adolescent or young adult usually has for dating and marriage is chiefly a reflection of this need to feel essential, individual, inexchangeable. In serious dating, for example, each person becomes so significant to the other in terms of emotional need satisfaction that the experience

may constitute a new dimension of awareness. This is essentially what is meant by being in love. In short, the paired relation, established in serious dating and marriage, integrates with the depersonalization of our highly urbanized and industrialized mass society by fulfilling the need for meaning and emotional satisfaction and by restoring an "input-output emotional balance" for the individual in a culture which is chiefly impersonal and in which most relations are interchangeable (Goode, 1964). The person who receives little recognition of his individuation in most relations will restore the balance through a relation in which intimacy is taken for granted and the person is important for himself.

Summary

A universal need of the individual in all societies and in all segments of society is the need to "belong" and to have a *significant other* who "belongs" to him. It is probably essential for the average person's well-being that he maintain *primary relations* and the ultimate of these relations, the *paired relation,* with significant others. A primary relation is one in which the person is important as an individual and in which the person is provided intrinsic satisfaction. A *secondary relation* is one in which the person is important chiefly because of the function he is fulfilling. This kind of relation is not intrinsically satisfying.

The person's behavior in this paired relation is a function of his own unique individuation and his cultural conditioning, or socialization. One important

roommates"). (2) Trial marriage (many young couples feel that if they live together for a year or so, they will know whether they really want to marry or not—if they are still in love, they marry; if they are not still in love they are spared the trauma and expense of a divorce). (3) Idealism, or defiance of convention, or rejection of what the couple regard as a dishonest and outmoded institution. A homosexual relation may also be as enduring, as responsible, and as loving as a heterosexual relation, even though the couple are not held together—indeed, are discouraged—by the conventions of society.

element in cultural conditioning is the level of social stratification to which he belongs, as indicated by his social class.

In our mass society, the person experiences a relative lack of primary institutions and relations, with most of his interactions chiefly functional, impersonal, and anonymous. He is perpetually once-removed from the sources of gratification; he is often fragmented and compartmentalized by his roles in the society; and he experiences a conflict between the society's values of doing and producing and the humanistic values of loving and being loved, of caring and being known and cared for. He thus places a great importance on the primary institutions and relations that do remain — especially in the paired relations of dating and marriage — and expects to receive from them the companionship, the emotional support and security, and the affection and love that are necessary for his confirmation of himself as a unique and valued individual.

Questions

1   What fundamental human needs must all societies provide?
2   What is the emphasis in a primary relation? In a secondary relation?
3   "Things actively wanted" in our society are? "Things actively avoided" in our society are?
4   Of what use is the concept of social class?
5   What are the major characteristics of
    (a) the upper class?
    (b) the upper-middle class?
    (c) the lower-middle class?
    (d) the upper-lower class?
    (e) the lower-lower class?
6   How important are anatomical and physiological variables in observable differences of behavior?
7   What are some of the psychological variables among individuals?
8   Discuss the need to form a paired relation.
9   What distinguishes a paired relation from other primary relations?
10   What do secondary institutions provide for in our society?
11   How is a mass society distinguished from a simple society?
12   How would you describe "fragmentation of the individual" in a mass society?
13   What rewards has the depersonalized emphasis on mass production brought to the individual?
14   Explain "other directed."
15   What happens to a person who cannot achieve either the personal needs or the achievement needs without sacrificing one or the other?
16   How are secondary relations "safer" than primary relations?
17   How is a socialized person in a society still an individual?
18   How does the paired relation integrate with the depersonalization of our mass society?
19   What is one of the most valuable functions of dating and marriage?

References and Selected Readings

Ardrey, Robert. *Social Contract.* New York: Atheneum, 1970.

_____. *The Territorial Imperative.* New York: Atheneum, 1966.

Bach, George R., and Ronald M. Deutsch. *Pairing.* New York: Wyden, 1970.

Bell, Earl H., and John Sirjamaki.
*Social Foundations of Human
Behavior,* 2nd ed. New York:
Harper, 1965.

Berelson, Bernard, and Gary A.
Steiner. *Human Behavior.* New York:
Harcourt, 1964.

Blitsten, Dorothy R. *The World of
the Family.* New York: Random
House, 1963.

Brown, Ina Corrinne. *Understanding
Other Cultures.* Englewood Cliffs,
N. J.: Prentice-Hall, 1963.

Channels, Vera. Family Life
Education through the Use of
Novels. *The Family Coordinator,*
July 1971, Vol. 20, pp. 225–230.

Coleman, James C. *Psychology,
Dynamics and Effective Behavior.*
Chicago: Scott, Foresman, 1969.

Coles, Robert. *Erik H. Erikson: The
Growth of his Work.* Boston:
Little, Brown, 1970.

Dreger, Ralph Mason. *Fundamentals
of Personality.* New York: Lippincott,
1962.

Duvall, Evelyn Millis. *Family
Development,* 3rd ed. Philadelphia:
Lippincott, 1967.

Dyal, James A., ed. *Readings in
Psychology: Understanding Human
Behavior.* New York: McGraw-Hill,
1962.

Erlich, Paul R. and Anne H.
*Population, Resources, Environment:
Issues in Human Ecology.*
San Francisco: Freeman, 1970.

Fromm, Erich. *The Art of Loving.*
New York: Bantam, 1970.

Gesell, Arnold, and Catherine
Amatrude. *The Embryology of
Behavior.* New York: Harper, 1945.

Goode, William J. *World Revolution
and Family Planning.* New York:
Free Press, 1970.

——————. *The Family.* Englewood
Cliffs, N. J.: Prentice-Hall, 1964.

Hobart, Charles W. Commitment,
Value Conflict, and the Future of
the American Family. *Marriage and
Family Living,* November 1963, Vol.
25, pp. 405–412.

Jay, Phyllis C., ed. *Primates:
Studies in Adaptation and
Variability.* New York: Holt, 1968.

Kagen, J. The Concept of
Identification. *Psychology Review,*
1958, Vol. 65, pp. 296–305.

Kaplan, Louis. *Foundations of Human
Behavior.* New York: Harper, 1965.

Kephart, Wm. M. *The Family, Society,
and the Individual.* Boston:
Houghton Mifflin, 1961.

Kroeber, Alfred L., and Clyde
Kluckhohn. Culture: A Critical
Review of Concepts and Definitions.
Papers of the Peabody Museum, 1952,
Vol. 47, No. 1a, pp. 456, 636–644.

Laing, R. D. *The Self and Others.*
Chicago: Quadrangle Books, 1962.

Lasswell, Harold D., and Abraham
Kaplan. *Power and Society: A
Framework for Political Inquiry.* New
Haven: Yale University Press, 1950.

Leeper, Robert Ward. *Toward
Understanding Human Personalities.*
New York: Appleton-Century-
Crofts, 1959.

Lehner, George F. J. *Explorations
in Personal Adjustment.* Englewood
Cliffs, N. J.: Prentice-Hall, 1969.

Lindgren, Henry Clay. *Psychology of
Personal Development,* 2nd ed. New
York: Van Nostrand, 1969.

——————. *Readings in Personal
Development.* New York: Van
Nostrand, 1969.

Lorenz, Konrad. *On Aggression,*
trans. by Marjorie K. Wilson.
New York: Bantam, 1970.

Marcuse, Herbert. *One-Dimensional
Man.* Boston: Beacon, 1964.

Martindale, Don. *Institutions,
Organizations, and Mass Society.*
Boston: Houghton Mifflin, 1966.

_____. *American Society.*
New York: Van Nostrand, 1960.

Maslow, A. H. *Motivation and
Personality.* New York: Harper,
1970.

_____. Deficiency Motivation
and Growth Motivation. In Marshal
R. Jones, ed., *Nebraska Symposium
on Motivation,* University of
Nebraska Press, 1955, pp. 1–30.

Mayer, Albert J., and Philip M.
Hauser. Class Differences in
Expectation of Life at Birth. In
Reinhard Bendix and Seymour M.
Lipset, eds., *Class, Status and Power:
A Reader in Social Stratification,* rev.
ed. New York: Free Press, 1966.

McKinley, Donald Gilbert. *Social
Class and Family Life.* New York:
Free Press, 1964.

Mead, George H. *Mind, Self and
Society.* Chicago: University of
Chicago Press, 1934.

Mills, C. Wright. *The Sociological
Imagination.* London: Oxford, 1967.

Money, J. Developmental
Differentiation of Femininity and
Masculinity Compared. In Seymour
M. Farber and Roger H. L. Wilson,
eds., *Man and Civilization: The
Potential of Women.* New York:
McGraw-Hill, 1963, pp. 51–65.

_____. Psychosexual
Development in Man. In Albert
Deutsch, ed., *The Encyclopedia of
Mental Health.* New York: Franklin
Watts, 1963, pp. 1678–1709.

Montagu, Ashley. *Sex, Man, and
Society.* New York: Putnam, 1969.

_____. *Man and Aggression.*
London: Oxford, 1968.

Queen, Stuart J., Robert W.
Habenstein, and John B. Adams.
The Family in Various Cultures, 3rd
ed. New York: Lippincott, 1969.

Reich, Charles A. *The Greening
of America.* New York: Random
House, 1970.

Riesman, David, *et al. The Lonely
Crowd.* New York: Doubleday
Anchor Books, 1956.

Rogers, Carl R. *On Becoming a
Person.* Boston: Houghton
Mifflin, 1970.

_____, and Barry Stevens.
*Person to Person: The Problem
of Being Human.* La Jolla, Calif.:
Real People, 1967.

Rogoff, Natalie. Local Social
Structure and Educational
Selection. In A. H. Halsey, *et. al.,*
eds., *Education, Economy, and Society.*
New York: Free Press, 1961.

Sawrey, James M. *Frustration and
Conflict.* Dubuque, Iowa:
Brown, 1969.

_____, and Charles W.
Telford. *Dynamics of Mental Health.*
Boston: Allyn and Bacon, 1963.

Saxton, Lloyd, and Walter
Kaufmann, eds. *The American Scene:
Social Problems of the Seventies.*
Belmont, Calif.: Wadsworth, 1970.

Shaffer, Laurance Frederic, and
Edward Joseph Shoben, Jr. *The
Psychology of Adjustment,* 2nd ed.
Boston: Houghton Mifflin, 1956.

Shibutani, Tamotsu. *Society and
Personality.* Englewood Cliffs, N. J.:
Prentice-Hall, 1961.

Stephens, William N. *The Family in
Cross-Cultural Perspective.* New York:
Holt, 1963.

Warner, W. Lloyd. *American Life:
Dream and Reality,* rev. ed. Chicago:
University of Chicago Press, 1962.

Williams, Roger J. The Biological
Approach to the Study of
Personality. In James A. Dyal, ed.,
*Readings in Psychology: Understanding
Human Behavior.* New York:
McGraw-Hill, 1962, pp. 375–385.

Wynne-Edwards, V. C. Population
Control in Animals. *Scientific
American,* August 1964, Vol. 211,
No. 2., pp. 68–74.

Part Two

A Background for Marriage

Chapter Two

Love in a Paired Relation

*Love grants in a moment
what toil cannot achieve
in an age.*

Schopenhauer

t he word *love* is extremely difficult to define; for although it is very widely used, it is used in so many different ways it can mean almost anything. For the same reason, we cannot simply assume that everyone intuitively knows what is meant by love. We must attempt to capture it in as accurate and useful a definition as possible. For love is a very real and extremely important element in all primary relations and especially in the paired relations of dating and marriage; and if we are to understand the formation and interactions of these relations, we must understand the concept of love.

In order to reach a shared definition, we will begin with an examination of some of the commonly agreed-upon characteristics of love:

First, the ability to feel and express love apparently is learned through cultural conditioning, although the need to experience demonstrations of love is innate and essential to survival in infancy and to well-being in adulthood.

Second, love is not an all-or-nothing phenomenon; it can exist in many different degrees. It may be simply the ultimate of "like," or it may be the type of passionate, totally absorbing attachment celebrated in literature and the arts.

Third, love may have many different forms. The *love-object*[1] may be concrete (a person, animal, or thing) or abstract (liberty, justice, adventure, art, mankind, God), and the motivation for love is as diverse as human personalities. The chief components of love that are manifested in dating, mate selection, marriage, and the family are *altruistic love, companionate love, sexual love,* and *romantic*

---

[1] A term derived from *goal object*, which in psychological terminology means anything providing need satisfaction.

love.[2] The love of marital partners is most often a blending of these four components, while the love of a dating couple may well emphasize the romantic and sexual elements. The love of parent for child is mainly altruistic.[3]

Finally, love has objective reality; it is not a myth. The experience of love is among the most powerful experiences of man. Love has at its basis some unknown "force" or "energy" which is real, although it as yet has not been isolated and identified by science. Sorokin (1967) suggests that the energy of love is of a different order from physical energy (physical energy may be used up, whereas the more love one uses, the more one has): The energy of love is a powerful creative, recreative, and therapeutic power, which generates a response of energy in the recipient and thus creates a chain reaction of "love-energy" exchanges between the two persons in a love relation (p. 643; see also Sorokin's other works listed in the bibliography for this chapter, and Kropotkin, 1955).

Perhaps the concept of love as a force or energy may ultimately prove to be the most accurate definition, but in light of present knowledge, and for our purposes, we will treat this energy as simply an aspect of love. For our operational definition of love, we will subsume all of what we can consider its various aspects and conclude that love is a vital and profound emotion[4] which is experienced as a result of a significant need satisfaction. In other words, a person "in love" derives a deep, compelling persistent, and positive emotional satisfaction from the love-object—a satisfaction that may be the most significant and highly motivating experience known to man.

The Learning of Love

The emotion of love is first experienced in infancy as a result of receiving nurture, usually from the mother. As the infant passively receives food, and as he is

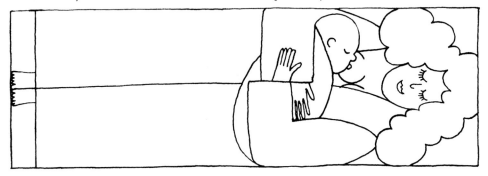

---

[2] These aspects of love in the paired relation were recognized as far back as the ancient Greeks. Whereas we use one word—love—to cover these components, the Greeks used three: *philos* (deep, enduring friendship), *eros* (passionate sexual attraction), and *agape* (non-demanding, self-sacrificing, spiritual love). (The concept of romantic love did not become institutionalized in the Western world until the eleventh century.)

[3] Romantic love with one's own child may also occur (and is a favorite theme in literature), but it is considered a perversion of love. Sexual love with one's own child (incest) is, of course, both illegal and culturally proscribed in all societies.

[4] An emotion—whether love, hate, fear, anxiety, disgust, joy, or elation—comprises four different types of response: subjective feeling, physical action, physiological change, and motivation, or stimulus to action, which is probably the most significant aspect of emotion because it arouses and directs the person's activity.

held and fondled, he comes to identify the resultant satisfaction *with himself* and to perceive himself as an object of worth—an object that is associated with the experience of deep and positive need satisfaction. It may be said that he comes to love himself—in the sense that we have defined the term *love* (a positive emotion which occurs when an important need is gratified). Apparently an infant must have this first experience of *himself* as a love object before he can experience love in relation with another.

The person who lacks this initial experience of love will, as he matures, try to compensate for his lack of self-love by demonstrating a greedy self-interest—by perceiving others chiefly in terms of their usefulness to him, and by manipulating them for his own gain. This is termed *selfishness*, which is the antithesis of self-love.

Close observation shows that while the selfish person is always anxiously concerned with himself, he is never satisfied, is always restless, always driven by a fear of not getting enough, of missing something, of being deprived of something. He is filled with burning envy of anyone who might have more. If we observe [him] still closer . . . we find that this person is basically not fond of himself, but deeply dislikes himself (Fromm, 1970, p. 115).

In contrast, a person operating from a firm base of self-love will extend his sense of self-acceptance and self-regard to the acceptance and regard of significant others.

The infant's first significant other, or love object (other than himself), is usually the mother, who is of course the figure he most closely and most often experiences in receiving nurture. Other members of the immediate family and other persons who actively provide nurture will also become love objects as the experience of the child broadens. In addition, inanimate objects (stuffed animals, dolls) and pets may receive the child's early feelings of loyalty, devotion, and concern and may provide him with intense satisfaction.[5]

The infant is completely dependent in his love relation, supplying nothing and taking everything. But as he perceives others as loving, he begins to perceive others as lovable and to provide these others with the nurture and regard that he himself first received. Extending his sense of self-acceptance or self-love to include a wider social environment than his family, he begins to demonstrate an independence in relations which becomes increasingly manifest from ages 3 to 5. Dependency needs will remain, but they decrease in relative importance. He comes to accept age mates and to form bonds of affection and regard with them. At first sexually neutral, his love for age mates soon focuses especially on like-sexed companions, because in our society boys are encouraged

---

[5] Animal experiments have demonstrated that the infant rhesus monkey will not survive when reared alone unless he has a soft cloth which he may cling to and fondle. Even when the cloth is removed only briefly for laundering, the monkey becomes very disturbed (Harlow, 1959). Parallel behavior may be observed in human infants and children.

to play with boys, and girls with girls. With the advent of puberty, this pattern is expected to change; and the adolescent usually begins to form other-sexed primary relations whose intensity of emotional involvement will gradually increase, becoming, through dating, deeply significant paired relations. These relations often are marked by an upsurge of dependency needs that occur simultaneously with the adolescent's strong need for independence from the family environment.

With adulthood, the focus of relations shifts to the need for interdependency. The young adult is then expected to fall in love exclusively with one other-sexed person, abandoning, for the most part, his like-sexed paired relations of childhood and early adolescence, and beginning the cycle again by marrying and providing his offspring with the love that he received as a child. Thus, all three needs — dependence, independence, interdependence — are present in a person from early childhood, but the emphasis in these needs shifts from dependency to independency to interdependency as the person proceeds through the developmental stages from infancy to adolescence to maturity. "Infantile love follows the principle: 'I love you because I need you.' Mature love says: 'I need you because I love you'" (Fromm, 1970, p. 34).

In Freud's psychosexual theory of personality development, the earliest stage of development, which chiefly entails self-love, is known as the *narcissistic* period, after the Greek myth about Narcissus, who fell in love with his own reflection in

SATISFACTION IN GIVING   SATISFACTION IN RECEIVING

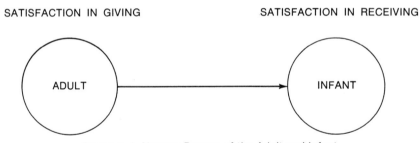

Figure 2–1. Nurture Pattern of the Adult and Infant

the still waters of a pool. In the second stage, which Freud termed the *Oedipal* period, after the ancient Greek myth of Oedipus, love is focused chiefly on the mother, and the father is seen as a rival.[6]

The stage when love is experienced chiefly with members of the same sex is known as the *homosexual* period and extends from about the ages of 8 to 12 years. It is followed by the *heterosexual* period, which extends from adolescence through maturity. The *adult* period, characterized by "mature" love — with the emphasis on giving, or providing, rather than receiving — completes the circle, with the adult now providing nurture and affection for his mate and children.

---

[6] See the classic Greek play, *Oedipus Rex*, by Sophocles. For a fuller account of Freudian terms and their meanings, see Mullahy, 1952; Thompson, 1951; English and Pearson, 1945; and Freud, 1938. For an excellent brief discussion, see Crawley *et al.*, 1964, pp. 88–135.

A person may be fixated at any of the psychosexual stages and remain oriented chiefly to the characteristics of that stage. This is termed *fixation*. For example, the adult, though fully developed physically, socially, and economically, may still be narcissistic, or incapable of any but self-love (while the severely disturbed adult may not be capable even of that). Or a person fixated at the homosexual stage may never proceed to the heterosexual stage. Similarly, a fixation at the heterosexual stage may limit the capacity of a person for mature love. (This is not to imply that mature love is the exclusive province of the heterosexual; both the homosexual and the heterosexual are capable of proceeding to mature love, if mature love is defined as an emphasis upon giving rather than receiving.)

It must not be assumed, of course, that a person proceeds from stage to stage in discrete jumps. Each stage blends into another. Moreover, as the person proceeds through the psychosexual developmental stages, it is the emphasis upon experience which changes; elements of all preceding stages remain. Thus the adult characterized by mature love still retains the elements of narcissistic love, for example, as a base upon which other elements are established—love of mother, family, friends, mate, and children.

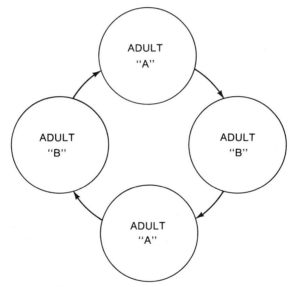

Figure 2-2. Nurture Pattern of Adults—Alternate Mutuality

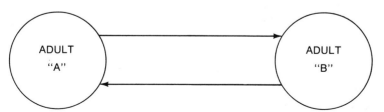

Figure 2-3. Nurture Pattern of Adults—Simultaneous Mutuality

The Four Faces of Love in a Paired Relation

Earlier in this chapter, we briefly stated that love, especially in dating and mating behavior, comprises four components: altruism, companionship, sex, and romance. Let us now return to these "four faces of love" and examine them in detail.

Altruistic Love

As we have seen, altruistic love implies an emphasis in the relation upon the well-being of the love object. If providing nurture brings the provider an intrinsic satisfaction, this emotion (especially when sustained and enhanced) may be defined as altruistic love. Providing for another may bring a person more satisfaction than providing for his own physical well-being. This is so because needs exist in a hierarchy, and the need to provide nurture for another person may take precedence over the need to provide for one's own welfare. In lower animals, the manifestation of altruistic love is reflexive-instinctive, so that mother love is literally blind, the female being impelled to "mother" (give nurture, care, and protection) mainly as a function of hormonal activity. "In the laboratory, maternal behavior can be induced in the female animal simply by hormonal injections — and it can be terminated in the same manner" (Kephart, 1961, p. 50). In the higher animals, and especially in the human being, the need to demonstrate maternal love is less reflexive and more diffuse; it is also somewhat less ubiquitous. The evidence from Harlow's studies (1962) with the rhesus monkey indicates that maternal care in the primate is a learned phenomenon, occurring as a result of having *received* maternal care in one's own infancy.

Sorokin (1961) suggests that the basis of altruistic love is a need for living organisms to be helpful to one another. Life either could not occur at all, or could occur only at the unicellular level, if this behavior were not characteristic of all life forms. Interaction and symbiosis occur from the unicellular level on up and are manifested in "innumerable reactions of cooperation and aid, at least as frequent and common as the actions-reactions of the struggle for existence" (Sorokin, p. 641). Among all organisms, altruistic tendencies and egoistic tendencies occur in a relatively close balance, with the need to interact in an integrative, unifying, harmonious way balanced against the need to demonstrate aggression, antagonism, destruction, and self-interest. Species compete with species for available living space, oxygen, water, and food; and individuals compete with other individuals in most environments for the basic goods of life. In human societies, then, "brotherhood tempered by rivalry" is the foundation of most social behavior (Wynne-Edwards, 1964).

Companionate Love

The relation between "liking" and "loving" is essentially one of degree; both are aspects of the same emotion of attraction and positive need fulfillment. However, the liking aspect of this emotion is probably more characteristic of more paired relations more of the time than is the deeper, more demanding involvement of ultimate like, or love. Married couples normally live at the more modest emotional levels of mutual respect, affection, and companionship than they do on the exalted heights that are celebrated by poets and song writers. This is not to say that the idealistic cultural expectations for ecstatic marital love are never fulfilled; such dreams may be not only fulfilled but surpassed. But the compan-

ionate component of love, although the least dramatic, is probably the most commonly and frequently experienced (and thus, in a sense, the most important) aspect of married love, despite mass-media emphasis on romance and sexuality.

Sexual Love

Love is frequently associated with the experience of sex, or with sexual attraction and fulfillment. This is not to say that love always involves sex; obviously it does not. It is equally obvious that sex does not always involve love. However, some measure of emotional involvement—or sexual love—usually occurs in all but the most cursory sexual relations. Sexual love, or the emotion which a person experiences when the love object is also the sex object, is characterized by (1) strong feelings of tenderness, admiration, and esthetic appreciation, and (2) a strong need for tactile and, usually, genital contact. Sexual participation then becomes an extension of the intimacy and communication of the relation. When a person experiences sexual arousal and orgasm with his love object, he may feel a satisfaction and depth of involvement that is almost mystical in its intensity— although the capacity for sensory and emotional involvement varies among individuals just as does the capacity for love (and, for the matter, all other capacities).

One aspect of sexual love which is especially important in contemporary American marriages is its function in the marital interaction as a confirmation of the love relation and of the mate as a significant other. Like such non-sexual marital activities as preparing and eating a meal, conversing, or providing solace, sex can be a love offering; or it can be a strategic move in a marital power struggle, which is the conflict over dominance in a marital relation.[7] But because

---

[7] See *The Power Struggle*, in Chapter Seven, for a full description of power struggle in marriage. Mays (1969) points out that sex may also be utilized as a flight from sexual *love*. "We [may] fly to the sensation of sex in order to avoid the passion of *eros*" (p. 65).

sex is unique among marital activities in (1) its inherent motivational strength and (2) its deep emotional effect, a non-reciprocal or resentful or unloving sexual relation is usually much more destructive to the happiness and stability of a marriage than divisive behavior in non-sexual areas. Further, the societal expectation of sexual loyalty to a mate places even greater responsibility on sex as a component of marital success. In contrast, food is also a powerful motivational force, and the role interactions in the preparation, serving, and eating of a meal may involve a good deal of emotional fulfillment; but there are no societal sanctions that motivate a person to eat solely with his mate.

Thus when sex functions in a marriage as a chief confirmation of love, it is sometimes enough to keep a couple happy, even if there is no significant congruence in other important areas of their marriage. But *without* sexual love, a marriage will be successful only if sex is not significant in the perception of *both* individuals (an unlikely happenstance in the American culture) and if both of them receive important mutual confirmation from each other in significant non-sexual areas—for example, companionship, or extreme altruism and dependency.

It is important to point out again that this stress on sexual love in marriage is largely a trait of the Western, and particularly the American, society. In other societies, where marriages are arranged, and in simple societies, where the woman's role is chiefly homemaking and child bearing, sexual love plays a smaller role in marriage.

Inasmuch as the identification of sex and love is so prevalent in our society, it must be emphasized that sex and love are not the same, although they share many important characteristics. Both demonstrate (1) physical, (2) physiological, (3) motivational, and (4) emotional aspects (the reproductive aspect of sex is physical and physiological, but its pleasure-giving aspect is emotional); yet it is possible to experience (1) sex without love, (2) love without sex, or (3) sex and love together.

Romantic Love

A final important component of love, especially in dating and mating, is that of romance—the idealization of the love object. Romantic love falls within the generic definition of love, yet possesses characteristics that serve to differentiate it from companionate love, altruistic love, and sexual love. Romantic love is a very complex and subtle aspect of the emotion, and observers are by no means in agreement in defining the dynamics of romantic love, or even in accepting its validity as an operational element in mate selection or marriage.

Some observers (Allport, 1924; Young, 1943) have suggested that romantic love occurs as a result of blocking the drive for sexual expression. From this point of view, since sex is usually readily available in marriage and a married person cannot therefore be presumed to be sexually frustrated, it would be impossible for him to be romantically in love. Critics of this view consider such a hypothesis much too ingenuous. Their own explanation is that romantic attraction can occur as an end in itself, independent of sexual needs or frustrations (see Ellis, 1949; Sears, 1943; Moll, 1925; and Bell, 1902). Malinowski (1929), for example, found that strongly individualized, passionate, and enduring romantic attractions occur among the Trobriand Islanders, whose society openly accepts sexual activity.

The prevailing opinion in our society regarding romantic love seems to be that it may occur, and persist, and even deepen in a relation characterized by sexual satisfaction rather than by sexual frustration. This view accepts two separate and distinct needs, sexual and romantic, but hypothesizes that these two needs are closely related and ultimately interdependent in love affairs or in marriage. The sex need is chiefly physical, the romantic need chiefly emotional; but both needs may be satisfied by the same person, who is then the sex object *and* the romantic love object. Thus the gratification resulting from sex will also be an emotional satisfaction, which will reinforce feelings of love and the need for romantic involvement. This kind of sexual contact will produce an intense intimacy and immediacy of communication and will strengthen a couple's mutual commitment to each other.

As with all love, romantic love apparently originates in the nursery, in the comfort and support and fondling that the child receives from his mother. Thus, the chief focus of affectional life in infancy is the mother, and affectional life is paramount in the infant's awareness. As the infant grows to be a child, and as the child matures, other interests crowd in upon his attention: the need to develop mastery and manipulative skills, to acquire esteem, to actualize his potentialities. Affective life does not necessarily diminish, but a variety of other concerns also become important. With adolescence, however, affective needs once again become central. The drive to satisfy them is generally no more self-consciously sexual than it was during infancy; rather, the adolescent's preoccupation with love may be almost entirely asexual and romantic. But from the middle teens to the mid-twenties, this preoccupation shifts to a fusion of sex and romance. And from the mid-twenties on, the preoccupation is probably chiefly sexual.

In mature romantic love, a person enters a state in which the supreme motivating factor in his life is his devotion to another person and, of equal or greater importance, his personal satisfaction from this devotion and the response to it (Cavan, 1969). Not only does each person see the other as an idealized version of his need but each tries in turn to fulfill the ideal of the other. In dating and all other romantic interactions, the principal role each person plays is to fulfill the romantic expectations of the other (as well as his own), in order that, as a pair, both people will conform to the romantic pattern as they have learned it. They wish to be alone with each other because "privacy and secrecy make identification easy, and the two build up a feeling of oneness and of separateness from the world. They create and exist in a little world of their own, furnished with their shared memories" (Cavan, p. 386). This kind of intense emotional response and great preoccupation and involvement may occur with little or no physical contact; merely talking, holding hands, or lightly kissing may be experienced as deeply satisfying.[8] Also, the person in love with someone who is not physically available may forego sex with another who *is* available in order to remain faithful to the romantic ideal.

Romantic love places the highest value on personal characteristics. A person is more discriminating in his choice of romantic love object than in the choice of a sex object, because the sex object need not have the many specialized requirements of the romantic love object. Romantic love is focused on the nature of the goal object; sexual attraction is concentrated essentially on the strength of the drive for sexual release. An initial attraction may be sexual and then develop into romantic love, or the relation may at first be a romantic one which later comes to include sexual love. In either case, in our contemporary society, the expected outcome of this attraction would be marriage.

The social setting of Europe, in which the concept of romantic love developed,[9] clearly separated romance from the institution of marriage (and still does to some extent). Marriage was arranged by families and was based upon practical considerations unrelated to whatever personal attraction a young man and woman might or might not feel toward each other. Marriage was not an institution to provide for the fulfillment of personal desires but rather was a sober relation that provided for societal and economic needs and for the establishment and maintenance of a family.

---

[8] Many engaged couples, especially in the middle class, limit their premarital sexual experiences to light petting, believing that copulation or intimate petting will spoil their idealized romantic attraction and that such intimacy should be saved for marriage, where the combination of romance and sex is institutionalized. (See Chapter Four, *Human Sexuality: Behavior and Attitudes*, for a discussion of premarital sexual patterns.)

[9] Romantic love, in its classical form, was asexual. It emphasized loyalty, service, and devotion to the ideals of feminine beauty and masculine chivalry and has had enormous influence on the manners and morals of European society from its inception in the eleventh century as a literary conceit right up to the present. This concept of romantic love persisted in much the same form well into the 1960s, as embodied in nursery tales, song lyrics, comic strips, movies, and novels. *Tarzan of the Apes* and *Flash Gordon* were direct lineal descendents of *Sir Launcelot*, for example. Since the mid 1960s, the popular emphasis in romantic love has shifted somewhat, toward an acceptance of sexuality as a concomitant of the romantic ideal; and this version is reflected in current mass media —*James Bond* is a good example.

Marriage and sex relations were contained within an official relationship, whereas romantic love . . . remained outside of marriage on an individual basis. Marriage was the public and responsible one. Marriage was permanent and stable, a means of conserving property and rearing children . . . romantic love lasted only so long as the personal preference for each other was fervid (Cavan, p. 383–384).

Contemporary American society makes romantic love a primary basis for marriage; and once married a person is expected to derive his personal and romantic satisfaction from within the framework of his marriage. If extramarital romantic involvement does occur, the cultural expectation is that it must be either discontinued or institutionalized by divorce and remarriage. (If children are involved, this may lead to exchanging whole families as well as spouses.)

Contemporary romantic love, then, is characterized by three distinctive elements: (1) the traditional asexual idealism of service, chivalry, devotion, and exaltation of feminine beauty and virtue, (2) the acceptance of sexuality as an extension (or concomitant) of this ideal, and (3) the emphasis upon marriage (or at least a fairly permanent paired relation) as the ultimate expression of this ideal.

Many observers have pointed out that the values of romantic love seem to contradict those of marriage. The emphasis in romance is upon freedom; the emphasis in marriage is upon responsibility. Values in romantic love are personal—in marriage they are familial. Romance is private, tumultuous, idiosyncratic, and characterized by an intensity of experience and heightened awareness; but marriage is public, stabilized, routine, and often mundane.

Despite many contradictory characteristics between romance and marriage, romantic love is not necessarily opposed to married love. Romantic love may not only continue after marriage but conceivably may even be enhanced by it— although such an occurrence is unfortunately rare (see Chapter Seven, *Conflict and Adjustment in Marriage*). If a person identifies with his mate as a real person, rather than as a projection of his own idealized needs, marital interaction can deepen the romantic love of dating and courting. But if identification is not founded upon reality, disillusion will inevitably occur because the close and constant everyday contact characteristic of marriage forces an acknowledgment of the reality of the person rather than the idealized vision.

Love and Infatuation

It is useful to employ the term *infatuation* to distinguish an emotion which in many respects is similar to love (especially romantic love), but which should be differentiated from love. Both infatuation and love are based on a need to experience an intimate emotional and tactile relation with the goal object. But infatuation has little to do with the reality of the personality of the highly idealized goal object, since the idealization is based chiefly on fantasy.

There are two types of infatuation object: (1) the distant infatuation object, whom the person knows not at all, or knows just slightly (for example, political or entertainment figures, or school athletic heroes), and (2) the associative infatuation object, whom the person knows and dates. An associative infatuation can involve a very deep intimate relation which nonetheless is not love.

Infatuation tends to focus on a single perceived characteristic of the infatuation object, such as voice or appearance, which in some cases may even acquire the force of a fetish. Love, however, focuses on the whole person as a love object. Whereas an infatuated person tends to relate to the object of his infatuation *as* an object, which is to be manipulated, controlled, or used, a person in love relates to his love object by identifying himself with it. Further, this identification with the love object tends to be persistent and enduring, while the relation to an infatuation object tends to be fickle and rather short-lived.

Infatuation is self-centered; love is other-centered. An infatuated person tends to be preoccupied with himself and with his own feelings; he often feels awkward, constrained, self-conscious, and unfulfilled, fragmented and insecure. He may withdraw from sensory experience and contact with others, becoming less and less aware of incoming stimuli (he may daydream, stay away from friends, be unable to eat). On the other hand, a person in love is oriented toward the well-being of the love object and tends to be less self-conscious or concerned with himself and with feelings of difficulty and inadequacy. He feels relatively more self-assured, secure, and personally adequate. He is active and open to sensory experience. He feels healthy and alive. He delights in all aspects of his environment — food, friends, sights and sounds. He is moved to put his dreams into action. In other words, infatuation binds energy, love releases energy. The person in love functions more efficiently, with greater drive, increased awareness, and an eagerness for achievement.

Because of our society's emphasis on the importance of romantic love, the young person of our society (especially in the middle class) dreams of the fulfillment of love long before he is ready for or even encounters an appropriate object of romantic love. Flaubert expressed this hauntingly in his autobiographical novel, *November:*[10]

> *The puberty of the heart precedes that of the body: I had more need of loving than of enjoying, more desire for love than for pleasure. Today I cannot even imagine the love of first adolescence, when the senses are nothing and the infinite alone holds sway. Coming between childhood and youth, it is the transition between them and passes so quickly that it is forgotten.*
>
> *I had read the word "love" so much in the poets and had repeated it to myself so often to charm myself with its sweetness that to every star that shone in a blue sky on a gentle night, to every murmur of the stream against its banks, to every ray of sun on the dewdrops I would say "I am in love! Oh, I am in love!" And I was happy, I was proud, I was ready for the finest acts of devotion, and above all, when a woman brushed me in passing or looked into my face, I wished I might love her a thousand times more, be even more at her mercy than I was; I wished my heart would throb so violently as to burst my breast asunder.*

---

[10] Serendipity Press, New York, 1966. Reprinted by permission.

There is an age, as you will remember, when you smile vaguely as if there were kisses in the air. Your heart swells in the fragrant breeze, your blood beats warm in your veins. You wake up happier, richer than the night before, more lively, more excited . . . As you walk in the evening and breathe the scent of cut hay and listen to the cuckoo in the wood and watch the racing stars, is not your heart purer, more bathed in air, in light, in blue than the peaceful horizon when the earth meets the sky in a tranquil kiss? Oh, the fragrance of women's hair! The softness of the skin of their hands, the penetration of their gaze!

Thus the person will often experience infatuation as a temporary fulfillment of his culturally conditioned need for a romantic love experience. And since the emotional and physical manifestations of love and infatuation are, on the surface, comparable, he is able to define his experiences as love.

These initial infatuation experiences also provide a kind of training ground for love. The young person is able to experience and assess first the vicarious fulfillments of a distant infatuation object, who is safely remote, anonymous, and undemanding, and second, the problems, disappointments, and fulfillments of an associative infatuation object, who is available and who makes demands. In the second real experience, he usually discovers eventually (and to his disappointment) that the infatuation object is not a love object; that he has created

this object out of his own self-centered fantasies, that he is unwilling and indeed unable to fulfill the demands and needs of the object, and that he is merely exploiting this object for the fulfillment of emotions that are immature. He discovers that romantic love, unlike infatuation, involves a *paired* relation, which is intimate, personal, giving as well as receiving, and real. The other in a love relation is an individual rather than the personification of a fantasy ideal.

Thus, infatuation will often precede love. With increasing maturity, a person may shift from the energy-binding, self-centered, withdrawn, unrealistic, and manipulative characteristics of infatuation to the energy-releasing, other-centered, outgoing, unself-conscious, and altruistic characteristics of love.

Love and Marriage

In marriage there is usually a fairly constant interplay of altruistic, companionate, sexual, and romantic love. The relative importance of these four components will, of course, vary for any given couple, with altruism or companionship or sex or romance being more prominent in some marriages than in others. The relative importance of these four components also varies for any couple with the duration of their marriage. In the very early stages of marriage, for example, the sexual and romantic components are generally predominant.

Obviously, the most significant influence on the relative prominence of one or another of the components of married love is the immediate love need of one or both of the persons in the relation. The love needs of a person will vary from time to time in a marriage, and these needs will not always coincide with the needs of the other person. But the societal expectation is that each will fulfill the particular need of his spouse, not because he shares that particular need at that particular time but because he recognizes the need in the other. He provides the need as a love offering. On occasion such provision will be simultaneous and mutual; but more often it is alternate.

So long as, in the long run, there is a balance of at least the alternate form of love fulfillment in marriage—so long as a person feels that he is getting as much as he is giving and that the spouse is giving because he wants to rather than because he feels he must—the marriage should be happy and fulfilling.

Despite the mass-media emphasis on sex and romance, the companionate side of love—shared dependence, mutual respect, and "belonging"—probably has more to do with what the average couple experiences as conjugal love than does the passionate romantic attachment of a Romeo and Juliet. We must remember that part of the essence of the romantic attachment of Romeo and Juliet was its brevity. The modern Romeo has to go to work and expend most of his time and energy performing all the various routine, mundane, and non-romantic activities necessary to meet the obligation of supporting Juliet and their children. Juliet, in turn, must also work until their first child is born, after which most of her time and energy is absorbed by various child-care and household obligations. Their marital relation may continue to include the passion and idealism of the romantic, sexual love of their youth—at least on occasion—but an increasingly important factor in their relation would be the satisfactions of shared responsibilities and experiences in meeting the practical demands of daily circumstance, in providing support and companionship to one another, and in loving and launching their children. These satisfactions would not only assume an added importance but might even come to constitute the chief basis of their relation. This fusion of romantic love (idealization of the love object), altruistic love (desiring the well-being of the love object), sexual love (in which the love object and the sex object are the same), and companionate love (or friendship) is the contemporary ideal of conjugal love in our society.

Summary

Love is a very complex emotion that has fascinated man since his earliest speculations, but it has only recently been subjected to scientific scrutiny. Whatever his viewpoint, every observer agrees that love is important, and that it is apparently necessary for infant survival and adult well-being. A person develops his innate capacity to love as the result of receiving nurture and altruistic love in infancy. Experiencing himself as loved, he perceives himself as lovable and significant others as loving. In other words, only after he has learned to love himself can he love others.

According to current theories of personality development, a person loves first himself, then his mother, then like-sexed and other-sexed friends, until finally he is capable of a mature love experience, in which he derives greater satisfaction from providing nurture than from receiving it. He reaches this kind of maturity by incorporating each new developmental stage into his experience.

In addition to being the ultimate of "like," love comprises four major components: altruism, companionship, sexuality, and romance. Companionate love is the aspect most frequently experienced by most married couples; the amount of time they spend "just being together" is far greater than that which they spend in nurturant, sexual, or romantic activity. Any one of these four components of love may be enhanced or diminished by satisfaction or deprivation of any of the other components. Sexual frustration, for example, may decrease companionate love; or sexual fulfillment may enhance it.

Altruistic love, or the provision of kindness, aid, compassion, and concern, operates in only one direction in the adult-infant relation, with the adult providing it and the infant receiving it. In adult-adult relations, however, nurture-need provision is characterized either by the person providing on one occasion and receiving on another, or by both people simultaneously giving and receiving.

Sexual love is the fusion of love and sex, or the combining of the sex object and the love object. So great are the psychological ramifications of both love and sex that when the two are combined the result may be an extraordinary intensity of experience. Romantic love, the idealization of the love object, is particularly important in adolescence, though it often persists into young adulthood and is one of the chief elements in mate selection.

Some observers have suggested that romance is blocked sex and is therefore diametrically opposed to marriage. Other observers have taken a different position; namely, that sexual fruition may reinforce, and thus deepen, the initial attraction of asexual romantic love. This latter opinion seems to be substantiated by learning theory, which finds that rewarding a response tends to reinforce it.

To sum up: Love is a learned emotion, usually profound, which is related to significant need fulfillment involving a goal object which may be either concrete or abstract. In addition to being the ultimate of "like," love may also have such other important components as altruism, companionship, sex, and romance. The psychological manifestations of love are exceedingly subtle and complex, compelling and persistent, with its energy and its motivational aspects among the most powerful that man may experience.

Questions

1   What is love?
2   Define *philos, eros,* and *agape.*
3   What are the four aspects of love manifested in dating, courtship, and marriage?
4   How does the energy of love differ from physical energy?
5   What different types of responses comprise an *emotion?*
6   How will a person behave who lacks the initial experience of love?
7   How does a person operating from a firm base of self-love view others?
8   How does the emphasis on dependence, independence, and interdependence shift from infancy to adolescence to maturity?
9   What are the stages described in Freud's psychosexual theory of personality development?
10 Describe altruistic love. Give an example of this kind of love.
11 In what way is altruistic love characteristic of all life forms?
12 Explain "brotherhood tempered by rivalry."
13 What is the most commonly and frequently experienced aspect of married love?
14 What characterizes sexual love?
15 What characteristics are shared by sex and love? What about them is not the same?
16 What characterizes contemporary romantic love?
17 How would you differentiate between love and infatuation?
18 What is the ideal of conjugal love in our society?

References and Selected Readings

Allport, F. H. *Social Psychology.* Boston: Houghton Mifflin, 1924.

Bell, Sanford. A Preliminary Study of the Emotion of Love between the Sexes. *American Journal of Psychology,* 1902, Vol. 13, pp. 325–354.

Bibby, Cyril. The Art of Loving. In Albert Ellis and Albert Abarbanel, eds. *The Encyclopedia of Sexual Behavior,* 2nd ed. New York: Hawthorn, 1967, pp. 657–662.

Biegel, H. G. Romantic Love. *American Sociological Review,* 1951, Vol. 16, pp. 326–334.

Blood, Robert O., Jr. *Love Match and Arranged Marriage.* New York: Free Press, 1967.

Cavan, Ruth Shonle. *The American Family,* 4th ed. New York: Crowell, 1969.

Clark, Le Mon. *Enjoyment of Love in Marriage.* New York: New American Library, 1969.

Coulton, G. G. *Life in the Middle Ages.* London: Cambridge University Press, 1930.

Crawley, Lawrence Q., *et al. Reproduction, Sex, and Preparation for Marriage.* Englewood Cliffs, N. J.: Prentice-Hall, 1964.

D'Arcy, Martin C. *The Mind and Heart of Love.* New York: Meridian, 1947.

Dell, Floyd. *Love in the Machine Age: A Psychological Study of the Transition from Patriarchal Society.* New York: Farrar, 1930.

Denenberg, Victor H. Early Experience and Emotional Development. *Scientific American,* June 1963.

De Rougement, Denis. *Love in the Western World.* New York: Pantheon, 1956.

Durant, Will. *The Story of Civilization,* Vol. 4: *The Age of Faith;* Vol. 5: *The Renaissance;* Vol. 6: *The Reformation.* New York: Simon and Schuster, 1950, 1953, 1957.

Ellis, Albert. *The Art and Science of Love.* New York: Lyle Stuart, 1960.

_____. A Study of Human Love Relationships. *Journal of Genetic Psychology,* 1949, Vol. 75, pp. 61–71.

English, O. Spurgeon, and Gerald H. J. Pearson. *Emotional Problems of Living.* New York: Norton, 1945.

Freud, Sigmund. *The Basic Writings of Sigmund Freud,* A. A. Brill, ed. New York: Modern Library, 1938.

_____. *Group Psychology and the Analysis of the Ego.* London: International Psychoanalytic Press, 1922.

Fromm, Erich. *The Art of Loving.* New York: Bantam, 1970.

Goode, William J. The Theoretical Importance of Love. *American Sociological Review,* 1959, Vol. 24, pp. 38–47.

Grant, Vernon W. Sexual Love. In Ellis and Abarbanel, eds. *The Encyclopedia of Sexual Behavior.* New York: Hawthorn, 1967, pp. 646–656.

Graves, Robert. Are Women More Romantic than Men? *Life,* October 15, 1965.

Harlow, H. F. The Heterosexual Affectional System in Monkeys. *American Psychologist,* 1962, Vol. 17, pp. 1–9.

_____. Love in Infant Monkeys. *Scientific American,* June 1959.

_____, and Harlow, Margaret Kuenne. Social Deprivation in Monkeys. *Scientific American,* May 1962.

Hess, Eckhard H. Imprinting in Animals. *Scientific American,* March 1958.

Howard, George E. *A History of Matrimonial Institutions.* Chicago: University of Chicago Press, 1904.

Hunt, Morton M. *The Natural History of Love.* New York: Funk and Wagnalls, 1967.

Kephart, William M. *The Family, Society, and the Individual.* Boston: Houghton Mifflin, 1961.

Knox, David H., Jr. Conceptions of Love at Three Developmental Levels. *The Family Coordinator,* April 1970, Vol. XIX, No. 2, pp. 151–157.

_____, and Michael L. Sporakowski. Attitudes of College Students Toward Love. *Journal of Marriage and the family,* November 1968, Vol. XXX, No. 4, pp. 638–642.

Kropotkin, Peter. *Mutual Aid, A Factor of Evolution.* Boston: Sargent, 1955.

Malinowski, Bronislow. *The Sexual Life of the Savages in Northwest Melanesia.* New York: Eugenics Publishing, 1929.

May, Rollo. *Love and Will.* New York: Norton, 1969.

Moll, Albert. *The Sexual Life of the Child.* New York: Macmillan, 1925.

Montagu, Ashley. *The Meaning of Love.* New York: Julian, 1955.

_____. *On Being Human*. New York: Abelard, 1950.

Mullahy, Patrick. *Study of Interpersonal Relations*. New York: Science House, 1967.

_____. *Oedipus, Myth and Complex*. New York: Hermitage, 1952.

Murstein, Bernard I., ed. *Theories of Attraction and Love*. New York: Springer, 1971.

Ortega y Gasset, José. *On Love*. New York: Greenwich Editions, 1957.

Prescott, Daniel A. Role of Love in Human Development. *Journal of Home Economics*, March 1952, Vol. 44, pp. 173–176.

Reiss, Ira L. Toward a Sociology of Heterosexual Love Relationships. *Marriage and Family Living*, May 1960, Vol. 22, pp. 139–145.

Robie, Walter F. *Art of Love*. New York: Paperback Library, 1969.

Rogers, Carl R. *On Becoming a Person*. Boston: Houghton Mifflin, 1970.

Sears, Robert R. *Survey of Objective Studies of Psychoanalytic Concepts*.

New York: Social Science Research Council, 1943.

Sorokin, P. Altruistic Love. In Ellis and Abarbanel, eds., *The Encyclopedia of Sexual Behavior*. New York: Hawthorn, 1967, pp. 641–645.

_____, ed. *A Symposium: Explorations in Altruistic Love and Behavior*. Boston: Beacon, 1950.

_____, ed. *A Symposium: Forms and Techniques of Altruistic and Spiritual Growth*. Boston: Beacon, 1954.

Suttie, Ian D. *The Origin of Love and Hate*. London: Julian, 1935.

Thompson, Clara. *Psychoanalysis: Evolution and Development*. New York: Hermitage, 1951.

West, Jessamyn. *Love Is Not What You Think*. New York: Harcourt, 1959.

Wynne-Edwards, V. C. Population Control in Animals. *Scientific American*, August 1964.

Young, P. T. *Emotions in Animals and Man*. New York: Wiley, 1943.

Chapter Three

Human Sexuality: Basic Responses

In the culture in which we live it is the custom to be least informed upon that subject concerning which every individual should know most, namely the structure and functions of his own body.

Ashley Montagu (*Anthropology and Human Nature*)

h

human sexual behavior has two major functions: *reproduction*, and immediate need satisfaction, or, more simply, *pleasure*. The primary biological function of sex is, of course, reproduction; it can scarcely have a more profound significance for the individual and for his society. However, sex also acts as a powerful drive in its own right, having nothing to do with reproduction. In fact, a person may take elaborate precautions to see that reproduction does *not* occur.

In lower animals, most sexual behavior is reproductive. The female in the lower primates, for example, is sexually receptive only when she is pregnable — about 3 percent of the time (Jay, 1963, p. 3) — and the male is sexually interested in her only during this time. In man, however, the reproductive aspect of sex is almost negligible, both in the subjective meaning of the behavior to the average individual and in the amount of sexual activity that may be defined operationally as reproductive.

Unlike the lower animals, only a tiny fraction of man's sexual behavior produces offspring. For example, the average man may experience 6,000 ejaculations during his lifetime, and the average married couple may have 3,000 copulations for each one that results in pregnancy.[1] Thus, as vital as reproduction is, both to the individual and to the society, most human sexual activity is non-reproductive. From a person's own subjective concern, sex occupies his consciousness

---

[1] These are median figures according to Kinsey's data (1948 and 1953). Dr. Kinsey was the first man to do a major taxonomic study of human sexuality. Prior to the publication in 1948 of his *Sexual Behavior in the Human Male*, very little was known about the general sexual-behavior patterns and the individual differences in these patterns in the human species. (His study of the sexuality of the human female was published in 1953.) Kinsey and his associates accomplished their comprehensive research by means of exhaustive interviews with a scientific sampling of the population.

primarily as a drive for immediate physical, emotional, or societal satisfaction; and human sexual needs and sexual satisfactions must be understood chiefly in terms of their pleasurable rather than their reproductive function.

In addition to reproduction and immediate need satisfaction, sexual behavior is also profoundly involved with much of man's nonsexual interests and activities (not only in marriage but in nonmarital activities), so that sexuality and sexually neutral behavior become very complex and interrelated. It is probably not an exaggeration to say that the average person's general life style—his activities, interests, values, and ambitions—is significantly involved with sexuality. So great is the importance of sexuality in personality structure that sex has been recognized as one of the chief forces in man's nature, not only by behavioral science but also by all philosophical systems and all religions in all known societies. Thus, to try to discuss and understand human sexuality solely in terms of its reproductive, biological function would be distressingly naive and misleading.

Marriage is in part a sexual relation between two persons, and this sexual relation is one of the most significant aspects of their life-long interaction. It is essential to an understanding of this relation that sex be seen in clear perspective. Each person in a marital relation has very real and very demanding physical and psychological needs involving sex. Further, the psychological, or emotional, aspects of sex are closely related with those of love. Thus, sex and love together form one of the cornerstones of marriage; and the person who lacks basic information about fundamental physical and psychological sexual characteristics is going to be more than a little handicapped in attempting to establish a satisfactory marriage relation for himself or for his mate. The person who not only lacks information but also holds harmful *mis*information is in an even worse predicament.

Masters and Johnson, who published the first objective experimental study of human sexuality, *Human Sexual Response* (1966), lamented in their preface this far-too-common ignorance of sex and the reluctance of the scientific and educational communities to do something about it:

How can biologists, behaviorists, theologians, and educators insist in good conscience upon the continued existence of a massive state of ignorance of human sexual response, to the detriment of the well-being of millions of individuals? Why must the basics of human sexual physiology create such high levels of personal discomfort among the very men and women who are responsible for guiding our culture? There is no man or woman who does not face in his or her lifetime the concerns of sexual tensions. Can that one facet of our lives, affecting more people in more ways than any other physiologic response other than those necessary to our very existence, be allowed to continue without benefit of objective, scientific analysis?

Why then must science and scientist continue to be governed by fear—fear of public opinion, fear of social consequence, fear of religious intolerance, fear of political pressure, and, above all, fear of bigotry and prejudice—as much within as without the professional world? (pp. vi–vii).[2]

The Biological Aspects of Sex

Human reproduction requires the fusion of one male and one female *gamete* in the female *Fallopian tube.* The male gamete is known as the *sperm*, and the female gamete is known as the *ovum*, or *egg*. Each of the gametes is a single-celled creature which is produced in organs called *gonads*. With fusion (*fertilization*, or *conception*), the two gametes become a single cell, a *zygote*, which contains the blueprint for the formation of the entire biological structure of a human being.[3]

Male Anatomy and Physiology

In the male, the gonads are ovoid-shaped organs called *testicles*, of which the normal male has two. The testicles vary in size but are generally about two inches long and an inch and a half in diameter. Because the testicles must be maintained at a temperature lower than the body cavity, they are enclosed in a sac called the *scrotum*, which hangs outside the body, between the legs, at the base of the abdomen. Within the testicles are several *lobules*, small divided areas which contain several winding and tightly-coiled *seminiferous tubules* in which the sperm are produced. Each testicle has some 300 to 600 tubules, each one a foot or two long when uncoiled, with an aggregate length of about half a mile. The sperm are produced in the germinal tissue which lines the walls of the tubules. This production of sperm, although seasonal in some animals, is continuous in man after *puberty.* The process of sperm production from *parent germ cells* is known as *spermatogenesis.*

The *penis* is the organ through which the sperm are *ejaculated.* The penis is situated at the base of the abdomen, and in its flaccid state it lies limply upon the scrotum. The loose skin of the penis is a continuation of the skin of the scrotum. The penis consists chiefly of spongy tissue surrounding the sperm- and urine-carrying tube, the *urethra.* The opening to the urethra at the tip of the penis is called the *meatus.* The main body of the penis is called the *shaft*, which extends about three fourths of the length of the penis. The smooth, cone-shaped head at the end of the shaft is called the *glans*, which is covered with both a very thin, sensitive skin and a heavier, retractable *foreskin,*[4] which is an extension of the loose skin covering the shaft.

---

[2] Masters and Johnson compiled their research for *Human Sexual Response* by observing and measuring the sexual characteristics and responses of a number of volunteers.

[3] For a more detailed discussion of reproduction, see *Pregnancy*, in Chapter Eleven. The prevention of pregnancy is also discussed in Chapter Eleven in the section *Birth Control.*

[4] Without *circumcision*, which consists of trimming away the foreskin, the glans is normally exposed

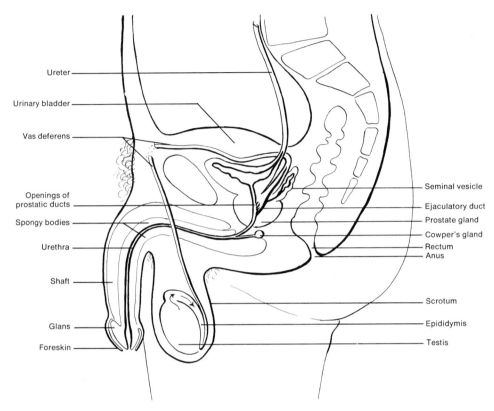

Figure 3-1. Male Urinogenital System

For sexual arousal, the glans is by far the most sensitive and excitable part of the average man's body. Its surface contains a high concentration of nerve endings, especially at the *corona*, the crown-like ridge at the back of the glans. An especially sensitive area of the corona is the *frenum*, the thin tissue on the lower surface of the glans, where the foreskin is attached. Although there is, as in all human organs, great individual difference, the average length of a penis is three to four inches in the flaccid state; the average diameter is slightly less than one inch. With erotic stimulation, either psychic or tactile, there is an involuntary response in the penis. Blood flows into its spongy tis-

---

only during erection. Circumcision is a fairly common practice in many societies and cultures. In some societies it is performed at puberty as a symbol of a boy's new maturity. In other societies, like our own, and in other cultures, like Judaism, circumcision is performed for hygienic reasons (it also has religious significance for the Jews). Just behind the glans, under the corona and on each side of the frenum, are *Tyson's glands*, which secrete a substance known as *smegma*. This substance may collect under the foreskin, if it is retained, and may act as a breeding ground for irritants and infection.

Circumcision is generally performed in our society a few days after birth, while the male infant is still in the hospital. The foreskin may be clipped off at this age with very little discomfort. Contrary to a widespread belief, circumcision does not enhance sexual sensitivity.

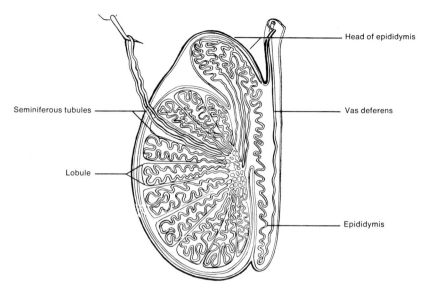

Head of epididymis

Seminiferous tubules

Vas deferens

Lobule

Epididymis

Figure 3–2. Cross Section of Testicle

sue faster than it flows out, until the spongy tissue becomes engorged with blood and the penis grows large, stiff, and hard. When fully erect, the penis projects outward from the body, pulling the now-taut scrotum upward. In this condition, which is termed an *erection*, the penis is usually about six inches long and about an inch and a half in diameter.

When the male becomes very sexually aroused, the erect penis may secrete a few drops of a clear, viscous fluid. It is assumed, but not definitely known, that this *pre-ejaculatory fluid* is produced in the *Cowper's glands*, two small bodies, each about the size of a pea, which are situated internally at the base of the penis.

Semen, which is ejaculated at orgasm by the mature male, is the fluid that carries the sperm through the urethra. The semen may contain something like 200 to 500 million sperm, within about a teaspoonful of the fluid. (One ejaculation *may* contain as many as a billion sperm cells.) Semen is usually rather viscous and milky, but it may vary normally from being very thick and gelatinous to being rather thin and watery. Semen is produced chiefly in the *seminal vesicles* and in the *prostate*, both of which are glands near the surface of the rectal wall. During ejaculation, the muscles of the penis contract to force the semen, in a series of spurts, into the urethra and through the meatus. It is released into the urethra simultaneously with the release of the sperm from the testicles. Before the sperm reach the urethra, they pass through the *epididymis* (a maturation chamber over the back and upper part of each testicle), through the *vas deferens*, a small tube about 18 inches long. The *ejaculate*, or semen, emerges from the erect penis in a series of jets. If not impeded, it may spurt three or four feet, although the ejaculatory action differs among individuals, and in some men the semen may seep from the penis with little force. Once ejaculated, the

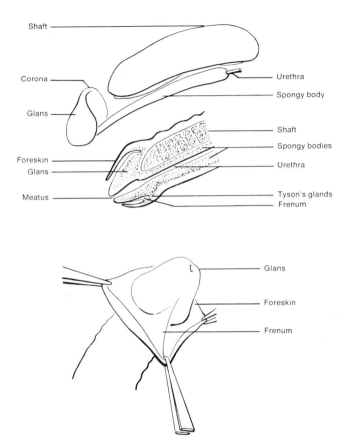

Figure 3–3. The Penis

sperm will die almost immediately unless they are ejaculated during copulation and are able to make their way to the female's Fallopian tubes, where they may survive for two or three (but possibly as long as five) days.

Puberty for the male occurs when he first ejaculates, generally between the ages of 11 and 14. However, the male can and usually does experience erection and orgasm (without ejaculation) from early childhood.

Female Anatomy and Physiology

The female gonads, the producers of the female gamete, or ovum, are called the *ovaries*. Just as the male has two testicles, the female has two ovaries, situated deep in the pelvis, below and to each side of the navel. The ovary, like the testicle, is small, ovoid in shape, and about an inch and a half in diameter. It is made up of glandular tissue and egg sacs, or *follicles*. The female has about 50,000 or more follicles in each ovary, but only about 250 of them ever

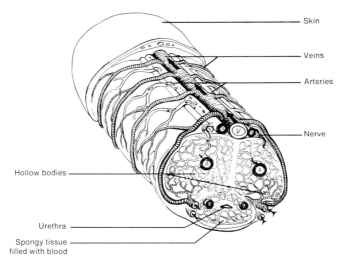

Skin

Veins

Arteries

Nerve

Hollow bodies

Urethra

Spongy tissue
filled with blood

Figure 3–4. Cross Section of Erect Penis

become active and produce an ovum, or egg. Unlike the mature male, who continuously produces sperm cells and may ejaculate two or three billion a week, the female produces only one egg about every 28 days, from about her 14th to her 45th to 50th year. At the appropriate time, a follicle wall in one of the ovaries bursts; a newly produced egg emerges and enters that ovary's Fallopian tube—a small tube that partially encircles each ovary and leads from that ovary to the *uterus* (also called the *womb*), the thick-walled, expandable organ that contains and protects the developing embryo and fetus. (For a detailed description of pregnancy, see Chapter Eleven.) This rupture of the follicle and release of the egg is called *ovulation*.

The external genitalia—the pubic mound, or *mons*, and the *vulva*, or *vestibule*— are at the base of the abdomen and between the legs. They consist of outer lips (*labia majora*) and inner lips (*labia minora*), which close the entrance to the *vagina*, the *urethra* (which in the female simply conducts urine and has no role in reproduction), and the *clitoris*. The *vagina* is a very thin-walled elastic organ which extends from the inner lips of the vulva to the *cervix*, the opening between the uterus and the vagina.[5] The clitoris, although it has no role in reproduction, is

---

[5] Just inside the entrance to the vagina is a membrane known as the *hymen*, or *maidenhead*, which may partially close the entrance to the vagina in some individuals or may be nearly absent in others. The hymen has no role in either reproduction or sexual pleasure; but if it does partially close the vaginal entrance, and if it is rather tough and has not been ruptured by active sports, by digital exploration and masturbation, or by insertion of tampons, it may act as a barrier to the insertion of the penis in copulation. Thus, initial copulations may be accompanied by a stretching or a rupture of the hymen, which can result in some bleeding and some discomfort or pain. A stubborn hymen will, of course, hinder pleasurable copulation for both the man and woman; and if, as in some rare cases, it does not give way after a few attempts, the woman should consult her doctor about the necessity for a simple and painless surgical perforation of the hymen.

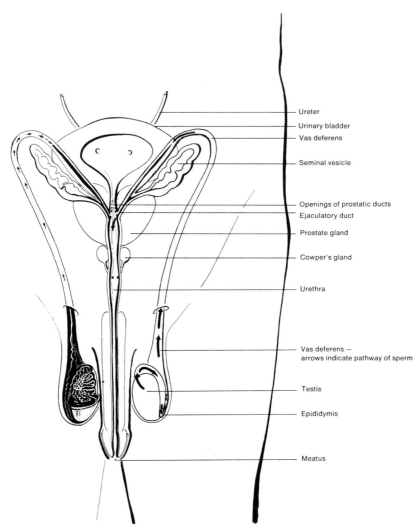

Figure 3-5. Cross Section of Male Genitalia (front view) Showing Movement of Sperm

extremely important to the sexuality of the female. It is the homologue of the male penis and consists of a shaft and a glans. It is situated just under the upper part of the labia minora, where the two lips join to form the clitoral *prepuce*, analogous to the male foreskin. Unlike the penis, the shaft of the clitoris does not hang free, however, and only the glans is exposed. With sexual excitement the clitoris becomes erect, though only the glans, usually about the size of a pea, may be felt. Like the glans of the penis, the clitoris has an abundance of nerve endings and is the most sexually excitable part of the average woman's body.

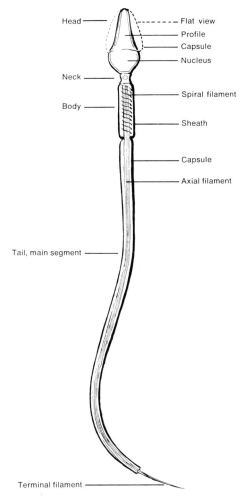

Head ———— ------- Flat view
 ———— Profile
 ———— Capsule
 ———— Nucleus

Neck ————

 ———— Spiral filament
Body ————

 ———— Sheath

 ———— Capsule

 ———— Axial filament

Tail, main segment ————

Terminal filament ————

Figure 3–6. The Sperm

During copulation, the penis is inserted into the vagina; and the male semen, containing millions of sperm cells, is ejaculated against the cervix. The sperm then make their way through the cervix, through the uterus, and into the Fallopian tubes by lashing their tails in a swimming motion. They are able to travel about an inch in 20 minutes. Fertilization, or conception, takes place in a Fallopian tube, where one of the sperm meets and fuses with the egg to form a zygote. Like the egg, the zygote is immobile and is propelled by the cilia of the Fallopian tube, by peristaltic action of the walls of the tube, and by a flow of fluid through the tube and into the uterus, the wall of which has been thickened and engorged with blood in preparation for receiving it. In the uterus, the new organism

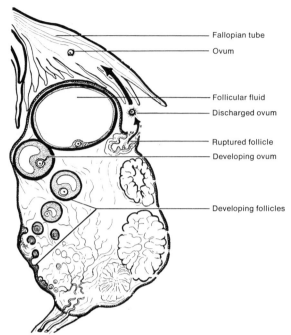

Fallopian tube
Ovum

Follicular fluid
Discharged ovum

Ruptured follicle
Developing ovum

Developing follicles

Figure 3–7. Ovulation

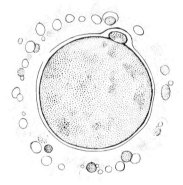

Figure 3–8. The Ovum

develops, over a period of about nine months, through the stages of embryo and fetus. If no sperm is present to encounter the egg as it floats and is propelled by the cilia through the Fallopian tube, the egg simply disintegrates.

If no fertilization occurs — that is, if copulation does not occur or if the sperm fail to reach the ovum in the Fallopian tube — blood and other material are sloughed off through the vagina. This process is called *menstruation* and usually lasts about four days. The cycle of ovulation, of engorgement of the uterine

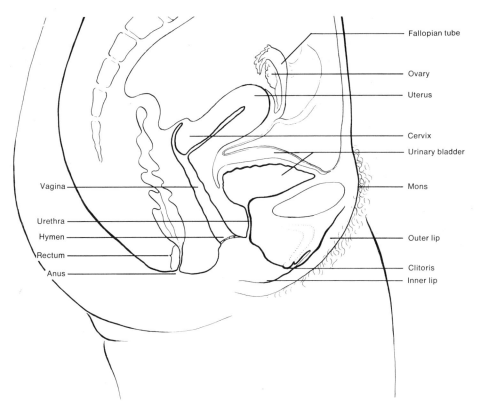

Figure 3–9. Female Urinogenital System

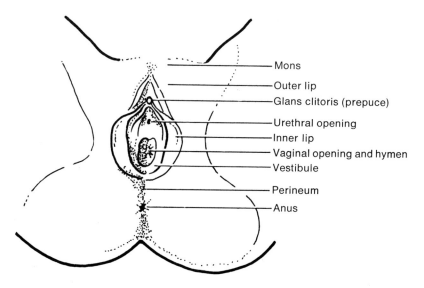

Figure 3–10. External Female Genitalia

1. Ovum ripens within the follicle. Womb lining is smooth and gradually thickening.

2. Ovulation: The ovum is released from the follicle. Womb lining thickens, preparing for possible zygote.

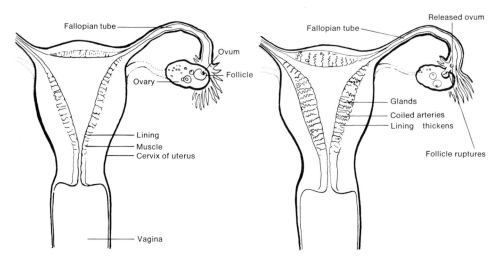

3. Ovum travels through tube.
   Lining thickens with more fluid in glands and more blood in coiled arteries.

4. Unfertilized egg disintegrates. Lining sloughs off and leaves the body.

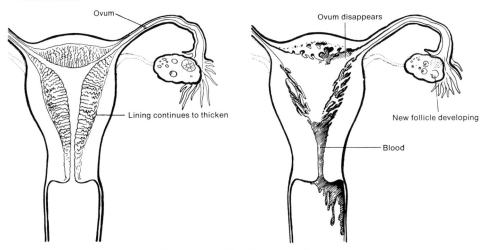

Figure 3–11. The Menstrual Cycle

wall with blood, of menstruating, and of another ovulation is called the *menstrual cycle*. This cycle repeats itself every 28 days, in the average female, although the cycle may occasionally be interrupted or delayed by factors such as fatigue, diet, hormonal factors, the pill, or emotional stress. Conception, of course, always interrupts the cycle; ovulation and menstruation cease, while the fetus develops in the uterus. (For a discussion of *parturition*, or the developments of pregnancy, as well as a more detailed description of conception—and contraception—see Chapter Eleven, *Reproduction: The Biological Basis of the Family.*)

At about age 45 to 50, in the average female in our society, ovulation and the menstrual cycle cease to occur. This cessation of ovulation and of fertility is known as the *menopause*. The menopause merely halts fertility in the female; it does not normally affect her sexuality—that is, her desire and her ability to have and enjoy sexual relations. (There is no menopausal experience for the male; the average male continues to produce sperm and to be capable of ejaculation throughout most or all of his lifetime.)

The beginning of ovulation and the menstrual cycle is known as the *menarche* and is the beginning of puberty for the female. In our society, girls experience the menarche at about 12 to 14 years. *Our* society is stressed because there is some evidence that puberty in girls may occur much earlier (at 9 or 10 years) or somewhat later (at 15 or 16 years) depending on various conditions of the society—the climate, altitude, diet, and prenatal care. The advent of ovulation and puberty is only one aspect of sexuality of the girl; she is capable of arousal and orgasm from infancy. Also, the girl may menstruate for two or three years before she is fertile—either because the ovum is not capable or because she may not have the hormonal development for implantation to occur. This is called *adolescent sterility* (Montagu, 1957).

The Three Modes of Sexual Expression

There are three possible modes of conscious sexual expression: *masturbation, petting,* and *copulation.*[6] Masturbation is erotic behavior which is *autosexual;* that is, it involves no one but the person himself. Petting is erotic behavior which involves physical but not necessarily genital contact between two (or more) individuals,[7] with stimulation either alternate or mutual. It may be either *homosexual* or *heterosexual*. Copulation is erotic behavior which involves penile-vaginal intromission. It is therefore, by definition, heterosexual, limited to two persons, and mutually stimulating. Both the masturbatory and petting modes are solely pleasure-giving, since reproduction cannot occur. However, petting often precedes copulation and accompanies copulation and may therefore be indirectly involved with reproduction. From this point of view, masturbation also is indirectly involved with reproduction inasmuch as it acquaints the person with the anatomy and physiology of erotic response, leads to the awakening of sexual interest, and normally leads to a pursuit of the other modes of petting and copulation. The average person's first acquaintance with sex is usually through masturbation.

---

[6] The so-called *nocturnal emission*, or *wet dream*, of the male is in a special category of unconscious sexual expression.

[7] Sexual behavior is not limited to activity between human beings, of course. Both petting (homosexual and heterosexual) and copulation may occur between a person and an animal—a practice that is termed *bestiality*.

Masturbation

Masturbation is the most frequent form of premarital sexual behavior in our society.[8] It is usually accomplished in the male by manipulating either the shaft or the glans of the penis until orgasm is imminent, pausing, and then resuming the manipulation until finally control is lost and orgasm occurs. Most males masturbate to orgasm rather quickly (between two and three minutes) but many prolong the pleasure for several minutes, half an hour, or even an hour or more (Kinsey, 1953, p. 163). Masturbation is usually accomplished in the female by clitoral, labial, or mons massage, although, generally, "the primary focus for sensual response in the human female's pelvis is the clitoral body" (Masters and Johnson, 1966, p. 60). Unlike the male masturbatory techniques, which are consistent in all males, the female techniques include great individual differences. In the Masters and Johnson study (p.63), no two women were observed to masturbate in identical fashion. This finding is very important to our understanding of sexual harmony in marriage. If a husband is not aware of his wife's uniquely individual requirements for sexual pleasure and orgasm (or, indeed, if the wife is unaware of these requirements or if she fails to acquaint her husband with these requirements), the wife may find little or no satisfaction in their sexual relations.

Females, like males, usually masturbate to orgasm rather quickly (the median figure is just under four minutes), and those who take longer do so deliberately to prolong erotic arousal and derive maximum enjoyment (Kinsey, 1953, p. 163). The rather widespread notion that the female is slower than the male in her orgasmic response is not consistent with Kinsey's data. This notion probably derives from the need in most females for a more adept and deliberate tactile stimulus than is necessary in the male (see pp. 69 – 72 , in this chapter). It may also derive from the apparent need in most females for more than one orgasm before their sexual fulfillment is complete.

Masturbation, as a sexual mode, is universally practiced by the males of the mammalian kingdom. (Because all female mammals except the human species are limited in their sexuality to the periods of "heat," or *estrus*, they rarely experience unfulfilled sexual needs and thus do not normally masturbate.) Most male mammals lick their genitalia for sexual pleasure. And those who are unable to accomplish this form of stimulation will find inventive methods for masturbation. For example, male porcupines have been observed straddling and rubbing against a stick, bull elephants will use their trunks to masturbate, and porpoises have been observed suspending their penises in jets of water (Ford and Beach, 1970).

Petting

Petting includes all physical contact between two or more persons which is specifically directed toward sexual arousal and which does not involve intromission

---

[8] For data, see *The Taxonomic Data on American Sexual Behavior*, in Chapter Four.

of the penis into the vagina.[9] By some definitions, petting also includes penile-vaginal penetration, so long as ejaculation does not occur. The techniques of petting are nearly unlimited and can include kissing, biting, licking, caressing, manipulating, and massaging all portions of the body. There are, of course, certain erogenous zones which generally receive the greatest attention in petting — the mouth, the neck, the breasts, the thighs, the feet, the anus, and the genitalia — but the whole body is generally responsive when there is erotic arousal.

The various petting techniques are usually acquired gradually through pre-pubertal and adolescent affectionate and sexual activity. The techniques usually evolve, with increasing experience, from hand-holding and simple kissing to deep kissing, breast contact, and genital contact. There are great differences in individual response to petting, depending upon such variables as the degree of attraction each person has for the other, the individual's biological charac-teristics and capacity, his psychological characteristics and capacity, his social expectation, his acceptance of sociosexual taboos, and his past experience. An individual might be extremely aroused by very slight physical contact with one person; with another person he may be only slightly aroused, even after pro-longed erotic stimulation. Petting may be relatively brief and casual, or it may be quite lengthy and deliberate; arousal from petting may be very minimal or may proceed to orgasm.

Petting not infrequently begins at a high level of erotic arousal and reaches orgasm within a minute or two. More often it is deliberately extended . . . It may be carried on for hours or through the whole of a night (Kinsey, 1953, p. 259).

Petting as a sexual mode is almost universal in the animal kingdom. Reptiles and birds may be observed to demonstrate the petting characteristics of crowd-ing together, grooming, and extensive tongue-to-tongue contacts.

Among most species of mammals there is . . . a great deal of sex play which never leads to coitus. They make lip-to-lip contacts and tongue-to-tongue contacts, and use their mouths to manipulate every part of the companion's body, including the genitalia . . . and repeatedly mount without, however, making any serious attempt to effect genital union. Such activity may continue for a matter of minutes, or hours, or even in some cases for days before there is any attempt at coitus (Kinsey, p. 229).

---

[9] Kinsey found that, among the college population, "in a surprising number of instances, the male genitalia was placed directly against female genitalia . . . during . . . petting . . . without any attempt to penetrate the vagina. In some instances this failure to effect actual coitus had de-pended upon the female's refusal to allow the male to go any farther; but in a larger number of instances, it had depended upon a mutual decision . . . that there should be no penetration" (1953, p. 258).

In all mammals there is great individual difference in duration of petting. Some individuals in almost all species enjoy petting for hours, whereas others limit their petting and proceed directly to copulation with little preparatory caressing, nuzzling, or fondling. "Just as in the human male, the noncoital sex play among other mammals may sometimes lead to ejaculation before coitus has been effected or even attempted" (Kinsey, p. 229).

In most petting, lower mammal and human being alike, the male directs the activity toward the female. Most females, however, reciprocate to some extent, and some females are more aggressive than the male in initiating and continuing sexual contacts.

Kinsey expressed the belief that petting is an important and even essential component of successful marital copulation. He also felt that petting is significant in educating adolescents in sociosexual relations and in assisting the young adult in his choice of a mate.

Petting provides a great deal more than experience in orgasm. It introduces the person to the physical, psychological, and social problems that are involved in making emotional adjustments to other individuals. As a socializing agent, premarital petting has . . . considerable significance (Kinsey, p. 269).

Copulation

Copulation consists of intromission of the erect penis into the vagina, after which there is an in-and-out movement of the penis which, with the friction on the glans of the penis and the warmth and pressure of the vaginal walls, leads almost inevitably to orgasm and ejaculation by the male. The movement of the penis against the sensitive external genitalia and the clitoris of the female may also arouse her to orgasm although, most often, simple copulation without preliminary petting or masturbation will not be sufficient for female orgasm. The size of the penis and the depth of its vaginal penetration have no relation to erotic response with most women, because the vagina itself has little erotic sensitivity and the responsive external areas of the female genitalia (the vulva, labia minora and majora, and clitoris) are stimulated regardless of penile size.

The duration of copulation varies from a few seconds to an hour or more, although in our society it is generally no more than five to ten minutes. The duration is almost always dependent on the male's willingness and ability to delay his orgasm, since most men will lose their erection for a varying period of time (the *refractory period*) after the initial orgasm and ejaculation while most women are capable of multiple orgasm without intervening rest periods.[10]

---

[10]The refractory period, during which the person is incapable of erotic response, is not a characteristic of the female but is universal among males. The duration of the period for the male may vary, however, from minutes to days, depending on the person's age, the degree of stimulation, and various other individual factors.

Copulation is, of course, universal among mammals, being the sexual mode for reproduction. It is also, again of course, one of the most significant pleasures in the animal experience. In the human species, particularly, in which copulation is not limited to the female estrous period, and in which the intense sexual experience can be combined with a deep emotional and affectional involvement, the pleasure and satisfaction that accompany copulation can assume monumental proportions.

A rear-entry position in copulation is used by all primates except man. Among the societies of man, the favored copulative position varies a great deal, with the crouching face-to-face position the most common (Ford and Beach, 1970). In our society, the most common position has the female supine and the male prone on top. Many other positions are practiced, and literally hundreds are possible;[11] but despite the recommendations of sexologists and marriage manuals, many people in our society believe that copulation in a position other than what the Tahitian natives call the "missionary position" would be a perversion

The Four Phases of Erotic Response

There are four phases of erotic response—*excitement, plateau, orgasm,* and *resolution*—which result from erotic stimulation and arousal. In both sexes, the end organs of touch are the chief sensory sources of erotic arousal, with no basic difference between the sexes in their responses to tactile stimulation. Other (non-tactile) senses—smell, taste, sight, and hearing—are also involved, of course, but to a lesser degree in most persons. Psychological non-sensory factors, such as attitude, interest, expectation, and specific sexual attraction, are of prime importance in sexual arousal because they can either negate or amplify a sensory stimulation.

Areas of the body capable of responding with sexual excitement are termed *erogenous zones*. The chief erogenous zone in most males is, of course, the penis, especially the corona and the frenum. The chief erogenous zone in most females is the clitoris, although the mons and the entire vestibule, especially the labia minora, are equally sensitive. All areas of the mouth—lips, tongue, and interior—are richly supplied with nerve endings and are primary erogenous zones, surpassed only by the genitalia. This is true not only in man but in all mammals. Almost all mammals tend to place their mouth on their partner's body during copulation, and mouth-to-mouth contact during petting may continue for hours (Kinsey, 1953, p. 588).

---

[11]The ancient Hindu love manual, the *Kama Sutra*, shows 30 basic positions and many more variations.

Even such large animals as the stallion, which are ill-equipped to make contacts with their mouth, keep their lips in constant motion during sexual activity and constantly attempt to nibble or bite over the surface of the body of the mare (p. 588).

It is not surprising, therefore, that in all animals "the two areas of the body which are most sensitive erotically, namely the mouth and the genitalia, should frequently be brought into direct contact" (p. 588). Oral-genital contact in which the male stimulates the labia, the vestibule, the clitoris, and the *perineum* (the area between the anus and the vulva or, in males, the base of the scrotum) of the female with his lips or tongue is known as *cunnilingus*. "Women who have experienced oral-genital stimulation report that the method is overwhelmingly pleasurable . . . both as sex foreplay and as the primary avenue to achieving orgasm" (McCary, 1967, p. 158). Oral-genital contact, in which the female stimulates the scrotum, shaft, and glans of the penis and perineum with her lips and tongue is known as *fellatio.*

The breast of both the male and female is also a primary erogenous zone for about half the population, with some individuals responding all the way to orgasm with no contact except breast stimulation (Kinsey, 1953, p. 587). The entire breast in the female is richly supplied with erogenous nerve endings; response in the male breast is usually limited to the *nipple* and the *areola,* the area immediately surrounding the nipple.

When a man's breast is stimulated by gently rolling the nipple between the thumb and finger, or by . . . oral contact . . . he quite likely will experience the same sort of sexual desire and excitement that women do from the same techniques (McCary, p. 154).

The perineum in both male and female contains a rich supply of nerve endings and may provide considerable erotic excitement. Many males, for example, respond with rapid erection to pressure on the perineum (Kinsey, 1953, p. 585). The anus is also richly supplied with nerve endings and is a primary erogenous zone to about half the population of males and females alike, some being more intensely aroused than by genital stimulation (Kinsey, pp. 585–586).

Although the genitalia, mouth, breast, perineum, and anus are chief erogenous zones, almost any area of the body surface—the ear, thigh, nape of the neck, throat, feet, fingers, toes, and even eyebrows—may also be a source of erotic excitement.

It is important to note that the vagina itself is almost devoid of nerve endings and is *not* an erogenous zone in most females. Less than 14 percent of women have tactile sensation at all in the vagina (Kinsey, p. 580). Moreover, the cervix has virtually no tactile nerve endings and is almost completely insensitive. Of course, sexual response is psychological as well as physiological, so the satisfactions derived from the pressure of deep penetration of the vagina provide erotic stimulation for some women and may even bring orgasm.

The Excitement Phase

The most obvious and significant aspect of the excitement phase in the male is the penile erection. There are two major determinants of erection: psychological stimuli, which cause the *cerebral erection;* and tactile stimuli, which cause the *reflex erection* (Kelly, 1967, p. 517; Hastings, 1963, p. 54).[12] The cerebral erection is characteristic of the male throughout childhood and adolescence and into the twenties. After this time, it begins to occur less and less frequently. The reflex erection, on the other hand, is the almost invariable response to tactile stimulation throughout most of the lifetime of the male (Kelly, 1967, p. 517). This is an extremely important point, since many males mistakenly believe that they are becoming impotent when the cerebral erection begins to occur less frequently. Genuine impotence (a physiological inability to obtain erection) is almost unknown for men in their 20s, very rare in the 30s, and occurs in only one male in twenty in the 40s. Nine in ten males are still potent at age 60, and two in three are still potent at age 70 (Kinsey, 1948, p. 236). However, most older men experience an erection more slowly and less frequently than younger men and require a few minutes or more of tactile stimulation (compared to the few seconds for young men). The older male may also experience a somewhat shorter orgasm, and he usually ejaculates with less force and about half the quantity. On the other hand, the older man will often be able to prolong the pre-orgasmic, or plateau, phase of sexual response for a considerable longer period of time than can a young man.

The most obvious and significant physiological response of the female is *vaginal lubrication*, or the "sweating" of the vaginal walls. This lubrication occurs within 10 to 30 seconds of adequate erotic stimulation (Masters and Johnson, 1966, p. 69) and is a sure sign that a female has entered the excitement stage. Conversely, the absence of vaginal lubrication is a sure sign that she has not. With the sweating of the vaginal walls, the clitoris becomes erect, the labia swell, and the inner two thirds of the vagina expands. The female body cannot be physiologically receptive to copulation until this first phase of erotic response is entered. Copulation prior to this response may be uncomfortable and even painful for the female; it is certain not to be pleasurable.

The role of psychological stimuli in effecting erotic excitement in the female varies greatly from individual to individual—in contrast to the male who can almost always be aroused by non-tactile psychological stimuli. Some females experience virtually no erotic response to non-tactile stimuli, whereas others may actually fantasy to orgasm. Psychological arousal in the female, especially when it results in the sweating of the vaginal walls, may be analogous to the cerebral erection in the male.

Other responses, which occur in the excitement phase in both sexes, include an erection of the nipples, a contraction of involuntary muscles, an increase in the pulse rate and the blood pressure, and a flushing of the body surface.

---

[12]The *morning erection* apparently fits neither of these classifications. Although it has been traditionally ascribed to the pressure of a full bladder, the cause of the morning erection is simply unknown (Hastings, 1963, pp. 57–58).

The Plateau Phase

In the plateau phase, all physiological behavior of the excitement phase continues, and some additional changes occur. In the male, the coronal ridge of the
glans enlarges even more, and the color of the glans deepens; also, a few drops
of pre-coital fluid may appear at the meatus. In the female, the outer third of
the vagina contracts, while the inner two thirds balloons even more than in the
excitement phase. The uterus becomes enlarged, and the clitoris elevates. The
labia minora change to a deeper red—a sign that orgasm will occur within a
minute or two if proper stimulation is continued.

In masturbation, petting, or copulation, the person may proceed swiftly
to orgasm, or he may prolong arousal almost indefinitely at the plateau phase
by slacking off stimulation when he enters the plateau phase, returning to the
excitement phase, and repeating stimulation until he enters the plateau phase
again. Once the orgasm phase starts, however, all control is lost. In the male,
it is more difficult to delay or otherwise control orgasm in copulation than it is
in petting or masturbation.

The Orgasm Phase

The orgasm is the climax of erotic arousal. Orgasm begins with a sensation of
suspension, or stoppage. This sensation lasts only an instant and is immediately
followed by an intense sensual awareness, which may range in degree from mild
pleasure to acute physiological shock. Physiological changes during orgasm
are quite pronounced. The pulse rate may increase from its norm of 70 to 80
beats per minute to more than double that, or 180 beats per minute.[13] Blood
pressure may double. The breathing pattern also changes markedly, becoming
deeper and faster; and in most persons, orgasm is accompanied by increasing
anoxia (shortage of oxygen) which causes the person to gulp and gasp for air.
The senses of smell, taste, hearing, sight, and feeling are temporarily diminished,
the degree of loss paralleling the intensity and the duration of the orgasm.
Involuntary neuromuscular responses consume the entire body, with muscles
rhythmically tensing and relaxing and the facial expression typically becoming
tortured (Masters and Johnson, 1966, pp. 127–140; Kinsey, 1948, pp. 567–641).

There are three major differences between the characteristics of the orgasm
in the mature male and that in the mature female:[14] (1) In the male, the orgasm

---

[13]A pulse rate of 180 is comparable to that of an athlete at the peak of his effort. The Mercury and
Gemini astronauts displayed a similar increase during orbital mishaps.

[14]The prepubertal male and female are capable of orgasm, and the male, especially, will normally
experience it during childhood in masturbating and petting. The average male child experiences
hundreds of orgasms before ejaculation finally takes place. (In prepubertal orgasm, the male is
often capable of several orgasmic responses in rapid succession.) The female prepubertal orgasmic
experience is less common and much less frequent than that of the male (see Chapter Four for
data and a discussion of the reasons). In both the male and female, the prepubertal orgasmic experience is identical physiologically (except, of course, for male ejaculation) with the mature orgasm.

is almost always accompanied by ejaculation of semen. (2) The female is often capable of a rapid return to a second and even third orgasm; the male usually is not, but must go through a refractory stage of a few minutes to several hours, depending chiefly upon his age, before he is capable of entering the excitement phase again. (3) The female is occasionally capable of a much longer orgasm than the male—as long as 20 to 60 seconds (Masters and Johnson, p. 131). The average duration of orgasm in both male and female is three to four seconds.

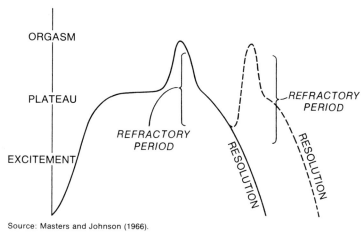

Source: Masters and Johnson (1966).

Figure 3–12. The Male Sexual Response Cycle

Masters and Johnson have laid to rest, once and for all, the myth of the "vaginal orgasm." Prior hypotheses (especially those of the Freudian persuasion) postulated that there were two types of female orgasm, the "clitoral" and the "vaginal," and that the "vaginal" orgasm was characteristic of emotional maturity. A "vaginal" orgasm was defined as one that occurs *solely* as a result of penetration of the vagina and stimulation of it and the cervix, whereas a "clitoral" orgasm was contrasted as an orgasm occurring *solely* as a result of clitoral stimulation. Masters and Johnson (1966) were unable to determine any measureable physiological difference in orgasm no matter how it was induced in their subjects and concluded that "an orgasm is an orgasm."[15] The revelation of this fallacy is a matter of some importance since countless women (and their marriages) have been disturbed because they thought that by their preference for clitoral stimulation, they were sexually immature. On the contrary, a "vaginal" orgasm, *per se*, amounts to a biological impossibility for most women.

---

[15]As we have noted, the vagina is almost devoid of the necessary nerve endings for erotic response, although in many women psychological variables (and referred sensations) make vaginal penetration especially stimulating and satisfying, and some individuals may require penetration for orgasm. (It is possible, of course, even to *fantasy* to orgasm.) For further discussion, see Masters and Johnson, 1966, p. 66; Brown, 1966, pp. 139–147; Clark, 1970; and Belliveau and Richter, 1970.

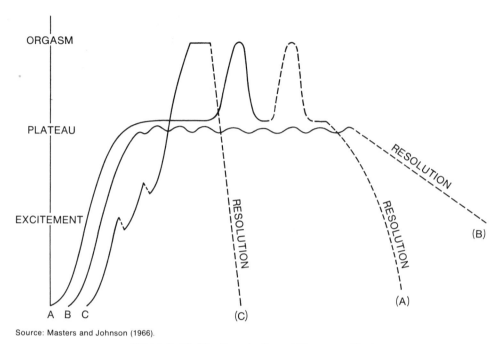

ORGASM

PLATEAU

EXCITEMENT

RESOLUTION

RESOLUTION

RESOLUTION

RESOLUTION

A B C

(C)

(A)

(B)

Source: Masters and Johnson (1966).

Figure 3–13. The Female Sexual Response Cycle

Capacity for orgasm and need for orgasm are both highly idiosyncratic, and very little is known about the long-range function that orgasm serves. The short-range function of the orgasm is quite clear: Once the plateau level of erotic arousal has been reached, the importance of the orgasm in returning the person to a normal state is unquestionable. For example, with one female in the Masters and Johnson study (p. 119), the plateau stage was repeatedly obtained for a period of six hours, after which no sexual stimulation was permitted for another period of six hours. The subject complained of "pelvic fullness, pressure, cramping, moments of true pain, and a persistent, severe, low backache." The uterus was enlarged to two to three times its unstimulated size, the walls of the vagina were engorged with blood, and the labia were swollen to two or three times their normal size. After the termination of the observation period, the subject masturbated to orgasm and the physical distress disappeared immediately. The physiological symptoms disappeared within ten minutes.

Speculation about the long-range function of the orgasm ranges from the rather questionable hypothesis that abstaining from orgasm will bring all manner of physical and spiritual reward (the doctrine of *sublimation*) to the hypothesis that failing to experience a patterned frequency of orgasm will bring all manner of personality disintegration and leave the person a neurotic wreck. The truth probably lies somewhere in between. The Kinsey data (1948) indicate that the male, particularly, establishes a pattern of frequency of orgasm with puberty, and that this pattern is maintained throughout his life whether he is married, unmarried, separated from his wife, or whatever his circumstances. Although the available demographic data on the female sexual behavior (Kinsey, 1953) indicate that women are not nearly so regular and persistent in their pattern of orgasmic experience as men in our society, many observers, from the *Kama Sutra* to Masters and Johnson, have suggested that the orgasm is equally important to the female. This indicates the importance, in marriage, of the two persons' meeting one another's sexual needs and patterns. Particularly, if the wife fails to recognize and cooperate with the husband's consistent orgasmic pattern, it may be inferred from the Kinsey data that the husband will fulfill his own particular pattern anyway, presumably through either masturbation or extramarital copulation.

A sidelight on the grudging acceptance of sexuality in our society is the curious folklore that orgasm is tiring or depressing, or that the person feels dejected after orgasm. This is nonsense. There is no psychological theory that could reconcile an alleged universal depression, sadness, or fatigue after orgasm with the strong need to experience orgasm. The average person feels content after orgasm. The person who does feel depressed or sad is reacting, not to the orgasm itself but to an anxiety occasioned by guilt feelings about his sexuality. If he thinks sex is wrong, dirty, sinful, or immoral, he might well feel depressed after copulation, petting, or masturbation. Obviously, such anxiety is going to be much more common with the non-culturally accepted behaviors of masturbation and of illicit (non-marital) petting and copulation than with petting or copulation within marriage, which, for the most part, is culturally accepted.

The Resolution Phase

In the resolution phase, the person returns to normal functioning. Pulse rate, blood pressure, breathing, and muscle tension all revert to their pre-excitement characteristics. The clitoris returns to its unstimulated size and position, and the erection of the penis subsides. After effects of orgasm usually include profound well-being, tranquility, and contentment, with the person often falling into brief but deep sleep. The sense of euphoria often persists for some time after the orgasm.

The female typically is able to experience another orgasm immediately if stimulation is resumed. In fact, the typical female will not be satiated until she *has* experienced more than one orgasm.

The human female frequently is not content with one orgasmic experience during episodes of automanipulation involving the clitoral body. If there is no psychosocial distraction to repress sexual tensions, many well-adjusted women enjoy a minimum of three or four orgasmic experiences before they reach apparent satiation . . . (Masters and Johnson, 1966, p. 65).

This important finding of Masters and Johnson is obviously extremely significant for understanding sexual interaction and satisfaction in marriage.

The male, on the other hand, must always go through a refractory period
before he is again physiologically capable of the sequence of erotic responses
beginning with the excitement phase. The refractory period may be very short—
a few minutes—but is usually an hour or more in males over age thirty. The
resolution phase almost always immediately follows the orgasm in the male.
However, if the plateau stage was deliberately prolonged, with orgasm delayed,
the erection tends to be maintained for some time after orgasm (Masters and
Johnson, p. 185). In the young male (under 25), the experiencing of very short
refractory periods and two or more orgasms before entering the resolution
phase is not unusual; it becomes rare over this age. (For precise data, see
Taxonomic Data on American Sexual Behavior, in Chapter Four.)

Male–Female Psychological Differences in Erotic Interest and Arousal

Although the biological factors of erotic response are nearly identical for males
and females, there is a considerable difference between males and females in
their psychological response to erotic stimuli. In lower animals, this difference
is apparently a function of hormonal factors and is species-wide. Among both
domestic and wild animals, males are characteristically interested in looking at
and attending to the female genitalia and in viewing the copulation of others,
whereas females typically are not. Similarly, during copulation, the male is
usually perceptually focused upon sexual responses, whereas the female's attention is easily diverted.

> . . . *cheese crumbs spread in front of a copulating pair of rats may distract the female
> but not the male. A mouse running in front of a copulating pair of cats may distract the
> female but not the male. When cattle are interrupted during coitus, it is the cow that is
> more likely to be disturbed while the bull may try to continue* (Kinsey, 1953, p. 669).

In man, similar differences in male-female psychological responses to erotic
stimuli may be observed. In our own society, for example, Kinsey (pp. 651–
683) found that while more than half the male population was stimulated to the
excitement phase of erotic response by viewing a picture of a nude female, and
fully one third were both regularly and considerably aroused simply by "girl-
watching," only about one sixth of the females were aroused simply by looking
at males and only about one in ten were aroused to the excitement phase by
viewing a picture of a nude male. He found, further, that almost all males but
very few females were stimulated by observing the genitalia of the opposite

sex. Indeed, most males were aroused by viewing their own genitalia, which was true of only about one in ten females in Kinsey's sample. Most males in the Kinsey study were also aroused by imagining sexual activity (and the higher the educational level of the male, the richer his sexual fantasy life), whereas fully one third of females had no erotic thoughts at all.

The male is aroused by observing his potential sexual partner, as most females are not . . . The male is aroused by anticipating new types of experience, new types of sexual partners . . . new opportunities to experiment with new techniques . . . None of these factors have much significance for the average female (Kinsey, p. 683).

In short, males in our society think and talk more about sex, are more promiscuous both in their attentions and their actions, and are more responsive to the idea of sex in all its various artifacts than females.[16] Almost all pornography (of which there is a vast amount) has been written for male consumption by other males. "In all the published material there are probably not more than two or three documents that were actually written by females" (Kinsey, p. 672).

As a result of his study more than a generation ago, Kinsey came to the conclusion that, like the lower animals, human males and females were *inherently* different in their response to psychological erotic stimuli—although he also pointed out that these innate differences were enhanced or diminished by a society's sexual attitudes and, thus, by societal conditioning. He was apparently only partially right; for intercultural sexual studies and the more precise physiological and psychological experiments that have followed his taxonomic research now suggest that these male-female differences are entirely cultural in origin.

---

[16] Kinsey, 1953. It must be borne in mind, of course, that we are speaking of the average male and female in our society, in terms of actuarial expectations; this tells us nothing about the characteristics of any given individual. There is a wide range of sexuality, both among males and females; and any specific female may be much more ardent than any specific male, responding to a wider variety of psychological stimuli, with a greater intensity, a greater preoccupation, and a greater interest. (For data, see Chapter Four.)

For example, a very significant study at the University of Hamburg (Schmidt and Sigusch, 1970) found that, contrary to the Kinsey hypothesis, males and females are *not* innately different in their erotic responses to viewing sexual pictures. In a carefully controlled experiment, men and women students were matched in terms of marital status, church denomination and attendance, political attitudes, attitudes toward premarital copulation, and copulatory experience. They were then shown slides and movies depicting six sexual themes: masturbation to orgasm, both male and female; petting, both with and without orgasm; and copulation, both with and without fellatio and cunnilingus. The research found no significant differences in erotic response between the group of males and the group of females.[17] In addition, the study found that a large percentage of the women (about 40 percent) even showed a slightly more intense sexual arousal than did the average man — a complete reversal of the Kinsey expectation. And as an example of a recent intercultural study, Marshall (1971) found that in Mangaia (an island of the Polynesian group), the experiencing of orgasm with copulation is universal among women, with frigidity an unknown concept. Moreover, the female *and* the male expectation is that the female will experience orgasm at least three times during copulation before the male ejaculates. In other words, the female is just as sexually responsive as the male in the Mangaian society.[18] Marshall also found that the Mangaian female was fully as erotically interested as the male.

These recent data suggest that the relative antisexuality of females in our society occurs only because, from childhood, the female is treated differently from the male in regard to *expectations* for erotic response. She is reared to be relatively sexually aloof; consequently, the average female rarely or never responds to psychological sexual stimuli. (For further data, see *Influence of Social Class upon Individual Sexual Behavior*, in Chapter Four.)

The average male in our society has been bitterly disappointed, depressed, puzzled, and hurt by his wife's lack of interest in sex. His adolescent dreams of a sexually fulfilling marriage have been shattered by the reality of his wife's apathetic or negative attitudes toward sex. The average female, on the other hand, has been outraged, bewildered, and herself hurt at her husband's preoccupation with sexuality and with feminine beauty and sexuality in its own right — having no comparable experience of her own. Not a few wives think of this male psychological involvement with sexuality as a kind of infidelity. Even the Victorian concept that the wife merely "submits" while the husband copulates is still perseverated among the lower and lower-middle classes.[19] Among

---

[17]Subjects were rated in terms of their physio-sexual reaction during the experiment, their subjective verbal responses immediately after and 24 hours after viewing the films, and their sexual behavior and reactions during the 24 hours following the experiment.

[18]It is interesting to note again that Masters and Johnson's research (1966) corroborated this need for multiple orgasms among sexually responsive women in our society.

[19]Rainwater (1964), for example, found that the poverty culture believes that women have no sexual desire at all. He hypothesizes that inasmuch as lower and lower-middle class husbands and wives tend to separate their work and recreational activities from those of their partner, this segregation and lack of mutuality extend to their sexual relations as well.

the middle class as well, according to Masters and Johnson (1970), more than half of marriages are characterized by sexual dysfunction.

Still, it must be pointed out that the Kinsey data regarding the sexual dis- interest of American females are now nearly 20 years old, and there have been gradual but considerable changes in sexual attitudes in our society during this time. These changes are reflected both in popular media and entertainment and in professional literature. What effect these changes have had on the sexual attitudes and responses of the individual female, or what percentage of females have been affected, we simply cannot say, given the limited data available. There are some indications, however, at least in some areas of the country, that the present young generation of girls, for example, are somewhat freer and more responsive sexually than were their mothers at the same age. Kinsey demon- strated that sweeping sexual changes occurred among women in the 1920s and 1930s; it is conceivable that although no further changes were demonstrated to occur in the era between the 1930s and the mid-1960s, a "sexual revolution" may again be changing female attitudes and responses in the post-pill decade of the 1970s. (We shall explore this question *Sexual Behavior in the '70s — A Sexual Revolution?* in Chapter Four.)

Fetishism

Fetishism is a complex in which the person's erotic arousal is focused on some specific object that represents to him the ideal or personification of sexual attraction.

Each individual has a private cluster of stimuli that possess a greater response value for him than the same stimuli do for others. Some of these may be quite specific . . . and the absence of them may cause the person to have reduced or no arousal feelings irrespec- tive of how sexually attractive the same person might be to another observer with different stimuli values (Hastings, 1963, p. 17).

Fetishism occurs on a continuum from very slight emotional involvement to very great, even compulsive emotional involvement with particular erotically arousing psychological stimuli. These stimuli may range from a focus of sexual interest on a *particular anatomical feature* of a person — for example, the female breast — to a focus upon a *representation* of these features — photographs or draw- ings — to a *displacement* of the focus onto normally non-sexual objects — for example, clothing.

The displacement of sexual focus onto a symbolic sexual object, when that focus and the involvement is so compulsive that the person is impotent in its absence, may be characterized as an aberration. The less compulsive forms of fetishism are quite common — especially in males. Most males are fetishists to some extent in their capacity for response to symbolic (but not displaced) repre- sentations of sexuality and to particular anatomical features. A response to symbolic representations is not so common among females, but many or even most females will probably respond in some degree to particular anatomical features of the male.

Objects that are typically experienced in *displacement* of sexual interest range from seemingly sexless items like shoes or gloves or certain fabrics to more specifically intimate objects like lingerie or underwear. Objects that are most typically experienced as *representations* of sexually arousing anatomical features are photographs or drawings depicting nudity. An aspect of an involvement with representative fetish objects is the capacity of some males to be more readily sexually aroused when the female is partially clothed in a particular way. For example, erotic arousal may be quicker and more pleasurable if the female is nude except for hose and garter belt or if she is wearing a filmy negligee. There are, of course, many magazines that specialize in publishing pictures of women clothed for typical fetishist tastes.

The focus of most persons on particular anatomical features—their "private cluster of stimuli"—is extremely common and almost universal. Most males in our society are extremely erotically responsive to the female breast—bare, partially concealed, or clothed; and many males are aroused by legs, bare or sheathed in nylon or net, and are strongly responsive to certain nuances of the female leg, like contour and texture. There are no available data on the response of females in our society to specific male features, but it is likely that females, like males, form their cluster of stimuli around the structure, line, texture, and general attractiveness of the male body. Specific features that will interest and arouse both sexes include the complexion, hair, neck, mouth, eyes, arms, feet, shoulders, hands, voice, and muscular definition or line and shape of the limbs and torso.

In most societies the beauty of the female receives considerably more attention than the handsomeness of the male. The attractiveness of the male usually depends less upon specific anatomical features and more upon his skills and abilities and social status.

Societies vary widely in the aspects of the female that they find attractive and erotically arousing, although the majority of societies prefer plump females to thin ones, and broad hips to narrow hips (Ford and Beach, 1970). The ideal of feminine sexual attraction in our society, along with regular features, emphasizes youth, long legs, slender figure, large conical or hemispherical breasts, and oval faces. Curiously, at least from our point of view, the size and shape of the breast are considered unimportant in most societies; and in societies that *do* focus attention on the breast, the admired shapes vary widely, from small and upright to long and pendulous (Ford and Beach). For centuries, the Oriental cultures have considered large breasts an *anti*-erotic feature. (The Japanese feel that the nape of the neck is especially important as an object of erotic stimulation, and the kimono was designed accordingly.)

Sexual Dysfunction

The inability to function sexually may be considered either in terms of *infertility*, the temporary inability to produce viable sperm or eggs,[20] or in terms of *impotence* in the male and *frigidity* in the female, neither of which is necessarily related to infertility. Both frigidity and impotence refer to an inability to proceed through the excitement and plateau phases of erotic response to orgasm. (For a discussion of the infertility aspect of sexual dysfunction, see Chapter Eleven.)

Impotence

The impotent male is one who does not experience an erection, although he may demonstrate all the other characteristics of the four phases of erotic response. Without erection, of course, he cannot copulate. Fortunately, true impotence is so rare that an eminent sexologist has stated that he has never encountered it in his practice (Hastings, 1963, p. 16). Almost all impotence occurs because of temporary psychological factors (Kinsey, 1948; Hastings, 1963; Masters and Johnson, 1966). Physiological or anatomical determinants of impotence, such as organic anomaly, injury, or disease, are possible, of course. Also, such factors as hormone deficiency, poor nutrition, fatigue, alcohol,[21] or drugs can cause temporary impotence (Hastings, pp. 43–67). In general, however, impotence may become a problem only with (1) ignorance or misinformation about the physiological characteristics of erection, or (2) a deep-seated disinclination to accept or participate in an intimate sociosexual relation.

Many males are woefully ignorant or misinformed about the nature of the erection and mistakenly believe that they are temporarily impotent when the cerebral erection does not occur. But the erection is involuntary and if psychic stimulation does not bring about a cerebral erection, tactile stimulation will

---

[20] If infertility is permanent, it is termed *sterility*.

[21] A small amount of alcohol usually acts as a psychological relaxant and thus has a salutary effect upon the erectile functioning of the average male; too much alcohol, however, will render him temporarily impotent — as many have discovered to their chagrin and dismay.

bring about a *reflex* erection unless there is a strong psychological disinclination.

The reasons for psychological disinclination are many. A male's generalized anxiety or tension about the possibility of interruption or discovery, apprehension that he might not *get* an erection, fear of displeasing the female, or fear of conception or disease may all impede the erection. Culturally conditioned feelings of guilt or shame about sex or copulation may also be involved. It is also possible that the male may require a type of erotic stimulation which he is reluctant to suggest or which his partner is reluctant to provide, or that he may have fetish needs that are not present in the partner or in the situation.

Other possible reasons for a male's impotence include hostility or indifference toward his partner, an insecurity and a shyness that also hinder his effectiveness in other sociosexual relations, or an unusual attachment to his mother (or to another older female), which makes him feel disloyal. Also, an impotent male may have primarily homosexual interests, so that he is impotent with females but not with males. Very rarely, he may be impotent with both males and females but quite potent autosexually.

Frigidity

Unlike impotence, frigidity is very common in our society, with fully one fourth of the married female population never having experienced orgasm by age 25, and as many as one in ten *never* experiencing it at any time during their married lives.[22] Kroger and Freed (1950) find that "frigidity is one of the most common problems in gynecology. Gynecologists and psychiatrists, especially, are aware that perhaps 75 percent of all women derive little or no pleasure from the sexual act.[23] Many women not only experience no pleasure but actually suffer pain and revulsion."

Anatomical anomalies are possible causes of permanent frigidity, but they are almost unknown. Physiological causes of permanent frigidity—hormone deficiencies, poor nutrition, fatigue, alcohol, or drugs—are also rare (Hastings, 1963, pp. 77–96). As with impotence, frigidity usually occurs (1) because of ignorance or misinformation about the anatomical and physiological characteristics of erotic arousal and orgasm or (2) because of a deep-seated disinclination in the female to accept her sexual nature, or the sexual nature of the male, or to participate in a sociosexual relation with the male.

The female may be frigid simply because she is ignorant of the details of her own erotic anatomy and physiology. In most women, simple copulation, with no specific mons, vestibule, labial, or clitoral stimulation, is inadequate to produce either pleasure or orgasm and may quite frequently be uncomfortable, unpleasant, or even painful. If both she and the male are unaware of this simple fact, she may be "frigid." Further, Masters and Johnson (1966, pp. 63–67) found that adequate and proper erotic stimulation is apparently a matter of great individual difference in the female. Thus, even the most experienced male may

---

[22] For statistics and references, see *Taxonomic Data on American Sexual Behavior*, in Chapter Four.
[23] Presumably, the writers refer to copulation.

be unable to relate effectively to the female in copulative behavior if she herself is unaware of the precise requirements for her own erotic arousal and is unable to communicate these requirements to the male.

Many professional observers have advocated a training procedure in which the woman first experiences orgasm through her own manual manipulation, then experiences orgasm with the cooperation of her husband, utilizing the same technique, and finally experiences orgasm through copulation (Hastings, 1963; Calderone, 1960; Ellis, 1960; Clark, 1967; Kelly, 1967; Brown, 1966; Masters and Johnson, 1966).

Having accomplished the desired threshold lowering by self-stimulation, she may then enlist the husband's cooperation to accomplish the same end through manual stimulation by him, subsequently attempting to achieve the same results with coitus. Apparently once the desired response pattern has been achieved, it tends to remain a stable one (Hastings, 1963, p. 93).[24]

Frigidity is more often involved with various other psychological factors than it is with simple ignorance or misinformation. When the female dreads or avoids copulation, either deliberately or unconsciously, the basis for this dread or avoidance is usually not specifically linked to the erotic experience itself. Instead, the basic problem is usually her attitude toward herself, toward the male, or toward sex in general.

Unlike the male, the female may participate in copulation without erotic arousal.[25] If she does, however, she is almost certain to develop an avoidance response. This will inevitably be apparent to the male; and each may then come to feel devalued, angry, and resentful and may lose interest in sexual participation.

A female may be frigid because she is so emotionally immature or has such an inadequate personality that cooperating with another person, even for her own pleasure, is beyond her capability. She might find herself unable to participate in the sociosexual interaction with the abandon, freedom, relaxation, or unselfconsciousness necessary for deep erotic arousal, especially if this would give another person pleasure. Her selfish need to dominate, to demonstrate independence, might cause her to feel that participating in the total involvement of orgasm would render her too vulnerable.

Frigidity may occur if the female is unaware of her anatomical sources of erotic response and is also reluctant to experiment with these sources, either autosexually or heterosexually, because of culturally induced attitudes that any sexual behavior except penile-vaginal intromission is perverted, immoral, or even sinful. Or she may know what stimulus would bring her to orgasm, yet be

---

[24] For a more detailed resume of recent findings and a discussion of training procedures in the treatment of frigidity, see Daniel C. Brown, "Female Orgasm and Sexual Inadequacy" in Brecher and Brecher (1966).

[25] The male must have an erection in order to copulate and so *must* be in the excitement phase of erotic response. The female, of course, need not be aroused at all.

reluctant to suggest it to the male. Or she may have conscious or unconscious fetishes that are not being fulfilled.

Culturally conditioned feelings of guilt or shame about sex are probably the most frequent sources of frigidity; the female may consciously or unconsciously feel that enjoying sexual participation is self-devaluating or shameful. She may be quite alarmed, consciously or unconsciously, at the first stirring of erotic sensations and may therefore be reluctant to experience their "base" nature. Or she may be romantically in love and, therefore, feel that sex would "spoil it." This attitude is the societal persuasion with which many females are reared in our society. They are constantly warned to resist the advances of the male, and their conditioning may persist after marriage.

She may also, of course, be sexually inhibited with some specific male because she feels that he does not love her, that he is just exploiting her, or that she does not love him. She may have a deep-seated, conscious or unconscious attachment to her father, or another older male, which causes her to feel disloyal in giving herself to another man. Or she may be hostile toward all males, consciously or unconsciously; and by maintaining control and not yielding to the tumultuous flood of the intense, uncontrollable feelings in orgasm, she can remain untouched, detached, disdainful, and remote. By not having orgasm she is demonstrating her innate resentment and establishing her independence: She doesn't need the male the way he needs her; she is strong where he is weak.

A woman may be frigid in premarital copulation particularly because she fears the possible consequences: anticipated guilt feelings, anticipated rejection by the male after copulation (the destruction of the romantic image), anticipated social damage to her reputation, the danger of venereal disease, or the danger of conception. Or, with the circumstances under which premarital copulation often occurs, she may fear a sudden, disastrous interruption.

Homosexuality is less common in the female than in the male,[26] but a woman may be frigid with males and not with females. Or, very rarely, she may be frigid with both males and females but perfectly responsive autosexually.

Treatment of Sexual Dysfunction

Laymen and professionals alike have assumed until recently that sexual difficulties in marriage were usually symptoms of deep-seated psychological problems and were resolvable, if at all, only through lengthy psychotherapeutic treatment. However, Masters and Johnson found in their eleven-year definitive study of sexual inadequacy (*Human Sexual Inadequacy*, 1970) that "sociocultural deprivation and ignorance of sexual physiology, rather than psychiatric or medical illness, constitute the etiological background for most sexual dysfunction" (p. 21). In short, misinformation and ignorance about the physiological and psychological aspects of sexuality form the bases of most sexual difficulties,

---

[26] See *Taxonomic Data on American Sexual Behavior*, in Chapter Four.

and these difficulties may be resolved rather quickly and easily with well-motivated subjects. Masters and Johnson found that most of the married couples who came to their clinic responded very satisfactorily within a short, two-week period of treatment.[27]

Their treatment program consisted of helping the couple arrive at (1) an understanding of their own and each other's sexual anatomy, physiology, and psychology, and (2) a mutual understanding of each other's attitudes and feelings about sex and about each other. In addition, they devised specific sexual techniques for resolving certain common sexual problems, such as temporary impotence and premature ejaculation in the male and failure to respond erotically or to reach orgasm in the female.

In treating their clients, Masters and Johnson found that, for males and females alike, one of the most damaging barriers to an individual's sexual adjustment is his assumption of a *spectator role.*

Instead of getting involved, instead of forgetting everything else and letting sexual arousal happen naturally, this person mentally sets himself apart and observes his own responses (Belliveau and Richter, 1970, p. 80).

Usually, a person will assume this spectator role because he is afraid of failing sexually. Ironically, this fear itself can block erotic response. One of the most important steps, then, in resolving sexual dysfunction is that of removing the pressure to perform, or produce, or achieve sexually. These concepts, so endemic to our culture, are very destructive to the fabric of harmonious and rewarding sexual interaction. For example, the wife who compliments her husband's sexual "performance" may by her well-meant gesture impede it instead; for this gesture shifts the emphasis in their sexual interaction from spontaneous natural happening to a kind of formal event involving standards or tests of proficiency and achievement.

With the male, fear of failing — either to experience erection in the first place or to satisfy the female once he does — is apparently the chief cause of temporary impotence. Every man will have the experience of not having an erection just when it would be most opportune that he should. If he then begins to worry that he is impotent, the worry itself can impede the possibility of an erection at that moment as well as in the future.[28] A pattern of sexual dysfunction may then be established. The solution, of course, is for him to reverse the pattern by relaxing, forgetting the unnecessary concern, taking his time and employing tactile stimuli, letting his partner guide him as to what pleases her, and, finally, simply

---

[27] For precise data regarding percentage of change in various categories, together with a description of the treatment procedures, see Masters and Johnson, 1970, and Belliveau and Richter, 1970.

[28] This pattern is often extremely destructive to the self-image. Masters estimates, for example, that "about 20 percent of impotent males attempt suicide before they reach 35" (in *Vogue,* August 15, 1971, p. 89).

enjoying himself. He may do this if he understands the naturalness and inevitability of occasional erectile failure (as well as the naturalness and inevitability of the erection when it does occur), and the importance of not being concerned about it.

Other [sexual] therapy has usually been directed at teaching the individual to do something . . . We insist he doesn't have to do *anything! All we really do is remove him from the spectator role first—we're banking on mother nature. We let her run the show. Nobody really appreciated that sex is a natural function until we went into the laboratory and found it out. We had no concept of this either. We always thought we should be teaching something. It just isn't so. A man is born with the ability to achieve an erection. The first time he had one he didn't think about it; he found himself with it.*[29]

Another of Masters and Johnson's discoveries regarding male sexual dysfunction was a technique for resolving the problem of premature ejaculation—the single most common male complaint. This technique for achieving ejaculatory control is simple, easily learned, and effective. If the penis is squeezed with considerable pressure for 3–4 seconds—with the thumb on the frenum, the forefinger on the glans just ahead of the coronal ridge, and the middle finger on the shaft just behind the coronal ridge—the male will immediately lose his urge to ejaculate. He will also temporarily lose 10–30 percent of his erection. After a few moments, penile stimulation can be resumed, and the full erection will return. Then the squeeze technique can be employed again when orgasm again becomes imminent. In this way, ejaculation can be delayed for a half hour to an hour or more.

Regarding female sexual dysfunction, the Masters and Johnson study found that their clients were most often blocked from orgasm by their fears that they are not attractive enough or that something is wrong with their sexual technique or responses. This problem among females parallels the problem of temporary impotence in the male brought on by fear of impotence or worry about occasional erectile failure. The study found, further, that very often the husbands of wives who are troubled by blocked sexuality contribute to the problem instead of relieving it.

Our cultural demand on the male to "do something" makes him feel responsible for her non-orgasmic state. He asks himself why he can't satisfy her and inevitably worries so much about his own performance that he can't allow himself the intensely pleasureable personal involvement that would lead to climax for his wife (Belliveau and Richter, 1970, p. 82).

The female is in a somewhat different situation from the male in that she has probably not had the masturbatory experience of erotic arousal and orgasm that

---

[29] Dr. Masters, as quoted in Belliveau and Richter, 1970, p. 81.

he has had, and so she may not know herself what sexual stimulation she finds pleasureable. (For data in this regard, see Chapter Four.) Furthermore, unlike the impotent male, the female may copulate without even entering the first stage of erotic arousal. This very important female characteristic may lead to a reinforcement of her feelings of sexual disinclination, since copulating without erotic arousal may be uncomfortable, perhaps painful, and probably boring.

According to the Masters and Johnson research, the most effective solution to the problem of frigidity among females (and in almost all other problems of sexual dysfunction) is a thorough understanding by both the male and female of their physiological and psychological responses to sexual stimuli, experimentation to discover the specific female's response pattern (what arouses and pleases her), and a relaxed, loving, and pleasureable approach to sexual encounters.

What about Venereal Disease?

Venereal (sexually related) *disease*, or *VD*, is an increasingly serious problem in this country. In fact, the two major venereal diseases of *gonorrhea* and *syphilis* are now, after the common cold, the chief infectious diseases in the United States. After remaining at a steady rate for decades, the incidence of gonorrhea

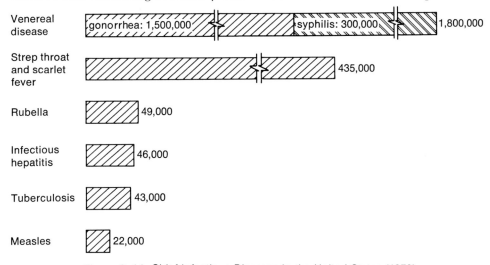

Figure 3–14. Chief Infectious Diseases in the United States (1970)

Sources: The American Social Health Association, 1971; U. S. Bureau of the Census, Department of Public Health, 1971.

began to climb in the 1960s at an annual rate of 15 percent, to reach an estimated 1.5 million new cases during 1970. Similarly, the incidence of syphilis, after declining from 1965 to 1969, increased nearly 9 percent during 1970, to an estimated 300,000 new cases (The American Social Health Association, 1971; Kaye, 1971). Experts in communicable disease warn that gonorrhea has now passed epidemic proportions to become a national pandemic. If the present trend continues, by 1980 one in every two high school students will have contracted gonorrhea (Public Health Services Center for Disease Control, 1971). Even now, teenagers in many of the major cities of the United States have a one-in-five chance of contracting gonorrhea before being graduated from high school (Osborne, 1970).[30]

No one knows why VD is rising at such an alarming rate after a long period of remaining fairly steady, but several reasons may be hypothesized. Chief among them is probably our society's new sexual permissiveness, which is reflected in a higher incidence of premarital copulation;[31] while a second major contributing factor is probably the contraceptive pill, which has largely replaced the prophylactic condom as a contraceptive and which has contributed, as well, to the changing societal attitudes toward sexuality.

Another probable reason for the growth of VD is the fact that the diseases are often very difficult to detect. A blood test for gonorrhea has yet to be developed, and fully 80 percent of women who are infected with gonorrhea show no symptoms, although they are highly infectious (Public Health Services Center for Disease Control, 1971). Similarly, most people, men and women alike, have no easily recognizable symptoms in the infectious stages of syphilis, and the disease often escapes detection unless a specific blood test for syphilis is administered. With gonorrhea, treatment is a problem as well, since virulent penicillin-resistant strains of the disease have recently developed, and fully 10 percent of new cases do not respond to penicillin treatment (Public Health Services Center for Disease Control, 1971).

Still another probable cause for the high incidence of VD is the reluctance of private physicians to report treated cases of the diseases to public-health officials. Although physicians are required by law to report all cases of VD so that public-health personnel can trace a patient's sexual contacts and limit the spread of the disease, only about one in nine privately treated cases are actually reported (The American Social Health Association, 1971). This reluctance among some doctors to deal openly with the problem of venereal disease reflects, of course, our society's general attitude of shame and squeamishness about the subject of VD. And this attitude, together with the lamentable ignorance of most people about venereal diseases, contributes to the rising incidence by making many infected persons either unaware that they are infected or unwilling to seek medical help.

---

[30] VD is primarily a disease of the young (and sexually active); most cases occur in persons 15 to 24 years of age (Kaye, 1971). Despite the commonly held belief that prostitution is a chief cause for the incidence of VD, public-health officials find that sources of the disease are much more likely to be acquaintances or casual pickups. For example, less than 2 percent of VD infections treated in clinics in California have been traced to prostitute contact (Ketterer, 1971, private communication). Nevertheless, 10 to 33 percent of prostitutes have VD; and since the chances of a client picking up VD from an infectious person are about 50-50, the likelihood of contracting VD from a prostitute is 5 to 16 percent (Kaye, 1971). Homosexuality is also often blamed for the spread of VD; but homosexual sources of the diseases account for only 12 to 18 percent of infectious syphilis among males and about 3 percent of gonorrhea, and the incidence of VD among females is rarely the result of homosexual contact (Ketterer, 1971).

[31] See *Sexual Behavior in the '70s—A Sexual Revolution?* in Chapter Four.

Although many public and private groups have attempted to institute widespread public-information campaigns about the problem of VD, their efforts have been seriously limited by the taboo nature of the topic. To speak openly about preventive measures, symptoms, and treatment for VD is often impolitic; for in the minds of the public and of many public officials, such a frank acknowledgment of the problem would seem to imply an acceptance of the behavior (premarital and extramarital sexual contacts — heterosexual and homosexual) that is the source of the infections. As a result, there is a serious lack of public funds for disseminating knowledge about venereal disease.

It is important to emphasize that both gonorrhea and syphilis may usually be cured quickly with prompt diagnosis and treatment and that most cities have free public-health clinics where the patient is treated efficiently and with the utmost discretion. Public-health officials (and most private physicians as well) are interested solely in curing and controlling the VD, and they take no moral position regarding its acquisition. Any moralizing on their part, or any violation of the trust and privacy of the patient, would make their task of combatting venereal infections virtually impossible.

It is also important to emphasize (1) that there is no effective home treatment for VD; (2) that once tissue damage occurs it is irreversable, so early diagnosis and treatment is important; (3) that although urethral gonorrhea in males is usually unmistakable, 80 percent of infected women have no gonorrheal symptoms and half of all persons with syphilis will have no easily recognizable symptoms for several years (until the disease enters its final and crippling stage); (4) that contracting and then being cured of syphilis or gonorrhea does not provide immunity from the diseases (a person may contract each any number of times); and (5) that it is quite possible to have both gonorrhea and syphilis at the same time.

The rules in dealing with the problem of VD are very simple: First, since these diseases are widely prevalent and can be highly destructive, a person should take every prophylactic measure possible in order to lessen his chances of infection. Second, it is mandatory that a person who is not sexually monogamous (or the equivalent) should have periodic checkups (every six months) specifically for gonorrhea and syphilis, even in the absence of any signs or symptoms. Third, he sould seek diagnosis and treatment *immediately* if he suspects that he may have been exposed to infection, or if there are any suspicious signs or symptoms. And, finally, in order to be able to take all of the measures listed above, a person must become familiar with the clinical characteristics of gonorrhea and syphilis, how each is contracted, and what prophylactic measures may be helpful.

Syphilis

Syphilis is a chronic infectious disease which goes through four stages and may affect any part of the body. It is caused by a corkscrew-shaped micro-organism called a *spirochete* and is acquired when spirochetes from the serum of an infectious *lesion* invade the bloodstream of a new host through either the mucous membrane (particularly of the glans or vagina but also of the labia, rectum, or lips, tongue, and mouth) or through broken skin on any bodily surface.[32] Because the spirochetes are fragile and can live for only a short time outside the host's body, it is highly unlikely for syphilis to be transmitted through a secondary source, such as a drinking glass, soiled towel, doorknob, or toilet seat— though it is theoretically possible.[33] The physiological secretions (salivary, vaginal, seminal fluid) of a diseased person are non-infectious in all stages of the disease.

The incubation period of syphilis, during which there are no signs or symptoms of infection, lasts for about three weeks (with limits of from ten to sixty days). At the end of this time, the disease enters the first stage, which is signalled in about half the cases by the appearance of a syphilitic lesion, called a *chancre*, at the site of the infection. The chancre has no typical appearance; it may resemble a simple abrasion, a pimple, acne, a blister, or a cold sore. It is painless, does not itch, and may be very inconspicuous. If it is hidden inside the vagina or rectum, it may easily escape detection even during a medical examination. The chancre usually clears up within a few weeks, with no treatment. The disease is highly contagious during the first stage, if the chancre is present.

The only certain evidence of syphilis during this first stage is a positive reaction from a serologic (blood) test, which will react to the presence of spirochetes in the blood stream anytime after four to six weeks from the time of infection.[34] Before the completion of this period of time, a blood test will be negative despite the presence of the infection.

The second stage of syphilis usually begins about two to six months after infection and is sometimes signaled by the appearance of a rash almost anywhere on the body, but most frequently on the palms of the hands or soles of the feet, the genital areas, the face, abdomen, or legs, or inside the mouth, vagina, or rectum. When this rash does appear (in less than half the cases), it is neither itchy nor painful, usually clears up quickly without treatment, and may easily be mistaken for a heat or drug rash. In something less than half the cases, this second state of syphilis is also accompanied by such symptoms as a slight feeling of illness, a slight fever, a headache, a sore throat, swelling of the lymph

---

[32] Another form of syphilis—*congenital* syphilis—is acquired by a fetus directly from the bloodstream of the mother, when the spirochetes penetrate the placental defenses. This invasion of the placental defenses will occur only after the fourth month of pregnancy (Brown, 1963). Since congenital syphilis may be prevented if the syphilitic mother is diagnosed and cured before this time, prenatal blood tests are required in forty-five of the fifty states. A baby who has contracted congenital syphilis in the early stages of pregnancy will show characteristic signs of the disease in infancy and early childhood; if the mother contracts syphilis late in the pregnancy, however, and is untreated, the baby may appear to be healthy at birth but will develop signs of syphilis in later months or years.

[33] Survival of spirochetes outside the host's body is usually limited to a few minutes and never exceeds an hour or two, even under ideal (warmth and dampness) circumstances.

[34] A serologic test, such as the Wassermann, is the most common technique for diagnosing syphilis. Other techniques include microscopic examination, either of the fluid from lesions during the first and second stages, or of a tissue specimen from an enlarged lymph node during the second stage, or cerebrospinal fluid tests, which are useful during the fourth stage of the disease, in differentiating symptomatic neurosyphilis from other diseases of the central nervous system.

glands, or hair falling out in patches. In addition, lesions, which are highly infectious, may appear on mucous membranes or where the skin is warm and moist.
These lesions may take almost any form—a crack on the corner of the mouth or
nostril, a small pimple or ulcer, acne-like abrasions, cold sores—and are painless
and do not itch. In the majority of cases, however, either these secondary symptoms do not appear at all or they are so mild or brief that they are unrecognized
or unnoticed. Both the rash and the secondary lesions clear up without treatment in from four to six weeks, although they may be recurrent for as long as
two years. Because of the possible appearance of the highly contagious lesions
during these first two stages, syphilis is termed "infectious" in this period.

The third stage of syphilis, which may last from two to thirty years, is called
the "latent period," because the infected person has no recognizable symptoms
at all (except for a positive reaction to laboratory tests). During this period, the
spirochetes tend to leave the bloodstream and lodge in the tissue of the host,
notably in the nervous system, the blood vessels, and probably in all major organs. During this latent period, a person may feel fine and go along for years
thinking he is healthy.

The disease finally breaks into the open again in the fourth stage, usually
ten to twenty years after the initial infection. Tissue destruction in this fourth
stage may be quite sudden, quite severe, and quite extensive, involving almost
any area of the body—the joints, musculature, heart, eyes, circulatory system,
nervous system, or brain. One of three of those persons initially infected and
untreated are now seriously incapacitated by the disease, experiencing severe
crippling, heart trouble, paralysis, blindness, insanity; and one in ten are killed
by the disease (Guthe, 1971). Since treatment cannot repair damage that has
already occurred but can almost always halt a further destruction by the disease,
the importance of early diagnosis and treatment cannot be overemphasized.

Treatment of syphilis is usually by a schedule of penicillin (or other antibiotic)
injections in the buttocks for eight to ten days, with periodic follow-up blood
tests for two years. This penicillin treatment is virtually 100 percent effective
(Ketterer, 1971). All spirochetes in any infectious lesions are usually destroyed
within twenty-four hours of the first injection, rendering the patient non-
infectious and halting the development of the disease.

. Effective prophylactic measures for the prevention of syphilis are quite
limited, since an infectious lesion may occur anywhere on the body and may
infect the new host through any mucous membrane or broken skin. The condom
provides some protection, of course, and urinating immediately after sexual
contact is a good prophylaxis, since this helps flush out the urethra. Also, since
the spirochetes are especially susceptible to heat and dryness, washing all exposed areas with soap and hot water immediately after sexual contact is a very
good prophylactic measure. Douching also has some limited prophylactic value.
With all these measures, speed is of the essence; for penetration of the new host's·
tissue by the spirochetes will take place within minutes after contact with the
serum of an infectious lesion.

Gonorrhea

Gonorrhea (commonly called *"clap"*) is an infectious disease caused by a micro-organism called a *gonococcus* and limited mainly to the mucous membrane of the urethra, although it may also involve the deeper genitalia or the rectal tissue.[35] The gonococci do not infect the vagina of the adult female[36] but may be harbored there to infect the male. The gonococci also do not establish themselves well in oral or throat tissue; hence, oral-genital contact rarely transmits gonorrhea (Ketterer, 1971). Infection through contaminated articles is theoretically possible but highly unlikely, since, as with the spirochete, the gonococcus lives for only a short time outside the host's tissue. Thus, gonorrhea is almost always contracted through either copulation or anal coitus.[37]

Gonorrhea affects men and women in quite different ways because of their different anatomy, and the symptoms in the male are usually different from those in the female. For example, in the male, gonorrheal infection of the urethra (gonorrheal urethritis) is unmistakable. The mucous membrane lining the urethra becomes inflamed, swollen, and painful within two to eight days after acquiring the disease, and urination causes a sharp burning pain. During this time, a highly infectious yellow discharge is exuded from the penis.

In the female, however, gonorrheal urethritis is completely free of symptoms in 80 percent of the cases, as we have seen, but is still highly contagious. Infection of the cervix often gives rise to a yellow discharge, but this discharge is usually scant and may be disregarded or attributed to ovulation (with its increased mucous flow) or to other sources of vaginal irritation, such as nervousness or fatigue.[38] The vagina will not become infected; but the complex folds of the vaginal lining may harbor the gonococci for months with no symptoms at all, and during this period any sex partner may be infected.[39]

Gonorrheal urethritis in both the male and female is usually self-limiting and will clear up without treatment in about three weeks. However, the infection may also spread into the deeper tissues of the prostate, the epididymides, or the

---

[35] Although gonorrhea is one of the most universal and widespread of all diseases that affect mankind, it is one of the few such diseases that does not also infect laboratory animals, so that medical research has been very limited.

[36] A female under five years of age (but rarely older) may acquire a vaginal form of gonorrhea (gonococcal vulvovaginitis) from contaminated articles, such as bedclothes or towels, but the vaginal tissue of older females is not usually susceptible to this form of the disease.

[37] A person may also acquire a form of gonorrheal infection of the eye (gonorrheal ophthalmia) if his eye comes into direct contact with an infectious gonorrheal discharge. Newborn babies are especially subject to this form of the disease because they may acquire it in their passage through the cervix of a gonorrheal-infected mother. Until about 1950, more blindness (10 percent) in the United States was caused by congenital gonorrheal ophthalmia than any other single cause. Now, because of this danger—for example, 6 percent of women delivering babies in Los Angeles county have gonorrhea—the eyes of newborn infants are routinely treated with a 1 percent silver-nitrate solution or a penicillin ointment, a precaution that has virtually eliminated this form of the disease (Public Health Services Center for Disease Control, 1971).

[38] Vaginal yeast infections, which are quite common among women who are taking the contraceptive pill, may also mask a gonorrheal infection.

[39] Rectal gonorrheal infections in both sexes are similarly symptom-free, although some discomfort and mucous discharge may develop if the infection persists.

testicles of the male, causing pain and swelling of the scrotum, or into the Fallopian tubes of the female, causing pain and swelling in the lower abdomen. These deeper infections are also usually self-limiting, but, especially in the female, the healing process may leave fibrosis and adhesions that obstruct the reproductive passages and cause sterility. The deeper infections are just as contagious as gonorrheal urethritis. For example, if the disease settles in the prostate, a microscopic examination of penile discharge may reveal no gonococci, but they will be present in the ejaculate and infect a sex partner.

With either the male or female, gonococcal invasion of the blood occurs only very rarely; but when it does, the disease may spread throughout the body to cause infection of extra-genital tissue. Joints are the most frequent sites of such infection, and painful arthritis may occur within one to three weeks after the initial infection of the genital tract. Other such infections may be skin lesions, tenosynovitis (inflamation of the tendon and its sheath), endocarditis (inflamation of the lining of the heart, which may be fatal), and meningitis (inflamation of the membrane of the spinal cord and brain).

Because a blood test for gonorrhea has not yet been developed, diagnosis must rely upon a microscopic examination of either a penile, vaginal, endocervical, or rectal smear for the presence of gonococci or a culture growth from the discharge of these areas. For the male, these tests are quite reliable, and in 90 percent of the cases the smear test alone, which takes just two or three minutes, is sufficient for diagnosis. In the female, however, fully 60 percent of tests for gonorrhea are inconclusive, because the gonococci quickly migrate into the Fallopian tubes (Private Correspondence, S.F. Public Health VD Clinic, 1971).

With men, a single massive intramuscular injection of penicillin will cure 90 percent of acute gonorrhea. Women are more difficult to cure, however, and often require a week of such treatments, with follow-up examination and treatment extended indefinitely in some cases. Although penicillin-resistant strains of gonorrhea are increasing, other anti-biotics are usually effective.

The condom is an excellent prophylactic against gonorrhea, since infection is almost invariably through copulation or rectal coitus. All other prophylactic measures mentioned with regard to syphilis are equally effective against gonorrhea.

What about Aphrodisiacs?

Although contemporary medical opinion feels that there is no such thing as a *true* aphrodisiac—in the sense that a certain food or chemical will alone bring about an erotic response—man, in his drive for sexual satisfaction and in his search for sexual power and endurance, has developed an extensive mythology about aphrodisiac substances (Hastings, 1963).[40]

---

[40] There is a similar folklore about powerful chemical *an*aphrodisiacs. Perhaps the most persistent and popular fallacy is that *saltpeter* (potassium nitrate) is used in prisons, hospitals, colleges, and the armed forces to lower libidinous impulses. Saltpeter is a diuretic, but it is not an anaphrodisiac. Some drugs, such as heroin, are sexually debilitating, and poor nutrition or fatigue will impair sexual functioning; but there is no specific anaphrodisiac, just as there is no known specific aphrodisiac.

Foods commonly thought to be aphrodisiacs are those which in some way resemble sexual organs or the physiological products of sexual excitement; examples of such foods include oysters, clam juice, raw eggs, and even squash and bananas. Many Chinese consider powdered rhinoceros horn a powerful aphrodisiac; and as a result of this myth the rhinoceros has been hunted to near extinction. An herb, gensing, also has had a long reputation as an aphrodisiac in the Far East. African natives attibute aphrodisiac qualities to yohimbine, a derivative of the yohimbe tree.

Probably the most widely known alleged aphrodisiac is "Spanish fly," or cantharides. Taken internally, cantharides will cause acute irritation of the genitourinary tract and may thus produce vasocongestion and erection; but this response is usually not accompanied by sexual desire; and, in excess, it may be dangerous and even fatal. Alcohol actually decreases sexual functioning physiologically; but in relatively small amounts, it may act *psychologically* as a stimulant, by reducing anxiety, fear, and tension and thus making the person less inhibited than he would otherwise be. Marijuana is reputed to increase sensuous awareness and bring a feeling of well-being. It, like alcohol, may act as a psychological stimulant. Similar claims have been made about LSD, but even less is known about its properties than is known about marijuana; and much controlled research remains to be done.

Because sexual interest and sexual performance are closely related to other physiological functions as well as to psychological functions, many stimuli may bring about an erotic response. For example, smells, fantasies, music, erotic art, and erotic literature may bring about an immediate and intense physiological excitement, as may textures and tastes of certain foods. But none of these can properly be designated as aphrodisiacs, since an erotic response to them is very much an individual matter — the "private cluster of stimuli" that we referred to in our discussion of fetishism. The chief ingredients of successful sexual functioning are good nutrition and health, pleasant surroundings and agreeable companionship, a positive attitude, and freedom from tension, fear, or guilt.

Summary

Human sexuality has two basic functions: reproduction and immediate need satisfaction. Although sexual behavior in lower animals is almost entirely reproductive, in man most sexual behavior is communicative and pleasure seeking — in fact, the couple may often take elaborate precautions to insure that reproduction does *not* occur.

There are three conscious modes of sexual behavior: masturbation, petting, and copulation. Of these, masturbation (or autosexual behavior) is by far the most frequent prior to marriage, and generally serves as the training ground in which almost all males and most females are introduced to their sexuality and to their own particular pattern of erotic response.

All individuals, male and female alike, go through the same four phases of erotic response: excitement, plateau, orgasm, and resolution. Males in our society are quite different from females, however, in terms of erotic interest, usually being responsive to a wider variety of psychological stimuli. This lack of interest and response by females is apparently a result of societal conditioning, and it may be less operative in the present generation.

The mature male ejaculates with orgasm; the ejaculate (semen) contains the sperm cells (the male gamete) which during copulation are deposited by the penis into the vagina of the female. If the mature female is ovulating at the time of copulation, a single sperm may unite with the gamete (ovum or egg) of the female in the Fallopian tube to create a new single-celled organism, the zygote, which will grow and develop into the billions of cells that make up a new human being.

Both males and females may be troubled with sexual dysfunction. The most common dysfunctions are premature ejaculation and temporary impotence in the male and physiological unresponsiveness and inability to experience orgasm in the female. Recent research indicates that sexual dysfunction is usually based upon ignorance and misinformation about the physiological and psychological aspects of sexual response. Masters and Johnson found that most sexual problems are rather quickly and easily resolved with accurate information and a relaxed and affirmative attitude.

Questions

1 Why is it naive to try to understand human sexuality in terms of its reproductive, biological function?

2 How is the person who lacks basic information about fundamental physical and psychological sexual characteristics handicapped in marriage?

3 What are the three modes of conscious sexual expression?

4 What is the average person's first acquaintance with sex?

5 Why and when is circumcision generally performed in our society?

6 How many sperm cells may be contained in one ejaculation?

7 How long do the sperm live once they are ejaculated?

8 What is ovulation?

9 What is the homologue of the male penis?

10 Explain the menstrual cycle.

11 What are the four phases of erotic response? Describe each.

12 How important are psychological factors in erotic arousal?

13 What are the two major determinants of erection? What causes each?

14 How common is genuine impotence?

15 What causes temporary impotence?

16 What are the three major differences between the characteristics of the orgasm in the mature male and that in the mature female?

17 Discuss male-female psychological differences in erotic interest and arousal, comparing the Kinsey data with the Schmidt and Sigusch study.

18 Which categories of sexual dysfunction respond readily to treatment with well-motivated persons?
19 Discuss what is meant by the *spectator role* being a damaging barrier to an individual's sexual adjustment.
20 What is fetishism?
21 Discuss the reasons for female psychological disinclination toward copulation in our society.

22 Why does frigidity usually occur?
23 What are the probable causes of the rapidly rising incidence of VD in our society?
24 What are the simple rules for dealing with the problem of VD?
25 How may syphilis be acquired? Describe each of its four stages.
26 How may gonorrhea be acquired? Describe its clinical symptoms in the male and in the female.

References and Selected Readings

Baruch, Dorothy W., and H. Miller. *Sex in Marriage.* New York: Harper, 1970.

Belliveau, Fred, and Lin Richter. *Understanding Human Sexual Inadequacy.* New York: Bantam, 1970.

Benedek, T. Panel Report: Frigidity in Women. *Journal of the American Psychoanalytic Association,* 1961, Vol. 9, pp. 571–584.

Bliss, E. L., ed. *Roots of Behavior.* New York: Hafner, 1969.

Brecher, Edward M. *The Sex Researchers.* Boston: Little, Brown, 1969.

_____, Ruth and Edward, eds. *An Analysis of Human Sexual Response.* New York: New American Library, 1966.

Brown, Daniel C. Female Orgasm and Sexual Inadequacy. In Brecher and Brecher, *An Analysis of Human Sexual Response,* pp. 125–133.

Brown, William J., and M. Brittain Moore, Jr. Congenital Syphilis in the United States. *Clinical Pediatrics,* 1963, Vol. 2, pp. 220–222.

Calderone, M. S. *Release from Sexual Tensions.* New York: Random House, 1960.

_____. Sex Education for Young People—and for Their Parents and Teachers. In Brecher and Brecher, *An Analysis of Human Sexual Response,* pp. 267–273.

Clark, L. Is There a Difference between a Clitoral and a Vaginal Orgasm? *Journal of Sex Research,* February 1970, Vol. 6, pp. 25–28.

_____. Sexual Adjustment in Marriage. In Albert Ellis and Albert Abarbanel, eds., *The Encyclopedia of Sexual Behavior,* 2nd ed. New York: Hawthorn, 1967, pp. 710–717.

Duffy, J. Masturbation and Clitoridectomy. *Journal of the American Medical Association,* 1963, Vol. 19, pp. 246–248.

Eichenlaub, John E. *New Approaches to Sex in Marriage.* New York: Dell, 1970.

Ellis, Albert. *The American Sexual Tragedy,* 2nd ed. New York: Lyle Stuart, 1962.

_____. *The Art and Science of Love.* New York: Lyle Stuart, 1960.

_____, and Albert Abarbanel. *The Encyclopedia of Sexual Behavior,* 2nd ed. New York: Hawthorn, 1967.

_____. Frigidity. In Ellis and Abarbanel, *The Encyclopedia of Sexual Behavior*, pp. 450–456.

Ford, C. S., and F. A. Beach. *Patterns of Sexual Behavior*. New York: Harper, 1970.

Friedan, Betty. *The Feminine Mystique*. New York: Harper, 1963.

Goldman, George D., and Donald S. Milman, eds. *Modern Woman: Her Psychology and Sexuality*. Springfield, Ill.: Thomas, 1969.

Guthe, Thorstein. Syphilis. In Paul B. Beeson, and Walsh McDermott, eds., *Textbook of Medicine*, 13th ed. Philadelphia: Saunders, 1971, pp. 655–668.

Hampson, J. L. and J. G. The Ontogenesis of Sexual Behavior in Man. In William C. Young, ed., *Sex and Internal Secretions*. Baltimore: Williams & Wilkins, 1961.

Hastings, D. W. *Impotence and Frigidity*. Boston: Little, Brown, 1963.

_____. Can Specific Training Procedures Overcome Sexual Inadequacy? In Brecher and Brecher, *An Analysis of Human Sexual Response*, pp. 221–235.

Havemann, Ernest. *Men, Women, and Marriage*. Garden City: Doubleday, 1962.

Heiman, M. Sexual Response in Women. *Journal of the American Psychoanalytic Association*, 1963, Vol. II, pp. 360–384.

Hendrick, I. Psychosexuality. In A. M. Krich, ed., *The Anatomy of Love*. New York: Dell, 1960.

Hirsch, A. H. *The Love Elite*. New York: Julian, 1963.

Holmes, K. K., *et al*. Studies of Venereal Disease. *Journal of the American Medical Association*, 1967, Vol. 202, pp. 461, 467, 474.

Jay, Phyllis C. The Female Primate. In Seymour M. Farber and Roger H. L. Wilson, *The Potential of Woman*. New York: McGraw-Hill, 1963.

Kaye, Donald. Gonococcal Disease. In Paul B. Beeson, and Walsh McDermott, eds., *Textbook of Medicine*, 13th ed. Philadelphia: Saunders, 1971, pp. 537–541.

Kelly, G. Lombard. Impotence. In Ellis and Abarbanel, eds., *The Encyclopedia of Sexual Behavior*, pp. 515–527.

Ketterer, Warren A. Homosexuality and Venereal Disease. *Medical Aspects of Human Sexuality*, March 1971, Vol. 5, pp. 114–129.

Kinsey, A. C., Wardell B. Pomeroy, and Clyde E. Martin. *Sexual Behavior in the Human Male*. Philadelphia: Saunders, 1948.

_____, Wardell B. Pomeroy, Clyde E. Martin, and Paul H. Gebhard. *Sexual Behavior in the Human Female*. Philadelphia: Saunders, 1953.

Koble, Wendell M., and Richard Warren. *Sex in Marriage*. New York: Academy Press, 1970.

Kroger, W. S., and S. C. Freed. Psychosomatic Aspects of Frigidity. *Journal of the American Medical Association*, 1950, Vol. 171, p. 469.

Lehrman, Nat. *Masters and Johnson Explained*. Chicago: Playboy Press, 1970.

Lloyd, C. W., ed. *Human Reproduction and Sexual Behavior*. Philadelphia: Lea & Febiger, 1964.

Lowen, Alexander. *Love and Orgasm*. New York: New American Library, 1967.

Macdougold, Duncan, Jr. Aphrodisiacs and Anaphrodisiacs. In Ellis and Abarbanel, eds., *The Encyclopedia of Sexual Behavior*, pp. 145–153.

Marshall, Donald S. Too Much in Mangaia. *Psychology Today,* February 1971, pp. 43–44, 70–75.

Masters, William H., and Virginia E. Johnson. *Human Sexual Inadequacy.* Boston: Little, Brown, 1970.

_____. *Human Sexual Response.* Boston: Little, Brown, 1966.

_____, and Virginia E. Johnson. Orgasm, Anatomy of the Female. In Ellis and Abarbanel, eds., *The Encyclopedia of Sexual Behavior,* pp. 788–793.

_____. The Physiology of the Vaginal Reproductive Function. *Western Journal of Surgery, Obstetrics, and Gynecology,* 1961, Vol. 69, pp. 105–120.

McCary, James Leslie. Myths About Sex. *Sexual Behavior,* April 1971, Vol. 1, pp. 24, 56–61.

_____. *Human Sexuality.* New York: Van Nostrand, 1967.

Money, John. *Sex Errors of the Body: Dilemmas, Education, Counseling.* Baltimore: Johns Hopkins Press, 1968.

_____. Components of Eroticism in Man: Cognition Rehearsals. In J. Wartis, ed., *Recent Advances in Biological Psychiatry.* New York: Grune & Stratton, 1960.

_____, ed. *Sex Research: New Developments.* New York: Holt, 1965.

Montagu, M. F. Ashley. *Anthropology and Human Nature.* Boston: Porter Sargent, 1957.

Osborne, Charles, ed. *Nature-Science Annual.* New York: Time-Life, 1970.

Rainer, J. and J. *Sexual Pleasure in Marriage,* rev. ed. New York: Simon & Schuster, 1969.

Rainwater, Lee. Marital Sexuality in Four Cultures of Poverty. *Journal of Marriage and the Family,* November 1964, Vol. 26, pp. 457–466.

Robertiello, Richard C. The "Clitoral Versus Vaginal Orgasm" Controversy and Some of Its Ramifications. *Journal of Sex Research,* November 1970, Vol. 6, pp. 307–311.

Schmidt, Gunter, and Volkman Sigusch. Sex Differences in Responses to Psychosexual Stimulation by Films and Slides. *Journal of Sex Research,* November 1970, Vol. 6, pp. 268–283.

Sigusch, Volkman, Gunter Schmidt, and A. Reinfeld. Psychosexual Stimulation: Sex Differences. *Journal of Sex Research,* February 1970, Vol. 6, pp. 10–24.

Stone, Hannah Mayer, and Abraham Stone. *A Marriage Manual,* rev. ed. by Gloria Stone Aiken and Aquiles J. Sobero. New York: Simon & Schuster, 1968.

Taylor, Donald L. *Human Sexual Development: Perspectives in Sex Education.* Philadelphia: Davis, 1970.

Top, Franklin H., ed. *Communicable and Infectious Diseases,* 6th ed. St. Louis: Mosby, 1968, pp. 260ff.

Watts, Alan W. *Nature, Man and Woman.* New York: Random House, 1970.

Wilcox, R. R. *Textbook of Venereal Disease and Treponemiasis.* Springfield, Ill.: Thomas, 1964.

Wilson, Robert Anton. Modern Attitudes toward Sex. In Ellis and Abarbanel, eds., *The Encyclopedia of Sexual Behavior,* pp. 186–192.

Winokur, George, ed. *Determinants of Human Sexual Behavior.* Springfield, Ill.: Charles C Thomas, 1962.

Young, Weyland. *Eros Denied: Sex in Western Society.* New York: Grove Press, 1964.

Chapter Four

Human Sexuality: Behavior and Attitudes

*Nothing is so firmly believed
as what we least know.*

Montaigne

 ex, being the very source of life, has always been shrouded by fear, superstition, mystery, and cultural sanctions.

The story is told of a German headmaster named Sprengel who published in 1787 an essay entitled "The Newly Revealed Mystery of Nature in the Structure and Fertilization of Flowers." In it he described quite precisely the sexual nature of reproduction in the higher plants. So shocking was this to his contemporaries that he was dismissed from his teaching post and his book was withdrawn from circulation (Calderone, 1960, p. 273).

Although this anecdote strikes us as quaint and old-fashioned, the general attitude that it reveals—the fear and horror of anything connected with sexuality—persisted for a very long time and has not totally disappeared even today.

Many educational, religious, and scientific communities still exhibit anxiety, ignorance, fear, and prejudice when they are confronted with learning and teaching more about human sexuality. Hastings (1963) states that in his four years of medical school, one hour of one course (obstetrics) was devoted to a discussion of sex—"and contained little that we had not read within an hour or so of purchasing our new obstetrical textbooks." Lief (1963) states that as of 1962 only four medical schools in the United States offered regularly scheduled courses dealing with sexual behavior. He goes on to say that "Doctors are woefully ignorant about sex." Wilson (1967) found that even professionals in the field—for example, instructors in marriage and family courses—are often uninformed, prejudiced, reluctant to discuss sex, and even afraid of the topic. Surely neither ignorance nor personal antipathy would be tolerated in an instructor in any other curriculum specialty.

Taxonomic Data on American Sexual Behavior

Considering the taboo nature of the subject, it is not surprising that man's sexual behavior has only recently been subjected to taxonomic investigation.[1] Prior to 1948, when Dr. Alfred Kinsey published his *Sexual Behavior in the Human Male*, only nineteen studies that were in any way taxonomic had been made of human sexual behavior, and each was very limited in its approach.[2] And although some criticism[3] has since been leveled at the Kinsey study of 12,000 native, white, American males and at his later study of 8,000 American females (1953), these two works remain, a full generation later, the main source of all of our knowledge and data about the sexual behavior of American males and females. Before Kinsey, we literally knew less about the sexual behavior of our own species than we did about the mating behavior of the stickleback, a species of fish. Kinsey himself had previously devoted his painstaking, dispassionate investigatory techniques to the study of the gall wasp (he was a zoologist before he became well known as a sexologist).

Other researchers followed Kinsey, of course, but a second great milestone in the study of human sexuality was not achieved until 1954, when Drs. William Masters and Virginia Johnson began an unprecedented study in the laboratory of the physiological processes involved in human erotic arousal and response. Until the publication of Masters and Johnson's results (*Human Sexual Response* in 1966 and *Human Sexual Inadequacy* in 1970), the physiology of human sexuality was largely a matter of conjecture, misinformation, and folklore. There still remains much to be learned about erotic response, of course—especially its psychological ramifications—but the taxonomic study by Kinsey and the physiological research of Masters and Johnson have made a very significant beginning.

The American Male

The most significant thing about male sexual behavior is its regularity. "More than 99 percent of the boys begin regular sexual lives immediately after the first ejaculation"[4](1948, p. 192). And from the time of this intitial ejaculatory ex-

---

[1] Taxonomy, the oldest branch of biological science, names, classifies, and attempts to account for differences among individuals. An understanding of the behavior of any species must rest upon a taxonomic study that uses a sample sufficiently representative and sufficiently large to be validly extrapolated to the population at large.

[2] For the reference to these studies (23 titles) and for a detailed criticism of their techniques, coverage, and scientific rigor, see Kinsey (1948, pp. 24–34).

[3] For example, see Wallis (1949), Wallin (1949), Bergler and Kroger (1954), and Himmelhoch (1955), who attack Kinsey's choice of samples, his interviewing techniques, and/or his generalizations and statistics. For Kinsey's own detailed discussion of the difficulties inherent in the interview technique, the problems in seeking statistical conclusions when there is such a mass of data and so many interrelated variables, and the probable validity of his data, see Kinsey (1948, pp. 35–153).

[4] The material for this first half of the chapter is drawn chiefly from the Kinsey samples (1948 and 1953). A convenient and precise factor which correlates highly with social class is education. For this reason, Kinsey used the educational categories of college and non-college or, sometimes, college, high school, and grade school as useful designations of the social level of the interviewees in his samples, whatever their ages at the time of the interview.

perience, which occurs for the average boy at about age 13, the average adolescent and young adult male in our population will experience a regularity of
orgasm (with ejaculation) of about three and a half times a week, or just about
every other day (pp. 195, 205, 266). Eight males in ten fall within this range of
one to seven orgasms per week; the other two males in ten fall either over or
under this range, with one of them ejaculating oftener than once a day and the
other less than once a week (p. 198). (About 10 percent of the male population,
ages 13 to 30, have one or more orgasms in a day, and a smaller percentage
experience twenty-five to thirty orgasms per week over a thirty-year period
(pp. 198, 216). On the other hand, their extreme opposite may experience as
few as one or two orgasms per year, although only one male in a hundred will
go for as long as five years without an orgasm (p. 268).)

Whichever orgasmic pattern an individual male falls into—whether daily,
weekly, or yearly—he will persist in this patterned regularity of orgasm and
ejaculation with only a very gradual decline from adolescence to old age. For
example, from age 20 to 30, the average number of orgasms per week for the
unmarried male is three; if he is married, it is four. From age 30 to 40, the unmarried average is about two; the married average, three. Over age 40, there is
very little change in this average; and there is little difference between the
bachelor and the married man (pp. 266–268). This astonishing regularity of
sexual performance is apparently characteristic of the male, before marriage,
during marriage, and after marriage (whether separated, widowed, or divorced).
Within his own characteristic degree of sexuality, the male inexorably continues
his ejaculatory schedule, regardless of his marital status, from the time of his
first ejaculation in about the eighth grade until he is retired and living on a
pension.

Sexual behavior in the prepubertal male. Most boys in our society experience
orgasm long before adolescence. Indeed, based upon the limited data available,[5]
it would seem that fully one third of all males have experienced orgasm by the
time they are a year old, more than half by the time they are 5 years old, and
more than three quarters by age 13 (1948, p. 178).

Prepubertal orgasm is not accompanied, of course, by ejaculation because the
prostate and the seminal vesicles are not yet functionally developed. The prepubertal orgasm is, however, identical to the postpubertal orgasm in all other
respects. In later childhood, a year or two before puberty, a drop or two of
pre-ejaculatory fluid may appear with extended masturbation. This presages
the development of the sex glands; and usually within a few months, the young
male will suddenly ejaculate.

The prepubertal male is, in many respects, actually more sexual than the
postpubertal male. For example, prepubertal erections occur more quickly and
last longer than the erections of older males.[6] Similarly, most prepubertal boys,

[5] Kinsey's sample of the preadolescent male was much smaller than the samples of other categories
in his total research population.
[6] Duration of erection declines from an average of nearly an hour for the 20-year-old to 45 minutes

unlike the adult, will maintain an erection after orgasm (pp. 178–180). Fully two thirds of prepubertal males remain erect after orgasm, and all are able to induce a second orgasm almost immediately, or after a wait of from ten seconds to thirty minutes. A number of prepubertal males characteristically achieve five or more orgasms in rapid succession, with a mean interval of about six minutes. The average duration of stimulation before orgasm occurs in the prepubertal male is about three minutes (p. 179).

This high degree of sexuality in the prepubertal male is not limited to our species but has been noted in many other mammals as well (Beach, 1947). Although the prepubertal male is more sexual than older males in his almost universal capacity for multiple orgasm, enduring erections, and fast stimulation, his sexuality is apparently not as regularly patterned as that of the postpubertal male.

Prepubertal erections are generally stimulated by cerebral arousal, although tactile contact, either in masturbation or in sex play (petting) with peers, also often induces arousal. Nearly all prepubertal boys experience some sexual play, either with other boys or with girls. The average age for beginning sexual play is about 9 years old. About half of the boys attempt copulation in their sex play with girls; the remainder limit their play to manual exploration and various "doctor" games (Kinsey, 1948 pp. 167–173).

Sexual behavior in the postpubertal male. When an ejaculation containing viable sperm occurs with orgasm, the pubescent male begins a measure of biological and physiological adulthood — in that an *adult* is defined as an individual capable of reproducing his own kind. Although still immature, or underdeveloped, in many biological, physiological, and psychological characteristics of adulthood, the male in his early teens is sexually adult. Further, he is at the most sexually active period of his life. Most of our societal institutions either deny the existence of this adolescent sexuality or ignore it, failing to recognize that the pubescent male has already established his characteristic pattern of regular ejaculation. It is ironic that although the sex life of the average teenager has no formally recognized existence in our society, the average high school boy is experiencing a higher frequency of orgasm, with a greater variety of modes of response, than are his teachers. Yet, under the assumption that the young person is not yet "ready," schools and parents rarely provide meaningful sexual education.

The sexual behavior of the postpubertal male population may be examined in terms of many variables, and Kinsey has done just this in several hundred pages of data. In order to formulate a profile of typical male sexuality, we must abstract his findings into just a few paragraphs — a process that necessarily leaves many questions unanswered. However, even with the briefness and limitations of the following description, we will be able to get a useful and illuminating view of sexual man.

---

for the 30-year-old, to 30 minutes for the 40-year-old, to 20 minutes for the 50-year-old, to 7 minutes for the 70-year-old. Under prolonged erotic stimulation, the teenage male may maintain a constant erection for several hours, even after two or three ejaculations (pp. 230–231).

Not surprisingly, masturbation is the most common mode of sexual expression before marriage (1948, p. 379). About two thirds of all males experience their first orgasm in masturbation, the techniques of which they usually learn from another male (p. 190). Although the practice of masturbation is almost universal among males, incidence varies slightly from group to group. For example, middle-class males masturbate more than lower-class males; 96 percent of college-level males masturbate, compared to 84 percent of lower-level males, who believe masturbation is harmful or unnatural (pp. 507–508). After marriage, masturbation becomes much less frequent, but by no means ceases. About 10 percent of the ejaculations of college-level husbands occur through masturbation (p. 508).

Heterosexual petting is the second most common mode of sexual expression for the unmarried male, although copulation is more frequent in some groups — for example, unmarried males with no more than eighth-grade education. Nearly all males pet, but petting never accounts for more than 3 percent of the ejaculations of any segment of the total male population (except that of the unmarried male in his thirties, who experiences fully 10 percent of his ejaculations while petting). Sixty percent of college graduates, 32 percent of high school graduates, and only 16 percent of those with only an eighth-grade education pet to orgasm. Frequency of petting reaches a height between ages 21 and 25, when those who are active in the petting mode will reach orgasm about once every three weeks (pp. 537–539).

Homosexual petting involves some 27 percent of unmarried males between puberty and age 15, 39 percent by age 36, and 50 percent by age 50. By contrast, homosexual petting occurs among only 10 percent of married men at age 20 and drops steadily to about 2 percent by age 45 (p. 285).

Premarital copulation is experienced by most males in our society and actually provides the *first* ejaculation for nearly one in five boys who will not go beyond grade school, one in eight who will not go beyond high school, and only one in 100 who will go to college. The cumulative incidence of premarital copulation is 98 percent of the males who never go beyond the eighth grade, 84 percent of those who finish high school, and 67 percent of those who are college graduates. Frequency of premarital copulation also varies considerably among the different educational levels: for the person who will go to college, premarital copulation never amounts to more than 21 percent of his total ejaculations; for the person who will not go to college, premarital copulation makes up 68 percent of his total ejaculations. For the total population of males, frequencies of premarital copulation average about twice a week from age 16 to the early 20s. The lower-class average is perhaps twice this, while the average at college level is about once every three weeks (pp. 549–552). (For further data, see pp. 112–115 in this chapter, Influence of social class upon individual sexual behavior.)

Marital copulation is, naturally, the most frequent source of orgasm for married males of all groups. It is also, of course, the only mode of conscious sexual expression not considered illicit by our moral codes. Incidence of marital copulation is virtually 100 percent from adolescence through the 30s, 98 percent in the 40s, and 94 percent in the 50s. Marital copulation provides about 85 percent of the average husband's ejaculations. Frequency of marital copulation declines from four to three to two to one per week for the population as a whole in the succeeding decades after marriage, although many individuals copulate regularly with their wives an average of one to three times per day during the early years of marriage, and some continue this schedule into the 30s and 40s (pp. 565–569). A separated, divorced, or widowed male continues the copulative sexual pattern of the married male, despite inconvenience, social taboos, moral suasion, religious condemnation, and legal dangers (p. 289).

Extramarital copulation is usually sporadic within all social groups in our society, "occurring on occasion with this female, a few times with another, a few times with the next partner, not happening again for some months or a year or two, but then occurring several times or every night for a week or even for a month or more, after which that affair is abruptly stopped" (p. 588). The institution of the mistress, so widespread in other societies, is rather rare in our own. Extramarital copulation accounts for something like 5 to 10 percent of the total ejaculations of about 50 percent of the married males in our society. The college-level group tends to have an extramarital affair with a single partner over a relatively protracted period of time; the lower levels are more likely to have regularly distributed experiences with a variety of females (pp. 585–588).

A comparison of two generations of males. Is the younger generation of males more active sexually? Is there more masturbation, petting, premarital copulation, or extramarital copulation? Does the younger generation experience a higher incidence of orgasm?

Kinsey was able to make a precise comparison between the generation born around 1905 and that born around 1925. At the time of his research, the younger group had a median age of 21 years; the older, a median age of 43 years. In the years separating these two generations, as many significant economic, technological, political, educational, and social changes occurred as perhaps in any other twenty-year period in this or any other century. Yet the pattern of sexual behavior of these two generations of males changed so little during this time as to be inconsequential.

In general, the sexual patterns of the younger generation are so nearly identical with the sexual patterns of the older generation in regard to so many types of sexual activity that there seems to be no sound basis for the widespread opinion that the younger generation has become more active in its sociosexual contacts (1953, p. 397).

This lack of change in sexual patterns provides a graphic illustration of the stability of the sexual needs and performance of the male.

The American Female

The combination of variables deterministic of sexual behavior in the female is so complex that any statement regarding an "average" female is almost meaningless. Unlike the male, the sexuality of each individual female is so unique that there is little chance that her own particular characteristics have ever existed before or will ever exist again (1953, p. 543). Kinsey felt that this discovery was the most important finding in his research on female sexuality. The variation in sexual responsiveness is so great among females, and the frequencies of sexual activity so diverse, that even females may be incapable of understanding the meaning of sex for other females—whereas even the least sexually responsive male can understand something of the meaning of sex for other males.

Although there is apparently no average female insofar as taxonomic data are concerned, and although each female is a unique sexual creature, taxonomic data do provide information about the characteristics of female sexual behavior in general, and about the range of female response, and about differences between male and female behavior.

Fully one third of all females in our society rarely respond to any sexual stimuli; they live in another world, sexually, from nine tenths of all males—as well as from the other two thirds of females. Most of the two thirds of females who do respond to sexual stimuli do so only rarely, and with no regularity; they are seldom if ever aroused by anticipation of sexual behavior. The range of sexuality among the females who are sexually responsive is enormous, with some individuals responding far more regularly, intensely, and frequently than any male.

The most obvious observation consistent with these data is, of course, that the chance of the average husband being matched sexually with his wife is rather remote. Some "goodnesses of fit" will inevitably occur, and some wives will be more sexual than some husbands; but most husbands will enter marriage with the sexual and romantic fantasies of adolescence, only to be bitterly disappointed at the sexual indifference of their wives. Even a woman who responds with ardor in the romantic atmosphere of premarital petting will sometimes find, after she is married, that copulation just isn't that rewarding; she will be puzzled by her husband's preoccupation with sex. About one in four of all married females at age 25 have not experienced orgasm; and one tenth of all married females will probably never experience orgasm during their entire married lives (p. 513). In contrast, the average male, by his wedding day, has already had 1,523 orgasms, 330 in copulation (p. 520). Not until age 29 is the number of the female population experiencing orgasm in any way comparable to the number of males currently experiencing orgasm (1948, p. 187). It is not surprising, then, that the average male often feels betrayed and dejected by the indifferent sexuality or antisexuality of his wife.[7]

---

[7]Since the female erotic physiology is almost identical with that of the male, and since the female is

Sexual behavior in the prepubertal female. Although the average female is much less of a sexual creature than the average male in our society, a small number (perhaps 4 percent) of females experience orgasm by three to five years of age (1953, p. 104). Kinsey reports such an experience in a 3-year-old girl, whose mother observed her sex play with a doll. The following description of the experience illustrates that the prepubertal orgasm is identical to the orgasm after puberty.

Lying face down on the bed, with her knees drawn up, she started rhythmic pelvic thrusts, about one second or less apart. The thrusts were primarily pelvic, with the legs tensed in a fixed position. The forward components of the thrusts were in a smooth and perfect rhythm which was unbroken except for momentary pauses during which the genitalia were readjusted against the doll on which they were pressed; the return from each thrust was convulsive, jerky. There were 44 thrusts in unbroken rhythm, a slight momentary pause, 87 thrusts followed by a single momentary pause, then 10 thrusts, and then a cessation of all movement. There was marked concentration and intense breathing with abrupt jerks as orgasm approached. She was completely oblivious to everything during these later stages of the activity. Her eyes were glassy and fixed in a vacant stare. There was noticeable relief and relaxation after orgasm. A second series of reactions began two minutes later with a series of 48, 18, and 57 thrusts, with slight momentary pauses between each series. With the mounting tension, there were audible gasps, but immediately following the cessation of pelvic thrusts there was complete relaxation and only desultory movements thereafter (pp. 104–105).

About 16 percent of females experience orgasm by 10 years of age, and about 25 percent by puberty. Most of this orgasmic experience occurs through masturbation. Eighty-six percent of first orgasms for the prepubertal female occur through masturbation. The other 14 percent are distributed as follows: 7 percent through homosexual petting, 2 percent through heterosexual petting, 2 percent through petting with a dog or cat, 2 percent through "unusual circumstances" (such as climbing a rope), and 1 percent through copulating (pp. 103–106). The ratio of preadolescent heterosexual play which reaches orgasm is thus about seven to one for males and females (p. 110). Moreover, most girls who do experience orgasm through heterosexual petting or copulation do so only once or twice. Therefore, to account for the seven to one difference between the occurrence of male and female prepubertal orgasms, we must assume that there are a few very sexually active girls, experiencing a high frequency of orgasms with a number of different boys.

Sexual behavior in the postpubertal female. Unlike the male, the female does not experience a marked upsurge in the incidence or the frequency of orgasm at the onset of puberty; most females do not reach a maximum of erotic interest and fulfillment until the mid-20s or 30s (1953, p. 125). Most adolescent girls are

just as *capable* of erotic response as the male, the sexual indifference of females is more often caused by socially conditioned attitudes and by female *and* male ignorance of the special requirements of each female for successful erotic arousal and response.

sexually unawakened. For example, more than one in four females in a sample of graduate students did not know that masturbation was possible until they had discovered it in their own experimentation after age 30. Contrast this with the experience of the males, most of whom had been masturbating regularly several times a week for ten to twenty years before their female teachers and female peers were even aware that there was such a thing. Moreover, some females, even after orgasmic experience in petting, did not realize that masturbation could effect similar results. Most females learn to masturbate through self-exploration, rather than by instruction from a peer (which is the way that most males learn the technique). Ironically, those females who did not learn about the possibility of masturbation through their own experimentation usually first heard about it from a moral or religious lecture designed to discourage the practice (pp. 137–140).

Most of the females in Kinsey's sample began to masturbate soon after they learned of the possibility, and most of these (95 percent) soon learned to proceed to orgasm. Ultimately, some 58 percent of females masturbate. However, the frequency of masturbation among this 58 percent is much less than for the male, with the average single woman masturbating only once every two to three weeks and the average married woman about once a month. Within these data, there are great individual differences, of course, and some females regularly masturbate several times a day or even several times an hour (pp. 140–146).

Masturbation provides the greatest number of orgasms for the unmarried female, accounting for something like 85 percent of the total number of orgasms from puberty to age 15, 60 percent from age 15 to age 20, and 46 percent from age 20 to age 25 (p. 178). By age 25, premarital copulation runs a close second to masturbation as the primary mode of orgasm in unmarried females (p. 291). By age 15, 10 percent of females are masturbating; by age 20, 40 percent; and by age 35, nearly 60 percent (p. 143). The female almost always reaches orgasm in masturbation.

About 90 percent of all females, and nearly 100 percent of those who marry, have some heterosexual petting experience. Ninety-seven percent of those who experience petting become erotically aroused to some extent, and 40 percent become aroused to the point of orgasm. The median frequency of petting to the point of orgasm is about four to six times per year, although there are great individual differences, with some females averaging seven to ten petting-induced orgasms per week and with others experiencing orgasm only once or twice in the same five-to-ten-year period (pp. 234–237).

Homosexual petting among single females is much lower than among single males, with only 3 percent experiencing it between ages 16 and 30. Between ages 36 and 40, this incidence has risen to 10 percent; and by age 40, it is 19 percent (pp. 487–489). Homosexuality among married females is negligible, as it is among married males.

Premarital copulation occurs for about half the females in our society but usually only in the year or two prior to marriage. The median frequency of premarital copulation among females is much lower than that of the male. For example, for those females who do participate in premarital copulation, the median frequency, for those under age 20, is only once in five to ten weeks; for those over ʌge 20, it is once in three weeks. Again, there are great individual differences; for example, about half of all sexually active unmarried females copulate as often as two or three times per week. However, this high frequency is usually sporadic and is interspersed with periods of inactivity (pp. 286, 289).

The percentage of females experiencing premarital copulation, by age group, is 3 percent by age 15 (compared to 40 percent for all males), 20 percent during ages 16 to 20 (compared to 71 percent for all males), and 35 percent during ages 21 to 25 (compared to 69 percent for all males) (p. 330). Orgasm is experienced by the female in premarital copulation about 40 percent of the time, although there is a wide range of individual experience, with some females never reaching orgasm, others always reaching orgasm, and some having two or three orgasms with each copulation (pp. 290, 330). About 14 percent of females regularly experience multiple orgasm (p. 290). Nearly one third of the females who experience premarital copulation do so fewer than ten times; and in many instances, the experience has occurred only once. Of those females who participate in premarital copulation, about a third to a fourth express feelings of regret (p. 332).

Nearly half of the females confine their premarital copulating to the year before marriage and to their fiancé (p. 291). In a sample of married females, about half of those who had had premarital copulation had performed it with only one partner, about a third had performed with two to five different partners, and about 13 percent had performed it with six or more different partners (pp. 291–292).

Marital copulation is, of course, the most frequent mode of sexual expression for the married female, just as it is for the male. Within one month of marriage, about half of all females have experienced orgasm in copulation with their husbands; about three fourths have reached orgasm within the first year; about 90 percent have reached orgasm by the fifth year; and the remaining 10 percent probably never will experience orgasm (p. 349). The percentage of wives reaching orgasm is also correlated with age of the female as well as with length of marriage. For example, only 71 percent of wives reach orgasm between ages 16 and 21, although nearly 100 percent are copulating several times per week; and the highest incidence of orgasm occurs between ages 31 and 40, when 90 percent are reaching orgasm at least occasionally (p. 352). In very general terms, there is a gradual increase of incidence of orgasm in the female to about age 35, after which there is a gradual decline. But inasmuch as there is no "average female" (in terms of taxonomic data), no statement, such as "three and a half orgasms per week are the median during a given age period," may be provided for the female, as it may for the male.

Extramarital copulation is ultimately experienced by about one fourth of all wives: 7 percent of wives in their late teens, 14 percent during their late 20s, and 17 percent during their late 30s. After the late 30s, the incidence of extramarital copulation drops, until by the 50s only 6 percent are involved (p. 417).

Unlike the male, there is a significant difference in the frequency of orgasm among unmarried and married females. Females who become separated, widowed, or divorced change from the sexual behavior characteristic of the married group to that of the unmarried group.

The aging female experiences menopause at about age 45 to 50. This biological change does not affect her ability to experience orgasm; nor does it have a measurable physiological effect upon her erotic response. However, the psychological ramifications of menopause can, in some females, alter sexual interest.

A comparison of two generations of females. Although Kinsey discovered no appreciable changes in the sexual behavior of the older and younger generations of males, the sexual behavior of the two generations of females (one born about 1905, the other about 1925) demonstrated quite marked changes. For example, during this period, the number of females masturbating to orgasm increased 10 percent (1953, p. 153) and the number of females petting increased nearly 20 percent. Also, the age at which petting began to occur dropped from 18 to 16 (p. 244). The number of females participating in premarital copulation actually doubled — from 25 to 50 percent (p. 330). The number of women experiencing orgasm also increased: The percentage of wives experiencing orgasm in copulation rose from 72 to 80 to 87 to 89 percent during the successive decades from 1920 to 1950 (p. 538).

To have frigidity so reduced in the course of three decades is a considerable achievement, which may be credited in part to the franker attitudes and the freer discussion of sex which we have had in the United States during the past 20 years, and to the increasing scientific and clinical understanding of the basic biology and psychology of sex. There were wives and husbands in the older generation who did not even know that orgasm was possible for a female; or if they knew it was possible, they did not believe that it could be pleasurable, or that it was proper for a well-bred female to respond, even in a marital relationship. The average female and male today are more often aware of the significance of mutual relationships in marriage and increasingly desirous of making such relationships satisfactory (p. 358).

The emergence of the institution of dating, the increased knowledge and availability of contraceptive devices, the anonymity that accompanied the rapid growth of urbanization and the mass society, the development of the automobile (a "mobile parlor" away from the surveillance of the family) and the motion picture (vivid romantic and sexual role models), the changes in attitude of popular media (such as women's magazines), and the political, economic, and social emancipation of women — all contributed to the marked changes in female sexuality which are reflected in the Kinsey (1953) data.

Influence of Social Class upon Individual
Sexual Behavior

A person's sexual behavior, like his behavior in other aspects of his existence, is learned in his particular environment. Thus, a person's sexual behavior is both a reflection and a result of his position, or social class, in the strata of his society. Although the incidence of orgasm among both males and females is about the same in all social classes, the mode of sexual expression leading to orgasm differs enormously (Kinsey, 1948, p. 336; 1953, p. 520).

Social class and masturbation. Masturbation is most frequent among college-level males and least frequent among grade-school males, with the high-school level falling halfway between (1948, p. 341). The college-level male usually feels that masturbation is perfectly acceptable and not so immoral as copulation; the non-college male often views masturbation as a dangerous perversion which may lead to disastrous physical effects. In the late teens, masturbation provides two thirds of the college-level male's sexual activities but less than one third of the non-college male's activities. Moreover, 60 to 70 percent of college-level males continue to utilize masturbation as a significant mode for orgasm after marriage, whereas only 20 to 30 percent of the non-college males masturbate after marriage (p. 339). (There are no comparable data on social class and female masturbation.)

Social class and petting. With the male there is as great a divergence of sexual experience between social classes in heterosexual petting as there is in masturbation. Petting to orgasm is a substitute for copulation for fully two thirds of the male college population, whereas less than one third of the high-school-level males and only 16 percent of the grade-school-level males have ever petted to orgasm. Moreover, frequency of orgasm from petting is *five times higher* for the college-level male than for the non-college male.

Among females, there seems to be no difference in incidence of heterosexual petting among the different social levels. Some 95 percent of all females, of all social classes, pet before marriage. Among those who experience orgasm, there is a frequency of orgasm of about once every five to ten weeks (1953, pp. 240–241).

Deep kissing is accepted as commonplace among the college-level group and is a prime source of erotic arousal for them. The lower-level group considers deep kissing a perversion and a source of disease (1948, p. 369). Caressing the breast is accepted as commonplace by the college level and it is often viewed as a perversion ("the breast is for babies") by the lower level (p. 371). Oral-genital erotic stimulation is about twice as frequent in the college level as it is in the grade-school level (72 percent vs. 40 percent), with the high-school level about midway (65 percent) (p. 371). The lower-level attitude toward most petting techniques is reflected in marital copulation. Often, at this level, copulation is performed with a minimum of preliminary and accompanying petting.

Homosexual petting is much less frequent for the college-level male than it is for the non-college population. Only about 20 percent of college-level males have experienced orgasm in homosexual petting before marriage; and after marriage, this figure drops to about 2 percent. In contrast, about one half of the non-college males experience orgasm in homosexual petting before marriage; and about 10 percent have such experience after marriage (p. 357).

Homosexual behavior among females is correlated more highly to social level than is any other mode of female sexual expression. By age 30, 10 percent of the grade-school level, 18 percent of the high-school level, 25 percent of the college level, and 33 percent of the graduate level have experienced some homosexual erotic response; and of these groups, 5 percent, 5 percent, 10 percent, and 14 percent, respectively, have continued to orgasm (1953, p. 459).

As these statistics demonstrate, the human species cannot be divided into two discrete populations—heterosexual and homosexual. Among males, for example, only about one half are exclusively heterosexual in their sexual behavior and only a few percent can be termed exclusively homosexual. "It would encourage clearer thinking on these matters if persons were not characterized as heterosexual or homosexual, but as individuals who have had certain amounts of heterosexual experience and certain amounts of homosexual experience" (1948, p. 617).

Social class and copulation. With the male, the social levels are farthest apart in the experience of premarital copulation. In the later teens only 42 percent of college-level males experience premarital copulation, as compared to 84 percent of the high-school-level and 98 percent of the grade-school-level males (1948, p. 347). Ultimately, however, 60 percent of college males experience premarital copulation.

So nearly universal is premarital intercourse among grade-school groups that in two or three lower-level communities . . . we have been unable to find a solitary male who had not had sexual relations with girls by the time he was 16 or 17 years of age (p. 381). Lower-level males are likely to acquire weekly or more than weekly frequencies in intercourse soon after they start in early adolescence, or at least by the middle teens . . . Some lower-level males may have premarital intercourse with several hundred or even a thousand or more different girls before marriage, and here their behavior is most different from the behavior of the college-bred males (p. 383).

A good many college males never have premarital intercourse with more than the one girl whom they subsequently marry, and very few of them have premarital intercourse with more than a half-dozen girls or so. College males are very slow in arriving at their first premarital intercourse, and they do not have their first experience until five or six years after the lower-level males start (p. 349).

Frequency of premarital copulation varies between social levels even more widely than occurrence. Grade-school-level males experience a frequency that is seven times that of the college-level males; the high-school-level males experience a frequency that is six times that of the college-level males (p. 347).

The lower-level female marries much earlier than the college-level female; and thus fewer lower-level females copulate before marriage.[8] Only 30 percent of the grade-school-level and 50 percent of the high-school-level females copulate before marriage, as compared to 60 percent of the college-level females. However, at any given age under 20, a higher percentage of non-college-level females are experiencing premarital copulation. For example, nearly one in five of grade-school-level females have premarital copulation by age 15, as compared to only one in one hundred at the college level. Between the ages of 16 and 20, 38 percent of the grade-school level, 32 percent of the high-school level, and 18 percent of the college level are experiencing premarital copulation. By age 20, incidence of unmarried copulation is the same for all levels—about 50 percent (1953, p. 295).

Most female premarital copulation, with all social levels, occurs the year or two before marriage. The college-level females marry and begin copulating later, but more of them ultimately experience premarital copulation.

Frequency of premarital copulation is about the same for females of all social levels, in contrast to the one to six differential between the frequency of college and non-college males.

The incidence of marital copulation is about the same at all social levels (p. 354). The non-college level tends to use only one position in copulation—the female supine beneath the male—with other positions considered perversions. Variations from this position occur among about two thirds of the college-level population (1948, p. 373).

Participation in extramarital copulation ultimately involves about half of all husbands and about one fourth of all wives. In the college group, the incidence of extramarital copulation rises after age 40; in the non-college group it drops. Between the time of marriage and age 40, about 15 percent of the college-level male's sexual activity is extramarital; after age 40 this more than doubles to about 33 percent. Between marriage and age 40 about 20 percent of the non-college male's sexual activity is extramarital, but this incidence drops to 10 percent after age 40 (p. 355). The trend of participation in extramarital affairs is thus actually reversed for the two classes. For the female, class level seems to have no significant effect in the incidence of extramarital sexual activity (p. 440).

Social class and psychological stimuli. The college-level male is more responsive to psychological stimuli than the non-college male. He is much more inclined to think about girls, talk about them, watch them, look at photographs of them, and read stories and articles about sexual behavior with them (1948, p. 363). Presently available data indicate that there is no difference in females of different social levels in their erotic response to psychological stimuli (1953, p. 685).

Social class and attitude toward nudity. The attitude toward nudity differs sharply with social class. For both males and females, nudity is accepted as commonplace

---

[8]Given the incidence of premarital copulation among lower-level males, the females who do participate must maintain a very high level of incidence in order to account for the differential of experience between the two.

in the college group. Nudity is almost universal in the home, and virtually all this population pet and copulate nude, except in situations which are semi-public (1948, p. 366). At the high-school level, only a little more than half of the population ever pet or copulate while nude; and at the grade-school level nudity is very unusual both in the home and in petting or copulation.

In the lower levels, nudity is virtually taboo, being considered obscene or dirty. Many of the lower-level population actually take pride in having never seen their mate unclothed; they often "acquire considerable knack of removing daytime clothing and putting on night clothes without ever exposing any part of their body" (p. 367). The human body is considered "dirty" and an object of shame at this level. The furor over the topless bathing suit for women in 1964 is a case in point. In a trial in Chicago the prosecutor told the jury that the defendant's behavior in wearing a topless suit was "like throwing dirt in the police officer's face and in your faces."

Sexual Behavior in the '70s—A Sexual Revolution?

An exceedingly important event that occurred in the early 1960s was the development and availability of the contraceptive pill for women.[9] It is still too early to assess the consequences that this discovery may have upon American sexual patterns and attitudes, but there is every probability that the pill is bringing enormous and far-reaching changes. Before the advent of the pill, copulation was obviously the concern of the entire society; for it was inseparable from the possibility of pregnancy. Now that copulation can be solely a function of individual need fulfillment—whether for pleasure, communication, or love—it may be argued that it is the concern of no one but the couple involved. This argument provides, of course that each person in the relation is physically, socially, and emotionally mature enough to accept the responsibility for what he is doing.

We can only speculate whether the social repercussions of the pill itself led to the increasing sexual candor characteristic of the late 1960s, or whether that candor would have developed anyway with the rapid social changes during that decade. But signs are clearly evident everywhere that sexuality has become more respectable—from movies, magazines, and the Broadway stage, where nudity, Anglo-Saxon words, and even the explicit depiction of various sexual activities (marital, premarital, extramarital, group, and homosexual) became commonplace, to such exalted levels as the Supreme Court, with their decisions regarding obscenity, and the President's Commission on Pornography (1970), which found no evidence that any harm whatever comes from the most explicit of sexual portrayals and advised that censorship laws be reexamined in this light.

We have noted that there was no significant change in male sexual behavior between Kinsey's "older" and "younger" generations (those maturing in the 1920s and 1940s). All published research since Kinsey agrees that male sexual

---

[9]See Chapter Eleven for a discussion of the pill and other birth control measures.

behavior also remained substantially unchanged in the 1950s and 60s. Unlike the male in this regard, however, female sexual behavior changed quite markedly between the 1920s and 40s. It then remained at the 1940 level for 20 years,[10] until the late 1960s—when once again significant changes, at least among college girls, apparently began to occur. Robinson (1968) found, for example, that 29 percent of the coeds in Georgia had experienced premarital copulation; Luckey and Nass (1969) found the figure to be 43 percent for college girls in 21 colleges in the United States;[11] Davis's (1970) figure for girls age 19 and over at Kansas State University was 37 percent and at the University of Colorado, 56 percent; Kaats and Davis (1970) found the figure to be 41 percent for coeds enrolled in a psychology course at the University of Colorado.[12] In the writer's classes at the College of San Mateo (California), the incidence of premarital copulation among coeds has risen to 40 percent in 1970. Cannon and Long (1971) in reviewing the most recent literature summed up their findings as follows:

Apparently there is not a single major study that has been made in the late 1960s that has found premarital coital rates that were the level of those found in the late 1950s and early 1960s (p. 40).

In examining the incidence of premarital copulation in regard to the depth or permanence of the ·relation between the girl and her partner, Bell and Chaskes (1970) found that in comparing 1958 to 1968 data, the percentage of coeds having premarital copulation had risen in casual dating from 10 to 23 percent, in steady dating from 25 to 28 percent, and in engagement from 31 to 39 percent.

Further examination of the data suggests that in 1958 the relation of engagement was very often the prerequisite to a girl having premarital sexual intercourse. Engagement often provided her with a high level of emotional and future commitment which she often felt justified her having coitus. However, in 1968 it appeared that the need to be engaged and all it implied was much less a condition the coed thought necessary before sexual intercourse . . . To put it another way, if in 1958, the coed had premarital intercourse, it most often occurred while she was engaged. But in 1968, girls were more apt to have their first sexual experience while dating or going steady (Bell and Chaskes, p. 82).

---

[10]Estimates of incidence of premarital copulation among coeds varied from 13 to 25 percent during the 1950s and 60s, but most researchers reported a figure close to 20 percent (Smigel and Seiden, 1968; Leslie, 1967; Bell, 1966, 1967; Reiss, 1966, 1967; Kephart, 1966; Freedman, 1965; and Ehrman, 1961).

[11]Luckey and Nass (1969) also surveyed cultures outside the United States and found the percentage of coeds reporting premarital copulation to be 35 percent for Canada, 55 percent for Germany, and 63 percent for England. In a similar study, Christensen and Gregg (1970) found the figure in Denmark to be 97 percent!

[12]In an attempt to relate personal attributes to incidence of premarital copulation among college girls, Kaats and Davis (1970) also found that among the "most attractive" group, 56 percent had experienced copulation, as compared to 37 percent for the "least attractive" group. The most attractive group also had the greatest number of sex partners. The assumption is that "the more attractive girls will be exposed to more sustained and convincing romantic behavior by suitors, and hence are more likely to have the opportunity to engage in 'lovemaking' with partners who care for them" (p. 92).

It has been popular in recent years to maintain that there has been no significant change in sexual behavior in college females despite the obvious changes
in the sexual attitudes of the mass media, the increasing incidence of venereal
disease among adolescents,[13] the increasing number of illegitimate births,[14] and
the growing number of unmarried couples openly living together. As late as
1967, a survey taken by the Institute for Sex Research among nearly 1,200 male
and female college students found no significant change from the Kinsey data,
and Reiss stated in 1968 that "the popular notion that America is undergoing a
'sexual revolution' is a myth." Perhaps in 1968, it was still a myth, but the my-
thologies of yesterday's mass media often predict and precede today's facts.

The previous decade was a time of wide-spread youthful rebellion toward
many of the norms of our society; it would be surprising if this rebellion did not
include impatience with the sexual proscriptions of our society:

*While there has always been rebellion by the younger generation toward their elders,
it probably never has been as great in the United States as it has been since the mid
1960s . . . Many college students now believe that a number of the norms of adult institutions are not only wrong but also immoral. This is the view held by many college students
toward the treatment of the blacks, toward the war in Vietnam, [and] toward American
political procedures . . . It therefore seems logical that if many of the norms of these institutions are viewed as wrong and immoral by large numbers of the younger generation, they
are also going to be suspicious and critical about other norms in other adult controlled
institutions. Certainly a social institution that one would expect the younger generation
to view with skepticism would be that concerned with marriage and sexual behavior (Bell
and Chaskes, 1970, p. 81).*

Furthermore, as Bell and Chaskes point out, the rebellion of the younger
generation has been given both implicit and explicit approval by many of the
older generation. It has become, then, a rebellion not so much of youth against
age but of the forces of humanity against those of restrictive conformity and
Victorian prudery.

These, then, are the various factors that seem to be creating what may be a
sexual revolution in our society: the very deep-seated disillusionment and skepticism of college youth toward societal institutions; the changing status of women,
with college girls, especially, demanding to have the same status and privilege
as the male in the society; the growing sexual candor at all levels of society; and,
finally, the advent of the pill, which gives sexuality a completely new meaning
by making the separation of sex and pregnancy possible — a possibility that now
occurs for the first time in the history of humanity.

The so-called "new morality" of the 1960s and 1970s no longer accepts the
concept that premarital copulation is immoral, *per se* — though this is certainly

---

[13]See the section *What about Venereal Disease?* in Chapter Three.
[14]The number of illegitimate births in our society doubled between 1950 and 1970. In California,
for example 46,000 babies, or nearly 13 percent of all live births, were illegitimate in 1970, and about
half of these were to mothers under age 20 (California Health Department, *Study on Illegitimacy,
1971*).

still the view of much of our establishment institutions, both religious and secular. The "new morality" maintains the essential desirability of the pleasure-giving aspect of sex, viewing sex as an essential way of relating which can be good or bad, depending upon the meaning of the relation to the couple. In other words, the "new morality" takes the position that sexual behavior is essentially a private matter between responsible, mature individuals. Sexual cruelty, sexual callousness, sexual exploitation (or sexual indifference for that matter) are viewed as deplorable—but only in the same way that cruelty, callousness, exploitation, or indifference are deplorable in any area of human interaction. Sex is seen as a natural extension of the intimacy, understanding, cooperation, and kindness of a relation, rather than as a separate and distinct human function to be performed and sanctified only within marriage.

This naturalistic view of sexual relations is still a minority point of view, of course, among the population as a whole and even among the young. Whether the changes in sexual attitudes and behavior that we have noted among some of the young are a "sexual revolution"—that is whether we will see sweeping *institutional* changes throughout our society in this regard—it is, of course, impossible to say as yet.

Societal Attitudes toward Sexuality

Man's sexual behavior, like his behavior in general, is acquired through his experiences as an organism with certain biological and psychological capacities and through his experiences as a unit of his society. At the biological-psychological level, sexual behavior is affected by the individual's general health—his glandular functioning, his diet, his level of energy—and by the psychological characteristics that make up his unique personality structure (see Chapters One and Three). As a unit of society, the individual learns to behave in ways that his society (or subsociety) considers "right" or "moral" and to avoid the "wrong" or the "immoral"; his sexual behavior, therefore, "is always shaped in a particular cultural milieu and oriented by the values of the society maintaining that milieu" (Frumkin, 1967, p. 439).

In short, though individuals may differ markedly in sexual capacity and interest, each individual's sexual behavior is determined to a very considerable extent by the social values and attitudes that he has learned—and incorporated into his own value system. Within a society, attitudes toward sex will differ, then, to the extent that segments within that society have different attitudes and that individuals differ in their perception, and introjection, of these attitudes.

All societies make some institutional provision for acceptable reproductive behavior, providing for copulation and pregnancy, and protection of the female and offspring, within a comparatively stable framework. In addition, all societies seek to control the purely pleasurable aspects of sexual expression (particularly when youth are involved). However, societies vary tremendously in the extent and rigorousness of their control. At one extreme, the *antisexual societies* look upon sex as degrading and immoral. At the other extreme, *prosexual societies* exalt sex as a source of delight. Although most societies fall somewhere between the extremes of sexual permissiveness and stringent sexual proscription, primarily antisexual and primarily prosexual societies do exist; and in our own society the two extremes frequently conflict.

Antisexual Societies

One basically antisexual society, the Manu of New Guinea, regards sex as a necessary evil, an unpleasant chore that men and women must perform for the sake of reproduction (Frumkin, 1967). There is no word in the Manu language for love; there are no romantic stories, no songs or dances. "Kissing is unknown, and breast stimulation and similar forms of love play . . . are generally lacking . . . . To the Manus sex is a sin" (p. 441).

In other antisexual societies, sexuality is accepted for males but proscribed except as a function of reproduction for females. Saudi Arabian girls, when they are about eight years old, are required to undergo a clitoridectomy (surgical amputation of the clitoris); since the clitoris has no function in reproduction but is the chief organ of sexual response, the girl can still reproduce but is less likely to enjoy sexual activity. The Sudanese not only amputate the clitoris but sew up the opening to the vagina at the same time, removing the sutures only at marriage.

Other societies (for example, Brazil, Spain, Sicily, and Mexico) are somewhat less extreme, in that they do not resort to anatomically crippling the girl, but do rigorously chaperone unmarried middle-class girls until marriage. In Greece, Sicily, Italy, and eastern Europe the bride may be required to prove her virginity in rural areas by flying a blood-stained sheet from the window the morning after the wedding night, as witness to her premarital chastity.

Prosexual Societies

Most human societies accept in varying degrees the pleasure-giving aspect of sex within marriage and permit some degree of sexual intimacy to children and adolescents. In fact, "in nearly every culture in the world there is at least some acceptance of coital activities among unmarried adolescent and teenage youth, both female and male . . . [and] in the majority of instances it is considered socially desirable that there *should* be premarital coitus" (Kinsey, 1953, p. 284).

However, probably the most openly and uninhibitedly prosexual peoples are those who inhabit the various tropical islands. For example, among the Trobriand Islanders of the South Pacific "children become acquainted with sex at a very early age by witnessing their parents in sexual intercourse and by imitating with their playmates their parents' sexual behavior. The art of love is gradually developed from the sexual games and play of Trobriand children into the passionate liaisons and partnerships of adolescence and adulthood" (Frumkin, 1967, p. 444). Among the Marquesans, also of the South Pacific, "regular coitus is begun before puberty . . . and sexual play is a favorite form of activity. . . .

[Among adults] exclusive sexual possession is socially disapproved. Sexual jealousy is considered in poor taste" (p. 443).

Polynesians encourage free sexual experimentation and play among their children, who observe nude dancing and demonstrations in techniques of copulation. Masturbation is either ignored or encouraged (Danielsson, 1961); and as soon as the boys have reached physical maturity and undergone the circumcision rite (at about age 14), they are instructed sexually by an older woman. "He is taught to perform cunnilingus, to kiss and suck breasts, and to bring his partner to climax several times before he reaches orgasm" (Marshall, 1971, p. 44). Girls are expected to develop an appetite for sex at about the same age, when they start to menstruate.

Until the present century, when American culture infiltrated the cultures of many Pacific Island peoples, there was no word in the Tahitian language for *immoral* and no word corresponding to *illegitimate*. The word for *fun* was the same as that for *copulate*, and adolescents were encouraged in sex play. Pregnancies were welcomed, and babies were absorbed into the households of the grandparents. Thus, the young adult was permitted full sexual freedom when his sex drive was the highest; he was not tied down by the responsibility of caring for offspring until he was well established in middle age and was happy to welcome children into his household.

Most prosexual societies, however, encourage early marriage — at least as soon as the female becomes pregnant.[15] When pregnancy occurs, the couple are expected to marry — forming a permanent social unit and providing for the protection of the mother and the child and the stability and continuation of the group.

The American Society

Until the present century, our society was avowedly antisexual — or, at least, closer to the antisexual than to the prosexual end of the continuum. Elements of prosexuality, which had always been present, became increasingly evident during the first third of the century; and, as we enter the last third, the two forces are vying with almost equivalent effect.

Our sexual heritage stems from the traditional antisexuality of the medieval church, when such writers as St. Augustine stated categorically, "The act of generation is sin itself" — a sin transmitted *"ipso facto . . .* to the new creation." This doctrine of the sinfulness of sex, even when limited to reproduction, has been remarkably persistent. As recently as the nineteenth century the Surgeon General of the United States wrote that "nine tenths of the time, a *decent* woman does not feel the slightest pleasure in intercourse," and eminent gynecologists

---

[15] An adolescent girl is not necessarily fertile just because she is menstruating — a phenomenon known as *adolescent sterility* (Montagu, 1957). She *may* menstruate for two or three years before ovulation occurs or, if ovulation does occur, before the ovum is capable of being fertilized or before she has the hormonal development necessary to become pregnant.

labeled sexual desire in young women as "pathological" (Hunt, 1959, p. 319).

In our contemporary society, a "naturalistic-acceptance" approach to sex is vying with this traditional approach. The naturalistic view regards both the reproductive and the pleasure-giving aspects of sex as normal, natural, healthful, and good — in any case, of no concern to society as long as the two persons involved are mature enough to accept the responsibility for their behavior.

Sex is thus viewed primarily as a method of relating, which can have many meanings and many consequences. If people relate to each other sexually in ways that are selfish, exploitative, ruthless, or callous, such a relationship is "bad" — just as a similar type of asexual relationship is bad. On the other hand, sexual — or asexual — relationships that are warm, friendly, and understanding, that deepen intimacy and communication, are defined as "good."

This naturalistic-acceptance view of sex is now quite widely held as legitimate within marriage, even by such staunch traditionalists as the Catholic Church, within which the doctrine of St. Augustine originated. For example, in 1951 Pope Pius XII affirmed that "the husband and wife shall find pleasure and happiness of mind and body." However, our formal institutions still forbid all forms of non-marital sexuality. And despite the wide incidence of sexual activity among the population, before and outside of marriage, most people continue publicly to uphold the institutional sanctions against such activity while they also continue to violate these sanctions privately. In general, the naturalistic-acceptance view of sex is probably still not as widely held as the traditional view, especially among females.[16] In many respects we still remain an antisexual society.

Identification of sex with dirt. In our society, sexual matters, whether anatomical or behavioral, are commonly associated with the concept of "dirt."[17] A "dirty" joke is almost always a sexual joke; a nude photograph, however artistic, becomes a "dirty" picture; a story about sex, even if it has literary merit, is a "dirty" story. Most striking in this regard is our identification of certain words as "dirty" — words associated with sex. So rigorous is this taboo that even textbooks and professional journals use such euphemisms as "the sex act," "having relations," "having intercourse," or "being intimate" — or, at best, the Latinate "copulation" — rather than the more familiar, concrete, and graphic Anglo-Saxon words. Admittedly, the very text you are reading, although it does shun the euphemisms, uses the Latin "copulate" rather than its Anglo-Saxon equivalents. The problem is that neither the so-called "gutter talk" nor the sterile scientific terminology properly *communicates* the facts: The Anglo-Saxonisms are too morally and emotionally loaded to be useful and usable; the Latinisms are cold, clinical, and

---

[16]For an excellent summary of present sexual attitudes in the United States, see Grunwald (1964). For a discussion of America's position on the prosexual-antisexual continuum, see Frumkin (1961).
[17]"One reason why genitality is considered to be 'dirty' may be guilt by association. The organs concerned are recognized and identified first as producers of urine, that is, as producers of dirt. Later it is discovered that (copulation) is performed by the same dirt-producing instrument. Here is dirt by association" (Dundes, 1966, p. 103).

unfamiliar to most people. The paucity of appropriate words available for discussing sex stems from the fear and sanctions that have surrounded sexuality.

The autosexual taboo. A society's attitude toward masturbation is perhaps the
most significant index to its position on the prosexual-antisexual continuum, inasmuch as masturbating has neither a reproductive nor an interpersonal function but must be viewed solely as pleasurable. Prosexual societies are not only
permissive toward masturbation but actually encourage it on the grounds that it
is an important training procedure for copulation. Antisexual societies, on the
other hand, find it an obvious target and condemn it as repulsive, degenerate,
immoral, and perverted "self-abuse."

The totally unsubstantiated notion that masturbation is harmful began in the
eighteenth century with Tissot, a French physician, who ascribed most known
ills to masturbation (Tissot, 1764, pp. 57–67). Insanity was soon added to Tissot's
list; and by 1839, the belief that maturbation caused insanity as well as countless
other diseases was held to be medical fact (Dearborn, 1967).

Representative of this attitude was an enormously popular book, Dr. Kellogg's
Plain Facts for Young and Old, published in 1879. It sold over a million copies and
was both quoted and imitated widely. Dr. Kellogg was no quack. He was a distinguished physician—a Fellow of the Royal Society of Medicine, a Fellow of the
American College of Surgeons, and an honorary Doctor of Laws. "Of all the
vices to which human beings are addicted," he writes, "no other so rapidly un-
dermines the constitution and so certainly makes a complete wreck of an individual. . . . It wastes the most precious part of the blood, uses up the vital
forces, and finally leaves the poor victim a most utterly ruined and loathsome
object." He cites the case of one "poor victim," a boy "addicted to the loathsome
vice"; this boy's father—after all remonstrance had failed—seized his son and
cut off his testicles. In Dr. Kellogg's view, the father was to be commended for
thus saving the boy from the "inevitable consequences of a practice he was
powerless to stop."

Other medical literature of the period advocated amputation and cautery of
the clitoris as an acceptable measure to combat female masturbation, as well as
suturing the labia, handcuffing, and a number of other practices and devices
(Levine and Bell, 1956).

The tenure of this doctrine is an indication of our societal willingness to accept it. Not until the present century did opinion begin slowly to change. By the 1920s, the 1930s, and the 1940s many leading theorists were not only questioning the doctrine that masturbation is physically harmful but were citing beneficial effects of masturbation. Kinsey (1948), for example, found that those who most actively masturbated in adolescence remained the most active in heterosexual behavior, and were among the most creative and productive in his sample. During the 1950s and the 1960s this shift in attitude led Dearborn, in surveying the recent literature, to conclude: "There is a growing body of opinion that masturbation (for the release of tension and for the emotional and physical satisfaction involved) is not only normal but carries with it positive values, which in many instances make it desirable and beneficial" (Dearborn, 1967, p. 206).[18]

Orgasm is now generally considered a natural biological phenomenon, however it is induced. According to a leading gynecologist, "If one is dealing with a female who has never achieved orgasm . . . it does occasionally occur that she has never experimented with masturbation. . . . Extended psychotherapeutic management is usually required in such a case, and it is an indication for psychiatric referral" (Hastings, 1963, p. 92).

The doctrine of conservation of sexual energy. Another curious, and implicitly antisexual, concept is that the person has a finite amount of sexual energy and therefore that "excessive" orgasm, whether masturbatory or copulatory, is a reckless squandering that will result in temporary or perhaps permanent impotence, as well as leaving the person a nervous wreck. This notion that "wastage of the vital fluids" will cause debility was widespread in our society until shortly after the turn of the present century (Hall, 1909; Dickerson, 1930) and is by no means unfamiliar today. The concept that sexual energy may be either conserved or wasted is not a product of our own civilization, however; it can be traced as far back as the early Greek period, where it was supported by such eminent philosophers as Empedocles, Diocles, and Plato. These classical Greek philosophers believed that semen originated in the brain and that "excessive" ejaculation would injure the central nervous system and thus impair the senses.

Not only is there no evidence that sexual energy may be husbanded, or conserved, but apparently quite the opposite is true: Those who have a high frequency of orgasm in early years, whether masturbatory or copulatory, continue a high frequency of orgasm, and those of low frequency maintain that pattern (Kinsey, 1948). Apparently a characteristic frequency of orgasm is usually established fairly early in life (at least for the male), and this pattern of ejaculatory frequency tends to persist, whether the incidence is high or low.

---

[18]See O'Hare (1950), Kinsey (1953), Kelly (1959), Ellis (1960), Calderone (1960), Hastings (1963, 1966), and Masters and Johnson (1966).

When the male is stimulated to high sexual output during his formative years and a similar tenor of activity is established for the 31–40-year range, his middle-aged and involutional years usually are marked by constantly recurring physiologic evidence of maintained sexuality. . . . It does not appear to matter what manner of sexual expression has been employed, as long as high levels of activity are maintained (Masters and Johnson, 1966, pp. 262–263).

The doctrine of sublimation. Closely related to the notion of conservation of sexual energy is the notion that any utilization of sexual energy must be compensated for by a lessening of non-sexual energy. According to this view, a person who "sublimates" his sexual drive to non-sexual behavior diverts energy that he would otherwise expend in orgasm into such productive and creative tasks as athletics, study, or creative expression.[19] Kinsey discovered, however, that the sexually active male apparently has *more* energy for other non-sexual activities and that the sexually non-active male has a generally low energy level in all categories of behavior. (There are no available data for the female in this regard.) Every individual in Kinsey's "low-incidence group" was relatively inactive non-sexually as well as sexually, and none showed the slightest sign of "sublimation" (Kinsey, 1948, pp. 208–211, 213). If sublimation occurs, there should be a correlation between low incidence of sexual activity and high incidence of non-sexual activity; but Kinsey found quite the opposite.

It is still conceivable, of course, that *temporary* sublimation might occur. Kinsey did not control for temporary sublimation, and no other research evidence is available. If temporary sublimation occurs, a sexually active person might occasionally divert into non-sexual pursuits energy he would otherwise spend in orgasm. There is a good deal of folklore to support this notion. It is very popular among coaches, who like their athletes to abstain from copulation before competition (and from masturbation at all times); and countless writers, painters, and musicians have remained celibate during artistic or creative efforts on the assumption that they would thereby have more energy. During various periods of history warriors have abstained from copulation on the eve of battle. However, although it is possible that the person who is temporarily deprived sexually may be more energetic, it is equally conceivable that—unless the deprivation is so short-lived as to be negligible—he may be preoccupied with sexual needs and thus *less* able to perform non-sexually than if he were sexually gratified and fulfilled. (This is analogous to the hungry man thinking of nothing but food.) Until further research evidence is available, the doctrine of temporary sublimation must be regarded as highly speculative.

---

[19]This doctrine was formalized as a psychoanalytic concept by Sigmund Freud (1938), but extends back into Christian, Hebrew, Greek, and even more ancient asceticism.

Concepts of perversion. Whether a specific sexual act is considered a perversion depends upon the attitude of society, and even of the subsociety in which the behavior takes place. The few exceptions to this are noted below. The concept of perversion may depend upon the idosyncrasy of the observer: The most arbitrary definitions imaginable, including everything that is even remotely sexual—except copulation in a specific position, under specific circumstances, with a specific person— is on someone's published list as a perversion. The most important point to make regarding perversion is that most marriage manuals, from the *Kama Sutra* to the present, agree that *any* behavior which is pleasurable to both parties and is not injurious is normal and desirable.

There are actually three categories of definitions of perversions: the biological, the societal, and the religious. The *biological* definition is behavior that is organically injurious. For example, sadism—an abnormality in which the person gets sexual pleasure by physically or psychologically hurting someone—is considered a perversion in all but its mildest (and relatively normal) forms. Similarly, masochism—sexual satisfaction from undergoing punishment or pain—can be biologically damaging and may therefore be considered a perversion. Any type of rape in which the victim is injured is very often a form of sadism and would be considered a biological perversion.

Once we leave those few aberrations which involve biological harmfulness, we enter the no-man's-land of *societal* and *religious* proscriptions, where almost anything might be considered a perversion. Lists of societally or religiously defined perversions fill whole volumes. A societal definition of perversion would include everything in the biological category and would add sexual behavior that is taboo within the particular societal group. The religious definition of perversion is really a subdivision of the societal definition, but adds further restrictions based upon theological convictions. Of course, a list compiled in one society or church is very likely to be completely different from a list compiled in another. The one exception is incest, which all societies define as a perversion, although there is little biological justification for this attitude.[20] The sexual activity defined as incestuous varies from society to society, but all societies consider copulation between parent and child and grandparent and grandchild incestuous, and most societies also include copulation between brother and sister.

With this one exception, there is no agreement upon what constitutes unacceptable behavior; not only from society to society, but in such a large and complex society as our own, behavior considered a perversion by one group may be perfectly acceptable to another group. Nudity is considered a perversion by the lower class, for example, but is generally acceptable in the middle class. Homosexuality is considered a perversion according to our statutory laws but is not

---

[20]It is true, of course, that incest may lead to a perseveration of genetically undesirable traits—for example, hemophilia. It is also true, however, that inbreeding may enhance desirable genetic traits. In fact, in animal communities inbreeding and selective breeding are the two methods used to obtain a genetically superior strain.

considered a perversion by many psychologists and biologists.[21] Masturbation is considered a perversion by most of the lower class and by many of the middle class but is regarded as normal by some people in all classes and as desirable and beneficial by sexologists. Cunnilingus, fellatio, and a variety of copulatory positions are regarded as perversions by our legal system but are recommended by most marriage manuals. Exhibitionism—displaying the genitals—is often listed as a perversion, is illegal in public, and is considered inappropriate by the lower class. Yet middle-class couples often prefer a lighted room for copulation and may display the genitals quite casually in the privacy of their home. Nudists display the genitals in public within the colony, and in California nude bathing is commonplace on many beaches which are not part of any nudist colony. Even voyeurism, obtaining pleasure from viewing a nude figure or sexual activity, often makes the list, although Kinsey found that almost all males are voyeurs.

Most lists of "perversions" or "aberrations" are ridiculous and are simply a perseveration of earlier lists. They have no relation whatsoever to biological normalcy, or to the way most people behave, to say nothing of accepted behavior in other societies.

Sex Myths in Our Society: A Summary

A *myth* is an invented story, an imaginary or fictitious thing, or a collective belief that occurs as part of the culture of the society. Sex myths in our society include the following:

1. "Sexual energy may be conserved." (Not true. Masters and Johnson found, as did Kinsey, that regular sexual activity in youth and middle age is the single most predictive factor of sexual activity in old age.)

2. "Sexual energy may be not only conserved but permanently diverted (sublimated) to other activities." (Not true. Kinsey found that all subjects in his "low-incidence group" in sexual performance (orgasmic experience) demonstrated a characteristic lack-luster performance in all other areas of life as well.)

3. "Sexual energy may be temporarily diverted." (The question of temporary sublimation must still be left open; however, there is no direct evidence to support it and some direct evidence to contradict it. Masters and Johnson, for example, found no evidence that even continued and persistent ejaculation in the male is followed by any subsequent physiological debilitation.)

---

[21]Some religious bodies still consider homosexual relations as "unnatural and sinful," but others have subscribed to the view that homosexuality is merely an alternate form of natural sexual expression. An influential statement by British Quakers in 1963, for example, held that "homosexual affection can be as selfless as heterosexual affection" and therefore is not necessarily "a sin." At a 1967 symposium on homosexuality sponsored by Manhattan's Cathedral Church of St. John the Divine, 90 Episcopal priests agreed that the church should classify homosexual acts between consenting adults as "morally neutral" in themselves and that they should be judged by the results, which may very well be good. The reverend Walter D. Dennis, Cannon of St. John, said "A homosexual relation should be judged by the same criteria as a heterosexual marriage—that is, whether it is intended to foster a . . . relation of love" (Auchincloss, 1968, p. 74).

4. "Masturbation is physically harmful." (Not true. There is no evidence to support this statement.)

5. "Excessive masturbation is physically harmful." (In the opinion of Masters and Johnson, among others, this notion is no longer tenable: In the female multiple orgasm is normal, and in the male the ability to ejaculate is self-limiting.)

6. "A person may be oversexed or undersexed." (There are great individual differences in both the capacity for sexual arousal and the capacity for sexual performance. However, a person can be considered oversexed or undersexed only in relation to a specific sex partner. The terms "nymphomania," high drive levels for the female, and "satyriasis," high drive levels in the male, no longer carry pathological meaning; see Hastings, 1963, p. 15.)

7. "There is widespread impotence in the male." (Persistent impotence is so rare as to be almost mythological, although occasional failure of erection under apparently optimal circumstances does occur. Ignorance of the reflex erection — the all-but-inevitable result of persistent penile massage — has led to a very widespread acceptance of this notion.)

8. "Size of the penis indicates virility." (Not true. Masters and Johnson found no relation between penile size and virility.)

9. "A large penis is more satisfying to the female." (Not true. Masters and Johnson found no relation between penile size and female satisfaction.)

10. "The pubic bone of the female may seize the penis." (Not true. This notion is probably based upon the phenomenon of "locking" that occurs in dogs, which is a consequence of the shape of the canine penis, with its bulbular end in erection. "Locking" does not occur in human beings. The rather rare occurrence of a vaginal sphincter muscle spasm gives support to this belief.)

11. "Female homosexuality is more common than male homosexuality." (Not true. Male homosexuality is about double that of the female.)

12. "A ruptured or absent hymen is proof that the girl is not a virgin." (Not true. Many girls are born without the hymen; moreover, the hymen may be ruptured by non-sexual activity.)

13. "The female is slower than the male in responding to erotic stimuli." (Not true. The lubrication of the vagina, which results from the "sweating" of the vaginal walls during the first phase of erotic response occurs within 10–20 seconds of erotic stimulation and is a sure sign that the female is aroused.)

14. "The female does not experience orgasm." (Not true.)

15. "The female ejaculates with orgasm." (Not true.)

16. "The female's orgasm is different from the male's." (Not true. It *is* true that the female does not ejaculate, but neither does the preadolescent male. It is *also* true that there are great individual differences in the experience of orgasm. There are no greater differences in this respect *between* males and females than there are *among* males and females, however. These individual differences are based upon biological factors, upon the situation, and upon the partner — and upon such psychological factors as expectation and past

conditioning experiences; they are *not* based upon whether the individual is a male or a female.)

17. "There is a vaginal orgasm and a clitoral orgasm—the vaginal orgasm being characteristic of emotional maturity." (Not true. Masters and Johnson were able to lay once and for all the stubborn ghost of the vaginal orgasm. An orgasm is an orgasm, regardless of the stimulation which produces it. The chief areas of erotic arousal are the mons, the labia, and the clitoris. Occasional women do prefer vaginal stimulation—and may even dislike clitoral manipulation; but this is very rare and can probably be explained as a function of cultural conditioning. Vaginal penetration is usually pleasurable and may induce orgasm, even though the vagina is relatively poorly supplied with nerve endings. Possible explanations involve various psychological factors associated with penetration: "referred" sensations; incidental clitoral, mons, and labial stimulation; and generalized bodily contact.)

18. "Multiple orgasm in the female is a myth." (Not true. Masters and Johnson found that the typical female reaches satiety only with three to four orgasms; some are capable of thirty to forty.)

19. "It is important for copulating couples always to experience simultaneous orgasm." (While this can be very gratifying, taking turns is much more practical, with the occasional simultaneous orgasm occurring spontaneously. Being compulsive about this can make nervous wrecks out of both parties, with each failure inducing guilt feelings and anxiety.)

20. "Simultaneous orgasms are necessary for conception to occur." (Not true. Conception may occur—and usually does in our society—with the female *not* experiencing orgasm.)

21. "The person is tired, or depressed, after orgasm." (Not true. This is perhaps the most curious myth of all. The typical psychological consequence of orgasm is a feeling of profound tranquility and contentment.)

22. "The menopause terminates a woman's sex life." (Not true. It is true that the reproductive aspect is terminated; but the pleasurable aspect—e.g., the physiological sequence to orgasm—is not affected.)

23. "A hysterectomy will terminate a woman's sex life." (Not true. As with menopause, the reproductive aspect is terminated, but not the pleasurable aspect.)

24. "Men and women alike lose their sex drive after age 50." (Not true. Nearly all husbands and wives copulate regularly after this age, and most copulate regularly into the 60s and 70s.)

Summary

The male is much more a sexual creature than the female in our society; from his initial ejaculation at about age 13, he demonstrates a universality and a regularity of sexual arousal and orgasm. There is, however, a gradual decline—from about four to three to two to one ejaculation per week, as he ages from

20 to 30 to 40 to 50, so that by age 60 ejaculatory frequency is less than once per week. He usually continues to be sexually active until his death, however.

The most important observation that may be made about female sexuality is that, unlike the male, there is no such thing as an average female. Sexuality in females is interrelated with so many deterministic factors—biological, psychological, and social—that the likelihood of any individual female being sexually like any other is exceedingly remote insofar as taxonomic data are concerned. Most females (perhaps two thirds) rarely experience sexual arousal, one fourth never experience orgasm before age 25, and one tenth never experience orgasm during the course of their lifetime. On the other hand, there are females more ardent than most males, and some females are more ardent than *any* male.

Inasmuch as females in other societies do not demonstrate this relative antisexuality, and the Kinsey data indicate a marked change in many aspects of female response between the older and younger generation, it seems reasonable to assume that cultural attitudes and expectations are significantly involved in female sexuality.

Our society is close to the antisexuality pole of the prosexual–antisexual continuum, although we appear to be moving away from the traditional (sex is dirty) persuasion toward a naturalistic-acceptance persuasion, and this movement is apparently being accelerated. Examples of implicit antisexuality are our identification of sex with dirt, our autosexual taboo, and the widespread acceptance of the doctrines of conservation of sexual energy and sublimation—neither of which has any demonstrable scientific validity.

As for concepts of sexual perversion—they are largely societal. What may be considered a perversion in one society may be perfectly acceptable in another. Actually, there are three definitions of perversion: biological, social, and religious. The biologist defines as a perversion only that behavior which is harmful to the individual or to another; the social definition includes numerous taboos, which are often extremely arbitrary; the religious definition adds theological proscriptions.

The subject of human sexuality, although extremely important (and extremely complex), is often ignored as a profound and sacred mystery which should not be openly discussed. The result is a very widespread acceptance of sexual myths, sexual ignorance, sexual stupidity. People are sexual; they do have sexual lives; and the more that is known about sexual behavior the greater the likelihood that there will be sexual harmony and satisfaction within marriage.

Questions

1 What are the two main sources of our knowledge about sexual behavior of American males and females?
2 What is most significant about male sexual behavior?
3 What did Kinsey feel was the most important finding in his research on female sexuality? Why?
4 What percent of married females at age 25 have not experienced orgasm?

What percent during their entire married lives?

5   Why does the average male often feel betrayed and dejected by the antisexuality of his wife?

6   What is the cause of the sexual indifference of females in our society?

7   At what age do most females reach a maximum of erotic interest? What factors are involved?

8   How do (a) most males in our society learn to masturbate? (b) most females?

9   What changes were demonstrated by Kinsey in the sexual behavior of the two generations of females? Of males? How does this compare with recent data?

10 Why has frigidity been reduced in

the U. S. during the last four decades?

11 Discuss the popular notion that America is undergoing a sexual "revolution."

12 How does the advent of the pill give sexuality a completely new meaning?

13 Where is the emphasis in the "new morality" of the 1960s and 1970s?

14 Describe the doctrine of conservation of sexual energy. What did Kinsey discover about the energy of the sexually active male?

15 What are the three categories of definitions of perversion? How do they differ?

16 What are some of the sex myths in our society?

References and Selected Readings

Auchincloss, Douglas. The Gay Crowd. In Joe David Brown, ed., *Sex in the Sixties.* New York: Time-Life Books, 1968, pp. 65–75.

Beach, Frank, ed. *Sex and Behavior.* New York: Wiley, 1965.

Beigel, H. G., ed. *Advances in Sex Research.* Scranton, Pa.: International Textbook Co., 1970.

Bell, Robert R. *Premarital Sex in a Changing Society.* Englewood Cliffs, N. J.: Prentice-Hall, 1966.

_____, and Jay B. Chaskes. Premarital Sexual Experience among Coeds, 1958 and 1968. *Journal of Marriage and the Family,* February 1970, Vol. 32, pp. 81–84.

_____, and Leonard Blumberg. Courtship Intimacy and Religious Background. *Marriage and Family Living,* November 1959, Vol. 31, pp. 356–360.

_____. Courtship Stages and Intimacy Attitudes. *The Family Life Coordinator,* March 1960, Vol. 8, pp. 61–63.

Bergler, Edmund, and W. S. Kroger. *Kinsey's Myth of Female Sexuality: The Medical Facts.* New York: Grune & Stratton, 1954.

Bibby, Cyril. The Art of Loving. In Albert Ellis and Albert Abarbanel, eds., *The Encyclopedia of Sexual Behavior,* 2nd ed. New York: Hawthorn, 1967.

Birenbaum, Arnold. Revolution without the Revolution: Sex in Contemporary America. *Journal of Sex Research,* November 1970, Vol. 6, pp. 257–267.

Brecher, Edward M. *The Sex Researchers.* Boston: Little, Brown, 1969.

Brecher, Ruth and Edward, eds. *An Analysis of Human Sexual Response.* New York: New American Library, 1966.

Burr, Wesley R. *Premarital Attitudes and Behavior.* Unpublished manuscript, available in mimeograph form. Child Development and Family Relations Department,

Brigham Young University, Provo, Utah.

Calderone, Mary S. *Release from Sexual Tensions.* New York: Random House, 1960.

Cannon, Kenneth L., and Richard Long. Premarital Sexual Behavior in the Sixties. *Journal of Marriage and the Family,* February 1971, Vol. 33, pp. 36–49.

Christensen, Harold T., and Christina F. Gregg. Changing Sex Norms in America and Scandinavia. *Journal of Marriage and the Family,* November 1970, Vol. 32, pp. 616–627.

Crawley, Alfred E. *Studies of Savages and Sex* (Landmarks in Anthropopogy Series). New York: Johnson, 1969.

Danielsson, Bengt. Sex Life in Polynesia. In Ellis and Abarbanel, eds., *The Encyclopedia of Sexual Behavior,* pp. 832–840.

Davenport, William. Sexual Patterns in a Southwest Pacific Society. In Brecher and Brecher, eds., *An Analysis of Human Sexual Response.* New York: New American Library, 1966.

Davis, Keith E. Is There a Revolution? *Medical Aspects of Human Sexuality,* Winter 1970.

Dearborn, Lester W. Autoeroticism. In Ellis and Abarbanel, eds. *The Encyclopedia of Sexual Behavior,* pp. 204–215.

——————. Masturbation. In Fishbein and Kennedy, eds., *Modern Marriage and Family Living.* New York: Oxford University Press, 1957, pp. 484–497.

DeMartino, Manfred F., ed. *Sexual Behavior and Personality Characteristics.* New York: Grove, 1966.

Dickerson, R. E. *So Youth May Know.* New York: Association Press, 1930.

Duffy, J. Masturbation and Clitoridectomy. *Journal of the American Medical Association,* 1963, Vol. 19, pp. 246–248.

Dundes, Alan. Here I Sit—A Study of American Latrinialia. *The Kroeber Anthropological Society Papers,* Berkeley: Dept. of Anthropology, Spring 1966, No. 34, pp. 93–103.

Ehrman, Winston. Changing Sexual Mores. In E. Ginzberg, ed., *Values and Ideals of American Youth.* New York: Columbia University Press, 1961, pp. 53–70.

Eichenlaub, John E. *New Approaches to Sex in Marriage.* New York: Dell, 1970.

Ellis, Albert. *The Art and Science of Love.* New York: Lyle Stewart, 1960.

——————, and Albert Abarbanel. *The Encyclopedia of Sexual Behavior,* 2nd ed. New York: Hawthorn, 1967.

——————, and Roger Conway. *Art of Erotic Seduction.* New York: Ace, 1970.

Ford, C. S., and F. A. Beach. *Patterns of Sexual Behavior.* New York: Harper Row, 1970.

Freud, Sigmund. *The Basic Writings of Sigmund Freud,* A. A. Brill, ed. New York: Modern Library, 1938.

Frumkin, Robert M. Sexual Freedom. In Ellis and Abarbanel, eds., *The Encyclopedia of Sexual Behavior,* pp. 439–449.

Gagnon, John H., and William Simon. Prospects for Change in American Sexual Patterns. *Medical Aspects of Human Sexuality,* January 1970, Vol. 4, pp. 100–117.

Glasner, Rabbi Samuel. Judaism and Sex. In Ellis and Abarbanel, eds., *The Encyclopedia of Sexual Behavior,* pp. 575–584.

Grunwald, Henry Anatole, ed. *Sex in America.* New York: Bantam, 1964.

Hall, W. J. *From Youth into Manhood.* New York: Association Press, 1909.

Hastings, Donald W. *Impotence and Frigidity.* Boston: Little, Brown, 1963.

_____. Can Specific Training Procedures Overcome Sexual Inadequacy? In Brecher and Brecher, eds., *An Analysis of Human Sexual Response.* New York: New American Library, 1966.

_____. *Doctor Speaks on Sexual Expression in Marriage.* Boston: Little, Brown, 1966.

Hegeler, Inge and Sten. *An ABZ of Love.* Trans. David Hohnen. New York: Crown, 1970.

Himmelhoch, Jerome. Kinsey's Research Design and Statistical Methods. In Sylvia Fleis, ed., *Sexual Behavior in American Society.* New York: Norton, 1955.

Kaats, Gilbert R., and Keith E. Davis. The Dynamics of Sexual Behavior of College Students. *Journal of Marriage and the Family,* August 1970, Vol. 32, pp. 390–399.

Kellogg, J. H., M.D. *Plain Facts for Young and Old.* Burlington, Iowa: Segner & Condit, 1879.

Kinsey, A. C., *et al. Sexual Behavior in the Human Female.* Philadelphia: Saunders, 1953.

_____. *Sexual Behavior in the Human Male.* Philadelphia: Saunders, 1948.

Kirkendall, L. A. *Premarital Intercourse and Interpersonal Relations.* New York: Julian, 1961.

_____, and R. W. Libby. Interpersonal Relationships — Crux of the Sexual Renaissance. *Journal of Social Issues,* 1966, Vol. 22, pp. 45–59.

_____, and Robert N. Whitehurst, eds. *The New Sexual Revolution.* New York: Brown, 1971.

Krich, Avon M., ed. *Sexual Revolution,* 2 Vols. New York: Dell, 1967.

Kronhausen, Phyllis and Eberhard. *Erotic Fantasies: A Study of the Sexual Imagination in Underground Literature.* New York: Grove, 1970.

Levine, M. I., and J. I. Bell. Psychological Aspects of Pediatric Practice: Masturbation. *Pediatrics,* 1956, Vol. 18, p. 803.

Lief, Harold Isaiah, *et al.,* eds. *The Psychological Basis of Medical Practice.* New York: Harper, 1963.

Luckey, Eleanore B., and Gilbert D. Nass. A Comparison of Sexual Attitudes and Behavior in an International Sample. *Journal of Marriage and the Family,* May 1969, Vol. 31, pp. 364–379.

Marshall, Donald S. Too Much in Mangaia. *Psychology Today,* February 1971, Vol. 4, pp. 43, 44, 70–79.

Masters, William H., and Virginia E. Johnson. *Human Sexual Inadequacy.* Boston: Little, Brown, 1970.

_____. *Human Sexual Response.* Boston: Little, Brown, 1966.

Mead, Margaret. *Coming of Age in Samoa.* New York: Dell, 1967.

_____. *Growing Up in New Guinea.* New York: Dell, 1967.

_____. *Male and Female.* New York: Dell, 1967.

_____. *Sex and Temperament in Three Primitive Societies.* New York: Apollo, 1963.

Middendorp, C. P., W. Brinkman, and W. Koomen. Determinants of Premarital Sexual Permissiveness: A Secondary Analysis. *Journal of Marriage and the Family,* August 1970, Vol. 32, pp. 369–379.

Money, John, ed. *Sex Research: New Developments.* Baltimore: Johns Hopkins University School of Medicine, 1965.

Montagu, Ashley. *Sex, Man, and Society.* New York: Putnam, 1969.

_____. *Anthropology and Human Nature.* Boston: Porter Sargent, 1957.

O'Hare, Hilda. The Normal Woman. *International Journal of Sexology,* 1950, Vol. LV, pp. 117–118.

Packard, Vance. *The Sexual Wilderness: The Contemporary Upheaval in Male-Female Relationships.* New York: Holt, 1968.

Rainer, Jerome and Julia. *Sexual Pleasure in Marriage,* rev. ed. New York: Simon & Schuster, 1969.

Reiss, I. L. How and Why America's Sex Standards Are Changing. *Trans-action,* March 1968, Vol. 5, p. 26.

_____. *The Social Context of Premarital Sexual Permissiveness.* New York: Holt, 1967.

_____. *Premarital Sexual Standards in America.* New York: Free Press, 1960.

Riegel, Robert E. *American Women: A Story of Social Change.* Rutherford, N. J.: Fairleigh Dickinson Press, 1970.

Robinson, Ira E., Karl King, Charles J. Dudley, and Francis J. Clune. Change in Sexual Behavior and Attitudes of College Students. *The Family Coordinator,* April 1968, Vol. 17, pp. 119–123.

Rubin, Isadore, and Lester Kirkendall, eds. *Sex in the Childhood Years.* New York: Association Press, 1970.

Schwabacher, Albert E., Jr. The Repository of Wealth. In Seymour M. Farber and Roger H. L. Wilson, eds., *The Potential of Women.* New York: McGraw-Hill, 1963, pp. 241–254.

Smigel, Erwin O., and Rita Seiden. The Decline and Fall of the Double Standard. *Annals of the American Academy of Political and*

Social Science, March 1968, pp. 6–17, 376.

Suggs, Robert C. *Marquesan Sexual Behavior.* New York: Harcourt, 1966.

Taylor, G. R. *Sex in History.* New York: Vanguard, 1955.

Tissot, S. A. *Onanism: A Treatise on the Diseases Produced by Onanism.* Lausanne: Marc Chapius et Cie, 1764.

Vatsyayana, Maharishi. *Kama Sutra,* circa 460 A.D. New Delhi: Kiram Publications, 1959.

U. S. Task Force on Pornography and Obscenity. New York: Stein and Day, 1970.

Vincent, Clark E., ed. *Human Sexuality in Medical Education and Practice.* Springfield, Ill.: Thomas, 1968.

_____. *Unmarried Mothers.* New York: Free Press, 1961.

Wake, F. R. Attitudes of Parents toward the Premarital Sex Behavior of Their Children and Themselves. *Journal of Sex Research,* Vol. 5, 1969, pp. 170–171.

Wallin, Paul. An Appraisal of Some Methodological Aspects of the Kinsey Report. *American Sociological Review,* 1949, Vol. 14, pp. 197–210.

Wallis, W. A. Statistics of the Kinsey Report. *Journal of the American Statistical Association,* 1949, Vol. 44, pp. 463–484.

Watts, Alan W. *Nature, Man and Woman.* New York: Random House, 1970.

Wilson, Robert Anton. Modern Attitudes toward Sex. In Ellis and Abarbanel, eds., *The Encyclopedia of Sexual Behavior,* pp. 186–192.

Wyden, Peter and Barbara. *Inside the Sex Clinic.* New York: World, 1971.

Young, Weyland. *Eros Denied: Sex in Western Society.* New York: Grove, 1964.

Chapter Five

Dating and Mate Selection

Those marriages generally abound
most with love and constancy that
are preceded by a long courtship. The
passion should strike root and gather
strength before marriage be grafted on it.

Joseph Addison *(The Spectator)*

a

ll societies must make some institutional provision for the fact that males and females, when they reach adolescence, become interested in one another sexually and seek to express that interest. Societies vary in their attitude toward premarital copulation, as we have seen; but no society permits completely free, unstructured adolescent relations. Even the most sexually permissive societies have highly rigorous patterns of expectation, and only within these patterns, or rituals, are couples permitted sexual freedom. These courtship rituals are universal; they appear not only in all human societies but in animal and insect societies as well. Casual pairing and copulation are unknown (Ardrey, 1966).

In short, all societies have developed some means for channeling the emerging heterosexual interest of their youth. This channeling takes the form of an institution, which — emerging from the interaction of the needs and structure of the *individual* and the needs and structure of the *society* — provides for mate selection, for courtship, and eventually for marriage and the establishing of a family. In our society this institution is dating.

In virtually all human societies except our own, and in our own society until after the turn of the century, courtship rituals presupposed a careful segregation of the adolescent female, with all her sociosexual activities rigidly supervised; courtship was not entered into until the parents were first consulted and their approval secured.[1] The chance of a girl's even meeting an unsuitable prospect in the first place was exceedingly remote; not only were "pickups"

---

[1] In the eighteenth century, when a young man even asked for permission to call on a girl, he was in effect asking for permission to marry her; in the nineteenth century, convention had relaxed somewhat; but the first call was still considered a public indication of interest in marriage.

almost unknown (at least in the middle class), but casual meetings even at supervised social affairs were almost as unlikely. Approved potential suitors were
introduced to the girl, usually by some member of her family. She was, most
emphatically, never left on her own to meet boys casually and indiscriminately.
Even engaged couples attended social affairs in the company of friends or
relatives and were not supposed to be alone together. Some lovemaking, with
mutual caressing and petting, undoubtedly occurred; but, because of the rigid
chaperonage, such behavior must have been relatively infrequent. Occasional
instances of strong attraction have, of course, always occurred (in all societies
and in all eras) between couples who were not formally introduced; but such
instances were in defiance of the societal norm. Until the present century no
institutional provision was made in our society for unarranged meetings of
young people.

Dating emerged in our society only about fifty years ago (Mead, 1959, p. xv)
and differs essentially from prior sociosexual behavior between heterosexual
adolescents in several important ways: (1) An introduction of the young man to
the young woman by a member of the family is not considered necessary. (2)
There is no chaperone. (3) There is no commitment or obligation, either public
or private, on the part of either the male or the female to continue the relation
beyond the actual time of the date itself. (4) The date is planned by the adolescents themselves, rather than arranged by elders. (5) Physical intimacies are
expected rather than forbidden (with the degree of intimacy depending upon
length of acquaintance, age, social class, educational level, religious affiliation,
and various personality elements).

With the emergence of dating, the importance of romantic attraction between
the young couple not only obtained formal societal recognition but actually
assumed institutional status. Prior to the present century romantic attraction
was recognized but was thought to be an aberration, and no provision was made
for romantic attraction in mate selection. Rather, the young couple were paired
on the basis of such practical considerations as money, property, health, skills,
vocational training, and family name, with mate selection carefully supervised
by both sets of parents. (For a detailed discussion of mate selection, see Chapter Six.)

Social Changes Underlying the Emergence of Dating

The basic change, from which all the others ultimately arose, was the advent of
the Industrial Revolution, which eventually produced changes in the entire
structure of our society. Until the late nineteenth, and even the early twentieth
century, the adolescent girl was expected to stay home and help her mother
with the housework and care of the younger children. What was meant by
"housework" then is quite different from what is meant today; "housework"
included the washing of clothes by hand, the preparation of food from garden

to table, the manufacture of clothes from raw material to finished product, and even the making of soap and candles. With the advent of the Industrial Revolution, women's functions in the home were supplemented by the artifacts of a mass society—commercial bakeries, laundries, clothing manufacturers, canneries. Women then began to move outside the home to participate in the production, marketing, and advertising of these products, even as male artisans were moving from early functions in workshops and farms (Riegel, 1963). Moreover, as our society shifted from predominantly agricultural to predominantly industrial, the population began to shift from isolated rural areas to crowded urban industrial centers, where young men and women lived and worked in close and casual circumstances.

Changes in Male–Female Relations

These changes in work patterns and consumption patterns were inevitably reflected in changes in male-female relations. As methods of mass production developed during the late ninteenth and early twentieth centuries, the female began increasingly to shift to occupations which brought her, for the first time, into casual contact with populations of males without the formality of introductions. At about the same time, coeducation in high schools and colleges became the fashion; and, for the first time since the days of the Roman Empire, girls were admitted to the same schools as their brothers.

During World War I, women began to move into the business world; and by 1920, when men returned from overseas, women were being employed in offices as commonly as they were in factories. The admission of girls into coeducational colleges was followed by the advent of women into the professional world. Meanwhile, American feminists became active in obtaining political rights for women.

In all strata of our society, as we moved into the 1920s, the role of the female was undergoing a profound change. The "ideal girl" of the Roaring Twenties was the Flapper, a thoroughly urbanized and industrialized product. In keeping with her emancipated place in society, she wore her skirts above the knee (they had been ankle-length for centuries); she shingled, bobbed, and marceled her hair (which had once reached her waist); and she replaced the old whalebone corset with brief panties. Moreover, she became acquainted with young men outside the family circle and felt free to "go out" with them. Commercial establishments soon arose in response to a developing need; and within one generation, age-old rituals of courtship had been abandoned, and the pattern of dating had emerged.

Developments in Transportation
and Communication

Occurring side by side with the growing emancipation of the female were the inventions of the telephone, the automobile, and the cinema, and other mass media. The telephone provided a means of close personal communication which reached right inside the home. A young man could communicate directly with a girl without going through the formality of being welcomed into the home. The automobile provided transportation to the roadhouses and nightclubs that were springing up and also served as a small, intimate,

mobile parlor where couples could easily obtain privacy. The cinema provided young dating couples with a dark and relatively secluded place to go and with matinee idols whose romantic behavior they could emulate. Newspapers, comic books, magazines, and eventually radio and then television further publicized the romantic ideal—so that young couples were provided with role models on every hand. The "old-fashioned girl" was soon regarded as a "flat tire."

The Sexual Philosophy of Sigmund Freud

The emancipated society of the 1920s was ready to seize a formalized justification for reversing the clandestine philosophy of sex and embracing a philosophy of naturalistic acceptance. The pronouncements of a Viennese doctor named Sigmund Freud provided precisely this.

By 1920, Freud's doctrines (mainly his doctrines of infant sexuality, female sexuality, and the normality of sexuality[2]) were rapidly replacing those contained in such texts as *What Every Young Man Should Know*—all of which advocated chopping wood to reduce sexual tension, solemnly warned about the dangers of "self-abuse," urged "conservation of the vital fluids," and counseled young people to keep their minds on "higher things."[3] And although marriage manuals

---

[2] These are not all, or even necessarily the most important, of Freud's contributions. Freud established an entire system of thought (psychoanalytic theory) and invented the means for implementing it (psychoanalysis). But these are beyond the scope of our discussion.

[3] To give some idea of how far ahead of his own era Freud was, it might be pointed out that medical orthodoxy still held that many female ills were caused by the uterus wandering about the body—one of the notions that Freud successfully refuted.

continued to be mailed out in "plain wrappers," the manuals themselves reflected the new morality—a morality in which sex was brought out in the open and made academically and philosophically respectable.

Freudian doctrine was especially appealing to the "image makers"—the talented and influential young men and women who wrote plays, novels, stories, songs, and advertising copy. Thus, Freudian doctrine spread—not through the lecture halls, though he was by no means ignored by professionals, but through Broadway plays, Hollywood movies, best-selling novels, lyrics of hit songs, and advertisements on billboards and in magazines.

Depersonalization and the Need for Primary Relations

Finally, of course, the growing urbanization brought depersonalization; and the growing freedom and independence for women brought a loss of primary function for men and women alike. Individuals became interchangeable in our mass society, almost like the industrial products they were producing and advertising. It was inevitable that, with the needs of the individual in a depersonalized society, the institution of dating, which emphasizes personal values, or a primary relation, would emerge. (See *The Nature of a Mass Society*, in Chapter One.)

As dating became the new pattern for ritualized mate selection and courtship, parental concern with adolescent heterosexual activities came to be regarded by the young people themselves as interference with their personal freedom and pursuit of happiness; and the single most important factors in mate selection became romantic love and personal choice.

The Importance of Dating

A solemn discussion about the important needs fulfilled in dating probably seems incongruous to the adolescents most actively engaged in dating. Most young people date because dating is expected behavior, because it's fun, and because it is a mark of status. Mate selection does not become important as a conscious function of dating until the late teens and early 20s. And personality development is not a reason for dating; it is simply an inevitable result.

However, whether or not it is so recognized by the young people involved, dating as an institution has profound significance for them and for their society.

Dating and Mate Selection

With a few isolated exceptions, dating has replaced all other institutions for mate selection in our society. The institution of dating provides a series of other-sexed companions with whom a person will relate socially and from whom he will eventually select a mate. The casual contacts of a rural community, where friendships and social interaction between the sexes may take place on the informal basis of daily routine, are not the norm in an urban population. The person must deliberately seek out other-sexed friends. Casual encounters usually do not provide sufficient basis for learning patterns of intimate sociosexual behavior—either in amount of time spent together or in depth of emotional interaction.

For the average person, the dating sequence begins with casual, random, group, and double dating at about age 14 (Landis and Landis, 1967, p. 48); then choice of dating partners narrows down to "going steady"; after which comes "pinning," engagement, and marriage, although terms like "going steady" and "pinning" are not always used and the engagement need not be formal. Very often, this dating sequence may be gone through more than once.

The person who rarely dates is seriously handicapped in the marriage market. He may have a very unrealistic, highly romanticized notion of what the person he marries is really like, as well as only a very limited idea of his own sociosexual needs. He may put too much or too little emphasis upon sex. Ultimately, with increasing sexual pressure untempered by contact with sociosexual reality, he may make a disastrous choice of mate.

As important as dating is, it usually occupies only a very short period of the life cycle—since half the female population is married by age 20, and half the male population by age 23.[4] Occasionally the person may fail to date in adolescence but may date as an adult—sometimes having his first heterosexual experience at age 30 or 40. Such instances are, however, extremely rare.

Dating and Sociosexual Development

Dating serves what LeMasters (1957, p. 96) calls the "entry point" whereby the adolescent begins to assume adult sociosexual roles. Until adolescence, young people generally relate most easily with members of their own sex. With adolescence, however, the biological drive for sexual experience reaches a peak; therefore, the average young person becomes interested in establishing relations with members of the opposite sex. At first, he may not feel comfortable and self-assured with an other-sexed person; very simply, he may not know what to talk about or what to do with this person. However, despite often painful social difficulties, he makes the adjustment from like-sexed to other-sexed social activities.

The following is a particularly clear and illuminating statement of the feelings an adolescent girl has in first essaying unfamiliar sociosexual roles.

At these dances I found out that if I started to dance with one of my girl friends, pretty soon a boy would cut in and although I was horrified at the thought I decided I could

---

[4]*Current Population Reports*, Population Characteristics, March 25, 1970, Series P-20, No. 198.

stand it. It seemed to me that the boys didn't exactly converse with me, or [with] any of the other girls for that matter . . .

To associate with a group where boys were present presented no real problem for I felt perfectly at ease with them. Whether it was in the classroom or at a social function I mingled freely with the fellows as well as the girls. But it was the thought of spending an entire evening with a member of the opposite sex that suddenly made me conscious of how clumsy my feet seemed to be and how cold and clammy my hands were . . . By the end of my sophomore year, I began realizing that boys could be fun on a date . . . and the more dates I accepted, the more adequate I began feeling in this thing called dating (Martinson, 1960, pp. 75, 76).

Males and females are conditioned from infancy to have somewhat different attitudes, interest, and skills. They are dressed differently, given different toys, and encouraged to play different games. The person is made aware very early in life of his sex-role characteristics. The adolescent male, who has been conditioned to be submissive to females during childhood and even in early adolescence, is expected to assume the adult masculine role of dominance in male-female relations. During childhood his mother and his generally female teachers are dominant figures. In early adolescence his female contemporaries are bigger and more aggressive than he.[5] By mid-adolescence, however, he has passed the female in physical size and strength and, in his dating behavior, is expected to assume a dominant role, reflecting his new status as an adult male. Thus, through dating experiences, he must try to resolve the conflict between his childhood subservience to dominant females and the expectation that *he* will play the dominant role as an adult. An interesting sidelight to this conflict is the tendency of the male to prefer females who are smaller, younger, less intelligent, and less well educated than he (this contributes to the phenomenon known as the *dating differential*, discussed later in this chapter).

The adolescent female also must learn new patterns of behavior in her social interaction with males. Although she has been trained for dominance in like-sexed groups and has perceived older females as dominant to her male age-mates, she is now expected by the society to be docile in sociosexual relations with males. She must resolve the conflict between being aggressive in other situations and docile in dating, or she will be threatening to the young male, who is unsteady at best in his new and unfamiliar adult role. (See also the discussion of *The Power Struggle*, in Chapter Seven.)

An exception to this female role of relative docility occurs in the sexual aspect of a dating relation. The female is expected to retain control in limiting the

---

[5] Girls mature two to three years earlier than boys and are often taller than boys of the same age; in social relations girls are often the aggressors in early adolescence, being more self-assured. In junior high school, for example, girls are much more socially active than boys. Boys are more unsure of themselves socially and are accustomed to female dominance. At school dances the girls will often dance with one another, while the boys huddle together in clumps.

sexual advances of the male. (After marriage, she is expected to reverse her role again and encourage and approve the sexual advances of the male.) The young male, on the other hand, often tends to feel that the other activities of the date are more or less a means to an end of sexual fulfillment and attempts to be dominant here too. He often wants and plans to end the date, if at all possible, with petting — and, ideally, with copulation.[6] Thus, another dimension — sexual conflict — is added to the dominance-submission conflict of the adolescent dating couple, but with the normal dominance — submission roles reversed. This conflict — the expectation for female reserve in the sexual interaction of dating and the sexual aggressiveness of the average male in dating — is primarily the result of different male-female values (the "double standard"), which have been conditioned from childhood. Also, the intense sexuality of the adolescent male and the relative asexuality of the adolescent female contribute to this conflict.

Because teenagers are for the most part still dominated by and dependent on their parents, the average dating couple can utilize dating to resolve various adolescent dominance-submission conflicts in socially acceptable ways; that is, without the danger of a serious breach in an already existing and important primary relation. For example, a serious conflict in role dominance with a parent would be much too threatening and could be disastrous, whereas the young person is able to work through such conflicts in a dating relation without nearly so much consequence riding on the outcome. The adolescent thus is able to approach increasingly satisfactory divisions of sociosexual role dominance in dating interaction. They each try, usually for the first time, to communicate with an other-sexed person of the same age about the things that are most important to each of them. In exploring their own innermost feelings, ideals, and convictions in the intimacy of a person-to-person relation, each can grow significantly as a person — incorporating new values, experiencing new emotions, finding new depths in old emotions, discovering an enormous expansion of perception. This kind of growth — the growth that occurs when a person seriously attempts to understand his convictions, his ideals, his philosophy, his ambitions in the intimacy of dating — is extremely important in the formation of his adult personality structure. The date therefore fulfills important needs for each person and becomes a mutual experience, providing physical, social, and psychological entertainment, adventure,[7] and exploration.

---

[6] In the lower class, almost *all* males and about half of the females, under age 20, experience premarital copulation. With the male, premarital copulative experience correlates with social class. With the female, it correlates with age: one half of both lower-class and middle-class girls copulate the year or two before marriage; for lower-class girls this is before age 20; for middle class girls this is after age 20. See Chapter Four for references and for further details.

[7] Another view of the dating function is the Waller theory (1937, 1952), which has been the subject of controversial discussion among sociologists for more than 30 years. According to Waller, dating is *primarily* a competitive game, engaged in for adventures and thrills and without emotional involvement. Thus, dating provides training only for future thrill seeking and not for future marriage; and a person shifting from dating to courtship would have to develop a radically different pattern of behavior.

Since initial dating is usually random, and a variety of partners are available, not too much is at stake on any one date. If mistakes are made, they are not really disastrous (though they may haunt the person for years). Often, they are even helpful, since they teach the individual through concrete experience what behavior is pleasing, what is displeasing, and what is not tolerated. A mistake on one date may be rectified on succeeding dates, until the person gradually approaches a pattern of acceptable behavior and overcomes his diffidence in heterosexual relations.

In the absence of any other institution to accomplish the establishment of a heterosexual pattern of behavior, failure to utilize dating for this purpose during the adolescent years may have a profound consequence in the adult. If heterosexuality is not accomplished during these years, it may never be accomplished.

Despite the very vital functions which dating serves in our society, the number of adolescents who do not date is rather high. For example, in one classic study, Burgess and Wallin (1953, p. 119) found that nearly half of the high school boys and more than a third of the girls had rarely or never dated.

Dating Patterns in Contemporary America

A "date," as the term is used in our society, is a planned event involving any shared activity between two persons (usually young unmarried persons of opposite sexes).[8] It may be planned many months or just minutes in advance; it may involve only the one couple or another couple as well, or it may take place within a group. In any case, an event becomes a "date" only when one person (usually but not necessarily the male) asks the other to share in the activity. They then form a paired relation, publicly recognizable, for the duration of the event. The pairing may be loose, casual, and tentative; or it may be highly tenacious and exclusive.

When the male asks the female for a date, no matter how commonplace the activity, it is implied that he feels an emotional interest in her as a person; the relation is always, to some extent, *primary*. Thus, a request for a date, as well as acceptance or refusal of it, usually involves a heightened awareness by both parties. The couple are at once established to some extent in a relation that is different from casual encounters: Each has accepted a measure of responsibility for the other; each assumes a special significance for the other. The degree of involvement increases, of course, through random dating to going steady to

[8]Although the institution of dating is specifically an instrument which introduces the adolescent to heterosexual social behavior and serves as the culturally accepted method for mate selection, it is by no means limited to these functions. A date may also serve the function of mate selection (as well as fun, sex, or romance) for older people, either those who have not married for one reason or another or those who have been divorced or widowed. The date may be between a single person and a married person, or between two people who are married to others, although both situations are usually considered illicit in our society, and the latter is not recognized as part of the culturally accepted institution of dating. And, finally, the date may be homosexual, with all the social and emotional concomitants and overtones of a similar heterosexual relation.

engagement, but is always present to some extent—and is quite marked in the experience of the youthful dater.

As mentioned, the male is expected to take the initiative throughout. If he does not, the childhood pattern of female dominance is simply carried over into dating. Thus, the male is expected to (and usually does) request and plan the date, open and close doors, light cigarettes, pay for food and entertainment, and take the lead in affectionate and sexual activity (although the female liberation movement is now questioning the validity of these gestures and assumptions by the male).

Dating Status

Some persons have a higher dating status than others: They date more often with a wider variety of partners. However, the lower-status person may with practice acquire skills and attributes that raise his dating status.

What determines dating status? Conversational skills usually are important, as are physical attractiveness, self-assurance, and an ability to put the other person at ease. Being oneself is important. Skill in dancing may be important in some groups; other skills, such as surfing, skating, tennis, swimming, diving, or bowling, may be important in other groups. Prominence in campus politics or campus sports also may be important. However, idiosyncratic factors may operate in an individual case; consequently, what is attractive, or "high status," for one person may not be so for another. Furthermore, although the two subpopulations of male and female sort themselves out operationally by dating, the idiosyncratic factors that apparently lead two persons to have a mutually high status for each other are by no means clearly understood.

One way of ascertaining factors that determine dating status is simply to ask subjects to rate status factors in a questionnaire. Opinions given in a questionnaire do not necessarily correlate very highly with operational behavior (what the person *does*). Nevertheless, responses to questionnaires do provide *some* information about "wanted," or high-status, factors in dating.

In a study in 1970 at the College of San Mateo (California), 350 randomly selected males and 350 randomly selected females were asked to write down (1) the three qualities he (or she) most valued in a date, and (2) the three qualities he (or she) would most value in a spouse. The qualities mentioned are listed below in rank order.

Qualities boys valued most highly in girls for a date:	Qualities girls valued most highly in boys for a date:
1. *Looks*	1. *Looks*
2. *Personality*	2. *Personality*
3. *Sex appeal*	3. *Thoughtfulness, consideration*
4. *Intelligence*	4. *Sense of humor*
5. *Fun, good companionship*	5. *Honesty*
6. *Sense of humor*	6. *Respect*
7. *Good conversation*	7. *Good conversation*
8. *Honesty*	8. *Intelligence*

Qualities boys valued most highly in girls for a spouse:	Qualities girls valued most highly in boys for a spouse:
1. *Looks*	1. *Love*
2. *Love*	2. *Honesty*
3. *Compatibility*	3. *Compatibility*
4. *Sex appeal*	4. *Understanding*
5. *Personality*	5. *Loyalty, faithfulness*
6. *Understanding*	6. *Intelligence*
7. *Intelligence*	7. *Sense of humor*
8. *Honesty*	8. *Responsibility*

Note that contrary to the other earlier studies "looks" appears first on both lists as a quality rated high for dating appeal. It is also first on the list of qualities the male would most like to have in his wife but does not even occur on the list the female would most like to have in her husband. Sex appeal is among the highly valued qualities in both categories of dating and marriage for the male but absent in both categories for the female. "Love" is a very highly valued category in anticipating marriage for both male and female but is not a necessary concomitant to dating.

The Dating Differential

Males tend to "date down" and females tend to "date up," the average male apparently preferring a female who is younger, smaller, somewhat less intelligent, less well-educated, and of a somewhat lower social status than himself. He may even feel insecure or threatened by a woman who is large, aggressive, older, brighter, better educated, and of a higher social class. Conversely, the average female apparently prefers a male who is somewhat older, bigger, more intelligent, better educated, and of a somewhat higher social status than herself.[9]

Since there are about equal numbers of males and females of the same age and of the same social class, and since most husbands are taller, older, better educated, and of a somewhat higher social status than their wives, an undating and unmarrying residue from the upper-status population of females and from the lower-status population of males is left outside the dating and mating system. Thus, a tall woman, or a woman with an advanced degree, or a woman of high professional or social status, or a woman who is unmarried by age 30, for example, is likely to be in the residue who seldom date and don't marry, as is a man who is short, poorly educated, and of low social status.

The dating differential helps to explain why many attractive, bright, and well-educated females remain unmarried. The factor of age alone is very significant

---

[9] Only 1 percent of the women in a study by Landis and Landis (1967, p. 97) said they would prefer husbands with less education than themselves; fully 83 percent preferred husbands with *more* education. Berelson and Steiner (1964) found that "upper-class men are more likely to marry than lower-class men, and upper-class women are less likely than lower-class women" (p. 307). Carter and Glick found that men with advanced degrees are much more likely to marry than similarly educated women (1970).

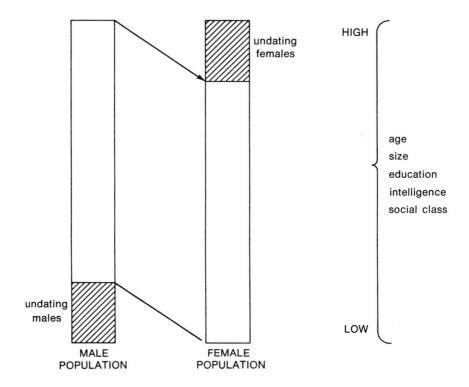

Figure 5–1. The Dating Differential

in this regard. The female who remains unmarried at age 30 generally looks for
a mate among the unmarried males of 30 to 45, and there simply aren't many
suitable candidates available. The 30-year-old bachelor, on the other hand, can
choose among females from 18 to 30, with a large number of suitable candidates
available. This tendency of men to date and marry younger women leaves an
increasing residue of undating and unmating females.

Social-class Differences in Dating Behavior

The sociosexual mores of dating vary considerably with social class; for the
values that young people bring to their dating relations inevitably reflect the
values of their parents, and the values of their parents inevitably reflect their
social-class position. Thus, a young person's attitude toward the opposite sex and
his experiences in dating are a function, to a considerable extent, of his social-
class membership.

Our upper-class population (about 3 percent of the entire population) exercises more control over the dating activities of its youngsters than do members
of the lower or middle class. The upper class maintains cultural unity largely
by withdrawing from middle-class public institutions.

The class tends to form an isolated social world, protecting its isolation by a system of exclusive social contacts. Nurses, tutors, governesses, and maids stand as a bulwark, both physically and in the training they give. . . . Later the children attend private day or boarding schools, which only admit children of the upper social classes. . . . Clubs, large and small, to which membership may be gained only upon election, also support the social isolation. . . .

Long before children are mature enough to think logically of their future the son knows what school and college he is destined to attend, what occupation the family has planned for him; the girl knows the kind of training she will receive and the type of young men she will meet at her debut, one of whom will become her husband (Cavan, 1969, pp. 90, 96).

Isolation is relatively complete until college. The upper-class children rarely know any other children than those of their own class. With college, there is some break in the cultural wall, permitting social contact with those of other classes. Even in traditional upper-class colleges and universities part of the student body is drawn from the middle and even the lower class; and occasional interclass dating, and even marriage, does occur. The usual pattern, however, is for the young adult to fulfill the expectation of his family and choose a mate from within the formal structure of family-supervised and family-approved eligibles.

Though exceptions do occur, the pattern of upper-class dating is characteristically class-linked: Young people attend supervised dances and parties, "going steady" is considered "common," and the high-status person prefers a wide variety of partners. There is great discretion in necking and petting. Dates are all drawn from school acquaintances and from friends known to the family. At 18, the girl is "presented" to society, enters the adult world of clubs and committees, and is introduced to eligible males from whom she will select a husband. Interclass dating may take place by college age, but family influence remains very great. Engagements are announced formally. Weddings also are formal. The median age at marriage is 27 for professional men, four years older than the national median (Carter and Glick, 1970).

There is more freedom of activity and freedom of choice of partner (insofar as the family is concerned) in the lower class than in either of the other two classes.

The date usually occurs in a place of commercial entertainment. Very little family-organized dating activity exists in the lower class; the family dwelling is too small and crowded and the mother is too tired and preoccupied with money problems to provide entertainment for her teenage children and their friends. School social events, popular with the middle class, are not utilized because they require clothes that the lower-class student doesn't have. Moreover, he is often looked down upon as inferior and is shunned by his middle-class age-mates. Nor is he familiar or comfortable with the social rituals and manners of the middle-class society.

Thus the lower-class young tend to "hang around" popular gathering places—drive-ins, skating rinks, bowling alleys, pool halls, dance halls, certain restaurants and movie houses—which are viewed as slightly less than respectable by children of the middle class. In these places lower-class boys and girls may meet without prearrangement and pick one another up. Sexual experience including copulation is virtually universal among the males of this group,[10] and among half of the females under age 20 (see Chapter Four).

Most members of this population drop out of high school before graduation—becoming clerks or waitresses or unskilled laborers. Occasionally, a boy may enter the field of entertainment, sports, or politics; or he may raise his status through higher education. Usually, however, by the time he is in his late teens or early 20s, the boy is working at a more or less steady job, unskilled or semiskilled. He begins serious, unsupervised, "steady" dating very early and takes copulation during these dates for granted; he also marries very early (Carter and Glick, 1970).

The lower-class boy rarely dates outside his social class. The girl, however, occasionally dates one or two classes above her own. A lower-class girl of exceptional physical attractiveness may interest a boy from the lower-middle or even the upper-middle class. She must have other qualities as well, however; and she must acquire the middle-class mores, manners, dress, and language if these forays are to be other than sporadic.

Although mobility does occur, the pattern of behavior in dating is characteristically class-linked: There is casual dating and picking up of girls. "Going steady" is the equivalent of courtship in this group, and it is assumed that the couple will soon marry. Engagements are not announced formally. Copulation is accepted as a normal part of dating for the average "steady" couple. Copulation is usually engaged in without the prelude of petting (extended petting without copulation may even be considered a perversion in this group).[11] When the girl becomes pregnant, marriage takes place. There is no formal wedding. Parents are often informed *after* the ceremony. The age at marriage is the mid-teens for the girl and the early 20s for the boy.

Unlike the lower class, in which little family organization of dating occurs, middle-class parents actively foster many formal events for adolescents. In addition, other middle-class institutions (schools, churches, and civic organizations) devote a great deal of time to providing events in which teenagers can meet and relate to one another. Adolescence is prolonged, as it is in the upper class, and young people are expected not only to finish high school but to attend college. Long after the age when lower-class young have entered a social life of their own, middle-class adolescents continue to be economically dependent on their parents.

---

[10] A lower-level male, by the time he becomes an adolescent, has learned that it is possible to josh any passing girl, ask for a simple social date, and inside of a few minutes suggest intercourse (Kinsey, 1948, p. 267). Such an approach is impossible for the average middle-class male.

[11] "Many a college male will have kissed dozens of girls, although he has had intercourse with none of them . . . the lower-level male is likely to have had intercourse with hundreds of girls, but he may have kissed few of them" (Kinsey, 1948, p. 369).

The pattern of middle-class dating characteristically includes tentative approaches, with some prior assurance of acceptance; school-oriented (or church- or family-oriented) functions, with classmates or friends; and random dating, followed rather quickly by "going steady," which has high prestige for this group but carries no implication of permanent alliance—although loyalty of partners is respected for its duration. Sexual standards are rather restrictive (compared to the lower class). As we noted in Chapter Four, only about 60 percent of college males experience premarital copulation, and the most recent estimate for college females is about 40 percent.

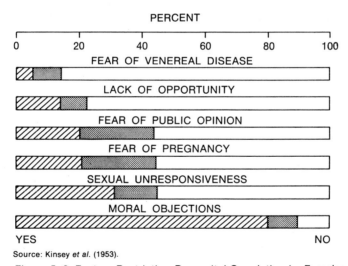

Source: Kinsey et al. (1953).

Figure 5–2. Factors Restricting Premarital Copulation by Females

Petting, however, is virtually universal among middle-class dating couples and is very protracted and intimate, serving to some extent as a substitute for copulation. Control is vested in the girls, with parental concern but little direct parental supervision of the last hour or two of each date. Engagement often occurs and is often announced in the press. There is a formal, though not elaborate, wedding. Marriage occurs in the early 20s for the female and in the mid-20s for the male.

College dating follows a somewhat different pattern from high-school dating, though the same middle-class values — quite different from either the lower-class or the upper-class pattern — continue to prevail there. Most college students are away from home and have somewhat more freedom. They are also older and more mature and are approaching the middle-class age for marriage; therefore, their dates tend to slip into courtship patterns, especially during the later years of college, when the "marketing" aspect of dating becomes quite pronounced — especially for the female.

Strategies of Sexual Conflict in College

The young college male has various techniques for attempting copulation. They depend upon his own characteristics, the characteristics of the female, the physical setting, and various idiosyncratic impulses of the moment which defy categorization. He urges her to go "all the way" on various grounds — not necessarily mutually exclusive. In a study among the author's students at the College of San Mateo, the males submitted the following as the arguments they used most often:

(1) It's a natural expression of love or affection; (2) it's abnormal not to want to; (3) it will release your inhibitions; (4) it will fulfill your personality; (5) it's advocated in most of the world's societies; or (6) everyone else does it, so why shouldn't we?

The young female may respond sexually for the following variety of reasons — if the physical opportunities of safety from discovery and pregnancy are present:

(1) If she loves the boy and thinks of copulation as an expression of love; (2) if she merely likes the boy but accepts copulation as a normal biological function and expression of affection;[12] *(3) if she hopes to discover through copulation whether she is in love; (4) if she is curious or in a mood for adventure; (5) if she needs affection and is using copulation as a means of achieving it; (6) if she is frightened, lonely, or insecure, and thinks sex might be the answer; (7) if the petting gets out of hand and she can't stop; (8) if she is using copulation as a tool to achieve popularity or dominance; (9) if she finds it easier than continued resistance, and, in that sense, is being coerced (a degree of rape); (10) if she is hostile (perhaps unconsciously) toward her parents or society and is using copulation as a gesture of defiance; or (11) if she is not quite sure what he is up to (unlikely but still possible).*

Once she has made the decision to succumb to the male's overtures, or has been swept along into participation, she is much more likely to repeat the experience on subsequent occasions; for succeeding petting and copulative

---

[12] This reason is much more prevalent now than it was prior to the mid-1960s, as we have seen in Chapter Four.

experiences are less a departure physically, psychologically, and socially than the initial experience. About one third of unmarried females (from all social levels) regret premarital copulation, but about one half intend to repeat the experience (Kinsey, 1953, p. 316).

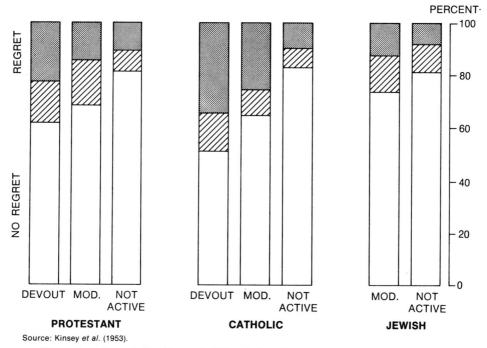

Source: Kinsey et al. (1953).

Figure 5-3. Regret after Premarital Copulation, Related to Religious Background

Of course, the female may act as the aggressor and seduce the young male, initiating him into more and more elaborate petting techniques, and finally copulation. She may use the same verbal techniques as the male, persuading him to deliberately proceed to copulation. In the *usual* dating situation, however, the male makes the advances and the female sets the limits.

The strategies and counter-strategies described above are all within the normal range of sexual interaction in a dating relation. However, some sexual behavior in dating is chiefly exploitive, on either the male's or the female's part, and is usually a manifestation of a maladjusted or immature personality. An encounter with such a personality in the average adolescent's and adult's dating experience is common enough to make a description of two such personalities worthwhile to this discussion of dating.

Two examples of persons who utilize dating solely for sexual exploitation are the male with a *Casanova complex* and the female with a *castration complex*. The male "Casanova" regards women solely as objects of conquest. After he has made his conquest, he becomes cool, uninterested, and remote. This kind of man, before he can be sexually satisfied, must win the female's love and affection and then spurn it. His counterpart, the "castrating" female, similarly seeks to conquer the male and then scorn him—making him feel impotent, symbolically "castrated." This type of female apparently likes men, is very feminine, and dates (and often marries) widely; but usually she is sexually frigid.

Mate Selection

Methods of mate selection vary from society to society—from *mate selection by parental arrangement,* in which, in its most extreme form, the couple have nothing to say about the matter, to *mate selection by mutual choice,* in which, in its extreme form, the parents are not consulted or even informed. The extremes of these methods are rare in all societies. In most societies, some degree of parental arrangement is involved in the mate selection: but there is generally at least some consultation with the couple (they usually have the choice of refusing to marry the person selected for them). In a very few societies, the couple make the choice but the parents retain a veto power. The method which characterizes our own contemporary society—mate selection by mutual choice with no parental veto power—is almost unknown throughout the rest of the world (Stephens, 1963). Of course, parents in our society often are consulted and almost always are informed.

In either method of mate selection, and in all societies, two cultural forces work to delineate the *field of eligibles,* the population within which mate-selection choices can and will be made. These forces are *endogamy* and *exogamy.*

Endogamy, the inclination or the necessity to marry *within* a particular group, is opposed by *exogamy,* the inclination or the necessity to marry *outside* a particular group. Thus, societies and subsocieties place endogamous restrictions on the field of eligibles, limiting marriage (legally or culturally) to members of a particular race, for example, or a particular religion, ethnic group, or social class. At the same time, the societies and subsocieties oppose this force for endogamy with exogamous proscriptions—prohibiting marriage between parents and children; usually between brothers and sisters; often between first cousins (such marriages are illegal in most of our states); and sometimes between all blood relatives, no matter how far removed.[13] In short, endogamy ensures certain specified similarities between married couples; exogamy sets certain specified limits to these similarities.

In our own society, two additional forces—*homogamy* and *heterogamy*—influence mate selection. *Homogamy* is similar to but somewhat broader than endogamy. When we state that mate choice is influenced by homogamous factors, we mean that the two persons have many things in common—not only the endogamous factors of blood, race, tribe, or clan but also such personality factors as

---

[13] An extreme form of endogamy is exemplified by the custom among the ancient Egyptian nobility of marrying only a sibling. Exogamy, in its extreme, is exemplified by the proscription during the T'ang dynasty in China against marrying anyone with the same surname.

similar level of intelligence, formal education, and social class, as well as shared interests and abilities. *Heterogamy* refers to the phenomenon of attraction and compatibility between individuals with different personality traits that complement each other. For example, if one person is relatively dominant and the other is relatively submissive, they will interact more effectively than if both are essentially dominant. Dominance-submission, then, is one trait where heterogamous rather than homogamous factors are probably operant in mate selection. These personality-trait aspects of mate selection are of interest only in societies where mate selection is chiefly by mutual choice. In societies where mate selection is chiefly by parental arrangement, personality factors are of little significance.

Mate Selection by Parental Arrangement

In societies with a strong family structure (that is, in all but the large industrial societies — and even in these societies until the nineteenth century), mate selection is almost invariably based upon parental arrangement. In such societies, the family is the chief or only source of employment; and marriage is seen primarily as a means of providing for the continuity and economic and status growth of the existing family, rather than as a means of establishing a new one. Thus, title to property usually is held by the family, and marriage contracts often are made in the names of the two families, with the signatures of the bride and groom not even required (Mace and Mace, 1960).

In most such societies, the family is perpetuated through the marriage of its sons (the daughters becoming members of their husbands' families). Families therefore are concerned mainly with making an advantageous (for them) marriage for a son and with seeing a daughter happily and comfortably married before she has passed the prime of her marriageable age.[14]

In societies where the female is considered an economic liability — supported by her family until marriage, and then by her husband — the institution of the *dowry* prevails. A dowry is any medium of exchange or any kind of property

---

[14]Under the law of the Chinese Empire (c. 1700), a father who failed to provide a mate for any nubile female within his family was legally liable to severe punishment (Wahn, 1933).

(whether stocks and bonds, a goat, a castle, or a hardware store) given by the parents of a bride to her husband, either to become solely his or to be shared by him though remaining legally his wife's. In many societies the dowry is indispensable. In contemporary Greece, for example, it is all but impossible for a girl to marry without sufficient dowry; and the father and brothers together assume the responsibility of providing one. It is a cardinal rule in these families that no male may marry until every girl has been provided with a husband.

In some societies, however, the female is considered an economic asset (that is, she contributes to the family's income by her own skills and labor). In these societies, mainly in Africa, the groom's family, instead of being offered a dowry, is asked to pay a *bride price*. The bride price is intended as partial compensation to the girl's family in societies where her loss actually means a certain economic hardship. Elaborate techniques and precise property evaluations, usually involving livestock, have long been established in many communities of Africa in regard to bride purchase.

In selecting an appropriate bride, then, the groom's family considers such assets as the girl's genetic characteristics (good health, intelligence), her family name, the value of her dowry or the cost of the bride price, the effect of the alliance on merging lands or properties or loyalties, and, finally, her own skills. Above all, she must be a member of the "community," however it is defined, but outside the proscribed "taboo" areas; and she must emphatically be a member of the same social class. Romantic considerations, or personal compatibility of the couple, usually are given a minimum of attention.

In many societies in which marriages are arranged, the parents will often utilize the services of a *marriage broker*. In fact, his information, skills, and resources are usually indispensable. The marriage broker seeks out and tentatively approaches the parents of a marriageable son or daughter who might be acceptable to his client. He vouches for the prospective spouse's age, health, education, skills, training, social status, and appearance; and, if the client is a male, the marriage broker negotiates for the dowry. If the parents are interested, very cautious formal exchanges will begin — with no commitment implied. If both families wish to pursue the possibilities after these initial exchanges, conferences are arranged which lead to formal engagement.

Often each family will employ a broker, so that the maneuvering takes place between two professionals. A family that does not utilize a broker sometimes is at a serious disadvantage and may be deluded by misrepresentations; if two professionals negotiate, both families are protected. If the marriage broker makes a mistake, his reputation suffers, and future clients will be scarce.[15]

Young people in these societies do not seem to resent arranged marriages but, rather, approve of them. For example, Mace and Mace (1960) found that

---

[15] The profession began to decline in Europe during the latter part of the nineteenth century. However, it is still widely practiced in Asia, in non-urban Europe, and among a few American subcultures (such as first-generation Chinese and Jewish immigrants). See Bernard Malamud's *The Magic Barrel* for an intriguing and perceptive description of the institution of the marriage broker in contemporary New York.

contemporary girls in India are delighted to be relieved of the pressures and responsibilities of selecting a mate and entering marriage.

We girls don't have to worry at all. We know we'll get married. When we are old enough our parents will find a suitable boy, and everything will be arranged. We don't have to go into competition with each other. . . . Besides how would we be able to judge the character of a boy? . . . We are young and inexperienced. Our parents are older and wiser, and they aren't deceived as easily as we would be. I'd far rather have my parents choose for me. It's so important that the man I marry should be the right one. I could so easily make a mistake if I had to find him for myself (p. 131).

In most such societies, the couple are at least consulted about the arrangement; and their own inclinations are, to some extent, respected—that is, they may exercise some veto power if their parents' choice is totally unacceptable to them. In addition, a young man sometimes may be allowed to court a girl of his choice—once both families have approved his choice.

After a marriage has been arranged, the engaged couple are regarded as unalterably committed to each other, so that engagements are as binding as marriage itself. In contemporary Spain and Sicily, for example, if the girl's fiancé attempts to break the engagement, it is not only culturally acceptable but almost mandatory that he be hunted down, and even murdered, by her father or brothers. Engagements, in fact, are so important that the celebrations accompanying them are far more elaborate than the wedding celebration is in our society. Ryan (1958) describes one such engagement ceremony, in contemporary Ceylon:

The prospective bridegroom, accompanied by all his male relatives, all dressed up in the best clothes they possess or can borrow, walks in procession to the house of the girl, where her relatives, also decked in finery, receive them formally. Tea, rice and curries are served. Then the agreement, in involved legal language, is read out, and the astrologer announces in detail the propitious times for the various stages of preparation, and for the wedding itself. Now the prospective bride and groom solemnly exchange rings, flowery speeches are made by the representatives of both families, and half of the promised dowry is handed over (p. 75).

There is very little data on the success or failure of parentally arranged marriages, mainly because "failure" (that is, termination) is seldom a considered possibility. Nor is personal happiness a factor in "successful" marriage; marriage is meant primarily to fulfill societal and economic needs. Each spouse has certain minimum standards of role performance (income provision, protection, home making, and child bearing); and so long as these standards are maintained, the marriage is successful.

Because the standards are so strongly culturally conditioned, only a social renegade or incompetent would violate them. When, on rare occasions, these standards are violated—for example, if a husband deserts his wife or fails to provide a minimum income, or, in some societies, when a wife cannot bear children—the only recourse for the injured spouse generally is his family, who will assess the problem and decide whether the marriage contract has been breached. If personal unhappiness is a cause of marital problems, usually the two persons must simply adjust to the unhappiness. (In India, an unhappy wife often must make a serious suicide attempt before her family will be moved to intervene on her behalf.) In all such cases, a marriage can be terminated, but only with great shame to both families and, particularly, to the family of the irresponsible or inadequate or unhappy spouse.

Mate Selection by Mutual Choice

With the development of industry in the nineteenth century, the family structure of Western Europe and the United States began to weaken and change. As other institutions emerged to provide or significantly augment many of the services hitherto performed chiefly by the family—such services as education, training, employment, protection, and security—the familial pattern increasingly shifted to that of the *nuclear family*, which consists of the father, mother, and offspring in a common residence which does not include the husband's or wife's family. Upon marriage the young husband was expected to establish his own household, creating his own family rather than perpetuating and enlarging the existing one. Moreover, as the female increasingly approached the economic, political, legal, and finally the sociosexual position of the male, the institution of dating emerged as a means of mate selection by mutual choice.

At the same time, with the relative decline of primary institutions and primary relations, and the relative proliferation of secondary institutions and secondary relations (see Chapter One), the remaining primary relations—most notably, dating and marriage—became increasingly significant for the individual. Thus, not only did the institution of mate selection chiefly by parental arrangement give way to a pattern emphasizing mutual choice, but this choice began increasingly to be based upon the personalities of the young couple. That is, the basis for mate selection shifted from such objective considerations as family name, income, property, vocational training, health, and heredity to subjective and personal factors—namely, compatibility and romantic attraction.

Although mate selection by mutual choice is the pattern utilized by all lower mammals, this pattern is very rare in human societies. And an emphasis upon esthetic or romantic attraction between individuals is even rarer—occurring perhaps only in northwestern Europe, in Polynesia, and in the modern urban United States (Goode, 1951). Even in these societies, despite the emphasis on compatibility and romantic attraction, mutual choice is not really entirely free, or dependent solely on personal whim, but is determined by many forces outside the individual's control—forces he is not always conscious of. These deterministic factors—both conscious and unconscious—are (1) his own biological needs and capacities; (2) the attitudes and values he has learned, or introjected; (3) immediate pressures from his family and friends; and (4) the opportunities offered by his physical and social surroundings.

In our society, the single most important factor in mate selection is what we perceive as "love." That is, we marry someone whom we perceive as possessing desired and desirable personality, status, and physical attributes which promise to fulfill our needs for companionate, sexual, romantic, and nurturant satisfactions. Nevertheless, what we call "love" usually occurs between two persons who are matched in some important areas of *homogamy* (similar background and traits) and *heterogamy* (complementary personality characteristics). When a mismatching occurs in one area, it must be balanced out by an especially strong match in another area. Similarly, persons who are apparently "made for each other" in terms of many homogamous and heterogamous factors may not appeal to one another as lovers in any one or all of the aspects of love as we have defined it (see Chapter Two).

Homogamous factors in mate selection. In our society, as in other societies, endogamous pressures encourage selection of a mate from within the "community." In our society, the "community" usually refers not only to people of the same race and ethnic groups but also to people who work at the same occupational level, live in the same environment, attend the same school, and have the same general background. Thus, the important homogamous factors of mate selection in our society are social class, propinquity, intelligence, age, race, ethnic group, and religion.

Social-class determinants in mate selection are mainly the occupation, income, area of residence, and education of the couple and their parents. Mate selection is limited by social class in two significant ways. In the first place, since a person associates mainly with people in the same social class, he is more likely to meet a prospective mate from within his class than outside it. In addition, since speech patterns, dress, educational level, interests, and even jokes vary considerably from class to class, the person is usually more confortable, self-assured, and compatible with a potential mate from his own social class.

Specifically, then, though we marry for love, we generally manage to fall in love with a person from our own social class. Most notably, we choose mates of about the same educational level (although, as we have seen, men tend to marry "down" and women tend to marry "up"—the phenomenon of the *dating differential*).

Propinquity, the proximity of geographic location, can be merely another reflection of social-class membership; but in our highly mobile and rather casually class-structured society, propinquity can work in mate selection as a factor which is independent of or overcomes social-class differences. For example, most people in our society attend public schools, which are, of course, highly mixed in the social classes represented. Similarly, many communities and neighborhoods, particularly in and around urban centers, contain persons from all social-class levels except, perhaps, the very highest and the very lowest.

Propinquity has a high correlation with mate selection by mutual choice. Clarke (1952) found in a study of married couples that mate selection quite frequently occurs with someone who lives nearby. For example, 53 percent of his subjects had lived within sixteen blocks of one another at the time they applied for a marriage license, and almost the same percentage lived within the same dis-

tance at the time of their first date. Similarly, 51.9 percent of the 5,000 married couples studied by Bossard (1932) lived within twenty blocks of one another, 23.2 percent lived within two blocks, and 12.6 percent lived at the *same address* at the time they applied for a marriage license.

Of course, propinquity also works as a factor in mate selection for people who attend the same school or club, who work in the same business or factory, or who play tennis at the same courts or swim at the same beach.

Intelligence acts as a factor for homogamy because two people of disparate intellectual ability usually cannot communicate easily with each other. A close heterosexual relation may exist on many bases: mutual physical attraction, interests, friends, etc.; but without a similarity of intelligence levels between two people, their relation will cease unless one of them is uniquely attractive to the other in terms of a significant status attribute which is especially important in the perception of the individual. Going steady, courtship, and marriage require intensive communication; the "identification" that takes place at each stage of a developing relationship is not only physical and emotional but intellectual as well. If there is a wide difference between intelligences, this identification will almost certainly fail to occur (Smith, 1941; Richardson, 1939; Terman, 1938).

Mate selection in our society usually occurs between two persons of about the same *age,* although the man is almost always slightly older than his wife. The slightly higher age of the husband is one aspect of the dating differential and correlates with the economic advantages of the vocational skills and training of an older male.

The median age for first marriage in our society is 20 for the female and 23 for the male.[16] College attendance delays the age of marriage about four years, so that the most frequent age of marriage for college graduates is 22 for women and 25 for men. Women who do not attend high school marry, on the average, at about age 15. (Landis, 1965, estimates that throughout the world, the average age at marriage is 24 for the bride and 27 for the groom.)

The older the groom in our society, the greater the age spread between the man and his bride, although the respective ages of the couple still remain fairly close. The highly publicized marriages between men in their 60s and 70s and girls in their teens and 20s are statistically insignificant. They are usually noted widely in the press because the men have exceptionally high prestige, wealth, and renown (characteristics, of course, which enable them to attract much younger females).

Race is an obvious factor in mate selection; interracial marriages rarely occur in our society and were even illegal in some states (with different states restricting different races) until 1967, when a United States Supreme Court decision invalidated existing state miscegenation laws.

The highest rate of interracial marriage occurs with servicemen stationed overseas. Between 1947 and 1961, for example, more than 46,000 servicemen married Japanese girls (Landis and Landis, 1967); and many others married Chinese and Koreans. Interracial marriages also take place occasionally on college campuses, where students from many different nationalities and racial and ethnic groups are brought together without the customary pattern of parental supervision and without the usually provincial and prejudiced environment and pressures of the home community.

Largely because of social pressure, interracial couples who live in this country face problems that intraracial couples do not encounter. Probably for this reason, there is a statistically higher rate of marriage failure, and a lower birth rate, among interracial couples than among intraracial couples (Landis, 1965). (For a fuller discussion of race in marriage, see *Interracial Marriage*, in Chapter Eight.)

An *ethnic group* is a subsociety which shares the same cuisine, language, dress, religious observance, and, to some extent, recreational interests and which is embedded in a larger and ethnically distinct society. Thus the Chinese communities of American cities make up a subsociety which is *both* racially and ethnically distinct, whereas the Italian or Polish communities in our society are ethnically different from but racially indentical with the larger society.

Ethnic characteristics, when they do not also include a racial distinctness from the major portion of the society, are not often restrictive upon mate selection.

---

[16] *Current Population Reports*, Population Characteristics, March 25, 1970, Series P-20, no. 198.

Except in the case of separatist subsocieties like the Amish and unusual religious congregations like the Mormons, most ethnic groups intermarry widely with the majority population and with each other. The mass media and the public school system in our culture virtually eliminate significant ethnic differences within a generation or two.

Most ethnic groups are far more *like* other groups in their particular geographic location and social level than they are unlike them. Consequently, information about a person's residence and educational level usually reveals more about his cultural pattern than does information about his ethnic group. If any ethnic characteristic restricts interethnic marriage, it is most likely to be differences in religious observance. (For a fuller discussion of marriage between members of different ethnic groups, see *Interethnic Marriage*, in Chapter Eight.)

Religion is among the most significant of the forces for homogamy. Of all marriages in the three major religions of the United States, less than one in ten is interfaith: 91.4 percent of all Protestants marry other Protestants; 78.4 percent of all Roman Catholics marry other Roman Catholics; and 92.8 percent of all Jews marry other Jews (Carter and Glick, 1970). (For a fuller discussion, see the section *Interfaith Marriage*, in Chapter Eight.)

Heterogamous factors in mate selection. Persons with *different* characteristics, drives, or needs in certain specific parameters seem to select one another as mates, with attraction being based upon heterogamous, or complementary, factors rather than homogamous, or similar, ones. In other words, within the field of eligibles — as defined and limited by the opposing forces of endogamy and exogamy and narrowed down by the homogamous factors of similar age, intelligence, and social class — mate selection is further influenced by the *complementariness* (or "oppositeness") of certain specific personality traits or needs (Winch, 1958, 1967).

Do the complementary needs explain why a person will be initially attracted to another? Probably not. Initial attraction probably is based upon similarities, upon the homogamous factors of shared interests, values, and backgrounds. Complementary needs are significant mainly in reinforcing and perpetuating the relation after it has been initiated. If these complementary needs are not satisfied in a relation — even though the factors of shared interests and background and romantic attraction are present — the relation probably will be discontinued. The complementary needs that seem to be the most forceful in a marital relation are *dominance-submission, nurturance-dependence, achievement-vicarious achievement,* and *hostility-abasement.*

A person who needs to be *dominant* in personal relations usually will regard a relatively *submissive* companion as compliant and agreeable; the submissive person, in turn, will look upon the dominant one as dependable and decisive. On the other hand, two equally dominant people may consider each other bossy, opinionated, and competitive. Thus, couples with opposing needs will be drawn together in mutual satisfaction, and people with similar needs usually will either be driven apart or will have constant clashes. Two primarily dominant people, for instance, if they have somehow been drawn into marriage, may engage in a perpetual cold war—vying with each other for dominance, unconsciously attempting to undermine each other, and eventually involving children and other family members in an unending and stressful power struggle.

Generally in our society the male is expected to be the dominant partner, providing for and protecting the female and the children. On certain occasions, and even in certain relations, the female may openly play the dominant role. Usually, however, if the female has the "masculine" trait of dominance and the male has the "feminine" trait of submission, dominance-submission needs are satisfied in a covert way; that is, the male makes the dominant gestures but the female makes the actual decisions.

Of course a person may be dominant in one area and submissive in another. The husband may be dominant in making decisions concerned with where the family should live; the wife may be dominant in deciding upon the living-room drapes. Usually, however, each person demonstrates a characteristic dominance or submission in most matters, as a reflection of his total personality structure; and in most paired relations—whether friendship or marriage—reciprocal role interaction will not occur unless there is a relative balance of dominance and submission, so that each is able to relate to the other in this regard in ways that are mutually satisfactory.

A *nurturant* person derives satisfaction primarily in giving sympathy, emotional support, and aid; a *dependent* person derives satisfaction primarily in receiving sympathy, emotional support, and aid. Although everyone is both nurturant and dependent to some extent, in any relation one person usually will be characteristically nurturant most of the time; and the other will be characteristically dependent.

In all societies the female role in the family is primarily that of being nurturant, while the male role is that of providing protection and dominance. The expectation is that the husband (and the children) will receive nurture, while providing material satisfactions; the wife will receive material satisfactions and provide nurture.

But in our mass society, the sex-role divisions are not so clear-cut; and the "working wife" is often expected to fulfill the traditional male role outside the family at the same time that she is providing comfort and solace within it.

Some persons have a strong need, or capacity, to derive *vicarious satisfaction* from the achievements of another. In contrast, some people have high *achievement* needs. The person who obtains satisfaction from identifying with another and vicariously experiencing his triumphs can form a complementary relation with a person who is achievement-oriented.

Vicarious achievement is by no means experienced solely by women in relation to their husbands; on the contrary, a woman may resent or be indifferent to her husband's achievements and more interested in her own, and many husbands are genuinely more pleased with the accomplishments of their wives than they are with their own. Pleasure in achievement is, in short, a matter of individual personality rather than sex; one either has high personal-achievement needs or is characteristically satisfied by vicarious achievements. If both people are achievement-oriented, however, there may be rivalry; similarly, if they are both high on the dimension of vicariousness, there will be little in the other for each to identify with.

One final example of a trait which may be complementary is that of *hostility-abasement*. If one person demonstrates a relatively high hostility need in relation to another's relatively high abasement need, the two persons will be able to form a satisfactory interaction, at least in this one dimension. Cuber and Harroff (1965), for example, found that one of the common categories of successful marriage is the conflict-habituated relation, in which the marriage actually depends upon a continuing series of conflicts. This type of relation is illustrated in Edward Albee's play *Who's Afraid of Virginia Woolf?* In the play, the need of the dependent husband to be abased is matched by the need of the dominant wife to be hostile (although these needs were sometimes interchanged). The marital interaction is thus one of mutual role reciprocation, with equivalence of need satisfaction on the part of both spouses.

When sexual satisfaction is involved in hostility-abasement needs, the hostile person is termed a *sadist*, and the abased person is termed a *masochist* (see Chapter Four).

Factors Contributing to Marital Success

Observers by no means agree on the reasons for marriage failure and consequently do not pretend to make infallible predictions. But despite disagreements about the causes of marriage failure, certain factors contributing to the success of a marriage can be isolated.[17] These contributing factors are childhood background, age at marriage, vocational preparedness, emotional maturity, present interests and values, and length of the engagement. In addition to these factors, which are discussed below, the homogamous and heterogamous factors discussed earlier (race, ethnic group, social class, dominance-submission, etc.) all correlate with marital success.

Childhood Background

Major studies since 1937 have agreed that a person's background is the single most important factor determining marital success (Popenoe and Wicks,

---

[17] Interestingly, women apparently are much more sensitive in predicting the potential success or failure of their marriages than are men (Burgess and Wallin, 1953). In addition, the predictions of parents (especially the girl's parents) and the predictions of friends (especially the girl's close friends) have a high degree of accuracy.

1937; Terman, 1938; Burgess and Cottrell, 1939; Burgess and Wallin, 1953). Specifically, the person most likely to have a successful marriage has the following background: (1) parents who are happy in their marriage, (2) a happy childhood, (3) lack of conflict with the mother, (4) home discipline that was firm but not harsh, (5) strong attachment to the mother, (6) strong attachment to the father, (7) lack of conflict with the father, (8) parental frankness about sex, (9) infrequency and mildness of childhood punishment, and (10) an attitude toward sex that is anticipatory and free from disgust or aversion. In contrast, a person whose parents were unhappily married and who was himself unhappy as a child is unlikely, statistically speaking, to make a successful marriage. In other words, marital happiness, as well as marital unhappiness, seems to run in families.

Age at Marriage

Personality changes occur with the passage of time. New interests emerge and new skills are developed. The mate a person would choose in adolescence might not be the one he would choose at age 20; and the one he would choose at age 20 might not be the one he would choose at age 25, or again at age 30. In general, however, he is better equipped to make such a choice in his 20s than he is in his teens. The person in his teens usually has not yet had the experience of being an independent adult, whereas the person in his 20s usually has acquired some concept of himself, is aware of his chief values, and is generally better equipped to choose a mate.

In a study which has long been accepted as classic, Burgess and Cottrell (1939) found that men who marry between the ages of 28 and 30 have the lowest divorce rate. More recent studies find that girls who marry before they are 18 are nearly three times more likely to be divorced than girls who marry when they are 22 to 24, and those that marry before age 20 are twice as likely to be divorced as girls that marry after 20 (Glick, 1957; Carter and Glick, 1970).

Why are early marriages generally less stable than later marriages? No one knows for sure, but there are several possible interpretations.

1. Early marriages most frequently occur in the lower class, and their relative instability may simply reflect the socioeconomic pressures of this group.

2. Chronologically immature people are likely to be emotionally immature also and, in consequence, to make unsound mate selections.

3. Early marriage usually curtails the husband's education (or vocational preparedness); consequently, there would be greater economic pressures in early marriages than in later marriages.

4. If the husband *does* continue his education while his wife works, he is likely to "outgrow" her; that is, he may acquire the subculture of a higher stratum and discover that his wife has "lowbrow" tastes or is intellectually his inferior (Winch, 1964).

5. In many young marriages, the wife was pregnant before marriage, and premarital pregnancy is correlated with a relatively high divorce rate (Christensen, 1963; Pratt, 1965).

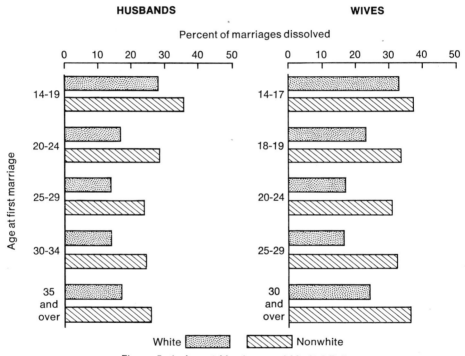

Figure 5–4. Age at Marriage and Marital Failure

Source: U. S. Bureau of the Census, *Subject Reports, Age at First Marriage*, 1960, Final Report PC(2)-4D, tables 8.11, 8.12.

Vocational Preparedness

Vocational maturity is attained when a person is educated and trained sufficiently to undertake the support not only of himself but also of a family. Certainly, this kind of maturity is one of the most significant factors in marriage readiness, one of the most obvious and easily recognized, one of the simplest to utilize as a factor in deciding to marry—and one of the most commonly ignored. No state requires a statement of financial responsibility when marriage licenses are issued. Yet a leading cause of marital unhappiness and failure is economic difficulty.

The importance of economics to marriage cannot be overemphasized (see Chapter Nine). If neither spouse (but usually the husband in our society) has the training or education to provide satisfactorily for the family, no amount of personal compatibility or emotional maturity is likely to save them from marital problems.

Emotional Maturity

The emotionally mature person is relatively independent and self-directed. Self-direction and independence imply a good deal more than freedom from outside authority; a willingness to make decisions and to abide by their consequences is also involved. The emotionally immature person tends to rely upon others for his behavior (and then to blame others for his failures). All decision-making involves risk, of course, but the emotionally mature person will use failure as experiential information which provides data that he can use in making future decisions.

The emotionally mature person is other-centered rather than self-centered; he is able to accept responsibility for the well-being of others as well as of himself. He is able to work toward group goals as well as individual ones. He also is *reality-oriented* rather than *defense-oriented* (see Chapter Seven). That is, he is able to acknowledge the reality of present difficulties and to make realistic (or appropriate) efforts to resolve them. He is able to sacrifice short-term goals in order to achieve long-term goals. He is able to make heavy emotional investments in relations that are important to him, and yet he is able to recover quickly from failure or disappointment. He can accept himself and others as he and they are *in reality*, rather than insisting upon maintaining an idealized version of himself and those around him.

In short, in the emotionally mature person, the two-valued system of childhood is progressively replaced by a recognition and acceptance of the many-valued complexities of real people living in a real world, where compromise is inevitable. The achievement of a full measure of emotional maturity is rare, of course. Emotional maturity, like all other aspects of the personality, exists on a continuum—from the egocentric, black-and-white perception of the child to the other-centered, self-directed wisdom of the fully matured adult, with most adults falling somewhere on the continuum between these two extremes.

We can readily see that the pathway to maturity does indeed involve a growing ability to perceive and cope with the demands and limitations of the "real world." . . . This means the individual must learn to delay immediate pleasures and gratifications—even to forego certain ones altogether—in order to achieve goals that are more important to him . . . And it is by no means always easy to develop and maintain the self-discipline that is required. Each individual learns that the realities of adulthood require that he sacrifice many of his own desires—that he learn to share, to cooperate, and even sometimes to put the needs of others before his own . . . The maturing individual learns to take in stride the many inevitable delays, frustrations, failures, hurts, disappointments of living. . . . this does not mean, of course, that adults are so emotionally insulated from life that they do not suffer hurt. Rather it means that they have learned to take most of the inevitable frustrations of life in stride and to show good resiliency when stress situations do hurt and disturb them (Coleman, 1969, p. 74).

Emotional support within marriage not only enhances the marital relation itself but also enhances accomplishment in other activities. Thus the husband-wife relation may become a source both of personal growth and material accomplishment (Blood, 1963). Conversely, *failure* to experience emotional support in marriage may spread to all other — non-marital — activities, with a resultant stunting of personality and increasing difficulties in all aspects of the person's societal activities (Dentler and Pineo, 1960).

In short, emotional maturity involves a twofold awareness: an awareness of one's own needs and values, and an awareness of the needs and values of other people and of the society at large. The emotionally mature person is able to fulfill his needs in ways that are appropriate to the situation. The more emotionally mature a person is, the greater the likelihood of a successful marriage.

Emotional maturity may occur at a very early age; it may occur quite late in life; or it may never occur. Some persons remain moral Peter Pans, never maturing ethically, never putting the rights or needs of others before their own immediate sensual gratification. This immature, inadequate personality is scarcely able to provide for himself, and he is totally unable to provide for the emotional support and stability and economic needs of a wife and children.

Present Interests and Values

Benson (1952) analyzed the effect of certain mutual interests and values on marital success. Some of his findings are a little surprising. For instance, mutual interests "in home, children, romantic love, sex, and religion," and mutual *lack of interest* in a "good time, commercial entertainment, and companionship to avoid loneliness" are highly correlated with success in marriage. However, contrary to common sense and public opinion, shared interest in leisure activity has no correlation with marital happiness. Moreover, mutual interests in community activity, money making, and material comfort are correlated with *poor* marital adjustment — as are mutual interest in fame and success, travel, dancing, and drinking.

Somewhat less surprising is Benson's finding that selfishness, cruelty, apathy, chronic illness, alcohol and drug addiction, and the premarital expectation that marriage will change one's chosen mate for the better are characteristics contributing to marriage failure.

Length of the Engagement

The institution of engagement in our society serves chiefly to help the couple determine whether or not they should marry. As such, it is an invaluable contributor to eventual marital success. During the engagement period, each person has a chance to explore the other's unique qualities and to consider whether those qualities are compatible with his own. In addition, the engaged couple learn new meanings of loyalty to each other and new kinds of social interactions with relatives and friends, acquaintances and future in-laws. Finally, the couple are given time to recognize that they have significant differences (if they have) and to break the engagement. Skipping the engagement and marrying immediately is highly inadvisable and very risky in terms of the success of the marriage and the happiness of the individuals.

If the engagement period is to be most effective, it should be comparatively long—from six months to two years. A classic study (Burgess and Cottrell, 1939) found that more than half of the couples who had been engaged for less than three months prior to their marriage rated their subsequent marital adjustment as "poor." Among those who had been engaged for two years or more, only one in ten rated their marital adjustment as "poor." A year's engagement yielded an 80 percent chance of either "good" or "fair" marital adjustment.

Landis (1970) estimates that one fourth of all engagements among college students are broken. Causes for breaking engagements include loss of interest, separation, incompatibility, contrasts in family background, influence of family and friends, and various personality difficulties. Of these, loss of interest accounts for most broken engagements. According to Landis, "Engagements after a short acquaintance are often based upon some superficial attraction which may wear off as the couple becomes better acquainted" (p. 229).

Landis found that young people usually recover quite quickly from a broken engagement and that the "broken-heart" hypothesis has very little foundation in fact. Only 12 percent of the students he questioned reported emotional involvement lasting more than two years after a broken engagement. Two thirds of his subjects had recovered from the trauma of the broken engagement within six months; fully one third had recovered within *one* month.

Final Preparations for Marriage

Presumably the person has been "preparing" for marriage, in a sense, throughout the engagement. Indeed, much of the "preparation" has been going on all his life, is embedded in every facet of his personality structure, and is beyond conscious awareness or recall. The engagement period is specifically a "preparation" for marriage, however, in that it provides the final opportunity to test the compatibility of the couple, their "goodness of fit," before the irrevocability of the wedding.

Thus, final preparation for marriage should include an *assessment of just how closely related are the couple's long-term interests, life goals, anticipated way of life, moral standards, and philosophical values.* Do they respect each other's ideals, or feel they are trivial? Do they agree upon vocational choice? Do they agree upon residence, or does one like the suburbs and the other the city? Do they accept each other as they are, or anticipate an important change? Does each feel proud of the other, or does one feel constrained to excuse or explain the other's appearance or conduct?

Final preparation for marriage should also include an *assessment of the compatibility of their likes and dislikes.* If each were to list the things he most likes to do, for example, or would be most reluctant to give up, how many activities would occur on both lists? A unanimous correlation would be unlikely, but a completely dissimilar list brings up the question of just how compatible their likes and dislikes really are. Do they like each other's close friends, or are they bored by them? Do they like each other's close relatives? In a very real sense, the person marries not just an individual, but a family; two families are joined by marriage.

Final preparation should include an *assessment of the compatibility of their personality characteristics.* How does each feel after they have been together — elated or depressed, relaxed and confident or moody and uneasy? Can they be together with no sense of strain? After a date does the person find himself reminiscing with pleasure or brooding over what he might have said to make a point? Is their satisfaction with each other broad enough to sustain through marriage? For example, a specific satisfaction like dancing or even sex, which might be a focal point in their relation *before* marriage, may well occupy much less of their time together *after* marriage.

Some awareness of the mundane necessities of allocating income among the necessary expenditures — an evaluation of what is available to spend and what each wants to spend it on — should certainly also be included in their assessment of their compatibility and should be given some weight in their marital considerations. The young couple may regard a discussion of the *economic aspects of marriage* as a crassly commercial invasion of their romantic, emotional, and spiritual orientation. However, more marriages founder in the shoal waters of inadequate finances, and the difficulties which stem from this inadequacy, than perhaps in any other single area (see Chapter Nine).

Attitude toward religion is also important in assessing compatibility, since religion often plays a very significant role in marital interaction. Many clergymen, priests, and rabbis refuse to marry a couple until they have had premarital religious instruction; and when a mixed marriage is contemplated, the premarital religious counseling often includes a series of interviews with the person not of the faith within which the ceremony will be performed (see *Interfaith Marriage,* in Chapter Eight).

Final preparation for marriage should also include *premarital medical counseling* which extends beyond the cursory examinations required by the states.

A complete physical examination may disclose defects and problems which the person should be aware of before making a final commitment to the marriage. The medical examination may determine, for instance, that one of the couple is unable to have children.[18] Whether or not a person decides to go through with marriage to a sterile or otherwise handicapped partner, he should at least have information enabling him to make such a decision.

The couple also should obtain information about the anatomy, physiology, and psychology of copulation, information available in a number of excellent marriage manuals.[19] If the couple are contemplating planned parenthood, they should acquire the necessary contraceptive information, techniques, and equipment. (For a discussion of birth control, see Chapter Eleven.)

Final preparation for marriage should include, of course, the *wedding plans and a public wedding ceremony*. Research indicates that secret weddings, or elopements, are statistically correlated with a higher incidence of marriage failure than weddings that are publicly planned and celebrated (Landis and Landis, 1967).

In the case of parental objection, the couple should still try to have a planned and public wedding and should attempt to win the parents over and have them attend the wedding and at least give token approval. "Often the parents will consent when they see that the young people are determined to marry" (Landis and Landis, 1967, p. 251). If parental opposition resists all blandishments, the couple might consider the possibility that the objection is well founded. Locke (1968) found parental disapproval closely related to marital failure (and, conversely, parental approval related to marital success).

The most significant function of the wedding is the establishment of the new status of the couple in the eyes of the community and the public announcement of the couple's new relation. Thus, a "secret" wedding is almost a contradiction in terms. If, for reasons of economy, avoidance of publicity, parental objection, or pregnancy, the couple elect to be married secretly, or to elope, the possibility of marriage failure is apparently much higher. According to an early study by Popenoe (1940), for example, fully two thirds of marriages turn out badly when pregnancy is the reason for the secret wedding or the elopement; when parental objection is the reason, more than one third turn out badly; and when economy is the reason, nearly one third turn out badly. Later studies (Christensen, 1963, pp. 16–22; Pratt, 1965) confirm that the likelihood of divorce is significantly increased if the bride is pregnant.

---

[18]Causes of sterility are many and varied, and not all are determinable by such an examination; on the other hand, many *are* determinable — for example, through a "sperm count" in the male.
[19]*New Approaches to Sex in Marriage*, by Eichenlaub (1970), and *Sexual Pleasure in Marriage*, by Rainer and Rainer, (1969), are both highly recommended. See also Hastings (1963), Brecher and Brecher (1966), Masters and Johnson (1966, 1970), Belliveau and Richter (1970), and Kobel and Warren (1970).

Summary

Dating is the institutional provision which our contemporary society uses to provide for the emerging heterosexual needs of adolescents. It is virtually unknown in all other societies, and emerged in our own society only some fifty years or so ago. In almost all other societies (and in our own society until about 1920), the female is cloistered in the family and has no relations with young men to whom she has not been formally introduced. Even after an introduction, the relation is still carefully supervised.

Dating differs from all prior sociosexual behavior between adolescents in that the couple are not necessarily formally introduced, there is no chaperone, there is no commitment on the part of the couple to continue the relation, the event of the date is planned by the young couple themselves, and physical intimacies are not necessarily forbidden (the degree of intimacy varies widely, of course, from the most casual gestures of friendship to copulation).

In our society, dating fulfills several very important functions: (1) it provides entry into the adult pattern of sociosexual relationships; (2) it provides experience in adult sociosexual role interaction and the development of social skills; (3) it allows the person to work through conflicts of dominance-submission in other-sexed relationships; (4) it serves other needs for personality development; and (5) it provides a succession of other-sexed partners as a marriage market. The ritualized pattern of dating behavior is precise and specific, although it varies markedly from class to class.

Mate selection is based either chiefly upon parental choice or chiefly upon mutual choice. In either method, prospective mates are selected from a field of eligibles which is defined in a society by the opposing cultural forces of endogamy and exogamy.

Mate selection by arrangement, which usually occurs in societies with strong family structure, relies upon reason rather than emotion. Economic and political considerations and suitability in characteristics other than the couple's mutual esthetic and romantic attraction are the governing factors in making the selection within the field of eligibles. The marriage results from negotiations between the *family* of the bride and the *family* of the groom.

In mate selection by mutual choice, attraction within the field of eligibles is based upon such homogamous determinants as social class, propinquity, intelligence, age, race, and religion and upon such heterogamous determinants as dominance-submission needs, nurturance-dependence needs, and achievement-vicarious needs.

The almost unique system of mate selection in our society rests upon mutual choice, with no parental veto power; and the single most important factor is love, which will usually involve (though it can largely disregard) the propitious homogamous and heterogamous factors of mate selection by mutual choice.

Factors which tend to be predictive of marital success in our society include, in addition to the homogamous and heterogamous factors, (1) each person's having had a happy, well-disciplined childhood with happily married parents; (2) age at marriage; (3) vocational preparedness; (4) emotional maturity of each person; (5) present interest and values of the couple; and (6) length of the engagement — six months to two years is optimal. The favorable prediction of parents and friends (especially those of the girl) also correlate with marital success.

Questions

1   How does dating differ from prior sociosexual behavior between heterosexual adolescents?

2   Along with the growing emancipation of the female in the early twentieth century, what developments in transportation and communication occurred to further the romantic ideal?

3   By 1920, what doctrines of Freud were replacing the prior clandestine philosophy of sex? How did they spread?

4   How is the person who rarely dates handicapped?

5   Describe dominance-submission role conflicts for the male. For the female.

6   How does upper-class dating differ from that of the lower-class?

7   Discuss middle-class patterns of dating.

8   What is
    (a) a Casanova complex?
    (b) a castration complex?

9   What very important functions does dating fulfill in our society?

10 What two cultural forces work to delineate the field of eligibles in mate selection? Discuss these forces.

11 What additional two forces influence mate selection in our own society? Discuss.

12 In what type of society is mate selection almost invariably based upon parental arrangement? Discuss these marriages.

13 What advantage does the groom's family have in the marriage market of arranged marriages?
    (a) What are the assets of the prospective bride that the groom's family considers?
    (b) What considerations are given minimum attention?

14 What is a dowry? Compare its importance in different societies.

15 What is the role of the marriage broker in arranged marriages?

16 Discuss the emergence in Western Europe and the United States of mate selection by mutual choice.

17 What deterministic factors — both conscious and unconscious — are involved in mate selection by mutual choice?

18 In our own society what is the single most important factor in mate selection? Discuss.

19 What are the homogamous forces operant in mate selection in our society? Discuss.

20 How is mate selection influenced by the complementariness of specific personality traits or needs?

21 Discuss
    (a) dominance-submission needs in mate selection.
    (b) nurturance-dependence needs.
    (c) achievement-vicarious needs.
    (d) hostility-abasement needs.

22 Describe the emotionally mature person.

23 What are contributing factors in the success of a marriage of mutual choice?

24 Describe the background of a person likely to have a successful marriage.
25 Why are early marriages generally less stable than later marriages?

26 What functions does the engagement serve?
27 What is the most significant function of the wedding?

References and Selected Readings

Belliveau, Fred, and Lin Richter. *Understanding Human Sexual Inadequacy.* New York: Bantam, 1970.

Benson, Purnell. The Interests of Happily Married Couples. *Marriage and Family Living,* 1952, Vol. 14, pp. 276–280.

Berelson, Bernard, and Gary A. Steiner. *Human Behavior: An Inventory of Scientific Findings.* New York: Harcourt, 1964.

Bernard, Jessie. Present Demographic Trends and Structural Outcomes in Family Life Today. In James A. Peterson, ed., *Marriage and Family Counseling.* New York: Association Press, 1968.

Blood, Robert O., Jr. *Love Match and Arranged Marriage.* New York: Free Press, 1969.

_____. The Husband-Wife Relationship. In Nye and Hoffman, eds., *The Employed Mother in America.* Chicago: Rand McNally, 1963.

Bossard, James. Residential Propinquity as a Factor in Marriage Selection. *American Journal of Sociology,* September 1932.

Brecher, Ruth and Edward, eds. *An Analysis of Human Sexual Response.* New York: New American Library, 1966.

Brown, Helen Gurley. *Sex and the Single Girl.* New York: Pocket Books, 1963.

Burgess, E. W., and L. S. Cottrell. *Predicting Success or Failure in Marriage.* Englewood Cliffs, N. J.: Prentice-Hall, 1939.

_____, and Paul Wallin. *Engagement and Marriage.* Philadelphia: Lippincott, 1953.

Carter, Hugh, and Paul C. Glick. *Marriage and Divorce: A Social and Economic Study.* Cambridge, Mass.: Harvard University Press, 1970.

Cavan, Ruth Shonle. *The American Family,* 4th ed. New York: Crowell, 1969.

Christensen, Harold T. Child Spacing Analysis Via Record Linkage: New Data Plus a Summing Up from Earlier Reports. *Marriage and Family Lving,* August 1963, Vol. 25, pp. 272–280.

Clark, Vincent E. Interfaith Marriages: Problem or Symptom? In Jane C. Zahn, ed., *Religion and the Face of America.* Berkeley: University of California Press, 1959, pp. 67–87.

Clarke, Alfred C. An Examination of the Operation of Residential Propinquity as a Factor in Mate Selection. *American Sociological Review,* February 1952.

Coleman, James C. *Psychology and Effective Behavior.* Glenview, Ill.: Scott, Foresman, 1969.

Cuber, John, and Peggy B. Harroff. *Significant Americans: A Study of Sexual Behavior among the Affluent.* New York: Appleton-Century-Crofts, 1965.

Dentler, Robert A., and Peter Pineo. Sexual Adjustment, Marital Adjustment and Personal Growth of Husbands: A Panel Analysis. *Marriage and Family Living,* 1960, Vol. 22, pp. 45–58.

Ehrman, Winston. *Premarital Dating Behavior.* New York: Holt, 1959.

Eichenlaub, John E. *New Approaches to Sex in Marriage.* New York: Dell, 1970.

_____. *The Marriage Art.* New York: Dell, 1961.

Ellis, Albert, and Albert Abarbanel, *The Encyclopedia of Sexual Behavior,* 2nd ed. New York: Hawthorn, 1967.

Epstein, Cynthia Fuchs. *Woman's Place.* Berkeley: University of California Press, 1971.

Farber, Seymour M., and Roger H. Wilson, eds. *Teen-Age Marriage and Divorce.* Los Gatos, Calif.: Diablo, 1967.

Friedan, Betty. *The Feminine Mystique.* New York: Dell, 1970.

Frumkin, Robert M. *Sexual Freedom.* In Ellis and Abarbanel, eds., *The Encyclopedia of Sexual Behavior,* pp. 439–449.

Glick, Paul C. *American Families.* New York: Wiley, 1957.

_____, and Arthur J. Norton. Frequency, Duration, and Probability of Marriage and Divorce. *Journal of Marriage and The Family,* May 1971, Vol. 33, pp. 307–317.

Hastings, Donald W. *Impotence and Frigidity.* New York: Dell, 1963.

Jay, Phyllis C. The Experimental Study of the Female. In Seymour M. Farber and Roger H. L. Wilson, eds., *The Potential of Woman.* New York: McGraw-Hill, 1963.

Kinsey, A. C., *et al. Sexual Behavior in the Human Female.* Philadelphia: Saunders, 1953.

_____. *Sexual Behavior in the Human Male.* Philadelphia: Saunders, 1948.

Koble, Wendell M., and Richard Warren. *Sex in Marriage.* New York: Academy Press, 1970.

Landis, Judson T. and Mary G. *Building a Successful Marriage,* 5th ed. Englewood Cliffs, N. J.: Prentice-Hall, 1968.

Landis, Paul H. *Making the Most of Marriage,* 4th ed. New York: Appleton-Century-Crofts, 1970.

LeMasters, E. E. *Modern Courtship and Marriage.* New York: Macmillan, 1957.

Locke, Harvey J. *Predicting Adjustment in Marriage.* New York: Greenwood, 1968.

Mace, David and Vera. *Marriage: East and West.* New York: Doubleday, 1960.

Masters, William H., and Virginia E. Johnson. *Human Sexual Inadequacy.* Boston: Little, Brown, 1970.

_____. *Human Sexual Response.* Boston: Little, Brown, 1966.

Mead, Margaret. Introduction. In Ehrman, *Premarital Dating Behavior.* New York: Holt, 1959, pp. *xiii–xviii.*

Popenoe, Paul, and Donna Wicks. Marital Happiness in Two Generations. *Mental Hygiene,* 1937, Vol. 21, pp. 218–223.

Pratt, William F. *A Study of Marriages Involving Premarital Pregnancies.* Dissertation, Department of Sociology, University of Michigan, 1965.

Rainer, Jerome and Julia. *Sexual Pleasure in Marriage,* rev. ed. New York: Simon & Schuster, 1969.

Reiss, Ira L. *Social Context of Premarital Sexual Permissiveness.* New York: Holt, 1967.

_____. *Premarital Sexual Standards in America.* New York: Free Press, 1960.

Richardson, Helen M. Studies of Mental Resemblance between Husbands and Wives, and between Friends. *Psychological Bulletin,* January 1939, pp. 104–120.

Riegel, Robert E. *American Women: A Story of Social Change*. Rutherford, N. J.: Fairleigh Dickinson Press, 1970.

_____. *American Feminists*. Lawrence: University of Kansas Press, 1963.

Ryan, Bruce. *Singhalese Village*. Miami, Fla.: University of Miami, 1958.

Sheldon, Henry D. *Student Life and Customs*. New York: Arno, 1969.

Smith, Mapheus. Similarities of Marriage Partners in Intelligence. *American Sociological Review*, October 1941, pp. 697–701.

Stephens, William N. *The Family in Cross-Cultural Perspective*. New York: Holt, 1963.

Terman, Lewis M., *et al. Psychological Factors in Marriage Happiness*. New York: McGraw-Hill, 1938.

Turner, E. S. *A History of Courting*. New York: Dutton, 1955.

Udry, J. R. Personality Match and Interpersonal Perception as Predictors of Marriage. *Journal of Marriage and the Family*, 1967, Vol. 29, pp. 722–725.

_____. Complimentariness in Mate Selection. *Marriage and Family Living*, August 1963, Vol. 25, pp. 281–289.

Wahn, Nora. *The House of Exile*. Boston: Little, Brown, 1933.

Waller, Willard. The Dating and Rating Complex. *American Sociological Review*, 1937, Vol. 2, pp. 727–734.

Winch, Robert F. Courtship and Mate Selection. In Ellis and Abarbanel, eds., *The Encyclopedia of Sexual Behavior*. New York: Hawthorn, 1967, pp. 301–305.

_____. *The Modern Family*, rev. ed. New York: Holt, 1964.

_____. *Mate Selection*. New York: Harper, 1958.

Part Three

The Married Couple

Chapter Six

The Institution of Marriage

*Marriage is a thing you've
got to give your whole mind to.*

Henrik Ibsen (*The League of Youth*)

I n every known human society, some form of the institution of marriage exists, fulfilling the basic needs of the society and of the individuals in that society.

For survival there must be accommodation between the sexes. The accommodative relationship must be enduring enough to provide for protection, care, and reasonable security for the offspring . . . the institution of marriage and the establishment of an integrative system are imperative to man's very existence (Kephart, 1961, p. 64).

Thus, marriage provides the formal basis for stable heterosexual relations and for the formation of nuclear families. In addition, marriage institutionalizes and therefore aids the fulfillment of many basic individual needs (besides sex), such as the need for a paired relation with its concomitants of love, nurture, and verification of the self-image; the need for socialization of children; the need for status; and the physical needs (food, clothing, housing, etc.), which are shared and alternately or mutually fulfilled by the two persons in the marital relation. In short, the stability and continuity of the social order and the need satisfactions and achievements of individuals are dependent upon the marital institution.[1]

---

[1] In all parts of the world, married men and women have lower death rates than those in the same sex and age groups who are unmarried — whether never-married, divorced, or widowed (United Nations Statistical Office, 1969). As yet, there is no explanation for this phenomenon other than the fact that unmarried people die earlier.

In order to encourage and benefit from the social order provided by marriage, all societies control and regulate the marital institution by putting it into a legal or sacred framework that (1) makes it a liaison of expected permanence; (2) formalizes the reciprocal rights and obligations of the married couple; (3) requires the nurture, protection, and socialization of children; and (4) provides formal kinship relations and thereby establishes property rights and stable lines of inheritance from generation to generation. A society's legal institutionalization of marriage also traditionally protects the female from exploitation, although the importance of this function has progressively lessened as women gain increasing equality with men.

There are four possible forms of marriage: *monogamy*, one husband, one wife; *polygyny*,[2] one husband, two or more wives; *polyandry*, one wife, two or more husbands; and *group marriage*, two or more husbands and two or more wives. Of these, most marriages in all societies are monogamous, although fully four in five societies permit polygyny (Murdock, 1949).[3]

The reason that polygyny rarely occurs, even in the large number of societies that recognize polygyny and assign high status to the possession of many wives, is simply economic: Only a relatively few men of status and wealth can afford to maintain such a household. There is no society in which the cultural norm is polygyny; for if polygynous marriage *were* the cultural norm, most men would have to remain unmarried.

In our society, *polygamy*, whether polygyny or polyandry, is illegal in all states. Still, we practice a form of polygamy, *serial polygamy*, in that a large minority of about one in three of our population divorce and marry a second time.

The Character of the Institution

Despite the various forms of marriage in different societies, and despite the inevitable individual variations among marital relations within a single society, the institution of marriage has three universally applicable characteristics: (1) Marriage is a legitimate sexual relation between two persons, who recognize and agree to some form of a civil and/or sacred contract, which verifies the expected permanence of the relation and which spells out the reciprocal societal obligations of the couple toward one another and toward their future offspring. (2) The marriage and contract is publicly recorded with some ceremonial observance, usually a wedding and a feast. (3) The marital relation implies certain culturally prescribed tasks and roles which are to be fulfilled by either one or both of the spouses (see Stephens, 1963). These three characteristics are termed (1) the *binding contract*, (2) the *ceremony*, and (3) the *division of labor*.

---

[2] The term *polygamy* means either polygyny or polyandry.
[3] Polyandry and group marriage are very rare, almost ethnographic curiosities. When they do appear, they usually appear together; perhaps because, as Stephens (1963, p. 34) suggests, polygyny "is a very usual, 'natural' human condition" while polyandry "appears to be very unusual, very 'unnatural.'" Thus, "whenever men could bring themselves to share a common wife, they have done the 'natural' thing and added more wives. Polyandry begets group marriage. At least, so it appears."

The Binding Contract

Until the present century, in Western societies, marriage was viewed chiefly as an institution of divine significance, sanctified by God and contracted between the spouses and God's earthly representatives, the churches. The divinity of the marital contract began to change only toward the close of the nineteenth century, when the agnosticism of scientists and scientific discovery, the liberalism (non-fundamentalism) of theologians and religious institutions, and the secularization of most Western societies shifted the emphasis in marriage from a sacred institution to a civil institution.

In this century, the emphasis has shifted again, with marriage becoming more and more a *personal* matter, which is beyond and more significant than the religious and civil aspects of the marital contract. Contributing to this personalization of the marital relation was the increasing *de*personalization of industrial mass societies, which made the marital relation even more important to the needs of individuals (and thus even more subject to stress and disharmony) than it had been in the past. Further, the emergence of dating as the chief means for mate selection, the mass-media enculturation of the significance of romantic love, the increasing independence and self-sufficiency of women, and the emergence of divorce as a socially tolerated alternative to unsuccessful marriage made the personal covenant of marriage relatively more important than either the sacred or the civil.

Of course, contemporary marriage still generally includes the sacred contract[4] and always includes the civil contract; and the relative importance of either aspect of marriage, as well as the importance of the personal aspect, depends upon the viewpoints of the individuals in the relation and upon the different institutions of our society. For example, most churches continue to emphasize the sacred aspect of the marital contract; our courts make their judgments entirely on the civil or legal aspects of the contract; and our mass media stress the personal-happiness aspect of the contract.

An individual is not necessarily consistent in applying one particular meaning to all aspects of his marital relation. For example, a wife may feel justified in having her husband support her (the civil concept), but she may also feel that she should be free to live her own life (the personal-happiness concept).

Legal aspects of the marital contract. In our contemporary society, marriage is legally regarded as a contract in all states, although there is a good deal of variation from state to state in the tenets and prerequisites of that contract. All state marriage laws consistently state that marriage is a civil contract, and they consistently impose sanctions for violations of this contract (for example, bigamy, desertion, non-support). Unlike other contracts, however, the marriage contract

---

[4]Three fourths of all marriages are performed within a religious institution, under the auspices of a minister, priest, or rabbi. One in four persons have a civil ceremony—usually before a Justice of the Peace (Landis and Landis, 1967).

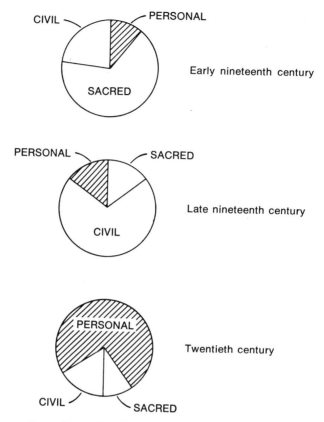

Figure 6–1.   The Change in Attitude toward Marriage

may not be broken by the will of either party; it may be set aside only by legal action.

Before the person may contract to enter into a marriage agreement, he must be of a certain minimum age, which varies from state to state. In most states, the age of eligibility is 18 for the male and 16 for the female with parental consent, and 21 for the male and 18 for the female without parental consent. In some states, parental consent is not required of a minor if he was previously married; other states allow a minor female to marry without parental consent if she is pregnant or already a mother. All states have incest laws prohibiting marriage between blood relations—father and daughter, mother and son, brother and sister, uncle and niece, aunt and nephew, and grandparents with grandchildren; and most states will not allow marriage between half-brother and sister and between first cousins. In a few states, the marriage of second cousins and in-laws also is forbidden. All states prohibit polygamy.

Before a couple may legally marry or be considered married, they must obtain a license from the appropriate governmental agency, or they must meet the requirements of a specific exemption to the marriage-license law. Examples of such exemptions are the recognition of common-law marriage[5] and the substitution of published banns for the marriage license in the cases of persons who cannot take out a license because of their religious beliefs.

In addition to a marriage license, a medical examination of the two persons who wish to marry is required; for in many states, if one of the persons is insane, mentally retarded, or epileptic, or if he has a communicable venereal disease, the license will not be issued. Also, some sort of delay (usually three days) is required between the time of the medical examination and the issuance of the license. This "cooling-off" period apparently prevents many hasty—and presumably ill-advised—marriages. In Los Angeles alone, for example, fully 1,000 couples per year who take the medical examination never return to pick up the license (Landis and Landis, 1967).

In order to be married, a couple must appear with their marriage license before an official or cleric who is legally permitted by the state to perform marriages. The wedding ceremony that follows must be witnessed by two persons of legal age; and certain portions of the ceremony, whether civil or religious, are prescribed by law. After the ceremony, the couple, the witnesses, and the officiator must sign the license, which must then be sent to the governmental agency where it is recorded and filed.

The marriage license, or contract, stipulates the minimum limits of marital satisfaction, below which the contract may be considered breached. For example, in most states, a person has the legal right to live with and copulate with his spouse when he wishes; a husband is required to support his wife; and a wife is required to function as a homemaker. These so-called "bed and board" rights are based, like most of American law, on the traditional English common law, which placed the essentials of marriage on the conjugal bed and on the homemaking functions of the wife and the bread-winning functions of the husband.

The married couple are legally required to provide certain minimum satisfactions of physical care and education for their offspring. Financial support of the child is required of the father in most states, and all states have property and inheritance laws determining the legitimate rights of people born of legally married parents. (It is in the case of inheritance rights and the legitimacy of offspring that the question of the legal recognition of common-law marriage most often arises.)

Sacred aspects of the marital contract. From the point of view of organized religions, the institution of marriage involves far more than a civil contract; it is a relation that is ordained by God. All three major religions in the United States emphasize marriage as an important spiritual relation and refer to it as "holy matrimony," "the holy estate," or "God's holy ordinance" in their formal references. Marriage, in religious terms, is a sacrament, "an outward and visible sign of inward and spiritual grace." The religious doctrine of marriage as a sacrament emphasizes the sacred tie, or contract, between the couple and God.

---

[5] Common-law marriages are recognized in some states if the couple can prove that they have lived together as "man and wife" for 7 years.

Table 6–1. Summary of State Marriage Laws

State	Age at which marriage can be contracted with parental consent		Age below which parental consent is required		Physical examination and blood test for male and female		Waiting period	
	Male	Female	Male	Female	Period between examination and issuance of license	Scope of medical examination	Before issuance of license	After issuance of license
Alabama	17 (a)	14 (a)	21	18	30 da.	(b)	—	—
Alaska	18 (c)	16 (c)	21	18	30 da.	(b)	3 da.	—
Arizona	18 (c)	16 (c)	21	18	30 da.	(b)	—	—
Arkansas	18 (c)	16 (c)	21	18	30 da.	(b)	3 da.	—
California	18 (a, d)	16 (a, d)	21	18	30 da.	(b)	—	—
Colorado	16 (d)	16 (d)	21	18	30 da.	(b)	—	—
Connecticut	16 (d)	16 (d)	21	21	35 da.	(b)	4 da.	—
Delaware	18 (c)	16 (c)	21	19	30 da.	(b)	—	(e)
Florida	18 (a, c)	16 (a, c)	19	19	30 da.	(b)	3 da.	—
Georgia	18 (c, f)	16 (c, f)	19 (f)	19 (f)	30 da.	(b)	3 da. (g)	—
Hawaii	18	16 (d)	20	18	30 da.	(b)	3 da. (h)	—
Idaho	18 (d)	16 (d)	21	18	30 da.	(b)	—	—
Illinois	18 (c)	16 (c)	21	18	15 da.	(b)	3 da.	—
Indiana	18 (c)	16 (c)	21	18	30 da.	(b)	3 da.	—
Iowa	18 (c)	16 (c)	21	18	20 da.	(b)	3 da.	—
Kansas	18 (d)	18 (d)	21	18	30 da.	(b)	3 da.	—
Kentucky	18 (a, c)	16 (a, c)	18	18	15 da.	(b)	3 da.	—
Louisiana	18 (d)	16 (d)	21	21	10 da.	(b)	5 da.	72 hrs.
Maine	16 (d)	16 (d)	21	18	30 da.	(b)	5 da.	—
Maryland	18 (c)	16 (c)	21	18	—	—	48 hrs.	—
Massachusetts	18 (d)	16 (d)	21	18	30 da.	(b)	3 da.	—
Michigan	(i)	16 (c)	18	18	30 da.	(b)	3 da.	—
Minnesota	18 (a)	16 (j)	21	18	—	—	5 da.	—
Mississippi	17 (d)	15 (d)	21	21	30 da.	(b)	3 da.	—
Missouri	15 (d)	15 (d)	21	18	15 da.	(b)	3 da.	—
Montana	18 (d)	16 (d)	21	18	20 da.	(b)	5 da.	—
Nebraska	18 (c)	16 (c)	21	21	30 da.	(b)	—	—
Nevada	18 (a, d)	16 (a, d)	21	18	—	—	—	—
New Hampshire	14 (k)	13 (k)	20	18	30 da.	(b)	5 da.	—
New Jersey	18 (d)	16 (d)	21	18	30 da.	(b)	72 hrs.	—

New Mexico	18 (c)	21	18	30 da.	(b)	72 hrs.
New York	16	21	18	30 da.	(b)	–
North Carolina	16 (c)	18	18	30 da.	(m)	24 hrs. (l)
North Dakota	18	15	21	30 da.	(o)	(n)
Ohio	18 (c)	21	18	30 da.	(b)	5 da.
Oklahoma	18 (c)	21	18	30 da.	(b)	72 hrs. (p)
Oregon	18 (j)	21	18	30 da. (q)	(r)	7 da.
Pennsylvania	16 (d)	21	21	30 da.	(b, m)	3 da.
Rhode Island	18 (d)	21	18	40 da.	(s)	–
South Carolina	16 (c)	18	18	–	–	24 hrs.
South Dakota	18 (c)	21	18	20 da.	(b)	–
Tennessee	16 (d)	21	21	30 da.	(b)	3 da. (h)
Texas	16	14	19	15 da.	(b)	–
Utah	16 (a)	21	18	30 da.	(b)	–
Vermont	18 (d)	21	18	30 da.	(b)	–
Virginia	18 (a, c)	21	21	30 da.	(b)	–
Washington	17 (d)	21	18	–	(o)	3 da.
West Virginia	18 (a)	21	21	30 da.	(b)	3 da.
Wisconsin	18	21	18	20 da.	(b)	5 da.
Wyoming	18	21	21	30 da.	(b)	–
District of Columbia	18 (a)	21	18	30 da.	(b)	3 da.

Source: U. S. Women's Bureau, 1970.

Note: Common law marriage is recognized in Alabama, Colorado, Georgia, Idaho, Iowa, Kansas, Montana, Ohio, Oklahoma, Pennsylvania, Rhode Island, South Carolina, Texas, and the District of Columbia.
(a) Parental consent not required if minor was previously married.
(b) Veneral diseases.
(c) Statute establishes procedure whereby younger parties may obtain license in case of pregnancy or birth of a child.
(d) Statute establishes procedure whereby younger parties may obtain license in special circumstances.
(e) Residents, 24 hours; nonresidents, 96 hours.
(f) If parties are under 19 years of age, proof of age and the consent of parents in person required. If a parent is ill, an affidavit by the incapacitated parent and a physician's affidavit to that effect required.
(g) Unless parties are 21 years of age or older, or female is pregnant, or applicants are the parents of a living child born out of wedlock.
(h) Unless parties are 21 years of age or over.
(i) No provision in law for parental consent for males.
(j) Parental consent and permission of judge required. In Oregon, permission of judge required for male under 19 years of age or female under 17.

(k) Below age of consent parties need parental consent and permission of judge.
(l) Marriage may not be solemnized within three days from date on which specimen for serological test was taken.
(m) Venereal diseases and mental incompetence.
(n) Forty-eight hours if both are nonresidents.
(o) Feeblemindedness, imbecility, insanity, chronic alcoholism, and venereal diseases. In Washington, also advanced tuberculosis and, if male, contagious venereal diseases.
(p) If one or both parties are below the age for marriage without parental consent.
(q) Time limit between date of examination and expiration of marriage license.
(r) Venereal diseases, feeblemindedness, mental illness, drug addiction, and chronic alcoholism.
(s) Infectious tuberculosis and venereal diseases.
(t) If female is nonresident, must complete license five days prior to marriage.

The relation of the couple is "elevated to the divine and the union thus created is to be a constant bridge between this world and the Kingdom of Heaven" (Rheinstein, 1963, p. 444).

The Roman Catholic Church is far more rigid than the various Protestant sects or the Jewish faith in regarding marriage as a divine function that is not to be tampered with by man. Civil divorce is not recognized by the Catholic Church; once established, marriage is under the jurisdiction of God and no human agency except the church can alter the relation. In many Catholic countries, the state also forbids divorce, and the only recourse for the termination of marriage is a change of citizenship or an appeal to the church hierarchy for annulment of the marriage.

Protestants and Jews accept civil divorce. They take the position that the marital vows for lifelong fidelity are expressions of solemn intent made with all sincerity at the time of the wedding. But although marriages should not fail, they sometimes do; and the persons involved should not be punished for their fallibility.

The Ceremony

In all societies, marriage is publicly recorded with a wedding ceremony of some kind, which is accompanied by a feast or celebration (Stephens, 1963). In state weddings, the feasting may go on for days; in simple weddings, the celebration may be nothing more than a wedding breakfast.

The wedding ceremony marks the transition of the person from single to married; it signifies his new status, new obligations, and new privileges. His relation to society is changed physically, psychologically, and legally. Most wedding ceremonies have a tone of irrevocability about them; and the vows taken during the ceremony reflect an anticipation of permanence:[6] ". . . to have and to hold from this day forward, for better or worse, for richer, for poorer, in sickness and in health, to love and to cherish,[7] till death do us part." Religious ceremonies additionally emphasize the sacred quality of the union: In most Christian ceremonies there is a phrase "Those whom God hath joined together let no man put asunder."

The Division of Labor

In almost all societies, the female fulfills roles that are related to her capacity for bearing and nursing children (for example, housekeeping and cooking, child

---

[6] The average person marries for life. At the time of the wedding, the actuarial expectation is that the marriage will last for 31.5 years, until the death of the male. The median duration of marriages which end in divorce, however, is seven years, and the ratio of divorces to marriages is one to three (U. S. Bureau of the Census, *Statistical Abstracts*, 1971).

[7] Until recently most ceremonies contained the phrase "love, honor, and *obey*," which the bride was to affirm as part of the ritual. The phrase has now been changed to "love and *cherish*," reflecting the changing status of the female in our society.

nurture and rearing) that allow her to remain near the home (or do not take her away for extended periods), and that do not call for great physical strength (for example, food gathering, planting, sewing and weaving). Murdock (1937) discovered, in surveying 224 societies, that females tend to prepare and preserve food, gather fuel, and harvest.

The male usually fulfills roles which call for mobility, extended absence from the home, and physical strength. Thus in most societies, the male will hunt, trap, journey over land and sea, make war, and protect the community from attack from roving bands of males from other communities (Stephens, 1963).

This pattern of male-female division of tasks and roles is all but universal and apparently reflects the biological differentiation between the sexes: The woman gets pregnant, bears children, and nurses and rears them; and to do all of these things she must be relatively close to the home most of the time. The man's biological role in reproduction is limited to a few moments; and although it is theoretically possible for the male to rear the child once the woman has given birth, there is no society in which this is the dominant cultural pattern.

The traditional male-female division of labor in marriage is no longer biologically based in large industrial societies, since the woman is no longer limited to spheres of activity centered chiefly around childbirth and nurture. In our own mass society, the sex-role characteristics of marriage are very much complicated by the near equality of the sexes, by the technological advances which have made homemaking easier, and by the peculiarly American values involved in the role interaction of marriage. But although the division of labor in our society is no longer necessarily sex-linked, some kind of division is still essential for marital stability. Harmony in marriage will not occur unless each spouse provides need fulfillment equivalent to that which he is receiving in the relationship. (For a further discussion, see the later sections *Role Behavior in Marriage* and *The Peculiarities of American Marriage*.)

The Decision to Marry: The Fulfillment of Individual Needs

Marriage is extremely popular in our contemporary society — fully 92 percent of males and 95 percent of females born in 1948 will be married. In contrast, as recently as 50 years ago, only about 80 percent of the population married. From the individual's point of view, of course, marriage is an extremely personal relation; and his interest in the fulfillment of societal needs is naturally somewhat limited. He sees marriage as a compelling source of intimacy and personal need satisfaction; and in our society, he probably sees it, further, as nobody's business but his own. What motivates the person to voluntarily, even eagerly, accept the responsibilities implicit in the marriage contract? Presumably, he is motivated to marry because he anticipates more satisfaction of material, sexual, and psychological needs within marriage than without it.

Material Needs

In our society, with its ready availability of supermarkets, laundromats, restaurants, and other services, a person can be perfectly comfortable unmarried, at least in the fulfillment of the material needs of creature comforts. Still, it is likely that he will be even more comfortable if he is married and is able to benefit from a division of labor between bread winning and homemaking, with the male chiefly responsible for the one and the female chiefly responsible for the

other. Benson (1952), for example, found that two out of three factors which correlate highest with marital happiness are (1) the husband's providing satisfactory economic support and (2) the wife's ability in homemaking.[8]

Sexual Needs

Marriage is the only institution in our society that makes provision for a couple to live together in a legitimate sexual relation. Although the incidence of couples openly living together without being married has been increasing in America since the mid-1960s, this practice has received no institutional status and at the most, only grudging societal acceptance. Couples who do so are often regarded as having dubious morals, and they are usually subjected to the societal pressure of disapproval, especially if they have children. If children are born to an unmarried couple, the children are considered to be illicit, with all the legal and societal handicaps that this implies. Moreover, the legal position of the woman and the children regarding property and inheritance rights becomes highly complicated and expensive to untangle if the father should desert the family or

---

[8] The third factor was complementary personality characteristics or needs, which are discussed in the later section *Psychological Needs.*

die. For all of these reasons, most couples expect and prefer to fulfill their sexual needs in marriage.

Psychological Needs

Complementary personality needs. In our society, the single most compelling need which the person seeks to satisfy, first in dating and then in marriage, is the need to form a paired relation, an intimate primary relation with a significant other. True, other needs are operant—societal pressure and material, sexual, and nest-building needs—but in our contemporary mass society with its dearth of primary relations for the adult, the need to form a paired relation of some permanence, stability, and intimacy is probably paramount.

What, precisely, is this need for a paired relation? It can be broken down into five component parts: the need for love and affection, for romantic fulfillment, for companionship, for emotional support (loyalty), and for emotional stability (security). It is a universal phenomenon, but it has acquired prominence in our society only recently as one of the basic functions of marriage.

> . . . *throughout most of man's history, people did not marry for happiness as they do to-day. Marriage was thought of as a necessary part of the business of living. Women were needed as homemakers and helpmates for their husbands . . . [but in present-day America] it seems only natural that before marrying, a boy and a girl should have compatible interests and personality traits (Kephart, 1961, pp. 11–12).*

The fact that complementary personality needs are now equally as significant in marriage in our society as material and sexual needs may be attributed to four main circumstances in our society: (1) the development of the relatively depersonalized American mass society, in which the average adult usually is able to maintain significant primary relations only within marriage; (2) the emancipation of the American female; (3) the shortening of the working hours and the increase of leisure in our society; and (4) the mass-media emphasis upon the significance of romantic love in courtship and marriage.

As we have seen, Benson (1952), in his research on the areas of need fulfillment which correlate significantly with happiness in marriage, found that one of the values[9] that correlates highest with marital happiness is "complementary personality characteristics." These complementary personality characteristics imply that a couple relate satisfactorily as a paired relation, that they provide one another with love and affection, romantic fulfillment, companionship, emotional support, and emotional security.

Blood and Wolfe (1960), in a similar study, found that the single most important ingredient of marriage is companionship, with 48 percent choosing "companionship in doing things together with the husband" as the most valuable aspect of marriage. According to the same study, the chief source of recreational

---

[9] Benson listed three values. The other two were income provision and homemaking.

activity during adolescence is heterosexual dating, so that a pattern of heterosexual leisure activity persists after marriage for the average couple.

Blood and Wolfe also found that "emotional support" ranked third as an
important ingredient of marriage for wives (after "companionship" and "opportunity to have children"). The person expects his mate to encourage him in
difficulty, sympathize with him in failure, and celebrate with him in success;
to embrace his friends and defy his enemies; to be calm when he is angry and
patient when he is bewildered — in short, to provide understanding and acceptance. Setbacks in the outside world are much less harrowing if he can receive
this emotional support at home. More precisely, the person's self-image is significantly affected by the reflection of his self in the perception and responses
of the significant other, the mate. Conversely, of course, failure to find this
support at home may render success in the outside world much less rewarding;
and rejection or belittling of the self-image by the significant other can be extremely corrosive to individual self-esteem and happiness and achievement.
(For further discussion of the self-image and marital adjustment, see *The Maintenance of the Self-image*, in Chapter Seven.)

Emotional security is an aspect of emotional support and stems from it: If
emotional support can be counted upon, it becomes emotional security. In a
mass society of anonymity, complexity, and uncertainty, marriage may provide
an oasis of certainty and permanence. It is anticipated that marriage will fulfill
the need for a person to belong, to feel that someone of primary emotional significance belongs to him, and that this relation will endure, that it will be stable
and dependable.

Opportunity to have children. Blood and Wolfe found that the "opportunity to
have children" occurred second in the choice of important ingredients of marriage, coming only after "companionship." In higher organisms, the need to suc-
cor offspring will often take precedence over the need for personal survival; and
the focus of a society is often on the mother and her offspring. In most human
societies, the birth of a child (especially a male) is regarded as an extremely
significant event; and this concept is formalized in our own society in the doctrines of all three major religions. Indeed, the Catholic church regards the procreation of children as the chief function of marriage.

It must be noted, however, that despite our biological heritage, our formal societal attitude, and the opinion of the subjects in Blood and Wolfe's study, a
substantial minority of American married couples do not have children (fully
15 percent in 1969, according to the Bureau of the Census).[10] It must be noted
further that Locke (1968) found, in comparing happily married and divorced
couples, that there was no significant correlation between having children and
being happily married or divorced. This discrepancy between the stated desire
for children and the actual practice is puzzling, although it is obvious that
children are no longer an economic asset to a marriage as they were in the past.

Acquiring adult status. All societies grant more status to the adult, and all societies recognize marriage as one of the important steps in the transition from
adolescence to adulthood. The person may feel a great need to establish his independence, demonstrate his maturity, and establish his adult status. Thus,
this need may participate in his decision to marry.

Conforming to societal expectations. Society expects a person to marry, as a gesture
of conformity to normative patterns and to the maintenance of the social order
and as a concomitant of maturity. To be unmarried is a social anomaly. The unmarried adult is placed in a minority group; and as with all minority groups, he
is subjected to some scapegoating. For example, many executive positions in
government and industry are refused bachelors; and terms for a single woman—
"spinster," "old maid"—carry unpleasant connotations.

The social pressures to marry are considerable, so that, unquestionably, the
need to fit into the social pattern, to do the expected thing, is operant in the
final stages of dating.

Male-female differences. There are some reasons for marrying which are more
characteristic of the female than the male. For example, the female apparently
marries more often for the immediate purpose of establishing a family; her
nest-building tendencies are more pronounced. The female also more often
marries for economic gain, or to be able to stop working; and she marries more
often to escape the domination of her family of origin than does the male.
Moreover, marriage is a more important status factor for the young female adult
than it is for the male. The societal expectations for marriage of the female occur earlier and are more pronounced. For example, a mother may become quite
upset if her daughter does not "move" on the marriage market; whereas a bachelor has a much longer period of time in which to select a mate (see *The Dating
Differential,* in Chapter Five).

There are important social-class differences in this male-female differential
in motivation for marriage. For example, in the lower class, the female typically pushes for marriage in her middle teens. Motivation includes wanting to escape from home and the domination of her parents, wanting to improve her
lot economically, and wanting a home of her own with the independence that
this implies. The lower-class male, on the other hand, actually loses a measure of

---

[10] *Current Population Reports,* Series P-20, 1969.

independence by marriage; in addition, he acquires added economic responsibility, which he is usually ill-equipped to meet.

The need for the female to escape parental domination and gain freedom of action is usually not a predominant reason for marriage in the middle and upper class: the middle- and upper-class girl is about four years older at marriage than the lower-class girl, is probably vocationally trained, and has already established a measure of independence. The middle-class male is also about four years older than his lower-class contemporary, is much better trained vocationally, and will not experience anywhere near the same degree of economic inadequacy.

The Reasons for Not Marrying

There are so many possible reasons for not marrying that with any given individual a generalization may prove to be more misleading than informative. However, inasmuch as the unmarried constitute a rather large minority group, it is appropriate to hypothesize about their motivations.

Why does a person remain single despite the acknowledged rewards of marriage, on the one hand, and the societal pressure for marriage on the other? One possible reason is that when (or if) marriage is delayed past the young-adult stage, a satisfactory pattern of need fulfillment is often well established and a person may be reluctant to relinquish his established pattern for the unknown quantity of marriage. He may have passed the marriageable stage because he lives in an area where one sex outnumbers the other, or where there is a disproportionate distribution of the sexes within his own social class and his own racial, ethnic, religious, educational, age, or other group. The very real problem of meeting an appropriate prospect, especially for the female (because of the dating differential), can be quite formidable.

A person may not marry because he is single-mindedly pursuing a career with such zeal that he does not have the time to engage in the preliminaries of dating and courting or because marriage is simply not important to him. Or a person's standards might be so high that he rejects one possible mate after another. Quite often, a person will not feel free to marry because he is supporting an ill or aging parent.

Finally, of course, the unmarried adult may be hostile, either consciously or unconsciously, toward the opposite sex, he may prefer the companionship of his own sex. This may occur with or without overt homosexuality; in fact, only about 50 percent of unmarried males at age fifty are homosexual, and the number of homosexual unmarried females at that age is much smaller. There is also the residue of the unmarriageable because of physical disability, mental deficiency, or social disorientation; but the number of such persons is small.

The male who remains unmarried does so more often from choice than does the female. More facilities are open to him as a single male; he is more socially mobile and is able to take the initiative in dating and seeking a mate. Also, the dating differential gives him a large pool of eligible females from which to draw.

Whatever the reason, or combination of reasons, marriage simply does not attract everyone. And in a world that has benefited immensely from persons who do not marry—for example, Plato, Newton, Leonardo da Vinci, Jonathan Swift, John Keats, Henry David Thoreau, Elizabeth the First, Florence Nightingale, Emily Dickinson, Mary Cassatt, Willa Cather—it would be fatuous to suggest that unmarried people make no contribution to society.

Role Behavior in Marriage

The concept of role is a very useful one in analyzing marital relations. As we have seen in Chapter One, *role* is the culturally conditioned behavior of a person in a relation with another person. There are three aspects of role which are important for an understanding of the interaction in a marital relation: (1) Role interaction must be *reciprocal*. (2) The *perceptions* of role and role interaction in marriage must be *congruent*. (3) The need fulfillments of the role interaction must be *equivalent* in value.

Reciprocity

Obviously, two people cannot interact unless each responds reasonably closely in the way the other expects. You can't play tennis with someone who doesn't at least try to bat the ball back across the net to you; moreover, you can't play tennis unless he also agrees to abide by the same rules of "in" and "out," "volley" or "single bounce," and scoring. All interactions, therefore, call for *reciprocity*, or mutuality of response-counterresponse. Furthermore, responses must conform to certain shared expectations, although *within* these expectations, there is room for almost infinite variation—as in the difference between a duffer and a professional tennis player. Occasional failure in reciprocity is inevitable in any interaction; but unless reciprocity usually occurs, a relation and its interaction must disintegrate. You can't continue a conversation, for example, with someone who persists in giving monosyllabic replies—unless this type of limited response constitutes the *expected* role interaction.

Congruence of Perception

The reciprocity of role interaction in a relation rests upon the *congruence* of four different perceptions—each person's perception of his own and the other's role. Obviously, unless each person perceives his own role in roughly the same way as the other person perceives it, interaction cannot occur. Successful marital interaction is impossible unless the wife perceives her own role in matters that are important to her husband in about the same way that he perceives her role (and vice versa). For example, if he expects his wife to look attractive and she does not, if she expects him to be cheerful and comforting and he is irritable and impatient, or if he expects an active sex partner and she is indifferent, there is no reciprocity of interaction. And the reason for this lack of reciprocity may be a lack of congruence in a person's perception of his role and his perception of the other's expectation for that role.

There cannot be an essential reciprocity of interaction until each one perceives his own role and the other's expectations for that role in about the same way. If a husband expects his wife to be a superb homemaker, and if she sees herself as a community political leader with no time for the drudgery of housekeeping (or if she simply finds homemaking intolerable and disregards his expectation), there is, of course, a lack of congruence in their role perceptions; and their relation is in trouble. A marital relation will eventually break down if the lack of congruence in a husband's and wife's role perceptions (and, therefore, the lack of reciprocity in their role interactions) continues without an adjustment on the part of one of the spouses. The extent of the disintegration of the relation will depend upon two factors: (1) the importance, in each one's perception, of the need not being fulfilled; and (2) the extent of the departure of the incongruent behavior from the expected role behavior. Behavior that may marginally satisfy one person may be totally unacceptable to another.

Role behavior is so *internalized* (that is, learned at such a very early age that the basis and the process of the learning is forgotten) that each person tends to regard his role expectation as inviolable — or "right" — with little or no recognition that the other person might legitimately have quite a different perception of his own and the other's roles. In a relation such as marriage, which is characterized by a great depth of emotional involvement and an exceptional vulnerability of the self to the significant other, even a slight incongruence of the role perceptions of the partners may lead to great difficulty, disappointment, and bitterness in their interaction. In short, a good deal of marital discord may be traced to confusion and misunderstanding over just who expects whom to do what.

Equivalence

The final ingredient of satisfactory marital interaction is so obvious that it is often overlooked. *The resources, or need satisfactions, that each provides in role interaction with the other must be of about equivalent perceptual value.* In other words, the role fulfillments must *seem* equivalent in the perception of each person in the relation. In any interaction which is one-sided, with one person giving more satisfaction than he receives, the dynamics of interaction are such that (1) a shift in role or in role perception will occur, so that a balance is established; or (2) the relation will cease. Each person in a marital relation must fulfill a series of roles which provide important need satisfaction for the other; and these roles, which were termed *labor* earlier in this chapter, must balance out in an equivalent division of labor, if a marital relation is to be viable and harmonious. This division of labor is, as we have seen, a universal characteristic of marriage in all societies. (For a discussion of just what this balance means in contemporary marriage in our society, see the later section *Division of Labor in Contemporary Marriage*.)

Role Performance

Ritual, procedure, operation. In operational terms, role behavior consists of activity, or performance—something a person *does*; and what he does in interacting with another is usefully analyzed in terms of three categories of role behavior: ritual, procedure, and operation.[11] A fourth category, intimacy, can characterize the behavior in any of the other three categories, which then take on a new quality that is essential to deeply fulfilling and happy marital interaction.

Response to the role expectations of another person in a relation is always done within the scope of one of the three categories, unless the person engages in *game* (see Chapter Seven). Thus, in order to analyze the role reciprocation, congruence, and equivalence in a marital relation, we must be able to recognize the category into which the activity falls.

Ritual is the simplest of all interactions—so simple that its importance may be overlooked. It consists of a prescribed format for a brief exchange of recognition and confirmation in a relation. Ritual enables people to relate to one another without inventing new responses for each occasion for such an exchange.

Saying "good morning," "hello," "thank you," "please," "pardon me," "how are you?" are all examples of rituals, as are such brief exchanges as announcing one's arrival and departure or describing something of one's most immediate experiences ("I had a rotten day today" or "Yes, I'm feeling better now"). Smiles, nods, reassuring expressions are also rituals. These ritualistic exchanges are extremely important in marriage (as they are in all interactions), since much of our marital interaction probably falls into this category and the harmony of a marriage may be more often damaged by daily mundane interactions than by unusual crises.

So long as ritual is reciprocated, interaction will proceed smoothly, with each person barely aware of the observance and of the importance of the observance. If a ritual is *not* observed, however, the interaction of a relation usually is immediately interrupted; and it may be very difficult to reestablish the interaction because of the defensive behavior which almost automatically occurs. The person who feels slighted by another's failure to engage in a ritual exchange often either will withdraw into apathy or sullenness or will attack the other. Often this defensive behavior, and the break in the interaction, will occur without either person realizing that the source of the conflict was the non-observance or non-reciprocation of ritual.

Procedure is simply a type of ritual in which some physical object is manipulated in the performance of a ritual. Shaking hands, lighting another person's cigarette, pouring coffee, opening the door for another, kissing one's spouse good-bye are all procedure. Like verbal ritual, procedure is important to a marital

---

[11] Another category of behavior, the *psychological game*, is examined in *The Power Struggle*, in Chapter Seven. All of these categories are adapted from Berne (1967).

relation, in that such behavior is constant, relatively automatic, and universally expected in a paired relation. And like ritual, a continual non-observance of expected procedure can be very damaging to a marriage.

If behavior has a *specific* purpose, it becomes *operation*. Thus, any type of work is operation. Doing housework, serving a meal, repairing an appliance, drying the dishes, holding a job are all operation. Often, sexual relations, protective gestures, nurture, and many other of the more basic and personal modes of interaction in a marital relation are also operation. The fulfillment of the most basic operational needs are, of course, inestimably significant to harmonious marital interaction. And even the more ordinary forms of operation — bread winning, housekeeping, and the sharing of household functions — are absolutely essential to the existence and the workings of a marital relation.

Ritual, procedure, and operation are not mutually exclusive, of course. On the contrary, they usually follow the same patterns and blend into one another. For example, a husband who always walks on the outside when he is with his wife may merely be performing procedure. But if she places great store in this procedure and would be disturbed or annoyed by his not observing it, the procedure then becomes operation — that is, he performs it because she considers it necessary and because it pleases her. Thus although the performance of ritual and procedure is very important to the day-to-day interaction of marital relations, the performance of operation ultimately affects the maintenance of the relation more.

Intimacy in marital interaction. Intimacy can occur with any of the aforementioned activities. It is characterized by a spontaneous and complete absorption with the reality of a present experience — whether in working, watching a play, listening to music, reading, or relating to another person. Intimacy in a relation with another person must be non-manipulative, and it depends upon the awareness, the abandonment of defenses, and the genuine, transparent behavior of both persons (Rogers, 1970). Intimate behavior is its own reward — it is satisfying in itself — because it is freely and spontaneously performed.

Intimacy implies complete freedom. The unfree person will, for example, maintain some defenses and will be very self-conscious about the purposive function of his activity. The free, fully functioning person, on the other hand, will engage in behavior for no other purpose than simple confrontation with the need for response. He will do precisely what he wants to do at the moment, as a spontaneous expression of his awareness and acceptance of his own feelings and the feelings of the other (Maslow, 1970).

Examples of intimacy in the marital relation would be any shared activity — conversation, copulation, or work — that is engaged in with a totality of unselfconscious involvement, attention, and participation.

Although intimacy is the most satisfying of social interactions, within marriage or without, it is also probably the least frequently experienced. The typical adult in our society is often so fully occupied with material needs, with manipulation of people and things for goal accomplishments, and with verification of the self-image that he rarely experiences an interaction with another for no other purpose than because the present activity is intrinsically attractive and satisfying.

Of course, the ideal of any paired relation is frequent intimacy. So long as intimacy often occurs, the relation will remain primary, or intrinsic. This is the basis of friendship, whereas a business relation is based upon the satisfactory performance of an operation (together with appropriate observance of ritual and procedure). Marriage is a blend of friendship and practical concerns and is thus more complex than either friendship or business. As well as providing greater rewards than either friendship or business, marriage also makes greater demands.

Division of labor in contemporary marriage. So long as the marital paired relation and the family were essentially the centers of production in society, the important equivalence of role fulfillment was accomplished by the traditional division of labor into "men's work" and "women's work"—the husband doing the "outside" work that called for mobility and extended absence; the wife doing the "inside" work of homemaking and child care. The questions of personal satisfactions and the equivalent fulfillment of interpersonal, non-material needs never arose in such marriages; one married (without too much personal say in the mate selection) and one stayed married unless the traditional division of labor was not fulfilled by one or the other in the relation.

With the shift of the marital relation and the family to consumption rather than production roles, and with the whittling away of the significance of many housekeeping functions and the entry of women into the world of outside employment, interpersonal satisfactions joined the material and sexual ones as significant aspects of marriage. Thus, in contemporary marriage, the areas of important need fulfillment are, in addition to those of income provision, housekeeping, and sex, the interpersonal satisfactions of the needs for love, companionship, and emotional support and security.

The income-provision function (usually of the husband), the housekeeping and child-care functions (usually of the wife), and the sexual fulfillments of each are widely acknowledged as essential for the success of a marriage. Interpersonal needs are equally important. *If any one of these four areas of need satisfaction is not fulfilled, a marriage is likely to fail.*

The importance of the income-provision and housekeeping functions to marital success or failure should be obvious to a couple. But the importance of reciprocal sexual fulfillment often is not so obvious in a marital relation, since people tend not to acknowledge sexual problems. If a wife fails to have dinner on the table, each knows and acknowledges her failure as the reason for a husband's discontent; whereas if she refuses to copulate, he is likely to deny that sexual frustration is the basis of his anger—and she is likely to pretend that she doesn't know why he is angry. They argue at cross purposes. Failure in sex-role reciprocation is thus more complex than failure in material-need provision because the person often denies, or fails to acknowledge, his sexuality; and sexual dissatisfaction is simply not faced or discussed as candidly or frankly as other problems by the average American couple.

In a society such as ours, in which we marry for happiness—or interpersonal need satisfaction—failure in the love, companionate, or emotional-support aspects of need fulfillment is just as significant as failure in the other three areas of marital need provision. But the importance of satisfactory interpersonal role participation is even more often overlooked or denied than the importance of sexual fulfillment. It is ironic that we often take liberties within our marital relation that we would not dream of taking in the outside world.

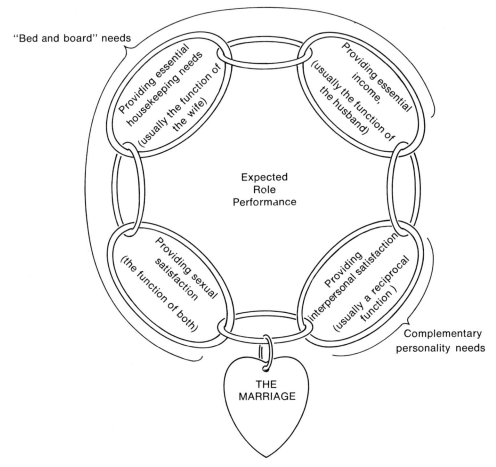

"Bed and board" needs

Providing essential housekeeping needs (usually the function of the wife)

Providing essential income, (usually the function of the husband)

Expected Role Performance

Providing sexual satisfaction (the function of both)

Providing interpersonal satisfaction (usually a reciprocal function)

Complementary personality needs

THE MARRIAGE

Figure 6–2. The Links of a Successful Marriage

For example, a secretary will usually be courteous to her boss and will observe the patterns of socially acceptable and admired interaction; and the boss will similarly put forth a good deal of effort being graceful and charming with his staff and with his sales prospects. Yet this same secretary may be rude to her husband, and the boss will go home and ignore or snarl at his wife.

If each person in a relation first understands the roles expected of him and then strives to fulfill these roles gracefully and spontaneously, whether as an operation or as intimacy, the relation will be at least marginally satisfactory. An ideal relation occurs, of course, if much of this role fulfillment is intimate. This ideal usually occurs in dating and generally leads to mate selection. It is too much to expect, however, that in the enduring relation of marriage a person will continue to fulfill all of his mate's needs solely as a demonstration of intimacy. By analogy, even the person who likes his job and enjoys his work most of the time (as an experience of intimacy) may not always feel like getting up and going to work in the morning; but he gets up anyway and performs his job as an *operation* simply because he knows he must—if he is to keep a job that is intimately fulfilling most of the time.

Similarly, so long as married persons perform the expected roles in all four areas of essential need fulfillment always as operation and occasionally as intimacy, their marriage will be successful.[12] The person cannot always feel like performing such role expectations as washing the dishes, cooking dinner, going to work in the morning, participating actively as a sex partner, or fulfilling interpersonal needs of encouragement and affection. And occasional non-observance of roles and need fulfillment will not unduly affect a marriage, if each person has sufficient perspective of the importance of these functions, and if each *usually* performs the expected role behavior anyway as an operation. Of course, if too much of the interaction becomes operational and intimacy disappears, a marriage will often not be successful even though it is functioning well in terms of role reciprocation. (For a discussion of conflict and adjustment in marriage, see Chapter Seven.)

Power structure in marital interaction. Another important aspect of the role interaction of marriage is power structure—the dominance and deference of each person in various aspects of their relation. The power structure of a marriage apparently stems from three factors: (1) the functions which each person fulfills within the marriage and the resources which each contributes; (2) the personality needs of each person; and (3) the objective characteristics of each person and of the relation—for example, income, race, social class, education, age difference, participation in community activities, church attendance, and occupation.

---

[12] To give one brief example: A young man came for marriage counseling because his marriage was failing and the only solution seemed divorce—even though he still loved his wife and was distressed about the effects of a divorce on his children. We found that he was extremely successful in the income-provision, companionship, and emotional-support aspects of his role fulfillment and that his wife was a good housekeeper and good companion. The one aspect of their relation which apparently had brought their marriage to the brink of failure turned out to be his perception of his role as a sex partner. He felt that he should not satisfy his wife sexually except when he felt like it; that is, when he felt romantically inclined. In other words, he believed that copulation should occur only as *intimacy* and never as an *operation*. This romantic illusion of his did not fulfill his wife's perception of his role as husband; she felt frustrated and cheated. To her, it seemed too much to expect that she should provide the romantic illusion every time she simply wished sexual satisfaction.

The person who contributes the greater resources to the marriage tends to dominate and maintain control in the relation. Of course, one obvious difficulty in analyzing the lines of power according to this formulation is that the contributions of each person are often in different categories, so that their relative values may not be precisely compared. For example, if one hunts the game and the other cooks it, who has provided the greater resource? Similarly, if a husband values beauty and charm and provides status, and if a wife values status and provides beauty and charm, it would be difficult to assess either person's provision of resources as more valuable. Nevertheless, if the resources provided by each person are *not* continuously perceived by each as being more or less equal in value, the power and dominance in the relation will almost inevitably rest with the one providing the greater resources.

Marriage . . . may be thought of as an institution designed to meet certain vital needs of the participants . . . Both partners hope to attain these goals through the same marriage . . . As one partner is able to contribute more than his share to the marriage, he acquires the basis for a more than fifty-fifty say in decisions (Blood and Wolfe, 1960, p. 12).

Personality is also significantly involved in the distribution of power in marriage, with some individuals simply being more dominant than others *despite* the relative value of the resources they each provide. Thus a person with pronounced dominance needs may hold the reins of power within marriage (or in other relations) even though the resources he provides in the relation may be almost negligible. The one yielding power under these circumstances probably has pronounced submissive needs. (This type of interaction may form a very sound basis for marriage—see *Heterogamous Factors in Mate Selection*, in Chapter Five.)

If a marital relation develops into a power struggle (see Chapter Seven) as a result of personality needs for dominance on the part of *both* persons, the one who stands to lose less in the interaction is obviously in a better bargaining position than the one who stands to lose more. Thus, each person may utilize his area of least involvement in order to force the capitulation of the other. For example, the husband may not provide sufficient household allowance until his power to make decisions is acknowledged; or the wife may withhold sexual participation until the husband gives in on a question which is in dispute. This type of interaction is called the "principle of least involvement."

Various objective characteristics of the persons and the relation, such as income, race, social class, education, relative age, participation in community activities, church attendance, and occupation have been investigated by Blood and Wolfe (1960) in terms of their relation to the power structure of marriage. They found that the greater the husband's income the greater his power, with relatively low-income husbands having very little power within the home, and the working wife having more power than the non-working wife.

Blood and Wolfe also concluded that black husbands have less power than white husbands. Low social-status husbands have less power than high social-status husbands. A husband who is eleven years or more older than his wife wields more power in the marriage than a husband who is closer to his wife's age; conversely, if the wife is four or more years older than her husband, she will wield more power than a wife who is the same age as her husband. If there is a discrepancy in the educational level of a couple, the better-educated of the two wields more power. Participation in community activities may also affect the balance of power, the shift being toward the more active member. Finally, the one who attends church more often wields more power.

The Peculiarities of American Marriage

Despite the common ethnocentric attitude that our marriage pattern is the normal one or, at any rate, the best of all possible patterns, the fact is that our views of marriage are almost unique. According to a comprehensive review by Stephens (1963) of all available ethnographic data on marriage in various cultures, "we are peculiar."

Not only are our methods of courting and mate selection, our attitudes toward sex, and our emphasis upon romantic love different from almost all other cultures; but also our pattern of deference, our power structure in marriage, our kinship patterns, and our methods of child rearing are almost unique. It seems that almost all the rest of the world approaches these matters in one way while we approach them in another.

The Blurring of Roles

There is little intercultural variation between "men's work" and "women's work" in the marital relations of different societies. But in our society, technological development has made the traditional strength of the male almost functionless, with 99 percent of work output being obtained from inanimate energy rather than from human muscles (Martindale, 1960). Even greater changes have occurred in the traditional female role of our society. In contrast to most societies, where the female is until menopause almost perpetually either pregnant or nursing a newborn child,[13] the female in our society still bears children, but in a much shorter time span — namely, from about age 20 to age 26 (Nye and Hoffman, 1963). Moreover, her lactation function is much less significant: The infant usually obtains much of his nourishment from a bottle, with the feedings routinely administered equally well by either parent; and foods for the older baby are commercially prepared.

---

[13] In our own society, the average number of children in a family in 1790 was eight. In 1971, it was two, with one fourth of college-educated wives having no children at all. Women who do not graduate from high school tend to have more children and have them earlier than high school graduates, who in turn have more children and have them earlier than college graduates (*National Center for Health Statistics, 1971*).

Until the present century, the role of the wife in our society was clearly defined: "She was faced with no decision as to whether she would train to be a nurse, a secretary, a biochemist, or a dentist, since such occupations either did not exist or were not open to women" (Riegel, 1963, p. 1). Now, with the development of home appliances and services, with the shift of many functions from the family to other agencies, and with the utilization of women in the work world, the wife's role has become much more diffuse; and, consequently, so has her husband's. Women may now do "men's work," and men may do "women's work." In our contemporary society, the married couple must discover for themselves what roles are appropriate for each of them; the husband may be more competent and more fulfilling in the relation if he performs many household tasks, and the wife may be more fulfilling and fulfilled in the business or professional world.

The Working Wife

A special manifestation of this blurring of male-female roles in our society is the "*working*" *wife*, who, as recently as 1940, was a negligible social phenomenon. The overall labor-force participation of married women living with their husbands increased from 15 percent to 37 percent from 1940 to 1969. During this period of drastic change, the proportion of married women with children under 18 who were in the category of the working wife rose from 9 percent to 60 percent.[14]

Prior to 1950, the working wife was chiefly a phenomenon of the lower class, with the employed woman providing essential income for the family. By 1960, the trend had extended into the middle class; and present data indicate that the working wife and mother tends to be of a higher social status than those who are not employed, with the middle class having the largest proportion of working wives. In fact, the higher the annual income (up to $25,000), the greater the likelihood that the wife is working, rising from 14 percent in families with incomes below $2,000, to fully 53 percent in families with incomes of between $15,000 to $25,000.[15] An increasing share of family income is earned by women;

---

[14] U. S. Department of Labor, Bureau of Labor Statistics, *Special Labor Force Reports*, 1969.
[15] *Special Labor Force Reports*, 1969.

indeed, the entire growth of the American labor force in the late 1960s can be accounted for by married women.[16]

In short, in a very brief period—from 1940 to 1970—a profound social revolution has apparently taken place. The massive realignment of marital roles has occurred in conjunction with three factors: (1) smaller families and the development of the pill and other effective birth-control measures, which enable women to plan careers; (2) an emerging cultural acceptance of complete female equality; and (3) mass production, marketing, and manipulation of tastes, which have combined to move many functions formerly served by the wife within the household into factories and service establishments.

Hoffman (1963) points out that among the motives for a wife's going to work are: (1) money;[17] (2) the Protestant ethic—"If the mother and wife roles do not fill the working day, it is increasingly felt that this time should be spent in gainful employment"; (3) the lack of creativity in housework—"There is very little skill demanded and very little room for excellence . . . If cooking is no longer creative, what is dusting, vacuuming, turning on the washing machine, running the drier, ironing, making beds, and doing 3,500 dishes every month?"; (4) housework usually involves a lack of interaction with other adults; (5) going to work usually gives her greater control over her own decisions; and (6) the working wife usually has somewhat greater success in obtaining her husband's participation in household tasks.

Many aspects of the traditional female role of mother and homemaker now approach the trivial; and the traditional "sole-provider" role of the male is, in many marriages, no longer applicable. This blurring and realignment of male-female roles in our society have profound effects on the behavior patterns of the contemporary marital relation.

The structural impact of the wife's employment on marriage seems well established. (a) The wife decreases her housekeeping activities while the husband increases his . . . by helping with the feminine tasks. (b) In an appreciable number of families, the pressure for revising the division of labor results in conflict between husband and wife over marriage roles. (c) The power structure of marriage shifts in the direction of a greater voice for the wife in major economic decisions and a lesser voice in routine household decisions (Blood, 1963, pp. 303–304).

---

[16] The number of men who entered the labor force during this period were outnumbered by the men who dropped out (U. S. Bureau of the Census, 1969).

[17] As the Female Liberation Movement has emphasized, however, women's pay averages only about 60 percent of men's pay. Government reports for 1970 show the median full-time earnings of men at $9,130, and women at $5,440. This earnings gap spreads throughout a wide range of jobs. Women sales workers, for example, had a median full-time income of $4,174 in 1970, as compared to the male's $9,765; for professional workers, it was $7,850 against $12,255. Women university professors were earning $11,649, as compared to the male professor's median of $12,768. Chemists were earning $9,000 if they were women, $13,500 if they were men. Only 3 percent of working women earned more than $10,000 for the year, as compared to 28 percent of men (*Current Population Reports,* Consumer Income, Series P-60, No. 78, May 20, 1971).

However, according to the study by Blood and Wolfe (1960), the husband does not participate in the household tasks as fully as might be predicted. Although the contemporary husband usually does the tasks that demand strength or mechanical aptitude, such as shoveling snow or making repairs, the contemporary wife, in common with wives in almost all other societies, still does everything else, whether she is a housewife or a working wife. Blood and Hamblin (1958) found that the housewife performs about 85 percent of the household tasks; if she goes to work outside the home she still continues to perform 75 percent of these tasks. Explanations for this include (1) the traditional societal assumption, implicitly accepted by the couple, that the male's outside function is more important than that of the female and that despite her outside employment, she should still function in the home; (2) the assumption that the wife's employment is only temporary; and (3) the husband's employment is usually more significant in identifying the pair's social status.

Research data have not kept pace with the very rapid emergence of the working wife as a social phenomenon so that the continuing effects of such a pronounced cultural shift in male-female roles are highly conjectural at this point. It is clear, however, that the traditional ideology which defined the male role as the dominant member in family decision making and the provider of family income is passing through a redefinition; just what this redefinition will finally result in is not yet clearly established.

The employment of mothers may be seen as part of a general trend toward a decrease in the differentiation of sex roles. Other variables that might be included in this trend are: the increased participation of fathers in routine household tasks, a change in power relations from male dominance toward husband-wife equality, and the corresponding changes in ideology about sex roles in the family (Hoffman, 1960, p. 27).

The Power Structure

One of the greatest peculiarities of American marriage, as compared to almost all other societies, is the relative dominance of the American wife. In almost all other societies, the male is dominant over the female. Stephens (1963), for example, found in his cross-cultural study that the more important honorific jobs and offices are the usual province of men, and women are actively excluded from them. Furthermore, in many societies, women are not only excluded from public life but also barred from public gatherings. Naturally this male dominance extends into the marital relation.

In contrast to this intercultural norm, Blood and Wolfe (1960) found that in our society only about one marriage in five is male-dominant; an equal number are female-dominant. The remaining three in five marriages are "democratic," with decision making, dominance, and deference either mutually or alternately shared. According to the Blood and Wolfe study, the greatest satisfaction in the marriage, according to both partners, was with a husband-dominant or democratic structure. Dissatisfaction with the marriage correlated with the wife-dominant structure.

"Togetherness" and the Romantic Illusion

Another aspect of contemporary American marriage which is almost unique in world societies is our expectation for husband-wife "togetherness" in all of their activities. The person in our society is conditioned from early childhood to anticipate an encounter with a significant other who is ideally appropriate to mutual romantic need fulfillment. In other words, the expectation is that to marry is "to live happily ever after" in mutual companionship and emotional support. This cultural ideal of togetherness, which is especially prevalent in the middle class, is a romantic illusion in that it emphasizes unrealistic goals: the exclusive possession of the love object and an almost complete identification with it.

Once the realization is accepted that even between the closest human beings infinite distances continue to exist, a wonderful living side by side can grow up, if they succeed

in loving the distance between them which makes it possible for each to see the whole against the sky (Rainer Maria Rilke, Letters).

In other societies, and in prior generations of our own society, the togetherness pattern is unknown:

Traditional barriers frequently stand between husband and wife, curtailing their intimacy, sharing, and togetherness. They usually observe avoidance customs while in public; they may sleep in separate beds, live in separate houses, own separate property, eat separately, go separately to community gatherings, and . . . usually work at separate tasks . . . In our present-day American society, for some reason, these traditional barriers have largely disappeared (Stephens, 1963, p. 270).

One of the chief reasons for marrying in the United States today, as we have seen, is in anticipation of this interdependence of activities and emotional fulfillment. This emphasis upon togetherness in American marriage increases both the number and the complexity of the roles involved in the relation—it is easier to learn to make light biscuits than it is to learn to be a good companion. The American view of marriage involves a greater investment of personal resources, as well as a greater yield of personal benefits, than does marriage in other societies. This has, of course, led to greater risk and a higher incidence of marital failure in our society. As more is demanded of marriage, more marriages may be expected to fall short of the expectations. (See Chapter Seven.)

Summary

In every known human society, some form of marriage exists. It is apparently essential for survival of man as a species; for marriage provides for a stability and continuity of the social order and for a regulation of kinship relations. It serves as the nucleus of the family.

Marriage makes the paired relation of the couple a socially acknowledged, legal, relatively permanent bond, which provides not only for reciprocal obligations between the married couple but also for the rights of offspring. It provides a formal and legal link to the extended family, or kinship relatives, and thereby establishes property rights and stable lines of inheritance from generation to generation.

There are four possible forms of marriage: monogamy, polygyny, polyandry, and group marriage. Polygyny is the most often permitted in the world's societies, but monogamy is the prevalent form in practice. Group marriage is the rarest form.

Marriage has three meanings: sacred, social, and personal. Until the present century, it was viewed chiefly as an institution of divine significance; at the close of the nineteenth century its meaning began to shift to that of a civil institution; and contemporary marriage is viewed chiefly in our society as a vehicle for personal satisfaction. The increasing emphasis on the personalization of marriage has occurred hand-in-hand with the depersonalization of many of man's other institutions as our culture has adopted the characteristics of a mass society.

All societies observe a division of labor in marriage. The male traditionally performs tasks that call for physical strength, mobility, and extended absence from the home; and the female performs the tasks that are related to her capacity for bearing and nursing children, that allow her to remain near the home, and that do not call for great physical strength. This traditional sex-linked division of labor is no longer functional in our contemporary society. The physical strength of the male is no longer absolutely necessary for making a living, and the female is no longer restricted to activities which are congruent with child bearing and rearing. Indeed, most American wives work outside the home, just as do American husbands. Thus, each couple must establish for themselves a satisfactory division of labor.

The tasks which must be performed in marriage are those of (1) income provision, (2) housekeeping, (3) sexual fulfillment, and (4) psychological need fulfillment. If one of these essential tasks is not characteristically performed, the relation will break down. The degree of failure will depend upon the extent of departure from the anticipated need fulfillment and the perceptual importance of the category within which the role failure occurs. These tasks are fulfilled in terms of role performance.

There are three important aspects of successful role interaction: (1) reciprocity, (2) congruence of role perception, and (3) equivalence of value. There are four factors involved in congruence of role perception: each person's perception of his own and of the other's role.

Role performance occurs in terms of ritual, procedure, and operation. Intimacy occurs when the behavior is a reaction to the immediacy of the present experience, so that the person is totally and unself-consciously absorbed. Intimacy is the most rewarding of all behavior but also the rarest. Intimacy in marriage is the ideal, but the marriage relation will succeed, even though most interaction is not intimate, so long as the four essential tasks of marriage are performed at least as operation and occasionally as intimacy.

Questions

1 How does society benefit from the social order provided by marriage?

2 What are the four possible forms of marriage found in different societies? Describe.

3 What are the three universally applicable characteristics of the institution of marriage?

4 In this century, what has made the emphasis in marriage shift from a civil institution to a more personal matter?

5 Explain the "bed and board" rights of the marriage contract.

6 From the point of view of organized religions, what more than a civil contract does the institution of marriage involve?

7 Explain the significance of the transition of the person from single to married.

8 Describe the division of labor in marriage.

9 What motivates a person to marry?

10 Which factors correlate highest with marital happiness?

11 What are the five component parts of the need for a paired relation?

12 Why are the complementary personality needs now as significant in our society as material and sexual needs?

13 How is the person's self-image affected by the responses of his mate?

14 Discuss
    (a) the importance in our society of the opportunity to have children.
    (b) the correlation between being happily married and having children.
15 What are some of the social pressures to marry?
16 Discuss the social-class differences in the male-female differential in motivation for marriage.
17 Discuss why a person might not marry.
18 What are the three aspects of role which are important for understanding of the interaction in marriage?
19 What does the reciprocity of role interaction in a relation depend upon? Discuss.
20 What can even a slight incongruence of the role perceptions of the marital partners lead to?
21 What happens in any interaction which is one-sided, with one person giving more satisfaction than he receives?

22 What are the three categories of role behavior? Define each and give examples.
23 Discuss intimacy in marital interaction.
24 What are the four areas of need satisfaction that must be fulfilled for a marriage to succeed?
25 How is failure in sex-role reciprocation more complex than failure in material need provision?
26 What three factors does the power structure of a marriage apparently stem from?
27 Describe and give an example of the type of interaction called the "principle of least involvement."
28 Discuss the peculiarities of American marriage.
29 Discuss a wife's motives for working outside the home.
30 Discuss the effect of the blurring and realignment of male-female roles in our society on the behavior patterns of the marital relation.
31 Discuss "togetherness" and the romantic illusion.

References and Selected Readings

Bardwick, Judith M. *Psychology of Women.* New York: Harper, 1971.

Bell, Robert R. *Marriage and Family Interaction,* 3rd ed. Homewood, Ill.: Dorsey, 1971.

_____, ed. *Studies in Marriage and the Family.* New York: Crowell, 1968.

Benson, Purnell. The Interests of Happily Married Couples. *Marriage and Family Living,* 1952, Vol. 14, pp. 276–280.

Berne, Eric. *Games People Play.* New York: Grove Press, 1967.

_____. *Sex in Human Loving.* New York: Simon and Schuster, 1970.

Biddle, Bruce J., ed. *Role Theory.* New York: Wiley, 1966.

Blood, Robert O., Jr. *Marriage,* 2nd ed. New York: Free Press, 1969.

_____. The Husband-Wife Relationship. In Nye and Hoffman, eds., *The Employed Mother in America.* Chicago: Rand McNally, 1963.

_____, and Robert L. Hamblin. The Effect of the Wife's Employment on the Family Power Structure. *Social Forces,* 1958, Vol. 36, pp. 347–352.

_____, and Donald M. Wolfe. *Husbands and Wives: The Dynamics of Married Living.* New York: Free Press, 1960.

Carter, Hugh, and Paul C. Glick. *Marriage and Divorce: A Social and Economic Study.* Cambridge, Mass.: Harvard University Press, 1970.

Cavan, Ruth Shonle. *The American Family,* 4th ed. New York: Crowell, 1969.

Christensen, Harold T. Child Spacing Analysis Via Record Linkage: New Data Plus a Summing Up From Earlier Reports. *Marriage and Family Living,* August 1963, Vol. 25, pp. 272–280.

_____, ed. *Handbook of Marriage and the Family.* Chicago: Rand McNally, 1967.

Clinebell, Charlotte H. and Howard J., Jr. *Intimate Marriage.* New York: Harper, 1970.

Cox, Frank D. *Youth, Marriage and the Seductive Society.* Dubuque, Iowa: Brown, 1968.

Davis, Maxine. *Sexual Responsibility in Marriage.* New York: Dial, 1963.

Dentler, Robert A., and Peter Pineo. Sexual Adjustment, Marital Adjustment and Personal Growth of Husbands: A Panel Analysis. *Marriage and Family Living,* 1960, Vol. 22, pp. 45–58.

Ditzion, Sidney. *Marriage, Morals and Sex in America: A History of Ideas.* New York: Octagon, 1970.

Eichenlaub, John E. *New Approaches to Sex in Marriage.* New York: Dell, 1970.

Eshleman, J. Ross. *Perspectives in Marriage and the Family, Readings.* Boston: Allyn and Bacon, 1969.

Farber, Seymour, and Roger H. L. Wilson, eds. *The Potential of Women.* New York: McGraw-Hill, 1963.

Goode, William J., ed. *The Contemporary American Family.* New York: Times Books, 1970.

Hadden, Jeffrey K., and Marie L. Borgotta, eds. *Marriage and the Family.* Ithaca, Ill.: Peacock, 1969.

Hoffman, Lois Wladis. The Decision to Work. In Nye and Hoffman, eds., *The Employed Mother in America.* Chicago: Rand McNally, 1963, pp. 18–39.

_____. Parental Power Relations and the Division of Household Tasks. *Marriage and Family Living,* 1960, Vol. 23, pp. 27–35.

James, Edwin O. *Marriage Customs through The Ages.* New York: Collier. Macmillan, 1965.

Jay, Phyllis C. The Experimental Study of the Female. In Farber and Wilson, eds., *The Potential of Women.*

Kephart, William M. *The Family, Society, and the Individual.* Boston: Houghton Mifflin, 1961.

Kirkendall, Lester A., and Wesley J. Adams. *The Students' Guide to Marriage and Family Life Literature.* Dubuque, Iowa: Brown, 1971.

Klemer, Richard H. *Marriage and Family Relationships.* New York: Harper, 1970.

Landis, Judson T., and Mary G. Landis. *Building a Successful Marriage,* 5th ed. Englewood Cliffs, N. J.: Prentice-Hall, 1968.

Lobenz, Norman M., and Clark W. Blackburn. *How To Stay Married; A Modern Approach to Sex, Money, and Emotions in Marriage.* New York: Cowles, 1969.

Locke, Harvey J. *Predicting Adjustment in Marriage: A Comparison of a Divorced and a Happily Married Group.* Westport, Conn.: Greenwood, 1968.

Martindale, Don. *American Society.* New York: Van Nostrand, 1960.

Maslow, Abraham, ed. *Motivation and Personality*. New York: Harper, 1970.

Masserman, J. H., ed. *Dynamics of Work and Marriage*. Science and Psychoanalysis Series, Vol. 16. New York: Grune, 1970.

Murdock, G. P. Comparative Data on the Division of Labor by Sex. *Social Forces*, 1937, Vol. 15, pp. 551–553.

_____. *Social Structure*. New York: Macmillan, 1949.

Nimkoff, M. F. Marriage. In Albert Ellis and Albert Abarbanel, eds., *The Encyclopedia of Sexual Behavior*, 2nd ed. New York: Hawthorn, 1967, pp. 663–671.

Nye, F. Ivan, and Lois Wladis Hoffman, eds., *The Employed Mother in America*. Chicago: Rand McNally, 1963.

Parke, Robert, Jr., and Paul C. Glick. Prospective Changes in Marriage and the Family. *Journal of Marriage and the Family*, May 1967, Vol. 29, p. 256.

Peterson, James A. *Counseling and Values*. New York: Intext, 1970.

_____. *Marriage and Family Counseling: Perspective and Prospect*. New York: Association Press, 1968.

Popenoe, Paul. *Marriage Is What You Make It*. St. Meinrad, Ind.: Abbey, 1970.

Rainer, Jerome, and Julia Rainer. *Sexual Pleasure in Marriage*, rev. ed. New York: Simon & Schuster, 1969.

Rheinstein, Max. Trends in Marriage and Divorce Laws of Western Countries. In Marvin B. Sussman, *Sourcebook in Marriage and the Family*, 3rd ed. Boston: Houghton Mifflin, 1968.

Riegel, Robert E. *American Feminists*. Lawrence: University of Kansas Press, 1970.

Rogers, Carl R. *On Becoming a Person*. Boston: Houghton Mifflin, 1970.

Rubin, Isadore, ed. *Sexual Freedom in Marriage*. New York: New American Library, 1969.

Russell, Bertrand. *Marriage and Morals*. New York: Liveright, 1970.

Saxton, Lloyd, ed. *The Individual, Marriage, and the Family: Current Perspectives*. Belmont, Calif.: Wadsworth, 1970.

Stephens, William N. *The Family in Cross-Cultural Perspective*. New York: Holt, 1963.

_____, ed. *Reflections On Marriage*. New York: Crowell, 1968.

Sussman, Marvin B. *Sourcebook in Marriage and the Family*, 3rd ed. New York: Houghton Mifflin, 1968.

Tegg, William. *Knot Tied: Marriage Ceremonies of All Nations*. Detroit: Singing Tree, 1970.

Udry, J. R. *The Social Context of Marriage*. Philadelphia: Lippincott, 1966.

Wake, Charles S. *Development of Marriage and Kinship*. Chicago: University of Chicago Press, 1967.

Westermarck, Edward. *Short History of Marriage*. New York: Humanities, 1969.

Winch, Robert F., and Louis W. Goodman. *Selected Studies in Marriage and the Family*, 3rd ed. New York: Holt, 1968.

Chapter Seven

Conflict and Adjustment in Marriage

Man is astonishingly good at dealing with the physical world, but he is just as astonishingly bad at dealing with human nature.

Arnold Toynbee

djustment is a sequence of behavioral response which resolves a perceived need. So long as a person has only himself to consider when he adjusts—for example, in drinking when thirsty or sleeping when tired—the process of adjustment is fairly straightforward. But when another person becomes involved, the needs of both people must be taken into account; and adjustment for one person may well be *deprivation* for the other. The resultant *conflict* of each person's needs may then cause a multitude of associated problems in their relation. Thus, *resolution of this conflict* and *mutual need fulfillment* are what we refer to when we speak of "good" *marital adjustment.* In contrast, "bad" marital adjustment may resolve an immediate conflict, but the resolution involves only one of the spouses; and the lack of mutual fulfillment usually sows the seeds of further conflict (see the later section, *Adjustive Responses to Marital Conflict*).

Internal and External Conflict

Viewed psychologically, there are two categories of marital conflict—*internal* and *external*—although marital conflict is invariably on several levels and generally involves interacting elements of both categories. *Internal conflict* is so named because the two opposing needs that produce the conflict are felt by one person only, although the conflict will affect both persons in the relation. For example, internal conflict would occur in a wife who wishes (1) to please her husband by copulating with him, but who also wishes (2) to control and therefore to dominate her husband by withholding sexual participation and thus using her sexuality as a bargaining instrument in a struggle for power in the relation.

Usually, a wish like the latter is an unconscious one, and this unconsciousness adds to the difficulty of resolving the conflict. For, obviously, if both conflicting needs are clearly seen, the need with the greater value will be chosen and the conflict will be resolved. But if, as frequently happens, the wife is unaware of or has repressed one or the other of the conflicting needs, the internal conflict cannot be resolved until the nature of the conflict is sought and acknowledged. So long as the wife does not recognize that by denying her husband the fulfillment of a basic need she is attempting to alter the balance of power and resource provision and thereby perhaps destroy the relation, there is little likelihood of a resolution of her conflict. And if there is no resolution, the marriage is likely to fall apart on many levels in addition to its sexual aspects. But if she is able to reduce her internal conflict to its essential ingredients — that is, if she is able to ask herself, "Why am I denying my husband sexual satisfaction, when I know how important it is to him?" — she may be able to identify her conflicting needs and allow the more important of the needs to take precedence.

The resolution of her conflict, then, would involve a kind of self-assessment, with the goal of isolating the real nature of the conflict:

"I want to satisfy my husband, and I know that I should; nevertheless, I don't. Why? When I reject his overtures, I sense that he is unhappy, frustrated, and powerless. But I want to please him and make him happy and fulfill his needs. Therefore, his powerlessness must be what I am seeking. But do I want a contented husband and a happy marriage, or do I want to wield power — to be able to turn him on and off?"

Thus the conflict is resolved into an essential question;[1] and with the answer to that question, the wife clarifies the alternatives and then makes her adjustive response. If she answers the question by fulfilling her husband's needs and providing reciprocal and equivalent role resources in the relation, her adjustment is a good one.

Adjustment of an internal conflict need not be (and, ideally, should not be) a one-sided process. If both spouses agree to explore an immediate problem (for example, her sexual disinterest), they will have taken an important step toward resolving the immediate problem and identifying the underlying conflict (her struggle for dominance). For by candidly and democratically sharing the problem and by clearing away surface difficulties (for example, his resentment and doubts about her love for him and her fear and resentment of his dominance), they will not only expose and perhaps resolve the underlying conflict but also reestablish the intimacy and trust and balance of their relation.

External conflict involves two opposing needs that arise between two people rather than within one person. One person wants what the other does not want —

---

[1] Of course, in any internal conflict, many needs (not merely two) oppose and modify one another. The example we provide is a useful simplification.

for example, an open window at night, a vegetarian dinner, a baby.[2] If a wife wants the bedroom window open and her husband wants the window closed, an external conflict of needs is occurring. If the husband is to be physically well adjusted — that is, warm — the wife must be poorly adjusted.

An external conflict may be resolved in four ways: (1) *by a unilateral and authoritarian decision*—the husband wants the window closed and closes it; (2) *by a permissive acceptance of the other's demand,* regardless of one's own need — "whatever you say, dear"; (3) *by an internal compromise,* in which the external conflict is transformed into an internal conflict for one or both of the spouses and, thereby, into a decision by either spouse to sacrifice his immediate need satisfaction for what he perceives to be a greater satisfaction — the fulfillment of the other's need; (4) *by creative problem solving,* in which the couple identify and discuss the conflict and then agree upon a creative solution — for example, the window stays open but they agree to purchase an electric blanket with dual controls.

Either the *authoritarian* or the *permissive-acceptance* decisions will result in a resolution of the immediate conflict, but they invariably lead to further conflict over the same problem and over new and unrelated disagreements. For these solutions will generally provoke angry resentment in the person whose need is ignored and guilt (and, therefore, often a shifting of the blame) in the person who dictates the solution or who is automatically deferred to. As a result, the couple will tend to attack one another instead of attacking the problem, and the personal attacks may lead to a power struggle between the two persons, with continual sparring for dominance and emotional defeats. Of course, if the marital relation is substantially based on the dominance of one partner and submissiveness of the other, an authoritarian or a permissive-acceptance resolution of conflict will be the expected and patterned adjustive behavior in the relation. This pattern is typical of some marriages in our society and of the majority of marriages in many other societies — for example, where the husband is traditionally the dominant and deferred-to figure. However, in a society such as ours, with such a strong cultural orientation toward personal fulfillment in marriage, such a relation is considered less than ideal and is usually far less stable than a relation based on democratic decision making and mutual fulfillment.

Resolution of conflict by *creative problem solving* is, of course, the ideal mode of marital adjustment since it usually results in intimacy. However, it requires understanding, discussion, both a willingness and an ability to compromise, and a good deal of emotional maturity. Resolution of conflict by an *internal compromise* is also a reasonable (and, often, intimate) mode of adjustment, since it is generally an effective (and realistic) solution to the immediate problem and it leaves

---

[2] Another type of external conflict involves two persons openly vying for the same need satisfaction or resource. This type of conflict behavior occurs often among children and among lower animals (two children fighting over a toy or two dogs vying for the same bone) and among adults who are strangers or rivals (two women diving for the same bus seat or two salesmen after the same customer). It rarely occurs among adults in any social situation — and especially in a marital relation — since adults are more fully socialized, and the roles, the division of labor and resources, and the etiquette of social relations are strongly conditioned in them. Moreover, in any paired relation, there is almost always sufficient altruism to prevent this kind of conflict over a limited resource.

little or no residue of resentment or guilt in either person. This is especially
true if the resolution of the internal conflicts of either or both is openly discussed and shared by the marital partners.

Marital conflict — both internal and external — is inevitable; for the interaction of a
paired relation involves countless interrelated needs and roles and personality
and physiological variables which must be fulfilled and reciprocated and accounted for day after day and year after year. Most adjustments in marriage,
except for the simplest of physical satisfactions, are involved to some extent with
the needs of the other; and it is too much to expect that the needs of both will always coincide.

Displacement and Repression

Marital conflict often occurs over rather mundane matters that two close
friends would consider implausible and laughable as subjects for disagreement
and open conflict. Such conflicts arise in part because of the nature of the marital relation — the constantness of the interaction, the stresses of having to compromise one's needs and desires, and the vulnerability of a person in such an intimate relation. But such conflicts also arise because we tend to *displace* or *repress*
our internal conflicts instead of resolving them. Displacement and repression are

simply delaying tactics; the internal conflicts will remain and will induce anger
or resentment that will eventually explode into open conflict over small frictions.
For instance, an angry marital quarrel arises over a disagreement as to which
television program to watch; the husband wants to watch a ball game and his wife
wants to watch a soap opera. Finally, he retreats sullenly behind the newspaper
for the rest of the evening and/or she takes to her bed in tears. That both persons
are so bitter and resentful that they can fight over so trivial an issue as choice of
television programs is probably indicative of an underlying problem or conflict —
perhaps, as in the earlier example, over the wife's using her sexuality for dominance. The real issue — mutual sexual fulfillment — is displaced by a false and trivial issue — the television program. Displacement very often explains the surprising

emotionalism and involvement that a couple will exhibit in disagreements over matters which are in themselves of little consequence. Usually, after a day or two has intervened, the couple cannot even remember the reason for their quarrel.

In a viable marriage, as in any good working relation, there is mutual altruism and respect and mutual attempts to understand and adjust to the inevitable divergences of interests, values, and performances. Therefore, each will try to put the relation back on a mutually supportive basis as soon as possible in order to please the other and in order to maintain their relation, which is the source of much need fulfillment for them both. On the other hand, when a marital relation is disintegrating, one or both will sulk, bear grudges, continually attack and devalue the other, and resist any attempt to examine the basis of the difficulty — returning again and again to a position of outraged morality or wounded innocence.

One of the major techniques of quarreling in our convention-bound society is to manipulate the symbols of morality in such a way that the other person is put in the wrong. In marital quarrels each person pays a great deal of attention to the mores. They constitute the unspoken major premise of every complaint. Sometimes the air is full of such phrases as "I don't deserve that," or "You have no right to do this" (Waller, 1951, p. 302).

If a conflict is not isolated, or agreed upon, and resolved, it is likely to recur year after year, with the same ground fought over again and again. Such behavior is hardly conducive to the personal happiness of the married couple or to the stability of their relation. Waller points out that "habitual conflict is probably the most expensive in terms of the mental health of the partners" (p. 306).

One characteristic of such recurrent quarrels is what Folsom (1943) calls "alternate approach and withdrawal."

The partner who takes the initiative is rebuffed by the other, who feels a desire to inflict further punishment before yielding to reconciliation. The initiating party, being rebuffed, withdraws and waits for the next advance to come from the other. When that advance does come, he retaliates by rebuffing on his side. The result may be that the initiative zigzags several times from one side to the other before reconciliation finally occurs (p. 447).

With all marital conflict, the first step toward resolution is mutual agreement upon the problem and the second step is abandonment of the temptation to "win," to put the other in the wrong. When these two adjustive steps are accomplished, the underlying problem may then be approached and, hopefully, resolved. Thus, a good marital relation has to do not so much with avoiding conflict as with successfully exploring and coming to grips with the conflicts that do occur. If each partner is able to fulfill most of his needs most of the time in interaction with the other, the couple and the marriage are well adjusted. But if certain needs are irreconcilable or if certain unconscious mechanisms of conflict are unresolved and prevent the satisfaction of important needs, the couple is poorly adjusted and their marriage is unhappy and may ultimately be a failure.

The Sources of Conflict in Marriage

In order to understand the dynamics of marital conflict and the processes of adjustment by which we resolve such conflict and fulfill our needs, we will examine seven personality factors that underlie conflict in a paired relation: divergent feedback, differences in frame of reference, maintenance of the self-image, discontinuity of role conditioning, excessive expectations of togetherness, frustration, and defense-oriented behavior.

Divergent Feedback

Feedback is information received by a person about the effects of his behavior on his environment. Utilizing feedback, a person will either continue or modify his behavior to achieve the result he desires. Feedback, which is usually received and utilized unconsciously, is involved in almost all behavior, even of the simplest kind. For example, no one can sit on a chair without using feedback. Careful measurements taken in the laboratory reveal that even when a person believes himself to be sitting perfectly immobile, he is in fact constantly rebalancing himself. As he starts to fall in one direction, his central nervous system instantaneously receives the information, which then is utilized to correct his position. Then information about how he has corrected his position is, in turn, "fed back" to the central nervous system so that his correction can be further modified. The result of this latter modification is fed back also; and thus by a continual process of correction, of receiving and utilizing feedback, the person is able to remain seated upright in his chair.

In interpersonal behavior, the utilization of feedback works in the same way, except that the process is more complex — principally because another person, unlike an object, responds to us differently at different times and is, moreover, from his own point of view not an object to furnish us with feedback but the subject for whom we are the feedback-supplying object. A man learning to hit a golf ball utilizes feedback to correct his stroke, until he can send the ball straight down the fairway with a solid drive. Any failure to do so is not the fault of the club or the golf ball. In relating to another person, however, the man finds that the feedback he receives is inconsistent — that, for example, the flattery that evokes a warm response from his wife at lunch may make her angry at dinner. The wife is relating to her husband in terms of her own needs, which continually change, and in terms of the feedback she is receiving from him. Therefore, if she suspects that his flattery at dinner time is a coarse attempt to make up for his being inexcusably late, the repressed annoyance that she is feeling may break into open anger. The "behavior" of the golf ball, on the other hand, is consistent; it has no needs and it does not *utilize* feedback. Relating to another person would be analogous to "relating" to a golf ball, if the golf ball were able to change into a land mine in the middle of the stroke.

Information fed back to a person that his behavior is bringing him a result he desires is called *convergent feedback*. Information that his behavior is not bringing him the desired result is called *divergent feedback*, which is almost always a sign that there is a present conflict. If he receives divergent feedback, he must modify his behavior until he chances upon an action which produces convergent feedback. Thus, *divergent feedback provides information which, after processing, is acted on by the person in an attempt to receive convergent feedback.*

However, this important step—the effort to change divergent feedback into convergent—is not always taken in the emotion-laden, ego-involved interactions of two people in a marital relation. Spouses who, for whatever reason, are not getting along will receive divergent feedback from one another in most or all aspects of their interaction. But, instead of making realistic attempts to obtain convergent feedback, each may either explode in anger or withdraw into sullen silence, which worsens the marriage relation by producing even more divergent feedback. This they will interpret as further evidence that the other is being aggressively unpleasant and unreasonable, and each will grow even more resentful than he was before. Even when one of them makes an attempt to obtain convergent feedback, it may not be immediately forthcoming from the other. The other will say, in effect, "I'm not ready to make up yet—I'm not through being mad. I feel wronged, and I feel that you are not contrite enough or haven't been punished enough." This, of course, turns the first person off; so that when the second person *is* ready to make up (or seek convergent feedback), the first person is now nursing his renewed grievance. Often this "alternate approach and withdrawal" may go on for hours and perhaps days, even in a viable relation, before both persons are ready to seek convergent feedback (or reconciliation) at the same time and resolve the conflict.

In a disintegrating relation, each person becomes progressively less willing to seek convergent feedback after a conflict and more and more insistent upon having his grievance acknowledged. Obtaining a verdict of "you're right" from the other, or from parents or friends, then becomes more important than winning convergent feedback from the other. If this pattern persists, of course, the interaction of the relation may be entirely put off. And once the spouses cease to be "significant others" for one another, the intimacy that brought them into marriage in the first place is destroyed.

Feedback may be, besides convergent or divergent, *immediate* or *delayed* and *free* or *limited*. In the physical world of hitting golf balls and sitting on chairs, feedback is immediate and free (or unqualified by other factors); in the psychological world of relating to other people, feedback usually is delayed and limited. For example, the husband who perceives himself as the life of the party, a belief which his wife's smiles seem to support, may find after the two of them leave that (1) he was not really getting convergent feedback from her but was misinterpreting the *limited* feedback she was providing, and (2) the only reason that she was providing limited rather than divergent feedback was that she was trying to conform to the cultural expectations of emotional control in a public place and of harmony between a married couple. Only with the delayed and now free feedback of her explosion of anger on the drive home is the husband able accurately to process the information which may modify his behavior at future parties.

Thus, feedback from other people, and even from a significant other, is generally ambiguous because of the multitude of needs and possible responses that a person must sort out (internal conflict) in interacting with others. Marriage particularly complicates the problems of psychological feedback, since the roles of a marital relation require even greater skills in processing feedback than are demanded in relating to friends or to members of one's family. Because the marital relation is so enduring and intimate and because it is expected to provide so many satisfactions, ineffective utilization of feedback is far more devastating to marital relations than it would be to other types of relations. Moreover, the married couple are held to their relation in ways that people relating in business or recreation or even the family of origin are not. Thus, the married couple must be especially aware of the meaning of the feedback each one gets from the other and must attempt to resolve differences in ways that are in accordance with this feedback; that is, in accordance with the conditioned difficulties and inadequacies in each one's response patterns. If they are unable to do this to their mutual satisfaction, they will have a very unhappy marriage.

Differences in Frame of Reference

The *frame of reference* is the cluster of values, expectations, and factual assumptions which underlie most of a person's adult perceptions of his roles, his experiences, and the feedback he receives and utilizes. This cluster is based chiefly upon the new experiences of the first few years of the person's life. Experiences he has after he is about five years old will, for the most part, merely serve to reinforce or modify only slightly his already existing cluster of assumptions. A person's earliest sociosexual experiences, for example, including his observations of the interactions between father and mother, parents and children, and sisters and brothers and the interactions among peers and their families, will produce most of the sociosexual attitudes, expectations, and behavior that he will demonstrate as a married adult.

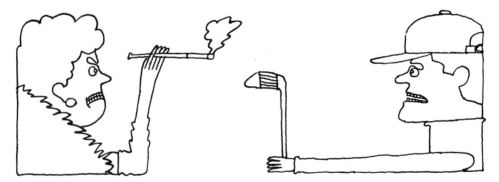

Clearly, then, in marriage, a reciprocity of role interaction will be dependent on the similarities of the frames of reference of the two persons. For feedback (and, thus, role perception and response) can be utilized only on the basis of a person's perception and interpretation of it—a process which is defined and limited by the individual's previous (and, usually childhood) experience, which has formed the basis for his frame of reference. Marital conflict very frequently arises from a disparity in some aspect of the partners' frames of reference, with each person unable to reconcile his point of view with that of his spouse. The likelihood of such conflict points up the importance of careful mate selection, of the engagement period, and of the homogamous and heterogamous factors that correlate with mutual attraction and successful marriage.

The Maintenance of the Self-image

The *self-image* is established as the person perceives his own experience and existence, utilizes feedback, and formulates a frame of reference from which he processes new experience and new feedback. The "core" of the self-image is formed with the frame of reference in early childhood and thereafter seldom undergoes any significant change, although it is constantly being modified slightly. Together with the frame of reference and the utilization of feedback, the self-image is a major force in marital conflict.

A great deal of a person's behavior is involved in his need to maintain or enhance his self-image. Indeed, after the basic physical needs have been met, the maintenance of the self-image is a principal human preoccupation. Much of social behavior consists of engaging in *reality testing*, or the sampling of other's responses and the subsequent modification of behavior in accordance with this feedback. A person will feel uneasy unless he is able to confirm "who he is" in terms of others responses to him. Such *confirmation* occurs almost automatically in a simple society, where each person makes a difference to the other, at least to some degree. In our mass society, however, this important function is fulfilled chiefly by the significant other in a paired relation and provides one of the relation's most essential aspects.[3]

Confirming responses (convergent feedback) of a significant other reinforce the self-image, make the person confident, secure, relaxed, and self-assured, and thus enhance his performance in all areas of life. On the other hand, negative responses (divergent feedback), which do not reinforce his self-image, cause him to become uneasy, tense, awkward, self-concerned, defensive, and even disoriented. Few persons can equably withstand direct and punishing assaults upon their self-image by a significant other; for in primary, and especially paired, relations, the self-image is almost completely vulnerable, since in these relations we necessarily drop the defenses we normally employ in our secondary relations with other people. We look upon an attack on our self-image by a significant other as betrayal; so that when a person's self-image is attacked in marital conflict, he must establish congruence between his self-image and the way he

---

[3] Confirmation of the self-image occurs in all relations, even the most casual, and the importance of such confirmation by colleagues, acquaintances, and business associates can scarcely be overemphasized. The significant other in a paired relation has unique strength, however, in his function of either confirming or denying the person's self-regard.

perceives a significant other as perceiving him, or he will remain seriously incapacitated.

Divergent feedback occurs often, of course, in marital conflicts; and if in the course of these conflicts the significant other resorts to or is provoked into personal attack—that is, attack on the other's self-image—the effect can be shattering and can provoke continuing conflict, permanent distrust, or a temporary breakdown of the relation. And if such an attack becomes a persistent pattern in the marital conflict, the relation may never recover and its disintegration may accelerate. For example, if the wife, during the inevitable marital quarrels, continually attacks her husband by calling him an incompetent clod, an inept lover,

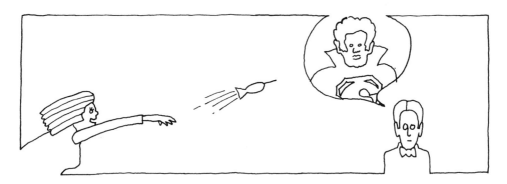

or a lazy provider, the relation must take one of three directions: (1) He will eventually *devalue* himself and be extremely dejected, defense oriented, and uninterested in the relation. Or (2), he will modify his behavior (if he can) in ways that will change her perception (he will be apologetic, and then will try to be charming, a consummate lover, or an energetic provider). Or (3), he will take the final step of ceasing to regard her as significant and thus downgrading their relation from primary to secondary. This step reduces his vulnerability to attack, of course; but marriage without a primary relation between the spouses is usually considered a "failed" marriage in our society. Inasmuch as marked modification of the self-image is relatively rare and behavior seldom changes for the better under the lash of self-devaluation, the third alternative—the downgrading of the relation—is often our societal norm.

In a well-adjusted marriage (or any enduring paired relation—whether friendship or business), each person supports and enhances the self-image of the other most of the time; and when one or the other's self-image *is* attacked during a quarrel, they characteristically move relatively quickly from the power-struggle zone of attacking one another to a creative zone of apology, mutual attack of the problem that caused the conflict, and mutual attempts to find a compromise solution. If they really care about one another, each will be moved to reestablish their close relation as quickly as possible. Each will try (after the initial impetus of anger has worn off) to understand the other's point of view and to resolve the conflict by changing one or the other's performance to meet the other's role expectations. For example, the husband, if his wife has been disappointed in a particular copulation – after his initial response of wounded ego and vanity has worn off – will try to be more sensitive to her needs and to fulfill them, or vice versa.

Discontinuity of Role Conditioning

Most role conditioning is continuous, so that the role behavior admired in the adult is expected of a child. Thus, there is no conflict between the role expectation of the child and that of the adult; and the transition from childhood to adolescence and adulthood takes place with no anxiety, confusion, or guilt. The Eskimo boy who carries a tiny spear when he goes hunting with his father and the little girl in our society who plays house are exemplifying the *continuity of role conditioning.*

However, in the very important parameters of sex, independence, and dominance, our society, particularly, is characterized by *discontinuity of role conditioning,* with the child expected to be asexual, dependent, and submissive and the adult expected to be sexual, independent, and dominant. Thus, in these three areas, the conditioning of a child does not prepare him for the role of the adult; and since discontinuity of conditioning occurs, there is a good deal of internal and interpersonal conflict involved in the transitions from childhood to adolescence to adulthood.

Adolescence is an especially difficult period precisely because of this discontinuity. The adolescent is generally expected to demonstrate *both* the asexuality, dependence, and submissiveness of the child and the sexuality, independence, and dominance of the adult. If the parents of an adolescent put too much emphasis on his conformity to childhood patterns, the adolescent may not be able to make the proper transition into adult patterns; and the ideals, attitudes, and expectations of childhood may be carried over into adulthood. For example, discontinuity in the role conditioning for sex commonly results in a husband who retains an attitude toward sex which is that of a "good" boy, or a wife who retains an attitude which is that of a model adolescent. In either case, the spouse is identifying with the asexual norms of the child rather than with the prosexual norms of the adult; and much of their marital difficulty stems from the feelings of guilt (on the part of the disoriented partner) and confusion (on the part of the relatively mature partner) which occur as a result of the sudden reversal of role behavior that is expected immediately after the marriage ceremony.

The resolution of conflict stemming from discontinuity of role conditioning is very difficult since the disoriented partner is not easily amenable to adult adjustive responses in the area in which he is immature. The more mature partner must either fulfill the role the other expects – for example, a wife's chief function may be to "mother" her husband and, perhaps, to disguise her sexuality by making it ritualistic and regularly scheduled – or he must exhibit exceptional patience and altruism in guiding his partner into emotional maturity and in avoiding serious conflict and resentment over the partner's difficulty.

Excessive Expectations of Togetherness

Despite the congruence of communication that is characteristic of the formation of a paired relation, and despite the intimacy of a couple's sexual and social interaction, each spouse will have inherently different needs, abilities, interests, attitudes, expectations, memories, and physiological and personality characteristics. Each is a unique individual with a unique background, frame of reference, and response pattern. Many of these factors will be similar, to be sure, or these two particular individuals would not have been drawn together in the first place, and their relation would certainly not have survived dating and engagement. However, inevitable dissimilarities will be present in the relation, and they will invariably be a source of some conflict.

The probability of such conflict is intensified when one or both of the spouses are excessively steeped in the romantic illusion of marital togetherness. Adjustment in marriage may become very difficult if one spouse expects the other to give up all interests, activities, and attitudes which he cannot share. Further, good marital adjustment is impossible if the couple do not realize and then structure their relation on the expectation that each must grow as an individual, maintaining the initial unshared interests and characteristics as well as developing new unshared interests and characteristics.

Couples must share their basic values and key activities, but this does not prevent them from going their separate ways the rest of the time. . . . Happy are those who find it possible to maintain a flexible bond between growing personalities. For them, marriage is a liberating force and a creative achievement (Blood, 1969, p. 292).

The vital importance and extreme necessity of achieving and maintaining a balance between individuation and togetherness has been stated most aptly by Gibran:

But let there be spaces in your togetherness,
And let the winds of the heavens dance between you.
Love one another, but make not a bond of love:
Let it rather be a moving sea between the shores of your souls.
Fill each other's cup but drink not from one cup.
Give one another of your bread but eat not from the same loaf.
Sing and dance together and be joyous,
*   but let each one of you be alone,*
Even as the strings of a lute are alone
*   though they quiver with the same music.*[4]

---

[4] Reprinted from *The Prophet* by Kahlil Gibran with permission of the publisher, Alfred A. Knopf, Inc. Copyright 1923 by Kahlil Gibran; renewal copyright 1951 by Administrators C.T.A. of Kahlil Gibran Estate and Mary G. Gibran.

Frustration

Frustration occurs when deprivation combines with self-devaluation. It is characterized by a feeling of either depression or anger and may result, on the one hand, in apathy, melancholy, or profound dejection or, on the other hand, in a verbal or physical attack of some kind. For the frustrated person to identify the cause of his depression or anger would necessitate admitting to himself his feeling of self-devaluation; and such an admission is, of course, extremely threatening to the self-image. Consequently, his emotional "misbehavior" appears to the other person—and sometimes even to himself—to be undirected, with no rational target on which to spend itself.

For example, a husband denied copulation by his wife may suspect that the tiredness she gives as her excuse is really a rejection of him; and his resultant self-devaluation may change his feeling of deprivation, which is occasionally tolerable in a relation, into genuine frustration, which is seriously damaging to the relation since it ceases all intimate and even operational interaction. An excellent illustration of the development of frustration occurs in a very perceptive passage in John Updike's *Rabbit, Run*.[5] The young husband wants to copulate with his wife and has been waiting to do so with increasing tension (and deprivation) throughout a long Sunday afternoon:

His wish to make love to Janice is like a small angel to which all afternoon tiny lead weights are attached . . . He has come home from church carrying something precious for Janice and keeps being screened from giving it to her . . . they blunder about restlessly through the wreckage of the Sunday paper . . . Rabbit, hoping to possess her eventually, hovers near her like a miser near treasure. His lust glues them together. When they are finally in bed together she refuses his advances.

"Harry, Don't you know I want to go to sleep?"
"Well, why didn't you tell me before?"
"I didn't know. I didn't know."
"You didn't know what?"
"I didn't know what you were doing. I thought you were just being nice."
"So this isn't nice."
"Well, it's not nice when I can't do anything."
"You can do something."
"No I can't. Even if I wasn't all tired and confused from Rebecca's crying all day I can't. Not for six weeks. You know that."
"Yeah, I know, but I thought . . . " He's terribly embarrassed.
"What *did* you think?"
"I thought you might love me anyway."
After a pause she says, "I do love you."

[5] From pp. 203–204, 206 of Updike's *Rabbit, Run* (1960). Reprinted by permission of the publisher, Alfred A. Knopf, Inc., New York.

Her total lack of understanding and awareness, or her deliberate misinterpretation of his need, using her recent childbirth as an excuse, leaves him with so great a feeling of vulnerability and frustration that he contains his resultant anxiety only by rising, dressing, and leaving the house. He needs her to respond to his need, and his need for response on her part is greater even than his need for sexual activity. He needs a congruence of communication, a demonstration of an essential similarity between her frame of reference and his, and at least an attempt at role reciprocation. When none of these non-physical needs are fulfilled, the self-devaluation that he feels is overwhelming.

Reaction to frustration may be either (1) *extrapunitive* (directed outward); (2) *intrapunitive* (directed inward upon oneself); or (3) *impunitive* (unaggressive). The frustrated husband who punishes his wife or smashes furniture is acting extrapunitively; the husband who gets nervous, sick, or despondent is acting intrapunitively; and the husband who sublimates his frustration by taking lonely walks, by reading, or by spending most of his time at work or in recreational activities is demonstrating impunitive behavior. No one's reaction to frustration is exclusively extrapunitive, intrapunitive, or impunitive but rather consists of a mixture of these responses, one or the other of which predominates at any given moment. However, one type of response usually is utilized by a person more frequently than either of the other two types and hence may be said to constitute his patterned response to frustration.

Defense-oriented Behavior

Defense-oriented behavior is an adjustment—that is, it is a response to conflict of needs and deprivation or to frustration—but it is an adjustment that is directed *not* toward satisfying the need but toward alleviating the tension and self-devaluation associated with the *failure* to satisfy the need. *Reality-oriented behavior*, on the other hand, successfully satisfies the need that initiated the behavior; for instance, drinking when thirsty, finding companionship when lonely, or resolving an inequivalence of role function by discussing the problem and changing the patterned behavior.

The defense-oriented approach to conflict and deprivation is commonly utilized by a person if his need is psychological (it rarely occurs if the need to be fulfilled is physical). For example, a thirsty person is increasingly motivated to find water until the search occupies his entire awareness, whereas a lonely person will often make a compromise adjustment which will lower his immediate tension but fail to resolve the basic need. A wife who does not feel that her husband is fulfilling her need for confirmation and emotional support (he spends most of his time working and shows little interest in her household problems and roles) may withdraw into apathy and solitude or may resort to drinking,[6] to ex-

---

[6] Alcoholism is a principal cause of marriage failure and divorce in the United States. One in three semiskilled workers names alcoholism as the cause of his divorce; so do one in five clerical and sales workers and about one in seven professional workers (Kephart, 1954). The alcoholic and the heavy drinker are reacting to pressures, frustrations, and conflicts by seeking temporary psychological release rather than realistic solutions.

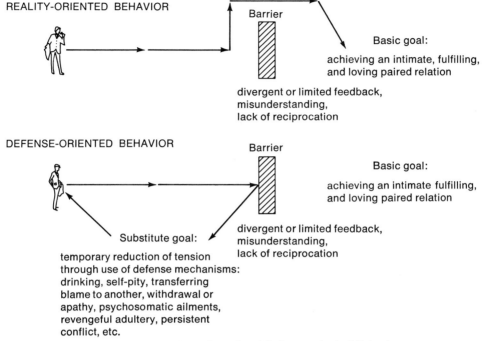

REALITY-ORIENTED BEHAVIOR

Barrier

Basic goal:

achieving an intimate, fulfilling, and loving paired relation

divergent or limited feedback, misunderstanding, lack of reciprocation

DEFENSE-ORIENTED BEHAVIOR

Barrier

Basic goal:

achieving an intimate fulfilling, and loving paired relation

divergent or limited feedback, misunderstanding, lack of reciprocation

Substitute goal:

temporary reduction of tension through use of defense mechanisms: drinking, self-pity, transferring blame to another, withdrawal or apathy, psychosomatic ailments, revengeful adultery, persistent conflict, etc.

Figure 7–1.   Reality-oriented and Defense-oriented Behavior

treme carelessness with the household, or to an extramarital affair. In none of these activities would she resolve the *basic need* (unless the effect of her withdrawal or unexpected behavior would shock her husband into changing his behavior pattern). However, by avoiding his rebuff through withdrawal of her concern for his response or by attacking him through nonconformist and self-devaluating behavior, she is resolving an immediate need—the temporary end to her stress—by substituting a secondary goal—emotional detachment or alcoholic escape or revenge.

Nevertheless, defense-oriented behavior does carry the reward of lowering tension, and it is therefore reinforced. Since reinforced behavior tends to be repeated, the person may develop a pattern of defense-oriented responses to psychological needs which he will utilize again and again under stress. This marginal adjustment is ultimately self-defeating, yet it can be very resistant to change. Not only is the immediate reduction of tension a powerful inducement to continue the behavior but because the person often is not fully conscious of the pattern of his behavior, he is not free to choose alternatives to it.

An outsider observing someone's defense-oriented response often reacts with puzzled impatience. Why, he may wonder, should anybody engage in defensive behavior when to do so obviously does not satisfy a basic need? If behavior is learned, and if learned behavior is based upon reinforcement, why doesn't everyone always behave in an optimal fashion, making the best possible adjustment? Can't the defensive person see that he's not getting what he really wants?

The answer, of course, is that needs do not exist in isolation and that, there-fore, a person's response to conflict, deprivation, and frustration depends upon which of his needs is taking precedence at the moment. Thus a person will utilize withdrawal, conversion of tension into physical illness, substitution, rationaliza-tion, excessive sleeping, fantasy, and other *defense mechanisms*[7] (modes of dis-placement and repression) to remedy the immediate need, the need to reduce tension, rather than to fulfill the more basic need. Such defense-oriented be-havior is normal, since it fulfills the function of satisfying one immediate need and since it "buys" time for the person while he further considers the means to satisfying the more basic need. But when defense-oriented behavior becomes the chief mode of response in marital conflict, the defense mechanisms become inadequate adjustments and the conflict, instead of being resolved or tempo-rarily delayed, looms larger, with an increasing tension, deprivation, and frus-tration.

Reality-oriented behavior in marriage requires trying to understand the basis of the conflict and attacking the problem rather than the spouse or oneself. When a husband comes home late and his wife is angry because of it, and when she says that she is angry, and when they both agree that coming home late creates a prob-lem which they must try to solve — this is reality-oriented behavior. But if she re-fuses to speak (*withdrawal*), shows no interest in his comings and goings (*apathy*), gets a headache (*psychosomatic ailment*), or punishes the children (*substitution*); or if he explains that he "couldn't reach a phone" (*rationalization*), dozes in front of the television set or goes to bed early when they are finally together (*escapist sleep*), or imagines that "next time" he will arrive home early bearing an expen-sive gift (*fantasy*) — this is defense-oriented behavior.

Adjustive Responses to Marital Conflict

There is no one type of happy or well-adjusted marriage; what one couple con-siders a reasonably satisfactory adjustive response to marital conflict, another couple may find unacceptable and tantamount to failure. A "good" adjustment is simply one which achieves a greater measure of satisfaction for both partners than does a "bad" adjustment. Needs in marriage are interrelated; the hungry husband who eats at a restaurant in the late afternoon and consequently can't eat the dinner his wife has prepared has made a good adjustment in satisfying his hunger but a bad adjustment in failing to support his wife's self-image and her expectation for role reciprocation. Each person (and each couple) has his own cluster of needs. Adjustments in marriage are good or bad only as they are so perceived by *both* partners.

A good adjustment is also dependent on the possibilities inherent in the rela-tion. One's spouse has both resources and lacks; and a good adjustment can be made only when both the attributes and the limitations of each person are ac-knowledged by both partners. In addition, each must recognize that there is no such thing as a final adjustment. Needs arise again and again and must be satis-

[7]For a fascinating discussion of these *ego-defense mechanisms,* see Coleman, 1969.

fied repeatedly. Every adjustment is related to countless needs of the individual and to numerous aspects of the environment in which he finds himself. A good adjustment maximizes gains and minimizes deprivations, but this process almost always requires relative deprivation in one area in order for satisfaction to be provided in another area.

Each spouse must have a clear understanding of which needs are important to him, of which are relatively unimportant, and of what choices of adjustive action are open to him. Such a clarity of perspective cannot be perfectly achieved, of course; but a person who is *reality oriented* about most things most of the time — that is, a person who clearly knows how he feels and who can satisfy his important needs without depriving the other of his important needs — such a person is unmistakably making a good adjustment. And two such people, functioning this way in their marital interactions, have a well-adjusted marriage.

Perhaps the principal element in good marital adjustment is the good will of the partners. If they have established and strive to maintain a viable and intimate primary relation, in which each *individual* is granted more importance than any function he may perform, conflict resolution and good adjustment will follow naturally. Such a recognition of one's mate works on many levels, verbal and nonverbal, physical and psychological. For instance, just as physical fondling is so necessary to the emotional well-being of an infant that a deprived infant will almost inevitably suffer psychological damage (Spitz, 1945), non-physical "handling" — that is, recognition of another by such means as smiles or conversation — is essential to the adult and may in fact be an essential substitute for the earlier physical comforting he experienced as an infant. The adult "learns to do with more subtle, even symbolic forms of handling, until the merest nod of recognition may serve the purpose to some extent . . ." (Berne, 1964, p. 14). Thus, if the marriage is to endure, a very large proportion of marital adjustment must be directed toward fulfilling the recognition need of one's mate. The actual methods — both good and bad — for achieving marital adjustment are discussed below.

Creative Problem Solving

Creative problem solving, in which there is no winner or loser, is the most reliably satisfying and complete mode of conflict adjustment. It may actually improve a marital relation by bringing the persons closer together. Creative problem solving involves the couple's ultimately agreeing to abandon their indignation and hurt feelings and to direct their argument toward cooperative examination of the problem. This approach not only avoids planting the seeds for future resentment but also leads to greater understanding and closer role reciprocation.

With this approach, then, the first step is to agree upon the problem. The **second step is to abandon the temptation to defeat the other person. And the third step is to mutually attack the problem and find out what the areas of dif-**ference are. The final step is to try to work out a compromise solution that satisfies both partners, so that "winning" for both people consists of defeating the problem (rather than attempting to defeat one another).

One major difficulty with creative problem solving lies in the fact that the method is not nearly so clear-cut and economical as either the authoritarian or the permissive resolution, in which a ready-made "solution" is always at hand no matter what the disagreement. With creative problem solving a new solution must be found for each new conflict.

The following deliberately oversimplified conflict situations illustrate the process of creative problem solving:

The wife is involved with numerous community activities and is frequently home too late to have a well-prepared dinner ready when her husband returns from work. The husband expects better treatment—especially because earlier in the marriage, when the children were young, his wife had devoted much of her time to domestic provisions. He becomes jealous of her outside activities and grows more and more annoyed. From the husband's point of view, this conflict could be resolved by an authoritarian demand— "From now on, my dinner will be ready or else"—or by permissive acceptance—"Don't worry about dinner; I'll have a glass of juice (or three martinis) while I'm waiting." Similarly, from the wife's point of view, the conflict could be resolved by her saying "I don't exist merely to provide you with dinner on time," or by her giving up the activities that are important to her fulfillment as an individual in order to meet his demand. It is obvious that none of these solutions would result in a more harmonious and fulfilling marriage.

With a creative compromise, however, they would first acknowledge and then discuss the problem in an attempt to resolve it in a mutually satisfying way. For example, they might agree that on certain specified days dinner would be late but the meal (say, a casserole) would have been prepared by the wife in the morning and would be put into the oven by the husband when he got home. Or they might agree to have dinner out on certain nights, or to employ a part-time maid (in return for which the wife would delay the purchase of the fur coat she had hoped to have someday), or to compromise their demands (she would give up some of her activities and he would fulfill the domestic function one night a week). The point is that they would each agree to an arrangement that would satisfy them both, although each would have to make some compromise.

The husband has become habitually preoccupied with his wife's activities. If he tries to call her at home and the line is busy or there is no answer, he later demands to know to whom she was talking or where she was. If she receives a telephone call while he is home, or if she receives a letter which she does not immediately show to him, he wants to know who the caller was or whom the letter was from. If she is going somewhere without him, he has to know with whom and at what time she got home. The wife has nothing to hide from her husband, but she resents her lack of all privacy and feels smothered by his attentions. The husband, on the other hand, does not perceive his behavior as jealous or possessive or in any way out of line with normal marital expectations.

If she insists upon her "rights"—an authoritarian solution—her attitude would lead to misunderstanding and frustration, with its inevitable concommitants. Likewise, a permissive solution, which would mean her putting up with what she perceives as his constant over-involvement in her affairs, would just as inevitably lead to resentment and dissatisfaction. A creative solution would require that the wife explain her annoyance at his interference and then listen to his explanations. When they understand each other's motivations and grievances, they may be able to compromise: He by expressing his interest and curiosity in less demanding ways and by consciously allowing his wife greater independence; she by accepting his need to be involved more in her life and graciously sharing more with him insofar as she is able.

A special technique of creative problem solving is that of *role taking*. With this method, the couple first agrees to cooperate in attacking the problem, then to limit the discussion to the problem they have agreed to attack. The role taking itself consists of four steps: (1) The husband states his grievance as fully and completely as possible, though limiting himself to the problem agreed upon. (2) The wife, who has listened without interruption, then takes *his* role; that is, she states his grievance, from his point of view, as he has just stated it. She must state his case to his full satisfaction. (3) She then states *her* grievance, fully and completely, while he listens carefully. (4) He then takes her role, stating her grievance from her point of view, until she is fully satisfied. Both people then examine the problem to see what points of agreement there are. By this time they understand each other's point of view so well that they usually find many points in common. Thus, they can isolate and identify their remaining differences to determine whether such differences may be resolved by compromise. If no compromise is possible—though it usually is—the couple may at least agree to disagree.

Internal Compromise

Internal compromise is another method of conflict resolution which generally leads to a satisfactory and relatively pervasive settlement. As we have seen earlier in this chapter, internal compromise is simply the identification and weighing of the alternatives in an internal conflict—"Which need satisfaction is more important to me?" Such a resolution involves altruism for one's spouse, a reasoned wish to avoid emotional stress, and a concern for the viability of the marital relation. When an external conflict is adjusted in this way, there is usually a mutuality of fulfillment and a minimal residue of resentment or guilt. And when such an adjustment is candidly shared by both partners, the possibilities of new and related conflicts are substantially reduced.

Authoritarian Resolution

An *authoritarian resolution*, which consists simply of the person's stating categorically what the decision is to be, is the method most often used upon inferiors, subordinates, and children. The authoritarian approach must, of course, rest upon authority; and authority, in turn, must rest upon physical strength, legal sanction, economic sanction, negotiated power, or tradition. The American husband until the present century was granted authority not only by tradition but also by legal and economic sanction. Today, however, authority in marriage is a result of negotiated power; and authority is assumed by as many wives as husbands.

Resolving a marital quarrel by the arbitrary assumption of authority always creates a winner and a loser. Thus, unless a marriage partner is content to surrender authority, he will, of course, inevitably feel resentment toward his authoritative spouse. The resultant tension will sooner or later lead to conflicts which are apparently totally unrelated to the initial disagreement.

Permissive Acceptance

Resolving a quarrel by *permissive acceptance* consists of voluntarily granting the spouse dominance and thereby responding to his needs rather than to one's own. Like the authoritarian approach, this method creates a winner and a loser. Thus, if the disagreement is over something that is important to the relation, such an approach may create more difficulties than it resolves. For if the subordinate partner is not really satisfied with the division of authority that exists in the marriage, there will rise an inevitable tension in the relation.

The Power Struggle

If husband and wife cannot resolve their conflicts in mutually acceptable ways, very often a *power struggle* will ensue, with each spouse battling for power and therefore dominance in a conflict situation (and in the relation). A winner and a loser will emerge from each conflict—the winner dictating the adjustment and achieving maximum need satisfaction, the loser grudgingly and temporarily accepting the solution and receiving no need satisfaction. Once it has begun, a power struggle is self-perpetuating and almost always involves personal attacks.

Since a spouse is especially vulnerable to personal attack by a significant other, and since a person cannot easily maintain in marriage the defenses that he employs in his secondary relations, the psychological damage that results from a demeaning personal attack can be so great that it persists long after the immediate conflict is over, haunting victor and vanquished alike. Unless a balance of power that is acceptable to both can be quickly reestablished, some disintegration of their relation is all but inevitable.[8]

Although a power struggle in marriage may be open and acknowledged,[9] the struggle between intimates—friendly colleagues as well as a married couple—most often operates in a covert, disguised form. This type of power struggle, which is basically dishonest and totally counterproductive, is called a *psychological game* (Berne, 1964). The psychological game almost completely disregards the goals of conflict resolution and, instead, emphasizes continuing competitive

---

[8]Although the struggle for power is characteristic of many marriages which end in divorce (Goode, 1965), a *balance* of power may be achieved which *includes* an unending struggle but which tries to avoid continual interpersonal devaluation (see p. 242, the conflict-habituated relation). It is also possible for a mutual adjustment to be reached as a result of the restructuring of a marital relation from a chiefly primary to a chiefly secondary one (see p. 242, the devitalized marriage).

[9]Within a family, this overt type of power struggle usually occurs only between a parent and child ("Be home by 11:30, or you can't have the car for two weeks") or between siblings. It rarely occurs in this way between spouses—or between any two adults, for that matter, except, occasionally, in the boss-employee relation.

conflict interaction and the demeaning of the other person. Such behavior is counterproductive not only because the basic conflict is unacknowledged (or even lost sight of) and therefore has no possibility of being resolved but also because the underlying element of struggle for dominance by demeaning the other person erodes meaning, trust, intimacy, and productivity in the relation.

The psychological game may take many forms, the most obvious of which is the direct personal attack which is devious in purpose. A more subtle form is the withholding of need fulfillment, again for an unacknowledged purpose. The game may also be even more subtly disguised as a ritual, a procedure, or an operation of role behavior in marriage.[10] In short, if in a power struggle the chief purpose is to demean the other person, and if this purpose is not openly acknowledged[11] so that it may be dealt with, then, whatever form it may take, the behavior is a psychological game.

The psychological game takes the form of a direct attack if, in an argument, one person shifts the focus of the discussion from the issue to the personality of the other. For example, say the conflict is over whether to send a child to an expensive summer camp and the wife shifts the discussion to a criticism of her husband's earning ability. She then has instituted a game, the purpose of which is to demean her husband. The merits of whether or not to send the child to camp are soon lost track of as the husband is provoked to shift to the new ground of personal attack as well. The discussion might then continue something like this:

Husband: *You knew how important the office party was to my commission the other night, yet you drank too much and insulted the buyer. You behaved like a fishwife!*
Wife: *Fishwife! A fishwife has a husband! You're a husband about twice a year!*

He then stomps out, and she wins—at least in the sense that her attack was more damaging and her statements of dominance more effective. The struggle then continues, over the same conflict or over new ones, until one or the other spouse is permanently defeated; that is, he breaks up the marriage, or he permanently accepts the dominance of the other, or he alters the relation so that the marriage is nothing more than two acquaintances living together and providing only the resources necessary for mutual survival—like two enemy soldiers left alone on a deserted island.

The use of attrition in a marital conflict—the *withholding of need fulfillment*—is a less overt and therefore less easily recognized form of the psychological game.

---

[10]See the section *Role Behavior in Marriage* in Chapter Six.
[11]Any game emphasizes competition and defeat of the other person, of course, but in the common understanding of the term "game" (for example, tennis, darts, or chess) the competitive aspect is straightforward and openly acknowledged, as are the rules and the score (who wins and who loses). Indeed, much of the satisfaction of such a game lies in this open acknowledgment of culturally acceptable and limited hostility. The dominant aspect of the *psychological* game, on the other hand, is that it is devious and covert. It is thus a perversion of the openness and honesty of the traditional game, to say nothing of the intimacy of a primary relation.

Moreover, with the withholding of need fulfillment there is even less possibility of dealing with the conflict honestly and openly in an attempt to obtain convergent feedback; for the withholding is usually presented not only as an absence of aggression but as a plea for sympathy and understanding. "I can't make love because I have a headache"; "I don't feel like talking because I'm exhausted from working hard at the office all day." The deprived person may suspect that the other's "headache" or "fatigue" is a disguised response to some earlier conflict or that the withholding of need fulfillment indicates either hostility or a lack of love, but he can't be certain. And if he even attempts to open a discussion about *this* problem, he makes himself extremely vulnerable to accusations of callousness and selfishness. The deprived person is thus caught in a classic double-bind: He is torn between anger and a feeling of guilt over his resentment, which he is not really sure is justified. The depriving person, on the other hand, will probably wear his triumph uneasily, because his victory in the game was achieved not only by cheating but by a betrayal of trust in a relation in which trust is essential.

The withholding of need fulfillment is a particularly insidious and damaging form of the psychological game and a very commonly utilized response to conflict within marriage. It is also very dangerous. For when this form of aggression becomes a patterned response in the relation, the erosion of intimacy is often irreversible.

An example of a psychological game disguised as an operation might be the washing of dinner dishes by a husband who comes home exhausted after a day's work. If he washes the dishes simply to get them done, with no overtones of criticism or complaint, he is performing an operation and accomplishing the dual purpose of doing a needed job and helping his wife. But if he is saying, in effect, "I work hard all day at the office to support both of us and then have to come home and do your work," he is playing a game, the purpose of which is to establish his wife as lazy and selfish and himself as noble, self-sacrificing and generous. Then, as a sort of bonus score, if she is not properly grateful for his sacrifice, she will have demonstrated for him that she is ungracious and presumptuous as well.

The wife will quite quickly pick up the "vibes" (and the challenge) if it is a game and may respond with an overt attack. A much more frequent response, however, is for her to regard this defeat simply as one move in a continuing struggle for dominance and then to try to win the next move. For example, she may devalue him before guests at the party they go to that night (but in a teasing way that would make him appear ungracious if he makes a rejoinder), or she might pretend not to understand his sexual overtures when they get home, or she could accidentally burn his bacon and give him warm coffee the next morning. The pattern of psychological game playing can thus become very persistent in the relation and, by its very nature, can inevitably destroy the possibility of intimacy.

A marriage cannot be a happy and rewarding one if it is characterized by psychological game playing (nor, for that matter, can any other relation, whether business, professional, or friendship). So long as the game playing remains peripheral to the main interaction of the couple, it may not be seriously damaging. The danger, however, is that their relation will move further and further into a game-playing interaction, until the chief preoccupation of each becomes the struggle for dominance and the covert scoring of points.

A person may detect that he is playing a pyschological game if he senses that something is wrong or less than candid and asks himself what he is really trying to accomplish. Is his activity involved solely with achieving a function of the marriage? If not, what additional benefit is he trying to achieve? Would it be possible to give up this additional benefit—such as sympathy for doing the dishes—in the interest of establishing intimacy with his wife? Understanding the pattern of game playing is extremely important in marital adjustment. A person who is unconsciously playing a game is helpless to change his behavior and to prevent the retaliation of his spouse. But once he understands what he is doing, he gains a measure of freedom to change. He may pull up short in the middle of a sentence, stop the game, and try to accomplish what is really important in the interaction: the awareness, understanding, and resolution of the conflict itself.

The difficulty of recognizing behavior as a game varies, of course. An apparent ritual or procedure when utilized as a game is usually quite obvious. Both ritual and procedure are highly stereotyped, and any departure from the conditioned pattern is usually crystal clear. For example, refusing to acknowledge a greeting or ignoring another person when he leaves are obviously game-playing moves designed to put the other person down. They can scarcely be understood to be anything else. The wife who says to her husband as he leaves for work on a rainy morning, "Darling, you must put on your rubbers; you aren't as young as you were" is obviously using ritual as a tactic of game playing.

Distinguishing operation from a marital game is very simple in theory, but it may be very confusing in practice because motivations for the activities are often deeply repressed. Berne (1964, p. 95) cites the example of "Lunchbag":

The husband, who can well afford to have lunch at a good restaurant, nevertheless makes himself a few sandwiches every morning, which he takes to the office in a paper bag. In this way he uses up crusts of bread, leftovers from dinner, and paper bags which his wife saves for him. This gives him complete control over the family finances, for what wife would dare buy herself a mink stole in the face of such self-sacrifice?

In a similar game, which Berne calls "Harried," the housewife simply attempts to do more than she can possibly accomplish and then blames the husband for her plight; her marriage disintegrates and self-reproaches are added to her misery.

In another game, "Look How Hard I Was Trying," the player justifies the seemingly irremediable conflict and collapse of his marital interaction by invoking self-righteous martyrdom—"Despite all my efforts look what you've done to me." In this game, the husband is told by his doctor that he has an ulcer, but he keeps the news from his wife.

He continues working and worrying . . . and one day he collapses on the job. When his wife is notified . . . she is supposed to appreciate him as she never has before, and to feel sorry for all the mean things she has said and done in the past. Unfortunately for the husband, her manifestations of affection and solicitude at this point are more apt to be motivated by guilt than by love. Deep down she is likely to be resentful because he is using unfair leverage against her, and has also taken unfair advantage of her by keeping his illness a secret. In short, a diamond bracelet is a much more honest instrument of courtship than a perforated stomach (p. 107).

Even when a game has been recognized, it may be difficult to abandon, because ceasing to play it necessitates breaking established behavior patterns and relinquishing secondary gains. However, the more earnestly each spouse tries to recognize and abandon game behavior, the more frequently will the couple's relation be characterized by candid operation and intimacy.

Categories of the Well-Adjusted Marriage

There are many degrees of successful adjustment in marriage, just as there are many degrees of marital failure; in between lie many gradations of marginal adjustment or unhappy compromise. In 1965, Cuber and Harroff made a study of the marriages of prominent people who would be considered by their society to exemplify the well-adjusted within marriage and without. They were all influential, socially active, economically successful, respected, policy-forming, "significant Americans." The subjects numbered 211; and all of them, in *depth interviews*[12] lasting from three hours to several days, described their marriage as happy, stating that they had never considered divorce or separation nor had they ever consulted a marriage counselor. The study showed that "five distinct life styles showed up repeatedly . . . in the way in which they lived together, found sexual expression, reared their children, and made their way in the outside world" (p. 43).

These five life styles break down into two categories of marriage: the *utilitarian* and the *intrinsic*. The utilitarian marriage, by far the more common of the two, comprises the "conflict-habituated," "devitalized," and "passive-congenial" relations. The intrinsic marriage includes two relations, "vital" and "total."

The Utilitarian Marriage

The *utilitarian marriage* is not a source of deep personal expression, and it is often characterized by such avoidance responses as working far from home; accepting traveling assignments; using one's leisure to engage in club or civic work, church activities, or hobbies; and sleeping in separate bedrooms. People who have a utilitarian marriage consider it to be very workable and rational as well as satisfying. It is maintained "for purposes other than to express an

---

[12] In a depth interview, a skilled interviewer asks many open-ended questions, in an attempt to obtain levels of information which are not usually revealed.

intimate, highly important, *personal* relation between a man and a woman."
(Cuber and Harroff, 1965, p. 106). Instead, such a marriage provides a "fitting
constellation for adult living, child-rearing, and discharging civic responsibility"
(p. 130).

Most utilitarian marriages are either *passive-congenial* or *devitalized*. "Utilitarian marriages, since they most perfectly encompass the passive-congenial
and the devitalized relation within the requirements of the monolithic code,
probably express the world of men and women for the clear majority of middle aged couples" (p. 196). The difference between the two is that the
passive-congenial relation never includes any depth of emotional interaction,
even during dating or early marriage, whereas the devitalized relation begins
as a vital relation with important interpersonal satisfactions. In the passive-
congenial marriage, neither partner *ever* intends that the marital relation include deep emotional involvement and interaction; the emphasis from the
first is on common sense, shared interests, and emotional and physical comfort, with each one's energies channeled into careers, community activities,
and, finally, rearing children. The couple in a devitalized marriage gradually
cease to share their interests and activities in a deep and meaningful way.
Sexual relations become far less satisfying than they once were; most of their
time together is occupied with the children, with guests, or with community
activities. Although there is little overt tension or conflict, role interaction is,
for the most part, apathetic or lifeless. Many couples interviewed felt that
their devitalized marriage was the most appropriate relation for the middle
years and that the vital personal interactions of youth should eventually give
way to "other things in life" which are "more worthy" of sustained effort.

A few utilitarian marriages are *conflict-habituated*. The dominant mode of
role interaction in such marriages is conflict and well-controlled tension, with
a private acknowledgment that incompatibility is both inevitable and pervasive. In these marriages, "the overt and manifest fact of habituated attention to handling tension, keeping it chained and concealing it, is clearly seen
as the dominant life force" (p. 46).

The Intrinsic Marriage

In contrast to the utilitarian marriage, the *intrinsic marriage* is characterized
by the intensity of the feelings each partner has for the other. Each spouse
believes his mate is indispensable to his own satisfaction in any activity, and
thus as many activities as possible are closely shared. In short, each depends
on the physical and psychological presence of the other.

*From this fountainhead flow positive influences for physical and mental health, as well
as creativity. A substantial professional literature in psychiatry confirms the testimony
of those in the intrinsic marriages that the vitality of their kind of relation radiates far
beyond the elemental ecstasy of the pairing (Cuber and Harroff, 1965, p. 141).*

This does not mean that the couple whose marriage is intrinsic have lost their separate identities or that they may not upon occasion be competitive. However, serious disagreements arise only about important matters and tend moreover to be settled rather quickly and to both partners' satisfaction. These disagreements may sometimes be settled by compromise, sometimes by one or the other partner's yielding, "but these outcomes were of secondary importance because the primary consideration was not who was right or who was wrong, but how the problem could be resolved without tarnishing the relation" (p. 58).

Sexual difficulties are almost nonexistent in the intrinsic marriage. Sex is usually very important for the couple, often pervading their whole relation.

Some couples . . . just seem to click. They love one another. They find fulfillment in their sexual relations, [as well as] mutual delight in [experiencing] no conflict between their sexual activities and their other human enjoyments . . . indeed, they make no sharp distinction between them . . . Let us call them, as does Professor Abraham Maslow, "the happy ones" (Brecher and Brecher, 1966, p. xii).

Despite its vitality, the intrinsic marriage may change, becoming either a utilitarian marriage or ending in divorce. "People who live in this way place enormous stress upon the personal relation–strains which are not present in the utilitarian marriage because of its avoidance devices and its modest expectations about feeling and mutuality" (Cuber and Harroff, 1965, p. 142). A personal merging so intimate and so encompassing as the intrinsic relation does not come about by drift or default, and it cannot be sustained by listless attention to a mate. "You either have the whole splendid edifice or the damn thing tumbles down on you. There's just nothing halfway about this kind of life" (p. 145).

Within the intrinsic marriage exist two kinds of relations, the *vital* and the *total*. The difference between them is essentially a matter of degree. The total relation is marked by more areas of interaction than are present in the vital marriage, and almost all activities in the total marriage are shared. Fewer total than vital marriages exist, of course; and those that do exist seem rather like the superb love matches described in romantic literature.

Our society considers total and vital relations to be more appropriate to dating and the early years of marriage than to mature adult behavior. Most couples interviewed by Cuber and Harroff doubted that intrinsic relations could or should exist after husband and wife enter their thirties. Those couples whose marriage was intrinsic recognized that they were in the minority and said that they had always taken pains to conceal the depth of the marital relation from their friends, in order not to be considered odd or deceitful. The norm, then, for the well-adjusted marriage in our society is apparently utilitarian rather than intrinsic.

Marriage Counseling

If a marital adjustment is very unsatisfactory, the couple may be moved to seek professional assistance from a marriage counselor, who will help them clarify their marital problems. Professional counselors may designate themselves solely as "marriage counselors," or they may be lawyers, psychiatrists, sociologists, social workers, or psychologists, as well. In addition, clergymen and family doctors often function as counselors; indeed, most troubled couples seek out these two professions first. The physician or clergyman, as well as lawyers and jurists, may then refer the couple to a professional counselor.

Although professional marriage counselors vary widely in their methods, it is a rare counselor who would take responsibility for deciding and telling the client what he should do. In general, most psychologically oriented counselors stay away from giving specific advice, mediating differences, or providing ready-made solutions to problems. Instead, the counselor's responsibility and expertise lie in exploring the couple's problems from their own point of view and trying to help them discover for themselves what seems the best course of action. This method is termed *non-directive*.[13] An exception to this essentially non-directive approach occurs only if a marital difficulty rests upon factual ignorance, such as lack of information about sexual anatomy and physiology. In this case, the counselor may either provide such information himself or recommend a source of information.

A typical counselor spends much of his time listening to the client. Occasional questions help stimulate self-analysis. From time to time he may interpret meanings and connections the client seems ready to understand. He may reassure the client about the value of expressing negative feelings in the interview situation. He may support the client in his desires to try a new course of action. Rarely, however, does the counselor take over responsibility for deciding what the client should do, despite requests to do so (Blood, pp. 265, 266).

By the time a person seeks out a marriage counselor, he is usually in extreme confusion about himself and is very reluctant to make any decisions. A failing marriage can be a bitter blow to one's self-respect, depriving a person of an important source of emotional support and need satisfaction in his life. Disillusioned and dissatisfied with himself, his spouse, and life in general, he regards the marriage counselor as a last hope. This hope is justified if and when the person is enabled to take steps to deal with his problem: either to change his behavior significantly in the direction of increased need satisfaction or to conclude that reconciliation is not realistic and that divorce is the best solution. *Successful* marriage counseling does not always lead to reconciliation.

Apparently marriage counseling is not yet as effective as is psychotherapy or counseling directed at non-marital problems. In one study, for example, about

---

[13] See Rogers (1951) for an explanation of non-directive therapy and Ellis (1958) for a more directive approach.

66 percent of the subjects who received marriage counseling reported the results "helpful"; in contrast, 88 percent of the subjects who sought help for personal non-marital problems reported the results as "helpful" (Gurin *et al.*, 1960). This finding is not surprising when we consider the fact that in marriage counseling the person must learn to utilize new patterns of adjustment without making any pronounced environmental change; whereas the person with non-marital, personal difficulties may be able to solve or alleviate his problem by changing his environment—that is, by getting a new job or moving to another neighborhood or city. Moreover, the person with marital difficulties has to consider not only his own personality structure and pattern of adjustive responses but also the personality structure and adjustive responses of his spouse—so that successful resolution of the difficulties depends upon changes in *both* individuals, and these changes must occur mainly within the same milieu that led to the difficulties in the first place.

As the various disciplines involved in marriage counseling learn more about the special problems of marital interaction, and as more basic information about human behavior is acquired from psychology and sociology, the incidence of successful counseling may be expected to increase. That this type of therapy as an independent discipline is coming of age may be seen in the establishment of the American Association of Marriage and Family Counselors, a national organization concerned exclusively with marriage counseling. Members in this association include physicians, ministers, social-service workers, sociologists, educators, and psychologists; and standards for membership are very rigorous—including graduate training, advanced degrees, and supervised experience in the field of marriage counseling.

Marriage Failure

The ultimate failure of a marriage usually stems from a multiplicity of factors, with the tangled skein of conflict so interrelated that every aspect of the couple's relation may be involved. As one divorce attorney put it, "Causes are jumbled, like a drop of bluing in a pail of water. You cannot tell where the bluing stops and the water begins" (Harmsworth and Minnis, 1955).

But despite this complexity, marriage failure can be viewed in an essentially simple framework: A marital relation will break down whenever marital conflict is the result of a patterned failure of one or both spouses to provide for the other the satisfactions that he expects in the three areas of material, sexual, and interpersonal needs. Thus, for a marriage to continue, the needs of each person in these three areas must be met. And they can be met only through (1) a congruence of each person's perception of his and the other's roles in the relation; (2) a reciprocation of each person's role performance in all important areas of need fulfillment; and (3) an equivalence of the values of the roles each person performs—that is, each must provide functions and resources that are approximately equal (perceptually) to those he receives. Therefore, although marriage failure can be correlated with such objectively determinable factors as childhood background, early marriage, short engagement, lack of educational or vocational preparedness, divorce of parents and/or grandparents, in-law objections to the marriage, elopements, marriage because of pregnancy, and lack of homogamy in education, social class, intelligence, interests, race, or religion — and although marriage failure can be traced to such subjective factors as physiological differences, housekeeping and money problems, sexual ignorance or inadequacy, character disorders (emotional immaturity, alcoholism, antisocial behavior), the romantic illusion of togetherness, an imbalance in the power structure, power struggle and game playing, and personality disorders (debilitating neurosis and psychosis) — all of these various factors arise from or contribute to the essential causes of failure: lack of role congruence, reciprocation, or equivalence within the marriage.

Incidence of Marriage Failure

In our society, as we all know, a very large percentage of all marriages fail. Probably the only marriages that can absolutely be termed failures are those that terminate in annulment, legal separation, or divorce. However, many couples may remain married — "for the sake of the children"; or because of the economic consequences of divorce; or because the laws of their state make divorce virtually unattainable; or because their religion prohibits divorce; or because of habit, inertia, social pressures, or fear of loneliness — without making any but the most marginal of adjustments to a continual pattern of marital conflict and unhappiness. Such marriages, when considered "very unhappy" by the couple themselves and by their friends, also would seem to fall within the category of failed marriages.

The rate of divorce in the United States has been rising rapidly since the early 1960s, from a rate of 2.2 per thousand in 1960 to a rate of 3.4 per thousand in 1970, making the ratio of divorce to marriage a little less than one in three (see Figure 7–2).[14] This one-in-three figure is misleading, however, if it is applied to

---

[14] Divorce figures usually include figures for annulment.

Rate per 1,000 population   Rate per 1,000 population

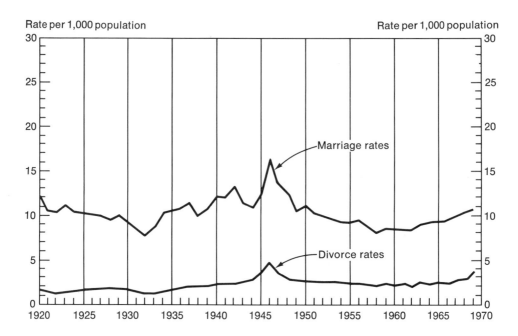

Figure 7-2. The Divorce Rate, 1920-1970

Source: U. S. Bureau of the Census, 1970; data from U. S. Public Health Service.

an *individual's* actuarial expectation for divorce. The rate of divorce among the non-white population is three to four times higher than it is for the white population at some age levels, for example (see Figure 7-3), and the divorce rate among lower-status whites is about the same as the divorce rate among non-whites (Winch, 1963). Thus, the actuarial expectation for divorce is much higher among that segment of the population which is non-white and/or lower-class.[15] Moreover, as we have seen in Chapter Five, the individual expectation for divorce also depends upon such additional factors as length of engagement, age at marriage,[16] and whether the person's parents or grandparents were divorced. Thus, if a person is white and middle-class, is engaged for a year or so before marriage, marries in his middle or late 20s, is in a business or profession, has a college degree and an about-average income,[17] and comes from an unbroken

---

[15] The economic and cultural pressures on the black or lower-status man and woman often interfere with the successful structure and functioning of the family unit. As a consequence, satisfactory marital adjustment becomes relatively more difficult, and the rates of divorce, separation, and desertion sharply increase in this group as compared to the white or middle-class marriage. For example, in 1968, 27 percent of all black families were headed by a woman, as compared to 9 percent of all white families (Current Population Reports, Bureau of the Census, 1969).

[16] For example, if a girl is white and middle-class but marries before age 18, she triples her actuarial probability for divorce; if she marries before age 20, she doubles it. (See *Factors Contributing to Marital Success*, in Chapter Five.)

[17] Glick and Norton (1971) found that income is more significant than education in determining which men obtain a divorce, particularly during the first 10 years of marriage. Men married less than 10 years were three to four times as likely to obtain a divorce if their income was under $3,000 than if it was $8,000 or more.

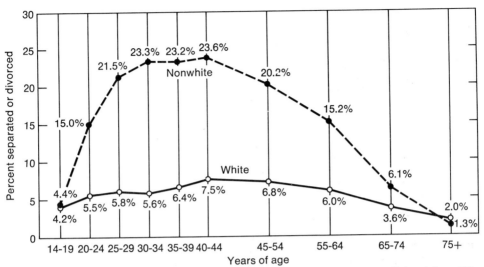

Figure 7–3. Percent of Ever-married White and Non-white Women, 14 Years Old and Over, Who Were Separated or Divorced in March 1968*

*Leaves out those who divorced and remarried the same man.
Source: Current Population Reports, *Population Characteristics*, Series P-20, No. 170, February 23, 1968.

home, his actuarial expectation for divorce is much lower than the one-in-three figure.

Furthermore, some geographic areas have a much higher rate of divorce than other areas, with the divorce rates by states generally increasing from east to west and from north to south (Fenelon, 1971). In San Mateo county in California, for example, the divorce-to-marriage ratio is fully seven to ten, although this county is predominantly middle-class and white and has one of the highest per capita income levels in the United States.

Given this multiplicity of factors affecting the divorce rate, it is possible to make only a very general statement about the relative probability of divorce for any given individual. Certainly, the probability is not necessarily the one-in-three figure.

Nevertheless, the overall figures for divorce in this country are extremely high, as we have seen in Figures 7–2, 7–3, and 7–4. In addition to this high rate of divorce, it is estimated that 3 percent of all marriages are terminated by "true separation" — that is, those couples with legal decrees of separation, those living apart with the intention of obtaining a divorce, and those permanently or temporarily separated because of marital discord.[18] Finally, numerous studies (Popenoe and Wicks, 1937; Terman *et al.*, 1938; Burgess and Cottrell, 1939; Chessar *et al.*, 1957; and Landis, 1965) agree that about 15–20 percent of all married couples can be classified as "unhappily cohabiting" (those whose marriage is considered very unhappy — both by the couple themselves and by their friends). The estimated rate of unhappy cohabitation is based solely on

[18] *Current Population Reports*, Bureau of the Census, Series P-20, 1969.

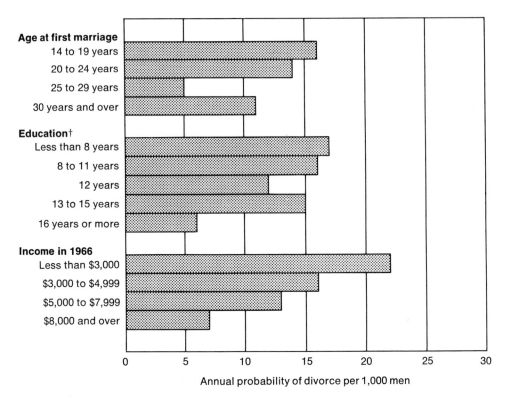

Figure 7–4. Annual Probability of Divorce by Selected Characteristics — Age, Education, and Income (1960–1966)*

*Estimates are for white men in their first marriage; a forthcoming report on blacks is not yet published.

†Note that although the college graduate has the lowest divorce rate of all reported categories, the college dropout (the "13-to-15 years" figure) has a higher divorce rate than a person who has never entered college. There is no explanation for this phenomenon, which contradicts the general trend that the higher the educational level the lower the divorce rate. One possible hypothesis: Perhaps the type of person who drops out of college also has a tendency to drop out of marriage.

Source: U. S. Bureau of the Census, 1967 Survey of Economic Opportunity.

studies done with the middle-class segment of the population. If we assume, however, that this unhappily cohabitating figure is no lower for blacks and lower-class whites (it is probably higher), we can conclude that the total estimated incidence of marriage failure in the United States is currently 50–55 percent — 15 to 20 percent unhappily cohabitating, 32 percent divorcing, and 3 percent ending in permanent separation of some kind, legal or otherwise.[19]

---

[19]It is interesting to note that in homosexual "marriages," which are sometimes quite enduring, the couple forms a paired bond that persists despite the forces of society — religious, social, legal, economic — that combine to drive the couple apart. With the heterosexual marriage, on the other hand, these same pressures, plus the needs of offspring, combine to encourage the couple to stay together. With no legal restrictions about separation and no child-care responsibilities — and with all the forces of society combined to separate them — the strength of the paired bond holding the homosexual couple together must be enormous.

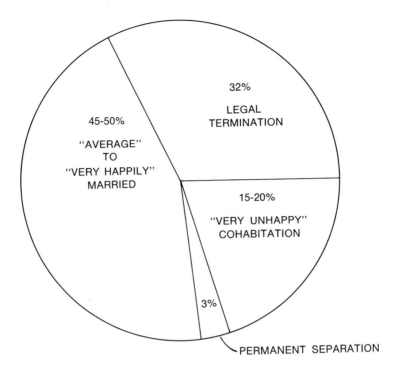

Figure 7–5. The Estimated Incidence of Marriage Failure (1970)

Why are these percentages so high? And why have they (most notably, the divorce statistics) increased during the past three generations? There is no one reason, in spite of attempts to blame it all on a "rising tide of immorality" or a "lack of respect for marriage." Rather, the sharp rise in divorce rates in our society must be seen as one consequence of our cultural revolution, which has brought about important social changes, many of them already discussed, and equally important changes in the roles of men and women and families:

1. By the twentieth century, marriage in our society was no longer regarded (except by the Catholic Church) as solely a sacred contract, indissoluble by its very nature. Divorce became the province of the civil courts.

2. Technological developments of the industrial revolution in the nineteenth century brought about a change in the function of the family. Resources and services previously provided by different members of the family began to be provided by specialized secondary institutions.

3. Women entered the vocational world, so that they were no longer dependent solely upon marriage for economic support. Also, more effective (and socially accepted) means of contraception made pregnancy a matter of choice, so that women were no longer tied to the home (or to a marriage) by the burden of many children and continuous pregnancy.

4. The process of mate selection passed from the control of the parents to the control of the unmarried generation, which developed the institution of dating. Marriage became a much more personal event. Two people married pri-

marily because each one expected the other to fulfill important personal needs —
not to further the family name or the family estate. And, just as personal needs
(numerous and not clearly definable) prompted marriage, non-fulfillment of
these needs became grounds for divorce.[20]

The median length of time between marriage and divorce is about 7 years —
giving rise to the expression "seven year itch" — but there are many variables,
especially age at marriage, educational level, and income (see Figure 7–6).

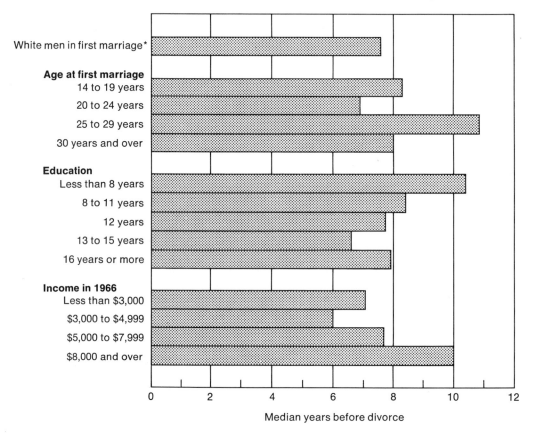

Figure 7–6. Median Duration of First Marriage—by Age at Marriage, Education, and Income
(1960–1966)

*Figures are for divorced white men; a forthcoming report on blacks is not yet published.

Source: U. S. Bureau of the Census, Survey of Economic Opportunity, 1967.

[20]In light of the contemporary emphasis on personal happiness and fulfillment in marriage, it is
interesting to note that most divorces occur during the first *two* years of marriage (Winch, 1963).

Legal Termination of Marriage

A marriage may be legally terminated in our society only by the civil actions of legal separation, annulment, or divorce.

Legal separation. A legal separation, which is not an alternative in some states, does not really "terminate" the marriage in that neither partner is permitted to remarry as long as the legal separation is in force. Legal separation merely limits the privileges of the two persons; for example, it provides for separate maintenance—the couple may not cohabit under penalty of law—but the husband is still financially responsible for the "separate maintenance" of his wife and family. In a sense, he has all the responsibilities of a marriage with none of the satisfactions. This arrangement, not surprisingly, is unappealing to most couples (except for those who, for social, religious, or professional reasons, need to retain their marital status but find it impossible to live together). The incidence of *legal* separation amounts to not more than 2–3 percent of the number of divorces.[21]

Annulment. The concept of annulment has its origins in the canon law of the Catholic Church—which takes the position that marriage is indissoluble except by death. Because of this position, the church had to have some means of ending a marriage that, in its view, was fraudulently entered into or maintained. Thus, annulment, which formally declares that the marriage never existed in the first place, was conceived. (Originally, this device was used to ensure that a European sovereign whose wife was barren could remarry and have an heir to his throne.) English common law, from which our own statutory law developed, adopted the church's concept; and therefore nearly all American states grant annulment, as well as divorce.

The grounds for civil annulment are based, in general, on impediments or irregularities preceding the marriage or during the wedding. (With divorce, the grounds usually occur after the marriage.) Thus, annulment may be sued for on the grounds that the marriage was contracted illegally (underage, consanguinity, bigamy) or with misrepresentation and intent to defraud or that the marriage is not properly consummated by copulation because of impotence or physical and psychological handicaps or because one of the couple did not intend to have children.

An annulment voids the marriage. All rights and obligations may be dissolved (although the law varies from state to state), and children may be declared illegitimate.

For all practical purposes, civil annulment is sought in our society only when divorce is not legally obtainable. In New Mexico, for example, where divorce may be granted on the grounds of "incompatibility," annulment is virtually unknown. Nationally, annulments represent only about 3.5 percent of the total number of marital dissolutions in our society.

---

[21] *Current Population Reports*, Bureau of the Census, Series P-20, 1969.

In the case of annulment, as in divorce, there is a marked discrepancy between the law on the books and the law in practice. Traditionally used to nullify marriages involving gross societal impediments (incest, prior marriage, underage) or a serious act of premarital fraud, annulment today is frequently . . . resorted to as a convenient circumvention of divorce (Kephart, 1961, p. 587).

Because the Catholic church remains unalterably opposed to divorce, a member must have his marriage annuled by the church if he is to free himself from his marriage, remarry, and still be in good standing as a Catholic. After a church annulment, he may then get a civil divorce, which defines his legal obligations and permits remarriage in the eyes of the state. The grounds for a church annulment, according to the most recent pronouncements of Pope Paul VI (*Apostolic Letter*, 1971), include incestuous marriage, impotence, non-consumation of the marriage, intent by a spouse not to have children, marriage under duress, and marriage under age 14 for a girl or age 16 for a boy. The new canonical law permits couples to get an annulment after a favorable decision by one local church court and ratification, without a trial, by another. The length of time for this procedure is estimated to be about seven months, as opposed to the three to seven years of heavy expenses and even a trip to Rome that a couple were forced to bear under the old law. The new law also grants bishops heading dioceses the right to annul a marriage under certain circumstances.

Divorce. Divorce, the legal abrogation of a valid marriage contract, not only ends the right of the couple to cohabit and limits the legal obligations of the husband but also permits remarriage. Property is divided by court action; and rights of visitation, physical custody, legal custody, and support payments for any children are assigned by the court. The husband may be required to pay alimony as well—either for a specified number of years or until the woman remarries. Alimony payments from the woman to the man are extremely rare.

Failure to meet alimony or child-support payments are the only debts for which a person may still be imprisoned in the United States. The husband who does not pay alimony or the father who does not pay the stipulated child support is in contempt of court and can be indicted on that basis. Such court action is usually slow and always expensive. In order to avoid clogging the courts, some states have found various ways in which the payments are made to the state and forwarded to the mother. Even so, there seems to be no really adequate means, as yet, of dealing with men who do not make alimony or support payments (Bohannan, 1970).

A divorce suit is a legal contest in most states. A husband or wife sues the other for one of the several kinds of acts or behaviors (for example, "mental cruelty," adultery, desertion) which constitute, depending on the particular state in which the suit is brought, legal grounds for granting divorce. If both husband and wife legally petition for divorce, it cannot be granted, because the legal view of a divorce contest is that one party is innocent and the other guilty.

Mutual agreement by husband and wife to divorce (called *collusion*) is legally punishable. However, in actual practice most divorces are decided on by both partners before proceedings are begun and little if any attempt is made by the courts to enforce the law against collusion. "The courts have . . . come to tolerate collusive practices through which consent divorces [that is, divorces mutually consented to by husband and wife] can be easily obtained in spite of their reprobation by the official law" (Rheinstein, 1953, p. 12). In fact, according to Kephart (1961), not more than 10 percent of all divorces are really contested; and the stated grounds for divorce have little relation to the actual reasons for the divorce.

There is now a growing tendency to get away from the legal-contest concept of divorce. In California, for example, the term "divorce" is no longer even used. Rather, the marriage is "dissolved," and only on the grounds of incurable insanity or "irremediable differences" (incompatibility). Instead of a contest, then, with one person suing the other, the couple must agree that their differences are irremediable, their marriage is legally dissolved, and the property is divided. Children must still receive child support, of course. (See Table 7–1 for the specific divorce requirements in each state.)

The ethics of divorce are by no means a matter of general agreement in the United States. One position holds that divorce cannot be justified under any circumstances, that marriage is irrevocable from the time it is contracted until one of the spouses dies. (Remarriage, in the view of many people who take this position on divorce, is also considered reprehensible.) Others believe that since marriage is, or should be, exclusively a private affair, divorce also should be a matter of mutual volition on the part of husband and wife; consequently, neither church nor state should interfere in this decision, and the court's sole function should be to legalize and record the couple's decision.

The trouble with the first position, that divorce should never be granted to anyone, is that it forces people to live together under perhaps intolerable conditions and therefore may be impracticable, if not inhumane. The difficulty with the opposite opinion, that divorce is strictly a private matter, is that often it is not true — for when children are involved, the marriage is *not* a private affair. In these instances, society, as well as the couple themselves, has a stake in the

Table 7–1. Divorce Laws, 1970

State or Jurisdiction	Residence Required	Adultery	Mental and/or Physical Cruelty	Desertion	Alcoholism	Impotency	Nonsupport	Insanity	Pregnancy at Marriage	Bigamy	Separation or Absence	Felony Conviction or Imprisonment	Drug Addiction	Fraud, Force, or Duress	Prior Decree of Limited Divorce	Other	Plaintiff	Defendant
Alabama	(1)	•	•	1 yr.	•	•	•(2)	5 yrs.	•			•	.		(3)	(4)	60 days (5)	60 days (5)
Alaska	1 yr.	•	•	1 yr.		•	•	18 mos.				•	.			(6)	—	—
Arizona	1 yr.	•	•	1 yr.			•					•	.			(7)	—	—
Arkansas	60 days (8)	•	•	1 yr.	•	•		3 yrs.		•	3 yrs.	•					—	—
California	(10)		—				•(9)									(11)	—	—
Colorado	1 yr. (12)	•	•	1 yr.	•			3 yrs.			3 yrs.	•	.		(3)	(13)	3 mos. (14)	3 mos. (14)
Connecticut	1 yr. (12)	•	•	2 yrs.	•			5 yrs.		•	7 yrs.	•				(15, 16, 17)	—	—
Delaware	2 yrs. (12)	•	•	1 yr.	•			5 yrs.	•	•	18 mos.	•	.			(17, 18)	—	—
Florida	6 mos.	•	•	1 yr.	•	•		3 yrs.				•	.				—	—
Georgia	6 mos.	•	•	1 yr.	•	•		2 yrs.	•	•		•	.				(14)	(14)
Hawaii	3 mos.	•	•	6 mos.				3 yrs.		•	3 yrs. (19)			.	(3)		(20)	(20)
Idaho	6 wks.	•	•	1 yr.	•			6 yrs.			5 yrs.	•	.			(21, 22)	—	—
Illinois	1 yr. (12)	•	•	1 yr.	•	•				•		•	.				(24)	—
Indiana	1 yr. (23)	•	•	2 yrs.	•	•		5 yrs.				•	.				1 yr. (5, 14)	1 yr. (5, 14)
Iowa	1 yr.	•	•	2 yrs.	•			5 yrs.	(25)		5 yrs.	•	.			(6)	60 days	60 days
Kansas	6 mos. (26)	•	•	1 yr.	(27)	•		3 yrs.		•	5 yrs.	•	.			(21, 28, 29)	wife, 10 mos.	wife, 10 mos. (1, 6)
Kentucky	1 yr.	•		1 yr.		•	•	5 yrs.		•	2 yrs.	•	.		(3)	(6)	—	—
Louisiana	(30)	•										•	.		(31)	(21, 28, 29)	—	—
Maine	6 mos. (12)	•	•	3 yrs.	•	•	•	3 yrs.				•	.				—	—
Maryland	1 yr. (33)	•		18 mos.		•		3 yrs.			18 mos. (34)	•				(34, 35)	—	—
Massachusetts	(36, 12)	•	•	2 yrs.	•	•	•					•	.				—	—
Michigan	1 yr. (12)	•	•	2 yrs.	•							•	.			(16)	—	(37)
Minnesota	1 yr. (12)	•	•	1 yr.	•			3 yrs.			2 yrs. (19)	•	.		(3)	(17, 18)	6 mos.	6 mos.
Mississippi	1 yr. (12)	•	•	1 yr.	•	•		3 yrs.	•	•		•	.			(7, 39)	—	—
Missouri	1 yr. (12)	•	•	1 yr.	•	•	•					•	.				—	(38)
Montana	1 yr.	•	•	1 yr.	•							•	.				—	—
Nebraska	2 yrs. (12)	•	•	2 yrs.	•	•		5 yrs.		•		•	.			(6)	6 mos.	6 mos.
Nevada	6 wks. (12)	•	•	1 yr.	•	•		2 yrs.			1 yr.	•	.			(6)	—	—
New Hampshire	1 yr. (12)	•	•	2 yrs.	•	•	•			•	2 yrs.	•	.			(28, 40)	—	—
New Jersey	2 yrs. (12)	•		2 yrs.								•	.				3 mos. (14)	3 mos. (14)
New Mexico	1 yr.	•	•	1 yr.				5 yrs.				•	.			(6)	—	—
New York	1 yr. (12)	•	•								2 yrs. (19)	•	.				—	—
North Carolina	6 mos.	•						5 yrs.			1 yr.						—	—
North Dakota	1 yr. (23)	•	•	1 yr.	•		•(9)	5 yrs.				•	.		(3)	(4)	(14)	(14)

Ohio	1 yr.	*	*	—	—	*	1 yr.	*	(16)	(41)	—
Oklahoma	6 mos. (26)	*	*	1 yr.	5 yrs.	*	—	—	(6, 16)	6 mos.	6 mos.
Oregon	1 yr.	*	*	1 yr.	2 yrs.	*	—	—	—	6 mos.	(32)
Pennsylvania	1 yr.	*	*	2 yrs.	—	—	—	—	(17, 42)	6 mos.	6 mos.
Rhode Island	2 yrs.	*	*	5 yrs. (33)	—	—	10 yrs.	—	(44, 45)	6 mos.	6 mos.
South Carolina	1 yr.	*	•	1 yr.	—	—	3 yrs.	—	—	—	—
South Dakota	1 yr. (12)	*	—	1 yr.	—	5 yrs.	—	—	—	—	(46)
Tennessee	1 yr.	*	—	1 yr.	—	—	2 yrs. (47)	—	(22, 42)	—	(32)
Texas	12 mos.	*	—	1 yr.	3 yrs.	—	3 yrs.	—	(48)	6 mos.	6 mos.
Utah	3 mos.	*	—	1 yr.	—	—	3 yrs. (19)	—	—	3 mos. (49)	3 mos. (49)
Vermont	6 mos. (50)	—	—	3 yrs.	5 yrs.	—	3 yrs.	—	—	6 mos. (14)	2 yrs. (14)
Virginia	1 yr.	*	—	1 yr.	—	—	2 yrs.	—	(51)	(54)	(54)
Washington	1 yr.	*	—	1 yr.	—	2 yrs.	2 yrs.	(52)	(4, 53)	6 mos.	6 mos.
West Virginia	1 yr. (12)	*	—	1 yr.	—	3 yrs.	2 yrs.	—	(55)	—	—
Wisconsin	2 yrs.	—	—	1 yr.	—	—	5 yrs.	—	—	1 yr.	1 yr.
Wyoming	60 days (12)	*	—	1 yr.	—	2 yrs.	2 yrs.	(56)	—	—	—
Washington, D.C.	1 yr.	—	—	1 yr.	—	2 yrs.	1 yr.	(57)	(7, 39)	6 mos.	6 mos.

Source: Women's Bureau, U. S. Department of Labor.

(*) Indicates ground for absolute divorce. (1) No specific period when court has jurisdiction of both parties, except 1 year when ground is desertion or defendant is nonresident, or 2 years if wife sues husband for nonsupport. (2) To wife, living separate and apart from husband, as resident of the State for 2 years before suit and without support from him during such time. (3) May be enlarged into an absolute divorce after expiration of 2 years; in Connecticut, any time after decree of separation; Hawaii, 2 years after decree for separate maintenance or divorce from bed and board; Minnesota, 5 years after decree of limited divorce. (4) Crime against nature. (5) Except to each other. (6) Incompatibility. (7) Crime before marriage. (8) In Arkansas, one must be a resident for 3 months before final judgment will be entered. (9) Also to husband in certain circumstances. (10) Effective January 1, 1970, no residence requirement before filing suit for divorce, but a final decree cannot be entered until party is a resident for 6 months. (11) Effective January 1, 1970, only two grounds of divorce: irreconcilable differences which have caused the irremediable breakdown of the marriage and incurable insanity. (12) Under certain circumstances a lesser period of time may be required. (13) Female under 16, male under 18, if complaining party under age of consent at time of marriage has not confirmed marriage after reaching such age. (14) In the discretion of the court. (15) Habitual violent and ungovernable temper. (16) Defendant obtained divorce from plaintiff in another State. (17) Relationship within prohibited degrees. (18) Mental incapacity. (19) Under decree of separate maintenance. In New York, also 2 years pursuant to a written agreement of separation. (20) Final decree is not entered until 1 year after interlocutory decree. In Hawaii, applies only where parties are under 18. (21) Loathsome disease. (22) Attempt on the life of the spouse by poison or other means showing malice. (23) Five years if on ground of insanity. (24) Two years where service on defendant is only by publication. (25) Unless at time of marriage husband had an illegitimate child living, which fact was not known to wife. (26) Five years if on ground of insanity and insane spouse is in out-of-State institution. (27) If on part of the husband, accompanied by wasting of husband's estate to the detriment of the wife and children. (28) Joining religious sect disbelieving in marriage. (29) Unchaste behavior on part of wife after marriage. (30) Must be domiciled in State and grounds occurred in State, except that 2 years separation need not have been in State. (31) One year after judgment of separation from bed and board decree becomes final; spouse who obtained judgment may obtain absolute divorce; other party may obtain decree 1 year and 60 days from date of separation decree. (32) When divorce is granted on ground of adultery, the guilty party cannot marry the accomplice in adultery during lifetime of former spouse. (33) No specific period required, except 1 year if cause occurred out of State and 2 years if on ground of insanity. (34) In Maryland, when the parties have lived separate and apart without cohabitation for 5 years. The 18 months separation listed must be voluntary. (35) Any cause which renders marriage null and void from the beginning. (36) If the cause occurred outside of Massachusetts, must be a resident for 2 years; if cause occurred in Massachusetts, no residence requirement. (37) Not more than 2 years in court's discretion. (38) When divorce is granted on grounds of adultery, court may prohibit remarriage. After 1 year, court may remove disability upon satisfactory evidence of reformation. (39) Husband a vagrant. (40) Wife's absence out of State for 10 years without husband's consent. (41) When husband is entitled to a divorce and alimony or child support from husband is granted, the decree may be delayed until security is entered for payment. (42) Incapable of procreation. (43) Or a lesser time in court's discretion. (44) Void or voidable marriage. (45) Gross misbehavior or wickedness; loss of citizenship rights of one party due to crime; presumption of death. (46) When divorce is for adultery, the guilty party cannot remarry except to the innocent spouse, until the death of the spouse. (47) To husband for wife's refusal to move with him to this State without reasonable cause, and willfully absenting herself from him for 2 years. (48) In Texas, if the marriage has become insupportable because of discord or conflict of personalities that destroys ends of the marriage relationship and prevents reasonable expectation of reconciliation. (49) In Utah, the decree does not become final for 3 months (court may extend to 6 months), thereby preventing remarriage until decree is final. (50) One year before final hearing, and 2 years if on ground of insanity. (51) Intolerable severity. (52) A limited divorce granted on the ground of cruelty or desertion may be merged with an absolute divorce after 1 year. (53) Wife a prostitute prior to marriage. (54) When divorce is granted on ground of adultery, court may decree the guilty party cannot remarry. After 6 months the court may remove disability for good cause. Remarriage of either party forbidden pending appeal. (55) Want of legal age or sufficient understanding. (56) Living entirely apart for 5 years pursuant to a judgment of legal separation. (57) Limited divorce may be enlarged into absolute divorce after 1 year. Also, absolute divorce may be granted for any cause arising after a divorce from bed and board, sufficient to entitle complaining party to an absolute divorce.

proceedings; and free divorce by consent would undermine the basic institution of the family, which is the cornerstone of society.

Thus, the institution of divorce, as it functions in the United States today, attempts to protect individual rights but also to preserve the institutions of marriage and the family by making divorce obtainable only with a measure of legal difficulty. Divorce may be seen, then, as a mechanism of adjustment which resolves the problems of an unsatisfactory marriage. While terminating the difficulties of adjustment *within* marriage, however, it brings other problems of its own — problems that are beyond the scope of our discussion.[22]

Summary

Adjustment is the pattern of behavioral responses which a person utilizes to resolve perceived needs. When the needs of one marital partner differ from those of his mate, an adjustment for one may mean deprivation for the other; and a conflict will result. Marital conflict is inevitable, but it may be satisfactorily resolved if the couple agree on the problem and make adjustive responses that are relatively mutually fulfilling. If the responses are arbitrary and unilateral or if the spouses attack one another instead of the source of the conflict, the immediate problem may be temporarily adjusted; but this adjustment will usually cause guilt, resentment, anger, and further and more intense conflict.

Thus, a well-adjusted marriage will involve altruistic and/or creative-compromise conflict resolution — which includes a mutual identification and acknowledgment of the problem, a mutual willingness to see the problem resolved, and a solution that adequately satisfies each one's essential material, sexual, and interpersonal needs.

In our society, most marriages which are described by the couple as "happy," fall into the *utilitarian* category, either conflict-habituated, devitalized, or passive-congenial; the *intrinsic* marriage, characterized by intensive interpersonal identification and satisfaction, is the ideal but is relatively rare after age 30.

If either person falls into a pattern of not fulfilling the expectations of the other in these important areas of need satisfaction, their marriage will fail. Thus, if a marriage, or any relation, is to be viable, there must be (1) a congruence of role perception, (2) a reciprocation of role performance, and (3) an equivalence of role functions and of resources.

Strictly speaking, a failed marriage will involve legal termination — annulment, legal separation, or divorce. However, those marriages that are characterized by chronic dissatisfaction and unhappiness but are not terminated because of children, religious proscriptions, and social pressures, etc., can also be described as failures, in that they provide only the most marginal of adjustments to conflict and fulfillment of needs.

---

[22]See William J. Goode, *Women in Divorce* (New York: Free Press, 1965); Morton M. Hunt, *The World of the Formerly Married* (New York: Doubleday, 1966); Paul Bohannan *et al.*, eds., *Divorce and After* (New York: Doubleday, 1970).

Termination may be the only solution for a marriage that not only fails to provide the essential need satisfactions but also has become a source of pain. Still, divorce is not a panacea. The divorced person is still faced with the same problems of adjustment — the necessity of obtaining his essential material, sexual, and interpersonal satisfactions. Thus, despite his bad marital experience, he usually attempts to achieve these satisfactions within the structure of a second marriage.

Questions

1   What is the psychological meaning of adjustment?

2   What happens when there is adjustment for one person and deprivation for the other?

3   What do we mean when we speak of (a) "good" marital adjustment? (b) "bad" marital adjustment?

4   Viewed psychologically, there are two categories of marital conflict — internal and external. Explain and give examples of each.

5   What are the four ways in which an external marital conflict may be resolved?

6   What is the ideal way of resolving external marital conflict, and why?

7   Why do conflicts arise in marriage that probably would not between two close friends?

8   In a viable marriage what will each person try to do following a quarrel?

9   In habituated conflicts, explain the characteristics of "alternate approach and withdrawal."

10   What may feedback be besides convergent or divergent? Give examples.

11   Why is feedback from other people, and even from a significant other, generally ambiguous?

12   What does convergent feedback of a significant other do to the person's self-image? Divergent feedback?

13   Divergent feedback often occurs in marital disagreements. If such attacks become a persistent pattern, what three directions will occur in the relation? Give examples.

14   What is meant by excessive expectations of togetherness? What is ideal in a marital relation?

15   What is the difference between defense-oriented behavior and reality-oriented behavior? Give examples.

16   If behavior is learned, and if learned behavior is based upon reinforcement, why doesn't everyone always behave in an optimal fashion?

17   What are six examples of defense mechanisms? What function do they all serve?

18   Is there such a thing as a final adjustment in a marital relation? Explain.

19   Explain internal compromise as a method of conflict resolution.

20   What must the authoritarian approach rest upon?

21   Explain how a quarrel is resolved by permissive acceptance.

22   What is meant by psychological game playing?

23   Why may it be very confusing to distinguish operation from a marital game?

24   What characterizes an intrinsic marriage?

25   What are the types of the well-adjusted marriages in our society?

26   For a marriage to continue, the needs of each person must be met in three areas. Explain.

27   Discuss why the estimated incidence of marriage failure in our society at the present time is so high.

28   Discuss social-class differences in incidence of marriage failure.

29   As it functions in the United States, what does the institution of divorce attempt to do?

References and Selected Readings

Adorno, T. W., *et al. The Authoritarian Personality.* New York: Harper, 1950.

Bach, George R., and Peter Wyden. *The Intimate Enemy: How to Fight Fair in Love and Marriage.* New York: Morrow, 1969.

Bell, Robert R. *Marriage and Family Interaction,* rev. ed. Homewood, Illinois: Dorsey, 1967.

Berelson, Bernard, and Gary A. Steiner. *Human Behavior.* New York: Harcourt, 1964.

Bernard, Jessie. Infidelity: Moral or Social Issue? *Science and Psychoanalysis,* 1970, Vol. 16.

_____. Factors in the Distribution of Success in Marriage. *American Journal of Sociology,* 1934, Vol. XL, pp. 49–60.

Berne, Eric, M.D. *Games People Play.* New York: Grove, 1964.

Blood, Robert O., Jr. *Marriage,* 2nd ed. New York: Free Press, 1969.

_____, and Donald M. Wolfe. *Husbands and Wives.* New York: Free Press, 1960.

Bohannan, Paul, *et al.,* eds. *Divorce and After.* New York: Doubleday, 1970.

Brecher, Edward and Ruth, eds., *An Analysis of Human Sexual Response.* Boston: Little, Brown, 1966.

Burgess, Ernest W., and Leonard S. Cottrell. *Predicting Success or Failure in Marriage.* Englewood Cliffs, N. J.: Prentice-Hall, 1939.

_____, and Paul Wallin. *Engagement and Marriage.* Philadelphia: Lippincott, 1953

Carter, Hugh, and Paul C. Glick. *Marriage and Divorce: A Social and Economic Study.* Cambridge, Mass.: Harvard University Press, 1970.

Chessar, Eustace, *et al. The Sexual, Marital, and Family Relationships with English Women.* New York: Roy, 1957.

Clarke, Carl. Group Procedures for Increasing Positive Feedback between Married Partners. *The Family Coordinator,* October 1970, pp. 324–328.

Coleman, James C. *Psychology and Effective Behavior.* Chicago: Scott, Foresman, 1969.

_____. *Abnormal Psychology and Modern Life,* 3rd ed. Chicago: Scott, Foresman, 1964.

Crow, Lester D. *Psychology of Human Adjustment.* New York: Knopf, 1967.

Cuber, John F., and Peggy B. Harroff. *The Significant Americans: A Study of Sexual Behavior Among the Affluent.* New York: Appleton-Century-Crofts, 1965.

Demographic Yearbook, 20th Issue. Marriage and Divorce Statistics. New York: Statistical Office of the United Nations, 1969.

Ellis, Albert. Rational Psychotherapy. *Journal of General Psychology,* 1958, Vol. 59, pp. 35–49.

Fenelon, Bill. State Variations in United States Divorce Rates. *Journal of Marriage and the Family,* May 1971, Vol. 33, pp. 321–327.

Folsom, J. K. *The Family, and Democratic Society.* New York: Wiley, 1943.

Glick, Paul C. Permanence of Marriage. *Population Index,* October-December 1967, Vol. 33, pp. 517–526.

_____, and Arthur J. Norton. Frequency, Duration, and Probability of Marriage and Divorce. *Journal of Marriage and The Family,* May 1971, Vol. 33, pp. 307–317.

Goode, William J. *Women in Divorce.* New York: Free Press, 1965.

Gordon, Albert I. *Intermarriage.* Boston: Beacon, 1964.

Gould Editorial Staff. *Marriage, Divorce, and Adoption Laws in the United States.* New York: Gould, 1970.

Gurin, Gerald, Joseph Veroff, and Sheila Field. *Americans View Their Mental Health.* New York: Basic Books, 1960.

Harmsworth, Harry C., and Mhyra S. Minnis. Nonstatutory Causes of Divorce: The Lawyer's Point of View. *Marriage and Family Living,* 1955, Vol. 17, pp. 316–321.

Harris, Thomas A. *I'm O. K. — You're O. K.* New York: Harper, 1969.

Hill, Reuben. Quarreling Comes into Its Own. *Parents' Magazine.* Sept. 1946, pp. 24 ff.

Hunt, Morton. *Affair: A Portrait of Extra-Marital Love in Contemporary America.* New York: New American Library, 1969.

_____. *The World of the Formerly Married.* New York: Doubleday, 1966.

Jackson, Joan K. Alcoholism and the Family. *Annals of the American Academy of Political and Social Science,* January 1958, pp. 90–98.

Jacobson, Paul. *American Marriage and Divorce.* New York: Holt, 1959.

Kagen, J. The Concept of Identification. *Psychological Review,* 1958, Vol. 65, pp. 296–305.

Kephart, William M. Drinking and Marital Disruption. *Quarterly Journal of Studies on Alcoholism,* March 1954, pp. 63–73.

_____. *The Family, Society, and the Individual.* Boston: Houghton Mifflin, 1961.

_____. Occupational Level and Marital Disruption. *American Sociological Review,* August 1955, pp. 456–465.

_____. Some Variables in Cases of Reported Sexual Maladjustment, *Marriage and Family Living,* August 1954, pp. 241–243.

Kinsey, Alfred C., Wardell B. Pomeroy, and Clyde C. Martin. *Sexual Behavior in the Human Male.* Philadelphia: Saunders, 1948.

Kirkpatrick, Clifford. Factors in Marital Adjustment. *American Journal of Sociology,* 1937, Vol. XLIII, pp. 278–283.

Klemer, Richard H., ed. *Counseling in Marital and Sexual Problems: A Physician's Handbook.* Baltimore: Williams and Wilkins, 1965.

Kohut, Nester C. *Complete Guide to Marital Reconciliations: Therapeutic Family Law,* 2nd ed. Chicago: Family Law, 1968.

Laing, R. D. *The Self and Others.* Chicago: Quadrangle Books. 1962.

Landis, Judson T. and Mary G. *Building a Successful Marriage,* 5th ed. Englewood Cliffs, N. J.: Prentice-Hall, 1968.

Landis, Paul H. *Making the Most of Marriage,* 4th ed. New York: Appleton-Century-Crofts, 1970.

Lanier, Roy H. *Marriage, Divorce, and Remarriage,* rev. ed. Shreveport, La.: Lampert, 1970.

Lederer, William J., and Don D. Jackson. *The Mirages of Marriage.* New York: Norton, 1968.

Leeper, Robert Ward. *Toward Understanding Human Personalities.* New York: Appleton-Century-Crofts, 1959.

Leslie, Gerald R. The Field of Marriage Counseling. In Harold T. Christensen, ed. *Handbook of Marriage and the Family.* Chicago: Rand McNally, 1964, pp. 912–943.

Locke, Harvey J. *Predicting Adjustment in Marriage: A Comparison of a Divorced and a Happily Married Group*. Westport, Conn.: Greenwood, 1968.

Maslow, A. H. *Motivation and Personality*. New York: Harper, 1970.

_____. Deficiency Motivation and Growth Motivation. In Marshall R. Jones, ed. *Nebraska Symposium on Motivation*. Omaha: University of Nebraska Press, 1955, pp. 1–30.

Mudd, Emily H. *The Practice of Marriage Counseling*. New York: Association, 1951.

_____. Psychiatry and Marital Problems. *Eugenics Quarterly*, June 1955, pp. 113–114.

Neubeck, G., ed. *Extramarital Sex Relations*. Englewood Cliffs, N. J.: Prentice-Hall, 1970.

Peterson, James A., ed. *Marriage and Family Counseling: Perspective and Prospect*. New York: Association Press, 1968.

Plescowe, Morris. *Sex and the Law*. Englewood Cliffs, N. J.: Prentice-Hall, 1951.

Popenoe, Paul, and Donna Wicks. Marital Happiness in Two Generations. *Mental Hygiene*, 1937, Vol. 21, pp. 218–233.

Rheinstein, Max. Trends in Marriage and Divorce Laws of Western Countries. In *Law and Contemporary Problems*. Duke University School of Law, Durham, N. C.: Duke University, 1953.

_____, ed. *Max Weber on Law in Economy and Society*, trans. Edward Shils and Max Rheinstein. New York: Simon and Schuster, 1967.

Rogers, Carl R. *On Becoming a Person*. Boston: Houghton Mifflin, 1970.

_____. *Client-Centered Therapy*. New York: Houghton Mifflin, 1951.

Sargent, S. Stanfeld. Reaction to Frustration—A Critique and Hypothesis. *Psychological Review*, 1948, Vol. 55, pp. 108–114.

Sears, R. R. Identification as a Form of Behavior Development. In D. B. Harris, ed., *The Concept of Development*. Minneapolis: University of Minneapolis Press, 1957, pp. 149–161.

Shaffer, Laurance Frederic, and Edward Joseph Shoben, Jr. *The Psychology of Adjustment*, 2nd ed. Boston: Houghton Mifflin, 1956.

Spitz, R. Hospitalism: Genesis of Psychiatric Conditions in Early Childhood. *Psychoanalytic Study of the Child*, 1945, Vol. 1, pp. 53–74.

Terman, Lewis M., *et al. Psychological Factors in Marital Happiness*. New York: McGraw-Hill, 1938.

Thomas, John L. Marital Failure and Duration. *Social Order*, Vol. 3, No. 1, p. 26.

Thurber, James. The Future, If Any, of Comedy. *Harper's Magazine*, December 1961, p. 44.

Waller, Willard. *Old Love and the New: Divorce and Readjustment*. Champaign, Ill.: Illinois University Press, 1967.

_____. *The Family: A Dynamic Interpretation*. Revised by Reuben Hill. New York: Dryden, 1951.

Warner, W. Lloyd. *American Life: Dream and Reality*, rev. ed. Chicago: University of Chicago Press, 1962.

Whitney, Elizabeth D. *Living with Alcoholism*. Boston: Beacon Press, 1968.

Winch, Robert F. *Modern Family*, rev. ed. New York: Holt, 1963.

Wyden, Peter and Barbara. *Inside the Sex Clinic*. New York: World, 1971.

Zimmerman, Carle C., and Lucius F. Cervantes. *Successful American Families*. New York: Pageant, 1960.

Chapter Eight

Marriage under Special Circumstances

*Better a dish of vegetables
stewed with love, than the best
of beef stewed with hatred.*

Proverbs 15:17

Certain categories of marriage are somewhat "special" in that they do not represent the average marital experience. These marriages—the *second marriage, intermarriage,* the *military marriage,* and the *college marriage*—have peculiar characteristics and success-failure probabilities that serve to distinguish them, to some degree, from the majority of marriages.

The Second Marriage

Most marriages in the United States take place between people who are marrying for the first time. However, about one in four of all marriages are second marriages for one or both of the couple.[1] This one-in-four ratio reflects the divorce to marriage ratio of the 1950s and 1960s. Now that this divorce to marriage ratio has risen to nearly one in three,[2] it may be predicted that perhaps one in three marriages may be second marriages in the next decade.

Barring marked change in current trends, it seems plausible to expect that, during the lifetime of those who are now entering marriage at . . . young ages [under 22 for men; under 20 for women[3]] close to one third of the whites and one half of the blacks will eventually end their marriages in divorce (Glick and Norton, 1971, p. 310).

It is estimated that about 20 percent of our current middle-aged population and nearly 30 percent of our current old-age population have been married at

---

[1]Since 1947, 30 percent of blacks and 17 percent of whites have been married twice (Glick and Norton, 1971).

[2]See *Incidence of Marriage Failure* in Chapter Seven.

[3]These are the average ages for first marriages for men and women.

least twice (Carter and Glick, 1970). Marriage for the third time is quite rare in our society, however, occurring among less than 3 percent of the married population.[4]

The group most likely to remarry are young divorcees (Carter and Glick, 1970). It is also interesting to note that the probability that a person will marry is higher for the divorced and widowed (men and women alike) at all age levels than it is for a never-married person of a comparable age (Carter and Glick, 1970).

Apparently, there is a slight tendency for the person who marries for the second time to choose a mate who has also been previously married. This is the case with 51 percent of remarrying females and 52 percent of remarrying males.[5] Whether or not a woman has had children by a previous marriage, and the number of children she may have had, apparently has little statistical effect on her chances for remarriage (Glick, 1957; and Goode, 1965). Glick found that the rate of remarriage for divorcees with children was only slightly lower (age for age) than the rate of divorcees without children.

Substantial numbers of those who remarry after their first divorce do so relatively soon. For example, among the white population, one fourth remarry within a year, one half within three years, and three fourths within nine years. Among blacks, the median interval is about half again as long as that for whites. Of the population who remarry after divorce, men remarry sooner than women (Glick and Norton, 1971).

In general, the dating and engagement periods leading to second marriage are shorter than those leading to first marriage (in fact, a formal engagement is somewhat unusual for remarrying people). A second wedding ceremony is usually quite simple, with few guests and often no formal reception. Honeymoons of second-marriage couples are simpler, shorter, and less expensive than those of the first marriage (Bernard, 1956).

There is a greater age difference between bride and groom in second marriages than in first marriages. A man of 30 marrying for the second time may

---

[4]Only 4 percent of blacks and 2 percent of whites have married three or more times since 1947 (Glick and Norton, 1971).
[5]*Vital Statistics of the United States,* 1959, Vol. 1, Section 2, pp. 2–9.

be expected statistically to marry a woman 23 years of age. In marriages which are the second marriage for both husband and wife, 35 percent of the husbands are 10 or more years older than the wife. In contrast, the modal age differences in *first* marriages for both persons is 2–3 years (Carter and Glick, 1970).

Prior to about 1920, neither divorce nor remarriage had achieved much public or institutional acceptance as a respectable alternative to unsuccessful marriage. And until about 1960, even sociologists and counselors discussed divorce and remarriage as "social problems." By the 1970s, however, both the professional and the general public's view had undergone a transformation, and divorce and remarriage are now generally regarded as *solutions* to a problem rather than as problems in themselves (Bernard, 1970).

This change in attitude toward divorce and remarriage has apparently come about as a result of the recognition of the importance of marriage in satisfying the basic affiliative needs for emotional security, understanding, acceptance, affection, and love within our mass society. More and more, our culture has adapted to the principle that if the first marriage fails in satisfying these needs, the person is justified in terminating this marriage in favor of a second—even when children are involved. This emphasis upon the personal-happiness concept of marriage is quite a departure, of course, from the earlier emphasis upon marriage chiefly as an institution which protects the property and inheritance rights of the female and offspring and which provides an essential stabilizing base for the society.

Remarriage, whether following divorce or the death of a spouse, is permitted by civil law in every state and recognized and accepted by all major religions in our culture except the Roman Catholic church. As we have noted, Catholicism still regards marriage as essentially indissoluble and does not recognize divorce (see Chapter Seven).

Motivation for Remarriage

The widowed person, who has experienced one successful marriage which terminated only with the death of the spouse, is understandably motivated to remarry for the same reasons that moved him to marry the first time. Similarly, the divorced person, despite the experience of an *un*happy marriage and the trauma of divorce, seeks in a second marriage precisely the same satisfactions that motivated him to marry the first time. Those needs which he expects to be fulfilled by marriage are apparently not diminished by the lack of reinforcement that results from a marriage failure. For example:

1. Sexual needs are fully as operant in middle age (when the average second marriage takes place) as they are in adolescence. In fact, the middle-aged female is usually far more awakened sexually than she was in adolescence.

2. The needs for love, affection, companionship, and emotional support— the need for a paired relation—are not abated in middle age.

Love in the middle years can . . . be as tumultuous and rapturous as youthful love . . . The joy and freedom of being able to act oneself with abandon, without reserve, with one's guard completely down, with the assurance of an absorbed and fascinated audience is as much a part of love in the middle years as it is of youthful love (Bernard, 1956, p. 121).

Companionship and emotional nurture from and for a significant other are perhaps even more important in the middle years than in young adulthood. The unmarried middle-aged person is far more vulnerable to intense loneliness than the young adult, who usually has more societal resources for companionship (such as school and sports activities) and a greater number of companions available.

3. Pressures for conformity to the societal expectation that everyone *be* married are no less in the middle years than earlier. Society generally views the unmarried person and the divorcee with some suspicion, considering such persons somehow incomplete or emotionally inadequate or nonrespectable. Further, if a divorced person has custody of the children born to his first marriage, there will be a good deal of pressure — both from the society and from the person's own feelings of responsibility — for remarriage in order to provide a proper familial environment for the children.

Success of Remarriage

Although there are no nationwide data, evidence from marital records of the state of Iowa (which require that the applicant for a marriage license state his marital status) indicate that second marriages involving a widowed spouse have a lower divorce rate than the first-married population. During the years 1953–1955, the divorce rate for the first marriages (in Iowa) was 17 percent; whereas for widows and widowers entering a second marriage it was 10 to 16 percent (Monohan, 1958). Second marriages for the divorced, on the other hand, had a much higher rate of failure than first marriages. If either or both of the couple had been divorced once, the rate of failure for the second marriage was 35–37 percent. If one had been previously divorced twice or more, the rate was 62 percent; and if both had been divorced twice or more, it was 79 percent (Monohan). According to these figures, a second marriage (for the divorced) is about twice as risky as a first marriage.

It is not surprising that the divorce rate in second marriages is somewhat higher than the rate for first marriages since persons who have already chosen divorce as the answer to the marital problems of their first marriage would tend to choose termination again if the marital problems of the second marriage become intolerable. Actually, according to one study, first-marriage divorce occurs after an average of 10 years of marriage, but second-marriage divorce occurs after an average of five years of marriage (Landis, 1970); so that the decision to divorce a second time is reached about twice as fast as the decision for first divorce.

Among the 60–70 percent of second marriages which do not terminate rather quickly in divorce, observers seem to agree that the expectation for a happy marriage is about the same for a second marriage as for a first marriage. Popenoe (1951), for example, finds that those who remarry after divorce have almost as high a percentage of happy marriages as those marrying for the first time. Terman (1938), in his classic study, found that "a majority of the divorced remarry and on the average are about as happy in their new marriages as those who have not been divorced." And Locke (1968), in the only study of its kind comparing happily married couples with divorced couples, found no significant differences between the adjustment of couples in first or second marriages.

The problems that the divorced person encountered in his first marriage as a result of his own personality and other needs will almost certainly arise again in a remarriage — he is, after all, still the person he was. But his new partner may be a very different kind of person from his first spouse, so that his need satisfactions now may produce little or no conflict. Of course, if either spouse brings children to the second marriage, the roles, role reciprocities, complexities of power structure, and intricacies of adjustment will be more delicate and difficult than they were in a first marriage that involved only the two partners.

The Decision Not to Remarry

Although the rate of remarriage is higher for all age groups than the rate of first marriages, not *all* persons remarry, of course, for a variety of reasons:

1. The widowed person may conceivably not remarry because of a feeling that this would be disloyal to the memory of the deceased spouse.

2. If children are involved, it is probable that some persons would not wish to take on the responsibility of being the father or mother of stepchildren. Also, some divorced or widowed persons with children may not wish to expose their children to the stresses of adapting to a new parent.[6]

3. Opportunities for meeting prospective mates are fewer in middle age than earlier, since there are simply fewer single persons available.[7]

4. The person who has made a satisfactory adjustment to being single may be reluctant to accept once again the responsibilities and restrictions and demands of marriage. The person who has a low sex drive or who has experienced bitter sexual frustration or dissatisfaction during the first marriage may not be interested in a second marriage.

---

[6]The creation of a stepchild–step-parent relation is difficult in American culture. Most children, at the time their divorced parents remarry, are old enough to have some very pronounced ideas about their parent's choice of a second mate. "One has only to turn to the writings about step-parenthood in the current etiquette books to learn that the American norm is either to disregard the subject completely or to assume that special care will be taken that no differences appear on the surface between step-parenthood and 'real' parenthood. Step-parents are not 'real' — and the culture so far provides no norms to tell us how they are different, or what ought to be done about them, or toward them" (Gebhard, 1970, p. 119).

[7]More specifically, there are fewer single persons available of the same age group. Of course, the person may marry someone younger than himself and thus dip into the pool of unmarried persons in their late teens and early and middle twenties. Generally, however, only the male is able to do this, since the cultural attitude toward older females marrying young men is more strongly forbidding than it is for the older male who marries a young girl. For a further discussion of this point, see *The Dating Differential*, in Chapter Five.

Intermarriage

Most marriages are homogamous. That is, although we marry for love, most of us fall in love with someone who is of the same race, religion, social class, and ethnic group. When a person marries someone of a different race, ethnic group, religion, or social class, the marriage is termed *intermarriage*.[8] Generally, an intermarriage involves the crossing of only one of these four homogamous factors. For example, a study of intermarriage among American servicemen stationed in the Philippines showed that the Filipino brides usually had the same religion and social status (and educational level) as their American husbands (Hunt, 1957). Similarly, interracial marriages occur frequently among college students, who—because they are college students—are usually of at least lower middle-class status.

Because a substantial minority of the American population does intermarry and because a mixed marriage often is involved with different interpersonal and social factors from a homogamous marriage, it is important that we explore the societal attitudes toward different types of intermarriage and motivations for incidence and success of these marriages.

Interracial Marriage

The nationwide incidence of interracial marriage in the United States is statistically negligible—probably amounting to fewer than four marriages per thousand (Carter and Glick, 1970).[9] However if we were to look at the ratio of interracial to racially homogamous marriages in the particular population groups of college students and servicemen stationed abroad, we would probably find a much higher incidence, although no comparative figures are presently available.[10]

Interracial dating on some college campuses is now not only acceptable but is often considered to be status giving. Contemporary college students are generally aware of the anomalies of racial concepts and are impatient with the provincialism of their society; and interracial marriage among this group probably accounts for much more than the national norm of interracial marriage, which is only .4 percent of all marriages—a figure that includes, of course, geographic areas where there is no opportunity for interracial dating, or where racial prejudice is pronounced.

---

[8]The concept of intermarriage, or "mixed" marriage, is sometimes interpreted more broadly. A marriage is sometimes considered mixed, for instance, if bride and groom belong to two different Protestant sects, or if one is "religious" and the other "non-religious," or if they belong to different age groups or have marked differences of intelligence or education (Landis and Landis, 1963). In sum, many marriages can be considered mixed in some way, and what is a mixed marriage for one observer may be a homogamous marriage for another observer—or may seem mixed to him for an entirely different reason.

[9]The racially mixed state of Hawaii is the exception, with the incidence of interracial marriage involving 29 percent of professional people and 51 percent of laborers (non-farm) in 1968 (Schmitt, 1971).

[10]Of the six categories of white–non-white marriage in the United States (black, American Indian, Chinese, Japanese, Filipino, and "others"), 31 percent are white-black (Carter and Glick, 1970).

Interracial marriage by servicemen stationed abroad is definitely much higher than the national norm. For example, servicemen stationed in Japan had married more than 45,000 Japanese women between 1949 and 1961 (Gordon, 1964). Between 1959 and 1961, more than 3,000 interracial marriages occurred in Tokyo alone.

The concept of race. The popular concept of race is based on skin pigmentation, so that the world's population neatly falls into a simple color spectrum of red, yellow, white, brown, and black. Like many popular concepts, this one is inaccurate and leads to many logical contradictions. Many "white" men have darker skins than many "colored" men. Moreover, genetic mixtures of skin pigmentation are usually identified with the darker race, although the converse is just as logical. A man with one sixteenth Negro background may be legally identified as Negro, whereas a man with one sixteenth Caucasian background is rarely called white.

The scientific concept of race is broader, using in addition to pigmentation such "racial" factors as hair, facial features and bone structure, teeth, and blood type; but the concept of race still remains contradictory and is by no means agreed upon by either biologists or anthropologists. Today scientific definitions of race range from a denial that races exist to a definition of race on an exclusively morphological basis. The majority of anthropologists acknowledge some racial divisions, but the number of races that they recognize varies from two to over one hundred. UNESCO issued a *Statement on the Nature of Race and Race Differences* (1952) which said: "There is no evidence for the existence of so-called 'pure races'"; and the eminent anthropologist Ashley Montagu writes that the entire concept of race is nonsense, based solely on *reification*, the process of regarding an abstraction as concrete.

Most readers will be aware that the social concept of race, the doctrine, to put it briefly, that there exist superior and inferior races, has long been unacceptable to anthropologists. What most readers may not be aware of is the fact that the biological concept of race has become unacceptable to a growing number of biologists on the one hand and to an equally increasing number of physical anthropologists on the other. . . . The probabilities are high that the concept will be afforded a status similar to that now occupied by the nonexistent substance known as "phlogiston."[11] . . . Race is the phlogiston of our time (Montagu, 1969, pp. xi–xii).

Societal attitudes toward interracial marriage. A large proportion of American society is racially intolerant or unqualifiedly racist, a situation that, of course, militates against acceptance of interracial marriage. As recently as 1958, more than 30 states legally prohibited interracial marriage, specifically stating that no Caucasian may marry a Negro. In many of these 30 states there were additional prohibitions against a Caucasian marrying an American Indian, a Chinese, Japanese, Mexican, Malaysian, or Hindu — in short, anyone not "white" or "pure white"

---

[11]*Phlogiston* is a hypothetical substance that was advanced in the late seventeenth century to explain combustion. The existence of phlogiston was accepted and examined for about a hundred years until the discovery (by Priestly) and the recognition (by Lavoisier) of the element oxygen.

(Gordon, 1964). Several states maintained these laws right up to the time of the United States Supreme Court decision in 1967 against such discriminatory statutes.

In almost every other large and racially mixed society in the modern world, interracial marriages are accepted, both legally and socially, with little or no disapproval. With the exception of the Republic of South Africa and possibly Great Britain, no other nation has ever been as determinedly race conscious as the United States.

The interracial couple is a target for bigotry and a cause for illogical fear. The couple will consequently experience problems with friends and relatives, with housing and employment. Husband and wife will be openly or tacitly rejected by most members of the white and non-white communities alike; and any chil-

dren born to an interracial couple will be publicly and sometimes legally classified as non-white—which in practical terms means that such children will find life in America difficult, to say the least. Their opportunities "for cultural, economic, political, and social advancement may, for some time to come, remain closed because of their color alone" (Gordon, p. 364).

The degree of difficulty which the interracial couple faces in America varies according to the couple's socioeconomic level, their place of residence, and the races of the partners. For example, a mixed marriage in which one person is Negro provokes more discrimination from the white majority than does a marriage in which one partner is Japanese. Mixed marriages between lower-class people sometimes meet with actual physical opposition from in-laws, friends, neighbors, and even strangers. A white student on a Boston or Los Angeles college campus who marries interracially is likely to be treated with respect, but a white student on a Mississippi college campus would find it very nearly impossible to marry (or even to date) interracially.

Yet despite the varying difficulties for interracial couples in America today, there seems to be some slight basis for hope for a normalization of their situation. America is witnessing a painfully slow and traumatic internal change of attitude toward the peoples of its many races, if only because nearly 50 percent of the population is under 25 years old[12] and young people are, in general, more intelligent about race than are their elders.

---

[12]The median age in the United States in 1969 was 26 years for males and 29 years for females (*Current Population Reports*, Series P-25, No. 441, 1971).

Motivation for interracial marriage. Many interracial marriages occur for the simple reason that the couple is in love. In this case, there is no motivational difference between an interracial marriage and a homogamous marriage contracted on the basis of love. But because an interracial couple is certain to be aware of the difficulties they will encounter, presumably other factors in addition to romantic attraction, propinquity,[13] shared interest, and personality compatibility will operate to bring about many interracial marriages. These factors seem to be clearly different for white and non-white people.

1. The "lure of the exotic" may induce a white person to be attracted to and marry a non-white person—in other words, the white person may experience a profound psychosexual attraction to the "otherness" of someone who is non-white (it works in the opposite direction, of course—from non-white to white). This kind of attraction—its existence and its repercussions—is described in the folklore and literature of many cultures, ancient and modern.

2. The white person may marry a non-white person for idealistic or liberal reasons; that is, to defy the prevalent cultural prejudice of his society. By intermarrying, he demonstrates that he refuses to identify himself with racial bigotry.

3. The white person may marry a non-white person to rebel against parental authority. This desire to hurt the parents may be conscious or unconscious; certainly it appears to be the principal motivation for interracial marriage (or even dating) among many young white Americans of the middle class.

4. The non-white person may marry a white person to achieve higher social status. Inasmuch as marriage is the most intimate of all social interactions, the non-white who marries a white may be demonstrating, in effect, that he is capable of being completely accepted socially—at least by the white person he marries, and therefore, by implication, by white society at large. The Negro community in general strongly disapproves of marriage to a white (see Risdon, 1954; and Drake and Clayton, 1945); but many Negroes nonetheless (and not unexpectedly, considering the racial inequalities in our society) regard marriage to a white person as status giving (Golden, 1953). Moreover, the high-status Negro—a successful entertainer, a sports figure, or politician, for example—who marries a socially desirable white person may be demonstrating not only his social equality with whites but also his superiority of status, as a Negro, to that of most whites.

5. Finally, the non-white person may marry a white person with the hope that to do so will somehow improve the social conditions and end the psychological suffering which, as a non-white in America, he has experienced all his life. The white mate in such a case represents for him the promise of a better life and an end to the futility he has found characteristic of many of his efforts to live a meaningful and satisfying life as a member of an American racial subculture.

---

[13]Propinquity, more than any other factor, is probably the basis of interracial marriages among servicemen overseas. The American soldier abroad is generally at the age when the males of our society are extremely "marriageable" and have intense romantic expectations for marriage. If his field of eligibles is almost completely limited to local girls of another race, it is not surprising that he would date one of these girls, discover for himself the foolishness of the American racial bias, and then marry the girl.

But such a hope is often disappointed. Interracial marriage, he discovers, does not solve his problems as a non-white, but rather, increases them: both he and his spouse are placed in a more socially vulnerable position, physically, emotionally, and psychologically, than either of them had experienced before marriage.

It must be emphasized that all of the above "motivations" are not necessarily involved in interracial marriage. As we have said, it is probable that in most interracial marriages the couple marry for precisely the same reasons that a racially homogamous couple would marry. Whatever the motives and/or attractions they can do their best to transform their new social vulnerability and difficulty into a social and a personal victory. And in the process of this attempt, they themselves will be presented with an opportunity to attain a kind of maturity that separately they would probably never have known—the kind of maturity that demands the intimate treatment of people as individuals, not as members of a group or as means to further one's own selfish wishes. This is one promise of interracial marriage; and regardless of the motivation that leads to the marriage, the final result is in many cases the fulfillment of this promise.

Success of interracial marriage. In all parts of the nation, considerably more interracial marriages than homogamous marriages terminate in desertion, annulment, separation, or divorce. In Hawaii, for example, the one state where data are presently available, the divorce rate for interracial marriages during the period 1952 – 1954 was 30 percent, as compared to 20 percent for homogamous marriages (Cheng and Yamamura, 1957). Interracial marriages also have a higher failure rate than other kinds of intermarriage.

Gordon (1964), in his very thorough study of the subject, suggests that the many manifestations of social and racial discrimination place a heavy burden upon the interracial couple and add special problems of adjustment which homogamous couples do not have to resolve. Further, he believes that the adjustment complications introduced by discrimination against the offspring of an interracial marriage are perhaps the most significant aspect of the couple's difficulties.

On the other hand, a study of Negro-white marriages in Indiana, when interracial marriage was illegal in that state, concluded that "the external pressures faced by the interracial couples are often great but certainly do not appear to be overwhelming" (Pavela, 1959). And two studies of Japanese-American marriages revealed that the mixed marriages examined were just as happy as homogamous marriages (Strauss, 1955; and Schnepp and Masoko, 1955).

Blood (1969), in discussing all kinds of mixed marriages, points out:

The very anxiety created by the prospect of a mixed marriage, the warnings of others, and the soul-searching deliberations guarantee that once the commitment to marriage is finally made, it is likely to be a firm one. To marry in the face of contrary advice is to make a public commitment which is unusually humiliating to break. Not only to outsiders but to oneself and to each other, the resolve to make a go of it is unusually explicit—and unusually necessary. Firm commitment will not guarantee success, but it helps mixed couples get through the crises they are bound to encounter (p. 98).

It is conceivable that the motivational factors for interracial marriage may in many cases balance the societal pressures and discriminations against the marriage. The very fact that an interracial couple go through with the marriage indicates the high motivation of both partners for facing societal obstacles and for marrying in spite of them. Thus the couple's compatibility may be so unusually high, in comparison to the compatibility of homogamous couples, that the marriage may succeed despite the social context in which it takes place.

Interfaith Marriage

An interfaith marriage is a marriage contracted by two persons of different religions. In the United States, the term *interfaith* usually refers to a marriage that "mixes" a Protestant, a Catholic, or a Jew (the three principal religions of the country), although marriage of a Methodist to an Episcopalian, say, or of a Conservative Jew to a Reform Jew, may also be considered interfaith — at least by the families of the married couple.

Interfaith marriages in the United States are more numerous than interracial marriages, but they are still somewhat rare. The national incidence of interfaith marriages is only 6.4 percent of all marriages performed in the United States. About 9 percent of Protestants marry non-Protestants, about 22 percent of Catholics marry non-Catholics, and about 7 percent of Jews marry non-Jews.[14] Conversely stated, 91.4 percent of Protestants marry other Protestants, 78.5 percent of Catholics marry other Catholics, and 92.8 percent of Jews marry other Jews (U.S. Bureau of the Census).

The incidence of interfaith marriage among the Protestant and Catholic groups appears to vary with such factors as residential area and the socioeconomic level of the persons. For instance, in Connecticut, where there are fewer Catholics per the total population than in the national average, more than 50 percent of Catholics marry outside their faith — which is more than twice the national figure for Catholic–non-Catholic marriages (Thomas, 1951). In general (and not surprisingly) it would seem that the lower the percentage of Catholics in the population, the higher the rate of Catholic interfaith marriage. The rate of interfaith marriages contracted by Catholics in Connecticut also was found by Thomas to vary according to socioeconomic level, with 8 percent among Catholics who lived in low-rent urban areas, 12 percent among Catholics who lived in middle-level urban areas, 18 percent among Catholics who lived in upper-level urban areas, and 19 percent among Catholics who lived in the suburbs.

The higher rate of interfaith marriages among the higher socioeconomic group suggests that the more "worldly" view that usually accompanies the better education, wider experience, and higher income of the upper social levels will tend to negate the traditional Catholic objections to interfaith marriage.

These same determinants of geographic location and socioeconomic level affect the interfaith marriage rate of Protestants; but, apparently, they do not hold

---

[14] A further breakdown of these figures reveals that 8.4 percent of Protestants marry Catholics, and 0.2 percent marry Jews. Of Catholic mixed marriages, 21.2 percent are with Protestants and 0.4 percent are with Jews.

true for Jews, who—although they are almost always a small minority in any particular community and although they are generally of the middle class or higher—have a low rate of interfaith marriage. This is probably explained by the strong ethnic and religious identification of many American Jews, by the significant differences between the tenets of Christianity and Judaism, and by the official discouragement by the Jewish religious leadership of interfaith marriage. Although the Catholic church has also always strongly discouraged interfaith marriage and makes such marriages difficult by demanding several difficult prerequisite agreements and procedures (see p. 337), the Catholic rate is considerably higher than that of either the Protestant or the Jew. It is probable that the reason for this higher rate is (1) the minority position of Catholics in the population of most American communities and (2) the ethnic diversity of the church membership—a diversity that prevents the kind of strong motivation for intrafaith marriage that the Jews experience.

The most recent available data indicate that interfaith marriages are becoming more numerous among all three major religions in our society (see Gordon, 1964), particularly among persons who have attended college—now about 45 percent of the population. A college background, in providing a humanistic perspective, tends to act as a leveler of racial, ethnic, and religious differences. Yet, interfaith marriages continue to be discouraged and, in some cases, even forbidden by official religious doctrine. Thus there is a growing conflict between institutional attitudes toward interfaith marriages and individual decisions to violate those institutional attitudes.[15]

Institutional attitudes toward interfaith marriage. Prior to the separation of church and state in western societies in the 18th and 19th centuries, interfaith marriage was not even a possibility. And even now, within all three major religions of the United States, there still exists an express opposition to interfaith marriage. This opposition is largely based on two fears: (1) that the family life of the couple may be disrupted if husband and wife do not belong to the same faith; and (2) that religious affiliation may weaken or dissolve as a result of interfaith marriage. As a matter of fact, from the point of view of institutionalized religion these fears are justified. For instance, between one third and one half of all American Protestants who marry people of other faiths subsequently withdraw from their congregations (Bossard and Boll, 1956; Pike, 1954); one third of all American Catholics who marry outside the church are lost to the church (Thomas, 1956; Bishops' Committee on Mixed Marriages, 1943); and, finally, a very large proportion of American Jews who marry outside their faith drop their active interest and participation in the faith (Barron, 1946; Slotkin, 1943). Thus, the major religions generally forbid the officiating of their ministers, priests, and rabbis at an interfaith marriage—unless a special dispensation has been granted or unless one of the partners converts.

---

[15]In a recent survey among college students, however, only 10 percent of the Jewish sample expressed a readiness to marry outside their faith, as compared with 27 percent of the Catholic sample and 45 percent of the Protestant sample (Berman, 1968).

The Protestant attitude toward interfaith marriage is summarized in the following:

Of the 250 varieties of organized Protestantism in America today, the vast majority have expressed their disfavor of interfaith marriages through church documents. There are even those denominations that oppose marriage between members of their own group and certain other Protestant sects. Fundamentalists and literalists most often urge their disciples to refrain from marriage with liberals (Gordon, 1964, p. 121).

The various Protestant denominations differ in the degree in which they oppose mixed marriage. For example, the Jehovah's Witnesses regard a marriage with anyone from outside their group as a mixed marriage (Gordon); and the theological differences, and therefore the biases, between some Protestant sects (say, Unitarians and Southern Baptists) are wider than those between some Episcopalians and Catholics.

The Catholic church is much more militant in its opposition to interfaith marriages than is the Protestant. Catholic law requires that its members be married in the church if a marriage is to be sanctioned and if the member wishes to remain in a state of grace and a member of the church. Catholic participation in a marriage before a civil official or a non-Catholic clergyman is expressly forbidden, and such a marriage, although legal in the view of non-Catholic clergy and civil authorities, is invalid in the view of the Catholic church. A Catholic who wishes to marry a non-Catholic must first receive dispensation from his priest and must make a "sincere promise" to remain steadfast in the Catholic faith and to do "all in his power" to have all the children baptized and brought up in the Catholic church.[16] The non-Catholic party must be informed of the promises that the Catholic party makes, and both parties are to be "clearly instructed on the ends and essential properties" of marriage, as they are perceived by the church (Pope Paul VI, *Apostolic Letter*, 1970). Since 1970, a Mass may be included as part of the marriage ceremony, subject to the local priest s consent.

Despite the promise to raise children in the Catholic faith, one study found that 50 percent of the offspring of valid Catholic–non-Catholic marriages are brought up as Protestants, and 5 percent are brought up "with no religion" (Gordon, p. 151). Another study of church-recognized mixed marriages revealed that 65 percent of male offspring and 75 percent of female offspring in such marriages follow the mother's faith—regardless of whether that faith is Catholicism or Protestantism (Landis, 1949).[17]

Judaism, like Protestantism and Catholicism, and for the same reasons, is opposed to interfaith marriage. It is also the most militant of all in its opposition.

---

[16] The hierarchy of the various territorial subdivisions of the Catholic church determine the way in which these promises, which are always required, shall be made—whether by word of mouth, in writing, or before witnesses.

[17] In both Catholic-Jewish and Protestant-Jewish mixed marriages, one study found that the offspring are most often brought up in the Jewish faith (Berman, 1968)

From its earliest history, Judaism has regarded interfaith marriage as a sin. Both the Talmud and the Rabbinical Codes declare that intermarriage is punishable by banning—the Judaic equivalent of excommunication. Various surveys show that Jewish identity is bound up with family loyalty and that Jews who intermarry demonstrate a history of alienation from their family. (On the other hand, Catholics who intermarry show a history of alienation from the church) (Berman, 1968).

> *Because of the special place that the home occupies in Judaism as a center of religious life and worship, almost co-ordinate with the Synagogue itself, Judaism holds it essential that both parties to a Jewish marriage be members of the Jewish faith. There is, of course, no objection to marriage with a sincere convert to Judaism. But it is not possible for the home to function in the manner prescribed by Jewish law unless both husband and wife are of the Jewish faith (Finkelstein, 1950, p. 1329).*

> *Our deep and abiding concern for the sanctity and the unity of the Jewish home, our profound commitment to the preservation of Judaism and the Jewish people make it imperative that the Reform Rabbinate do everything within its power consistent with the principles of liberal Judaism to discourage mixed marriages (Central Conference of American Rabbis, 1961).*

Unlike both Protestantism and Catholicism, Judaism has never proselytized; but any person who sincerely undertakes to study the history and theology of Judaism may become and may then be accepted as a proper mate for the Jew that he wishes to marry. The person who converts to Judaism in order to marry a member of the Jewish faith must promise to raise the children as Jews. Almost no orthodox and very few conservative rabbis will agree to or officiate at a mixed marriage. Some reform rabbis are more lenient, however, and Gordon (1964) estimates that as many as one fifth of reform rabbis perform the wedding without insisting upon the conversion of the non-Jewish partner, if that partner agrees to respect the other's faith and to raise the children as Jews.

Like Catholicism, Judaism does not recognize the legitimacy of civil marriage for its membership, and a Jew is properly married only when a rabbi has officiated. However, the Jewish faith does not forbid a dual ceremony in which the couple is married twice, once before a rabbi and then before a Christian clergyman. Since Catholicism specifically forbids such an arrangement, a Jewish-Catholic mixed marriage cannot be performed to the satisfaction of either religion and one of the partners would have to suffer excommunication or banning.

Motivation for interfaith marriage. As in any other kind of marriage, interfaith marriage may take place between two people simply because they fall in love and have complementary interests and needs. Other, less obvious, motives for interfaith marriage in the United States are suggested by Vincent (1959):

1. There may be a disproportionately small number of eligibles within a person's own religion as compared to the eligibles in other religions. For ex-

ample, two studies of Catholic interfaith marriage (Thomas, 1956 and 1951) revealed that in communities that are two thirds Catholic, less than one in five Catholics married outside the church; whereas in communities one twentieth Catholic, as many as three in four Catholics married non-Catholics. Thus, the distribution of Protestants, Catholics, and Jews in the total population of a community and the distribution of males and females within any one religious group will provide an obvious basis for interfaith marriage.

2. The pervasiveness of the middle-class culture in contemporary American society, along with the recent ecumenicalism of American religious bodies, has tended to blur religious differences — especially for young people. Thus, two people of different faiths may marry simply because they do not consider their religious differences to be a problem.

3. Marriage to someone of another faith may serve as a means of dissociating oneself from one's group or social class. Thus, lower-class and minority-group persons may drop their adherence to their own religion in order to marry someone of another, higher-status faith and, therefore, of a higher social rank. Indeed, interfaith marriage, particularly for females, is one of the commonest methods for moving up into middle-class membership.

4. An American male and female, whose religions are not the same but whose racial or ethnic membership is the same, may find that they have more in common than, say, a Chinese-American Methodist and a Scotch-American Methodist. In other words, two people of similar minority-culture backgrounds may be attracted to one another, despite their religious differences, because their homogamous cultural similarities carry more strength (see Hollingshead, 1959; and Williams, 1952).

5. What is popularly and officially classified an interfaith marriage may be no such thing; for the couple involved may be agnostic or may have very little commitment to religion, although each one is identified as a Protestant, Catholic, or Jew. Also, a person who falls in love with someone of another faith may find that the prejudice he feels toward the other's religion or the commitment he feels to his own religion is unfair or unrealistic or inconvenient.

6. Finally, adolescent rebellion may be a factor in many interfaith marriages of young people. The rebellious behavior may be directed against the parents; against the person's minority-group culture, which is strongly tied to a particular religion; against the person's majority-group culture, which he strongly identifies with intolerance for minority religions; or against society at large.

Success of interfaith marriage. No one really knows, or perhaps can ever know, whether a difference in the husband's and wife's religions is a more or less significant factor in the marriage than, say, a marked difference in metabolism, sexual appetite, or the various factors associated with social class. Religious leaders and counselors issue dire forebodings about the risks of interfaith marriages; but these opinions represent an unavoidable bias:

Ministers may emphasize that marital strife can result when husband and wife attend separate churches and seek to rear their children in different faiths. But do physiologists stress that marital strife can result when the cup of physical energy and health runneth over for one spouse, and runneth dry for the other? Or when 365 nights a year the husband wants three blankets — the wife but one? And when husband wants car windows closed — wife wants them open? (Vincent, 1959).

Objective research on mixed marriages is quite limited. There are no nationwide data, and we must rely upon regional and denominational research. The studies that are usually quoted in marriage-and-the-family texts agree that the percentage of marriages regarded as successful (did not end in divorce) in the sample populations was about 95 percent if the couple was religiously non-mixed and 85 percent if the mixture was Catholic-Protestant (Bell, 1938; Weeks, 1943; and Landis, 1949).[18] If each of the couple professed *no* religion, the number of successful marriages dropped to 82 percent for these populations. A more recent study (Zimmerman and Cervantes, 1960) also agrees with these earlier reports. Apparently, then, the actuarial expectation is that a Catholic-Protestant marriage has about a 10 percent greater possibility of ending in divorce than does a non-mixed marriage — that is, 85 percent of Catholic-Protestant marriages succeed, whereas 95 percent of religiously homogamous marriages succeed. This 10 percent difference is especially significant in that many texts cite the obverse — that is, that 15 percent of the mixed as compared to 5 percent of the non-mixed end in divorce — and conclude from this reversal of the statistics that the divorce *rate* of the mixed marriage is 3 times, or 300 percent, that of the non-mixed. This is simply not an accurate reading of statistics. (See Vernon, 1960, and Berman, 1968, for a further discussion of this point.)

The incidence of divorce in Christian-Jewish marriages is usually represented in texts as being higher than in Catholic-Protestant marriages. The study cited (Zimmerman and Cervantes, 1960) for this conclusion found that the divorce rate in Christian-Jewish marriages ranged from 25 percent (in Boston) to 62 percent (in Omaha). However, since this study was done on a different population (non-college instead of college) than that of the Catholic-Protestant study and since this study was not controlled for factors of income or social class, it may not really be validly compared to the Catholic-Protestant studies cited above.

A marriage between a member of a religion and a person who professes *no* religion was found in a study of the college population to have a slightly higher rate of divorce than a marriage involving different faiths. But this rate was no higher than when neither partner professed religious affiliation (Landis, 1949). This was confirmed by a study of the marriage-divorce records of the state of Iowa,[19] where it was found that although the divorce rate of religiously mixed vs. non-mixed marriages differed by only about 10 percent, the divorce rate of *non-affiliated* Protestants was 65 percent and the divorce rate of Catholic–*non-affiliated*

---

[18] Ironically, these data, which are so often utilized as demonstrating the high incidence of failure for *all* categories of interfaith marriages, are significantly lower than the national norm of failure for all marriages (25 percent) and *much* lower than the failure rates for low-income groups, early-marriage groups, and other categories.

[19] Iowa is the only state that requires a statement of religious affiliation on the marriage application.

Protestants was 71 percent (Burchinal and Chancellor, 1962)! Apparently the actuarial risk of marriage failure occurs not so much with *mixed* religions (although there seems to be some slight increase here) as it does with *non*-religious marriages — or marriages between persons who profess no church membership. There seems little question, in light of these recent data from Iowa, that the relative incidence of divorce is correlated more with the absence of religious affiliation than with degree of religious homogamy. Locke (1968) found, in comparing happily married couples with divorced couples, that controversy over religion was not specifically a factor in the failure of marriages.

It is probable, of course, that although an interfaith couple will not openly disagree with one another over their separate faiths, nor engage in discussions about comparative theology or the significance of the different religious rituals, they may feel resentment and uneasiness over such factors as the children's being indoctrinated into one or the other's religion, or the birth-control issue, or the particular religious practices that may affect or interfere with the daily routine of their marriage. And, of course, it is quite conceivable that differences in religious doctrine may be felt by the couple in many other areas, and in many divisive ways, without the couple's necessarily being consciously aware of the religious nature of their conflicts.

Finally, it must be emphasized that one of the crucial things in a mixed interfaith marriage is the degree of commitment which the person feels toward his faith.

A Catholic-Jewish marriage might have no strain if neither of them happens to be strongly committed to religion, whereas a Methodist-Baptist marriage could be marked by much religious friction if each is strongly committed. Similarly, friction could occur between two people of the same faith, if one is strongly committed and the other not.[20]

Interethnic Marriage

There are no figures available as to the extent of interethnic marriage in the United States. Evidence indicates, however, that there is far more interethnic marriage than there is interracial, or even interfaith. "Interethnic marriages among the American people are becoming more common as the years pass. The preservation of racial and religious ties, in that order, are definitely of much greater concern to us" (Gordon, 1964, p. 301).

Ethnic groups seldom persist beyond the first generation in the United States and almost never persist into the third.

There is evidence that the distinctive cultural ties of native-born Americans are not as strong as they were among their foreign-born ancestors. Mores and folkways are often ignored, national origins forgotten, and the desire to perpetuate distinctive languages, dress and value systems appears to be waning (Gordon, 1964, p. 296).

---

[20]Henry L. Manheim, Professor of Sociology, Arizona State University, 1967 (private correspondence).

The structure of our society is such that the immigrant family usually absorbs our language and cultural patterns by the second generation. The children of these families often consciously reject the ethnic identification of their parents.

The motivation for marrying across ethnic lines is probably the same as it is for homogamous marriage in most cases, although it is conceivable that such motives as the "lure of the exotic," "rebelliousness" (in the second-generation children), and "marrying up" may be operant.

There are no data available about the comparative divorce rates of interethnic marriages as compared to homogamous marriages, since marriage applications do not usually request ethnic information. However, we can hypothesize that the ethnic factors operant in the relative success of interethnic marriage are probably chiefly related to the attitudes of in-laws and friends rather than to any generalized discriminatory pressure of society.

Interclass Marriage

The category of interclass marriage is included among the categories of inter-racial, interfaith, and interethnic primarily to indicate its probable importance. Very little data may be cited. No state requires (or even requests) a marriage-license applicant to note his social class status. Moreover, there would be little agreement between a person and sociologists about his class status, even if he *were* required to note it on the application. (Most persons estimate their social class as being at least one step higher than a sociologist would estimate it.)

Nevertheless, it is conceivable that class differences may be as significantly cor-related with marriage difficulties as are differences of race or religion. Roth and Peck (1951), for example, found that in class-homogamous marriages, 53 per-cent make a "good" adjustment, that is, their marriage is successful. In mixed-class marriages which are husband-high, wife-low mixtures, 35 percent make a "good" adjustment; whereas in wife-high, husband-low mixtures only 28 per-cent make a "good" adjustment.[21]

Thus, there is considerable speculation that the cultural differences resulting from social-class membership are of considerable importance in marital adjust-ment.[22] However, the extent of this importance cannot even be estimated until further research is available.

---

[21] Roth and Peck analyzed marital and social-class data that were published by Burgess and Cottrell in 1939. Thus, the data they were working with are presently over 30 years old.

[22] For example, a few representative leading marriage-and-the-family texts contain the following *apropos* mixed-class marriage: Paul Landis (1970)—speculates about the importance of class (great) but gives no citation; Cavan (1969)—speculates about the importance of class (great) and cites Hunt (1949), who studied various factors but especially propinquity and mate selection, and Roth and Peck (1951), who are cited above; Peterson (1964)—speculates about the importance of class (great) and cites Centers (1949), who studied occupation and mate selection, and Cavan, who cites Roth and Peck. The Hunt and Centers data are interesting and support speculation on this topic but are not as pertinent as Roth and Peck's—which are, however, based upon data 30 years old (Burgess and Cottrell, 1939). None of these studies represent themselves as definitive, and Roth and Peck is the only one to address the problem of social class within marriage specifically. The others investigate class and mate selection.

Military Service and Marriage

The service marriage is of interest to more and more young adults in our society as (1) the "peacetime" utilization of the universal draft remains at an unprecedented high, and (2) the age at marriage continues to decline. As more and more young American men are being drafted into the armed forces, more girls are being faced with the question of whether to marry now or wait until their boyfriends have served their tours of duty and have returned to civilian life. The two young people confronted with impending separation may feel the need to bind themselves by marriage and thus avoid the risk of losing one another through the long separation. But to marry *because of* an impending separation is even more risky than marrying *despite* an impending separation (Bowman, 1965).

If a wife cannot follow and live with her husband, their marriage is similar to other marriages only in the formal sense of having been legally contracted. The social and interpersonal components of marriage — living together, providing resources and fulfilling needs for one another, sexual interaction, altruistic support, and establishment of a family — will be absent. On the other hand, if the wife is allowed to live with her husband on a military post, she will discover the role of a military wife to be somewhat different from that of a civilian wife, particularly in regard to the military caste system, which limits the possible social interactions; the residential impermanence, which results from the husband's periodic reassignments; the small income of servicemen; and the very limited leisure time in which a serviceman is able to be at home.

Most females who marry a young man entering the armed forces today are constrained to wait at home while he serves out his tour of duty. If the absence is extended, the wife may become bored and lonely and therefore decide to begin dating — merely as a social activity. But, often, the sexual and mate-

selection aspects of dating will, despite the girl's good intentions, become involved in the new relation — a circumstance that is, of course, frowned on by most of society and usually causes the girl to feel either disloyal and guilty or frustrated that she is tied down by her marriage. The husband, of course, is in a similar or perhaps even more difficult situation, since the social pattern of the soldier's life includes not only loneliness but also an especial focus on sexual activity, promiscuity, and "making it" with the local girls.

When the period of separation is over and husband and wife are reunited, they often find each other changed. Since enormous personality changes can occur with the transition from late teens to early twenties—from the end of adolescence to the onset of adulthood—often the romantic attraction of their earlier love vanishes and each may seem almost a stranger to the other. Even more importantly, the experiences each has known in his absence from the other may have been among the most significant experiences of his life; and their effect may be to create feelings of distance and incompatibility.

Many couples decide against marriage before their separation by military service. Although these couples are just as committed to each other as those couples who marry, and although they are just as eager to formalize their relation, they choose another, less risky, solution, that of formal engagement. This solution has the advantage of leaving the couple free from the possible later difficulties of trying to make successful a marriage that has already come to be regretted. And it has the further advantage that a "Dear John" letter is far less traumatic than divorce proceedings.

Marriage While in College

Campus marriages are a rather recent phenomenon in our society. Before World War II, many colleges and universities actually expelled students who married while in school; but with the return in the late 1940s of tens of thousands of veterans who attended schools all over the country on the GI Bill, the married student ceased to be a statistical rarity. In 1965, 22 percent of all college students in the United States were married and living with their spouses. For those attending college part time, 61 percent of men were married, as were 49 percent of women. Among full-time college students, 6 percent of women were married, as were 15 percent of men.[23]

Perhaps the central reason for this large percentage of student marriages is the increasing stresses associated with the contemporary American mass society. Among the present generation of young people, the need to belong—the need for emotional support and security, for companionship, for love, for a *permanent paired relation*—has become more pressing and significant in the context of our impersonal and materialist society. Marriage is the only primary institution in our society that can reliably and satisfactorily fulfill this need. The need and, in recent times, the expectation for a complete heterosexual life in early adulthood has also contributed to the increasing number of campus marriages.[24]

---

[23]U. S. Bureau of the Census, "School Enrollment," *Current Population Reports*, Series P-20, No. 162, 1967.

[24]With the development of the pill and the changing societal attitudes during the late 1960s, an increasing number of college students also began living openly together without marriage (see *Sexual Behavior in the 70s—A Sexual Revolution?* in Chapter Four).

The difficulty with these marriages was, and still is, that the expected roles and resource provisions of marriage usually cannot be fulfilled with the many interpersonal and economic stresses of student life. The husband, for example, who both works and attends classes knows that if he falls behind on his job he may be fired but that if he doesn't keep up his grades he will flunk out and probably have to accept a substandard income and an unwanted occupation for the rest of his life. On the other hand, if his wife works to support them and any children they may have, he may feel guilty or ashamed at not fulfilling what he considers to be the traditional bread-winning role of the husband. At the same time, the working

wife may resent the time her student husband devotes in the evenings and on weekends to his studies and may regret that she too cannot experience the social and intellectual stimulation of student life.

If the wife does not work but, like her husband, is a student, she may feel little incentive to continue with her education since she has already found the security and status of a husband; thus, with the first pregnancy, the student wife almost always discontinues full-time class attendance. Pregnancy and birth also create additional economic pressures on the marriage. Often with the birth of the first child, a husband's educational goal becomes a purely practical one of achieving job qualification, rather than the more general and beneficial goal of knowledge and self-development (Mead, 1960). This cessation of intellectual inquiry and its replacement by female housework and male vocational preparation will also commonly occur even when pregnancy or a child is not involved.

Intellectual life demands some kind of postponement of his early domesticity . . . which has always been characteristic of most savages, of most peasants and of the urban poor. . . . In European history it has been the young men of the elite class who have been permitted to postpone responsibility while they have had a chance in some reasonably protected environment to think, and to make friends . . . and discuss things, and develop and change their minds and explore. This is the thing we're cutting out in this country.

Early student marriage is domesticating boys so early they don't have a chance for full intellectual development. They don't have a chance to give their entire time, not necessarily to study in the sense of staying in the library . . . but in the sense that the married students don't have time to experiment, to think, to sit up all night in bull sessions, to develop as individuals. . . . There is a tendency to substitute easy domesticity for a period of stretching one's intellectual and ethical muscles before one settles down (Mead, 1960).

There are as yet no national data concerning the relative expectation for success of campus marriages as compared to post-college marriages. The few regional studies which have been done are of the questionnaire type (asking a married student if he is happily married), and in these studies one fourth of the students said that they would *not* marry while in college if they had it to do over again (Landis, 1948; Christensen and Philbrick, 1952). This figure is slightly less than the one in three national divorce rate but much higher than the divorce rate for college graduates. (There is no evidence, however, and this is not to imply, that the divorce rate for campus marriages is any higher than it is for college-educated couples who marry after graduation.)

Summary

Marriage for the second time, interracial, interethnic, interfaith, and interclass marriage, marriage while in the service, and marriage while in college are special circumstances which affect a rather sizable minority of our population.

About one in five of our married population are in a second marriage. Interracial marriage nationally involves only a fraction of all marriages but is much higher for college groups and servicemen stationed overseas. Interfaith marriage, although formally discouraged or opposed by all three major religions, involves about one in five Catholics, about one in ten Protestants, and less than one in ten Jews. Campus marriage, almost unknown just a generation ago, now involves one in five undergraduates and more than half of graduate students.

Although many second marriages succeed, the rate of failure is almost double that of first marriages. Very little is known of the success of interracial marriages. Although interracial couples face more problems than homogamous couples, research indicates that they may have compensating factors of motivation which may tend to equalize the difficulties to some extent. The person contemplating an interracial marriage should be well aware of the difficulties, however, especially for his offspring, and should be certain of his motivation. Most interfaith marriages succeed, although they have a somewhat higher rate of divorce (about 10 percent) than do religiously homogamous marriages. The degree of religious devotion may be a more significant success factor than formal membership in a particular church; and non-religious marriages have a significantly higher rate of failure than do mixed marriages. Interethnic and interclass marriages are much more frequent than any other type of intermarriage, but there is very little data available on the incidence of such marriages. Speculation would indicate that interethnic difficulties are probably negligible, whereas interclass difficulties may be quite pronounced.

Marriage while in the service imposes unusual hardships, whether the wife follows the husband from base to base or remains at home. If the couple wish to establish a permanent relation during his service they would be well advised to consider engagement rather than marriage.

Campus marriages limit freedom of inquiry and movement and impose the responsibilities of marriage and a family at the very time that a person can most profit from independence of societal and economic demands. There is little data about the success of campus marriages, but it is estimated that about one fourth of the persons involved in such marriages regret their early marriage to some extent.

Questions

1   What are some of the motivating factors for remarriage among widowed and divorced persons?
2   Why is the divorce rate somewhat higher in second marriages than the rate for first marriages?
3   Give four reasons why a person may *not* remarry.
4   What does the term intermarriage mean?
5   What is meant by the popular concept of race?
6   What is the scientific concept of race?
7   What is usually our society's attitude toward the interracial couple and their children?
8   What are some of the motivations for interracial marriage?
9   Discuss the successes of mixed marriages.
10 What does the higher rate of interfaith marriages in the higher socioeconomic group suggest?
11 Why is the Catholic rate of intermarriage considerably higher than that of either the Protestant or Jewish rate?
12 Discuss the Protestant attitude toward interfaith marriage.
13 Discuss the Catholic attitude toward interfaith marriage.
14 What is the attitude of Judaism toward interfaith marriage?
15 Discuss motivation for interfaith marriage.
16 Why is the interethnic marriage becoming more common in America?
17 How is a wife's role on a military post different from that of a civilian wife?
18 If a couple want to establish a permanent relation during the male's military service, what course of action would probably be best?
19 What is the main difficulty with campus marriages?

References and Selected Readings

Adams, Romanzo. *Interracial Marriage in Hawaii.* Reprint Series in Criminology, Law Enforcement, and Social Problems, No. 65. Montclair, N. J.: Patterson-Smith, 1969.

Baber, Ray E. *Marriage and the Family*, 2nd ed. New York: McGraw-Hill, 1953.

Barron, Milton J. The Incidence of Jewish Intermarriage in Europe and America. *American Sociological Review*, February 1946, Vol. 11, pp. 11–12.

_____. *People Who Intermarry.* Syracuse, N. Y.: Syracuse University Press, 1946.

_____. Research on Intermarriage: A Survey of Accomplishments and Prospects. *American Journal of Sociology,* November 1951, Vol. 57, pp. 249–255.

Bell, Howard M. *Youth Tell Their Story.* Washington, D. C.: American Council on Education, 1938.

Berman, Louis Arthur. *Jews and Intermarriage.* New York: T. Yoseloff, 1968.

Bernard, Jessie. Infidelity: Moral or Social Issue? *Science and Psychoanalysis,* 1970, Vol. 16.

_____. *Marriage and Family among Negroes.* New York: Prentice-Hall, 1965.

_____. *Remarriage.* New York: Dryden Press, 1956.

Bishops' Committee on Mixed Marriages. *A Factual Study of Mixed Marriages.* Washington, D. C.: National Catholic Welfare Conference, 1943.

Blood, Robert O. *Marriage,* 2nd ed. New York: Free Press, 1969.

Bossard, James H.S., and Eleanor Stoker Boll. *One Marriage, Two Faiths.* New York: Ronald Press, 1956.

Burchinal, Lee G., and Loren E. Chancellor. Survival Rates among Religiously Homogamous and Interreligious Marriages. *Agricultural and Home Economics Experiment Station Research Bulletin 512,* December 1962.

Burgess, E. W., and L. S. Cottrell. *Predicting Success or Failure in Marriage.* Englewood Cliffs, N. J.: Prentice-Hall, 1939.

Carter, Hugh, and Paul C. Glick. *Marriage and Divorce: A Social and Economic Study.* Cambridge, Mass.: Harvard University Press, 1970.

Cavan, Ruth S. *American Family,* 4th ed. New York: Crowell, 1969.

Centers, Richard. Marital Selection and Occupational Strata. *American Journal of Sociology,* 1949, Vol. 44, p. 533.

Central Conference of American Rabbis, eds. *Rabbi's Manual.* New York, 1961.

Chancellor, Loren E., and Thomas P. Monohan. Religious Preference and Interreligious Mixtures in Marriages and Divorces in Iowa. *American Journal of Sociology,* November 1955, Vol. 61, pp. 233–239.

Cheng, C. K., and Douglas S. Yamamura. Interracial Marriage and Divorce in Hawaii. *Social Forces,* October 1957, Vol. 36, pp. 83–84.

Christensen, Harold T., and Robert E. Philbrick. Family Size as a Factor in the Marital Adjustments of College Students. *American Sociological Review,* June 1952, Vol. 17, pp. 306–312.

Downs, Ivan. Black–White Dating. *Life,* May 28, 1971, Vol. 20, pp. 56–57.

Drake, St. Clair, and Horace R. Clayton. *Black Metropolis.* New York: Harcourt, 1945.

Dunn, L. C., and T. Dobzhansky. *Heredity, Race, and Society.* New York: New American Library, 1952.

Erlich, Paul R., and Richard W. Holm. A Biological View of Race. In Ashley Montagu, ed. *The Concept of Race.* New York: Macmillan, 1969.

Finkelstein, Louis, ed. *The Jews,* Vol. I, 4th ed. New York: Schocken, 1970.

Fox, Robin. *Kinship and Marriage.* Baltimore: Penguin Books, 1968.

Gebhard, Paul. Postmarital Coitus among Widows and Divorcees. In Paul Bohannan *et al.,* eds., *Divorce and After.* New York: Doubleday, 1970.

Glick, Paul C. *American Families.* New York: Wiley, 1957.

_____, and Arthur J. Norton. Frequency, Duration, and Probability of Marriage and Divorce. *Journal of Marriage and The Family,* May 1971, Vol. 33, pp. 307–317.

Golden, Joseph. Patterns of Negro-White Intermarriage. *American Sociological Review,* April 1954, Vol. 19, pp. 154 ff.

_____. Characteristics in the Negro-White Intermarried in Philadelphia. *American Sociological Review,* 1953, Vol. 18, pp. 177–183.

Goldstein, Sidney, and Calvin Goldscheider. Social and Demographic Aspects of Jewish Intermarriages. *Social Problems,* 1966, Vol. 13, pp. 386–399.

Goode, William J. *Women in Divorce.* New York: Free Press, 1965.

Gordon, Albert L. *Intermarriage.* Boston: Beacon Press, 1964.

Hathorn, Rev. Raban, Rev. William H. Genne, and Rabbi Mordecai L. Brill *et al. Marriage: An Interfaith Guide for All Couples.* New York: Association Press, 1971.

Heiss, Jerold S. Premarital Characteristics of Religiously Intermarried. *American Sociological Review,* 1960, Vol. 25, pp. 47–55.

Hollingshead, August B. Cultural Factors in the Selection of Marriage Mates. *American Sociological Review,* 1959, Vol. 15, pp. 619–627.

Horowitz, Irving L., and Lee Rainwater. Social Accounting for the Nation. *Trans-action,* 1967, Vol. 4, pp. 2–3.

Hunt, Chester L., and Richard W. Collier. Intermarriage and Cultural Change: A Study of Philippine-American Marriages. *Social Forces,* 1957, Vol. 35, pp. 223–230.

Hunt, T. C. Occupational Status and Marriage Selection. *American Sociological Review,* 1940, Vol. 5, pp. 494–504.

_____. Occupational Status and Marriage Selection. *American Journal of Sociology,* 1949, Vol. 44, p. 533.

Israel, Robert J. A Note on Counseling Young People Contemplating Intermarriage. *Campus 1966: Change and Challenge.* Washington, D. C.: B'nai B'rith Hillel Foundation, 1967, pp. 47–54.

Jacobson, Paul H. *American Marriage and Divorce.* New York: Rinehart, 1959.

Kohn, Melvin L. *Class and Conformity: A Study in Values.* New York: National Institute of Mental Health, 1969.

Landis, Judson T. and Mary G. *Building a Successful Marriage,* 5th ed. Englewood Cliffs, N. J.: Prentice-Hall, 1968.

Landis, Judson T. Marriages of Mixed and Non-Mixed Religious Faith. *American Sociological Review,* June 1949, Vol. 14, pp. 401–407.

_____. On the Campus. *Survey Mid-monthly,* January 1948, Vol. 84, pp. 17–19.

Landis, Paul H. *Making the Most of Marriage.* New York: Appleton-Century-Crofts, 1970.

_____. Sequential Marriage. *Journal of Home Economics,* October 1950, Vol. 42, pp. 626–628.

Larsson, Clotye Murdock, ed. *Marriage across the Color Line.* Chicago: Johnson, 1965.

Locke, H. J. *Predicting Adjustment in Marriage.* Westport, Conn.: Greenwood, 1968.

Mayer, John E. *Jewish-Gentile Courtships.* New York: Free Press, 1961.

Mead, Margaret. A New Look at Early Marriages. *U. S. News and World Report* (1960). Reprinted in Bowman, *Marriage for Moderns* (1965).

_____ et al., eds. *Science and the Concept of Race.* New York: Columbia University Press, 1968.

Merton, Robert K. Intermarriage and the Social Structure: Fact and Theory. *Psychiatry,* August 1941, Vol. 4, pp. 361–374.

Monohan, Thomas P. The Changing Nature and Instability of Remarriages. *Eugenics Quarterly,* 1958, Vol. 5, pp. 78–85.

_____. The Duration of Marriage to Divorce: Second Marriages and Migratory Types. *Marriage and Family Living,* May 1959, Vol. 21, pp. 134–138.

_____. How Stable are Remarriages? *American Sociological Review,* November 1952, Vol. 58, pp. 280–298.

Montagu, Ashley. *The Concept of Race.* New York: Macmillan, 1969.

Pavela, Todd H. *An Exploratory Study of Negro-White Intermarriage in Indiana.* Chicago Urban League, 1958–1959.

Peterson, James A. *Education for Marriage.* New York: Scribner's, 1964.

Polish, David. The Problem of Intermarriage—Will Moderation Help? *CCAR Journal,* 1964, Vol. 11, pp. 33–37.

Pope Paul VI. *An Apostolic Letter Determining Norms for Mixed Marriages,* April 29, 1970.

Prewitt, Kenneth. Institutional Racism in American Society. In Lloyd Saxton and Walter Kaufmann, eds., *The American Scene: Social Problems of the Seventies.* Belmont, Calif.: Wadsworth, 1970, pp. 195–211.

Prince, Alfred J. A Study of 194 Cross-Religious Marriages. *The Family Life Coordinator,* January 1962, Vol. 11, pp. 3–6.

Resnick, Reuben B. Some Sociological Aspects of Intermarriage of Jew and Non-Jew. *Social Forces,* October 1933, Vol. 12, pp. 94–102.

Risdon, Randall. A Study of Interracial Marriages Based on Data for Los Angeles County. *Sociology and Social Research,* 1954, Vol. 39, pp. 92–95.

Roth, Julius, and Robert F. Peck. Social Class and Social Mobility Factors Related to Marital Adjustment. *American Sociological Review,* 1951, Vol. 16, pp. 478–487.

Schmitt, Robert C. Recent Trends in Hawaiian Interracial Marriage Rates by Occupation. *Journal of Marriage and the Family,* May 1971, Vol. 33, pp. 373–374.

Schnepp, Gerald and Jui, and Agnes Masoko. Cultural and Marital Adjustment of Japanese War Brides. *American Journal of Sociology,* July 1955, Vol. 61, pp. 48–50.

Schnepp, Gerald. *Leakage from a Catholic Parish.* Washington, D. C.: Catholic University of America Press, 1942.

Simpson, George E., and J. Milton Yinger. *Racial and Cultural Minorities,* 3rd ed. New York: Harper, 1965.

Sklare, Marshall. Intermarriage and the Jewish Future. *Commentary,* 1964, Vol. 37, pp. 46–52.

Slotkin, J. S. Jewish-Gentile Intermarriage in Chicago. *American Sociological Review,* February 1943, Vol. 7, pp. 34–39.

Strauss, Anselm L. Strain and Harmony in American-Japanese

War Bride Marriages. *Marriage and Family Living*, 1954, Vol. 16, pp. 99–106.

Terman, L. M. *Psychological Factors in Marital Happiness.* New York: McGraw-Hill, 1938.

Thomas, John L. *The American Catholic Family.* Englewood Cliffs, N. J.: Prentice-Hall, 1956.

_____. The Factor of Religion in Selection of Marriage Mates. *American Sociological Review*, August 1951, Vol. 16, pp. 487–491.

Vernon, Glenn M. Bias in Professional Publications Concerning Interfaith Marriages. *Religious Education*, July–August 1960, Vol. 55, pp. 261–264.

Vincent, Clark E. Interfaith Marriages: Problem or Symptom? In James C. Zahn, ed., *Religion and the Face of America.* Berkeley: University of California Press, 1959.

Weeks, Ashley H. Differential Divorce Rates by Occupation. *Social Forces*, March 1943, Vol. 21, p. 336.

Williams, J. Paul. *What Americans Believe and How They Worship.* New York: Harper, 1952.

Winch, Robert F. *The Modern Family*, rev. ed. New York: Holt, 1963.

Zimmerman, Carle C., and Lucius F. Cervantes. *Successful American Families.* New York: Pageant Press, 1960.

Chapter Nine

The Economics of Marriage

Getting money is like digging with a
needle; spending it is like
water soaking into sand.

Japanese proverb

oney is a vital force in nearly every facet of man's life. More of his waking hours are engaged with the earning of it than with anything else, and his entire life style is tied to his pattern of spending it. From the very beginnings of civilization, money has been a major part of man's consciousness. Most people are concerned, more or less continually and both consciously and unconsciously, with the solution of their private money problems, and all ramifications of money have a powerful effect upon the person's inner feelings of satisfaction or anxiety. The psychological effect of money is such that spending it is often necessary to feelings of security and self confidence, just as the proper use of money gives a person a sense of well-being and emotional security.

All of this is not to imply, of course, that a fixation on the possession of money for its own sake, or for the objects that it can buy, is essential to the pursuit of a meaningful, productive, rewarding life.[1] The point is, rather, that a lack of sufficient money, or its improper use, can mean deprivations, indignities, anxieties, and conflict for the person as well as loss of opportunities for his children; while sufficient money, properly used, will bring much good for the

---

[1] The importance of money to the normal person is its use as a medium of exchange; love of money itself, or its accumulation for its own sake, is a deviant need. The respected and influential British economist Lord Keynes (1932) put this very strongly:

The love of money as a possession — as distinguished from the love of money as a means to the enjoyments and realities of life—... is a somewhat disgusting morbidity, one of those semi-criminal, semi-pathological propensities which one hands over with a shudder to the specialists in mental disease.

The same thought was summed up centuries ago in this often misquoted phrase from the New Testament: "The love of money is the root of all evil" (Timothy 6:10).

person—adequate medical and dental care, easy access to the material necessities and comforts of life, the benefits and pleasures of education, travel, and the arts, and, finally, the ability to launch his children successfully.

The importance of money and man's preoccupation with it is reflected in the enormous number of aphorisms on the subject:

"A heavy purse makes a light heart" (16th-century English proverb). "Lack of money is the root of all evil" (George Bernard Shaw). "Money is like a sixth sense without which you cannot make the most of the other five" (Somerset Maugham). "It's a kind of spiritual snobbery that makes people think they can be happy without money" (Albert Camus). "Wine maketh merry but money answereth all things" (Ecclesiastes 10:19). "There are three faithful friends—an old wife, an old dog, and ready money" (Benjamin Franklin).

And, finally, as Ogden Nash succinctly put it:

> *Certainly there are lots of things in life that money*
> *won't buy, but it's very funny—*
> *Have you ever tried to buy them without money?*

Despite the extreme importance of money—and, most important, the management of that money, or *personal finance*—the subject is quite often cloaked in virtually impenetrable silence. Most people are as secretive and ignorant about their financial situation as Victorian ladies were about their sexuality. Together, the two areas of money and sex form a twin dimension of ignorance and ineptness in American life, and particularly in American marriage. In fact, the average person knows even less about personal finance than he knows about sex; for the onus of dullness which surrounds the subject of money makes it even more forbidding to most people. Money is regarded, *per se*, as a boring subject. Economics is called "the dismal science."

It is curious that the study of money and how to handle it effectively is so often considered dull. Money should be one of the most fascinating subjects imaginable, involved as it is in almost everything we do. Moreover, the study of how to handle it effectively pays such immediate and rich dividends not only in directing cash flow in such a way as to enhance the person's life style but in greatly lessening the tension and anxiety of financial uncertainty. Mishandling money, on the other hand, will result in a depressed and deprived life style, and, far too often, an unhappy or ruined marriage.

Money and Marital Conflict

One of the obvious and most basic facts about marriage in the United States is that for perhaps 98 percent of the families there will never be enough money. Inevitably, families who have incomes of $6,000 per year believe that if they earned but $2,000 more their financial needs would be satisfied, while families with incomes of $8,000 feel themselves just as economically oppressed as those earning $6,000 and are convinced that if they were earning $10,000 they would be satisfied. Incomes of $10,000, $20,000, even $30,000 still do not seem to provide enough money for the family to do *everything* it wants; for as income increases, the family's perceived needs and its spending increase even faster so that high-income families are often in deeper debt than medium-income families, who are more in debt than low-income families. With about one in five families in the lower-lower class, the problem, of course, is chiefly that of subsistence[2] — finding shelter and getting enough food to stay alive and enough clothing to keep covered and warm. For the rest of the nation it's a question of continually opting for better—and more expensive—food, housing, clothes, education, medical and dental care, and recreation and entertainment.

Since there is never "enough" money for the average American family, whatever the income level, sound money management is essential to the achievement of personal fulfillment as well as good marital and family relations. Marriage counselors and family-service agencies agree that economic stress is the main cause of conflict in American families—despite the fact that ours is an "affluent society." All recent studies indicate that married couples quarrel over money more than anything else, that economic factors are closely related to marital stability and critical to marital adjustment, and that economic stress is a major cause of marital failure.[3] Married couples quarrel both about allocation of present spending—who should spend how much for what—and about how to pay

<hr />

[2] Poverty is much more widespread in America than is generally realized. For example, the *average* industrial worker in 1967 was earning $5,800 per year, whereas the U. S. Bureau of Labor Statistics estimated a "modest but adequate" budget for that year as $6,900 for a family of four and $7,900 for a family of five. Incidentally, contrary to popular opinion, a large proportion of the U. S. poor live in families whose heads work: in 1967, 57 percent of all the U. S. poor were in households headed by working men or women. The working poor remain the truly forgotten Americans; for despite their low incomes they are unaided by welfare programs (Population Reference Bureau, 1969).

[3] See, for example, Landis, 1968; Goode, 1965, Chapters 4 and 5; LeMasters, 1957; and Goode, 1951. (Earlier studies such as Burgess and Cottrell, 1939, and Terman, 1938, which found no correlation between financial difficulty and marital disharmony, were based on homogenous samples and are therefore regarded as misleading. For a discussion and critique of these early studies, see LeMasters, 1957.)

the monthly bills for things they've *already* bought. Quarrels stem especially from personal expenditures and those for the children which the husband or wife regard as unnecessary or excessive.

Usually, the young couple first come face to face with the harsh reality of economic necessity only with the birth of a child. So long as they have only themselves and their own needs to look after, they are relatively free from the grinding stresses of indebtedness. Children, however, bring certain minimum costs below which it is simply not possible for a couple to go, given the basic needs of growing offspring. Moreover, the wife's income is usually lost with the birth of a child, so that at the same time that the family's expenditures soar, their income is cut.

These, then, are the major sources of economic conflict in marital relations:

1. *Conflict over bills.* The struggle to pay bills, when the money simply won't stretch, often reduces the marital relation to one of haggling, recrimination, and bitterness, which gradually but inevitably erodes away the romance and intimacy of dating and early marriage.

2. *Conflict over the allocation of limited resources.* Such conflict, with each person vying for a share of a limited resource, is very destructive to any intimate relation. Usually, these conflicts in a primary relation are internal (with the same person wanting two mutually exclusive things) or are over a need that is adjustive to one but not the other (such as the "open-window, closed-window" controversy). Particularly when the conflict involves the latter—openly vying over a limited resource with satisfaction for one meaning deprivation for the other—the primary relation is finished.

3. *Conflict over power.* The *quid pro quo,* or "something for something," balance that any lasting relation must establish is always disturbed and must be reestablished when children are born. With the wife at home taking care of the children and with all resource provision stemming from the husband, new alignments must emerge, often involving controversy or a power struggle over male dominance with the cash flow as its focal point. Again, when the children are half grown and the wife returns to work, a second realignment must occur and a power struggle may ensue.

Such stress over money is by no means limited to the lower-lower and the working class (upper-lower and lower-middle), whose financial difficulties stem from a lack of sufficient funds for physical necessities as well as the careless or ignorant mismanagement of the funds that are available. The middle-middle and upper-middle class families are equally susceptible to financial difficulties. According to the Tracer Company of America, a firm that specializes in tracking down missing husbands, 99 percent of the runaway husbands traced by the company had skipped out not because they were dissatisfied at home, or found another woman more sexually responsive, or were tired of the routine and in need of adventure, but rather because of insoluble financial difficulties. Nor was the financial difficulty a simple lack of funds in most cases. The average missing husband traced by the company had a yearly income of between $12,000 and $18,000, was a college graduate, lived in an above-median home, drove an above-median car, and belonged to the usual clubs and organizations regarded as bastions of establishment respectability. The problem with these husbands, according to the company, was mismanagement of the considerable family funds available (Smith and Pratt, 1969).

The Problem of Money Management

Sound money management consists simply of allocating available funds in ways that maximize need fulfillment and minimize deprivation. Few people, however — even knowledgeable, well-educated, middle-income people — are able to do this. In fact, experts in personal finance agree that it is far easier to make money than it is to handle it wisely. Unless the person is a professional in one of the fields of money management, his economic affairs are likely to be pretty much of a jumble. Few people know with any accuracy, for example, even how much money they have to spend; and they are only vaguely aware of how they spend it. They regard a budget as an anathema, buy what advertising and convenience impels them to, pay what they can of their bills, and have little clear notion of what the flow of money means in their lives or how they could improve it. Studies show that today's typical middle-class family will pass something like a half a million dollars through its hands during the lifetime of the husband; yet this apparently affluent family is often deeply beset by financial troubles throughout most of its existence.

Virtually overnight, the average newly married couple become candidates not only for the day-to-day necessities of running a household and maintaining a family but for the "big ticket" items of furniture and appliances — all with little or no training in the basic principles and skills of successful money management and personal finance. Besides their lack of knowledge and skill, the young American couple are faced with a society in which it is very difficult to avoid overspending. For ours is a culture which emphasizes consumption and the flow of easy credit. Thousands of advertising appeals confront a person daily, demonstrating the affluence that others presumably have and that he should attain and urging him to buy. The young family that responds to these appeals, making use of "easy" (though very expensive) credit, can find itself hopelessly in debt within a very short time. The dangers of mismatching income and outgo and making careless choices in discretionary spending can be very insidious, and an enormous number of young families are trapped into needless, life-long peonage.

Three items that every newlywed couple should have are a commonsense book on sex, a practical cookbook, and a good book on personal finance.[4] Most marriages that founder do so in one or more of these areas; and if any two are a source of persistent tension (rather than of pleasure and satisfaction), the marriage has little chance of success. Generally, interest in sex, and in food as well,

---

[4] Highly recommended is Smith and Pratt's *The Time-Life Book of Family Finance*. New York: Time-Life Books, 1969.

will lead a couple to at least experiment, to search for knowledge and improved skills. Unfortunately, this rarely happens with what is often regarded as the difficult and boring subject of money.

As difficult as sound money management may be, however, the basic principles of good personal finance may be stated quite simply:

1. Directing cash flow. *You must direct your money where you most want it to go. This involves (1) knowing what your spendable income is and not exceeding it, (2) acknowledging that you can't buy everything you would like and making an attempt to define what you most want, (3) putting some money each month into a temporary reserve (savings), and (4) putting some money each month into a long-term investment. These accomplishments are usually made possible only with the use of a budget.*

2. Using Credit. *You must know the proper use of credit—how to let it work for you for your financial or personal gain. There are three good uses of credit, which will be explained in this chapter. You should know them and use them.*

3. Buying wisely. *You must work at getting the proper value-received for your money—a dollar's worth out of a dollar—whether you pay cash or use credit.*

The rest of this chapter will examine these basic principles of personal finance—budgeting cash flow for the best use of available funds, using credit wisely, and being a good consumer.

Relation of a Budget to Personal Finance

One of the brutal facts of life is that everything a person does involves (an often unconscious) choice between available alternates and that choosing one eliminates the possibility of choosing the other. If he chooses *A,* he may not have *B.* In the realm of personal finance, this means that a person can't buy everything he would like to buy. So long as his available income is limited (as it is for 98 percent of our population), diverting funds into one channel (buying *A*) automatically diverts them away from another (buying *B*).

This principle of *forced alternate choice* is extremely important to the management of personal finance; for sound money management rests upon the ability of a person to narrow the range of choices sufficiently for him to be able to recognize that by using his money for *A,* he will eliminate the possibility of using it for *B.* If he can narrow the myriad choices for which his money might be exchanged into logical and manageable small categories, the options become clear; and it becomes possible for the person to *plan* his spending—to weigh the choices and to select the one that is most important or advantageous to him at the time.

The technique or the mechanics for securing this clarity of choice, where the alternatives are clearly drawn and the choice can be carefully considered and planned, is called a *budget.* A budget is *not* a financial strait jacket designed to force a person to keep track of every penny he spends, although this is the very common misconception and probably explains why most people hate the idea of a budget and refuse to keep one. Rather, a budget is an informal plan for intelligent spending—a clear, uncomplicated way of helping a person spend his money the way he wants to and obtain the things he most wants to obtain.

Until the actual costs of whatever a person wishes to buy are written down and compared with the costs of other things he wants, it is impossible for him to make a considered choice, a clear-headed decision for the right reasons. If he wants to move to an apartment that will cost $50 more a month, what will this mean in terms of the sports or hobby equipment, the furniture, the clothing, the appliances, the vacation travel he also hopes to have? If he doesn't move to the costlier apartment, what will this mean to the need-satisfactions that he ful- fills through his home environment?

No one, certainly not a budget, can tell a person what to do with his money. But a budget can be an indispensible aid in clarifying just what the alternatives are and in providing a general record of where the money is going, so that the person can readily assess his spending pattern and change it if he wishes. A budget will even enhance a person's income by directing the outflow of his money into the most productive channels—productive in terms of providing the tool and the plan by which he can obtain more goods or satisfactions for his money and avoid impulsive or careless and therefore costly spending. The al- ternative to keeping a budget is for a person to let his money seep away in such a fashion that he knows only that he is continually broke, in debt, without the things he wants, and wondering where it all went. Sound money management cannot even be approached in a household that denies itself the use of a budget. It is an essential aid to personal finance.

Developing a Budget

The first step in setting up a budget is to list all monthly assets—that is all of a person's or family's spendable, or "take-home" income per month, from what- ever source (remembering that income tax, social security, and usually many other sums are withheld from the monthly pay check).[5] The second step is to list all of the *fixed,* or *non-discretionary,* expenses per month, averaging those that vary somewhat from month to month. These would be such items as rent, mortgage payment and home maintenance for home owners, taxes, utilities, insurance, automotive and other transportation costs, and medical and dental expenses[6]—all expenditures over which a person has little or no control every month.

---

[5] Although such a list can be made on any piece of paper, it is more practical to use a permanently bound budget book, with pages ruled into columns. Such a book is available in any stationery store for a nominal sum.

[6] Home maintenance is estimated at 2 percent annually of the worth of the house. Medical and dental costs average $497 for a family of four according to the Bureau of Labor Statistics (1971). The cost of driving a car (for 10,000 miles) is estimated at $1,550 per year if the car is standard size, bought new and traded in every four years—$1,125 for fixed costs (insurance, license, depreciation), and $425 for maintenance costs (gas, oil, tires, etc.); maintenance cost for each mile driven was estimated as 4.25 cents for the standard car, 3.65 cents for a "compact," and 2.60 cents for a Volkswagon (The American Automobile Association, 1971).

The third step is to list all of the *variable*, or *discretionary*, expenses — a list that would include food, clothing, household supplies, personal care and laundry, entertainment, contributions and gifts, a personal allowance ("pocket money"), savings and investments; in short, all those necessities and wants that are not fixed as a specific and unvarying monthly expense.[7] (See Figure 9–1 for a sample budget form.)

The total of monthly discretionary expenses must be the same or less than the difference between total income and total fixed expenses or the person is in trouble, of course. If the discretionary expenses are higher and he makes up the difference by going into debt, the following month he must add the repayment of the debt to his fixed-expenses column, and he will have that much less for the discretionary-expenses column. If he couldn't manage before on his total income, he will now have even greater difficulty; for he will have less to manage with. Eventually, of course, this kind of creeping indebtedness can so swell the fixed-expenses with debt repayments that there will not be enough money available for the discretionary column to cover the everyday expenses of sheer survival. Then when credit is withdrawn because the person is no longer able to meet both his debts and his everyday needs, he will be overcome with financial disaster — collection agencies, repossessions, evictions, lawsuits, the whole miserable dehumanizing lot. Moreover, long before this crisis is reached, the marriage is usually seriously undermined, if not destroyed, by the tensions, anxieties, and frustrations of insoluble financial pressure.

People without a budget can easily fall into this situation because they are not precisely aware of what financial experts call *cash flow* — exactly how much they are spending for what and how this total compares to their spendable income. A budget lays out the cash flow very simply and precisely in a brief page or two. When a person can see clearly just what his financial options are, he can begin to direct his financial destiny with certitude: He is much less likely to overspend when he sees precisely in what area the overspending lies, and he can make plans for modifying his *fixed-expenses column* in the future.[8] Moreover, he can see at a glance what indebtedness will do to his discretionary-expense funds and is able to consciously direct his cash flow into channels which will bring the most satisfaction.

Savings is a very important item in the discretionary-expenses column. Most experts in personal finance emphasize that 10 percent of a person's spendable income should be reserved. There is a good deal of confusion regarding the concept of saving. Actually, money which is "saved" is not *removed* from spenda-

---

[7] The National Industrial Conference Board estimates (1971) that the average person has available to him about one third of his spendable income for these discretionary expenses.

[8] Since two thirds of the average family's spendable income goes for fixed expenses, this is the area in which modifications must be made if any significant change is to be effected in the family's financial picture. An item that is "fixed" this year is not necessarily fixed forever if the person is conscious of the need for a reduction. Housing expenses and car expenses are the two chief fixed expenses, and both are generally subject to significant modification. The person should carefully examine and evaluate every item in his fixed expenses column to determine if he is spending his money where he really wants it to go.

```
Monthly Income

    Source                          Amount

    ----------                      ----------

    ----------                      ----------

    ----------                      ----------

                         Total:  ----------


Monthly Fixed Expenses

    Item                            Amount

    ----------                      ----------

    ----------                      ----------

    ----------                      ----------

    ----------                      ----------

    ----------                      ----------

                         Total:  ----------


Total Monthly Income               ----------

Total Monthly Fixed Expenses       ----------

                         Difference:  ----------
                         (amount available for all
                         discretionary expenses.)

Monthly Discretionary Expenses

    Item                            Amount

    ----------                      ----------

    ----------                      ----------

    ----------                      ----------

    ----------                      ----------

                         Total:  ----------
```

Figure 9–1. Sample Budget Form

ble income; rather, it is simply temporarily held for *deferred spending.*[9] If a person thinks of saving as an act of self-denial, he probably won't save. He *is* likely to save if he sees it for what it is — a means for buying wanted items in the relatively near future without incurring debts and costly finance charges, or a standby

[9] Another common understanding of the term "saving" is the putting away of a portion of one's income for a long-term program of growth. This is more properly called *investing.* Invested money

fund for unexpected family emergencies. In addition, saving can actually increase a person's discretionary funds by the amount of interest the savings will earn and by the bargains that he can take advantage of when he has cash at hand. The penalty for not having reserve cash to use for deferred purchases or emergencies can be substantial.

Another very important item in the discretionary-expenses column is the *personal allowance* category. The size of the personal allowance should be scaled to the overall budget, of course, but it should be generous enough that the person can avoid the feeling of being in some sort of financial strait-jacket. The personal allowance is a budgeted sum that the person may spend freely for whatever he wishes without making an accounting.[10] Experience has shown that a tight, overly detailed budget, which demands an accounting for every penny spent, will not work. If a person is forced to feel like a cheat or a miser everytime he contemplates buying something, he will soon abandon his budget with more relief than guilt.

A budget is not hard to set up, once a person decides to do it. And once this first vital step is taken, the actual mechanics are very easy. Most people even find to their surprise that they actually enjoy the mechanics of setting down the figures because of the confidence and security they gain by transforming what has always been vague and undetermined into precise and recorded figures and categories. Keep the budget simple; keep it flexible; keep it to a few manageable categories; allow an ample personal-expense category; allow a reasonable amount for deferred spending (or saving); provide something (however modest) for investment; and think of it as a tool. It will pay surprisingly rich dividends.

Involving the Whole Family in the Budget

Money and the goods money can buy have different meanings for different people, with each person having his own values and his own goals. For some, the acquisition of material things is important; for others, humanistic values and experiences — whether in travel, education, the arts, or recreation and entertaining — are more important than objects. A family budget should both acknowledge and attempt to harmonize these differences, so that each person in the family can feel that he has appropriate rights in the allocation of the family's spendable income. Any other policy of allocating available funds will breed dissension and resentment.

This doesn't mean, of course, that the children are going to have a determining voice in where the family will live or what car the family will drive. But

---

is usually not meant to be spent; the investor's anticipation is that his money will be left undisturbed, so that it will eventually provide income from the interest it earns. A regular sum for investment should also be included in the budget as a discretionary expense (see the later section *The Importance of Regular Investments*, for a discussion of investing).

[10] A child's personal allowance is no less important than the husband's or wife's, and, in some ways, it is more important; see the discussion of the child's personal allowance in the later section *Involving the Whole Family in the Budget.*

when they are old enough to understand and express their own consumer needs, children should be included in some of the budgetary discussions, so that they understand where the money is going and the various ways that they are benefitting from this cash flow. Certainly, with all matters that directly concern them (clothing, allowance, recreation, toys, etc.), they should be included in the family's budgetary problems, and a common consensus should be arrived at regarding the distribution and direction of cash flow.

If the attitude with which the family discusses the subject of money is one of practicality, reasonable optimism, and openness—a frank acknowledgement of the principle of forced alternate choice in the allocation of the limited funds— the children will gradually develop a healthy awareness of and competence in the dollars-and-cents world of economic reality. Discussions about the budget should ideally bring the family closer together as they share in money problems and their solutions. All spendable income should be treated as the *family's,* and all decisions should be made as a matter of concensus—directing cash flow where it best provides the greatest satisfaction for all concerned. Arguing over money or being secretive about it breeds resentments and bad spending habits, which create tension for everyone in the family—child and parents alike.

The child's ability to understand the uses of money does not emerge full-blown at any particular age. The average child can learn the principle of exchanging a nickle for a package of gum by the time he is five years of age; and for the next two or three years, he should be given money in appropriate amounts at the time he can use it—a dime for the ice cream vendor, 15 cents for popcorn at the zoo, etc.—until he is in the third or fourth grade and can grasp the concept of deferred spending and planning ahead. (Many people never do grasp this concept, of course.) At this point, when the child is eight or nine years old, he should be ready for a regular, fixed weekly allowance.

The size of the allowance should be determined by consultation. Decide with him how much he needs for his own personal expenditures, allowing an appropriate amount for "pocket money." Experience has shown that when their counsel is sought, children are very reasonable, even modest, in their demands. A child should learn from the outset, however that his allowance is a fixed amount. If he spends it before the end of the week and asks for more, he should be told that the amount he was given was the allowance agreed upon in the budgetary discussion. (He should *not* be told that there is no more money; for he will know that this is not the truth—a budget, by its very nature, is a series of *choices.*) If he can establish that he needs more, then his allowance should be raised; he should not be given "advances" or extra amounts. It is obviously a serious mistake to make the child feel as though he were a burden or a drain upon the family's finances; it is *equally* a mistake, however, to provide for all his wants as though the source of the family's funds was inexhaustible.

If his allowance is scaled properly, he will learn for himself, through his own experience and through the family's budgetary counsels, sound principles of money management—not spending more than he has, making choices wisely, and saving for things he wants and cannot afford right now. His initial purchases seem outrageous; it is important, however, that he be allowed to make—and

learn from—his own mistakes. After all, these mistakes cannot be too serious if they are kept within the bounds of a fixed allowance. The child's allowance should be his to spend with no necessity for an accounting.

A child should never be expected to earn his allowance with household chores. It is important that his allowance should be openly acknowledged as his fair share of the family's resources. If he does some work that an outsider would have had to be paid for, then by all means the child deserves to be paid as well. But this work-for-pay arrangement should be in addition to his allowance and to the simple household chores he is assigned as his role in fulfilling family functions.

Similarly, withholding the child's allowance as a disciplinary measure is never advisable; for such action will be perceived by him as being paid to be good, which is a very poor idea with which to indoctrinate a child. He should be good because he wants to be good and enjoys pleasing adults, and his allowance should be his by right.

It goes without saying, of course, that wives should have an appropriate say in all budgetary matters. It is a rare, authoritarian family in our society where one person (husband *or* wife) maintains power by absolute control of the purse strings. It is also, inevitably, an unhappy and resentment-ridden family.

Major Budget Problems in Different Stages of the Family

As the family develops over the years from a newlywed and childless couple, to a couple with their first child, to rearing growing children, to putting children through college, and, finally, to preparing for retirement, their financial pattern and problems change significantly. The first stage—from the wedding until the first child is born, a period of from one to three years for the average couple—is the most financially carefree stage, although it rarely seems so at the time. Even though the young couple face much uncertainty and have but limited resources and few belongings, they have no one to look after but themselves; and they most often have a double income with which to do it.

Most couples feel financially oppressed when they are first married because there are so many things they want—a home (or at least a better apartment), furniture, appliances, a second car, sports and hobby equipment, travel. However, it is during this period that a couple spend more money on pleasure, on leisure activities, and on personal items than they ever will again, unless they become relatively affluent by middle age. In fact, the double income and relatively cheap household and family expenses during this period often give the couple a false sense of financial security; for the fixed expenses and installment payments seem comparatively easy to make at this point, and the excessive debt they may incur does not become a source of stress until they enter the second stage of their marriage—when they have responsibility for children as well as for themselves.

With the addition of children, the costs of maintaining a family begin to soar, while the income is sharply reduced by the loss of the wife's paycheck. Medical care, food, clothing, baby sitters, the need for larger living quarters and more furniture and appliances contribute to a continually swelling family budget. Not surprisingly, during this period of the family, when the couple are plunged from relative prosperity into financial difficulties and even depression, money becomes the leading area of disagreement (Blood and Wolfe, 1960).

If a newlywed couple have the foresight to live in a furnished or modestly self-furnished apartment during the childless period and avoid buying an expensive car or spending beyond their means on clothes, recreation, vacations, eating out, and entertainment, they will be able to save a substantial amount for this second stage and continue their comfortable life style without becoming embroiled in debt and financial recriminations. Entering the second stage with no backlog of savings is both foolish and potentially disastrous.

The cost of rearing each child from birth to age 18, regardless of family income and price levels, averages about three years of the father's salary according to data accumulated by the Metropolitan Life Insurance Company. Thus, a family of five with an average income of $10,000 will spend $30,000 for each child, or a total of $90,000 to rear the three children to age 18—and few middle-class families stop supporting their children at age 18. Fortunately, as the children get older and more expensive, the mother is usually back at work, and the income of the father is reaching its peak, so that the family is able to keep pace with expenses.

A second major financial difficulty faces the family when the children reach college age. In the ten years from 1957 to 1967, the average cost of tuition (to say nothing of student living expenses) rose from $700 per year to $1,300. In 1967, for example, at the University of Chicago, the total of all of a student's expenses for four years was $15,000. Estimates indicate that the average cost of a college education in 1967 was at least $10,000, with some 40 percent of universities costing $12,000 or more, and another 20 percent costing $14,000 or more (Smith and Pratt, 1969). A family of five would therefore have to budget an average of $30,000 just to see their three children through college. In the future, these costs may be expected to rise considerably along with the increasing costs of living.

These are average costs, of course; they may be much higher, and they also may be somewhat lower. Many publicly supported universities, colleges, and junior colleges assess little or no tuition; and living at home while going to college is cheaper than paying board and room. Part-time jobs, summer jobs, and work-study programs for students from low-income families can help defray ex penses. A student who works ten to fifteen hours per week during the schoc year and full time during the summer may be able to contribute as much a $1,000 a year, or 40 percent of the annual cost of his education.

Despite the belief by many parents that various sources of help are available, this just is not so for the average family. In more than 1,200 universities and colleges surveyed by the College Board, only one student in five received any form of financial help outside of that supplied by his family. And for this one in five, the average scholarship grant was only $553 per year (Smith and Pratt, 1969). The moderately affluent family cannot even expect a one in five chance of aid; the average income of the families who *do* receive aid is well under $10,000 (Smith and Pratt).

Thus, it is often necessary for students or their parents to borrow in order to finance the extra expenses of a college education. Simply from a dollars-and-cents point of view—not taking into consideration the intellectual, social, and cultural values of a college education—this use of credit is one of the best pos-sible investments; for a college degree is worth a lot of money (see Figure 9-2). College graduates make about 65 percent more during their lifetime than do high school graduates, with about $200,000 added to the college graduate's lifetime earnings (U. S. Office of Education, 1970).

If necessary, any measure is justified—mortgaging the house or even taking out a personal bank loan at the exorbitant rate of interest that is required (18 percent in 1971). Other ways short of borrowing money should be sought by a student first, of course, and a mortgage or personal bank loan, especially, should be resorted to only as a last emergency measure. The reason for caution with the latter is, of course, the high interest and the timing of repayment. If the parents repay the loan, they will be seriously depleting funds they should be investing for retirement during their middle years. If the newly graduated stu-dent pays such a loan back, the repayments fall at a time when he is just moving into the heavy economic responsibilities of housing, marriage, and a family.

There are several special sources for student loans, all with very attractive interest rates. Repayment of United States government NDEA (National De-fense Educational Act) loans begins nine months after graduation (or with-drawal) from college and may be extended for as long as a ten-year period at 3 percent annual interest on the unpaid balance. A student may borrow up to $5,000 under this program and an additional $5,000 if he goes on to graduate school. If the student borrower joins the Armed Services, VISTA, or the Peace Corps after leaving school, he is granted a two- or three-year grace period before he must begin repayment. In addition, up to 50 percent of the NDEA loan may be cancelled if the student goes into teaching, and up to a 100 percent of the loan (and all interest) may be cancelled if he teaches for seven years in certain deprived-area schools that have a high concentration of enrollment from low-income families. To qualify for this loan, however, the student must show finan-cial need, which means, in effect, that his family must be unable to help him.

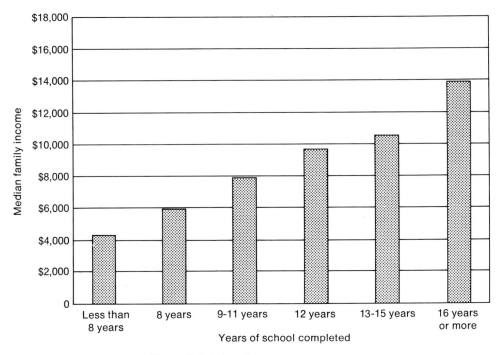

Figure 9-2. Education and Income

Source: *Current Population Reports, Consumer Income*, Series P-60, No. 79, July 27, 1971.

These NDEA loans are also limited in quantity and not always obtainable even if the student can meet the financial-need qualification.

Students who can't qualify for (or obtain) an NDEA loan may borrow a total of $7,500 through the Federally Insured Educational Loan Program, which makes no financial need requirement—although, as with the NDEA loans, funds are limited and the loan is not always available. The student must shop around at participating banks until he finds one that has the funds and is willing to grant him the loan. Interest rates on the loans are 7 percent on the unpaid balance, and repayment does not begin until nine months after graduation and may be extended for as long as ten years, with repayment deferred if the student joins the Armed Services, the Peace Corps, or VISTA. Applications for these loans may be obtained from offices of financial aid in all universities and colleges.

A third period of potential financial difficulty for the family occurs in the middle years, when they must prepare for retirement and old age. At this time, the couple are in their middle and late forties; they have discharged their obligations to their children; their home, furniture, and appliances are largely paid for; and the middle-class husband is reaching his peak earning years. This should be a second period of relative affluence and comfort for them. However, during this period, substantial sums must be budgeted for investment, since retirement is now only fifteen or so years away. If the couple are able to invest sufficiently during this time, they may have a graceful, dignified old age; if they are not, they may enter old age as another period of financial crisis, this time without the advantages of youthful resilience and promise. Fully one in four of our retired people have no resources beyond their social security payments — which have never been represented as being sufficient for even bare subsistence but were designed as a cushion to help stretch out other funds for the retired. (For a detailed account of investing for retirement, see the later section *The Importance of Regular Investments.*)

The Effective Use of Credit

Properly used, *credit* — "buying now and paying later," for that is what credit is — can make a person's life much richer and fuller. Improperly used, it can bring ruin. In order to take advantage of the good uses of credit (and to avoid its pitfalls), it is essential to know its various forms, to understand how each works, and then to use it — as one would any useful but dangerous tool — with caution and respect.

Three Sound Uses of Credit

There are three sound uses of credit. Two — *open credit* and *profit-making credit* — are obviously sensible and fairly safe if they are properly used. The third — *non-profit-making credit* — is only marginally safe or sensible and requires especially careful consideration. Let us examine these three categories of credit in detail (see Table 9–1 for a comparison of the three):

Open credit is the term used for credit advanced with no finance charges.[11] The old-fashioned grocer that kept an account of the items a person bought during the month and then settled the bill on payday was extending open credit. Today, open-credit opportunities occur with dairy- and bread-delivery companies, diaper services, the phone company, utilities, newspaper subscriptions, cable television, doctors and dentists, and many other businesses and stores that have the facilities for sending monthly statements to their customers and are willing to provide their services or products in advance of payment.

Department stores, gasoline companies, and multi-purpose bank credit cards also extend open credit if the charge customer or credit-card holder pays the bill in full at the end of the billing cycle (usually 30 to 60 days). However with these formalized charge accounts and with credit cards, if the user fails to pay the full bill within the billing cycle, his account will be financed — that is,

---

[11]Open credit is not really cost-free, of course, since the creditor's accounting costs are included in the purchase price. But because these accounting costs are buried in the price regardless of whether a person pays cash or defers the payment, he may as well have the advantage of the open credit. If pressed, some merchants make a 5 or 6 percent discount if a customer uses cash instead of a credit card.

Table 9–1. The Effective Use of Credit

Type	Cost	Risk	Use or Purpose	Advisability	Sources
Open	Free (that is, cost buried in the purchase price, whether or not the credit is used).	Safe—if monthly bills are paid in full.	Any purchase that a person wants, can use, and can afford.	Good—if the item satisfies the test of "forced alternate choice."	Revolving charge accounts, credit cards, medical and dental bills, etc.
Profit-making	Financed, but cost is temporary (that is, cost is free in the long-run, since cost of the credit is repaid by the use to which the credit is put).	Safe—if the income realized from the use of the credit will ultimately repay the cost of the credit.	Any purchase that can increase a person's income or reduce his living costs; for example, education, car, clothing, or tools for work, investments, etc.	Good—if the item satisfies the test of "forced alternate choice."	Any of the above, plus cash loans. If cash loans, finance charges should be kept low by shopping for money as one would for any other commodity.
Non-profit-making	Full finance charges.	Risky. Is the cost of the credit worth the need satisfaction? Costs can lead to reduced standard of living, continual financial difficulties and tensions, and repossession if payments are not kept up.	Anything a person would like to have but can't immediately afford; for example, hobby or sports equipment, recreation and pleasure, travel, new furniture, clothes, car, etc.	Questionable—even if the item satisfies the test of "forced alternate choice. May be good, however, if used with exceptional caution and with available alternates and all possible consequences clearly in mind.	Same as above.

charged with interest (usually a minimum of 1½ percent per month on the unpaid balance, which is 18 percent in true annual interest).[12] It should be clear that a person can use open credit wisely and properly only to the extent that he is certain of being able to settle his account in full at the end of the billing cycle. If he doesn't, the bills will mount rapidly and become more and more difficult to meet; and inevitably, he will be refused further service. If his open-credit account is a formal charge or credit-card account, he will also be charged with high interest rates (as well as service charges), so that the *real* price of his purchase will soar. On the other hand, if open credit is used properly, it is not only a great convenience but a real bargain in that the consumer has the use, almost indefinitely, of the cash he would have spent.[13]

---

[12] Some merchants with charge-account systems compute their interest charges from a different base than the monthly unpaid balance, so that the actual true annual interest rate is substantially higher than the 18 percent figure. Scaduto (1970), for example, points out that many large department stores charge 1½ percent interest on the previous month's balance rather than on the current unpaid balance, which may work out to a true annual interest rate of more than 18 percent, depending on the size of the current payment in relation to the unpaid balance. Many stores will charge interest on the original purchase price rather than on the unpaid balance; applied this way, the 1½ percent per month is a true annual rate of 36 percent (interest is often computed this way by car dealers).

[13] In other words, if a person makes a purchase for $100 on open credit, paying the $100 the following month out of his next paycheck, he has the use of that $100 (as well as the item purchased) in the meantime. He could be earning interest on the money in a savings account, or he could spend the money on something else. This process could continue indefinitely, with the person having the free use of an extra $100 for months and even years.

Open credit is also a cost-free way for a person to build up the credit references that become essential when he needs to borrow money for major purchases.
People often have the mistaken idea that they will be regarded as a good credit
risk if they have always remained solvent and paid cash for everything. The
opposite is true. A person is regarded as a good credit risk only if he has borrowed money (or used credit) and demonstrated his ability to repay it. Thus,
paying cash for everything can actually create unnecessary hardships for a
person when he wants to make a major purchase that requires credit financing
(appliances, furniture, a car, a boat, or a house, for example).

Profit-making credit—financed loans or credit purchases that promise a financial return—is a sound use of credit if the consumer will eventually profit more
from the use of the borrowed money or credit purchase than he will pay in
finance charges. An example of a good use of profit-making credit is borrowing
for an education, or for vocational training, thereby acquiring the knowledge
or skills that will enable the borrower to earn more. Similarly, good uses of
profit-making credit might be borrowing to buy tools that are needed to produce
income or to save money (a sewing machine, for example), borrowing to buy or
maintain a car that is needed to get to work or school, borrowing to buy work
clothes or an office space, or borrowing to move to a new locale and a better
job.[14] Businessmen, of course, use profit-making credit in borrowing to build
or to buy goods or labor or to make an investment, believing that these steps will
bring them more income than the costs of the credit. This use of financed credit
is the basis of all commerce.

Non-profit-making credit—the third category for the sound use of credit—is
that shadowy region of potential financial difficulty in which a person borrows
money or makes a financed-credit purchase to satisfy an immediate and non-
profitable need the satisfaction of which he values more than he does the cost
of the finance charges. This use of credit requires the greatest exercise of
judgment; the borrower must weigh the subjective value of the need satisfaction
against the considerable costs of the finance charges and the decrease of subsequent monthly discretionary funds as a result of these charges. This is not only a
"buy now and pay later" plan but a "buy now and buy *less* later" plan. If a person
makes too many purchases in this way, with each purchase reducing his future
spendable income by the amount which he will be paying for credit, he obviously
may eventually reduce his standard of living severely and find himself embroiled
in months and years of financial stress. It is generally far wiser to follow a de-
ferred-spending, or *saving*, plan.

An example of the sound use of this type of credit, however, might be buying
a refrigerator that provides more convenience in storing larger amounts of food,
thus allowing the person to shop less often. Similarly, this form of credit might
be used wisely in buying a vacuum cleaner that shortens housecleaning time as
well as making the time spent more efficient, in buying a piano with which the
person can start piano lessons at once instead of deferring them until he is able

---

[14]Buying a home, which utilizes financed credit in the form of a mortgage, may also be a profitable
and sound venture, but the ramifications of home buying are so complicated that the subject will
be treated separately in the later section, *Being a Wise Consumer*.

to save the purchase price, in buying a camera that will provide a great amount of pleasure and capture moments that will never return, or in providing for a vacation or travel opportunity which, once deferred, may not recur in just the same way. There are countless other examples that could be given; for the use of this category of credit is highly subjective. The important point is that the person knows what the costs of the credit are and weighs the relative values carefully; for the routine use of *non-profit-making* financed credit can be a serious drain on even a solvent family's spendable income. For example, the family that carries a continuous average of $1,500 of financed debts (not including a mortgage) — a rather modest amount by today's standards — will pay about $225 a year in finance charges, or $7,000 over its major buying years (Margolius, 1967).

Pitfalls of Credit-installment Buying

The use of *credit-installment contracts* rather than revolving charge accounts or credit cards is often required by stores and dealers when they sell what they call a *"big ticket"* (expensive) *item*, such as furniture, major appliances, carpeting, or a boat or automobile. Credit-installment contracts are a legal agreement between the consumer and the dealer for the financed purchase of a specific item. They provide for a delayed payment for the item on a weekly or a monthly basis for a specified period at the end of which the contract is retired. The payments generally include not only the cost (principal) of the item and the interest charges but also service charges and insurance coverage for the amount. These credit-installment contracts will almost always involve higher interest rates than almost any other source of financing.[15] From the consumer's point of view, therefore, the very worst place to get credit for his purchase is usually the store or dealer who is selling the item. The rule is simple: When buying a "big ticket" item, it is usually advisable to borrow the money[16] elsewhere and then pay cash to the dealer for the purchase.

With an installment-plan purchase, the customer must sign a contract which specifies that the item purchased may be repossessed by the seller if the customer fails to keep up the payments. If repossession occurs, the item may then be resold by the merchant, with the proceeds from the second sale used to cover the expenses of repossession and resale and the remaining indebtedness on the item. If the proceeds from the resale fail to pay everything off, the original customer owes the remainder — even though he no longer has the item. Thus,

---

[15] Dealers often charge rates as high as 4 percent per month on the unpaid balance of installment contracts, which comes to a true annual interest rate of 48 percent. In addition to this cost, service charges (credit investigation, accounting expenses, etc.) and insurance are often tacked on as well, so that the actual costs for the installment contract may range as high as 81 percent in true annual interest, according to Kenneth B. Wilson, president of the National Better Business Bureau. One workingman whose case was cited in the U. S. Senate hearings on unscrupulous credit bought a television set for $124 with a two-year contract calling for monthly payments of $17.50. These payments amounted to a total of $420 — a finance charge of 229 percent (Margolius, 1967).

[16] Money should be shopped for as carefully as any other item, since there are many sources of loans with interest rates varying from exorbitant to reasonable, see the later section on *Sources of loans.*

a credit-installment plan is risky, especially if the item involved is costly and depreciates rapidly as does furniture, any major appliance, or a car.

In addition to the repossession clause in installment-plan contracts, many of these contracts have an *"add on" clause*—a device by which all of the items purchased by a customer from one dealer over a long period of time are written on the *same* installment contract, with payments and charges pro-rated among *all* the debts outstanding and the repossession clause applicable to all the items. For example, suppose a person buys a stereo-television console on the installment plan, makes regular payments, and then, when the console is all but paid off two years later, he buys a small refrigerator from the same dealer. If the refrigerator is "added on" to the installment contract for the console, and if the customer is unable to make the payments for the refrigerator, the seller may then repossess not only the refrigerator but also the console. For according to the "add on" clause that was a part of the contract the customer signed, all payments that he had been making were pro-rated among both items, so that neither was paid off and both were subject to repossession. This "add-on" installment-credit trap is not limited to just two items, of course, but may be extended over an indefinite number of purchases.

Another perfectly legal and widely used device in installment-plan contracts is the *"holder in due course" clause.* This clause provides that the dealer may sell his contract with the customer to a finance company, which then becomes the "holder in due course." The new holder of the contract, the finance company, is under no obligation to guarantee the item sold and cannot be legally involved in any dispute between the seller and the customer regarding shoddy merchandise, failure to provide service, or misrepresentation of any type. This arrangement allows the dealer to realize a full return on the contract; it allows the finance company to collect the full amount of the bill or, if the payments are not made, to repossess the item; and it leaves the customer with no recourse but an expensive law suit against the dealer if the merchandise proves unsatisfactory.

Still another device found in installment contracts is the *"balloon payment" clause,* which requires a very large final installment payment on the contract. Such a clause is often added to a contract to make the monthly payments for an expensive item small enough to be within the present means of the buyer.[17] Then, with the final balloon payment, the buyer must make up the difference between the sum of the small monthly payments he has been making and the total cost (principal and finance charges) of the item. If the customer is careless about preparing for the final balloon payment, he can find himself faced with an impossible debt and no alternative but to refinance (at still further cost to him) or lose the item and the money he has already invested in it.

Other practices that plague the unwary consumer in installment contracts are being induced to sign *blank* contracts, not being told the full purchase price

---

[17]The small monthly payments also make little dent in the balance of the principal, so that the holder of the contract makes considerably more on the finance charges applied against the monthly balance than he would with a regular installment plan.

or finance costs by the salesman,[18] and not being given a copy of the contract. All of these practices are devised, of course, to keep the consumer ignorant of the real costs of a purchase. It certainly should go without saying that a person must (1) never sign a contract unless all of the spaces are filled in; (2) never sign a contract without reading and understanding it or having it explained by a reliable third party; (3) never sign a contract involving a substantial sum of money without having a lawyer check it; (4) always get a copy of the signed contract; (5) always know precisely what the credit is costing you in finance charges and true annual interest. A consumer should also keep in mind that any agreement that is not in writing is not binding; therefore, a salesman may verbally represent his product or the charges for that product almost any way he wishes without obligating himself legally to fulfill his promises.[19] Conversely, once a consumer has signed an installment contract, he is legally obligated to pay in full (even when the item is repossessed), and the seller may attach his wages if he fails to do so.[20]

Sources of Loans

As we have noted, it is generally inadvisable to use the installment-credit plan of the store or dealer selling the goods. Instead, the person should *borrow the money* from another source (at the best rate available, of course) and then *pay cash* for the goods. There are various sources for borrowing money, with a wide range of interest rates. The following sources of loans are listed in order from the most costly to the least costly:

1. A pawnbroker is a very poor source of money, not to be considered except in the most desperate circumstances. Besides the exorbitant interest-rate charges (36 to 50 percent), the borrower gets only a fraction of the worth of the article he has pawned, and he loses the use of the article for the time that the credit is extended.

2. The small-loan company is one of the worst sources of money, in terms of both cost and reliability. The actual charges for loans from such companies ran from 30 to 36 percent in true annual interest in 1971. In addition, unless the borrower goes to one of the large, nationally advertised companies (such as Morris Plan, Household Finance, etc.), he must be very wary of perfectly legal

---

[18]Some relief for the consumer was achieved with the passage by Congress of the Truth in Lending Act in 1968. The true annual interest rate for loans or credit purchases must now be shown prominently on the statement or contract. In addition, the statement or contract must now show clearly just what all of the other finance charges are—for example, fees for opening the account, carrying charges, bookkeeping expenses, fees for insurance against fire or theft, life insurance, etc.

[19]Automobile salesmen use this ploy almost as a routine procedure. They make an attractive offer; then they alter the agreement in the final contract that is presented, explaining that the sales manager wouldn't approve the deal as stated.

[20]It is legal in all states for an installment-contract holder to get a court order attaching the wages of the contractee if he fails to keep his terms of the contract. The amount or the percentage that may be *garnisheed* (attached) varies from state to state.

but shoddy practices which make the true interest rate far higher than even the exorbitant 30 to 36 percent.[21] The only advantage to the borrower offered by the small-loan company is that it will accept greater credit risks than banks, savings-and-loan associations, or credit unions.

3. The bank credit card cash-advance service is a relatively expensive source of money. Bankamericard, for example, charged 2 percent on the monthly balance (24 percent in true annual interest) for a cash advance in 1971. Most borrowers will use this source of money either because they are not aware of the high interest they must pay (the rate is clearly shown *only* on the statement at the end of the billing cycle) or because they can get the cash quickly and conveniently. Actually, however, this source is no faster or more convenient (and somewhat more expensive) than the "balance plus" type bank loan discussed below. The bank credit cards are very aggressive, of course, in promoting the use of their cards as a convenient source of cash. For example, every year, many of the card companies mail forms payable to the Internal Revenue Service, as well as to state and local tax collectors, to their cardholders. Then, to pay his taxes, all a cardholder need do is fill in the correct sum and sign the form — and pay the high interest on the money.

4. Borrowing money through bank "checkway credit," "instant credit," or "balance plus" plans is about as costly to the customer as a revolving charge account at a department store, usually $1\frac{1}{2}$ percent on the unpaid balance each month, or 18 percent in true annual interest.

5. A second mortgage is a good source of money; the charges average from 12 to 14 percent in true annual interest, and the borrower has the use of the money for a period of from 3 to 10 years. The borrower's home, of course, must be put up as collateral, and if the payments are not kept up, the mortgage may be foreclosed. Thus, there is a certain risk involved, and a second mortgage should never be undertaken without careful consideration.

6. Commercial banks are an excellent source for personal loans, since their charges are only 11.5 to 13.5 percent (in 1971). However, unless a person has collateral, an excellent credit rating, or a co-signer, this source of money is not available to him. The purchase of an automobile (or boat), which provides its own collateral, should usually be financed through a commercial bank (or credit union) rather than with a dealer (although comparative interest-rate charges should always be checked).

---

[21]One of the worst of these tactics is the procedure known as *"flipping,"* where the loan company charges interest on the total amount of the principal borrowed as new loans are granted (instead of writing a new loan contract for each additional loan). Sylvia Porter cites the example of a customer who borrowed $1,152 from a small loan company and signed a note for $1,632, which included the interest. During the following two years, while this loan was being repaid, the loan company granted the customer several small additional loans, bringing the total amount borrowed to $1,805. At the end of this two-year period the customer had paid off $1,405 but discovered that his outstanding balance was now $3,040! Following the practice of "flipping," the loan company had simply added on his later loans to the initial loan and continued to charge interest on the total sum of *all* the loans, so that it was costing this person $3,443 to borrow $1,805 for two years! (San Francisco Chronicle, February 18, 1971). This is a particularly graphic example of the vital necessity of knowing the meaning of any contract before signing it.

7. Credit unions are an ideal source of money for those who are eligible to become members. Their rates usually range from 10 to 12 percent a year. Personal loans are made on the member's signature, with no collateral, up to a maximum amount fixed by the policies of the union. Higher amounts may be obtained with co-signers or with collateral.

8. Refinancing a mortgage is an excellent way to obtain money, with the cost in 1971 running between $7\frac{1}{2}$ and 9 percent a year. A homeowner becomes eligible for this loan source—called "opening up the end of the mortgage"— when he has paid off part of his mortgage. He may then borrow more money on his home, with the amount of the mortgage increased and the payments extended. The difficulty here, of course, is that it is only the relatively affluent or the long-time home owner who can take advantage of this source of money.

9. Finally, if a person has a savings account, investments (stocks, bonds, or mutual funds), or a life-insurance policy with a cash-surrender value, he may borrow on these with very low cost. Borrowing money using one's own savings or investments as collateral cost 7 to 9 percent in 1971. This finance charge is offset, of course, by the interest of 4 to 6 percent that the bank, credit union, or savings-and-loan association is paying on the savings, or the dividends or interest that the stocks or bonds are earning. Thus, the actual cost to the borrower is no more than 4 to 6 percent in true annual interest. Generally, the banks will loan up to 50 percent of the current market value of stocks or mutual funds. The charge for borrowing from a life-insurance company on the cash-surrender value of one's policy is 5 to 6 percent per year, and the person may fix his own repayment terms.[22]

Questioning a Credit Rating

If a person is refused credit, a loan, insurance, or a job and has reason to believe that the refusal stems from a bad credit rating, he may do something about it under the federal Fair Credit Reporting Act, which took effect in 1971. Whoever turns down his request for credit (or whatever) must give him the name of the credit agency that made the negative report. This agency must, in turn, let the person see exactly what its files contain under his name. Should the information be inaccurate or include data that cannot be verified, the credit agency must promptly delete it from the file. Moreover, any information that is disputed must be checked again for accuracy by the agency. Finally, the person has a right to enter in his file an explanatory statement about any entries that he feels are misleading. (For example, the file might record late payment of a bill that the person deliberately held up because the merchandise was unsatisfactory.)

Even if the unflattering information is accurate, it cannot stay in the file forever under the 1971 act. Most adverse information, even criminal records, must be deleted after seven years; information on bankruptcy must be deleted

---

[22] In terms of overall money management, however, the cash-value type life-insurance policy is a very poor buy; see the later section *Buying Life Insurance.*

after fourteen years. If the agency's negligence in this regard causes a person financial loss or embarrassment, he may sue the credit agency.

Being a Wise Consumer

The decision of (1) whether to make a purchase and (2) whether to make it with credit or cash are only the first steps to sound personal finance. A third step consists of getting the greatest return for each dollar spent. The wise consumer gets more for his money by not wasting it on things that won't last or won't work or simply don't give full value proportionate to their cost.[23] He must know not only value and comparative prices but also how to distinguish quality merchandise from the cheap and shoddy.

The prices for the same or equivalent items often vary widely, depending on the store, the neighborhood, the season, or even the type of reduced-price sale in which the item is offered. The wise consumer must recognize misrepresented merchandise, inflated prices, phony markdowns, and fictitious discounts. Guarantees and warrantees are always limited in some way, the wise consumer will read the fine print and know precisely to what he is entitled if something should go wrong with the product.[24]

Such business-like attention to getting a dollar's worth out of a dollar is more difficult than one might think. The fact is that for a great number of young families especially, the money that is not drained off in excessive credit charges is lost through bad shopping.

Buying Food

Food has the aesthetic value of pleasure as well as the practical value of nutrition. The pleasures and amenities of food may be of such importance to a person that it is worth budgeting a relatively high proportion of his discretionary funds for it. This is perfectly sensible—so long as he has weighed the relative values and the alternatives and therefore knows what he is doing. To use his shopping dollar wisely, then, a person should buy food that meets his psychological as well as his nutritional needs at the best possible price. In short, buying food should rest upon a three-fold knowledge: (1) the personal factor of the psy-

---

[23] An immensely valuable source of consumer information is *Consumer Reports* magazine. The professional shoppers and evaluators of the staff carefully compare and evaluate packaged food, clothing, cameras, automobiles, all types of appliances, and many other consumer goods for durability, safety, effectiveness, and price value. *Consumer Reports* is published monthly by the Consumers Union, a nonprofit organization, at 256 Washington Street, Mount Vernon, N. Y., and may be obtained by subscription, on newstands, or in the public library. Consumers Union also publishes an annual digest, *Buying Guide,* which covers the most popular consumer items.

[24] Here, the use of open credit is an enormous advantage; for the consumer is in a much stronger position regarding exchanges or returns if he hasn't yet paid anything for the item (unless, of course, he has signed a contract). In general, paying cash in advance for anything is never a good practice. Whenever possible, get the item, try it out, and *then* pay cash for it.

chological meaning of food for the individual, (2) the nutrition factors, and (3) the purely monetary factor of getting full value for each dollar spent.

Consumer experts agree that when buying a large amount of groceries it is important to shop from a list that has been based in part upon pre-planned menus. Supermarkets make a science of inducing shoppers to buy more than they want or need. Packaging, lighting, displays, and other psychological lures are carefully designed by specialists in consumer practices to encourage shoppers to fill their carts. The person who just wanders about the market picking

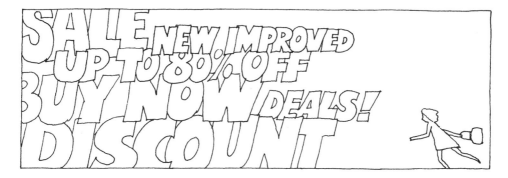

up anything that looks good—and, most especially, one who does this when he's hungry—will wind up with things that may be overpriced or that he doesn't really want. The wise shopper will first plan menus which, ideally, should provide a week's meals and be arranged to take advantage of left-overs and advertised sales and specials. Then he will prepare a shopping list mainly from these menus. The shopper should also be flexible enough to take advantage of on-the-spot bargains and to buy in quantity when he finds these bargains.

It is also important for a shopper to compare prices and to know and read labels, so that he is aware of what and how much he's getting and how much he's paying for it. In buying pre-packaged meat, for example, the wise consumer will read the price-per-pound figure on the label as well as the net price; a large steak with a lower price may actually cost more per pound of *meat* because of the bone, which must be paid for but can't be eaten. The wise consumer also knows that foodstuffs carrying the private label of the market or chain are usually of the same quality as the nationally known brands but significantly cheaper, that most fresh fruits and vegetables have a season in the year when they are in plentiful supply and therefore relatively cheap, and that buying at the small corner store or the late-night market is justified only in terms of convenience — for prices are inevitably far more than in large chain markets or co-ops. Contrary to common opinion, the prepared or "convenience foods" are not always bad bargains, since according to a marketing research report of the department of Agriculture, most convenience foods average only 2 percent higher in price than their unprocessed equivalent (Smith and Pratt, 1970, p. 55). On the other hand, some prepared foods can be enormously extravagant; frozen beef patties, for example, sometimes sell for as much as $2\frac{1}{2}$ times more than fresh ground beef which must be shaped for cooking.

Buying Clothing

As with food, clothing fulfills psychological as well as practical needs. Again, the wise shopper must know his values, weigh alternatives, and then try to get the most for his money. As with shopping for food, he should decide what he wants before he shops, so that he can resist the subtle pressures of skilled salesmen, clever displays, and phony (or even legitimate) sales on items that he doesn't really want. He should comparison shop, know values, and be certain that what he is paying for an item is what the item is really worth both on the market and to him personally.

Clothing expenses can be cut substantially by planning ahead and taking advantage of seasonal reductions. Winter coats usually go on sale the day before Christmas, with reductions of as much as one third or one half. All varieties of clothing go on sale in January,[25] before the stores make their inventories. Children's clothes are usually also on sale in September, just after school starts. Women's coats, woolen dresses, and men's suits and coats are often marked down in November, which is also the month for manufacturers' closeout sales of men's shirts. Men's and boy's suits and women's dresses and hats also go on sale after Easter, in late April. Ski sweaters and bathing suits sell for half their pre-season price, after the season.

Even during these seasonal sales, the shopper must always beware of phony markdowns and close-outs and the substitution by the stores of lower quality and shoddy sale merchandise for the store's regular fare. Most important of all, he should buy only what he would buy anyway, even it were not on sale. Buying something at a sale price that won't be used or isn't needed is certainly no bargain, no matter how cheap it is.

Buying the "Big-ticket" Household Items

Furniture is the one item for which buying top quality is the most *economical* as well as the most aesthetically satisfying. Poor quality furniture very quickly loses its appeal and is a constant source of irritation and expense as it breaks down or wears out and needs repairs or replacement. Good quality furniture, on the other hand, remains a continuing pleasure and will, with proper care, last a lifetime. If well-chosen, it may even grow in value.

There is generally no particular urgency in selecting furniture, so the shopper can take his time, choose carefully and watch for bargains. It is possible, for example, to save 15 to 30 percent on quality-furniture sales, usually in June.

Unless he is unusually knowledgeable about furniture standards and prices, it is risky for the consumer to shop for furniture in cut-rate stores, "discount"

---

[25] This is also the period of the traditional "white sales" on linens and bedding. The bargains available during the January "white sales" are so well-known that it is surprising that people would buy sheets, pillowcases, towels, etc., at any other time.

houses, or stores featuring distress sales. There are legitimate discount houses and distress sales that offer bargains on furniture, but it is important to be very sure that the furniture (or appliance) is a standard item and that the price is genuinely a bargain. Again, comparison shopping is an important prerequisite.

Used furniture can also be a very good bargain. Quality pieces can sometimes be picked up for next to nothing in thrift shops or through the classified ads in the newspaper. But again, the shopper must be wary, especially with the latter. There are people who make quite a good living by filling their house or apartment with junk from second-hand stores during the week and disposing of it through the Sunday want ads. It is vital to be skeptical and to compare values carefully.

One of the furniture-merchandising swindles that every consumer should be aware of is the type of store known in the trade as a *"borax" store*. Such stores specialize in selling furniture by the room. An ad typically reads something like "three rooms of furniture for $198." The person who responds to such an ad is shown the advertised furniture stacked in a dark, dusty corner. Then the salesman, with a mixture of contempt thinly overlayed with deference, leads him to a different area with better lighting and display—and higher prices. (This is called the "bait and switch" technique.) The store profits, of course, even if the customer insists upon buying the low-quality merchandise for the advertised price; but the store counts on the fact that many people are unable to resist the need to show the salesman that they can afford the better merchandise (which is either higher-priced junk or standard-quality merchandise outrageously over-priced).[26]

The electronics, jewelry, and appliance businesses frozen-food-and-freezer "bargain" plans,[27] and carpeting dealers also have their share of "borax" stores and swindles. Carpeting seems to lend itself particularly well to the "borax"-store racket, and the Sunday paper and late-night television programs are filled with ads for bargain carpeting "for your whole house." Area rugs are actually much more economical than carpeting; but if the consumer does decide on carpeting, he must be very wary of misrepresentation and outright rackets.

---

[26]"Borax" stores will charge two to five times the usual price for ordinary household furniture and appliances. One investigation, for example, cited a case where a customer was sold a Philco washer for $479, including finance charges. The same washer would have cost $250 with standard price and legitimate financing (Florence Rice, Consumer Education Director of the League of Autonomous Bronx Organizations). Mrs. Rice cites another typical example of a customer who was sold a double mattress and box spring in a "borax" store for $500; the same item was available in reputable stores in the same area for less than $100! Comparison shoppers in the government-sponsored "Project Money-Wise" found that people would pay $170 to $280 in a "borax" store for a standard-brand television set that could be bought in any legitimate store in the same area for $105 to $140 (Margolius, 1967).

[27]For example, beef is offered to freezer-plan clients at an incredibly low price (say, 29¢ per pound). When the client goes in to buy the beef at this price, the salesman shows him meat that is virtually inedible, then takes him into another freezer where the good meat is kept. This meat, at 70¢ to 80¢ per pound untrimmed, may still seem like a bargain. However, after the fat and bone is trimmed off, the price per pound is actually about 20 percent higher than the cost would be at the local super-market (Margolius, 1967). Finally, the meat is added on to the installment contract for the freezer, so that the customer pays a finance charge on both!

There is an enormous range of carpeting grades, and the unwary consumer can easily be sold an over-priced and inferior grade, which stretches, fades, and wears quickly. Some retailers will also advertise "free" installation, when actually the cost of installation ($2 to $2.50 per yard in 1971—a considerable amount) is made up by the profit in foisting an inferior grade of carpet upon the gullible buyer. It is especially important with carpets to deal only with reputable, conservative stores. The consumer should also take advantage of legitimate sales (usually in January and February), but he should expect to save no more than about 20 percent. With a discontinued mill end, the savings could go as high as 50 percent.

Consumer Reports magazine is a completely reliable source for the quality-rating of carpeting as well as for major appliances, bedding, radio/television/ stereo equipment, household tools, typewriters, and just about every other consumer item from swimming pools to shower stalls. There is no reason why a consumer should be swindled with cheap or faulty merchandise or inflated prices. Unfortunately, however, most consumers are willing cooperators in their own exploitation. We get taken not so much because we're gullible— although that certainly helps—but because we're trying to impress the hustler with our worth, our perspicacity in understanding what he is talking about, and our shrewdness in realizing that the once in a lifetime bargain he is offering is made only for the daring—and only the daring succeed in this world. We also get taken because everybody loves a bargain. Legitimate stores know this and offer us bargains hoping that we'll pick up something else along the way or that we'll return often for other items. Swindlers know this and play to our greed with glib promises and an air-tight procedure for taking our money without giving just value in return.

Here are some general principles for any kind of buying:

1. Don't be misled by the dealer who lures you into his place with an attractive ad and then tries to talk you into a higher-priced article.

2. Don't be blinded by "bargains" offered at impossible-to-believe prices.

3. Don't be fooled by phony mark-downs of overpriced items or the substitution of poorer quality merchandise during special sales.

4. Don't be rushed into making a decision by the salesman who talks about "the last chance to get in on a good thing," or the "golden opportunity" you might miss by not signing immediately.

5. Don't permit door-to-door salesmen to leave merchandise with you "on approval." You may find that you are obligated to pay, whether you keep the merchandise or not.

6. Never, never sign a contract that you do not understand or that has not been completely filled in.

Buying a Car

As with food and clothing, cars often serve more than practical necessity for the buyer, so that buying a car is not merely an operation in personal finance.

We enjoy driving cars. We use them to ease emotional tensions. They fill us with a sense of freedom, power, speed, and general well-being. They affect our jobs, our recreation, our love-lives, our social status, and the economy. They constitute a social force of roughly the same magnitude as the American Revolution or the invention of gunpowder. Throughout the lives of most of us, one car follows another like floats in a Rose Bowl parade. Models may differ with our circumstances — sports cars when we're young, station wagons in the family years, and sedate sedans in old age. But the question is never whether to buy, it is only what and when (Smith and Pratt, 1970, p. 105).

A car is the single most expensive thing the average person will ever own, unless he buys a house. The expense of a car is not only the initial purchase price but the license, insurance, maintainance, and operating expenses, which are a constant and unending drain on the car-owner's income. As we have seen, it costs the average person about $1,500 a year to drive a standard American car (see footnote 6).

A brand new car is very probably the worst investment it is possible for a person to make. The value of a new car drops 25 to 30 percent the first year. It then depreciates another 18 percent (of the original price) the second year, 14 percent the third year, 11 percent the fourth year, and 9 percent the fifth year. And at the end of ten years, it is valueless. In terms of cash, if one buys a new car for $3,000, it will drop $750 the first year, $540 the second, and $420 the third. If a person trades his car in every year for a new one, he will lose $7,500 in depreciation over a period of ten years.

In short, it is economical to buy a used car. But how used? — for with each succeeding year, although the depreciation is less, the maintainance costs of a used car are more. At what point is the saving the consumer makes by taking advantage of a car's depreciation balanced by the increasing costs of maintaining the aging car?

The answer is very clear statistically: On the average, annual maintainance costs become greater than the annual depreciation about half way through the fourth year. A two-year-old car, then, which a person should drive for about three years before trading it in on another two-year-old car, avoids both the enormous initial depreciation of the first two years and the rise in repair costs after the fifth year. Individual makes of cars vary, however, and no statistical rule-of-thumb can tell a consumer when to buy or when to trade-in a specific car. There are cars that give comfortable, trouble-free service for more than five years and cars that are lemons from the outset. An older car is an especially good bargain if the buyer is able to do the mechanical repairs himself.

The sticker price on the window of a car in the showroom is there because the law says it must be, but it is a naive buyer who accepts the sticker price as anything but a starting point for negotiations. A Federal Trade Commission survey made in 1969 showed that most new cars were sold at prices from $200 to $800 lower than the sticker price. During year-end sales in the late summer and fall, discounts are even higher than that. It helps in making a realistic offer for a car to know how much it cost the dealer. To find the dealer's cost, subtract the transportation charge from the bottom sticker price. Then, for an intermediate car, take $81\frac{1}{2}$ percent of the remainder; for standard-sized cars, take 78 percent of the remainder; and for compacts take 85 percent of the remainder. Then add the transportation charge back in. The result will be very close to what the car cost the dealer. Before he sells the car, of course, the dealer has to take into account his costs in preparing the car for delivery, the commission he must pay his salesman, his overhead, and the profit without which he is out of business. Usually, a dealer will be satisfied with a price of $150 to $250 above the cost of the car, rather than lose the deal.

A person can find what his old car is worth as a trade-in by checking either the *Bluebook*, which the salesman has in his desk (but may be reluctant to show you), or *Consumer Reports*, which lists the prices of cars for the last six years.

It is, of course, foolhardy in the extreme to make such an important purchase as a car without checking with expert opinion. New cars are reviewed in the annual "Auto Buying Guide" issue of *Consumer Reports*. Consumers Union also publishes a section on "How to Buy a New Car" in the year-end "Buying Guide" issue. This issue is also invaluable for detailed information on the precise steps to take in buying a used car. In the 1971 edition, for example, it specifies eight "On the Lot Tests" and eight "Driving Tests" that the shopper should make before purchasing a used car. It also has a table showing the "Frequency of Repair" record of various models of cars for the past six years and an analysis of year-old cars, specifically criticizing five factors: seating comfort, ride, handling and steering, brakes, and frequency of repair record. Another very useful source of information for the used-car buyer is an automotive diagostic center, which for about $25 will analyze the faults in a car and itemize the costs of repair.

A person should be very careful about buying a used car from a listing in the want ads or from used-car lots with signs advertising enormous discounts. And he should pay little attention to the mileage figure on a speedometer; it is a very simple matter to turn it back.

When the consumer has settled on the car he wants and agreed with the salesman on a price, he should have the dealer put the agreement in writing before he makes a deposit or gives up the keys to his old car. The order form that embodies this agreement should include a statement of the precise car being bought, the accessories agreed upon, the transportation charge, the sales tax, the registration fee, and the value of the trade-in. In addition, an officer of the firm must sign the order form, or it is valueless. The salesman's signature means nothing; and a buyer may find that when the time comes to actually close the deal, he has been "low-balled," promised a better deal than he is actually able to get, or "high-balled," offered more on his trade-in than he will actually get. A person may quite readily be both "high-balled" *and* "low-balled" during the course of the negotiations; both practices are very common among car salesmen.

The insurance for a car should be shopped for as carefully as for the car itself. Insurance is one of the most costly items of automobile operation, and without some comparison shopping, a car owner can spend a lot of money unnecessarily. Insurance should never be obtained from the dealer who sells the car; such policies are seldom the best or most economical. Similarly, in arranging for the money to buy a car, the consumer makes a serious mistake in getting credit through the dealer. He should borrow from a bank (or credit union) with the lowest possible interest rate and then pay cash to the dealer for the car.

Buying a House

A house is the single most expensive item a person will ever buy, unless he is in that very small minority which has enormous sums available for yachts, jewelry, or Picassos. Certainly, for the average person, a home is by far his most valuable possession. Experts on personal finance find that a person should pay no more than about one fourth of his monthly spendable income on rent and no more than $2\frac{1}{2}$ times his *dependable* yearly income on the purchase of a home. These are statistical generalities, however, and offer little more than rough guidelines for the individual. A person must look to his own budget to determine what *he* can afford to pay for housing. By subtracting the monthly total of all his non-housing expenses from his total monthly income, he will have the figure that is available for rent or mortgage payments.[28]

The young couple usually regard their initial apartment as only a temporary home and plan to move to better quarters as soon as they can afford it. Whether to buy a home instead of renting is a question that necessarily comes up only when they have the resources to make the down payment on a house. When the funds for a down payment are either at hand or within reach, there are two questions the couple must consider: (1) Do they prefer the life-style of apartment dwelling, with its convenience and relative freedom from responsibility, or would they find more satisfaction in the privacy and responsibility of a home? (2) What are the relative costs of renting and buying?

The life-style question is highly individual, of course. The second question must involve a comparison of the total costs of renting and the total costs of buying, not for the next year or two but for the next 30 years (assuming a 30-year mortgage for the house). Merely comparing one's present rent with the monthly mortgage payments for the house he wants is much too simplistic and may be very misleading—as many a dismayed buyer struggling with mortgage payments and home maintenance has found to his consternation.

Now, obviously, making such a comparison calls for the use of many assumptions about future income, future taxes and costs, future needs, and the future state of the economy. Making as accurate an *estimate* as possible, however, using the assumptions of experts in the field of personal finance and economics, is the only sound basis on which a person can decide whether to continue renting or to buy, and just what the true cost of home ownership will be compared to the cost of continued renting.

---

[28] The total monthly cost of buying a house includes, in addition to the mortgage payment, taxes, insurance, utilities, and the estimated annual 2 percent of the worth of the house for maintenance and repair; *minus* the income-tax benefits—a figure which may be obtained by multiplying the individual's income-tax bracket (the percentage of income he must pay) by the total amount paid monthly in interest, insurance, and other deductible costs (for example, using part of his house to produce income).

Again, then, comparing the costs of renting versus buying (over the lifetime of a 30-year mortgage) involves estimating the total costs of each for 30 years, as follows:

Costs of home ownership:
(1) Mortgage payments (annual total x 30).
(2) Maintenance and repair (2 percent of the cost of the home x 30).
(3) Utilities ($120 x 30 — utilities are always higher in a home and $10 more per month is a conservative estimate).
(4) Fire-insurance payments (annual cost x 30).
(5) Property taxes (annual cost x 30).[29]

Costs of renting:
(1) Monthly rent (increased 3 percent annually x 30 years).[30]

Now by subtracting from each total the financial benefits that may be gained over that same period by buying or renting, the person will have a rough but useful estimate of the comparative costs:

Financial benefits of home ownership:
(1) Income tax savings (each year for 30 years, the total figure of property taxes, home insurance, and that part of his mortgage payment that represents interest may be deducted from a person's taxable income by the percentage of his tax bracket that year, thereby lowering the amount he must pay annually in federal, state, and local income taxes. In other words, if he is in the 25 percent bracket, he may lower his annual income taxes by 25 percent of the total figure for property taxes, insurance, and interest.[31]

---

[29]This figure may change if the tax rate changes or the assessed evaluation of the property increases; the potential home buyer should check the assessment history of property in the area.

[30]Finance experts suggest that in a period of continuing inflation, a 3 percent annual increase in rent is a very modest estimate for the long run of 30 years.

[31]If a person is using part of his home for any income-producing activity he may also include this proportion of his mortgage cost as a deductible expense. For example, if he is a teacher and has a five-room house, and uses one of the rooms for grading papers, he may deduct one fifth of the cost of the mortgage from his taxable income; he may also, in this case, deduct one fifth of his home maintenance costs as well.

(2) Appreciation of the property (in a time of continuing inflation, the property may be expected to appreciate at a rate of about 3 percent annually,[32] so that its value should at least double during the 30 years).

Financial Benefits of Renting:
(1) Annual appreciation of the sum of the down payment if it were invested in conservative securities (9 percent per year, compounded for 30 years would be a modest expectation for an investment in blue-chip stocks according to Smith and Pratt) (1970, p. 339).

In short, whether the person will find renting or owning more economical depends basically upon the amount of his rent, the cost of the house he would buy, the amount of the down payment required, the costs of property taxes and home insurance, his income-tax bracket, and whether or not he can deduct part of the cost of the house as income-producing.[33] Having these specific figures, the comparative costs are not difficult to estimate.

There are many things to look for if a person does decide to buy a home — the neighborhood, whether to buy a new house or an old one or to have one built, design and construction features, etc. An excellent guide to shopping for a house may be found in Chapter Seven of Smith and Pratt's *The Time-Life Book of Family Finance* (1970), which includes a convenient check list for every aspect of shopping and buying. The legal ramifications of home buying and mortgages are so complex that no one should ever proceed beyond looking and discussing without the aid of an attorney. Certainly, one should never put anything into writing without an attorney's advice. Smith and Pratt give the following example of the kind of trap the unadvised buyer may unwittingly fall into:

A St. Louis couple particularly wanted a house with an oversized, heated garage. The husband needed it for the radio and TV repairs that were his hobby. They eventually found exactly what they were looking for in a nearby suburban town. Dan gave the owner $100 as "earnest money" and noted on the check, "Deposit toward purchase of property at 640 Maple Avenue at price of $23,750."

Dan consulted a lawyer during his lunch hour next day. The attorney asked if he'd checked zoning laws in connection with the intended workshop. No, said Dan, but the owner had assured him there would be no difficulty. On the contrary, said the lawyer, he knew about a complaint made by residents of the neighborhood involving a similar use of residential property; Dan would almost certainly run into trouble. Dan went back to the owner and explained that he'd have to back out. "A deal's a deal," said the owner. "All

---

[32]The rate of property appreciation will vary, of course, with the geographic area, the neighborhood, the type of property, the soundness of the construction, and how good a buy the person was able to get in the first place.

[33]It must not be overlooked, of course, that a similar part of his apartment rent may be deducted, if a room is used to produce income, so it would only be the *difference* between the apartment deduction and the home deduction that should be used in computing the difference between the costs of renting and buying.

*right, my tough luck," said Dan, and went home to give his wife the news that they'd kissed
$100 goodbye.*

*But that wasn't quite what the owner had meant. After some conversations between his
lawyer and Dan's, it turned out that Dan was going to buy the house, willy-nilly. That
notation on his check was as binding as a three-page contract (p. 198).*

The moral is, of course, that if a check is given for a deposit on a house, put
no notations on it. If a cash deposit is given as earnest money, the person should
take only a receipt for the amount, with no stipulations about why it was paid or
for what. But the best way to avoid such pitfalls is not to make any agreements
at all without consulting an attorney; his cost should be considered an essential
part of the cost of buying a house.

Buying Life Insurance

The basic purpose of life insurance is to provide *income protection* for the bene-
ficiary (the family of the deceased) in the event of the policy holder's death.
For a relatively modest sum, a person may *insure* that when he dies, he will leave
his family with an "instant estate" that can partially substitute for the loss of his
earnings. It is the only substantial estate that most people who die before their
children are grown will have. Thus, there is no question of the value and importance of this basic coverage for the breadwinner of a growing family.[34] He
should be insured for as substantial a sum as is appropriate to his income and
budget.

Again, however, as with all matters of personal finance, it is essential for a
person to get the best possible buy. In terms of life insurance, this means under-
star.ding the provisions and the purpose of a life-insurance policy and then
shopping around to get the greatest income protection possible for the size of
the premium, or fee, that is paid.[35]

There are basically two kinds of life-insurance policies: (1) *term insurance*,
and (2) *insurance-plus-investment*.[36] Term insurance, which is the least expensive
by far, guarantees the payment of the face value of the policy at death for a
prescribed period of time (a "term") from the signing of the policy contract.
That period of time is generally five years, after which the policy must be renewed (if it is "renewable") at a higher premium that reflects the advancing age

---

[34] Insuring children is a very poor use of money. The main purpose of life insurance is income protection. If a family's resources are limited—and they almost always are—the money available for
insurance premiums should be spent on maximum coverage for the wage earner.

[35] Of course, a person must also be certain that the insurance company is sound and has a good
reputation. There are many fly-by-night insurance companies that should be avoided no matter what
their rates.

[36] Insurance-plus-investment policies come under various plans and names—ordinary life, straight
life, 20-payment life (paid-up—that is, no more premiums after 20 years), 20-year endowment
(returns an income after 20 years), etc. Term insurance also comes under various names, such as
decreasing-term (the premium remains the same but the face value declines), renewable and con-
vertible-renewable term, mortgage insurance, etc.

and higher death risk of the insured. When the insured reaches age 65, the term policy is usually cancelled and non-renewable.

Insurance-plus-investment policies divide the premium into two parts, one of which pays for a life-insurance feature of the policy, while the other part is invested for the policy holder and earns interest and an increasing cash value. This type of insurance guarantees the payment of the face value of the policy throughout the lifetime of the insured. Unlike term insurance, the policy need not be renewed periodically, it is not cancelled at age 65, and the premiums generally remain the same rather than increasing with the years. The insured may borrow against the accumulated cash value of his savings (paying interest, of course, and depleting the face value of the policy by the amount borrowed), or he may terminate the policy and collect its cash value.

On the surface, it would seem that the insurance-plus-investment type policy is the better buy, since (1) it accumulates a cash-loan value from a part of the premiums that are paid; (2) it remains in force after age 65, when the insured is getting closer to death; and (3) its premiums and its coverage remain constant, in contrast to the five-year renewals and increased premiums of term insurance. Insurance companies and their salesmen go to some lengths to convince prospects that this surface comparison of the two types of policies is an accurate one and that insurance-plus-investment policies, though more expensive, are indeed the better buy. They have good reason to say this: Insurance-plus-investment policies pay a much higher commission to the salesmen and earn much more in profits for the company (chiefly because the higher premiums are reinvested by the company for a much better return than the policy holder receives).[37]

The fact is that the insurance-plus-investment type of policy is a very bad buy — one of the worst possible uses of money by a family that should be investing every insurance dollar available into the income-protection aspect of life insurance for the breadwinner.

Let us see why this is so. In the first place, the cash-value aspect of the policy is not really as attractive as it appears on the surface. The part of the premium that goes into savings for the policy holder collects only about $2\frac{1}{2}$ percent interest, compounded annually, which is less than half of what is available in a savings-and-loan account (in the form of an investment certificate) and is not even enough to keep pace with the current rate of inflation. (The insurance company, as we have noted, uses the person's savings for its *own* investments at a much higher rate of return and keeps the difference.) Moreover, the policy holder may not withdraw his money without losing the policy; that is, if he draws out his savings, the life-insurance part of his policy is cancelled as well. For all practical purposes, then, this places his savings beyond reach, unless he is willing to lose his insurance coverage. He may borrow his savings (paying 5 to 6 percent annual interest), but if he dies before repaying the loan, the face value of the policy is reduced by the unpaid remainder. In other words, his beneficiaries

---

[37] Insurance-plus-investment policies are the chief business of all life insurance companies, and most salesmen won't even discuss term insurance with a prospect; he must usually go directly to the company to get term-insurance coverage, unless it is part of a group plan.

will not get the full face value of his policy even though he has presumably been paying the insurance part of the premium *for* this face value (with the rest of the premium going to the savings account against which he has borrowed.) And finally, if he repays all loans and doesn't cash in his policy, his beneficiaries will be paid only the face value at his death. The cash value — the policy holder's accumulated savings plus $2\frac{1}{2}$ percent interest compounded annually — is kept by the insurance company. This might explain in part why insurance companies now have more total assets in the United States than all the giant industrial corporations combined.

So much for the cash-value aspect of the insurance-plus-investment policy. The second major selling feature of this type of policy is that the premiums remain the same for the ordinary life, whereas they rise every five years for the renewable term insurance. With term insurance, however, the policy holder pays only for what he is getting, based upon his actuarial life expectancy: If 7 out of every 1,000 in his age, sex, and racial group will die in the following year (according to actuarial expectations), then he must pay $7 for each $1,000 of insurance coverage (plus enough differential so that the company may pay its overhead and make a profit). As he grows older, the actuarial expectancy of death increases and his premium is raised accordingly. Ordinary-life premiums remain the same as he grows older simply because the risk is pro-rated, or spread over the life of the policy, with the policy holder paying a premium higher than his actuarial expectation during the first half of the life of the policy, and a premium lower than his actuarial expectation during the remainder. Since many policies are dropped by their holders before they reach this half-way point, the excess in premium charge is a bonus realized by the company (and it certainly is no bargain for the policy holder).

The third selling point is that with the ordinary-life type of policy, protection is not cancelled at age 65, whereas with term insurance the policy holder not only pays an increasingly high premium all his life but then is cancelled out when he is too old to get another policy. To take a closer look at this point — the permanence of protection — it is necessary to trace the relative value of the cash-saving-plus-insurance protection a person would have (1) if he bought a renewable term insurance policy and invested the difference in cost between that policy and an ordinary life policy of the same initial face value, and (2) if he bought an ordinary life policy, which does not cancel out at age 65 and has a cash surrender value and uniform premiums.

Suppose a 30-year-old man decides that he wants $50,000 worth of life-insurance income protection for his family. The premium for renewable term insurance at this age comes to about $3.85 per $1,000,[38] so his total premium comes to about $192.50 per year. On the other hand, ordinary life (the most common insurance-plus-investment plan) at his age would carry a premium of about $15 per $1,000, or $751 a year for $50,000 of insurance coverage. If the

---

[38] Premiums varied in 1971 from more than $8 down to $3.85 for each $1,000 of insurance coverage for a 30-year-old white male.

policy holder invests the difference between the $751 and the $192.50 premium for the renewable term insurance (a difference of $558.50 per year), he will accumulate $2,792.50 in 5 years.

If we assume that he can realize 5 percent interest on this money, compounded annually, he will have $3,349.42 in his savings account at the end of the five-year period. At this time, when his renewable term policy must be renewed, he will need only $47,000 of life-insurance coverage (to match the ordinary life), since he now has over $3,000 in investments. During the second 5-year period, following the same plan, he will accumulate $3,195 (at 5 percent interest, compounded annually), which when added to the prior savings (now grown with the compounded interest to $4,166) gives him a total cash savings of $7,361 ($47,000 of insurance coverage plus a total cash savings of $7,361). At the end of the second 5-year period, then, his total worth to his beneficiaries would be $54,361 ($47,000 of insurance coverage plus $7,361 in savings). For each succeeding 5-year term, he may continue to invest the difference between the cost of the two premiums and add the results to the prior accumulated savings.

The figures are easier to see and understand if we put them in the form of a table (see Table 9–2 – the figures are rounded off to the nearest dollar).

It should be clear that "buying term and investing the difference," even at the modest return of 5 percent, provides an equal or higher income protection for the policy holder's survivors at every period, from age 30 to age 65 and beyond. If the person dies before age 65, he has protection equal to that of ordinary-life insurance the first year of each 5-year term and much more protection during each succeeding year of every 5-year term. At age 65, he has the same protection ($50,000) but $22,270 more cash value, since with ordinary life the "cash surrender value" of a $50,000 policy taken out at age 30 is $27,300 after 35 years. Moreover, with each year after age 66, the $50,000 will continue to grow. He can either let it appreciate, or he can begin withdrawing the interest – $2,500 (at 5 percent) each year for the rest of his life – and still leave the $50,000 intact. With ordinary life, on the other hand, he would have to continue to pay the premium of $750 each year for the rest of his life just to maintain the $50,000 coverage.[39]

In summary, every person with dependents should have an income-protection, or life-insurance, plan and a regular savings and investment plan. With insurance, he should get the maximum possible coverage for his money; with investments, he should put his money where it will collect the best possible

---

[39] There are various limited-payment plans, with the insurance paid up after a specified time or at a specified age. With these policies, the insurance company calculates the premiums to age 100, and then bunches them into a shorter period of time (usually 20 or 30 years – called "20-pay life" and "30-pay life"). The annual premium is accordingly higher. The limited-payment plans are even worse buys than ordinary life; for (1) if the policy holder dies early, he has paid out more in premiums for the same coverage; and (2) because of continuing inflation, if he enjoys a long life, the money with which he paid up his policy is worth more than the money he would have paid if the premiums had been spread out over his entire lifetime.

Table 9–2. The "Buy Term and Invest the Difference" Plan

Age	Value of renewable term-insurance policy	Annual premium for renewable term-insurance policy	Annual premium for ordinary-life policy (with $50,000 face value)	Amount saved between ordinary-life and term-insurance policies	Accumulated savings during current 5-year period (at 5 percent interest compounded annually)	Total of all prior savings plus interest at 5 percent compounded annually	Total in cash savings*	Total face value of term-insurance policy, plus accumulated savings at end of period
30–35	$50,000	$192	$750	$558	$3,249	$ 0,000	$ 3,249	$53,249
35–40	47,000	202	750	549	3,195	4,166	7,361	54,361
40–45	43,000	240	750	511	2,974	9,437	12,411	55,411
45–50	38,000	298	750	453	2,634	15,912	18,546	56,546
50–55	31,000	359	750	392	2,282	23,777	26,060	57,060
55–60	24,000	421	750	330	1,922	33,409	35,331	59,331
60–65	15,000	395	750	356	2,074	45,296	47,370	62,370†

Source: After Smith and Pratt, 1969, p. 117.

* Sum of current 5-year-period savings plus all prior savings (both at 5 percent interest compounded annually).
† At age 65, the term insurance is cancelled and the plan is worth $47,370 (total of cash savings). One year later, at age 66, interest would bring this up to $50,000.

return consistent with safety. He accomplishes neither if he uses his insurance company as a bank.

Finally, he should be aware of the income protection provided survivors by the federal Social Security Administration. In many cases, social security provides benefits that it would take an estate of $200,000 to equal. He should know what these benefits are and how to take advantage of them.[40] He may find that his potential estate is much richer than he thinks.

Paying Income Tax

The U. S. Internal Revenue Service does not expect a person to pay any more in income tax than he is legally liable for; the taxpayer is encouraged to take advantage of all the opportunities for lowering his personal taxes that the tax laws make available. Yet the service can expect that as many as three out of four people who figure their own tax returns will overpay their taxes (Smith and Pratt, 1970, p. 279).

The biggest mistake that people make is using the *short form*, which allows only a 13 percent deduction (not exceeding $1,500) from a person's total income for all his legally deductible expenses.[41] Some 57 percent of the tax payers use this short form every year (Smith and Pratt, p. 28) because it is very simple and fast. They should be aware that it can also be very expensive. The average student who works only part time probably saves on the short form, of course, because he has very few deductions and a limited income. If he works full time, however, or is married and going to school while his wife works full time, or if both he and his wife are working part time, relying upon the short form is likely to be an expensive luxury. For in any of these cases, the standard 13 percent deduction provided for in the short form is usually a very conservative estimate of the deductions legally available during the course of the year.

The interest payments on loans and credit purchases, medical and dental expenses (in excess of 3 percent of the tax payer's adjusted gross income), contributions to organized charities, churches, and other non-profit organizations, and *all* taxes are deductible if they are properly itemized. A person may exclude "sick pay" (under certain circumstances and to a certain degree), unemployment assessments, and retirement-fund payments (under certain circumstances). If he has to move because of job relocation or for a new job, he may deduct the cost of moving (if the new job is at least 20 miles away and permanent for at least 39 weeks.) If he uses an employment agency to get a job, he may deduct the agency's fee. He may deduct educational expenses that are necessary to produce his income, union and professional dues, the tools, equipment, uniforms, and publications useful or required for his occupation. Finally, he may, of course, deduct all unreimbursed business expenses.

[41] In 1973, this deduction will be 15 percent, with a ceiling of $2,000.
[40] The *Social Security Handbook* is available for $2.25 from the Superintendent of Documents, U. S. Government Printing Office, Washington, D. C., 20402.

A complete list of all legal deductions, together with the circumstances under which they may be applied, is clearly beyond the scope of our discussion. The important point to emphasize is that the tax laws are very complicated and change periodically, and it is therefore very difficult for the average person to figure his own income tax and take advantage of all the legal deductions to which he is entitled. If his income is very modest and his deductions very few, he will profit by using the very uncomplicated short form. Otherwise, he will do better financially to pay a professional to make out his tax return. A tax expert is likely to find enough deductions that the average person hadn't thought of or doesn't know about to more than pay for the moderate fee the expert will charge — which is another deductible item, by the way. The tax expert must have something to work with however, and a wise consumer makes a practice of saving and then sorting into categories all sales receipts, cancelled checks, and records of unreceipted deductible expenditures for the year. The tax expert will make good use of this data.

Before taking his form and his records to the expert, a person should first try to compute the long form himself. He will then be much more knowledgeable in discussing the deductions and the problems with the tax expert — he also will be aware, then, of just how much the expert has saved him. In making this initial and informational attempt, the person will need a tax guide. A good manual, which is available for about a dollar, is the government's own *Your Federal Income Tax*, which can be ordered from the U. S. Superintendent of Documents, Washington, D. C., 20402. Lasser's annual *Income Tax Guide* is another good source of information, available at libraries and book stores.

The Importance of Regular Investments

Experts in personal finance distinguish between *saving* and *investing*. The emphasis with saving is threefold: (1) saving allows the person to buy the things he wants in the near future without letting part of his spendable income drain off in finance charges; (2) saving allows the person to buy things he otherwise wouldn't be able to buy — say, a house or a boat — because it is not possible to get a loan for a sizable purchase unless he has a down payment, which is accumulated by saving; and (3) saving provides protection against a sudden unexpected expense (a nest egg tucked away but easily accessible will create enormous peace of mind — if the inevitable family emergencies must be handled with borrowing under pressure at high interest rates, they can be financially ruinous.)

The emphasis with *investing* is on the distant future and upon long-term growth of the investment. The goal of investing is not deferred spending for the immediate future or an emergency reserve but rather upon removing the invested money from spendable resources and allowing it to grow — taking advantage of the "growth on growth" principle of capital funds. Eventually, of course, withdrawals are made — but only from dividends or interest, never, at

least ideally, from the principal. For example, if a person were to invest $100 each month for twelve years in an account that paid 6 percent interest compounded annually, he could then withdraw $100 each month from that account forever. He could do this without ever touching the principal or depositing another cent, so long as the account continued to pay 6 percent compounded interest.

Money reproduces itself in this way because of the system of *compound interest*, in which the interest that invested money earns, itself earns interest. Thus, if the investment of $100 a month is drawing 6 percent interest compounded annually, each dollar that is deposited doubles in twelve years. At the end of this time, *two* dollars are on deposit for each *one* that was put in twelve years previously, and the person can then withdraw one of these dollars, leaving the other to begin *its* cycle of doubling.

This "doubling time" of twelve years is very modest when compared to the potential of an investment in common stocks. Despite crashes and recessions, stocks have averaged a growth of 9.3 percent per year from 1926 to the present and 12 percent per year from 1945 to the present (Smith and Pratt, 1970, p. 339). Mutual funds have done even better than this, averaging an annual growth rate of 15 percent during the past decade (Smith and Pratt, p. 405; see also Figure 9–3). At this rate of 15 percent compounded annually, the doubling time is just 5 years.[42]

There are three factors which must be considered in any long-term investment program: *safety, yield,* and *growth.* A good investment balances these three factors. If an investment is safe but provides a yield less than the rate of inflation and no growth at all, it is obviously a poor investment (U. S. government series-E savings bonds, which yield only $3\frac{1}{2}$ percent, are an example). If the investment provides safety and a relatively high yield but fails to grow with the economy, it is also a poor investment (a savings and loan "certificate of deposit"

---

[42] A person who invested $100 at age twenty in a program which maintained an average growth rate of 15 percent compounded annually would have on deposit more than $44,000 by age 65.

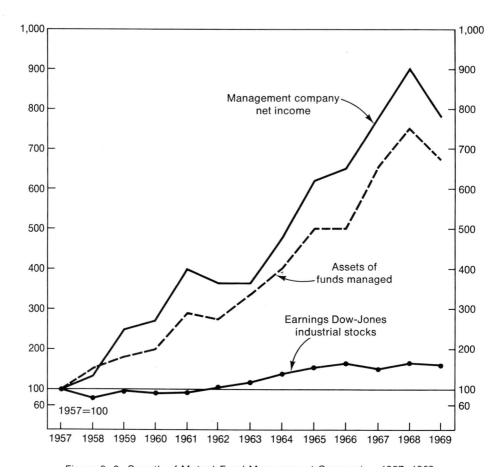

Figure 9–3. Growth of Mutual-Fund Management Companies, 1957–1969

is a good example).[43] Finally, if the growth is phenomenal and the yield out-standing but the potential too risky, it is obviously a poor long-term investment. (Buying this type of security is called "speculating" rather than investing.)

A point that is especially important is that any investment must especially consider the long-range trend of the American economy. If an investment does not even keep pace with inflation, the investor's funds will actually *lose* value (even while they are appreciating). Thus, when he withdraws his funds, they will be worth less in actual purchasing power than when he invested them.[44]

---

[43] While the "certificate of deposit," which paid 6 percent interest compounded annually in 1971, is a poor *investment* (not even keeping up with current inflation after taxes are paid on the earnings), it is a good depository for *saving.*

[44] It would take $100 today to buy what George Washington could buy for $1 and $10 to match the dollar of Abraham Lincoln's day. Since World War II, the decline in purchasing power of the dollar has *averaged* 2 percent each year. If costs continue to rise during the next 30 years as they have in the past 30, in the year 2000 a cup of coffee will cost 50¢, coffee and a doughnut $1.25, a glass of milk 75¢, a cocktail $4, a visit to a doctor's office $50, a hospital room $600, a standard-size new car $9,000.

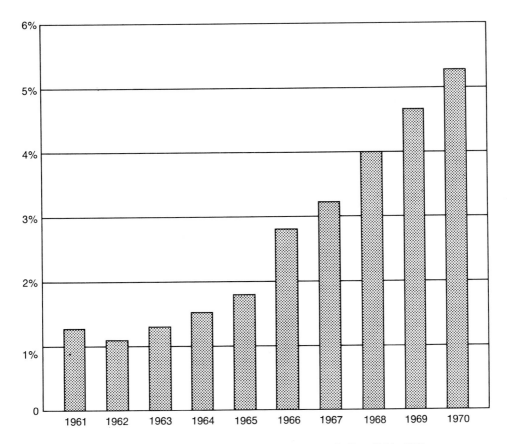

Figure 9–4. Decline in Purchasing Power of the Dollar, 1961–1970

The current inflationary decline in purchasing power is a little over 5 percent a year (see Figure 9–4). This means that an investment would have to yield at least 5 percent annually, after taxes, just to break even. Fortunately, long-range growth of industrial stocks has averaged a little better than 9 percent annually since 1900, even with the inevitable fluctuations (see Figure 9–5).

Picking a portfolio of stocks that will yield maximum growth and return consistent with safety is no task for the average person, of course, unless he is able to devote a good deal of time to the market and to investment principles. No one can buy an "average stock," which is why mutual funds are so popular. With a mutual fund, the portfolio of stocks is balanced for return, growth, and risk by the professionals who manage it; and the funds of the investor are spread over the contents of the many stocks in the portfolio. Even so, performance among mutual funds varies almost as much as among individual stocks; and some funds have actually lost money while the market was rising, while others have failed to pay even the 5 percent earnings available in bank savings deposits.

Still, it is much simpler for the average person to get reliable information on mutual funds than it is for him to evaluate stocks. *Forbes* magazine puts out an

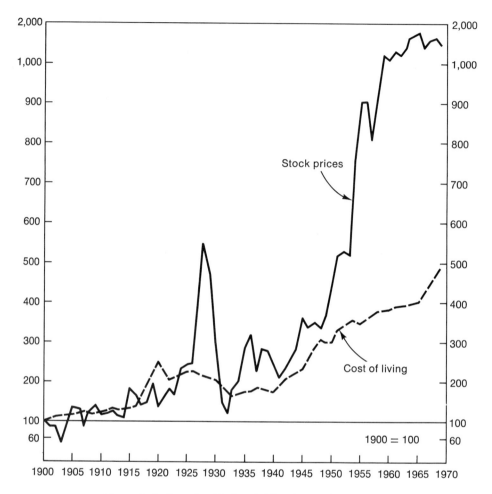

Figure 9–5. Growth of Industrial Stocks vs. Cost of Living

annual rating of mutual funds, analyzing their record during the prior decade. The "Wiesenberger Report,"[45] which costs $40 but is available in the public library, does the same in considerably more depth and detail.

The basics of investing, then, are simply stated: It is important (1) to start an investment program *immediately* (thus taking advantage of the "growth on growth" principle of capital funds; (2) to invest *regularly* (however modestly); and (3) to balance the three factors of safety, yield, and growth, choosing investments that will more than keep up with inflation in terms of both yield and

---

[45] Wiesenberger, *Investment Companies 1971: Mutual Funds and Other Types* (31st ed.). New York: Wiesenberger Services, Inc., 1971.

[46] According to this principle, for example, a mortgage is a good use of money: Value is received today and paid for in tomorrow's devalued dollars. (Conversely, an insurance-endowment policy is one of the worst possible investments: The premiums are paid with today's dollars and repaid in tomorrow's devalued dollars.)

growth.[46] To go beyond these basic elements into an in-depth analysis of the ins-and-outs of investing is, of course, beyond the scope of our discussion. There are many excellent and fascinating primers readily available, however.[47]

Summary

The "facts of life" that the young couple encounter when they strike out on their own is not only the birds-and-bees world of mature sexual relations but the dollars-and-cents world of hard economic reality. Research indicates that couples quarrel more about money than any other topic and that the various economic pressures on a family are among the major sources of marriage failure. The "real world" is the world of wresting a living from the culture, whether as the breadwinner or as a consumer. In the complex world of our mass society, wresting a living means, in essence, directing one's cash flow; for few of us can provide our own goods or services directly.

Keeping a budget is an enormous help in enabling a person to maximize his need satisfactions with available funds — that is, to maintain a cash flow that directs his spendable income where he most wants it to go. Since there is never enough money for everything a person needs or wants, he is always forced to choose between available alternates, whether or not he realizes it at the time. It is impossible to make these choices wisely if the alternates are not clear. The budget is an indispensable tool that clarifies these choices and puts them into perspective.

Credit is a potentially dangerous tool; yet it is a fundamental element of economic life in our society, and the wise use of it can provide significant enhancement of a person's life style. There are three major forms of credit: open credit (which is not financed and therefore "free" and a great bargain and convenience), profit-making credit (which *is* financed but potentially profitable), and non-profit-making credit (which is financed and costly). The wise consumer will be aware of the ways that each of these forms of credit can be used most effectively, as well as the risks inherent in each form. Credit-installment buying of a "big-ticket" item is expensive, risky, and usually an unwise use of credit. Instead, the person should borrow the money and pay cash for the item. He should shop for the money as carefully as for any other commodity, looking for the best "buy" — that is, the lowest interest rate.

A wise consumer not only understands the principles of budgeting (especially the concept of forced alternate choice) and the effective uses of credit; he also understands the principle of *value-return* — getting a dollar's worth out of a dollar. He knows what he wants and why he wants it; and he learns to comparison shop, to recognize overpriced or shoddy merchandise and faulty contracts, to distinguish the legitimate from the phony sale, to handle the smooth or bullying salesman who uses various high pressure techniques, and to recognize and

---

[47] An excellent and eminently readable analysis of the investment aspect of family finance may be found in Chapter Twelve of Smith and Pratt's *The Time-Life Book of Family Finance* (1970).

avoid completely the "borax"-type stores. He knows that he can't get something for nothing and is especially wary of offers of "free services" or unbelievable bargains.

Finally, sound personal finance requires that the breadwinner of the family has an income-protecting, renewable term life-insurance policy and a regular program of saving *and* investing. "Saving" is the term used for the accumulation of money for deferred spending and for an emergency reserve. "Investing" is the term used for a long-range program in which the money is left undisturbed to utilize the "growth on growth" principle of capital funds, doubling and re-doubling itself over the years.

Personal finance is one of the least understood and most neglected areas of family life, although it is at the heart and core of most familial interaction. Acquiring financial expertise will pay rich dividends far beyond the amount of time and attention it demands.

Questions

1 What is the main source of conflict in most marriages? Discuss the reasons why this is so.

2 What are the benefits of keeping a budget?

3 What are the basic principles of sound personal finance?

4 What is meant by the principle of *forced alternate choice?* Why is it so important to sound money management?

5 What are non-discretionary expenses? Discretionary expenses?

6 Discuss the importance of the personal allowance (a) for adults. (b) for children.

7 How does the advent of children into the family affect the family's expenditures?

8 What is the estimated cost of rearing a child to age 18 in terms of the father's annual income?

9 What are the chief sources for college student loans?

10 What is a college education worth in financial terms?

11 What are the three sound uses of credit? Discuss.

12 Explain the term *true annual interest rate.* How do you translate various other interest rates into true annual interest so that they may be compared?

13 Discuss the pitfalls of credit-installment buying?

14 What does "holder in due course" mean?

15 Explain the "balloon payment" clause in installment contracts.

16 What are some good and bad sources of loans?

17 What is a "borax" store?

18 How do most consumers cooperate in their own exploitation?

19 Discuss the economics involved in buying a car, whether new or used.

20 Discuss the economics involved in owning and driving a car.

21 What is the basic purpose of life insurance?

22 What is meant by *term insurance?* What is meant by *insurance-plus-investment?* Which is the better buy? Why?

23 What is compound interest? Explain the "growth on growth" principle of capital funds.

24 Discuss the difference between *saving* and *investing.*

25 What three factors must be considered in any long-term investment program?

26 How does *investment* differ from *speculation?*

References and Selected Readings

Arndt, Johan, ed. *Insights into Consumer Behavior.* Boston: Allyn and Bacon, 1968.

Bishop, James, Jr., and Henry W. Hubbard. *Let The Seller Beware.* Washington, D. C.: National Press, 1969.

Blood, Robert O., and Donald M. Wolfe. *Husbands and Wives: The Dynamics of Married Living.* New York: Free Press, 1960.

Boggess, Louise. *Your Social Security Benefits.* New York: Funk and Wagnalls, 1968.

Caplovitz, David. *The Poor Pay More: Consumer Practices of Low-income Families.* New York: Free Press, 1963.

Cobleigh, Ira O. *Building a Successful Family Investment Program.* New York: Association Press, 1967.

Consumer-information government pamphlets. *Be a Good Shopper* (1965). Catalog No. A43.2:SH7 − (5¢). Superintendent of Documents, Washington, D. C., 20402.

_____. *Consumer's Quick Credit Guide* (1964). Catalog No. A1. 11/3:C86 − (5¢). Superintendent of Documents, Washington, D. C., 20402.

_____. *Credit, Master or Servant?* (1966). Catalog No. D2.14:PA-10 − (25¢). Superintendent of Documents, Washington, D. C., 20402.

_____. *A Guide to Budgeting for the Family,* rev. ed. (1970). Catalog No. A.177:108/3-(10¢). Superintendent of Documents, Washington, D. C., 20402.

_____. *A Guide to Budgeting for the Young Couple,* rev. ed. (1968). Catalog No. A1.77:98/3 − (10¢).

Superintendent of Documents, Washington, D. C., 20402.

_____. *Helping Families Manage Their Finances,* rev. ed. (1968). Catalog No. A1.87:21/2 − (40¢). Superintendent of Documents, Washington, D. C., 20402.

_____. *Money Worries? A Credit Union Can Help,* rev. ed. (1969). Catalog No. HE3.302:M74/969 − (10¢). Superintendent of Documents, Washington, D. C., 20402.

_____. *Social Security Handbook* (1969). Catalog No. FS 3.52:135 − ($2.25). Superintendent of Documents, Washington, D. C., 20402.

_____. *When You Use Credit for the Family* (1965). Catalog No. A43.2:C86 − (10¢). Superintendent of Documents, Washington, D. C., 20402.

Consumer Reports. Buyers' Guide. Mount Vernon, N. Y.: Consumers Union, 1971.

_____. *How to Buy Life Insurance,* (Part 1), January 1967, Vol. 32, pp. 14−25. *Should Your Policy Also Be A Savings Account?* (Part 2), February 1967, Vol. 32, pp. 100−107. *Prices, Options, and Reading the Fine Print,* (Part 3), March 1967, Vol. 32, pp. 156−64. Mount Vernon, N. Y.: Consumers Union.

Cross, Jennifer. *The Supermarket Trap.* Bloomingdale, Ind.: Indiana University Press, 1970.

Cutright, Phillips. Income and Family Events: Family Income, Family Size and Consumption. *Journal of Marriage and the Family,* February 1971, Vol. 33, pp. 161−173.

Fromme, Allan. The Problems of Money and Work. In *The Psychologist Looks at Sex and Marriage,* Chap. 8. Englewood Cliffs, N. J.: Prentice-Hall, 1900.

Galbraith, John Kenneth. *The Affluent Society,* 2nd ed. Boston: Houghton-Mifflin, 1969.

Golde, Roger A. *Can You Be Sure of Your Experts? A Complete Manual on How to Choose and Use Doctors, Lawyers, Brokers, and All Other Experts in Your Life.* New York: Macmillan, 1969.

Goode, William J. Economic Factors and Marital Stability. *American Sociological Review,* 1951, Vol. 16, pp. 802–811.

Haines, George H. *Consumer Behavior.* New York: Free Press, 1969.

Hendrickson, Robert A. *The Future of Money.* Englewood Cliffs, N. J.: Prentice-Hall, 1970.

Herman, Robert O. Families in Bankruptcy. *Journal of Marriage and the Family,* August 1966, Vol. 28, pp. 324–330.

Katona, George. *The Mass Consumption Society.* New York: McGraw-Hill, 1964.

_____, and Eva Meuller. *Consumer Response to Income Increases.* Washington, D. C.: Brookings Institute, 1968.

Keynes, John Maynard. *Essays in Persuasion.* New York: Harcourt, 1932.

Knight, James A. *For the Love of Money: Human Behavior and Money.* Philadelphia: Lippincott, 1968.

Lasser, J. K. (J. K. Lasser Tax Institute). *Managing Your Family Finances.* Garden City, N. Y.: Doubleday, 1968.

Linder, Staffan Burenstam. *The Harried Leisure Class.* New York: Columbia University Press, 1970.

Margolius, Sidney K. *The Innocent Consumer vs. the Exploiters.* New York: Trident, 1967.

Markin, Ron J. *The Psychology of Consumer Behavior.* Englewood Cliffs, N. J.: Prentice-Hall, 1969.

Massy, William F., Ronald E. Frank, and Thomas Lodahl. *Purchasing Behavior and Personal Attributes.* Philadelphia: University of Pennsylvania Press, 1968.

Mayo, T. J. The High Cost of Parenthood. *This Week,* September 27, 1965, pp. 26–27.

McClellan, Grant S., ed. *The Consuming Public.* New York: Wilson, 1968.

Miller, Herman P. The Cash Value of Education. In *Rich Man, Poor Man.* New York: Crowell, 1971, pp. 166–194.

Nuccio, Sal. *The New York Times Guide to Personal Finance.* New York: Harper, 1967.

Paolucci, Beatrice, and Helen Thal. *Youth and Money.* Washington, D. C.: Department of Home Economics, National Education Association, 1964.

Reader's Digest, *How to Live on Your Income.* Pleasantville, N. Y.: Reader's Digest Association, 1970.

Ritter, Lawrence S., and William L. Silker. *Money.* New York: Basic Books, 1970.

Scaduto, Anthony. *Getting the Most for Your Money: How to Beat the High Cost of Living.* New York: David McKay, 1970.

Schottland, Charles I. Government Economic Programs and Family Life. *Journal of Marriage and the Family,* Vol. 28, August 1966, pp. 71–123.

Smith, Carlton, and Richard Putnam Pratt. *The Time-Life Book of Family Finance.* New York: Time-Life Books, 1969.

Springer, John L. *Consumer Swindlers and How to Avoid Them.* Chicago: Henry Regnery, 1970.

_____. *Financial Self-Defense.* New York: McGraw-Hill, 1969.

Terman, Lewis M., *et al. Psychological Factors in Marital Happiness.* New York: McGraw-Hill, 1938.

Unger, Maurice Albert, and Harold A. Wolf. *Personal Finance,* 2nd ed. Boston: Allyn and Bacon, 1969.

Part Four

The Family

Chapter Ten

The Nature of the Family

*"Home is the place where, when
you have to go there,
They have to take you in."*

Robert Frost ("The Death of the Hired
Man")

I n the bewildering complex of demands, needs, rewards, and interactions within which man must live, the *family* stands out as an institution that universally provides a nucleus of identity and reality for each individual. Whether in the *family of origin*, the family in which one is born and reared, or in the *family of procreation*, the new family that one establishes, an individual finds a protective and loving and specific kinship grouping in which he is accepted for himself and in which he is fulfilling a need that is as basic and as mysterious in its phylogenetic source as the need for a paired relation. Like the paired relation, some form of the family is repeated in every known human and mammalian society.

What distinguishes the family from the married couple is the presence of offspring. Although the term *family* can be applied to a variety of kinship groupings,[1] it is usually understood to mean parents and offspring, living in mutual interdependence within one household. Such a grouping, which will be the basis of our discussion of the family, is known as the *nuclear family*.[2]

---

[1] The U.S. Census Bureau defines a family as any two people who are related by blood or by marriage and who live in the same household. Thus, although a strict but commonly accepted definition of the family would demand the presence in the household of parents (or *a* parent, in the *broken family*) and offspring, most societies extend the definition to include innumerable combinations of relatives by blood or marriage. Even the childless couple, when they have passed well beyond the newlywed category, are often referred to as a family (of course, the couple whose children have grown up and left home are, by any definition, a family — the family of origin).

[2] The categories of kinship groupings known as the *family* are on a continuum, with the *nuclear family* at one end and, at the other end, the *extended family* — two or more nuclear families, together with other relatives, all in one household. The extended family is the ideal in most of the societies of the world (Murdock, 1949), but in actual practice it is a rarity since the large extended-family grouping is an economically and socially inefficient and stressful arrangement (Goode, 1964). (For example, in prerevolutionary China, which idealized the *corporate family*, a form of the extended

The family is, in a sense, an organism in itself—a living, growing, and malleable entity, which, once established, will take its own direction. Babies become children and children become preadolescents and preadolescents become adolescents and adults, who finally leave the family of origin to create a family of their own. Each member of a family interacts with the others in an exceedingly complex relation, which is perceived differently by each person according to his own unique frame of reference. Each child necessarily perceives himself as the center of the household, each adolescent perceives himself as autonomous, and each parent will find that the role relations that were established in early marriage between himself and his spouse will have irrevocably altered and will continue to change. As the family grows in size and in age, new role relations will be established and old roles will alter or fade. And as the offspring form their own nuclear families, the role interactions will become even more complex.

The Character of the Institution

The family is a societal institution that is, in addition to marriage, the most universal and basic of all human relations. As an institution, it fulfills the seemingly intrinsic need of man (and most of the higher animals) for economic and political organization (division of labor and social control) and stratification (status). The family, through its status position, its control of offspring, and its socializing function (which is discussed below), serves to fit the individual into the societal structure in a functional relation with the other members and other institutions of the society.

As a primary relation, the family fulfills certain intrinsic material and emotional needs which are essential to survival and normal development. The most obvious of the relational functions of the family is, of course, the care and protection of offspring. Some form of the family grouping occurs as a basic form in all species of animals in which the young are not immediately independent.[3]

---

family, the average family had only five members.) Similarly, the completely isolated nuclear family is unknown in all societies, since all peoples not only recognize but also interact frequently and extensively with the various members of their "extended" family—almost always with their parents and usually with their siblings (Reiss, 1965; Bell and Boat, 1957; Axelrod, 1956; and Greer, 1956).

In our society, we have the ideal of the nuclear family; but like all societies that hold this ideal, we extend our family grouping to include both sets of in-laws as well as various aunts, uncles, cousins, and great-grandparents. Often in our society, a single-household "nuclear" family will include a widowed mother or father-in-law. Occasionally, also, a newly married couple will live with one family of origin for a short time before they set up their own household. This American variation of the extended-family pattern was even more common and encompassing in the past in our society; for example, our literature (and television series like *The Virginian* and even *The Beverly Hillbillies*) contain many examples of single-household families that included cousins, maiden aunts, a second nuclear family, etc.

[3] Recent research in the behavior of birds and mammals (particularly, the primates) has confirmed the existence in most animal societies of the paired relation and functionally discrete family units. The major exception to this pattern is the ungulate species (the hooved animals) who relate chiefly as a herd. (See Ardrey, 1966, 1970; Altman, 1965; De Vore, 1965; Schaller, 1964, 1969; and Schrier et al., 1965.)

The mother devotes her attention to the care, training, and upbringing of her helpless offspring; the father usually protects and cares for his mate during this period and, in many species, assists the mother in protecting, caring for, and socializing the young (Lorenz, 1966).

Especially among the primates, whose offspring are particularly slow in maturing, the care and socialization of the young must be quite extensive, sometimes continuing for several years. The baboon baby, for example, remains in physical contact with his mother for a full two years following birth and then ventures only a few feet away for another year. During this time, he is provided with his needs by both the father and mother, and he is taught (mainly by the mother) the physical and social skills and knowledge necessary for survival— what food to eat and where to find it, what dangers to avoid, how to respond to and make the calls and gestures that provide communication for his species, and how to relate properly and effectively to the other members of the society. When the baboon baby is about three years of age (and until he is about five years) older peers take over this socialization process.

Even in contemporary human societies, where the socialization of the young is provided by various secondary institutions (schools, churches, the mass media), the family remains the most important agency for the socialization of children. It is within the family that the child learns the skills and attitudes which determine the manner and the extent of his utilization of the socializing programs of the secondary institutions.

The family is the only significant social institution charged with transforming a biological organism into a human being. By the time other institutions have begun to shape the individual in important ways, his family has already accomplished much of this transformation, having taught him to speak and to play out many social roles (Goode, 1964, p. 8).

In addition, evidence from a wide variety of sources—empirical and clinical— has established that the physical and psychological development of children, and consequent adult behavior, is closely related to the diversity and quality of intellectual and emotional stimuli provided during infancy and early childhood by the family group (see The Socialization of a Child, in Chapter Twelve).

Apparently, the provision of emotional stimuli, or nurture (both tactile and attitudinal), is the most basic and essential of familial functions. Without fondling and caressing, attention and emotional support—in short, loving behavior—infants suffer psychological damage and do not mature normally—neither physically, nor psychologically, nor socially. Numerous studies of early emotional deprivation in animals and children[4] have verified to the satisfaction of most behavioralists the significance of both physical *and* emotional nurture in normal development. Moreover, this nurturant function of the family, is also essential to the well-being of adults. The opportunity that the family unit provides for the *giving* of physical and emotional nurture is the chief source of fulfillment of the intrinsic altruism of the emotionally mature adult. The person who has not formed a relation in which there is someone who depends upon him (and upon whom he can depend) probably will experience an essential deprivation and frustration that will make it difficult and even impossible for him to function in an effective or satisfying manner. The family, based as it is upon the paired relation of marriage and upon the production, care, and socialization of off-spring, provides the opportunity for altruistic (and reciprocal) nurture in greater depth than does any other relation.

Finally, to come full circle in this discussion of the importance of the emotional-nurture function, there is considerable evidence that among the higher animal species, an individual who is deprived of proper emotional nurture experience in infancy will be psychologically unable to provide nurture as an adult to his own offspring (or to any other members of his society). The pattern of caring for and loving offspring is not so much instinctual as it is learned (Lorenz, 1966; Harlow, 1962)[5]; and therefore, the demonstration of this pattern varies in quality and degree, depending upon the quality and degree of each person's nurturant experience as an infant.

To sum up: The need to establish and live within a family is based chiefly upon (1) the inherent proclivity of man and the higher animals for interde-pendency, for order, and for status and social identity; (2) the physical helpless-ness of the newly born child and the culturally learned pattern of adult nurture provision, which is linked, of course, to our instinct for survival; (3) the social helplessness of the child and the societal need for socialized members; (4) the phylogenetic need of all higher creatures for receiving loving physical and emo-tional nurture in infancy and giving this nurture at maturity.

Because the family grouping is based chiefly upon conditioning which begins in an individual's infancy—when he himself is physically and emotionally nur-tured and taught to love and to reciprocate affection and support—the family

---

[4] The Harlow studies (1959, 1962), the Denenberg experiments (1963), Bettelheim in his article "Joey: A Mechanical Boy" (1959), and Axline in her book *Dibs: In Search of Self* (1964). See Chapter Twelve, the section entitled Emotional security.

[5] This is a rather recent hypothesis and it is still somewhat controversial, but there is an ever-increas-ing amount of supportive data. (See Scott, 1968; Stevenson *et al.*, 1967; Lorenz, 1966; Rheingold, 1963; Bliss, 1962; and Harlow, 1962. See also Chapter Twelve, Emotional security.) These studies also demonstrate that mating behavior and therefore the production of offspring (the foundation of the family unit) is also largely *learned* during the socialization process.

syndrome is very nearly impossible to escape unless a person is deprived of care and affection as an infant. Thus, no system for child care and socialization and the fulfillment of adult nurturant needs has ever emerged to replace the family as the dominant form in a society (Stephens, 1963). Other systems have been tried with little success;[6] and hypothetical systems have been explored by social scientists and science fiction writers, with much interesting speculation about the organization and the effects of such systems (see Huxley, *Brave New World;* Mead, *Male and Female;* Orwell, *1984;* and Zamiatin, *We*).

The Changing Character of the Family in the Mass Society

In this the final third of the twentieth century, the family's basic role—that of nurturing human beings through an exceptionally long childhood—remains intact; and the great majority of Americans continue to view the family as an institution that is indispensable to their way of life. Even so, the various roles played by the family in our society have shifted greatly in emphasis during the present century. The typical family of 1890 was a full-fledged economic unit in which children contributed to production as well as consumption. Under these conditions, having large families made a great deal of sense. The typical American family of the 1970s still consumes as a unit, but its productive functions have been largely replaced by various secondary institutions of our mass society. As a result the large family today is economically burdensome to the parents.

Three other aspects peculiar to our mass society have significantly altered the functions of the family: (1) the relative isolation of young children (especially in the middle class) from the socializing influences of their peer group and of the adults outside their nuclear-family group; (2) the increasing alienation of the individual from intimacy and intrinsic satisfactions in his social interactions; and (3) the increasing importance of leisure, recreation, and play in social interaction—within and outside the family—and therefore in emotional fulfillment, sex-role identification, and the learning of mastery skills and social competence. These manifestations of the mass society have made two essential functions of the family—early socialization of children and emotional support—more vital to the operation and harmony of the society than they had ever been in the past.[7]

---

[6] The closest any society has come to utilizing an institution other than the family as a basic socializing force is the *kibbutz* of Israel. However less than 4 percent of the Israeli society has been reared in the kibbutz, and as an experiment it seems to have been only marginally successful (Stephens, 1963). Experiments with state care of children and very restricted parental contact were carried out in the early years of the Soviet Union, but these experiments were omitted after a few years, apparently because the results were not satisfactory.

[7] One reason that these changes have occurred, and have had to occur, is the phenomenon of *differentiation*, or the specialization of institutional functions, which is a characteristic result of the complexity, urbanization, and unique economic pattern of the mass society. Differentiation occurs when two functions, previously performed by the same societal institution, are taken over by two separate, "differentiated" structures. This process allows each institution to concentrate more

In the past in our society, and in simple societies, the familial functions of early socialization and of emotional support were, of course, operational. But these functions were less vital for the following reasons:

1. Children were exposed, from the time they were mobile, to the socializing influences of their peers and the unrelated adults of a community. The women of a community shared the responsibility of child care and training, and the arduous housekeeping and agricultural duties of the mother restricted the time she could devote to her children. Also, the larger families of the past limited further the time that a mother could spend with an individual child and increased the probability of considerable socialization of the child by older siblings. In the mass society, the child spends most of his first few years almost exclusively with the mother and with, perhaps, one sibling; and the socialization and emotional-nurture processes are enduring and intensive.

2. Secondary relations and institutions were relatively few and thus intrinsic satisfactions were an integral part of the societal structure and were easily perceived and attained by a person in the society. The child was not faced with a bewildering array of roles and exchanges and institutional training. The easy perceivability and availability of role positions and intrinsic need satisfactions made the emotional condition of man less stressful and therefore his need to attain affectional satisfactions less urgent than in the mass society.

Further, the relatively authoritarian behavioral patterns of the society combined with the general acceptance of a rigid stratification system made identification of the self and interaction with others somewhat more straightforward. For example, the young man had no doubts about his position and roles in the family and in the society. He knew which decisions and interactions were his to make and which resided in the authority of the father or grandfather. He knew who was dependent upon him and whom he was properly dependent upon. He knew that his marriage was largely an economic arrangement. Finally, he perceived "emotional" support as the recognition and appreciation by his family of a "job well done."

This is not to say that there was no love involved in the interactions of the society but rather that love had more to do with propriety, duty, resource provision, and family loyalty, than with deep, unearned affection, value-free support, or romantic idealization. Mothers and fathers loved their children, of course, but the expression of this love (especially in the nineteenth century) was restricted in scope and manner by cultural standards ("Spare the rod . . ." and "Children should be seen . . ."). The involvement and intensity of parental love was probably also spread over many members of the very much larger families of the time. Also, the provision of material goods often was a struggle that left little time for interpersonal affectional nurture. By contrast, in our

---

freely and effectively on the remaining one or very few functions that each institution is left to perform (Parsons, 1961). Thus, as the family in our society lost the once-vital functions of vocational and intellectual education, protection, and sole occupational source, the functions of early socialization and emotional support became more important within the family and to the society.

contemporary society, which is relatively indifferent to the role of the individual in society, the American family provides an oasis of interpersonal awareness, affection, and confirmation.

3. In our mass society with the shortening of work hours, the labor-saving devices in the home, and the resultant leisure time available to most people, the role interactions and time structuring involved in *recreation* activities are becoming increasingly essential aspects of the interpersonal and societal functions of the family. People in general usually relate to one another only by performing a function together. Similarly, a family can interact only in terms of some activity they are mutually performing; and since economic production, child labor, and material self-sufficiency are virtually obsolete as familial functions, family members now relate to one another mainly in *conversation*, in the observance of *ritual*, in *parallel activity*, and in *play*[8] — whereas in the past they had related in economic production and homemaking.

Although homemaking is still a work function of the family, it is much less time-consuming than in the past and it does not often involve all the family members (children still have their chores but they are usually trivial and not vital to familial interaction). Similarly, income provision is now almost solely the function of the parents and does not involve the whole family. Furthermore, this work is generally done away from the home and is not shared by the children on even an intellectual level.

Thus, except for conversation, for parallel activities and ritual, and for minor homemaking functions (and such forms of "work" as shopping or schoolwork), the family members in our society usually have the opportunity to relate only in terms of play. And because play establishes a basis for doing something together and therefore for operational demonstrations of interest, confirmation, and affection, the structuring of recreational time by parents for themselves and their children is approaching equivalent importance with the provision of emotional support and socialization. Indeed, play is becoming a chief mode of the emotional-support and socialization functions of the family in our society. The achievement of intellectual and mastery skills and the confirmation of emotional support depend more and more in our society upon a parent's playing with his child. Play contributes significantly to the child's competence and to his self-image; he will perceive the world as friendly, supportive, and manageable, and he will perceive himself as a loved and loving, important and proficient individual.

The child who does *not* develop a sense of adequacy in interaction with the environment in early childhood is liable to see all challenge as a threat rather than as an opportunity, to be withdrawn and apathetic (or hostile and belligerent),

---

[8] *Parallel activity* (eating dinner, watching television) is not, strictly speaking, a form of interaction; but it occupies a large portion of the time a family spends together, and it is important as a catalyst or opportunity for interaction. *Play* is a form of interaction which, like ritual, is not specifically functional. Unlike ritual, the essential aspects of play are its voluntariness and its intrinsic pleasure and satisfaction. Play is, in short, a form of self-expression.

and to be unable to develop the early competencies (physical, psychological, and social) upon which all later competencies are based.[9] Similarly, the contemporary adult who is unable to play is seriously handicapped in most spheres of

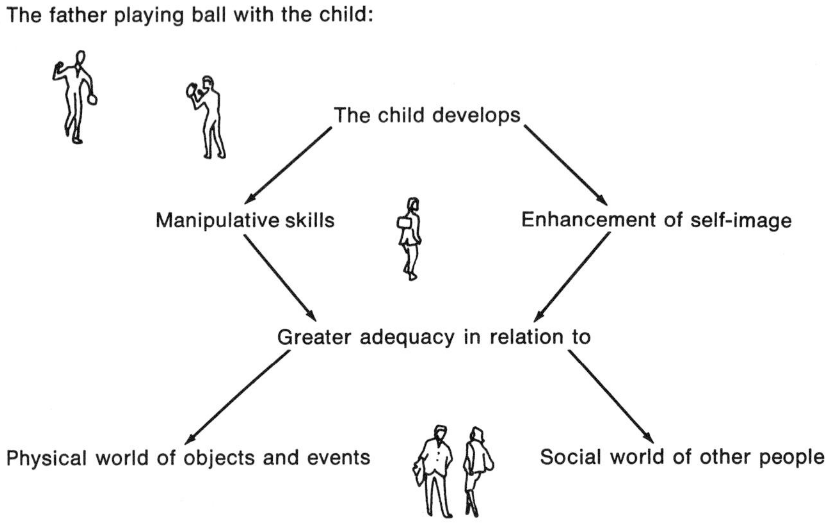

The father playing ball with the child:

Figure 10–1. The Importance of Play in Familial Interaction

his activity.[10] In his familial activities, the adult who cannot play is not only damaging the full development of his offspring but also restricting the quality and effectiveness and the fulfillments of his interactions with his spouse, his offspring, and his general social environment. Even in the sphere of work (income provision), play has become a part of most occupations, with business luncheons, club meetings, golf, and business junkets an important part of our economic system.

---

[9] Play is a natural expression of children and has always served, among young children, as an aspect of their socialization *through their peer group* (but less so, in simple societies and in our past society, through their parents or instructors). In all societies, past and present, "the playing child takes different roles and uses his own responses in building a self" and also in inventing conflicts and exploring the possible adjustive responses (Martindale, 1960, p. 437). This role-taking play of children, most of which is founded on their observation of adults (and, now, television), is important in the development of all social, psychological, and material skills. Play often "precedes the ability of the organism to function in a given way" and consists of the practice of capacities before they are actually required (Martindale, p. 436).

[10] Because the importance of play has arisen within the last twenty-five years, and because of the "all-work-no-play" Puritan ethic of our past society (when recreation was not possible except for the very rich), the inability of many adults to function in play activities is an aspect of the current generation gap.

Role Interaction within the Family

The theory of role and role interaction, and all of its various ramifications, has been discussed in Chapters One, Five, Six, and Seven. The role interaction of the family follows these same principles and utilizes these same dynamics — except that familial interaction is complicated by the involvement of more people (and the larger the family the greater the complication). Not only does each added member introduce another role relation, but the previous role relations are significantly altered.

To give an obvious example, when a couple are still childless, the husband may expect the wife to make him the center of her attention when he arrives home from work, and he may regard her as the center of his attention. But when they become a family and there are children clamoring to be fed or bathed, changed or petted, the husband and wife can scarcely expect to be the centers of one another's regard. The function of the person as a "father" or "mother" becomes central to each one's role relation with his spouse in most of their interactions.

Male Roles in the Family

In almost all societies, animal and human, the father-husband is expected to organize the family's food production or food gathering, to provide protection, and to solve the problems caused by physical environmental factors.

Apparently in all societies the privilege of major decisions is in the hands of men . . . Assumption of the adult status requires that the male be relatively independent, dominant, and instrumental in social interaction, and be able to discharge his obligations as head of the family (Goode, 1964, pp. 74, 78).

Even in our contemporary society, in which secondary institutions have created a distance between the male and his original familial roles, so that he no longer builds the shelter or hunts the food, the father-husband is still generally the head of the family and the *instrumental* figure in the social interactions of the family. He usually pays the rent, buys the life insurance, and deals with the host of external contingencies that indirectly threaten the welfare of his family.

Female Roles in the Family

The mother-wife's family roles have, in general, remained the same throughout all societies — animal or human, simple or mass, historical or contemporary. She has always dealt with the care of the offspring and with problems that originate within the household and not in the outside environment. In addition to her child-care and housekeeping functions, her roles are mainly *relational* and educational; she is expected to provide emotional and physical nurture, both to her children and to her husband, and also training for the children in the skills and roles appropriate to their socialization. The nurture and socializing roles are, of course, interrelated; the child who receives physical and emotional nurture from his mother also acquires some degree of socialization simply from the experience of nurture and from the patterning of his behavior after hers.

Very young girls and boys both identify chiefly with the mother. She is most often at hand during early socialization, and the child's earliest and most significant affectional relations are formed with her. She smiles as she nurtures her baby, and the baby learns to associate her smile with his feeling of pleasure and well being. He also learns that by smiling at her, he will further affection and nurture. His verbal patterns of response also are learned mainly from the mother. The experiences which gradually become connected to form the self are in infancy and early childhood usually provided by the mother.

In terms of *sexual* identification, or the learning of appropriate sex roles, the dominance of the mother in the socialization of the children may create a problem for the male children in our society. The mother is, of course, the role model for the female child; but male children must identify with a culturally defined masculine role, and since the father is often absent from the home, the masculine role must be learned chiefly from the male peer group. Male children, therefore, often achieve their sexual identification somewhat later in childhood

than female children. And if the father is totally absent (as in a broken family) or if the mother is careless in the socialization of her son into male roles, the male child may sometimes fail to identify himself adequately with male roles. This failure may then lead to inadequacy in coping with the exigencies of the physical and social environment (see Chapter Twelve).

The importance of sexual identification can scarcely be overemphasized; the sexual role behavior that every child learns to demonstrate will affect the success of his interactions with family members, peer groups, and adults. And his own adulthood will, in large measure, be shaped by these early childhood interactions.

Children's Roles in the Family

We will thoroughly explore the role reciprocation between child and parents in Chapter Twelve, The Family with Young Children. For the purpose of the discussion here, we will suggest simply that the child initially functions (in infancy) chiefly as a nurturant object for the parents. From this initial passivity, the child begins to develop in two directions: (1) He experiences the increasing necessity to control and manipulate his environment, both physical and social (to cry for attention; to tie his shoes; to ride a bike, to learn to read; to drive a car). (2) He experiences the increasing necessity to relate to other members of his family (and soon, others outside his family) in a manner other than simple passivity.

The child's role environment, after his first two years, extends beyond the family. His peer culture and peer relations become increasingly important as he plays with neighbors and enters school, until finally the peer relations supersede his family relations some time in late adolescence or early adulthood.

The Blurring of Family Roles in Our Society

With the structural and attitudinal changes in our society in the past fifty years, the familiar roles of male and female are becoming more and more interchangeable, although, in general, they follow the traditional divisions.[11] The numerous secondary institutions and services in our society and the increased leisure that has resulted from them have freed the mother-wife to work outside the home, have enabled the father-husband to perform household functions that no longer require special training or large allotments of time, and have freed both parents to spend more time in loving, playing with, and socializing their children. Similarly, the children, who no longer contribute economically to the family, have assumed a more important role in the social interaction within the family and in the enhancement or maintenance of the family's status position within the society. Children are no longer "seen but not heard." They are expected to interact socially with their parents and with other adults and to enrich the familial social environment with a strongly developed and individual personality and with suggestions, opinions, and humor. Also, by succeeding in school and in academic, social, and competitive activities, children are expected to verify or enhance the status of the family.

Role Failure in Familial Interaction

There are two sources of role difficulty in the interaction of a family group. One source is the aptitude or the ability of parents for fulfilling the roles appropriate to their positions as both husband and father or wife and mother. This combination of role positions requires a wide spectrum of skills, both in manipulative

---

[11] See *The Peculiarities of American Marriage*, in Chapter Six, for a fuller discussion of the difficulties in male-female marital roles in our society.

and mastery tasks and in relational ability; and these skills are mainly dependent upon the ability, frame of reference, and emotional maturity of the persons performing the familial tasks. Furthermore, even with the best of intentions, no one can be expected to function ideally in all situations at all times.

The other source of role difficulty is the occurrence of conflict between two roles, both of which are incumbent upon the person at the same time. For example, a parent often must relate to his children as "disciplinarian" when he would prefer to relate as "companion" or "confidant." Or a husband may wish to relate to his wife in the role of lover but must play with their children instead, thus experiencing deprivation simply because he is called on to perform roles

for more positions than he desires to hold at once. What is required in such role conflict is, first of all, a clear recognition of the various roles involved in any single position in the familial interaction and, second, the ability to shift flexibly from one role to another.

Examples of serious role failures are a husband-father's failure to provide income and material security or a wife-mother's failure to fulfill nurturant and household duties. Of course, temporary loss of employment or an occasional bad dinner would not be seriously disruptive to a family — unless the temporary behavior became relatively permanent. Also, in the instance of one parent's patterned role failure, the other parent may learn to perform dual roles — his own and that originally performed by his spouse — and to compensate for the failures of the other. For example, if the father fails to fulfill an instrumental role, the mother may manage to produce the necessary income (as well as fulfilling her housekeeping and relational roles) and thus prevent family disintegration. Or, on the other hand, the father may perform the nurturant role, serving as stabilizer and conciliator as well as the income provider in a family where the mother is inoperative in these roles.

The husband-father or wife-mother who can successfully discharge the role positions of both parents is relatively rare, however; and in the case of a major role failure by either spouse, the family is usually disrupted. Also, generally speaking, if the major bed-and-board roles are not fulfilled by parents, the offspring, deprived of their role models, will have considerable difficulty in achieving social maturity.

Family disorganization, which is the result of patterned role failure by one or both parents, is especially damaging to the offspring in the family.[12] The disorganized family which continues to live together is demonstrating merely the outward signs of a family; in reality its members are giving each other little or no emotional support and the socialization function becomes a travesty. Since the chief functions of the modern American family are its provision of early socialization and continual emotional support to its members, the family which fails to supply its members with intimacy, with role identification, with confirmation and emotional nurture can, more than any other institution in our society, create anxiety and personality and character disorders in its members — who in turn, of course, influence other people and thus the harmony and order of the society at large. (For additional discussions of various aspects of the American family and of its role dynamics, see Parsons, 1955 and 1965; Martindale, 1960; Duval, 1967; Goode, 1964; McKinley, 1964; and Winch, 1964.)

Summary

The term *family* is used principally to describe the nuclear group comprising parents and offspring who live together in physical, emotional, social, and economic interdependence. This definition, however, is usually considerably expanded by the closeness most people feel for relatives — whether by blood or marriage — who live outside the nuclear grouping. It is also expanded by the common recognition of such "family" groupings as the broken family and the childless couple.

As a societal institution, the family functions as the basis of a society's economic and political organization and its stratification. The family also serves (through its status position and its control and socialization of offspring) to "place" the individual into the societal structure in a functional relation with the other members and other institutions of the society.

As a primary relation, the family fulfills the relational functions of the care, socialization, and physical and emotional nurture of the offspring. The family also serves as an outlet for the adult's intrinsic altruism — his need to give physical and emotional nurture (and, with the raising of children, to ultimately have this nurture reciprocated).

The role interactions of the family follow the same principles and utilize the same dynamics as those in any primary relation, except that familial interaction is complicated by the involvement of three or more persons. In general, the husband-father fulfills instrumental roles and deals with problems of the outside environment, and the wife-mother fulfills the relational and socialization

---

[12]Carter and Click (1970) point out that more than half a million children under 18 years of age are affected each year by divorcing parents (sixty percent of divorcing couples report having at least one child). At present, 42 percent of black children and 11 percent of white children under 18 years of age do not live with both parents (*Current Population Reports,* U. S. Bureau of the Census, Series P-20, No. 189, 1969).

roles and deals with problems within the home. In the modern society, the familial roles of children are not economically productive, so that their familial interactions are limited to parallel activities and play—and to enriching the status and environment of the family group through their personalities and achievements.

The functions and the role interactions of the family are in large measure learned in infancy and early childhood and become part of each person's frame of reference. Thus the family is the most important of all social institutions, since a breakdown in the provision of essential functions and role performances is self-perpertuating: The deprived child grows up to make the same or worse mistakes in his own family.

Two functions in our mass society are particularly important to the development of offspring and the well being of the family. One of these is early socialization, which is almost exclusively the province of the family and which is the basis of a person's ability to function effectively and happily in society. The other is interpersonal emotional support, which is essential to personality development and emotional maturity and which must be provided in the family since there are very few other institutions in our mass society that are capable or willing to fulfill this nurture need. In both of these functions, the structuring of leisure time is becoming increasingly important in our society.

Questions

1 How would you define the *family*?
2 What is the difference between the *family of origin* and the *family of procreation?*
3 What do we think of as
   (a) the *nuclear* family?
   (b) the *extended* family?
4 What functions does the institution of marriage serve in our society? Discuss in detail.
5 What is the relation between the physical and psychological development of children and the consequent adult behavior?
6 What is considered to be the most basic of familial functions? Discuss.
7 What would a person's adult behavior probably be like if he were deprived of proper emotional nurture experience in infancy?
8 How successful have experiments been in utilizing an institution other than the family as a basic socializing force?

9 How has our contemporary mass society altered the functions of the family?
10 What is meant by the phenomenon of *differentiation?*
11 How has the status of "play" changed for every member of the family?
12 How would you define "play" as it is used in this chapter?
13 Discuss the importance of the parent's structuring recreational time for the child.
14 What functions does the parent accomplish while he plays with the child?
15 Play among children usually involves *role taking*. Discuss.
16 In our society what is usually considered the role of the male in the family? The female?
17 Why do male children often achieve their sexual identification somewhat later in childhood than female children?

18 What is meant by sexual identification? How important is it?

19 Discuss the blurring of family roles in our society.

20 Discuss the two sources of role difficulty in the interaction of a family group.

21 What are the *worst* role failures of the mother and father?

22 Describe the characteristics of the disorganized family which continues to live together.

References and Selected Readings

Altman, S. A. Primate Behavior in Review. *Science,* 1965,Vol. 150, pp. 1440–1442.

Ardrey, Robert. *Social Contract.* New York: Atheneum, 1970.

_____. *The Territorial Imperative.* New York: Atheneum, 1966.

Axelrod, Morris. Urban Structure and Social Participation. *American Sociological Review,* 1956, Vol. 21, pp. 13–19.

Axline, Virginia. *Dibs: In Search of Self.* Boston: Houghton Mifflin, 1964.

Bell, Robert R. *Marriage and Family Interaction,* 3rd. ed. Homewood, Ill.: Dorsey, 1971.

_____, ed. *Studies in Marriage and the Family.* New York: Crowell, 1968.

Bell, Wendell, and N. D. Boat. Urban Neighborhoods and Informal Social Relations, *American Journal of Sociology,* 1957, Vol. 43, pp. 381–398.

Bernard, Jessie. Present Demographic Trends and Structural Outcomes in Family Life Today. In James A. Peterson, ed., *Marriage and Family Counseling.* New York: Association Press, 1968.

Bettelheim, Bruno. Joey: A "Mechanical Boy." *Scientific American,* March 1959.

Biddle, Bruce J., and Edwin J. Thomas, eds. *Role Theory.* New York: Wiley, 1966.

Bliss, E. L., ed. *Roots of Behavior.* Darien, Conn.: Hafner, 1969.

Blitsten, Dorothy R. *The World of the Family.* New York: Random, 1963.

Cavan, Ruth Shonle. *The American Family,* 4th ed. New York: Crowell, 1969.

_____, ed. *Marriage and Family in the Modern World,* 3rd ed. New York: Crowell, 1969.

Clarke, Edith. *My Mother Who Fathered Me.* London: George Allen & Unwin, 1957.

Cunningham, Kenneth R., and Theodore B. Johannis, Jr. Research on the Family and Leisure: A Review and Critique of Selected Studies, *The Family Life Coordinator,* September and December 1960, Vol. 9.

Denenberg, Victor H. Early Experience and Emotional Development, *Scientific American,* June 1963, Vol. 208, pp. 138–146.

DeVore, Irven, ed. *Primate Behavior.* New York: Holt, 1965.

Dodd, Marjorie N., and Robert J. Havighurst. The Meanings of Leisure. *Social Forces,* May 1959, Vol. 37, pp. 355–360.

Duvall, Evelyn Millis, *Family Development,* 3rd ed. Philadelphia: Lippincott, 1967.

Foote, Nelson. Family Living as Play. *Marriage and Family Living,* November 1955, Vol. 17, p. 297.

Gerson, Walter M. Leisure and Marital Satisfaction of College Married Students. *Marriage and Family Living,* 1960, Vol. 22, pp. 360, 361.

Glasser, Paul H. and Lois N., eds. *Families in Crisis.* New York: Harper, 1970.

Glick, Paul C. *American Families.* New York: Wiley, 1957.

Goode, William J., ed. *Contemporary American Family.* New York: New York Times Book, 1970.

——————— *et al. Social Systems and Family Patterns: A Propositional Inventory.* Indianapolis: Bobbs-Merrill, 1970.

———————. *The Family.* Englewood Cliffs, N. J.: Prentice-Hall, 1964.

———————. Economic Factors and Marital Stability. *American Sociological Review,* 1951, Vol. 16, pp. 802–812.

Greer, Scott. Urbanism Reconsidered: A Comparative Study of Social Areas in a Metropolis. *American Sociological Review,* 1956, Vol. 21, pp. 19–25.

Hadden, Jeffrey K., and Marie L. Borgatta. *Marriage and the Family: A Comprehensive Reader.* Itsaca, Ill.: Peacock, 1969.

Harlow, Harry F. Love in Infant Monkeys. *Scientific American,* June 1959, Vol. 204.

——————— and Margaret Kuenne. Social Deprivation in Monkeys. *Scientific American,* November 1962, Vol. 207, pp. 137–146.

Heiss, Jerold, ed. *Family Roles and Interaction.* Chicago: Rand McNally, 1968.

Heron, Woodburn. The Pathology of Boredom. *Scientific American,* Vol. 196, January 1957, pp. 52–56.

Huxley, Aldous. *Brave New World and Brave New World Revisited.* New York: Harper, 1958.

Kaplan, Max. *Leisure in America.* New York: Wiley, 1960.

Kirkpatrick, Clifford. *The Family as Process and Institution.* New York: Ronald, 1963.

Lee, Richard B., and Irven DeVore, eds. *Man the Hunter.* Chicago: Aldine, 1968.

Leslie, Gerald. *The Family in Sociological Context.* New York: Oxford, 1967.

Litwak, Eugene. Geographic Mobility and Extended Family Cohesion. *American Sociological Review,* 1960, Vol. 25, pp. 385–394.

Lorenz, Konrad. *On Aggression.* trans. Marjorie Kerr Wilson. New York: Harcourt, 1966.

Marmon, Judd, ed. *Sexual Inversion: The Multiple Roots of Homosexuality.* New York: Basic Books, 1965.

Martindale, Don. *American Society,* Chapter 18, The Sociology of Play. New York: Van Nostrand, 1960.

McKinley, Donald Gilbert. *Social Class and Family Life.* New York: Free Press, 1964.

Mead, Margaret. *Male and Female.* New York: Dell, 1968.

Mudd, Emily, Mitchell Howard, and Sara Taubin. *Success in Family Living.* New York: Association Press, 1965.

Murdock, George Peter. *Social Structure.* New York: Macmillan, 1949.

Neumeyer, Martin and Esther S. *Leisure and Recreation,* 3rd ed. New York: Ronald, 1958.

Parsons, Talcott. The Normal American Family. In Seymour M. Farber, Piero Mustocchi, and Roger H. L. Wilson, eds., *Man and Civilization: The Family's Search for Survival.* New York: McGraw-Hill, 1965.

_____. The Stability of the American Family System. In Talcott Parsons and Robert F. Bales, *Family, Socialization, and Interaction Process.* New York: Free Press, 1955.

_____, and Robert F. Bales. *Family, Socialization and Interaction Process.* New York: Free Press, 1955.

_____, and Winston Wharton. The Link Between Character and Society. In Seymour M. Lipset and Leo Lowenthal, eds., *Culture and Social Character.* New York: Free Press, 1961.

Quarantelli, Enrico L. A Note on the Protective Function of the Family in Disasters. *Marriage and Family Living,* August 1960, p. 264.

Queen, Stuart A., Robert W. Habenstein, and John B. Adams. *The Family in Various Cultures,* 3rd ed. New York: Lippincott, 1969.

Rainwater, Lee. *Behind Ghetto Walls: Black Family Life in a Federal Slum.* Chicago: Aldine, 1970.

Reiss, Paul J. The Extended Kinship System: Correlates of the Attitudes and Frequency of Interaction. *Marriage and Family Living,* 1962, Vol. 24, pp. 333–339.

_____. Extended Kinship Relationships in American Society. In Hyman Rodman ed., *Marriage, Family, and Society.* New York: Random House, 1965, pp. 204–210.

Reynolds, Farley, and Albert I. Hermalin. Family Stability: A Comparison of Trends between Blacks and Whites. *American Sociological Review,* February 1971, Vol. 36, pp. 1–17.

Rheingold, H. L., ed. *Maternal Behavior in Mammals.* New York: Wiley, 1963.

Robins, Lee, and Miroda Tomanec. Closeness to Blood Relatives Outside of the Immediate Family. *Marriage and Family Living,* Vol. 24, pp. 340–346.

Rodman, Hyman, ed. *Marriage, Family and Society.* New York: Random House, 1965.

Scanzoni, John H. *Opportunity and the Family.* New York: Free Press, 1970.

Schaller, George B. *The Year of the Gorilla.* Chicago: University of Chicago Press, 1964.

_____, and Millicent Selsam. *Tiger: Its Life in the Wild.* New York: Harper, 1969.

Schorr, Albin L. Filial Responsibility and the Aging. In Hyman Rodman, ed. *Marriage, Family, and Society.* New York: Random, 1965, pp. 186–197.

_____. *Filial Responsibility in the Modern American Family.* Washington, D. C.: Social Security Administration Division of Program Research, 1961.

Schramm, Wilbur, Jack Lyle, and Edwin B. Parker. *Television in the Lives of Our Children.* Stanford, Calif.: Stanford University Press, 1964.

Schrier, Allan M., Harry F. Harlow, and Fred Stollnitz, eds. *Behavior of Nonhuman Primates.* New York: Academic Press, 1965.

Scott, John Paul. *Early Experience and the Organization of Behavior.* Belmont, Calif.: Brooks/Cole, 1968.

Shanas, Ethel. Living Arrangements for Older People in the U. S. *The*

Gerontologist, March 1961, pp. 27–29.

_____, *et al. Old People in Three Industrial Societies.* New York: Atherton, 1968.

_____, and Gordon F. Streib, eds. *Social Structure and the Family: Generational Relations.* Englewood Cliffs, N. J.: Prentice-Hall, 1965.

Sharp, Harry, and Morris Axelrod. Mutual Aid Among Relatives in an Urban Population. In Ronald Freeman *et al., Principles of Sociology.* New York: Holt, 1956.

Sheldon, Henry D. *The Older Population of the U. S.* New York: Wiley, 1958.

Skolnick, Arlene and Jerome H. *Family in Transition.* Boston: Little, Brown, 1971.

Stephens, William N. *The Family in Cross-Cultural Perspective.* New York: Holt, 1963.

_____, ed. *Reflections on Marriage.* New York: Crowell, 1968.

Stevenson, H. W., E. H. Hess, and H. L. Rheingold, eds. *Early Behavior: Comparative and Developmental Approaches.* New York: Wiley, 1967.

Strauss, Murray A., ed. *Family Analysis.* Chicago: Rand McNally, 1970.

Sussman, Marvin B. *Sourcebook in Marriage and the Family,* 3rd ed. New York: Houghton Mifflin, 1968.

_____. The Help Pattern in the Middle Class Family. *American Sociological Review,* 1953, Vol. 18, pp. 22–28.

_____. The Isolated Nuclear Family: Fact or Fiction. *Social Problems,* 1959, Vol. 6, pp. 333–340.

_____, *et al. Family and Inheritance.* New York: Russell Sage, 1970.

_____, and Lee Burchinal. Kin Family Network: Unheralded Structure in Current Conceptualizations of Family Functioning. *Marriage and Family Living,* 1962, Vol. 24, pp. 231–240.

_____. Parental Aid to Married Children: Implications for Family Functioning. *Marriage and Family Living,* 1962, Vol. 24, pp. 320–332.

Winch, Robert F. *The Modern Family,* rev. ed. New York: Holt, 1964.

Zamaitin, Eugene. *We.* New York: Dutton, 1959.

Chapter Eleven

Reproduction: The Biological Basis of the Family

You are the bows from which your children as living arrows are shot forth.

Kahlil Gibran (*The Prophet*)

the creation of a new human life remained a profound mystery for thousands of years. Not until the development of modern techniques of biological investigation did men learn that, in the first place, life is not really newly *created* but rather is passed on from one generation to the next through the living germ cells, or gametes (the ovum and sperm), which, in combination, form a new cell, the zygote, that *proliferates* and *differentiates* into the multicellular human organism. What was previously thought to occur spontaneously or through some mysterious intervention is now known to be simply another manifestation of the molecular combination, proliferation, and replacement that governs all living matter on this planet. The mechanisms of this process and of the inheritance of the previous generation's traits were, until this century and the development of sophisticated microscopes, unknown. With the discovery and study of subcellular, berry-shaped, biological bodies called *genes,* it was found that the complex and detailed biological instructions necessary for the building of a complete human body and the transmission of hereditary traits are carried in the genetic material contained within the nucleus of each germ cell—half of this material in the nucleus of the male gamete (sperm) and half in the female gamete (ovum). When the gametes combine during the fertilization process, the nuclei of the two gametes (and the genetic materials within them) also combine to form a single nucleus containing the precise number of genetic bodies found in every human cell (except, of course, in the gametes).

The genetic material includes the genes, the *DNA molecules*[1] within each gene, and the rod-shaped carriers of the genes, the *chromosomes.* Every creature that

---

[1] *DNA*, deoxyribonucleic acid, is the basis of all reproduction and therefore, apparently, the basis of continuing life. The DNA within the genes encodes the messages of heredity on long, extremely

reproduces sexually has paired sets of chromosomes in the nucleus of each cell of his body, one set inherited from each parent. In the nuclei of human cells, there are 23 such pairs, or 46 chromosomes. When a cell divides (*mitosis*), the 46 chromosomes split lengthwise; and the resulting 92 *chromatids* (split chromosomes) are shared equally between the two resulting cells. However, when *parent germ cells* divide to become sperm or eggs, the individual chromosomes do not split to become chromatids; instead, each of the 23 chromosome pairs simply separates, with one of the pair going to each new cell. (This process is termed *meiosis*, or *reduction division*.) The mature sperm or egg, then, contains 23 chromosomes, rather than the 46 characteristic of every other cell of the body; thus, when a sperm and an egg unite to form a *zygote*, the zygote will have 46 chromosomes, one half of them from each parent.[2]

Within each chromosome in the zygote, there are two genes for every hereditary trait — one provided by the male gamete, the other provided by the female. Certain traits will occur with ·the influence of only one of these genes, called a *dominant gene*; other traits, which are determined by *recessive genes*, occur only when both genes are recessive. Among human traits determined by dominant genes are such things as brown eyes, short stature, blood types A, B, and AB, high blood pressure, and allergies. Recessive genes determine such traits as blue eyes, normal vision, blood type C, and, possibly, left-handedness.

Thus, when a dominant gene is paired with a recessive gene, only the dominant trait is expressed; and a recessive trait will occur only when two recessive genes are paired. In addition, however, there are a number of traits that are partially dominant, so that a single gene produces an intermediate effect; for example, medium skin pigmentation or wavy hair. Also, some genes may be dominant in one situation and not dominant in another; for example, baldness is a dominant trait in men but a recessive trait in women (a woman must have two genes for baldness, a man but one). Thus, which side of the family the baby takes after depends upon a multiplicity of highly complex variables — all based on the mechanism of the gene. Even the observable genetic traits (*phenotypes*) are not predictably inheritable since the *genotype*, the underlying genetic makeup,

---

complex, chain-like molecules, which are able to replicate themselves precisely, and which therefore initiate asexual cell division.) Because the DNA molecule is capable of replication, it is able to direct the continuous and consistent development and reproduction of living matter (the cells). A form of DNA has already been synthesized, and it will be but a few months or years before science will have utilized this synthesis in "creating" life in the laboratory. The discovery by James Watson and Francis Crick of the structure of DNA was the key to our understanding of the borderline between life and non-life. See Watson's book, *The Double Helix* (1968); also, Watson (1965), and Whittinghill (1965).

[2] During meiosis of the germ cells, corresponding genes in a chromosome pair sometimes trade places with one another, so that the chromosomes themselves may change in character and each sperm or egg may represent a different sorting and shuffling of potentialities. Indeed, the possible combination of genes in any given gamete runs into the billions, and a certain amount of variation (within the limits set by the characteristics of the species) is inevitable. Moreover, the reshuffling of genes that occurs in the formation of the zygote makes possible combinations of variables truly enormous. Thus, the possibility that any specific pattern might be repeated is almost nonexistent, and variability (*individual differences*) between all members of a species that reproduces sexually is guaranteed.

does not necessarily correspond to the phenotype. Thus, two phenotypically brown-eyed parents may have blue-eyed children—if each parent carries a recessive blue-eyed gene and if these genes happen to combine at conception.

The sex of a baby is determined by a single set of the normal 46 chromosomes. These sex chromosomes are designated Y for male traits and X for female traits. The normal human sperm cell contains either an X or a Y chromosome, while the normal human ovum contains an X chromosome. If an ovum is fertilized by a Y-bearing sperm, the resulting baby has one X and one Y chromosome (XY) in each of its bodily cells and is chromosomally a male. If the ovum is fertilized by an X-bearing sperm, the resulting baby has two X chromosomes (XX) in each bodily cell and is chromosomally a female.[3]

There are also rare variations in this normal pattern. Some girl babies are born with three X chromosomes (XXX) instead of the usual two, and other girls are born with one X chromosome missing (XO). Some boy babies are born with one or more extra X chromosomes (XXY) or (XXXY), or with an extra Y chromosome (XYY). Very unusual cases of XXXXXY and XXYY have also been reported. With these and other rare variants, the Y chromosome is still apparently the determiner of maleness. Lacking a Y chromosome, the baby is a chromosomal female.

Pregnancy

Because the egg apparently remains capable of fertilization for no more than 18 to 24 hours after ovulation, and the sperm seldom live for more than 72 hours after ejaculation, fertilization and conception will occur only in the brief time span just before or soon after ovulation, which occurs at approximately the midpoint of the menstrual cycle.

Conception

At ovulation, a mature egg is released from one of the thousands of egg sacs (*follicles*) lining the walls of the ovaries.[4] In some way as yet only partially under-

---

[3] Development of male and female characteristics, both biological and social, also depends upon the functioning of the hormones and upon sex-role identification, or socialization. If hormone functioning is not normal, various types of *hermaphroditism* may occur—for example, chromosomal males with labia (unfused scrotal sac), undescended testicles, and a clitoris-like penis, or chromosomal females with fused labia suggesting a scrotum and a penis-like clitoris. Similarly, sex-role identification, especially as developed during the first five years of life, may result in biological (chromosomal and hormonal) males who identify as females, and vice versa. A person's sexual characteristics are therefore a blend of three factors—chromosomal pattern, hormonal functioning, and socialized role-identification—and may vary in many ways from what we would call normal. It is not always possible to define a person simply as a "male" or "female." For a further discussion of "hermaphrodites, tomboys, sissies, transvestites, transsexuals, homosexuals, bisexuals, and heterosexuals," see *Males, Females, and Others* by Brecher (1969), Chapter Seven.

[4] Normally only one egg is released in the ovary, but occasionally two or more are released and the result is a multiple birth. More rarely, a single egg divides at the zygote stage before proceeding

stood by scientists, this ovum travels through the ovary to the mouth of the *Fallopian tube* that joins each ovary to the uterus. The Fallopian tubes are between two and four inches long and are extremely narrow; at their ovarian ends, the diameter is about that of a whisker. The outer walls of the Fallopian tubes contain muscles which contract and relax rhythmically, creating a wave-like motion within the tube which helps to carry the egg toward the uterus. Also aiding this peristaltic movement are the *cilia*, hairlike structures lining the inner walls of the Fallopian tubes. Their constant undulation help to create a current which moves the egg through the tube. If sperm are present, fertilization usually takes place about one third of the way through the tube. If fertilization does not take place, the egg generally disintegrates before reaching the uterus.

The Germinal Period

The first two weeks of pregnancy — from the formation of the zygote to the time it is firmly embedded in the uterine wall — are called the *germinal period*.[5] During this period, the mother has no sign that she is pregnant and pregnancy cannot be reliably detected by laboratory tests.

By the time the zygote comes to rest in the uterus, it has become a multicellular hollow sphere with an outer layer of cells, the *trophoblast*, and growing inward from the trophoblast an inner cluster or lump of cells which contains the *germinal disc*, the developing organism, and the organs that will provide a protective and nurturant environment for the organism while it is in the uterus.

---

with its development, and two organisms develop from the single egg. Twins produced by the fertilization of two separate eggs are called *fraternal twins*. Although they may appear similar in some ways, fraternal twins are products of separate eggs, separate sperm, and thus separate sets of genes and are biologically wholly different individuals. Twins produced by the division of a single zygote are called *identical twins*. Since they are the products of the same set of genes, such twins are biologically wholly identical — although environmental factors may effect differences in their physical and psychological development. Triplets can result from three eggs, but usually they develop from two eggs, with one of the eggs dividing at the zygote stage. Similarly, quadruplets generally result from the division of two zygotes.

Twins occur once in every ninety births, triplets once in every eight thousand, and quadruplets once in every five hundred thousand (Crawley *et al.*, 1964). Multiple births generally result from an inheritable genetic pattern, so that in families with a history of multiple births the actuarial expectation for producing twins is usually exceeded.

[5]Although it is clear that a form of life begins at the instant of conception, there has always been legal, theological, philosophical, and biological disagreement as to precisely when the organism developing within the mother achieves the status of a person. Does the organism become a person prior to birth? If so, does it become a person as a zygote? As an embryo? As a fetus?

Oriental cultures consider a baby to be one year old at birth, reflecting a belief that the status of person is achieved at conception. Roman law, from which a large part of our own law comes, considered the fetus not a human being but a part or possession of the mother; abortion was punishable as "property damage." With Christianity came the idea that the fetus was a human being, but the precise stage at which it became a human being remained a matter of speculation. Saint Augustine distinguished between a "formed" and an "unformed" fetus and believed that the soul does not enter the fetus until it is formed. Thomas Aquinas felt that life occurred only at the moment of *quickening*, the first perceptible movement of the fetus; and this notion became part of the common law of England. Today the debate continues and has even been revitalized as a part of the controversy over liberalization of abortion laws.

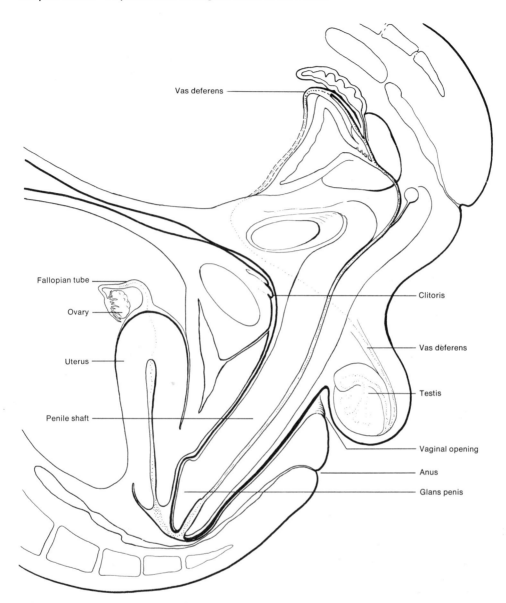

Vas deferens

Fallopian tube

Ovary

Uterus

Penile shaft

Clitoris

Vas deferens

Testis

Vaginal opening

Anus

Glans penis

Figure 11–1. Cross Section of Penis in the Vagina, Showing the Path of Sperm.

About seven or eight days after conception in the Fallopian tube, the zygote finally touches the uterine wall, which, since ovulation, has been thickening its mass with blood and enriching this mass with a supply of nutrients. Secretions of enzymes from the trophoblast erode in the uterine wall a cavity in which the zygote completely embeds and buries itself. By about two weeks after conception, tiny tendrils, called *chorionic villi*, have begun to extend from the tropho-blast, marking the beginning of the second stage of the organism, the *embryonic period.*

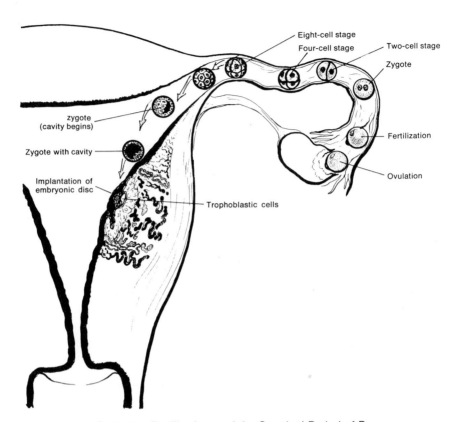

Figure 11-2. Ovulation, Fertilization, and the Germinal Period of Pregnancy.

The Development of the Embryo

From two to three weeks after conception, the germinal disc begins to assume an animal shape, although its length is still no more than one twelfth of an inch. A neural plate has formed in what will become the embryo's head; and *somites*, the spinal segments which will develop into vertebrae, have begun to appear. The heart, at first a single tube, also begins to develop by a process of looping and infolding and will soon begin to beat, even before there is any blood to be circulated. Often, at this time, a primitive digestive tract can also be distinguished.

The chorionic villi burrow into the blood-filled uterine tissue and by osmosis through their membrane walls, absorb food, oxygen, and immunizing agents from the blood of the mother and pass the waste products of the embryo back into her blood. (No blood is actually mixed between the developing fetus and the mother; all the blood of the fetus originates within the organism itself.)

The villi are connected to the fetus by the *body stalk*, which develops from the inner cluster of cells containing the germinal disc and which forms (by about the fifth week) the *umbilical cord*.[6] The body stalk, and later the umbilical cord, is the

[6]The umbilical cord, which contains the blood vessels linking the circulatory system of the embryo and fetus to the placenta, is a transparent and rubbery tube, containing two arteries and one vein.

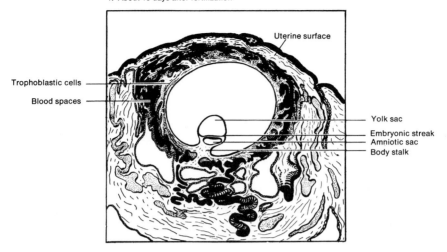

Uterine surface

Trophoblastic cells

Blood spaces

Yolk sac
Embryonic streak
Amniotic sac
Body stalk

2. Buildup of placental villi, about two and a half weeks after fertilization.

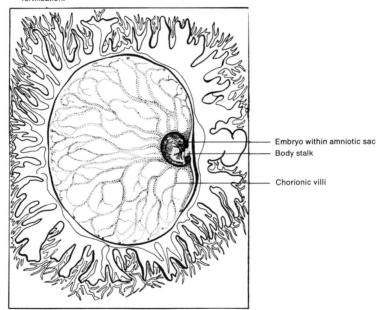

Embryo within amniotic sac
Body stalk

Chorionic villi

Figure 11–3. The Development of the Embryo

only direct connection between the organism and the uterus. The cluster of cells that develops into the organism and body stalk also forms in the embryonic period into the *amnion*, a protective sac of salty, watery fluid in which the embryo and fetus float—separated from the uterine wall, cushioned against injury and temperature change, bathed and perhaps partially nurtured by the soothing

---

The rush of blood (about four miles per hour) through the cord keeps it relatively stiff and prevents it from entangling and then strangling the fetus. At full term, the umbilical cord is about twenty inches long and about three quarters of an inch in diameter.

3. Dwindling of yolk sac; embryo about three weeks old. Umbilical vessels are forming.

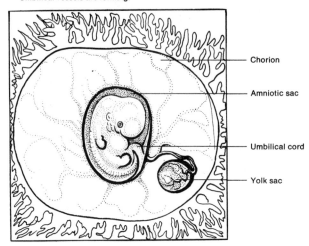

Chorion

Amniotic sac

Umbilical cord

Yolk sac

4. Embryo at about fourth week. Embryo and placenta well formed.

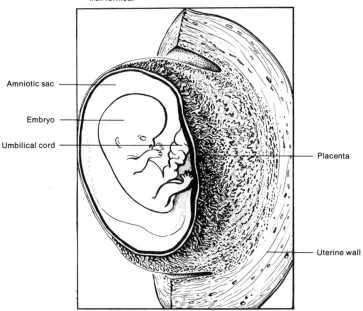

Amniotic sac

Embryo

Umbilical cord

Placenta

Uterine wall

Figure 11–3. *(Continued)*

solution, and free to flex its limbs and move its head.[7] The amniotic fluid is apparently manufactured by the organism.

---

[7] This cluster of cells also develops into the *yolk sac,* an organ that is largely vestigal among mammals. (Among birds and amphibians, of course, whose fertilized eggs are separate from the mother, the yolk sac serves as the source of nutrition for the developing organism.) At first, the yolk sac is a large protrusion from the midsection of the embryo, but it grows gradually smaller and is eventually integrated into the umbilical cord. For a brief period, it appears that the yolk sac aids in the manufacture of blood cells, a process that is gradually taken over by the developing liver and bone marrow.

By three weeks, the embryo's tissues have become specialized — differentiated into *mesoderm*, which will become bone, muscle, and supportive tissue; *endoderm*, from which the alimentary tract and digestive organs develop; and *ectoderm*, which becomes skin and neural tissue. Circulation of blood also begins in the embryo and into the body stalk, where the nutrition and oxygen of the mother and the wastes of the embryo are exchanged through the medium of the chorionic villi and the uterine wall. By the end of the third week, the embryo has grown to about one seventh of an inch in length and has a clearly distinguishable head and spinal cord and the buds of arms and legs. Lenses are forming in the eye areas, the location of the ears has been marked off, a few isolated nerves have appeared, and various other glands and organs are taking rudimentary shape.

About the fourth week, the mother becomes aware of the possibility that she is pregnant. Her menstrual period is now about two weeks overdue, and she may have noticed a heaviness and fullness of her breasts and an enlargement and darkening of her areolae and nipples (which also may exude a secretion when pressed). She may also have to urinate more often than usual because of the pressure on the bladder from the expanding uterus; and, in the early weeks of pregnancy, she may experience "morning sickness." All of these signs, however, can occur as symptoms of *false pregnancy*, a psychosomatic response to such psychological stimuli as fear of pregnancy. Occasionally, false pregnancy can counterfeit even gradual swelling of the abdomen for a full nine months.

Actual pregnancy, at least in the embryonic stage, can be determined beyond doubt only by laboratory tests, and these will be reliable only if enough time (from ten to forty days) has elapsed after conception to allow buildup of the *gonadotropic hormone (HCG)*[8] in the mother. It is this hormone whose presence in large quantities indicates pregnancy.

The pregnancy tests most commonly in use today are the *immunologic tests*, which because of their simplicity, economy, and speed have largely replaced the earlier biological tests[9] (Bermes and Isaacs, 1969). These immunologic tests are of two forms: (1) those performed in a test tube, which take about two hours for results to be obtained, and (2) the microscopic slide tests, which give results within minutes. Both the tube and the slide test depend upon the chemical principle of *agglutination inhibition.*

With the tube test, for example, two reagents (testing agents) are added to a specimen of the subject's urine. One reagent consists of erythrocytes (red blood cells) coated with HCG; the other reagent is anti-HCG. In the absence of HCG in the urine specimen, the erythrocytes will agglutinate (collect into clumps),

---

[8] HCG is an abbreviation for the full name of the gonadotropic hormone: human chorionic gonadotropic hormone.

[9] The biological pregnancy tests were developed in the 1930s and 1940s, starting in the early 30s with the *Ascheim-Zondek*, or *A-Z, test*, where the subject's urine is injected into a female mouse which has not had its first ovulation. If the subject is pregnant, there will be enough gonadotropic hormone in her urine to cause the animal's ovaries to mature and to form eggs within 24 to 48 hours. Numerous modifications of the A-Z test followed. The most well-known is the *Friedman, or rabbit, test*, which was also developed in the early 1930s. The two shortcoming of these biological tests are their need for trained laboratory personnel and for laboratory animals, which makes them relatively expensive and slow.

which is a negative result. The presence of HCG in sufficient quantity in the urine specimen will neutralize the anti-HCG, so that there is agglutination in-hibition, a positive test. The agglutination inhibition is indicated by the settling of the erythrocytes to the bottom of the tube in a characteristic ring. The slide test operates in the same way, utilizing latex particles as the reagent instead of erythrocytes. The slide test is much faster than the tube test; but it is not so sensi-tive to low concentrations of HCG in the specimen's urine, and it is more sus-ceptible to false positives.[10] Because of the possibility of false positives with both forms of immunologic tests, physicians generally recommend that both tests be used (Cabrera, 1969). When used together, these immunologic tests are better than 98 percent reliable.

The Development of the Fetus

The *fetal period* of development, from eight weeks to birth, is the time of the growth and refinement of the organs and structural systems that budded in the embryonic stage. During the third month, the fetus reaches a length of about three inches. The features of the face become more differentiated; the lips take shape, the nose begins to stand out, and the eyelids are formed, although they remain fused. The fingers and toes are well developed, and fingernails and toe-nails are forming. The primitive kidneys begin to secrete small amounts of urine. By the tenth week, the fetus begins to make breathing movements and reflex movements of the lips resembling sucking.

By the fourth month, the chorionic villi have disappeared, except for those that are functioning in direct contact with the uterine wall and the umbilical cord. These villi, together with the portion of uterine tissue in which they are embed-ded, become the *placenta*. The placenta holds the organism in place in the uterus while continuing and increasing the nurturant functions that the villi had served. On the side connected to the uterine lining, the placenta is a spongy mass of blood vessels; on the other side, to which the baby is connected by the umbilical cord, the placenta is smooth. At full term the placenta weighs about a pound and is about eight inches in diameter and one inch thick.

As the villi which are unconnected to the uterine tissue have disappeared, the trophoblast, now called the *chorion*, remains as a sac around the amniotic sac and gradually fuses with the amnion as the fetus and the amniotic sac grow larger.

In the fourth month, the fetus grows to about six inches and weighs about four ounces. Most of its bones have been formed, although they are still cartilage and will not be completely hardened into bone (*ossification*) until many years after birth. By the fourteenth week spontaneous movements of the fetus can be detected by stethoscope. However, the *quickening*, the first fetal movements of which the mother herself is aware, does not occur until about the seventeenth week. Also during the fourth month hormone secretion becomes greater as the body of the

---

[10]Recent data indicate that certain psychiatric drugs, excessive protein in the urine, the post-meno-pausal state, and, possibly, hyperthyroidism may cause falsely positive reactions. The oral estrogen-progestin contraceptive pill does not appear to affect the test results, however (Kerber, 1970).

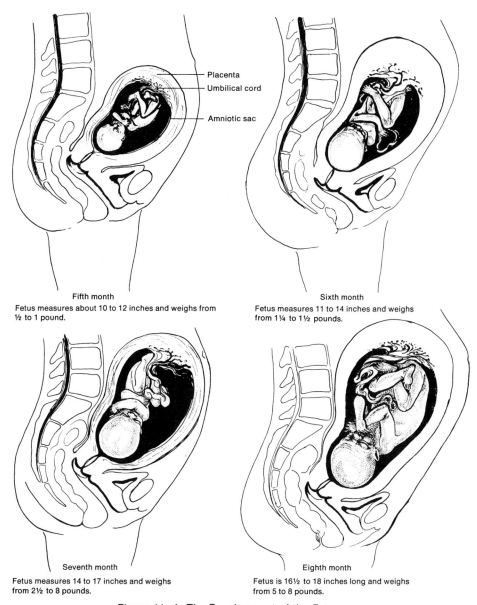

Placenta
Umbilical cord
Amniotic sac

Fifth month
Fetus measures about 10 to 12 inches and weighs from ½ to 1 pound.

Sixth month
Fetus measures 11 to 14 inches and weighs from 1¼ to 1½ pounds.

Seventh month
Fetus measures 14 to 17 inches and weighs from 2½ to 8 pounds.

Eighth month
Fetus is 16½ to 18 inches long and weighs from 5 to 8 pounds.

Figure 11–4. The Development of the Fetus

fetus takes on increasingly complex functions, including digestion and the secretion of bile by the liver.

In the fifth month, the fetus's heartbeat can be heard through a stethoscope and quickening becomes quite apparent to the mother, first as a mild fluttering and later as solid kicks against the inside of her abdomen. Any morning sickness she may have had is gone, and she is now in the most comfortable period of pregnancy.

During the sixth month, the fetus grows to a foot in length and about twenty ounces in weight. His eyelids are now separated, and he can open and close his eyes; eyelashes and eyebrows may have begun to appear; and he makes slight but *regular* breathing movements. By the end of this month, his essential anatomy and physiology are almost complete, and development from now until birth is largely a matter of increase in size and of stabilization of organic function. If he is born at this time, the baby will require constant medical attention and his chances of survival are slim.

By seven months the fetus is about fifteen inches long and weighs about two and a half pounds. If he is born now he will have a fair chance of survival, with the aid of specialized attention and equipment. A baby born in the eighth month of pregnancy, however, has a very good chance of survival, since his development is now virtually complete. In the eighth and ninth months, his growth consists mainly of a very rapid gain in weight, an average of nearly half a pound a week, the shedding of prenatal body hair, and the development of a less wizened appearance.

During the final months of pregnancy, the mother will probably feel generally healthy, but she is likely to be uncomfortable because of the crowding of her organs by her expanding uterus and because the increasing weight of the baby causes some problems in her movement and her equilibrium. Many women feel

awkward and cumbersome in these months and look forward to childbirth as liberation. Many others, however, report that the later stages of pregnancy are for them a time of unparalleled physical and mental well-being (Stone and Church, 1968).

Prenatal Influences

It has long been known that in the intimately symbiotic relation of mother to fetus, biological and physical factors affecting the mother's body will also have a profound effect on the development of the baby. The most obvious of these factors, of course, is nutrition. The mother's diet must enable her body to pass on to the fetus an adequate supply of the building materials necessary for its development. If the diet of the mother should contain, for example, too little calcium or vitamin A, the teeth of the baby will develop improperly and no amount of postnatal care will repair the damage. Moreover, since the placenta allows the passage, from the mother to the fetus, of drugs and many viruses and bacteria as well as food and oxygen, any illness contracted or drug taken by the mother during pregnancy is potentially harmful to the fetus. The effect of drugs was dramatically demonstrated in the case of Thalidomide, which in 1964-1965 caused thousands of babies to be born without limbs or with deformed limbs. It is now thought that even aspirin may be potentially dangerous to the fetus, possibly impairing its full potential for development.

Among diseases and illnesses afflicting the mother, typhoid, influenza, diphtheria, and syphilis may reach and damage the fetus. German measles is particularly dangerous, especially if contracted in the first three months of pregnancy; for it will almost invariably cause brain damage, deafness, or blindness to the unborn baby. Indeed, a woman should consult a doctor about any illness she contracts at any stage of pregnancy, no matter how mild the effects of the illness may seem to her. Similarly, x-rays and other forms of radiation are especially damaging to the fetus and must be avoided if possible—there is no safe range of exposure (Sternglass, 1963). Sometimes x-rays must be made to anticipate delivery difficulties.

Modern science is also learning more and more about psychological factors affecting the relationship of mother and fetus. Research into this relationship gives no credence to such folklore notions as that a pregnant woman who is frightened by a horse will have a child who looks like a horse or that by thinking pleasant thoughts she will have a cheerful baby or that by listening to classical music she will have a baby who is a musical prodigy. But research has revealed, for example, that emotional stress in the mother can alter her secretion of hormones that may be transmitted to the fetus and affect his development. Similarly, an emotionally content mother will be able to function optimally—given the significant relation between emotions and physiology—and will therefore provide maximum opportunity for realization of the fetus's full potential.

In short, although the relation between psychological factors in the mother and mental processes in the baby is still unclear, it is now acknowledged that if the mother is experiencing *both* physical and emotional well-being, the opportunity for the proper development of the fetus is optimal; conversely, if the mother is tense, worried, uneasy, or unhappy, the fetus might very well suffer for it.

Prenatal Tests

A very important prenatal diagnostic tool developed recently but already a routine procedure in many hospitals is the technique of *amniocentesis,* in which a long needle is inserted through the mother's abdomen into the amniotic sac, and a sample of the amniotic fluid is drawn off. Cells that have been sloughed off from the mucous membranes of the fetus are found in this sample of amniotic fluid; and these cells may be cultured, stained, and examined microscopically for the possibility of disease and birth defects. Before this technique was devised, couples who were known carriers of hereditary diseases could be given only the most limited statistical prediction of their chances of having a genetically damaged baby. Now, however, diagnosis by amniocentesis can provide 100 percent certainty for some types of diseases. Furthermore, because the fetal cells can predict the baby's sex, sex-linked hereditary illnesses can be forestalled (muscular dystrophy and some types of cerebral palsy are found only in males, for example). One of the most dramatic and important new uses for amniocentesis is in forestalling a dangerous respiratory disease (hyaline membrane disease) that strikes many premature infants immediately after birth and is the most common cause of death in premature infants. When fetal lungs are fully developed, the disease does not occur; thus, amniocentesis can measure precisely the maturity of the lungs in an unborn baby and tell obstetricians whether it is safe to deliver the premature infant or whether delivery should be delayed.

Childbirth

Toward the end of pregnancy, the fetus usually changes its position so that the head is in the lower part of the uterus. This may occur as early as four weeks before birth or it may not occur until the onset of *labor*, which is the process by which the baby is propelled from the mother's body. Labor consists of involuntary contractions of the longitudinal uterine muscles, voluntary contractions of the abdominal muscles, and relaxation of the sphincter muscles of the cervix. By these means the baby is gradually squeezed out of the uterus and through the cervix and vagina.

The beginning of labor is signalled by the onset of labor pains, which are produced by the recurrent contractions of the uterine muscles. Initially the pains occur at regular intervals of about fifteen to twenty minutes and are rather mild. As labor continues, the pains become more intense and the time between them shortens, eventually to about two or three minutes. The pains begin in the back and move toward the front of the abdomen.

Because uterine contractions occur all through pregnancy and, in the last weeks, may become quite intense and frequent, the mother, especially if she is having her first child, may mistake them for labor pains and enter the hospital prematurely. Three signals help to distinguish true from false labor pains. One is the regularity and increasing frequency of the pains. Another is called *show* and is the discharge from the vagina of a small plug of mucus spotted with blood, followed by varying amounts of a bloody discharge (the more imminent the birth, the more blood there is). This plug, which during pregnancy helps to prevent infection from entering the uterus through the cervix, is released in the early hours of labor, as the cervix begins to relax and dilate. The third signal is the *rush of waters* that occurs when the amniotic sac ruptures and releases the amniotic fluid. The rush of waters does not usually occur until the birth of the baby is imminent.

Obstetricians recognize three stages of childbirth. The first and longest stage begins with the onset of labor pains and involves the dilation of the cervix to permit passage of the baby's head. This stage lasts from about six to eighteen hours for first births and from about three to ten hours for subsequent births. When labor pains become very regular and are about five to ten minutes apart, the mother is usually taken to the hospital. There the cervix is watched closely until it reaches a diameter of about ten centimeters and the baby's head starts to enter it. At this point the mother is moved to the delivery room and the first stage of childbirth merges into the second.

The second stage lasts from less than 20 minutes to (rarely) more than 90 minutes and ends when the baby has emerged and been separated from the mother. During this stage especially, the mother's blood pressure is constantly measured and the fetal heart rate is watched. The mother can speed the birth process at this stage by tightening her diaphragm, abdominal, and back muscles so that the uterine muscles are aided in pushing the baby through the cervix. The mother's active participation at this point also seems to help reduce her pain.

When the baby appears at the vaginal opening, his head turns so that the back of his skull emerges first. If it appears that the size of the head will tear the vaginal tissues, the doctor makes an incision (*episiotomy*) at the top of the perineum to enlarge the opening (an incision heals more quickly than a tear). Once the back of the skull has been squeezed out, the rest of the head comes free, face down and draining. The doctor supports the head with one hand and draws gently on the baby as the shoulders, parallel with the vulva, slip out. With the other hand, he removes the mucus from the baby's mouth with his finger, so that the infant will not aspirate the mucus with his first breath.

Because the head and shoulders of the baby are the largest part of his body, once they have passed through the vagina the torso and legs slip out quickly and easily, followed by the umbilical cord, which is still attached to the placenta. The doctor suctions the remaining mucous out of the baby's mouth and throat with a small syringe and then places the baby on the mother's abdomen where his weight helps in the later expulsion of the afterbirth.

As the baby lies on the mother's abdomen, the doctor holds the umbilical cord between his fingers, feeling for the pulsations of its blood vessels to stop. When they do, he clamps off the cord an inch or two from the baby's abdomen, places a second clamp about four inches from the first, and cuts the cord midway between the two clamps. (The stump later dries out and drops off.) Penicillin ointment is applied to the baby's eyes to prevent infection, and an identifying band is fastened around his wrist and ankle. Usually the baby's footprint is taken on a card which also has the mother's thumbprints.

One minute after delivery and again five minutes after delivery, the baby is rated on an evaluation scale called the *Apgar Scoring System*. By this system he is given a rating of 0, 1, or 2 in five categories: heart rate, respiratory effort, muscle tone, reflex response, and color. Babies with a total score of five or more rarely need special attention; babies who score four or less need immediate special attention. Approximately 70 percent of newborn infants score 7 or better (Apgar *et al.*, 1958). The Apgar score is later useful to the pediatrician in observing and diagnosing a child's development and health.

The third and final stage of childbirth occurs from 2 to 20 minutes after delivery and consists of the expulsion of the *afterbirth*—the placenta, the amniotic

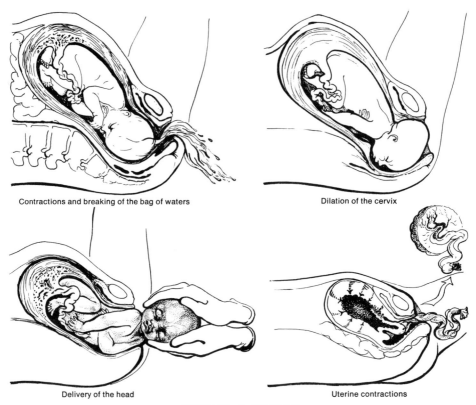

Contractions and breaking of the bag of waters

Dilation of the cervix

Delivery of the head

Uterine contractions

Figure 11-5. Childbirth

sac, the chorionic membranes, and the remainder of the umbilical cord. The afterbirth is carefully examined for signs of abnormality and to make certain that all of it has expelled. While this is going on the mother is usually given hormone injections[11] to hasten the shrinkage of her uterus and to stimulate her milk production. If she does not want to nurse the baby, she is given injections that will help to dry up the milk. Her abdomen may also be kneaded to help restore tone to the uterine muscles. Meanwhile, the baby is washed, wrapped in a warming blanket, placed in a crib, and taken to the nursery, where he is observed carefully.

Nearly 95 percent of births involve the normal *vertex presentation*, in which the baby's head emerges first (Crawley *et al.*, 1964). The remaining 5 percent are more difficult deliveries because the baby's buttocks (*breech presentation*) or shoulder (*shoulder presentation*) or foot (*incomplete breech*) or face (*brow presentation*) emerge first from the vagina. Oversized babies (the average baby weighs 7½ pounds) can also cause difficulty since the baby's head must pass between the bones of the pelvic arch of the mother. Only one baby out of one hundred, however, weighs over 10 pounds (Fitzpatrick, 1966).

---

[11] These hormone injections substitute for the eating of the hormone-rich afterbirth by other mammals—even those that are normally herbivorous.

If the baby is too large or if the mother's or baby's physical condition makes the stress of childbirth dangerous, the baby is delivered by *Caesarean section* (so called because Julius Caesar was supposedly born in this manner), an operation in which delivery is made by cutting through the mother's abdominal and uterine walls. Also, if uterine contractions weaken or stop during labor, the baby may have to be delivered by *forceps*, tongs that fit around the baby's head and enable the doctor to draw him out of the uterus. The use of forceps during the first or second stages of labor (high forceps) is very dangerous because the possibility of inaccurate placement and because the force that is necessary may disfigure the baby or cause brain damage. Nevertheless, for a time, high-forceps deliveries were popular because they shortened both the mother's and the doctor's labors; current practice, however, is to regard the use of high forceps as an emergency measure. *Low-forceps* deliveries, which occur only after the head of the baby has emerged from the vagina, involve much less risk. The frequency of forcep deliveries varies with the hospital and the doctor. According to one survey, the frequency in the United States varied from 1 to 85 percent of childbirths in different areas and with different doctors (New York *Times*, June 23, 1963, p. 54).

Childbirth does not have to occur in a hospital, of course, nor does it require the attendance of a physician. In many societies, even some in the Western world, most childbirths still take place in the home with only a midwife or a friend or relative to assist. In the United States, however, this rarely occurs.

Hospitalization and a doctor's assistance has, of course, contributed significantly to the sharp decrease in infant and maternal death during childbirth. But there has been a reaction in the past decade or two to the attitude (arising from the general atmosphere and procedures of hospitals) that childbirth is a medical problem rather than a natural procedure. Many doctors and expectant mothers are favoring *natural childbirth*, in the belief that delivery without forceps, heavy anesthetics, or other unnecessary medications is in the long run more emotionally satisfying to the mother and more physically beneficial to the child. (For example, a general or heavy anesthetic often affects the infant's alertness and general functioning for hours and even days after the birth.) With natural childbirth the mother is generally prepared with a course of breathing and muscular exercises that make labor easier and faster. She may go through the entire delivery without anesthetic or she may receive only a small dose of a local anesthetic during the final and most painful point in the labor. Often she is able to observe the delivery through mirrors mounted over the delivery table, and usually the father is also able to observe the precedure, either from an adjoining glassed-in room or in the delivery room itself.

Another procedure that provides more involvement for the mother in the birth and care of her child is what is called *rooming in*. With rooming in, which many new hospitals are adopting, the infant is placed in the mother's room a few hours after delivery and is kept there throughout their hospitalization so that the mother can immediately begin to care for the baby. This procedure has the advantage of allowing the mother to be active almost immediately after childbirth and helping her to recover rapidly; but, most important, it enables the infant to have more loving attention and care than is provided in a communal nursery.

Rooming in also allows the father to visit and to become involved with the baby. It is possible that the widespread use of natural childbirth combined with rooming in could mean significant advantages for the emotional development of the child and the psychological satisfaction of the mother in our overinstitutionalized mass society.

Infertility and Its Treatment

Every human being occupies a position on a scale from total sterility, which is fairly rare, to high fertility; moreover, his position on this scale varies from day to day with such factors as illness, fatigue, nutrition, drug consumption, and emotional stress. Because one out of eight couples in the United States find that despite repeated copulation the wife fails to become pregnant (Brecher and Brecher, 1966), a large proportion of married couples are concerned with the problem of infertility.

It is estimated that 20 to 50 percent of cases of infertility in the United States are due to male problems (Bowman, 1965). Treatment of male infertility includes various nutritional, hormonal, or surgical procedures, depending on the nature of the problem. The most readily determinable physical symptom of male infertility is a low number of sperm or a high proportion of inactive sperm in a man's ejaculate. It is estimated that in order for conception to be probable the male must produce an ejaculate containing at least 60 million to 100 million sperm per cubic centimeter of semen and that at least three quarters of these sperm must possess a sound structure and high mobility (Crawley *et al.*, 1964). A sperm count is used by physicians to determine whether these conditions are met.

If a sperm count reveals a deficiency in quantity or quality of sperm, and if the man does not respond to hormonal or nutritional treatment, conception is sometimes effected by *artificial insemination,* in which a physician accumulates several of the husband's ejaculations (which can be preserved through refrigeration) and injects them into the vagina of the wife at the time she is ovulating. The sheer quantity of the ejaculate introduced into the vagina may overcome the effect of sperm deficiencies.

If, however, diagnostic procedures reveal total sterility of the husband, or if repeated artificial inseminations using his sperm fail to result in pregnancy, sperm from a donor[12] other than the husband is sometimes obtained and mixed with that of the husband. When a donor's sperm is used the physician usually attempts to match physical traits, blood type, and general characteristics with those of the husband, so that fertilization by the husband's sperm will still seem

---

[12]Donors are usually medical students and interns who are paid between five and twenty dollars for a specimen. Physicians prefer to use fresh semen in artificial insemination and therefore the specimen is generally produced within an hour or two of insemination. The practice of artificial insemination provokes many legal, religious, and psychological problems. For an interesting discussion of some of these, see Monsma (1963).

a possibility. This possibility, that a child produced by artificial insemination may still be the natural offspring of the husband, naturally carries great psychological weight for couples who elect this procedure.

Most cases of infertility are traceable to the wife, whose conceptive processes are far more complicated than those of the male. While the male must simply produce viable sperm in sufficient quantity and then deposit them in the vagina, fertility in the female involves proper ovulation and passage of the egg through the Fallopian tube, maintenance of a chemically hospitable medium for the sperm and the zygote in the uterus and Fallopian tubes, and, possibly, a proper psychological preparation for fertilization (it has been suggested that proper ovulation may be inhibited by tension or stress). In examining for female infertility, a physician first tries to determine whether ovulation occurs, since without ovulation conception is impossible. The occurrence of ovulation is usually (though not always) indicated by regularity of the menstrual cycle and by the slight temperature change (.5 degree) that occurs with ovulation. If ovulation is presumed to occur (there is no way to know for sure), the next question is whether or not the egg can penetrate the Fallopian tube. It is possible to determine whether the Fallopian tubes are open by gently forcing a small amount of carbon dioxide through them or by filling them with an opaque liquid which will show up on an x-ray. Sometimes either of these procedures is sufficient in itself to open a blocked tube.

If an examination of sperm in the vagina immediately after copulation indicates that the sperm are not surviving their passage, the chemistry of the female genital fluid may be tested to determine if it is a hospitable medium for sperm. If the degree of acidity in the reproductive tract is found to be excessive, for example, chemical treatment is often possible.

Perhaps as many as half the couples who experience infertility problems are able to have children after proper medical or psychological treatment. For many of those for whom treatment is unsuccessful or for whom artificial insemination is an unsatisfactory alternative to childlessness, adoption is a solution. Federal welfare officials estimate that 142,000 childless couples each year solve their fertility problem by adoption through formal state or private agencies; and many more turn to the so-called "grey market" in babies and arrange for the adoption of an unwanted child through the mother, her physician, or an attorney. The adopting parents usually agree to pay the medical and legal costs of the mother and baby in return for the child. At present, something like eight million Americans under the age of 18 live with adoptive parents (*Time*, January 27, 1967). (For a further discussion of adoption, see Smith, 1963.)

Birth Control

In some societies, the possession of many children has a status or economic value and a wife is usually so often pregnant that menstruation is actually considered an abnormal phenomenon.[13] In our society, however, where no economic use is made of children and where, indeed, children are usually a serious economic liability, the average woman is pregnant only a tiny fraction of her lifetime. It is important to most couples that the number of their children be limited; and, as a result, birth control procedures or devices are very widely used. Research published in 1961 indicated that in the United States fully 92 percent of couples who had been married for several years had practiced some method of birth control in their marriage (Guttmacher, 1961).

Such widespread practice (and, apparently, acceptance) of birth control is a recent phenomenon, not only in our society but in most of the world.[14] The first birth control clinic in the United States was not established until 1917 (by Margaret Sanger, who was imprisoned for her efforts). Since then the problem of world population growth has become so pressing and the social and economic arguments for birth control have become so persuasive that contraceptive information and devices are now provided free of charge by public health clinics in every large city in the United States, by the American government in its foreign aid programs, by the United Nations in its assistance to developing nations, and by other governmental agencies around the world. There is a general belief among most world leaders and scientists that overpopulation, and its concommitant problems of starvation, mental illness, demagoguery, and international aggression, is the most dangerous problem facing the world in the next few decades.[15]

There are six general means to effect the control of pregnancy: (1) natural methods, (2) mechanical barriers, (3) spermaticides, (4) the douche, (5) physiological controls, and (6) anatomical alteration. Some are *contraceptives* and prevent union of the egg and sperm; others are *abortifacients* and prevent the successful implantation of the embryo in the uterine wall.

Natural Methods

The rhythm method. The rhythm method, which is considered natural because it requires no devices or specialized equipment, depends for its effectiveness on

---

[13] In such societies, menstruating women are considered taboo and must undergo a ritual cleansing before they are allowed to participate in the community. In the past in the Indian (Asian) culture, menstruation was considered a sin since it was believed that a discharged egg was equivalent to the loss of a person.

[14] Various forms of birth control and contraception have been practiced for centuries. For example, the ancient Egyptians are known to have used condoms made of animal membrane, and many societies have practiced infanticide and abortion. There is a story that Casanova for his many conquests devised the use of a half lemon as a kind of diaphragm. And a small sponge saturated with soapy water was a popular device that is still being used in many parts of the world. Except for infanticide and abortion, most historic birth-control methods were extremely unreliable and ineffective, and contraception was not widely practiced. (See Finch and Green, 1963.)

[15] In 1900, the world population was 1,550 million; in 1950 it was 2,497 million, and in 1970, it was 3,552 million. It is estimated that by 1980, it will be 4,500 million; by 1990, 5,800 million; and by the year 2000, 7,500 million (Erlich and Erlich, 1970, pp. 42–43).

the fact that the female can conceive only when an egg is within the Fallopian tube. Since an ovum may live in the Fallopian tube for as long as 24 hours and since sperm may live in the genital tract of the female for as long as 72 hours, the period during which safe copulation cannot take place extends from three or four days prior to ovulation to at least one day after ovulation. In other words, on all but the four or five days of her menstrual cycle when ovulation is likely to occur, the female may copulate without risk of conception.

Although theoretically sound, the rhythm method is not a highly reliable means of birth control. A recent study of birth-control methods in the United States found that about 24 percent of the couples using the rhythm method reported unwanted pregnancies (Cant, 1971). The difficulties with the rhythm method are both physiological and psychological. To begin with, not all women are so predictable in their menstrual cycle that the time of ovulation can be ascertained with the degree of accuracy the method requires. The period of ovulation is estimated as about fourteen days before the beginning of menstruation; but neither a conscientious calendar count nor daily temperature taking (the temperature usually rises about .5 degrees with ovulation) can be completely reliable.

Even in women whose menstrual cycles are very regular, any excitement, anxiety, illness, shock, or even copulation itself can precipitate sudden ovulation at unpredictable times. Furthermore, copulation on a time schedule is for most people an unsatisfactory pattern to maintain, fulfilling neither their physical nor psychological needs.

The rhythm method, because of its "naturalness," is the only method of birth control that is sanctioned by the Roman Catholic church. Because Catholic law considers reproduction the primary function of marital copulation, it forbids the use of all contraceptives, which, by their nature, interfere with this function. There is considerable pressure within the church for a modification of this position, and it is probable that eventually the canon law will accept the use of at least the pill. Some priests are already somewhat more tolerant than the church hierarchy. In their counseling of parishioners, these "liberal" priests emphasize the importance of individual conscience and circumstances in choosing birth-control methods.

Withdrawal. A second method of contraception which requires no devices or specialized equipment is simply the withdrawal of the penis from the vagina before ejaculation, so that no ejaculate is allowed to reach the vagina. The advantage of this method is that it obliges a couple to follow no set schedule for copulation, and sexual relations may be spontaneous. On the other hand, withdrawal eliminates the physical and psychological satisfactions of intravaginal ejaculation, which is a significant part of the pleasure of copulation. Indeed, to expect the male to always withdraw from the vagina just as the intensely pleasurable moment of ejaculation is approaching is unrealistic. And, in any case, even if he is able to withdraw each time, pre-ejaculatory fluid, over which he has no control, may contain sufficient sperm to effect conception.

In view of these shortcomings, it is not surprising that withdrawal is one of the least popular methods of contraception in our society. A recent study found it to be used by only about one couple in ten; and of those couples who practiced withdrawal, 18 percent reported unwanted pregnancies (Cant, 1971).

Mechanical Barriers

The condom. One of the most popular of all contraceptive devices, the condom is a sheath of thin rubber that is rolled over the erect penis before vaginal intromission to prevent the semen from being ejaculated into the vagina. (It is also a prophylactic device which protects against venereal disease.) The condom is inexpensive, readily available in any drugstore (about 750 million are produced annually in the United States), and quite reliable. The possibility of the condom leaking or breaking is very unlikely, and its major shortcomings are due not to the unreliability of the device but to its inconvenience. Couples using the condom as a regular birth-control measure occasionally find the interruption involved in getting and rolling on the condom too demanding, and so they copulate without it. Consequently, about 14 percent of couples using the condom reported unwanted pregnancies (Cant, 1971).

The condom was used by about 30 percent of married couples in the United States in the late 1950s (Freedman, 1959; Westoff, 1961). There are no more recent data, but it is quite possible that use of the condom declined during the 1960s with the development of the pill and the intrauterine device and then probably increased again with adverse publicity surrounding the pill in 1970.

The diaphragm. The diaphragm is a circular piece of thin rubber with a stiffened but flexible rim. It is designed to lie along the roof of the vagina, between its back wall and the pubic bone, and thus to cover the cervix. It must be fitted by a physician, who also instructs the user in its proper positioning. Usually spermaticidal jelly is used in conjunction with the diaphragm.

Before the Masters and Johnson research (1966), the diaphragm was thought to be the most effective and convenient of all contraceptive devices. Since it is inserted several hours before copulation and remains in place for several hours after copulation, it was thought that it eliminated all danger of conception as well as allowing uninterrupted petting and orgasm. Masters and Johnson discovered, however, that during the period of sexual excitement and petting, the vagina may double or even triple its normal diameter; and thus, although the diaphragm may have fit perfectly at the beginning of the sexual activity, it may, by the time ejaculation occurs in copulation, have slipped from its proper position. In eight out of thirty couples participating in a "diaphragm test" conducted by Masters and Johnson, diaphragms slipped, permitting sperm access to the cervix.

About 12 percent of the couples using a diaphragm reported unwanted pregnancies (Cant, 1971).

The cervical cap. The cervical cap is similar in construction to the diaphragm, but it is designed to cover only the cervix itself. (The cervix is about one inch in diameter and projects into the vagina about one inch.) Although frequently used in Europe, it is less popular in the United States and is reported to have a 12 percent failure rate (Cant, 1971).

Spermaticides

Spermaticides are chemical substances designed to immobilize or destroy sperm before they enter the cervix. They are available in a variety of forms, including creams, jellies, suppositories, and foam sprays. Spermaticides are usually used in conjunction with mechanical barriers, such as the diaphragm or condom, since used by themselves the substances are unreliable. The Masters and Johnson study found that a spermaticide used by itself was as little as 50 percent effective.

The Douche

One of the oldest methods of contraception, the douche, consists of flushing the vagina with water immediately after copulation.[16] (The *bidet*, which is a low basin specially designed for douching, is standard equipment in most European hotels and private homes. In the United States, a douche is usually administered with a syringe.) The water in douching acts as a mild spermaticide, but the primary contraceptive effect of the douche is mechanical—the removal of sperm from the vagina by rinsing. As a method of contraception the douche is highly unreliable, since no matter how soon after ejaculation the douche is performed, it is usually not soon enough. Within one minute after ejaculation, millions of sperm have found their way through the cervix. In the Freedman study (1959), only about one married couple in ten relied on the douche, and of these about 33 percent reported unwanted pregnancies. The Westoff study (1961) of the metropolitan areas found even fewer couples regularly using the douche—about one in twenty-five. In 1971, the douche was reported to have a 31 percent failure rate (Cant, 1971).

Physiological controls

Oral contraceptives (the pill). The oral contraceptive pill controls the female reproductive physiology by causing modifications in the hormonal activity and thereby preventing ovulation. The pill is composed of the female hormone estrogen and a synthetic substance called progestin, which is chemically similar to progesterone, a hormone produced in the ovaries. When the pill is taken for 20 consecutive days, beginning on the fifth day after onset of menstruation, the

---

[16]A folk method related to the douche is the practice of urinating immediately after copulation. This method is based upon a faulty knowledge of anatomy. While the penis conducts both sperm and urine, the vagina is a separate structure from the urethra and urination can serve no flushing function. Another method, shaking up a soft drink bottle and using it as a syringe is no more effective (and for the same reasons) than a douche with water.

combination of estrogen and progestin simulates the hormonal conditions of pregnancy and thereby suppresses ovulation.

There are various combinations and dosages of the two drugs in the different brands of the pill, but all of the brands fall into either of two general categories: (1) the combined form, in which both drugs are ingested throughout the cycle; and (2) the sequential form, in which the estrogen is administered alone during the early part of the cycle, and the progestin is added only during the latter part. Women respond differently to the different forms of the pill, and sometimes the occasional undesirable side effects of the pill[17] can be eliminated simply by changing brands.

Despite the controversy and fear that surrounded the pill in 1970, and although many medical questions regarding the pill remain to be answered, currently available evidence indicates that the pill is completely safe for fully 90 percent of women. In addition, most of the 10 percent for whom the pill is potentially dangerous may be detected in advance of their taking it—simply with a few minutes of questioning by a physician and a few easily administered laboratory tests (supported by regular six-month checkups). For a small minority of women—perhaps 1 percent—the pill carries risks that cannot be detected in advance with present medical knowledge. It should go without saying that because there is some slight risk, the pill should never be used without a physician's recommendation and continuing supervision.

The advantages of the pill are obvious. When taken properly, it is virtually 100 percent effective in preventing conception. Moreover, its use causes no inconvenience or delay or interruption to the sequence of behavior preceding, during, and following copulation. (In that sense, it is the most "natural" of all contraceptive devices.) It also has the effect of regulating the woman's menstrual cycle to exactly 28 days and reducing menstrual flow.

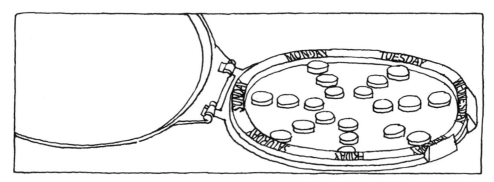

---

[17]The undesirable side effects that some women experience are similar to those accompanying pregnancy—tenderness and swelling of the breasts, weight gain and retention of fluid, nausea, headaches, depression, nervousness and irritability, and bleeding. The estrogen content of the pill causes a problem with blood clotting in an extremely small percentage of users. It must be pointed out, however, that even for susceptible women, a normal pregnancy is more dangerous to the mother's health than the pill. For a brief discussion of the possible hazards of the pill, see Erlich and Erlich, 1970, pp. 216–217; and Cant, 1971.

"Morning-after" treatment. A "morning-after" treatment that acts to prevent implantation of the embryo in the uterine wall has been available for some time, although it is not widely known among the general public. This treatment consists of heavy dosages of an estrogen compound (for example, stilbestrol or diethylostilbestrol pills, or premarin injection) for three to five days. Since it takes approximately four days from the time of conception for the fertilized egg to travel through the Fallopian tube and implant itself in the uterus, most physicians will begin this treatment as late as 72 hours after copulation, although they prefer to begin within 24 hours.

The prescription pills and injections are available from most private physicians and from the student health services at some colleges. The issue of side effects (possible nausea or prolonged menses) is considered inconsequential by physicians, since the treatment is used only as a "one shot" or emergency measure and even massive doses of estrogen taken occasionally are not considered harmful. The failure rate for this treatment is as yet undetermined. There are no figures available regarding the frequency or the extent of the treatment.

The intrauterine device (IUD). A third method which effectively controls the reproductive physiology of the female to prevent pregnancy is the intrauterine device, a plastic or stainless steel object that is inserted through the vagina into the uterus, where it may be left indefinitely. Such a device has been used successfully in animal husbandry for some time, but it has only recently been adapted for human use.

Just how the IUD works is still uncertain. It may be an abortifacient which acts as an irritant to the wall of the uterus and prevents the successful implantation of the embryo, or it may interfere with conception by causing the ovum to travel very rapidly through the Fallopian tube. The IUD comes in a variety of shapes, each one having advantages and disadvantages relative to the others. The most commonly used shapes include the loop, the ring, the spiral, the double coil, and the bow (see Figure 11–6).

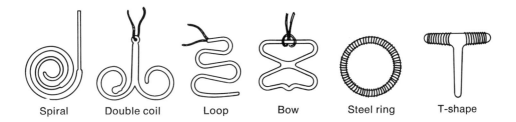

Spiral   Double coil   Loop   Bow   Steel ring   T-shape

Figure 11–6. Various Forms of IUDs

The IUD must be inserted by a physician (or by paramedical personnel) and should be checked by a physician every six months. Possible undesirable side effects include bleeding and discomfort, but the IUD is generally so safe and problem-free that it is recommended to women who cannot safely tolerate the pill. It is often not fitted on women who haven't had a baby, however, because it is more apt to cause discomfort and bleeding with these women than with those who have had a child.

The advantages of the IUD are, like the pill, obvious; once the device has been inserted, it may be ignored (except for regular checkups) and sexual behavior may be completely spontaneous and untrammeled. The failure rate—5 percent—is higher than the pill, but the higher rate of failure is thought to occur chiefly because the IUD may sometimes be spontaneously expelled without the woman's awareness. With normal precautions, the IUD should attain a contraceptive efficiency very close to that of the pill.

Because the IUD is cheap, simple, and highly effective, it is especially interesting to underdeveloped countries for distribution among their very rapidly growing populations.

Sterilization

Vasectomy. Vasectomy is a surgical procedure in which the vas deferens, the tubes through which the sperm pass from the testicles to the seminal vesicles, are cut and tied off or cauterized. This operation makes it impossible for the sperm to be included in the ejaculate; instead, they are absorbed into the tissue, once they reach the surgical barrier. The sperm are so infinitesimally small that the volume of the ejaculate is not diminished; in fact, the absence of sperm from the ejaculated semen can be detected only by a microscopic examination. It is important to emphasize that vasectomy does not interfere with the person's sex life in any way except to render him sterile. Sperm are still produced in the testicles, the hormone system is undisturbed, and erection and ejaculation occur exactly as before the vasectomy.

Vasectomy is a relatively simple and inexpensive procedure which may be performed in a physician's office under local anaesthesia in 15–20 minutes. The vas deferens lie close to the surface and may be reached through a small incision in the scrotum, which is then closed by a stitch or two. The person may copulate immediately after the operation; but some other birth-control precautions must be taken for a time, since sperm may remain in the male genital system for several weeks, and pregnancy may occur if they are ejaculated. A post-operative microscopic examination of the ejaculate will verify when the sperm are no longer present.

Since the vasectomy can be reversed only an estimated 50–80 percent of the time (Erlich and Erlich, 1969), sterilization should be utilized as a contraceptive measure only after a person is quite sure that he doesn't want further children.[18] Vasectomy is legal in all states, although it is restricted in Utah and

---

[18] Sperm banks are now being used in some areas to collect and store the husband's ejaculate prior to the vasectomy, in case he should change his mind about wanting more children If the sperm are stored at sub-freezing temperatures (minus 321 degrees), they may apparently be used for artificial insemination at a later date, with perfectly normal embryos resulting. A form of this method has been used satisfactorily with animal sperm for some time. The length of time human sperm may be safely stored has yet to be determined.

Connecticut to cases of "medical necessity." An estimated 750,000 American men had vasectomies in 1970, about three for every female sterilization (Association for Voluntary Sterilization, 1971).

Incidence of failure with vasectomy is, of course, virtually zero. Cenception could occur only if the sterilized male copulates without another contraceptive device too soon after the operation or in the highly unlikely event that the physician severs the wrong tube or the severed tubes spontaneously regenerate and realign.

Table 11–1. Principal Methods of Birth Control

Method	Percentage failure rate	Possible side effects	Special requirements
Sterilization	0	None.	Operation must be performed by physician.
The pill	0.3	Breast tenderness, weight gain, nausea, complexion changes, clotting.	Must be prescribed by physician (periodic check advised).
"Morning-after" treatment	Undetermined	Nausea, breast tenderness, prolonged menses.	Must be prescribed by physician.
Intrauterine devices	5	Irregular bleeding, discomfort (when first used).	Must be inserted by physician or trained technician (yearly check advised).
Diaphragm or cervical cap (with spermaticide)	12	Minor irritation (especially with spermaticide).	Must be fitted by a physician (a return visit may be required).
Condom (increased effectiveness if used with spermaticide)	14	Minor irritation (especially with spermaticide).	None.
Withdrawal	18	None.	None.
Rhythm	24	None.	Determination of "safe days" may require physician's advice.
Douche	31	None.	None.
Spermaticides (used alone)	50	Minor irritation.	None.

Salpingectomy. The female's sterilization operation is called a salpingectomy and consists of removing a section of the Fallopian tubes so that the ovum cannot pass through. The salpingectomy involves an internal surgical operation with the usual attendant risks, so it is generally performed only during a Caesarian operation, when the abdomen is already opened. Two new methods of salpingectomy, one involving an approach through the vagina and the other using an approach through the unbilicus, are now being pioneered, however. If either proves satisfactory, the operation will be as simple as the male vasectomy.

As with the vasectomy, salpingectomy has no effect whatsoever upon a woman s sex life, except for the psychological benefit of no longer having to worry about the possibility of conception. She continues to ovulate, her hormone system remains undisturbed, and the menstrual cycle goes on. The only change is that her ova never reach the uterus, nor can sperm travel up the Fallopian tubes to reach the ova. As with the vasectomy, reversal of the operation is difficult because of the minuteness of the structures involved and the technical difficulty of realignment. Success has been achieved in reversal operations in about 52 to 66 percent of the cases (Erlich and Erlich, 1969, p. 220).

Salpingectomy is legal in all states, although Utah and Connecticut restrict it to cases of "medical necessity." Inasmuch as there is no difficulty for the physician in identifying the Fallopian tubes, and since ova do not remain in the uterus after a salpingectomy, the probability of conception after a salpingectomy is zero. An estimated 250,000 American women had salpingectomies in 1970 (Association for Voluntary Sterilization, 1971).

Future Possibilities

The search for even more effective and safe methods of controlling conception is in progress; and many new methods have already been developed, although they are not yet commercially available. For example, a synthetic progesterone-only (progestin) "minipill" has proven quite successful in preventing pregnancy while allowing ovulation to continue and preventing the side effects (especially blood clotting) of the progestin-estrogen pill. Apparently the synthetic progesterone somehow prevents the sperm from proceeding into the uterus and Fallopian tubes. If scientists can isolate and then synthesize the element in the synthetic progesterone that stops the sperm, they should be able to develop a contraceptive pill that would be taken only once or twice a year.

Another recent development is a new family of drugs, *prostaglandin*, which may prove to be the basis for the long-sought, routine, "after-the-fact" pill, or chemical abortifacient, which will cause the implanted embryo to be sloughed off with menstruation up to a month after conception. Since the woman would need to take this pill only when she misses her menstrual period, and since the actuarial expectation for pregnancy in a woman copulating several times per week is four or five times per year, she would have to take the pill only at these times.

A new system of administering birth control hormones without the use of pills involves a chemically impregnated intrauterine device that would remain in place for a full year, releasing the female hormone progesterone into the uterus in minute quantities. Since the device employs extremely small amounts of this natural hormone (as much in a whole year as conventional pills contain in a single dosage), and since the hormone moves directly to the uterus without passing through any other part of the body, the system is expected to create none of the side effects associated with the pill. This new technique, called a Uterine Contraception System, involves a small, soft, plastic packet that is inserted directly into the uterus by a physician. Inside the uterus, the device floats freely, eliminating any possibility of pain, irritation, or bleeding. Tiny quantities of progesterone escape continuously from the plastic packet to the lining of the uterus, altering the hormonal balance and causing the lining to reject the implantation of the fertilized egg. The device would be replaced yearly and could be removed by a physician at any time.

A completely new IUD has been developed which virtually eliminates the pain and bleeding that some women experienced with earlier IUDs and which is apparently 100 percent effective in preventing pregnancy. This newly developed IUD is T-shaped polyethylene, with copper wrapped around the stem of the T. This type of IUD (called "the T") may prove to be the ideal birth control device — effective, economical, and trouble-free.

A new approach to vasectomy involves a tiny, T-shaped, metal device, called a Phaser, which is surgically inserted into each vas deferens. The device embodies an adjustable valve, the size of a pinhead, which a physician can open or close by twisting the upright that projects through the wall of the vas. This new device would avoid the tissue damage caused by cutting and tying the vas deferens and, presumably would make the sterilization easily reversible.

A totally new birth control concept, one that would have profound cultural implications because of its simplicity and permanence, is a method that would render a woman indefinitely sterile with a single injection. This method, now under active investigation, involves the discovery, isolation, and synthesis of an active agent in sperm cells that, researchers believe, will cause an allergic reaction to sperm in virtually all women. The injection of this agent would cause the woman's bodily chemistry to form antibodies that would either inactivate the sperm before fertilization of the egg or make the fertilized egg incapable of implantation. It is believed that this allergy to sperm would then continue indefinitely unless the woman avoided all contact with sperm through either total continence or the rigorous use of the condom for a period of nine months to a year.

Still awaiting development are a once-a-month pill that will either control ovulation or prevent the sperm from reaching the egg, a once-a-year pill that is implanted under the skin to release small measured doses of the drug throughout the year, and a male pill, which will render the male temporarily infertile.

Abortion

Contraception can prevent pregnancy, but once pregnancy occurs, only abortion can prevent birth. *Spontaneous abortion*, sometimes called *miscarriage*, occurs naturally rather than as a result of outside interference with the organism or the female's reproductive system; it is essentially the organism's way of terminating a biologically abnormal pregnancy. Spontaneous abortion occurs in about one in ten pregnancies in this country (Guttmacher, 1957).

Induced abortion, the deliberate surgical termination of pregnancy, is not a method of contraception, of course, but one of birth control, or family planning. One of the most striking medical and social phenomena of 1970 was the change in the United States in public attitudes and laws regarding abortion. Scarcely three years earlier, every state in our society had strict laws prohibiting abortion except in very special circumstances. In some states, the pregnant woman could not obtain a legal abortion even if conception was the result of rape or incest. But by 1970, a dozen states had substantially relaxed their restrictions, and three states—Alaska, Hawaii, and New York—had virtually eliminated them, making abortion a matter to be decided solely between a woman and her physician. (See Table 11–2 for a summation of current abortion laws.) New York passed the most liberal "abortion by demand" law of all, stipulating only that the operation be performed by a licensed doctor within the first 24 weeks of pregnancy, which is considered by physicians to be the outer limit of the time during which abortions are medically feasible. Theoretically that meant that from 1970 on, any woman could receive an abortion in the United States simply by traveling to New York and making the necessary arrangements—which could be as uncomplicated as spending a few hours in a doctor's office and paying a fee in the neighborhood of $50.

This very dramatic social and medical change was apparently a reflection of the sweeping cultural revolution which our society seems to be undergoing. Traditional moral and religious taboos are being eroded by a demand for ecological and humanitarian considerations as well as for freedom of individual choice in matters relating to sex and birth control. There are now many vocal and well-organized groups in this country who sincerely believe that population control and the right of women to control their own bodies are more important than the equally sincere beliefs of those who hold that a fetus has life which must be protected and preserved above all other considerations. These proponents of unrestricted abortion also point to the uncounted tragedies—death, serious injury, and sterility—that have resulted from women trying to abort themselves[19] and from the clandestine abortions performed by unqualified personnel with improper techniques. Until the dramatic changes in abortion laws occurred, it was estimated that fully one million criminal abortions were

---

[19]Many women have done injury to themselves in the belief that pregnancy can be terminated by some drug or by some physical means, such as pounding the abdomen or falling downstairs. In fact, there is no way short of surgery to induce abortion without seriously harming the mother. Any woman who is persuaded that she was aborted by means other than surgery was either not pregnant in the first place or would have undergone spontaneous abortion anyway. Equally fallacious are the beliefs that hot baths, steam cabinets, hot douches, or even skydiving will terminate a pregnancy. The most common myth about abortion (and one that is as dangerous as throwing oneself down a flight of stairs) is the belief that there is a "black pill" that will terminate pregnancy. There is, indeed, a black pill, *ergot,* that will terminate a pregnancy; but in order for it to be successful the mother must take a quantity that will also terminate her life. Taking less will make her violently ill but will not induce abortion. Ergot is an alkaline substance that is used in very mild doses to induce uterine contractions to tighten the uterus and abdomen after the fetus and afterbirth have emerged.

Table 11–2. Abortion Statutes, 1970

Statutory provisions, by states:
The statutes in Massachusetts, New Jersey, and Pennsylvania do not indicate legal circumstances for abortion. However, case law in Massachusetts[1] and New Jersey[2] has sanctioned abortion in certain instances.

To save woman's life: Every state except Massachusetts, New Jersey,[2] and Pennsylvania.

To preserve woman's physical or mental health: Alabama, Arkansas, California, Colorado, Delaware, District of Columbia, Georgia, Kansas,[3] Maryland, New Mexico, North Carolina, Oregon,[4] South Carolina, and Virginia (Washington[5]).

If there is indication of fetal malformation: Arkansas, Colorado, Delaware, Georgia, Kansas,[3] Maryland, New Mexico, North Carolina, Oregon, South Carolina, and Virginia.

In case of rape: Arkansas,[6] California,[6] Colorado, Delaware,[6] Georgia, Kansas,[3] Maryland,[6] Mississippi, New Mexico, North Carolina,[6] Oregon,[7] South Carolina,[6] and Virginia.[6]

In case of incest: Arkansas, California, Colorado, Delaware, Kansas,[3] Maryland, New Mexico, North Carolina, Oregon,[7] South Carolina, and Virginia.

Restrictions:

Time limit for performing abortion (duration of pregnancy): Alaska (30 days), California (20 weeks), Colorado (16 weeks in case of rape or incest), Delaware (20 weeks),[8] Hawaii (nonviable fetus), Maryland (26 weeks),[8] New York (24 weeks), and Oregon (150 days).[9]

Residency requirements: Alaska (30 days), Arkansas (4 months), Delaware (4 months)[10], Georgia (must be state resident), Hawaii (90 days), North Carolina (4 months), Oregon (must be state resident), South Carolina (90 days), and Virginia (120 days).

Authority for decision on whether to perform abortion:

Therapeutic abortion board: California, Colorado, Delaware,[11,12] Georgia,[11] Maryland,[12] New Mexico, and Virginia.

Consultation of physicians: Arkansas, Delaware,[11] Georgia,[11] Kansas,[3] Louisiana, Mississippi, North Carolina, Oregon, South Carolina, and Wisconsin. In Alaska and Hawaii, an abortion may be performed on a consenting female by a physician who agrees to conduct the operation, providing it is performed in "a hospital or other facility approved for the purpose . . ." (Alaska) or "in a hospital licensed by the department of health . . ." (Hawaii). In New York, an abortion may be performed on a consenting female by a physician who agrees to conduct the operation.

Hospital policy: In the following states, permission of either the Therapeutic Abortion Board or Consultation is not required but authority for decision rests with local hospital policy: Alabama, Alaska, Arizona, Connecticut, District of Columbia, Florida, Hawaii, Idaho, Illinois, Indiana, Iowa, Kentucky, Maine, Michigan, Minnesota, Missouri, Montana, Nebraska, Nevada, New Hampshire, New York, North Dakota, Ohio, Oklahoma, Rhode Island, South Dakota, Tennessee, Texas, Utah, Vermont, Washington, West Virginia, Wyoming.

Source: Association for the Study of Abortion, Inc.

[1] Commonwealth v. Wheeler (1944): The court held that an assumed danger to physical or mental health would justify abortion. [2] State v. Siciliano (1956): The court held that abortion "is authorized when necessary for avoidance of death or permanent serious injury to the mother." [3] Effective July 1, 1970. [4] In determining whether there is risk to woman's physical or mental health, account may be taken of her total environment—actual or reasonably foreseeable. [5] Case law sanctions abortion to preserve woman's physical or mental health. [6] Forcible. [7] "Felonious intercourse." [8] Not applicable when woman's life is in danger or fetus is dead. [9] Not applicable when woman's life is in danger. [10] Not applicable if woman or husband work in Delaware, if woman has previously been a patient of a Delaware physician, or if woman's life is in danger. [11] Both Board review and Consultation required. [12] Hospital Review Authority.

performed yearly in the United States, three quarters of them upon *married* women who felt that financially, physically, or emotionally they could not afford another child (Crawley, 1964). Calderone (1958) determined that about one in five married women had had an illegal abortion by age 45. Among unmarried pregnant women, an estimated 85 to 90 percent of the pregnancies were terminated by illegal abortion (Neumann, 1967).

An abortion performed by a competent physician in proper surroundings is a relatively minor surgical procedure, less dangerous than normal childbirth. In Czechoslovakia, for example, where abortion is legal, not a single death was reported in 140,000 abortions in 1963–64 (Lader, 1966).

Summary

A new individual is created with the fertilization of the ovum by a sperm and with the fusion of these two gametes (the sperm and egg) into a single-celled organism, the zygote. The zygote then multiplies and differentiates into the billions of cells that make up the human being. The direction of the reproductive process is governed by DNA molecules within the genes, which contain the coded information that determines the development and characteristics of the organism.

Conception (the fertilization of the egg by the sperm) is the beginning of pregnancy. Although there are many natural signs of pregnancy (cessation of menstruation, swollen breasts, darkening areolae, frequent urination, liquid exuding from the nipples, morning sickness), all these may be counterfeited by *false* pregnancy. The only way to determine for certain that conception has occurred is through an examination in the physician's office and a laboratory test. There are three stages of pregnancy: the germinal (the first two weeks, during which the zygote embeds itself in the uterine wall); the embryonic (the third to the eighth week, during which the organ systems are established); and the fetal (the third to the ninth month, during which growth and refinement of the organs take place). The new organism is especially susceptible to environmental imbalances (from hormones, chemicals, diseases) during the first three months.

At full term the baby's head drops to fill the cervix; and labor pains—regular muscular contractions which force the baby through the birth canal—begin. Labor consists of three stages. The first stage begins with the onset of labor pains and ends with the baby's head filling the dilated (to 10 centimeters) cervix. The second stage begins with the baby's head coming through the cervix and ends with the severing of the umbilical cord. The first stage may last several hours (6 to 18); the second stage lasts anywhere from a few minutes to an hour or so. The third stage is the expulsion of the placenta (afterbirth) and usually occurs within a few minutes after birth.

Contraception and birth control are the concern of nearly all married couples in our society. Contraceptive methods and devices were notoriously unreliable and inconvenient until our own era, when the development of the contraceptive pill (which prevents ovulation) and the development of intrauterine device (which prevents the lodging of the zygote) have rendered family planning virtually foolproof.

Questions

1 What was the significance of the discovery of the biological bodies called genes and of the DNA molecules?

2 Why does the mature sperm or egg contain 23 chromosomes, rather than the 46 characteristic of every other cell of the body?

3 How do you explain the probability that among all members of a species that reproduces sexually individual differences are guaranteed?

4 How many genes are there for each hereditary trait?
   (a) What do you understand of the dominant genes? Recessive genes?
   (b) Give two examples of dominant and recessive traits.
   (c) What are the characteristics termed phenotypes? Genotypes?

5 When an X-carrying sperm unites with the ovum, the resultant zygote is XX and develops into which sex? When a Y-carrying sperm unites

with the ovum, the resultant zygote is XY and develops into which sex?

6 What is the time span in which fertilization and conception can occur. Why?

7 What is the significance of two or more eggs being released in the ovary? Of two zygotes developing from a single egg?

8 Why are fraternal twins biologically wholly different individuals? Why are identical twins biologically wholly identical?

9 How do triplets result? Quadruplets? Are multiple births hereditary?

10 What happens during the germinal period of pregnancy?

11 By three weeks, the embryo's tissues have become specialized. What will develop from the
    (a) mesoderm?
    (b) endoderm?
    (c) ectoderm?

12 When may the mother first become aware of the possibility that she is pregnant? What is the only sure method of determining pregnancy?

13 What is the function of the placenta? How large is it at full term?

14 What is the difference between the fetus and the embryo?
    (a) How long is the fetal period?
    (b) How long is the embryonic period?

15 What does quickening mean? When does it occur?

16 Could the fetus survive if born at the sixth month? Discuss development at this stage.

17 How does the mother feel during the final months of pregnancy?

18 Discuss the importance of nutrition in the mother's prenatal diet.

19 Describe the three stages of labor.

20 What signals help the mother to distinguish true from false labor pains?

21 Why may a Caesarean section be done?

22 Why may a mother be interested in natural childbirth?

23 What is meant by infertility? What percent of cases in the United States are due to male problems? What treatments are available for the male?

24 What is meant by artificial insemination?

25 What factors are involved in female infertility?

26 What percent of couples who have been married for several years practice some method of birth control? What means are used to effect contraception?

27 What is the rhythm method? How reliable is it? What are its difficulties?

28 How is the diaphragm used in contraception? What was significant in the Masters and Johnson research in 1966 regarding its use?

29 Describe the intrauterine device for contraception. How does it act?

30 What is the physiological action of of the contraceptive pill? How reliable is it?

31 Describe the vasectomy. The salpingectomy.

32 What are some abortion myths?

References and Selected Readings

Apgar, V., *et al.* Evaluation of the Newborn Infant, 2nd report. *Journal of the American Medical Association.* December 13, 1958, Vol. 168, pp. 1985–1988.

Bates, Jerome E., and Edward S. Sawadzki. *Criminal Abortion.* Springfield, Ill.: Thomas, 1964.

Beadle, George and Muriel. *The*

Language of Life: An Introduction to the Science of Genetics. New York: Doubleday, 1966.

Bermes, Edward W., Jr., and John H. Isaacs. Evaluation of a Direct Agglutination Latex Particle Test for Human Chorionic Gonadotropin. *American Journal of Obstetrics and Gynecology,* May–August, 1969, Vol. 104, pp. 865–870.

Bing, Elizabeth D. *Adventure of Birth.* New York: Simon & Schuster, 1970.

_____, Marjorie Karmel, and Alfred Tanz. *A Practical Training Course for the Psychoprophylactic Method of Childbirth (Lamaze Technique).* New York: American Society for Psycho-Prophylaxis in Childbirth, 1961.

Blau, Saul. The Venereal Diseases. In Albert Ellis and Albert Abarbanel, eds., *The Encyclopedia of Sexual Behavior,* 2nd ed. New York: Hawthorn, 1967, pp. 1,023–1,032.

Brecher, Edward. *The Sex Researchers.* Boston: Little, Brown, 1969.

_____, and Ruth Brecher. *An Analysis of Human Sexual Response.* New York: New American Library, 1966.

Cabrera, Hugo A. A Comprehensive Evaluation of Pregnancy Tests. *American Journal of Obstetrics and Gynecology,* January–April, 1969, Vol. 103, pp. 32–38.

Calderone, Mary S., ed. *Manual of Contraceptive Practice,* 2nd ed. Baltimore: Williams and Wilkins, 1963.

_____. *Abortion in the United States.* New York: Harper, 1958.

Cant, Gilbert. Is The Pill Safe? *Nature/Science Annual.* New York: Time-Life, 1971, pp. 33–44.

Clemens, Alphonse H. Catholicism and Sex. In Ellis and Abarbanel,

eds., *The Encyclopedia of Sexual Behavior,* 1967, pp. 228–234.

Crawley, Lawrence Q., et al. *Reproduction, Sex, and Preparation for Marriage.* Englewood Cliffs, N. J.: Prentice-Hall, 1964.

Danielsson, Bengt. Sex Life in Polynesia. In Ellis and Abarbanel, eds., *The Encyclopedia of Sexual Behavior,* 1967, pp. 832–840.

Davis, Kingsley. Population and Sex. In Ellis and Abarbanel, eds., *The Encyclopedia of Sexual Behavior,* 1967, pp. 841–847.

Dunn, Leslie C. *Short History of Genetics.* New York: McGraw-Hill, 1966.

_____. *Heredity and Evolution in Human Population,* rev. ed. Cambridge, Mass.: Harvard University Press, 1965.

Duvall, Evelyn M., and Sylvanus M. Duvall. *Sex Ways in Fact and Faith: Bases for Christian Family Policy.* New York: Association Press, 1961.

Eastman, Nicholson J. *Expectant Motherhood,* 13th ed. Boston: Little, Brown, 1970.

Erlich, Paul R. and Anne H. *Population, Resources, Environment: Issues in Human Ecology.* San Francisco: Freeman, 1970.

Finch, B. F., and Hugh Green. *Contraception through the Ages.* Springfield, Ill.: Thomas, 1963.

Fischberg, M., and A. W. Blackler. How Cells Specialize. *Scientific American,* September 1961, pp. 121–140.

Fitzpatrick, Elise. *Maternity Nursing: Nurses' Handbook of Obstetrics,* 11th ed. Philadelphia: Lippincott, 1966.

Freedman, Ronald, Pascal K. Whelpton, and Arthur A. Campbell. *Family Planning: Sterility and Population Growth.* New York: McGraw-Hill, 1959.

Gardner, E. J. *Principles of Genetics.* New York: Wiley, 1960.

Gilbert, Margaret Shea. *Biography of the Unborn*, rev. ed. New York: Hafner, 1963.

Goode, William J. *World Revolution and Family Planning*. New York: Free Press, 1970.

Gould Editorial Staff. *Marriage, Divorce, and Adoption Laws in the United States*. New York: Gould, 1970.

Guttmacher, Alan F. *Birth Control and Love*. New York: Bantam, 1970.

_____, ed. *Case for Legalized Abortion Now*. Los Gatos, Calif.: Diablo, 1967.

_____, Winifred Best, and Frederick S. Jaffe. *Planning Your Family*. New York: Macmillan, 1964.

_____, and the editors of *Consumer Reports. The Consumers Union Report on Family Planning*. Mt. Vernon, N. Y.: Consumers Union of the U. S., 1962.

Hartman, Carl G. *Science and the Safe Period*. Baltimore: Williams and Wilkins, 1962.

Jones, Kenneth L., *et al. Marriage and Reproduction*. New York: Harper, 1970.

Kerber, Irwin J., *et al.* Immunologic Tests for Pregnancy, a Comparison. *Obstetrics and Gynecology*, July 1970, Vol. 36, pp. 37–43.

Lader, Lawrence. *Abortion*. New York: Bobbs-Merrill, 1966.

_____, and Milton Meltzer. *Margaret Sanger: Pioneer of Birth Control*. New York: Crowell, 1969.

Lehfeldt, Hans. Artificial Insemination. In Ellis and Abarbanel, eds., *The Encyclopedia of Sexual Behavior*, 1967, pp. 180–185.

Masters, William H., and Virginia E. Johnson. *Human Sexual Response*. Boston: Little, Brown, 1966.

Mittwoch, V. Sex Differences in Cells. *Scientific American,* July 1963, pp. 54–62.

Monsma, John Clover, ed. *Religion and Birth Control*. Garden City, N. Y.: Doubleday, 1963.

Montagu, Ashley. *Human Heredity*, 2nd ed. Cleveland: World, 1963.

_____. *Prenatal Influences.* Springfield, Ill.: Thomas, 1962.

Neumann, Gottfried. Abortion. In Ellis and Abarbanel, eds., *The Encyclopedia of Sexual Behavior*, 1967, pp. 35–43.

Nillson, Lennart. Drama of Life before Birth. *Life*, April 30, 1965, Vol. 58, No. 17, pp. 54–67.

Rainwater, Lee. *And the Poor Get Children*. Chicago: Quadrangle Books, 1960.

Rorvick, David M. *Your Baby's Sex: Select, Don't Settle*. New York: Dodd, 1970.

Rosenfeld, Albert. The Placenta. *Life*, April 30, 1965, Vol. 58, No. 17, pp. 70–71.

Smith, I. Evelyn, ed. *Readings in Adoption*. New York: Philosophical Library, 1963.

Sternglass, E. J. Cancer: Relation of Prenatal Radiation to Development of the Disease in Childhood. *Science*, 1963, Vol. 140, pp. 1102–1104.

Stone, L. Joseph, and Joseph Church. *Childhood and Adolescence: A Psychology of the Growing Person*, 2nd ed. New York: Random House, 1968.

Taussig, H. B. The Thalidomide Syndrome. *Scientific American,* August 1962, pp. 29–35.

Watson, James D. *The Double Helix*. New York: Atheneum, 1968.

_____. *Molecular Biology of the Gene*. New York: W. A. Benjamin, 1965.

Westoff, Charles F., and Leslie Aldridge. *From Now to Zero.* Boston: Little, Brown, 1971.

Westoff, Charles F., and R. H. Potvin. *College Women and Fertility Values.* Princeton, N. J.: Princeton University Press, 1967.

_____, et al. *Family Growth in Metropolitan America.* Princeton, N. J.: Princeton University Press, 1961.

Whittinghill, Maurice. *Human Genetics and Its Foundations.* New York: Reinhold, 1965.

Chapter Twelve

The Family with Small Children

The childhood shows the man,
as morning shows the day.

John Milton *(Paradise Regained)*

a fter the birth of a first child, a new and irrevocable life phase begins for husband and wife. They become father and mother, a fact which not even divorce will change. Entering parenthood, they are forced to take the final step into the adult world — to assume complete responsibility for the physical and emotional welfare of a new and helpless human being. They also undertake the socialization of their child — a teaching process that will continue for the next 20 years and that will be enormous in its scope and irreplaceable in its significance for them, for their offspring, and for society.

The Sequence of a Child's Behavioral Development

Relatively few elements learned in socialization are specifically the same among different cultures, but the developmental sequence and the basic needs of human offspring are the same in all societies. Children everywhere proceed from dependency to independency, from self-centeredness to an awareness of and responsiveness to others, and from responding only to immediate goals to planning ahead.

The Neonate

Because childbirth usually occurs in seclusion in our society, many people have never seen a newborn baby, a *neonate,* until they see their own; and they are frequently quite surprised at its appearance. The neonate is surprisingly small — the average weight is about seven and a half pounds — and because he keeps his legs drawn up he looks even smaller. His head makes up a quarter of his length and seems to rest almost directly upon his tiny shoulders.

His features are still largely undifferentiated: He seems almost chinless, his nose is nearly flat, and his head may be slightly misshapen as a result of his passage through the cervix and vagina (this molding of the head usually disappears within a week or two). Both eye and skin pigments are not developed at birth, so that virtually all babies are born with smoky blue eyes and pinkish skins (even Negro neonates may have light skins for the first few days). His skull has six soft spots (*fontanels*), where certain structural bones have not yet grown together. The most conspicuous of these, at the very top of his head, may not close over until he is a year or more old. The genitals of the neonate are quite prominent; and both boys and girls have enlarged breasts, which may temporarily secrete a milky substance (*witch's milk*). Girls may also have a brief "menstrual" flow just after they are born. Both the breast secretions and the bleeding are caused by hormones absorbed from the mother's bloodstream and will subside rapidly a few hours after birth.

The *neonatal period*, during which a complete transition takes place from fetal to postnatal ways of living, occupies approximately the first month of extrauterine life. The change from being a water-born physiological *symbiote* to being an air-born physiologically independent individual is extremely complex. While the fetus is maintained at a constant temperature and, through the umbilical cord and the placenta, receives oxygen, nutrients, immunizing agents, and hormones directly into his bloodstream (discharging the waste products of metabolism in the same way), the neonate, once the umbilical cord is cut, must quickly shift to a pattern of breathing, eating, digesting, urinating, defecating,[1] and providing for his own temperature control and immunilogical defenses.

The muscle groups active in breathing are poorly coordinated for some weeks after birth, and the neonate's respiration tends to be noisy, shallow, and irregular. Also, because the soft palate has not yet been integrated into respiration, his breath may rattle in his throat in a rather alarming way. The shift from fetal to postnatal blood circulation begins with the first breath, when the task of aerating the blood is taken over by the fetus's breathing mechanism (it has previously been provided by the oxygen contained in the pools of maternal blood in the placenta). The abdominal muscles surrounding the umbilical cord contract, and circulation through the umbilical artery and veins stops almost immediately (making it possible to tie and sever the cord). The shutting off of the umbilical arteries forces blood into the lungs, and the oxygen level of the blood reaches 90 percent of the normal level within three hours after birth. (The acid-alkaline balance of the blood is normal within a week or so; and blood pressure is normal within about ten days.)

The neonate's first attempts at eating (which consist, of course, of sucking) are very unskilled, and he loses weight for the first few days. When he is hungry,

---

[1] Once the fetus's kidneys are developed, it secretes small amounts of urine into the amniotic fluid. In addition, the fetus swallows mucus and amniotic fluid containing shed skin and hair, and these substances become solid wastes in the intestines, but they ordinarily are not defecated until after birth.

the neonate engages in complex *rooting* behavior, which stops only when the nipple is placed in his mouth. When he has found the nipple, he clasps and pumps the breast with his hands, even though at all other times he usually keeps his hands closed into fists and is unable to grasp things that he sees.

The intestinal bacteria necessary for digestion must be taken in from the environment (these bacteria also produce vitamin K, which is important for blood clotting; therefore any lesion during this time holds the grave threat of serious hemorrhage); thus the digestive system is slow in developing and rather delicate for the first few days. Mechanisms for internal temperature control also develop slowly, so that the neonate is at the mercy of changes in temperature and may easily become overheated or chilled. His sweat glands begin operating only when he is about a month old, and this delay makes it easier for him to conserve bodily heat (and bodily fluids). However, the inability to sweat also makes it hard for him to adjust to heat. (Parents often err on the side of keeping him too warm, which not only makes him uncomfortable but also may interfere with the normal development of temperature-regulating mechanisms.)

The immunity mechanisms which he has been receiving from the mother's bloodstream are no longer available to him, so he is very susceptible to infections, especially of the gastrointestinal tract, respiratory system, and skin. Overprotecting him in this regard, however, may have the paradoxical result of retarding the necessary formation of his own immunities and making him even more vulnerable to infection.

The neonate spends about twenty hours a day sleeping. During the first few weeks, in fact, waking and sleeping are really only a matter of degree—he is rarely fully awake except when hungry, startled, or otherwise distressed. When "awake," he is liable to stare fixedly and blankly at a face or spot of light that happens to fall within his field of vision. Asleep or awake, he is subject to fits and starts and tremors reflecting the spread of stimulation in his still immature nervous system. The sleeping neonate shows the same brain wave pattern and the rapid eye movements (REM) that accompany dreaming in adults—in fact, the neonate has a higher proportion of REM in his sleep than is characteristic of adult sleep.

For the most part, the neonate is blankly unemotional, although he may smile when contented, whether he is awake or asleep. There is no indication that the neonate feels affection toward anybody or anything, although such affection develops quickly in the first few months.

The neonate is also relatively insensitive to pain, but his sensitivity picks up rapidly in the first few days. Circumcision can be performed a few days after birth with no anesthetic and with apparently very little discomfort. However, internal pain (for example, from hunger cramps or colic) seems to distress him.

Individual differences are important from the very moment of birth. Some neonates, when they are held, are passive and seem disjointed; others are lively, active, and squirming. Neonates also are different in muscle tonus, the forcefulness or sluggishness with which they act and move (whether waving their arms and legs or crying), the vigor with which they root and suck, their sensitivity and responsiveness to light or noise, their irritability, and their alertness.

Of course, they will differ profoundly in such measurable anatomical and physiological modalities as size and shape of body organs, blood chemistry, and hormonal balance.

The Infant

The neonatal period ends with the first month of life after birth; with the
second month, the baby begins *infancy*, which ends when he is walking and
beginning to talk. In infancy, the child begins to look like a person. He gains
weight and develops the natural layer of fat that fills out his scrawniness; the
head and nose fill out to a normal shape; the skin loses its redness. He now has
a large forehead, large eyes, small nose, small chin, and plump cheeks. His
hands and feet are chubby and his abdomen is round.

During the 15 months or so of infancy, the child changes from being completely helpless — unable even to roll over or to brush a piece of tissue off his
face — to being a highly active, self-directed, willful pedestrian. His social behavior changes from the blank stare of the neonate to an active interchange of
smiling, laughing, making communicative sounds, demanding company, and
participating in games. By the time he is a year old, he can understand much of
the language of his culture, both verbal and non-verbal, and can communicate
his own feelings and needs to others in the same way. Thus, after the neonatal
period, when the child has only a rudimentary awareness of the world around
him, the infant develops to quite an elaborate awareness and interaction with his
surroundings. It is during this period that one of the most important elements
of his socialization is established: his *sense of trust*, upon which his *sense of autonomy* is built.

During the second month, the infant is more awake than he was as a neonate
and shows more sustained response to an increasing variety of sights and
sounds — vacuum cleaners, television programs, and ringing telephones. He
can usually raise his head slightly to look at something; and, although he still
cannot really change position, he can usually arch his back. Also, during the
second month, the infant's crying will stop at the sight of his approaching
mother, and most infants respond with a smile to a human face. At this age, the
infant still takes two or more night feedings.

Early in the third month, the baby is able to reach out and bat at dangling
objects, but he is not yet able to open his fingers to grasp them. (An institutionalized baby may not reach out to grasp until almost five months of age.)·
Accommodation of the lens of the eye is essentially complete by age three
months, and the eyes converge on an object as it approaches his nose. The infant is quite social at three months, gurgling and cooing in response to adult
overtures and even to music. He recognizes members of the family and smiles
and wriggles and gurgles at them, and he meets strangers with a solemn, reserved, watchful stare. He is now usually sleeping through the night.

The baby first laughs when he is about four months old. He can now be
propped in a sitting position for short periods and can half recline indefinitely
in a baby carrier. He begins to eat semi-solid, strained foods, although it will

be months before he eats without spluttering, choking, coughing, and spitting. He becomes able to grasp things that he first notices visually (until now he could just bat at them); but he still can't release anything, and if he really wants to get rid of something he has grasped, he will rub it against his body until it is loosed from his grip.

By age five months, he will study his fingers, pick up something to examine or taste, show preference when given different colored patches, and remain in a sitting position for some time before his head begins to loll and his body to slump. And, by the time he is six months of age, he is not only able to grasp, but to manipulate and release something he is gripping.

Between the ages of six and nine months, the baby is usually able to roll completely over. He is now on our culture's three-meal-a-day and sleeping schedules (with occasional snacks and naps). During this stage, the baby begins to hold out his arms to be picked up, and becomes highly responsive to the moods of those around him. His vocalization becomes more differentiated, with consonants emerging to break up the vowel sounds and babbling replacing the gurgling and cooing.

His first two teeth appear by about the seventh month (though some babies are *born* with teeth). He can usually sit up without support and can amuse himself with toys and noises and the movement of objects. The baby begins an early manifestation of the child's fascination with repetition, with imitation, with discovery, and with experimentation. Social games and learning evolve out of the baby's imitating what the parents do and the parents' imitating the baby.

Usually by about seven months, the baby begins creeping for short distances, and by eight months he can crawl. The baby also begins to feed himself with a spoon at about this age—developing the essential feedback for coordinating the muscle control necessary for contacting an object, his mouth, that he cannot see.

By about eleven months, he can creep or crawl up and down stairs and has learned to detour around obstacles in order to get something he wants. (In contrast, a chicken separated from food by a short length of wire fence may starve to death without even discovering that she has only to walk around the fence in order to get the food.) He becomes much less passive during this period and no longer lies quietly while being dressed. On the other hand, he learns to cooperate, holding out his hand for a sleeve or raising his head and shoulders to allow the shirt to pass behind his back. He recognizes himself in the mirror, plays pat-a-cake, works simple cupboard latches, turns electric lights off and on, regulates the volume on a television set, learns to distinguish between pictures of objects in books.

The Young Child

By the first birthday, most children are crawling and many are taking their first steps. They can also sit up, pull themselves up, and stand alone, and they can imitate sounds and words, follow simple instructions, and point out objects they are asked to identify. By the age of two years, they are walking, running, climbing stairs, opening doors, eating with a spoon, taking off their shoes and socks, and using a working vocabulary of about 25 words. By three years, they can play for short periods without supervision, coloring with crayons, dressing dolls, building with blocks. They can eat with a fork and get a glass of water from the kitchen faucet. Being toilet trained, they have only occasional daytime accidents.

Most four-year-olds can wash their hands and button their clothes. They show some sense of rhythm in running, skipping, and marching and are able to participate in simple group activities, such as kindergarten games. They can perform short errands and pick up after themselves if they are asked to. At five years of age, most children can dress themselves completely except for tying and lacing, can wash both face and hands, and are perfectly toilet trained. They can play in the immediate neighborhood untended and can maintain unsupervised group games with their peers and with older children. They also can draw recognizable objects: a house, a man, a landscape.

At five years, children have formulated a basic frame of reference. From their experiences, they build and act on assumptions of fact, assumptions of probability, and assumptions of value; and their subsequent experiences will be perceived largely in terms of these early expectations and assumptions.

From the ages six to twelve, children are extremely busy acquiring information and mastery skills. In the highly structured organization of the classroom, they learn to read, to write, and to resolve arithmetical problems. They absorb a very wide range of knowledge of many kinds: geographical, historical, grammatical, and so on. They also develop physical skills such as roller skating, bicycle riding, throwing and catching a ball, jumping rope. And they acquire the skills of social behavior — the skills of group participation and of interpersonal relating — that are as important to functioning in our mass society as harness mending and wool spinning were in the past. With more and more experience, they achieve an increasingly realistic — that is, accurate — frame of reference in regard both to their natures and to the nature of their environment. They develop competency in dealing with their culture, in acquiring the physical, intellectual, and social skills common to it. And finally, they learn, through meeting specific problems, what kinds of problems they are likely to confront in the future, and how they should prepare for and resolve such problems (see Coleman, 1969).

As the child grows older his behavior becomes successively more differentiated. The trend is from homogeneity, from undifferentiated and global capacities and activities to ever more finely differentiated and specialized ones, and from few-general to many-specific (Berelson and Steiner, 1964, p. 53).

In other words, the child learns at various points in the complex, multilevel processes of maturation and socialization to differentiate between his mother and father, to select a favorite toy and neglect the others, to like certain foods and certain people, and to develop certain skills. When he reaches adulthood, he will have refined these early differentiations of perception and behavior to an incredible degree: Perhaps he may be able to tell a genuine Van Gogh from a skillful copy, or distinguish easily the voices of two sopranos singing the same aria, or tune an automobile engine, or solve a problem in quantum physics. This differential development takes place as part of the essential socialization process for which the family in the early and most important stages is chiefly responsible.

The Socialization of a Child

We have been talking about the early developmental sequence of the child almost as though he were growing up in a vacuum, essentially unrelated to the world around him. Nothing, of course, could be further from the truth. From the first week of his life, the child exists in relation to his family with a closeness of interaction that is almost as symbiotic as was his relation to his mother while he was still in the uterus. Everything that he does affects his family, and everything his family does affects him. Thus, just as the physical development of the child depends upon the family's provision of adequate physical and material care, the social development of the child depends upon the family's provision of adequate socialization—the learning of competency and self-esteem in relational and mastery skills.

The socialization process can be divided into three key need provisions: (1) the provision of ample emotional security; (2) the provision of the information and opportunities necessary for the development of appropriate mastery skills; and (3) the provision of discipline, without which mastery-skill development would be quite limited. If parents provide these three necessities for child development, they maximize the probability that their child will become cheerful, self-respecting, self-assured, competent, creative, and productive—making the fullest use of his own unique potential as a human being (and, incidentally, being a joy in the family).

Emotional Security

Equally important with such physical needs as nourishment, sleep, and warmth are the child's innate psychological needs for response, for contact, for cuddling, for play, and for all the other various ways that affection and acceptance, understanding and respect are expressed. If these needs are met, his frame of reference and his self-image will include a sense of the world and most things in it as good, stable, pleasant, and—ultimately—manageable. Conversely, if these basic needs are *not* met, he will sense the world as unstable, unpleasant, and threatening, and himself as hopelessly inadequate in coping with environmental exigencies and demands.

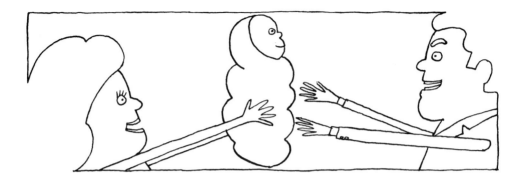

An attitude of basic trust permits the development of variegated emotional responding across a full range from pleasant to unpleasant, whereas serious basic mistrust keeps emotional response in the limited range from distress to dull apathy. And out of variegated emotional functioning we would expect the growth of openness to experience and of the ability to master reality (Stone and Church, 1968, pp. 108–109).

In addition, the baby whose needs are met becomes a *satisfying* baby, who calls forth an ever-growing abundance of love and attention; whereas the baby whose needs are not met becomes petulant, irritable, demanding, and hard to love.

The evidence for the importance of emotional support in successful socialization and in adequate personality development comes from several different kinds of sources and is now quite formidable.[2] The most obvious source is the studies that compare babies reared in institutions with babies reared within their families. All such studies agree that among the consequences of emotional deprivation are inconsolable distress, which in turn leads to perceptual retardation, blunted responsiveness, incommunicability, increased susceptibility to infection, impaired learning ability, ritualistic (and even bizarre) mannerisms, and a generalized apathy.[3]

Although these studies are all relatively recent, it is interesting to note that evidence was available as long ago as the thirteenth century, when a Prussian king instigated an experiment in which babies were deliberately subjected to institutional deprivations in order to determine what language children would develop if they grew up speaking to no one.

So he bade foster mothers and nurses to suckle the children, to bathe and wash them, but in no way to prattle with them, or to speak to them, for he wanted to learn whether they would speak the Hebrew language, which was the oldest, or Greek, or Latin, or Arabic, or perhaps the language of their parents, of whom they had been born. But he labored in vain because the children all died. For they could not live without the petting and joyful faces

[2] See Berelson and Steiner (1964), pp. 64–85, for a summary and a bibliography.
[3] See Cadden (1971), Pines (1971), Wyden (1971), Bowlby (1965), Ribble (1965), Provence and Lipton (1963), Ainsworth (1962), Stone (1954), Goldfarb (1945), and Spitz (1945 and 1951).

and loving words of their foster mothers. And so the songs are called "swaddling songs"
which a woman sings while she is rocking the cradle, to put a child to sleep, and without
them a child sleeps badly and has no rest (Salimbene, quoted in Ross and McLaughlin,
1949).

Berelson and Steiner (1964), in surveying the sum total of scientific findings
about the importance of providing emotional support and security for children,
agreed that prolonged separation from the mother and from a secure home environment seems to lead to serious intellectual and emotional retardation; that
the more isolated and deprived the child, the greater the deterioration; and that
people who have experienced such deprivation in childhood are as parents less
able than others to care for their own children properly.

The critical period for emotional-support provision seems to be from birth
to about five years of age; deprivation after this period does not seem to be so
damaging, especially if the early experience of parental care has been lavish.

The less the affection, satisfaction of dependence, or warmth the infant and child re-
ceives . . . (1) the less developed is his subsequent personality likely to be and the less
quickly he matures (in childhood) — i.e., the more he is apathetic, unresponsive, "vegeta-
tive," and incapable of independent action; and (2) the less strength of character and
sense of self he is likely to have, leading even to the development of a psychopathic per-
sonality that feels no responsibility to others . . .

In general, the unloved child tends to be an unloving adult, with a high degree of self-
hatred (i.e. unlovable) . . . Severity of socialization (i.e. highly rigid or highly critical
practices by parents) seems to make for generalized anxiety in later life . . .

The earlier and more severely the infant or child is forced to be independent, the
more concerned and even anxious he is about his independence in adult life (Berelson
and Steiner, 1964, pp. 75–79).

A second source for the importance of early emotional support comes from
longitudinal studies, or case histories of a single child. In all of the studies we cite,
the child was reared within his family, but by parents who were unconsciously
rejecting and who, though providing all material needs, failed to provide the
understanding, assurance, play, and loving contact that is apparently so essential
to optimal development.

For example, in *Dibs: In Search of Self* (1964), Virginia Axline recounts the
case history of a boy who was thought mentally deficient and who was so unsocialized that he was almost totally unmanageable in the expensive private
school where his professionally distinguished parents had placed him. In a
series of interviews with the mother, the therapist found that the mother was
harsh and rejecting of the child's emotional needs. During treatment, the therapist constantly sought to communicate to the boy an atmosphere of trust,
attention, confidence, and affectionate regard. As a result, the boy came to

regard himself more highly, and he emerged as actually being both extremely bright and unusually creative. In earlier studies, Dorothy Baruch (*One Little Boy*, 1952) describes a similar encounter, with very similar results, and Bruno Bettelheim ("Joey: A Mechanical Boy," 1959) describes the almost total withdrawal of a boy into machine-like behavior as a defense against the emotional deprivation that he had experienced as an unwanted baby who was totally ignored by his parents except in physical care, which they provided rigidly and mechanically. Countless other case histories have been documented, of course; these three are merely cited as representative.

The third source of evidence regarding emotional deprivation comes from animal experimentation in this field. Clearly there is a need to study the development of personality from infancy forward under experimentally controlled conditions; and since this may not be done with children, animals are used and the findings are extrapolated to human behavior. The most familiar of these studies is the trail-blazing work of Harry F. Harlow (1959, 1962) with the rhesus monkey—a course of experimentation which succeeded in demonstrating several far-reaching and significant relations between early tactile, companionate, and nurturant experiences and later adult personality manifestations in these animals. In the first phase of his study (1959) Harlow found that animals who were reared with two "mother" figures, one made of wire and one covered with a soft terry cloth, preferred the soft cloth figure, whether they were fed by it or by the wire "mother." This finding contradicts the theory that the need for tactile comfort is learned (as a result of receiving it together with food, protection, and other material support) and suggests that it is *innate*—a basic rather than a conditioned need.

Harlow also found that the baby monkeys would seek out the cloth "mother" and derive comfort and security from it in times of stress, whether they had been fed by her or by the wire mother. He put into a monkey's cage an unfamiliar and frightening object, such as a mechanical toy bear which would move forward, beating a drum. The terrified baby monkey would run screaming to the cloth "mother." After a few moments of clinging and rubbing the cloth, he would be calm and relaxed and would examine the toy bear.

In the absence of the cloth "mother," the terror and anxiety would persist, and the baby monkey would continue to scream in distress. The presence of the wire "mother" made no difference in this behavior, even though the baby monkey had been fed by it. The monkeys who from birth had known only the wire "mother" would run to the wall, clasp their heads, and rock convulsively. "Such activities clearly resemble the . . . behavior seen frequently among neglected children" (Harlow, 1959).

The second phase of Harlow's research (1962) had to do with the importance of peer contact. Harlow established that monkeys who were reared with no peer contact became severely psychologically disturbed; they sat in their cages and stared fixedly into space, occasionally chewing and tearing at their bodies until they bled. As adults, these monkeys never did engage in affectional or sexual behavior; and when the females were artificially impregnated, they rejected their offspring, failing to provide even minimal maternal care and affection.

The critical period of emotional deprivation was found to be the age of 6 months; beyond this time personality damage was both severe and irreversible. (This is the equivalent of 2 to 3 years in the human child.) Thus, Harlow concluded that normal personality development requires both (1) sufficient early bodily contact (warmth and cuddling) and (2) early companionate contact with peers. If both these experiences do *not* occur in infancy, the adult will be antisocial, asexual, aloof, and self-destructive. If we may extrapolate from monkey to man, the hypotheses which had been based on clinical observation of children and adults and were experimentally supported by the Harlow studies include the following:

1. Early nurture and companionate experiences are an innate need, and the lack of nurture or companionate experiences in infancy and early childhood will be reflected in an adult incapacity to relate normally and effectively in sociosexual situations.

2. The effects of early nurturant or companionate deprivation may be irreversible.

3. A critical period of time exists during which these irreversible effects of personality damage may take place.

4. In primates, "normal" heterosexual responses—whether reproductive, nurturant, or companionate—are not instinctive but rather are learned through affectional interaction in infancy and early childhood.

In short, Harlow was successful in demonstrating, once and for all, that maternal care is significantly related to adult personality in terms of sociosexual behavior, affectional behavior, and maternal behavior in the second generation.

Following Harlow's work, Denenberg (1963) reasoned that if tactile contact and support is indeed a basic need, it should persist throughout the mammalian world and be just as demonstrable in animals lower than the monkey. In an ingenious series of experiments with rats,[4] Denenberg succeeded in supporting Harlow's findings that early tactile deprivation is correlated with adult personality disturbance. He discovered further that (1) emotionally secure mothers will rear emotionally secure offspring; (2) emotionally disturbed infant rats, when given to an emotionally secure mother, will cause the mother to demonstrate emotional insecurity; (3) handling of the infants will affect their emotional development positively and decisively, whereas infants reared in isolation will be severely emotionally disturbed;[5] (4) a rich and complex en-

---

[4] The Denenberg study employed a brilliantly simple design. Denenberg separated his subjects into two groups: rats that were handled in infancy and rats that were not handled in infancy. The adult subjects were then individually placed in a large box with the floor marked off in 9-inch squares. A normal rat will explore its environment, and the extent of its activity can be quantified simply by counting the number of squares it enters in a given time. Thus, when the non-handled rats entered far fewer squares than did the handled group, Denenberg concluded that his experimental design successfully differentiated between the two groups. He then employed a second measurement, the number of boluses the rats defecated during the period in the box. The non-handled rats defecated a significantly higher number than did the handled rats. Therefore, because emotional disturbance in rats correlates with their exploratory behavior and their defecation pattern, Denenberg was able to conclude that the non-handled rats were emotionally disturbed.

[5] Thompson (1961) was among the first to show that daily handling of infant rats by the experimenter affected their personality structure as adults.

vironment has a therapeutic effect on the emotionally disturbed offspring;[6] and (5) the emotionally disturbed offspring will increase their insecure behavior if they are placed in the same environment with emotionally secure infants.

The Concept of "Spoiling"

There is a difference, of course, between providing *appropriate* nurture and *over*protecting; overprotection will lead to inadequate personality development just as surely as will emotional deprivation. However, the withholding of affection, either for punishment or as a "toughening" process in socialization, makes no more sense than the withholding of food. But because there is a strong historical tradition in our society (but rarely in others) that men are born with original sin which can be tempered only by discipline and control,[7] many parents still feel, despite the current child-rearing literature, that too much affection will "ruin" or "spoil" a child. With the best will in the world, they will deprive their baby of appropriate affectionate attention simply because they do not want to harm him. Inasmuch as the concept of spoiling has received a good deal of emphasis in older child-training theories — "If the crying baby is picked up he will be conditioned to expect his own way, and will be petulant, sulky, and spoiled if he does not get it" — it is worthwhile to examine the concept in some detail.

---

[6] A classic study by Forgays and Forgays (1952) preceded Denenberg in showing that rats brought up in an enriched environment (other young rats, mazes, ramps, exercise wheel, swings) are brighter than rats reared in a deprived environment. It also has been shown that the frequency of changing the cage-floor shavings can affect development (Hatch *et al.*, 1963).

[7] Because "the approved adult was industrious, pious, and, above all, self-denying . . . it seemed to follow that the child-rearing regimen should be one of sternness, work, and denial of the flesh" (Winch, 1964, pp. 457–459). The following admonition from colonial times is typical of our child-training heritage:

Never sit down at the table till asked, and after the blessing. Ask for nothing; tarry till it be offered thee. Speak not. . . . Sing not, hum not, wriggle not. Spit nowhere in the room but in the corner . . . When any speak to thee, stand up. Say not I have heard it before. Never endeavor to help him out if he feel it not right. Snigger not; never question the truth of it (quoted in Calhoun, 1945).

Even as recently as 1928, John B. Watson, one of the most distinguished psychologists of the period, provided the following advice for parents:

There is a sensible way of treating children. Treat them as though they were young adults. Dress them and bathe them with care and circumspection. Let your behavior always be objective and kindly firm. Never hug and kiss them, never let them sit in your lap. If you must, kiss them once on the forehead when they say good night. Shake hands with them in the morning. Give them a pat on the head if they have made an extraordinarily good job of a difficult task. Try it out. In a week's time you will find how easy it is to be perfectly objective with your child and at the same time kindly. You will be utterly ashamed of the mawkish, sentimental way you have been handling it. . . . In conclusion won't you then remember when you are tempted to pet your child that mother love is a dangerous instrument? An instrument which may inflict a never healing wound, a wound which may make infancy unhappy, adolescence a nightmare; an instrument which may wreck your adult son or daughter's vocational future and their chances for marital happiness (Watson, 1928, p. 87).

Watson saw as the ideal result of his child-rearing philosophy " . . . a child as free as possible of sensitivities to people and one who, almost from birth, is relatively independent of the family situation" (p. 186).

It is certainly true that there is such a thing as a *spoiled* child—that is, a child who expects to get his own way upon demand; who, when he does not get his way, sulks, pouts, and has temper tantrums. It is also true that the spoiled child will often develop into an adult who has unrealistic expectations of his environment and therefore is unprepared for coping with society and for relating to other people. However, the crucial question is how the syndrome of spoiling occurs; and current psychology, based on very solid evidence, suggests that it occurs not as a result of lavish affection and a relatively permissive and creative family environment, but rather from (1) a lack of emotional support and affection and (2) a family environment that is authoritarian or that fails to be demonstrative in its affectional interaction. An environment of emotional deprivation results in a child who lacks self-assurance, who perceives himself as inadequate in dealing with the world; and such a child is likely to manifest all the behavior patterns (in childhood and as an adult) that we recognize as "spoiled." Similarly, these patterns, and the same lack of self-assurance, will develop in children who are overprotected or smothered with inappropriate attention. A child who is not given the independence that he needs and who is sheltered from experience will, of course, lack a sense of adequacy and of self, just as will the child who is denied sufficient emotional support and affection.

It is important that the parents distinguish between giving security to the children and dominating them. Dominating parents undermine their child's self confidence and thus destroy his sense of security. They prevent his developing the resourcefulness and self-sufficiency necessary for the progressive steps toward maturity (Cavan, 1963, p. 457).

Thus, the rearing of a well-adjusted, happy, and competent child requires parents (1) to provide the child with the opportunity to develop appropriate mastery skills, (2) to give the child as much freedom as possible consistent with discipline, and (3) to find a balance between acceptant and loving regard, on the one hand, and overprotective, inappropriate indulgence, on the other. The finding of this middle ground of appropriate affection and attention is not so difficult as it may sound; for a child will not ask for more emotional support and affection than he, for the moment, requires. When an infant cries, he is seeking comfort or attention. When a baby lifts his arms, he is demonstrating a need for emotional support and cuddling. When a child follows his parent about or asks endless questions or cries over some frustration, he is usually seeking affection and assurance of his worth. And when a child struggles to get free or refuses to relate or wants to go out to play, he has had all the parental nurture that he needs and wants. When he wants more, he will return for it. In short, if a parent is sensitive to his child's needs, the child will be getting a proper balance of love and freedom.

This is not to say that a child should be able to do or have exactly what he wants at all times; but parental discipline should be consistent, reasonable, and accompanied by an affectionate explanation, if the child is old enough to understand, or a demonstration of affection, if he is not. Whenever possible, an attractive alternate to the unwanted behavior should be made available to him (If he *can't* write on the wall, he *may* write in a coloring book). Also, when the child is not old enough for explanation, the things he shouldn't have should be put out of his way, so that the occasion for a harsh confrontation simply never arises.

A child should never be allowed to feel that parental discipline is arbitrary, ill-considered, or—most important of all—*rejecting* of him as an individual. In other words: don't make love dependent upon approval for his actions. Criticize or correct the *action*, not the child. Say, in effect, "I love you, but that was a naughty thing to do." Do not say, "You are a naughty child; I do not love you when you do that."

Parents are individuals and have different ways of expressing their affection. Some parents are lavish with physical demonstrations of their feelings; others are not, but still manage to convey them. Some parents are soft and tender, some are bluff and hearty, some are sober, some ironic. Furthermore, nobody can love his baby equally at all times and in all circumstances. Babies are sometimes cranky and sometimes exasperating. They can destroy the parents' sleep or favorite treasure. What is important in terms of the baby's sense of trust is the reliability of his parents' love, the clarity with which it shows through transitory vicissitudes, through the inevitable strains and anxieties (Stone and Church, 1968, pp. 108–109).

Experience has shown that denying a child love because of his actions or making love conditional upon his good behavior is a very poor way to effect discipline. Instead of encouraging wanted behavior, the results are likely to be the opposite: defiance, perseveration of the "bad" behavior, lowering of the child's self-esteem and self-image, and, perhaps worst of all, a rift in the parent-child bond. These results inevitably lead to further scolding and condemnation, followed by further unwanted behavior, in a descending spiral of parental frustration and tension. Once this pattern is set up, it is very hard to reverse. It is much simpler to avoid it at the outset by following the few sound principles described above.

Thus, at the base of all socialization and child training there must be a foundation of love and respect—expressed as frequently and as intimately as is appropriate to the needs and circumstances of the child. A child whose needs for affection, attention, physical nurture, and creative and intellectual stimulation are adequately fulfilled will be a happy, good-natured, cooperative, and flexible child; and there will be few disciplinary demands with such a child. (For further discussion, see Discipline, in this chapter.) In short, fulfilling nurture needs will *not* cause spoiling; rather, the child whose nurture needs *are* fulfilled will be the child who is least likely to be spoiled and most likely to be sociosexually well adjusted and emotionally mature.

Children Learn What They Live

If a child lives with criticism,
he learns to condemn.
If a child lives with hostility,
he learns to fight.
If a child lives with fear,
he learns to be apprehensive.
If a child lives with pity,
he learns to feel sorry for himself.
If a child lives with jealousy,
he learns to feel guilty.
If a child lives with encouragement,
he learns to be confident.
If a child lives with tolerance,
he learns to be patient.
If a child lives with praise,
he learns to be appreciative.
If a child lives with acceptance,
he learns to love.
If a child lives with approval,
he learns to like himself.
If a child lives with recognition,
he learns it is good to have a goal.
If a child lives with fairness,
he learns what justice is.
If a child lives with honesty,
he learns what truth is.
If a child lives with security,
he learns to have faith in himself
and those about him.
If a child lives with friendliness, he
learns the world is a nice place
in which to live.

Mastery Skills

While emphasizing the significance of affectional need satisfaction in the socialization of children, we must not lose sight of the importance of providing the information, equipment, and opportunities necessary for the acquisition of *mastery skills,* which are the knowledge, intellectual and physical abilities, aptitudes, and attitudes necessary for coping successfully with the environment. As the child grows through infancy and into early and middle childhood, his early experience with manipulating objects in his environment (*environmental control*) will manifest itself either in increasing autonomy (independence and self-reliance) and the eager pursuit of further skills or in self-doubt, the perseverance of dependency needs, and the disinclination, or worse, inability, to acquire skills and competency. By age five, the competency and independency needs approach an importance equivalent to the affectional needs, and the failure of parents to provide for these maturational needs will be just as stultifying to the child's development as emotional deprivation.

The child who is prepared for nursery school by having an easy familiarity with everything he will be expected to manipulate there will get a "head start" that will affect his self-esteem and his accumulation of skills tremendously. Conversely, the child who is unfamiliar and ill-at-ease with the nursery school materials may be already one step behind most of his peers and will experience adjustment and learning difficulties that will hinder his progress and lead inevitably to anxiety, withdrawal, and poor performance.

Developmental readiness. In the learning of mastery skills, a happy and self-assured child is eager and tremendously capable, limited only by his innate capacities and stamina and by the precise period of *developmental readiness.* Developmental readiness, particularly, restricts the learning of skills, since an attempt to teach a skill before the child is ready—biologically (chronologically) or psychologically—will inevitably fail, meanwhile causing frustration and emotional difficulties. "When the time comes that the body is ripe for, culture is pressing for, and the individual is striving for some achievement, the teachable moment has arrived" (Duvall, 1967, p. 38). An example of the biological aspect of developmental readiness is toilet training. Before two or three years of

age, a child has no sphincter muscle control, and no amount of toilet training will prevent him from defecating in his diapers.

On the other hand, the teaching of a skill after the period of optimum developmental readiness may result in the learning of the skill, but the learning process will be much less economical and may also end in frustration and emotional difficulties. "If these tasks are *not* mastered at the appropriate stage of development, the individual may be at a serious disadvantage in making subsequent adjustment" (Coleman, 1969, p. 79).

Success experiences. Because a person's readiness to learn a new skill usually depends upon past learning experiences, it is important in the socialization of children that they are provided opportunities for experiences that they can *successfully* undergo at their particular period of biological and psychological development. In other words, it is important that as developmental readiness occurs, the parents set things up so that their child is likely to have a *success experience* (rather than a failure experience). The reason that the success experience is important in the socialization process is that it enhances the self-image and provides a picture of the world as controllable. Failure depresses the self-image and provides a picture of the world as unmanageable.

The importance of success experiences is so obvious that it should hardly be necessary to labor the point, but such experiences are so significant in determining the future *set* (or readiness to respond) within a child's frame of reference that they cannot be overemphasized. As a child becomes ready to develop a skill or acquire information, if his experience with the activity is successful he will be conditioned to persist; if it is not successful he may discontinue his attempts—depending upon the strength of motivation, of course, and upon the degree of his frustration (his feelings of inadequacy and threat associated with the failure). Of course, if the parent makes the activity *too* easy it will not provide enough challenge and may even be boring to the child. In short, if the parent provides the child with an activity which is just within his ability—neither so difficult that the child fails nor so easy that he becomes bored—the situation is conducive to maximal acquisition of mastery skills. For example, suppose the child is shown (at the appropriate stage in his motor development) the old puzzle of two interlocking nails which are to be separated. At first, the parent joins the child in examining the puzzle and in determining the challenge. The parent then lets the child play independently with the puzzle for a short time; and finally, while the child is still intrigued and has not yet given up (since to do so would make the experience one of failure), the parent demonstrates how to separate the two nails. Thus, the child's interest is sustained, and he is assured of a success experience when he finally solves the puzzle by himself. This type of success experience generalizes into ever more finely differentiated activities. Initial perceptions (for example, the experience with the puzzle) form the basis upon which the child's frame of reference toward his competence with the environment is established; subsequent perceptions (later experiences) merely serve to modify or elaborate the initial structure of his frame of reference. Thus, with significant and repeated success experiences—the puzzle, then a jigsaw, then a model airplane and a radio[8]—the core of the child's frame of reference will include a positive self-perception: an image of himself as someone capable

---

[8] Success experience is also important in the learning of roles and appropriate sociosexual behavior. If, for example, a child is accustomed to being treated as a significant entity in the family—if someone comes when the child calls him or if the child's opinion is acted on—he will experience success in his interpersonal relations and he will be open to the learning of more complex roles and behavior patterns.

of and accustomed to succeeding, and a concept of difficulties and problems as usually solvable and of the resolution of these problems as pleasureable.

The tension caused by the need to resolve a problem is usually a good thing for the child, providing that it does not continue too long, and that his frame of reference includes expectation of success. On the other hand, if the tension continues too long, or if he has an expectation of failure (based upon prior failure experiences), the resultant anxiety will often be too high; and he may direct his efforts toward alleviating this anxiety rather than toward trying to succeed in the activity. (See *Defense-oriented Behavior*, in Chapter Seven.)

Obviously not all of the child's experiences can be successful, but as a general rule, if the initial set is one of success, subsequent occasional failures will only act as stimuli to effort. Conversely, it is doubtful whether any number of subsequent success experiences can produce a habitual expectation of success if the initial set was one of failure.

The learning of mastery skills and the experience of emotional security are provided almost as concomitants to the success experiences of a child. Thus the child's learning to tie his shoes, go down stairs, or spell "cat" will be success experiences as well as the achievement of a skill. (Success experiences may also occur, of course, as a result of applying an already learned skill.) Moreover, when the success experience takes place within the family context, it is accompanied by the child's perception of his family as rendering him acceptance and respect, love and affection.

Implements of learning. In order to acquire mastery skills, children must, of course, have available the tools and information necessary for challenging their abilities and stimulating their interest in learning. Ideally, these tools and this information should be provided by parents when the child is developmentally ready—providing them too soon can be discouraging for the child and providing them too late is at best uneconomical.

To an infant, the appropriate implements of learning would be such objects as a rattle (for manipulative skills) and a rag doll (for relational skills). The small child can play with building blocks, a pull-toy, coloring books, and dolls, and with toys (a large ball, a tea set, miniature tools) that provide for the participation of parents or siblings. As he grows older he should be provided with dull, round-nosed scissors, cut-outs, colored paper, paste, smaller balls, puzzles, and the thousand and one items of play which reflect our cultural preoccupations. Picture books will lead to reading; building sets, balls and bats, and tricycles will lead to manipulative skills and interests, to neuromotor coordination and to a knowledge of spatial relationships. And all of these skills will lead to a self-image of adequacy in control of the environment and effectiveness in relating to others.

Similarly, the child who is stimulated to inquiry and who has his questions answered as candidly and thoroughly as he is developmentally prepared to cope with, not only acquires information but will be self-assured intellectually. Children want to learn—they are as eager to acquire information as they are to acquire abilities. All the parent need do is provide the raw material and the intellectual stimulus.

Discipline

All psychologists would agree that *discipline*, which is the setting of limits and the inducing of wanted behavior that will be self-perpetuating, is invariably good. Children need discipline, want discipline, and would be insecure and inadequate without discipline. Discipline is essential for a productive life—no less for children than for adults; for the undisciplined person is not only unsocialized but unfulfilled.

Briefly, there are two ways to accomplish socializing discipline—or, in other words, to control and guide the behavior of offspring. One way is *punishment*. (Punishment is not synonymous with, and should not be confused with, discipline;[9] punishment is merely one way—not particularly successful—of accomplishing discipline.) The other way of accomplishing discipline—*reward*, or *positive reinforcement*—is more conducive to discipline than negative reinforcement, since it tends to perpetuate wanted behavior more dependably, more effectively, and more economically. Wanted behavior is rewarded, and thus positively reinforced, by approval. The approval in most cases may be tacit, since most approved behavior has its own reward—the solid satisfaction of convergent feedback. Punishment, besides being less predictable and less effective, also may have the unwanted and unfortunate **side effects of** (1) **causing resentment and rebellion and therefore of** perpetuating the very behavior it expects to change; (2) causing possible personality damage because it involves self-devaluation for the person being punished; and (3) causing a breach in the essential bond of closeness between parent and child.

Under certain circumstances, punishment may result in a self-perpetuating learning or modification of behavior, but these circumstances must include all of the following four conditions:

1. There must be *no significant emotional involvement* with the behavior to be learned or with the punishment, so that resentment will not arise to reinforce the very behavior being punished.

2. The punishment must be *informative*, so that the person is able to relate the punishment to his behavior.

3. There must be *no strong motivation* for the behavior. (If motivation is strong and persistent enough, no amount or severity of punishment will change the behavior—as witness the Christian martyrs, for example.)

---

[9] Discipline and punishment were equated in most Western societies until late in the nineteenth century. Corporal punishment was maintained in the U. S. Navy, for example, under the impression that men who were not flogged for disobedience would be unruly and unmanageable, especially under enemy fire. The few officers and administrators who objected to flogging were ridiculed as "bleeding hearts." Flogging is no longer permitted in the navy, nor is any form of corporal punishment, and discipline has, of course, not suffered as a result of this more enlightened and logical view.

4. There must be a *clearly alternative course of action*, so that the person is able to behave in another way and therefore avoid the punishment.[10]
If all four of these factors are *not* present, the punishment may actually reinforce or perpetuate the unwanted behavior (instead of stopping or modifying it).

Insofar as the discipline and socialization of children is concerned, the utilization of punishment is a very tricky procedure and rarely will satisfy the above four conditions. For example, the very act of punishing, or inflicting pain or suffering, almost always involves significant emotional response, unless the punishment is very mild and non-threatening. Also, it is important to maintain the close bond of affection between parent and child and "punishment in any form tends to weaken this bond . . . There should be no violation of the intimacy and trust which exists between the child and the parent" (Landis, 1970, p. 636).

In socialization, positive reinforcement is much more efficient, much more predictable in its effects, and involves far fewer variables. Even when there is "no significant emotional involvement" and "no strong motivation," so that

punishment could be effective, a positive reinforcement would probably work just as well and be much better for the well-being of the child and of the familial relation. For the side effects of positive reinforcement are beneficial to the self-image of the child and to the affectional bonds of parent-child, whereas the side effects of punishment are almost invariably negative.[11]

---

[10] An illustration of a system that utilizes punishment very effectively is the tagging of cars for illegal parking. There is no significant emotional involvement; the tag is informative; and there is a clear alternate course of action available. Moreover, if there is no strong motivation, the negative reinforcement of the tag (the threat of the fine) will cause the motorist not to park illegally. However, if there *is* strong motivation, he will park illegally, despite the possibility of getting a ticket.

[11] Our society is one of the few that characteristically utilizes punishment in disciplining its children. Whiting and Child (1953) rated our society as far more severe in child-training procedures than the average. For many years, it was assumed in sociological circles that discipline in the middle-class family is relatively rigorous, whereas in the lower-class family, discipline was relatively permissive. McKinley (1964) discovered that the opposite is true: the lower-class father, beset by economic pressures and crowded living facilities, is generally harsh and rejecting, while the middle-class father is both less severe and more creative and affectionate in his discipline of offspring. Apparently the more severe child training practices in the lower class reflect the frustration (or "lack of gratification experiences") which the family experiences in everyday life. At any rate, middle-class children tend to be well disciplined but seldom punished (corporal punishment is very rare), while lower-class children tend to be poorly disciplined and frequently punished (corporal punishment is common).

The unhappy effects of punishment have run like a dismal thread through our findings. Mothers who punished toilet accidents severely ended up with bed-wetting children. Mothers who punished dependency to get rid of it had more dependent children than mothers who did not punish. Mothers who punished aggressive behavior severely had more aggressive children than mothers who punished lightly . . . Harsh physical punishment was associated with high childhood aggressiveness and with the development of feeding problems (Sears et al., 1967, p. 484).

Just where should the limits between permissiveness and discipline be set? In the first place, in most situations it is usually not necessary for there to be a conflict between discipline and permissiveness. The limits of permissiveness with children should be set at behavior that is dangerous or that infringes upon the rights of others. Such obvious potential dangers as matches, firearms, or knives should not be available to a child until he is old enough to handle them competently and to understand their potential danger. Similarly, in the second category of infringement upon the rights of others, certain common sense limits seem obvious. Destruction or defacement of property, deliberate rudeness, or overt physical attack will destroy the fabric of social interaction and prevent any cooperative ventures from occurring. Inasmuch as most satisfactions come from just such cooperative ventures, it will be the natural inclination of the child to learn to interact with others without violating *their* rights. Specifically, this means that he learns to say "hello," "please," "excuse me," and "thank you"; that he learns not to write on the wall (but to write on paper), not to cut the curtains (but to cut out patterns), and not to kick the baby (but to kick a ball). He will learn these things (or become socialized) most effectively through constant repetition, or *overlearning*, just as he learns the language. The positive reinforcements of warm acceptance and approval (as well as identifying with and copying his parents' behavior) are the most effective socializing instruments in teaching social roles. *Disapproval* (not punishment) is an effective negative reinforcement for the inevitable lapses.

When the behavioral limits set by parents are realistic and consistently enforced, the child will usually accept them—although he will occasionally test the boundaries. The limits should be as few as possible, and the child should be permitted as much freedom as is practical for exploration outside of these limits. Once a child eats a piece of soap or touches a hot stove, he is not likely to repeat his experience.

The more freedom the child has, the greater will be his potential for optimum development as a competent, creative, and emotionally mature person. "Since community organizations, handling children in large groups, often tend to enforce uniformity, it is all the more important for parents to permit as much freedom as possible" (Cavan, 1969, p. 458).

When the importance of freedom and permissiveness is emphasized in the classroom, someone inevitably asks "What are you supposed to do? Let him run hog wild?" The answer, of course, is no. The point at which the child may be considered to be infringing upon the freedom of others must be decided upon by each parent, of course, and will even vary with the same parent from time to time. The father who usually permits his small son to play "choo-choo" on the living room floor may find himself completely unable to cope with the noise if he is tired and distraught from a hard day at the office. Thus, each situation must be dealt with as it arises. A good rule of thumb is to ask oneself whether the limit being set is really necessary. If it seems so at the moment, set the limit; but be sure the child is able to divert himself with another activity equally attractive and that he does not feel rejected or resentful because of the diversion. Children will understand and accept occasional unreasonableness in their parents and not be harmed by it if they feel generally wanted, accepted, and respected; if they have enough acceptable activities which they *may* perform; and if they do not feel that the limits imposed upon them are unrealistic or unreasonable.

In the farm home of yesteryear, children were taught never to play with matches and were severely punished if ever caught with them. The usual consequence was that when parents were out . . . the child set the lace curtains on fire . . .

In the democratic family, children are as fascinated by matches as children ever were. Parents let them start the fire when a picnic fire is being lighted or when kindling in the fireplace is ready to be ignited. They light the candles on the birthday cake and the Christmas altar. Not having been taught never to play with matches, and having had experience in the correct use of matches, child-started family fires no longer occur with regularity (Landis, 1970, p. 648).

To sum up: (1) A child should be well disciplined within the limits set by danger to himself and the equivalent right of *other* people to enjoy freedom. (2) These limits should be realistic, however; and *they should be as few as possible*. Within these limits, he should be allowed as much complete freedom as possible. (3) The limits should be extended as quickly as possible—that is, the child should be allowed increased freedom of movement and access to possibly dangerous objects as soon as his developmental level is appropriate.

Summary

The optimum development of a person can take place only when, in the earliest years of childhood, he is provided with abundant physical care, love, and emotional support and he is socialized (taught the roles and attitudes appropriate to adequate interaction in his society). Love and emotional support must be operationally demonstrated with tactile support as well as understanding, respect, and acceptance. Socialization—which has as its ideal the development of a person who is able to make the fullest use of his own unique potential—is best accomplished, not by punitive methods but by positive guidance, encouragement, stimulation, and example by the parents and by the parental provision of success experiences for the child in his attempts to acquire the mastery skills necessary for successful adjustment in society. If parents are not conscious of the limits on the socialization process imposed by the child's biological and psychological developmental readiness, and if they fail to provide frequent and not unduly stressful opportunities for success experiences, a child will almost inevitably lack self-assurance and will suffer from fear and frustration.

This lack of self-assurance will also be manifested in a child who is spoiled by receiving insufficient affection and emotional support or by receiving more attention and protection than he wants or needs (the child must have some independence if he is to develop into a self-assured and self-reliant adult).

Thus, the socialization of children must rest upon a foundation of love and emotional support, which provides the child with a sense of himself as a competent and significant person. When the child has this self-assurance, and when he is provided with discipline (reasonable and consistent limitations), positive reinforcement (rather than the negative reinforcement of punishment), and a permissive and creative environment, he will develop into a competent, loving, emotionally mature, and resourceful person.

Questions

1 When is the neonatal period? What changes occur during this time?

2 Of what significance is the fact that the neonate's sweat glands don't begin working until he is about one month old?

3 Discuss some of the individual differences of neonates (such as activity, muscle tonus, etc.).

4 When does infancy begin? When does it end? Describe the changes in appearance when the neonate enters infancy.

5 Discuss the social behavior of the one-year-old infant. What two important elements of socialization are established during this first year?

6 At what age will an infant
(a) pick up something to examine or taste?
(b) roll completely over?
(c) get visible teeth?
(d) begin creeping for short distances?
(e) begin to feed himself with a spoon?

(f) creep or crawl up and down stairs?

(g) recognize himself in the mirror?

(h) learn to distinguish among pictures of objects in a book?

7   Discuss the mastery skills acquired by children from the ages of six to twelve.

8   What does the social development of the child depend upon? Discuss the three key need provisions into which this process can be divided.

9   How will the baby perceive the world if his basic needs are not met?

10   What is the most critical period for emotional-support provision?

11   What is the evidence that emotional deprivation in infancy causes irreparable damage?

12   What finding suggests that the need for tactile comfort is *innate* not learned?

13   Harlow concluded that normal personality development requires certain childhood experiences. What are they? How will the adult behave if these requirements were not met in his childhood?

14   Denenberg's experiments supported Harlow's finding that early tactile deprivation is correlated with adult disturbance. What else did Denenberg discover?

15   Discuss the difference between providing appropriate nurture and overprotecting.

16   Discuss how the syndrome of spoiling occurs.

17   Why is rearing a well-adjusted, happy, and competent child not so difficult as it may seem?

18   What are the most important aspects of parental discipline?

19   What is the basis of all socialization and child training?

20   What is meant by the term *mastery skills*? How will a child get a head start in nursery school?

21   Discuss the concept of developmental readiness.

22   Why are success experiences so important in a child's socialization?

23   What is discipline? Why is it essential? How is it accomplished?

24   What are some of the unfortunate side effects of negative reinforcement?

25   Punishment will bring about behavior change only if four conditions are present. What are they?

26   Why is the use of punishment a tricky procedure in the discipline and socialization of children? Would a positive reinforcement work just as well?

References and Selected Readings

Ainsworth, M. D. The Effects of Maternal Deprivation. *Public Health Papers, No. 14.* Geneva: World Health Organization, 1962.

Altman, S. A. Primate Behavior in Review. *Science,* 1965, Vol. 150, pp. 1440–1442.

Anthony, E. James, and Cyrille Koupernik, eds. *Child in His Family.* New York: Wiley, 1970.

_____, and Therese Benedek, eds. *Parenthood: Its Psychology and*

Psychopathology. Boston: Little, Brown, 1970.

Axline, Virginia. *Dibs: In Search of Self.* Boston: Houghton Mifflin, 1964.

Baruch, Dorothy. *One Little Boy.* New York: Julian Press, 1952.

Beach, F. A., and J. Jaynes. The Effects of Early Experience on the Behavior of Animals. *Psychological Bulletin,* 1951, Vol. 54, pp. 239–263.

Beadle, Muriel. *Child's Mind: How Children Learn During the Critical Years from Birth to Age Five.* New York: Doubleday, 1970.

Beck, Joan. *How to Raise a Brighter Child: The Case for Early Learning.* New York: Trident, 1967.

Berelson, Bernard, and Gary A. Steiner. *Human Behavior.* New York: Harcourt, 1964.

Bernard, Harold W. *Human Development in Western Culture,* 3rd ed. Boston: Allyn and Bacon, 1970.

Bettelheim, Bruno. Joey: A "Mechanical Boy." *Scientific American,* March 1959.

Birch, Herbert G., and Joan Dye Gussow. *Disadvantaged Children.* New York: Harcourt, 1970.

Bliss, E. L., ed. *Roots of Behavior.* Darien, Conn.: Hafner, 1969.

Bossard, James H., and Eleanor S. Boll. *Family Situations: An Introduction to the Study of Child Behavior.* Westport, Conn.: Greenwood, 1969.

Bowlby, John. *Attachment.* New York: Basic, 1969.

_____. *Child Care and the Growth of Love.* London: Pelican, 1965.

Cadden, Vivian. 'Yes,' to Love and Joyful Faces. In *Life,* December 17, 1971, Vol. 71, No. 25, pp. 93, 95.

Calhoun, A. W. *A Social History of the American Family.* New York: Barnes and Noble, 1945.

Calhoun, J. B. Population Density and Social Pathology. *Scientific American,* February 1962, pp. 139–148.

Cavan, Ruth Schonle. *The American Family,* 4th ed. New York: Crowell, 1969.

Child, Irvin L. Socialization. In Gardner Lindzey, ed., *Handbook of*

Social Psychology, 5 Vols. New York: Addison-Wesley, 1969.

Coleman, James S. *The Adolescent Society.* New York: Free Press, 1961.

_____. *Personality Dynamics and Effective Behavior.* Chicago: Scott, Foresman, 1969.

Deese, James E., and Stewart H. Hulse. *Psychology of Learning,* 3rd ed. New York: McGraw-Hill, 1967.

Denenberg, Victor H. Early Experience and Emotional Development. *Scientific American,* June 1963, pp. 138–146.

Duvall, Evelyn Millis. *Family Development,* 3rd ed. New York: Lippincott, 1967.

Epstein, William. *Varieties of Perceptual Learning.* New York: McGraw-Hill, 1967.

Finch, B. F., and Hugh Green. *Contraception through the Ages.* Springfield, Ill.: Thomas, 1963.

Forgays, D. G. and J. W. The Nature of the Affect of Free Environmental Experience in the Rat. *Journal of Comparative and Physiological Psychology,* 1952, Vol. 45, pp. 322–328.

Garrison, Karl C., *et al.* The Psychology of Childhood: A Survey of Development and Socialization. New York: Scribner's, 1967.

Glick, Paul C. *American Families.* New York: Wiley, 1957.

Goldfarb, W. Psychological Privation in Infancy and Subsequent Adjustment. *American Journal of Orthopsychiatry,* 1945, Vol. 15, pp. 247–255.

Gordon, Thomas. *Parent Effectiveness Training: The No-Lose Way to Raise Children.* New York: Wyden, 1970.

Gray, Philip H. Theory and Evidence of Imprinting in Human Infants. *Journal of Psychology,* 1958, Vol. 46, pp. 155–166.

Harlow, H. F. The Heterosexual Affectional System in Monkeys. *American Psychologist*, 1962, Vol. 17, pp. 1–9.

_____. Love in Infant Monkeys. *Scientific American*, June 1959, reprint.

_____, and Margaret Kuenne Harlow. Social Deprivation in Monkeys. *Scientific American*, November 1962, Vol. 207, pp. 137–146.

Hatch, A., *et al.* Long-term Isolation Stress in Rats. *Science*, 1963, Vol. 142, p. 507.

Hilgard, Ernest R., and Gordon H. Bower. *Theories of Learning*, 3rd ed. New York: Appleton-Century-Crofts, 1966.

Hurlock, Elizabeth B. *Child Growth and Development*. New York: McGraw-Hill, 1970.

Jones, Eve. *Natural Child Rearing*. New York: Free Press, 1959.

Kephart, William M. *The Family, Society, and the Individual*. Boston: Houghton Mifflin, 1961.

Landis, Paul H. *Making the Most of Marriage*, 4th ed. New York: Appleton-Century-Crofts, 1970.

Lee, Mark W. *Children Are Our Best Friends*. Grand Rapids, Mich.: Zondervan, 1970.

Leeper, Robert Ward. *Toward Understanding Human Personalities*. New York: Appleton-Century-Crofts, 1959.

Le Masters, E. E. *Parents in Modern America: A Sociological Analysis*. Homewood, Ill.: Dorsey, 1970.

Lipset, Seymour M. *Political Man*. Garden City, N. Y.: Doubleday, 1960.

Lipsitt, L. P., and C. C. Spiker, eds. *Advances in Child Development and Behavior*, Vol. 5. New York: Academy Press, 1970.

McCandless, Boyd R. *Childhood Behavior and Development*, 2nd ed. New York: Holt, 1967.

McClelland, David C., *et al. The Achievement Motive*. New York: Appleton-Century-Crofts, 1953.

McKinley, Donald Gilbert. *Social Class and Family Life*. New York: Free Press, 1964.

Montagu, Ashley. *Direction of Human Development*. New York: Hawthorn, 1970.

Montessori, Maria. *Child in the Family*, trans. by Nancy Cirillo. Chicago: Regnery, 1970.

_____. *Absorbent Mind*, trans. by Claude A. Claremont. New York: Dell, 1969.

_____. *The Montessori Method*. New York: Schocken, 1964.

Munn, Norman L. *The Evolution and Growth of Human Behavior*, 2nd ed. Boston: Houghton Mifflin, 1965.

Neill, A. S. *Summerhill: A Radical Approach to Child Rearing*. New York: Hart, 1960.

Nixon, Robert E. *The Art of Growing: A Guide to Psychological Maturity*. New York: Random House, 1962.

Parsons, Talcott. Foreword. In Donald Gilbert McKinley, *Social Class and Family Life*. New York: Free Press, 1964.

Pines, Maya. A Child's Mind is Shaped Before Age 2. In *Life*, December 17, 1971, Vol. 71, No. 25, pp. 63, 67, 68.

Provence, S., and R. Lipton. *Infants in Institutions*. New York: International Universities, 1967.

Queen, Stuart A., *et al. The Family in Various Cultures*, 3rd ed. New York: Lippincott, 1970.

Rheingold, H. L., ed. *Maternal Behavior in Mammals.* New York: Wiley, 1963.

Ribble, M. A. *The Rights of Infants,* rev. ed. New York: Columbia University Press, 1965.

Rogers, Carl R. *On Becoming a Person.* Boston: Houghton Mifflin, 1970.

Ross, J. B., and M. M. McLaughlin, eds. *A Portable Medieval Reader.* New York: Viking, 1949.

Scott, John Paul. *Early Experience and the Organization of Behavior.* Belmont, Calif.: Brooks/Cole, 1968.

Sears, Robert R., *et al. Identification and Child Rearing.* Palo Alto, Calif.: Stanford University Press, 1965.

Sirjamaki, John. *The American Family in the 20th Century.* Cambridge: Harvard University Press, 1953.

Spitz, Rene A. Hospitalization: An Inquiry into the Genesis of Psychiatric Conditions in Early Childhood. *Psychoanalytic Study of the Child,* 1945, Vol. 1, pp. 53–74.

_____. The Psychogenic Diseases in Infancy: An Attempt at Their Etiologic Classification. *Psychoanalytic Study of the Child,* 1951, Vol. 6, pp. 255–275.

_____. *The First Year of Life.* New York: International Universities, 1966.

Spock, Benjamin. *Baby and Child Care,* rev. ed. New York: Pocket Books, 1957.

_____. *Problems of Parents.* New York: Fawcett-World, 1970.

Stephens, William M. *The Family in Cross-Cultural Perspective.* New York: Holt, 1963.

Stevenson, H. W., *et al.,* eds. *Early Behavior: Comparative and Developmental Approaches.* New York: Wiley, 1967.

Stone, L. J. A Critique of Studies of Infant Isolation. *Child Development,* 1954, Vol. 25, pp. 9–20.

_____, and Joseph Church. *Childhood and Adolescence: A Psychology of the Growing Person,* 2nd ed. New York: Random House, 1968.

Stott, Leland H. *Child Development.* New York: Holt, 1968.

Thompson, W. R. Early Environmental Stimulation. In D. W. Fiske and S. R. Maddi, eds., *Functions of Varied Experience.* Homewood, Ill.: Dorsey, 1961.

Watson, John B. *Psychological Care of Infant and Child.* New York: Norton, 1928.

Whiting, J. W. M., and Irvin L. Child. *Child Training and Personality: A Cross-Cultural Study.* New Haven: Yale University Press, 1953.

Winch, Robert F. *The Modern Family,* rev. ed. New York: Holt, 1964.

Wyden, Barbara. Growth: 45 Crucial Months. In *Life,* December 17, 1971, Vol. 71, No. 25, pp. 93, 95.

Yarrow, L. J. Maternal Deprivation: Toward an Empirical and Conceptual Re-evaluation. *Psychological Bulletin,* 1961, Vol. 58, pp. 459–490.

Appendix One

An Annotated List of Readings

The interested student will want to pursue further many of the topics discussed in this text; and the following carefully selected and briefly annotated readings list provides many easily available and especially relevant and interesting titles, which will be useful to the student in expanding his intellectual horizons and in preparing papers and reports.

Ardrey, Robert. *The Territorial Imperative*. New York: Atheneum, 1966.
A fascinating account of animal societies, with special reference to the paired relation, mating, and familial solidarity.

Bach, George R., and Peter Wyden. *The Intimate Enemy: How to Fight Fair in Love and Marriage*. New York: Morrow, 1969.
A bright and useful exposition of psychologist Bach's theory of "constructive aggression" in marriage, with specific suggestions for identifying, understanding, and resolving the individual's own marital conflicts.

Belleveau, Fred, and Lin Richter. *Understanding Human Sexual Inadequacy*. New York: Bantam, 1970.
A clear, simple, and accurate explanation and analysis of Master's and Johnson's highly technical study of human sexual inadequacy.

Berelson, Bernard, and Gary A. Steiner. *Human Behavior: An Inventory of Scientific Findings.* New York: Harcourt, 1964. *A compilation of what is "known" in the social sciences, conveniently categorized.*

Bernard, Jessie. *Remarriage.* New York: Dryden Press, 1956. *A discussion of the demographic data and the personal experiences of second marriages.*

Berne, Eric, M.D. *Games People Play.* New York: Grove Press, 1964. *An intriguing examination of the psychological game—the covert and dishonest attempt to defeat the other, rather than to unite and attack the source of conflict in marriage.*

Biegel, H. G. Romantic Love. *American Sociological Review,* 1951, Vol. 16, pp. 326–334. *An examination of the origins, development, and significance of romantic love in our society.*

Blitsten, Dorothy. *The World of the Family.* New York: Random House, 1963. *A cross-cultural examination of the chief forms the family takes.*

Brecher, Edward M. *The Sex Researchers.* Boston: Little, Brown, 1969. *The first historical account of Western man's efforts to understand his sexuality within a scientific framework, evaluating a century of sex research in clear, non-technical language.*

——————, and Ruth Brecher. *An Analysis of Human Sexual Response.* New York: New American Library, 1966. *An inexpensive and readily available layman's version of the highly technical Masters and Johnson study.*

Brown, Ina. *Understanding Other Cultures.* Englewood Cliffs, N.J.: Prentice-Hall, 1963.

An excellent, short, clear account of the meaning and importance of culture to the individual in all societies.

Burns, Eugene. *The Sex Life of Wild Animals.* New York: Holt, 1953. *One of the few definitive accounts of sexual behavior among wild animals.*

Cavan, Ruth. *The American Family,* 4th ed. New York: Crowell, 1969. *Examines American family structure and dynamics with particular reference to social class.*

Coleman, James C. *Psychology and Effective Behavior.* Chicago: Scott, Foresman, 1960 *A readable account of such topics as feedback, frame of reference, self, and the interaction of the individual with the environment.*

Cuber, John F., and Peggy B. Harroff. *The Significant Americans: A Study of Sexual Behavior Among the Affluent.* New York: Appleton-Century-Crofts, 1965. *A study of marriage—the utilitarian and the intrinsic—among our most successful citizens.*

Denenberg, Victor H. Early Experience and Emotional Development. *Scientific American,* June 1963. *An ingenious experimental study which demonstrates that early tactile contact is important for normal development in the rat.*

Duvall, Evelyn. *Family Development,* 2nd ed. Philadelphia: Lippincott, 1962. *Examines the structure and dynamics of the family from the point of view of the life cycle—the important "tasks" that the individual must accomplish in each stage of his development.*

Eichenlaub, John E. *New Approaches to Sex in Marriage.* New York: Dell, 1970. *An excellent practical sex manual.*

Ellis, Albert, and Albert Abarbanel, eds. *The Encyclopedia of Sexual Behavior,* 2nd ed. New York: Hawthorn, 1967.

The most definitive study to date on sexual behavior. Each article is written by an expert in his field. Highly recommended.

Farber, Seymour M., and Robert H. L. Wilson, eds. *Man and Civilization: The Potential of Women.* New York: McGraw-Hill, 1963.
A critique and examination of the role of the female in our complex mass society.

Finch, B. F., and Hugh Green. *Contraception through the Ages.* Springfield, Ill.: Thomas, 1963.
A fascinating study, ranging from ancient Egypt to modern times.

Ford, C. S., and F. A. Beach. *Patterns of Sexual Behavior.* New York: Harper, 1970.
Definitive in its field. Covers both infrahuman and human sexual behavior.

Friedan, Betty. *The Feminine Mystique.* New York: Harper, 1963.
What is the place of woman in today's mass society? What are the "real values"? Intriguing and speculative.

Goode, William J. *Women in Divorce.* New York: Free Press, 1965.
One of the most comprehensive examinations to date of the experience of women following divorce.

_____. *The Family.* Englewood Cliffs, N.J.: Prentice-Hall, 1964.
A short but definitive account of the basis of family structure.

_____. *World Revolution and Family Patterns.* New York: Free Press, 1963.
A study of the impact of current sociological changes upon age-old familial patterns.

_____. The Theoretical Importance of Love. *American Sociological Review,* 1959, Vol. 24, pp. 38–47.
A thoughtful and penetrating study of the meaning of love.

Gordon, Albert I. *Intermarriage.* Boston: Beacon Press, 1964.
An exhaustive and authoritative examination of interclass, interfaith, and interethnic marriages in our contemporary society.

Graves, Robert. Are Women More Romantic than Men? *Life,* October 15, 1965.
Graves, after examining all the evidence, finds that they are not.

Grunwald, Henry A., ed. *Sex in America.* New York: Bantam, 1964.
A compilation of recent articles about sexuality in our contemporary society.

Guttmacher, Alan F., M.D. *The Complete Book of Birth Control.* New York: Ballantine, 1961.
A resumé of both demographic data and practical methods for contraception.

Harlow, Harry F. The Heterosexual Affectional System in Monkeys. *American Psychologist,* 1962, Vol. 17, pp. 1–9.
Affectional and sexual behavior in the monkey is learned, not instinctive — a finding which has extremely significant implications for all child-training theories.

_____. Love in Infant Monkeys. *Scientific American,* June 1959.
An attempt to reduce the concept of love to operational terms. An extremely significant study.

_____ and Margaret K. Social Deprivation in Monkeys. *Scientific American,* May 1962.
Early peer interaction is equally important with early nurturant behavior in determining later personality structure.

Hastings, Donald W. *Impotence and Frigidity.* Boston: Little, Brown, 1963.
A thorough and straightforward account of sexual difficulties, and their treatment.

Hegeler, Inge and Sten. *An ABZ of Love.* Trans. David Hohnen. New York: Alexicon, 1967.

An enlightened, witty, and informative glossary of human sexuality.

Hess, Eckhard H. Imprinting in Animals. *Scientific American,* March 1958.
A study of the importance of early experience.

Hunt, Morton M. *The World of the Formerly Married.* New York: McGraw-Hill, 1966.
A description of the experiences, expectations, attitudes, and opportunities of the separated and divorced in our contemporary mass society.

—————. *The Natural History of Love.* New York: Knopf, 1959.
Traces sex attitudes and concepts of love from classic Greece to the present.

Kephart, William M. *The Family, Society, and the Individual.* Boston: Houghton Mifflin, 1961.
One of the best standard works available on marriage and the family in our society.

Kinsey, Alfred C., Wardell B. Pomeroy, and Clyde E. Martin. *Sexual Behavior in the Human Male.* Philadelphia: Saunders, 1948.
A taxonomic examination of native, white, male sexual behavior in the United States.

—————. *Sexual Behavior in the Human Female.* Philadelphia: Saunders, 1953.
A taxonomic examination of native, white, female sexual behavior in the United States.

Lederer, William J., and Don D. Jackson. *The Mirages of Marriage.* New York: Norton, 1968.
An incisive analysis of contemporary marriage, and a discussion of practical approaches which the individual might take to help understand and improve his own troubled marriage.

Locke, Harvey J. *Predicting Adjustment in Marriage: A Comparison of a Divorced and a Happily Married Group.* New York: Holt, 1968.
The only study of its kind which compares the conflicts and difficulties of persons in these two groups.

Lorenz, Konrad. *On Aggression.* Trans. Marjorie Kerr Wilson. New York: Harcourt, 1966.
Many reviewers called this the most important book of our era. Has much about the paired relation and the importance of primary interaction.

McKinley, Donald G. *Social Class and Family Life.* New York: Free Press, 1964.
The influence of social class upon family life, both in terms of its structure and its dynamics.

Mace, David and Vera. *Marriage: East and West.* Garden City, N.Y.: Doubleday, 1960.
A cross-cultural study of contemporary mate-selection and marriage practices.

Martindale, Don. *American Society.* New York: Van Nostrand, 1960.
A thoughtful and penetrating analysis of the origins and structure of our mass society.

Maslow, A. H. *Motivation and Personality.* New York: Harper, 1954.
Explores the difference between physiological need fulfillment and "growth motivation" (or "self-actualization") in human volition.

Masters, William J., and Virginia E. Johnson. *Human Sexual Inadequacy.* Boston: Little, Brown, 1970.
A highly technical and detailed account of the authors' clinical research with sexually dysfunctional couples. Masters and Johnson's findings indicate that most sexual dysfunction may be rather quickly resolved.

—————. *Human Sexual Response.* Boston: Little, Brown, 1966.

The first study to subject human sexuality to objective, laboratory experimentation. Many valuable and pertinent findings.

Montagu, Ashley. *Anthropology and Human Nature.* Boston: Porter-Sargent, 1957.
A far-ranging discussion of the nature of man, in cross-cultural perspective.

_____, ed. *The Concept of Race.* New York: Free Press, 1964.
Explodes many myths about, and questions the very existence of, the concept of "race."

Queen, Stuart J., Robert W. Habenstein, and John B. Adams. *The Family in Various Cultures.* Philadelphia: Lippincott, 1961.
A study of a representative family in a few selected societies.

Rainer, Jerome and Julia. *Sexual Pleasure in Marriage,* rev. ed. New York: Simon & Schuster, 1969.
An excellent sex manual—practical, informative, and straightforward.

Riegel, Robert E. *American Feminists.* Lawrence: University of Kansas Press, 1963.
The history of the feminist movement in the United States, and an examination of its political and social significance.

Rogers, Carl R. *On Becoming a Person.* Cambridge, Mass.: Riverside Press, 1961.
What is man's real nature? How may he realize it?

Rosenfeld, Albert. The Placenta. *Life,* April 30, 1965.
Remarkable photos accompany this text of reproduction and gestation in man.

Schaller, George B. *The Year of the Gorilla.* Chicago: University of Chicago Press, 1964.
The first study of its kind made of the gorilla in his natural habitat. Shows the relational patterns of infrahuman primates.

Shibutani, Tamotsu. *Society and Personality.* Englewood Cliffs, N.J.: Prentice-Hall, 1961.
The relation between social structure and individual experience.

Spock, Benjamin. *Baby and Child Care,* rev. ed. New York: Pocket Books, 1957.
A modern classic of practical, down-to-earth manual of infant and child care.

Stephens, William N. *The Family in Cross-Cultural Perspective.* New York: Holt, 1957.
Easily the best in the field—well researched, thought provoking, clearly written.

Stone, L. Joseph, and Joseph Church. *Childhood and Adolescence: A Psychology of the Growing Person,* 2nd ed. New York: Random House, 1968.
A clear and concise statement of current psychological and sociological theory of the early developmental years.

Taylor, G. R. *Sex in History.* New York: Vanguard, 1955.
Sexual attitudes and behavior in historical perspective—from classic Greece to the present.

Turner, E. S. *A History of Courting.* New York: Dutton, 1955.
The processes of mate selection in the Western world, from the medieval period to the present.

Vatsyayana. *The Kama Sutra.* Trans. Sir Richard Burton and F. F. Arbuthnot. New York: Putnam's, 1963.
The all-time classic among sex manuals. Formerly unavailable in the United States.

Vincent, Clark. *Unmarried Mothers.* New York: Free Press, 1961.
A demographic and personal examination of the problem of premarital pregnancy.

Watson, James D. *The Double Helix.* New York: Atheneum, 1968.
A fascinating account of the discovery of how the DNA molecule directs the

division of the cell and encodes all
the information necessary for replication.

_____. *Molecular Biology of the
Gene*. New York: W. A. Benjamin,
1965.
*The mechanics of reproduction — with
special reference to the role of the DNA
molecule.*

Watts, Alan W. *Nature, Man and
Woman*. New York: Random, 1970.
*An unconventional and imaginative
contribution to the age-old problem of
male-female interaction.*

Winch, Robert F. *The Modern
Family*, rev. ed. New York:
Holt, 1964.
*One of the most complete recent studies
of family structure and dynamics.*

_____. *Mate Selection*.
New York: Harper, 1958.
*Does "like marry like" or do "opposites
attract"? Winch finds both these factors
operant in mate selection — with four
specific areas where complementary
personality characteristics determine
attraction.*

Wyden, Peter and Barbara. *Inside
the Sex Clinic*. New York: World,
1971.
*One half to three quarters of all
marriages have sexual problems.
This is a detailed (but fictionalized)
account of one troubled couple's
sexual difficulties and how they were
eventually resolved at the Masters and
Johnson clinic.*

Wynne-Edwards, V. C. Population
Control in Animals. *Scientific
American*, August 1964.
*A wild animal will not mate unless he
has room to establish a family — an
apparent built-in instinctual safeguard
against a population explosion, a
safeguard which man lacks.*

Young, Weyland. *Eros Denied:
Sex in Western Society*. New York:
Grove Press, 1964.
*A refreshingly frank exploration of
our sexual attitudes and behavior.*

Appendix
Two

A Guide to
Writing an
Autobiographical
Term Paper

Often one of the most heuristic experiences of a course in marriage and the family is the writing of an autobiographical term paper. Through such a paper, the student is able to relate the material he has learned in the classroom to experiences he has had in his own life and to attempt to explore his feelings and experiences as honestly as possible. In order to achieve the candor that is essential to such a term paper, the student should keep in mind (1) that the instructor will respect the anonymity of the papers and (2) that the instructor will assign a grade only on the basis of the sincerity and seriousness of the term paper.

The following questions are provided to guide the student in thinking out and structuring his autobiographical term paper.

1. What were your childhood experiences regarding sex? How did you acquire your sex education? What were the circumstances under which you began masturbating? What are your memories of early childhood sexuality (children's sex games, mutual exhibition, peeping, boy's bull sessions, etc.)? What were

your sexual experiences in adolescence (homosexual and heterosexual contacts, dating, etc.)? What are the nature and the extent of your sexual activities while in college? What is your attitude toward sex as you anticipate marriage? What experience and attitude do you expect your mate to have?

2. What were your early childhood experiences in your family regarding love? Was your early experience in your family one of affectionate acceptance or of rejection? Did your parents openly display love and affection for one another? For you and your siblings? Do you regard yourself as an outgoing, affectionate person or as a reticent, rather cold person? Is it more important that your mate be warmly affectionate or perceptive and practical? How do you look upon the responsibility of having and rearing children? Do you think you will be a good parent?

3. Would you categorize your parent's marriage as intrinsic or utilitarian? If utilitarian, was it conflict habituated, devitalized, or passive-congenial? If your parents are divorced, how did their breakup affect you? If you have a step-parent, how would you categorize the marriage? In general, what kind of home life did you have as a child? What were your most significant familial experiences between the ages of five and twelve? Between the ages of thirteen and eighteen? Since you have started college?

4. How did your parents tend to settle their quarrels? Would you categorize your parents' marriage as authoritarian or democratic? Do you tend to be authoritarian, permissive, or democratic in working out conflicts with your friends? In working out conflicts with you, are your parents authoritarian, permissive, or democratic? How would you anticipate settling conflicts in your own marriage? With your own children?

5. What were your relations to your siblings as a child? What are your re-lations to them today? Does your position in the family (whether oldest or youngest, male or female) bring any special strain or reward?

6. Were ceremonial observances important in your family when you were a child? Did these ceremonial observances have a significant influence upon your development and your present attitude? What ceremonial observances would you emphasize in your own family?

7. Describe the high points of your life, from earliest childhood to the present. How have these "significant experiences" contributed to your present frame of reference?

8. Is your approach to life, your "life style," essentially negative or essentially positive? Do you consider yourself to be essentially a rebel or essentially a con-formist? Are you essentially liberal or essentially conservative? Are you es-sentially practical? Religious? Iconoclastic? Humanistic? What kind of person

would you consider to be an ideal mate? Do you think this person would be attracted to you?

9.   Do you think you have self-understanding? What are the chief goals of your life? The chief values? The chief problems? What do you want most in life? Wealth? Power? To give service? To gain knowledge? What do you fear most? What do you hate most? What do you value most? Trace the development of your attitudes, interests, and values, from your childhood to the present.

10. In conclusion, describe the person you are today, the kind of person you were in the past—during your childhood and early and middle teens—and the kind of person you hope to be in the future. What are the realistic possibilities that you will accomplish this ideal? How important will your marriage be to you in accomplishing it?

Glossary

Abortifacients. Substances or objects that interfere with the implantation or development of the embryo. Such contraceptives as the prostaglandin ("morning-after") pill and the IUDs are examples.

Abortion. Separation of the embryo or fetus from the mother before the organism is capable of extrauterine existence. There are three categories of abortion: *induced abortion*, the surgical termination of a pregnancy; *spontaneous abortion*, or miscarriage, the natural termination of a pregnancy during the first 20 weeks, usually because the pregnancy or the organism is biologically abnormal; and *therapeutic abortion*, the surgical termination of a pregnancy that endangers the life of the mother—the only legal form of induced abortion in most of the United States.

Achievement need. The need to overcome obstacles, to exercise power, to gain high status.

Achievement—vicarious needs. An interaction in which the achievement need of one person in the relation will complement the vicarious-achievement need of the other.

Acquired need. A need that is learned in the environment (as opposed to an inherent psychological or physiological need).

Actuarial expectation. An expectation of behavior based on statistical probability, which is computed through the accumulation and comparison of relevant facts.

"Add on" clause. A device in some credit-installment contracts by which all items purchased by a customer from one dealer over a period of time are written on the same installment contract, with payments and credit charges pro-rated among *all* the outstanding debts and with the repossession clause applicable to all the items.

Adequacy. The ability and the self-assurance necessary for coping with problems, decisions, and stress in the environment.

Adjustment. A sequence of behavioral response which resolves a perceived need. In marriage, adjustment is the resolution of a conflict of needs between the marital partners.

Adolescence. The transition period between puberty and adulthood.

Adolescent sterility. The phenomenon of infertility that sometimes occurs with females during the first 2–3 years of menstruation and results from a temporary failure to ovulate or from an incomplete hormonal development which prevents implantation of the zygote.

Affect. Any experience of emotion or feeling.

Affectional needs. The inherent needs for receiving and giving love, confirmation, tactile contact, and nurture.

Afterbirth. The materials (placenta, amniotic sac, chorionic membrane, and umbilical cord) that are expelled from the uterus after the birth of a child.

Agglutination inhibition. The principle upon which immunilogic pregnancy tests are based. The presence of sufficient quantities of the pregnancy-indicating hormone HCG in the subject's urine neutralizes the anti-HCG testing agent and prevents a clumping (agglutination) reaction—a positive confirmation of pregnancy.

Alimony. The maintenance allowance set by a court and paid to a former spouse during the proceedings and after the decree of legal separation or divorce. The payments cease when the former spouse remarries or, in some states, after a specified number of years.

Altruistic love. The experience of a deep and intrinsic satisfaction as a result of providing nurture to and showing concern and affection for a love object.

Amnio centesis. An important prenatal diagnostic tool. A long hollow needle is inserted through the mother's abdomen and into the amniotic sac, where a sample of the amniotic fluid is drawn off. This fluid contains sloughed-off cells from the fetus which may be examined microscopically for signs of disease or birth defects, enabling early treatment to be instituted. This technique may also determine the baby's sex.

Amnion. The protective wall of cells surrounding the germinal disc and becoming the sac of salty fluid that cushions, bathes, and partially nurtures the embryo and fetus and also allows the organism to move about.

Annulment. The legal declaration that a marriage is invalid and therefore does not exist. As a mode of marital termination, annulment is chiefly utilized in our society in states where divorce laws are especially stringent and by members of the Roman Catholic Church, which takes the position that marriage is indissoluble except by death.

Apathy. A marked diminishment or absence of feeling in situations that would normally elicit an emotional response.

Apgar scoring system. A system of evaluating the condition of the new-born infant. The infant's score later serves as an aid to the pediatrician in following the development and diagnosing the health of the child.

Aphrodisiacs. Certain foods or chemicals that are fallaciously thought to induce erotic arousal or sexual endurance.

Areola. The pigmented area surrounding the nipples of the breasts and a significant erogenous zone for about half of the male and female population.

Artificial insemination. Introducing semen into the vagina by means of a syringe. Artificial insemination is utilized in combating a husband's sperm deficiencies; that is, his infertility. The husband's semen is either accumulated from several ejaculations in order to increase its quantity, or it is mixed with an anonymous donor's healthy ejaculate in order to ensure that fertilization will take place.

Ascheim–Zondeck (A-Z) test. A test for pregnancy in which the female's urine is injected into a female mouse that has not had its first ovulation. If the gonadotrophic hormone which is produced with pregnancy is present in the subject's urine, the ovarian tissue of the mouse will change, and the subject's pregnancy is confirmed.

Authoritarian decision making. An unsatisfactory mode of adjustment for conflict in a relation; consists of one person stating categorically what the adjustment will be (usually the fulfillment of his need). Such an adjustment creates a winner and a loser; and, in a marital relation, this often results in a power struggle.

Autosexual behavior. Self-gratification of sexual needs, or masturbation.

"Balloon payment." A device in some credit-installment contracts which requires a very large final installment payment on the contract. Such an arrangement is usually made to keep monthly payments small enough to be within the present means of the buyer.

Behavior. A complex pattern of response in which the individual interacts with his environment.

Behaviorists (behaviorism). Psychologists who regard objective, observable manifestations of behavior, such as motor and glandular responses, as the key to an understanding of human behavior and the only proper subject for psychological study. The subjective study of the phenomena of consciousness and feeling is rejected by behaviorists as unnecessary and unscientific.

Bestiality. Petting and copulation between a person and an animal.

Bigamy. The crime of marrying a person at the time that one is already legally married to another.

"Big ticket" item. Business jargon for expensive consumer items, such as major appliances, costly furniture, rugs or carpeting, automobiles, etc.

Body stalk. The early form of the umbilical cord, developing from the inner cluster of cells containing the germinal disc

"Borax" store. Consumer finance jargon for dishonest "cut-rate" stores selling furniture, carpeting, jewelry, electronic gadgets, and such.

Breast. In females, a milk-producing organ consisting of glandular tissue and fat. In both males and females, an erotically sensitive area.

Breech presentation. The birth of a fetus, buttocks first.

Bride price. Provided as an economic compensation to a bride's family in societies where a young girl is an economic asset to her family.

Brow presentation. The birth of a fetus, face first.

Budget. A record of income and expenditures, which clarifies the alternatives in directing one's cash flow for maximum return and minimum deprivation.

Caesarean section. The delivery of a baby by means of a surgical incision through the mother's abdominal and uterine walls. Caesareans are generally performed when the physical condition of the mother or the fetus is such that one or both might not survive the stress of vaginal delivery.

Cash flow. The relation between expenditures and income — how much a person makes and spends and how he spends it. A budget is

the best means for directing cash flow wisely.

Celibate. A person who abstains from all sexual behavior.

Cerebral erection. Penile erection caused by psychological stimuli.

Cervical cap. A contraceptive device similar in construction to the diaphragm but designed to cover only the cervix itself.

Cervix. A small, slightly protruding opening between the uterus and vagina.

Chancre. A lesion that develops at the site of syphlitic infection and signals the first stage of syphilis in about half the cases. It may resemble a pimple, cold sore, acne, ulcer, etc., does not itch, and is not painful. It is, however, swarming with spirochetes and highly infectious.

Chorion. The protective sac which develops from the trophoblast and surrounds the amnion and the embryo. As the fetus grows larger, the chorion gradually fuses with the amniotic sac.

Chorionic villi. The tendrils which extend from the trophoblast, burrow into the uterine tissue, and, by osmosis, absorb nurturant materials from the mother's blood and pass fetal waste products back into her blood. The villi nearest the uterine wall and the embryonic body stalk ultimately develop into the placenta.

Chromatids. The split chromosomes that occur as a cell divides itself into two (the process of mitosis).

Chromosomes. The rod-shaped carriers of the genes in the nucleus of each cell of a sexually reproducing creature. In human cells (except the germ cells), there are 23 pairs of chromosomes, or 46 chromosomes, each one of the pair contributed by one parent.

Cilia. Hair-like structures that line the inner walls of the Fallopian tubes and help to create the current that moves the egg or the zygote through the tube and into the uterus.

Circumcision. The surgical removal of the foreskin of the penis. It is generally performed for hygienic reasons a few days after birth.

Clitoridectomy. The surgical amputation of the clitoris. It is an unusual practice that occurs in Saudi Arabia and the Sudan, with the purpose of virtually eliminating sexual pleasure for the females and thus making premarital copulation much less likely.

Clitoris. The small organ situated just under the upper portion of the labia minora of the female genitalia. It is the homologue of the male penis, consists of a shaft and a glans, and becomes erect with sexual arousal. It is also the prime organ for erotic arousal in the female.

Coitus. Copulation.

Collusion. The mutual agreement by husband and wife to divorce—an agreement that is technically illegal according to the divorce laws of our society. One spouse must sue the other for divorce and must charge the other with some breach of the marital contract. No attempt is made to enforce the laws against collusion, so long as the couple pay lip service to the procedure of divorce suits.

Common-law marriage. A marriage which is based not upon legal ceremony but rather upon the tenure of the couple's living as mates in the same household. Such a marriage is legally recognized in many states if the couple can prove that they have lived together as man and wife for 7 years.

Companionate love. The sharing of interests, respect, friendship, goals, and companionship. It is the most commonly and frequently experienced aspect of married love.

Compatibility. The presence of complementation in a paired relation.

Compensation. Defense mechanism in which an undesirable trait is covered over by the exaggeration of a desirable trait.

Complementation. The balance of needs, attitudes, behavior patterns, and self-perceptions that is necessary if a paired relation is to be harmonious—that is, reciprocally and equivalently fulfilling.

Compound interest. Interest that itself earns interest.

Conception. The fertilization of the ovum by a sperm and the fusion of the two gametes into a single-celled organism, the zygote, which develops into a new human being.

Conditioning. The process of learning responses through experience and reinforcement or through repetition.

Condom. A thin rubber bag which is worn over the penis to contain the ejaculate during copulation and, thus, to prevent conception. It also serves as a prophylactic; that is, as a protection against venereal diseases.

Confirmation. Providing verification of the self-image of a significant other through positive feedback.

Conflict. The stress resulting from the occurrence of two or more needs in a situation in which only one of the needs can be fulfilled. Marital conflict, both internal and external, occurs when each spouse has a need and when the satisfaction of the need of one spouse leads to (or will lead to) deprivation for the other spouse.

Conflict-habituated marriage. The role interaction of the marriage is characterized by well-controlled tension resulting from continuing conflict of needs between the spouses. In such a marriage, there is an acknowledgment by the partners that incompatibility is pervasive in their relation. The conflict-habituated marriage is the most common type of utilitarian marriage.

Congenital. A condition existing at birth or before birth but not by heredity.

Congenital syphilis. A special form of the disease transmitted from an infected mother to her unborn child anytime after the fourth month of pregnancy. Treatment of an infected baby will cure the disease, but tissue already destroyed cannot be restored. For this reason prenatal blood tests are required by law in forty-five of the fifty states.

Congruence of role perception. A balanced, verifiable, and realistic perceptual interaction in a relation: Each person's perception of his own and the other's role is verified and fulfilled by each one's behavior.

Conservation of sexual energy. The fallacious belief that an "excessive" number of orgasms will result in temporary or permanent impotence.

Continence. Abstaining from sexual activity.

Continuity of role conditioning. The consistency of the role conditioning for a particular expected behavior from childhood through adolescence and into adulthood (as opposed to *discontinuity* of such role conditioning, which often results in conflict between the role expectations that a person values as a child and those that he must value as he matures).

Continuum. A continuous scale of measurement on which variables of, say, behavior are shown in a relationship from "least" (normal, important) to "most" but are not divided into discrete categories.

Contraception. A deliberate action to prevent fertilization of the ovum as a result of copulation.

Convergent feedback. Information that one's behavior is bringing a desired result.

"Cooling off" period. A legally required lapse of time (usually three days) between the premarital medical examination and the issuance of the marriage license.

Copulation. A mode of sexual expression involving penile-vaginal intromission. It is, by definition, heterosexual and limited to two persons.

Corona. The crown-like ridge which extends around the back of the glans of the penis and which is a primary source of erotic sensitivity and arousal.

Corporal punishment. The deliberate infliction of pain or suffering as a mode of changing behavior, bringing about remorse, or exacting retribution. It rarely is successful in perpetuating new behavior patterns.

Courtly love. A medieval code of behavior for lovers which advocated a chaste, self-sacrificing, and absolutely loyal relation between a man and woman outside of marriage. It also prescribed the idealization of women and chivalry toward them as the chief opportunity for a man's achievement of nobility and grace.

Cowper's glands. The pair of small, internal organs at the base of the penis. Their function is unknown, although it is suggested that they produce the pre-ejaculatory fluid.

Creative problem solving. A method of resolving conflict in a relation; consists of an identification and discussion of the sources of conflict and then an agreement upon a mutually acceptable solution—often a creative compromise of the conflicting needs.

Credit. Buying now and paying later.

Credit-installment contracts. A legal agreement between consumer and dealer for the financed purchase of an item on a delayed-payment plan (usually with a re-possession clause). These contracts will almost always involve higher interest rates than a direct cash loan from other credit sources, and they are therefore risky—especially if the item involved is costly and depreciates rapidly, which in the case of repossession would make it worth less than the consumer still owes.

Cultural conditioning. The process of learning the cultural patterns of behavior and the implements, information, values, and attitudes of the culture.

Culture. The way that the persons in a society or subsociety behave and the implements, artifacts, institutions, and concepts that they characteristically utilize in their behavior.

Cunnilingus. A technique of petting involving oral stimulation of the female genitalia.

Dating. The institutional mode in our society of (1) sociosexual contact and experimentation between male and female adolescents and young adults, (2) mate selection, and (3) courtship.

Dating differential. The tendency of the male in our society to prefer females who are smaller, younger, somewhat less intelligent and less educated, and of somewhat lower status than he is and the tendency of the female to prefer males who fulfill the converse of these qualities. This cultural phenomenon results in a residue of relatively high-status females and low-status males who do not date and often do not marry.

Defense mechanisms. Modes of displacement and repression—for example, excessive sleeping, fantasy, rationalization—which are utilized in the experience of deprivation or frustration to resolve the immediate need, the feeling of failure, rather than the more basic need, the achievement of a desired goal or fulfillment.

Defense-oriented behavior. That behavior which is directed toward alleviation of the stress and self-devaluation associated with the failure to achieve a basic need rather than toward the resolution of the basic need itself.

Deference need. The need to ask for and follow the opinions and decisions of another and therefore to subordinate one's own desires or values. This need is also termed a *submission need*. The person with such a need will often form a complementary relation with someone who has a strong dominance need.

Demography. The statistical study of the characteristics of human populations.

Dependency need. The need to receive emotional support and nurture from another person. In infancy, and also in early childhood, the satisfaction of this need is necessary for survival and normal development. In later childhood, adolescence, and adulthood, the satisfaction of this need is important in the maintenance of one's sense of being.

Depersonalization. The separation of man from the end product of his labor and from the intimacy and confirmation of primary relations—a condition which is characteristic of the mass society and which commonly results in the loss of a sense of personal identity.

Depression. An emotional state of dejection, usually accompanied by feelings of apprehension, worthlessness, and guilt.

Deprivation. The failure to experience need fulfillment.

Desertion. Abandonment of one's spouse—a violation of legal and moral marital obligations.

Developmental readiness. A concept that describes the optimal periods in an infant's and child's development when he has reached the neuro-motor maturity necessary for the learning of a particular skill. If he is not developmentally ready, he cannot learn the skill; and if the period of developmental readiness has passed, his learning of the skill is not economical.

Developmental sequence. The highly predictable sequence of growth and development in infancy and childhood.

Devitalized marriage. A utilitarian marriage in which the important interpersonal need fulfillments at an early stage in the marriage are no longer present in the interaction of the marital relation. In such a marriage, the spouses no longer spend much time together and no longer share interests and activities in a deep and meaningful way. Usually, the couple's sexual relation is less satisfying than it had formerly been.

Diaphragm. A contraceptive device consisting of a circular piece of thin rubber which is fitted by a physician so that it spans the back of the vagina and covers the cervix. Spermaticidal jelly often is used in conjunction with the diaphragm.

Differentiation. Specialization of function. With social structure, differentiation refers to the specialization of institutional functions, which is a characteristic result of the complexity, urbanization, and unique economic pattern of the mass society. With biological structure, the term refers, for example, to the specialization of the cells of a developing organism.

Discipline. Setting limits and providing guidance in order to induce and perpetuate self-directed, socialized behavior.

Discontinuity of role conditioning. The inconsistencies between the role behavior expected of a child and an adolescent and the role behavior expected of an adult. For example, the contradiction in our society in its expectation that a child will be asexual, dependent, and submissive and an adult will be sexual, independent, and dominant often causes a good deal of internal and interpersonal conflict in the self-perceptions and role behavior of children, adolescents, and even married adults. (In contrast, some societies have a *continuity* in these areas of sexuality, independence, and dominance; and the persons in these societies experience less stress and personality disorder as they mature.)

Displacement. The basis (along with repression) of all defense-oriented behavior, displacement involves the unconscious shifting of frustration and tension from an object or situation that is not controllable by the person to an object or situation upon which the person can safely or easily vent his hostility, guilt, or fear without having to recognize or cope with the true nature or source of his feelings and problems.

Divergent feedback. Information that one's behavior is not bringing the desired result.

Division of labor. The socialized pattern of male-female division of functions and roles.

Divorce. The legal abrogation of a valid marital contract and of the right of the couple to cohabit. A divorce decree also provides for property settlement between the couple, for custody and support of offspring, and, often, for alimony payments.

DNA molecules. Contained within each gene, these complex chainlike molecules encode the information of heredity. Because the substance of the molecules — deoxyribonucleic acid — is non-living matter which is able nevertheless to replicate itself precisely during the cell mitosis or meiosis which it directs, DNA is considered to be the basis of all reproduction and therefore the source of continuing life.

Dominance need. The need to influence or direct others. A person with a dominance need will often form a complementary relation with a person who has a submission or deference need.

Dominance–submission needs. An interaction in which the dominance need of one person in the relation will complement the submissive need of the other.

Dominant gene. Within each chromosome, there are two genes for every hereditary trait, one gene contributed by the germ cell of the mother and one gene contributed by the germ cell of the father. If one of these genes is dominant, the trait determined by the gene will occur regardless of the trait of the other gene, which is called recessive. Dominant genes determine, for example, brown eyes, short stature, and allergies.

Douche. A contraceptive technique which consists of flushing out the vagina after copulation.

Dowry. Money or property given by the parents of the bride to her husband, either to become solely his or to be shared by him though remaining legally his wife's.

Drive. The observable manifestations of behavior that stem from hypothesized motivations.

Ectoderm. The differentiated embryo tissue which will become skin and neural tissue in the fetus.

Ejaculate. Semen.

Ejaculation. The rhythmic discharge of seminal fluid from the penis during orgasm.

Embryo. The developing organism, from the second to the eighth week of pregnancy. During the embryonic period, the second stage of pregnancy, all the organs and tissue are differentiated into their human form.

Emotion. A response that comprises subjective feeling, physical action, physiological change, and motivation (stimulus to action). Motivation is probably the most significant aspect of emotion because it arouses and directs the person's activity.

Emotional deprivation. The lack of affectional support, confirmation, and tactile nurture—a condition that results in personality disorders, perceptual retardation, impaired physical and mental development, and a generalized apathy and inadequacy.

Emotional maturity. The capacity for deriving intrinsic satisfaction from the provision of nurture, emotional support, and need fulfillment to another person. The person who is emotionally mature is a self-actualized, competent, and loving individual.

Emotional security. An essential psychological need that is fulfilled by the nurture, affection, guidance, and confirmation of a significant other.

Emotional support. Providing nurture, affection, sympathy, and confirmation to a person.

Endoderm. The differentiated embryonic tissue which develops into the digestive organs and the alimentary tract of the fetus.

Endogamy. The inclination or the necessity to marry within a particular group.

Environmental control. The developing child's ability to cope with and manipulate his environment.

Epididymis. A sperm-maturation chamber in the testicle.

Episiotomy. A surgical incision which is made in the mother's perineum during childbirth in order to prevent tearing of the vaginal tissues.

Equivalence of role function. The necessary balance in the perceptual values of the *resources,* or need satisfactions, that each person provides in an interaction. This is especially essential in a marital relation.

Erection. The involuntary enlargement and stiffening of the penis (and clitoris) during erotic arousal. Erection is caused by the engorgement of the tissue with blood. There are two categories of penile erection: cerebral and tactile.

Erogenous zones. Certain areas of the human body—for example, the genitalia, the mouth, the breasts, the neck—that are particularly sensitive to tactile stimuli and that respond to such stimuli with sexual arousal.

Erotic. Pertaining to sexual stimulation and gratification.

Erotic response. The inevitable result of appropriate and sustained erotic stimuli. The sequence of erotic response is divided into four phases— excitement, plateau, orgasm, and resolution—each of which has predictable physiological characteristics.

Escapist sleep. The defense mechanism of excessive sleeping.

Estrus. The period of maximum sexual receptivity in the infrahuman female. It is also termed *heat* or *rut.*

Ethnic group. A subsociety which shares the same cuisine, language, dress, religious observance, and recreational interests and which is embedded in a larger and ethnically different society.

Excitement phase. The first phase of erotic response, which is characterized by several physiological manifestations—among them, vaginal lubrication and expansion; erection of the penis, clitoris, and nipples; increase in the pulse rate and rate of respiration; and a flushing of the body surface.

Exogamy. The inclination or the necessity to marry outside a particular group.

Extended family. Two or more nuclear families, together with other relatives, in the same household. The ideal form in most societies, it is a rarity in actual practice.

External conflict. A conflict between the felt or perceived needs of two or more persons.

Extramarital. Outside of the marital relation.

Extrapunitive reaction. The tendency to direct hostility outward in reacting to frustration.

Extrauterine. Outside the uterus.

Fallopian tubes. The tubes that link the ovaries to the uterus and move the ovum, by the peristaltic action and the cilia of the tubal walls and by the flow of the tubal fluid, into the uterus. Fertilization of the ovum and formation of the zygote occur in the Fallopian tube.

False pregnancy. A temporary psychosomatic response which can include all of the physiological manifestations of pregnancy, including cessation of menstruation and the swelling of the uterus.

Family. Operationally defined as a mother, father, and their offspring living in the same household. The family is, in addition to marriage, the most universal and basic of all human relations.

Family of origin. The family in which one is born and reared.

Family of procreation. The new family that a person establishes when he marries and rears his own offspring.

Fantasy. Behavior, generally defense-oriented, by which one indulges in imaginary solutions to a perceived need. Such behavior may be creative and lead to reality-oriented solutions.

Feedback. Information received by a person about the effects of his behavior.

Fellatio. A technique of petting involving oral stimulation of the male genitalia.

Fertility. The capacity for reproduction.

Fertilization. The union of the sperm and ovum and the formation of the zygote.

Fetishism. A complex of physiological and psychological responses in which a person's erotic interest is focused on and aroused by some specific object (an anatomical feature, a manner of dress, a symbolically sexual object) that represents to him the ideal or personification of sexual attraction.

Field of eligibles. The population within which mate selection can and will be made.

Fission. The division of a cell into two separate cells. It is also termed *mitosis* and *meiosis.*

Fixation. A rigid habit developed as a consequence of repeated reinforcement or frustration.

Fixed, or non-discretionary, expenses. All expenditures over which a person has little or no control every month — rent, mortgage payments, utilities, taxes, etc.

"Flipping." A tactic used by some small loan companies whereby the various loans to a client are written on the same contract, so that interest may be charged on the total amount of the principal borrowed over a period of time instead of on each new loan.

Follicles (egg sacs). The sacs in the ovarian tissue which nurture the maturing ova and which rupture (one every 28 days) during ovulation and release the ovum into the Fallopian tube.

Fontanels. The six soft spots in the skull of the neonate where the structural bones have not yet grown together.

Forced alternate choice. The ability of a person to narrow the range of choices sufficiently for him to be able to recognize that by using his money for *A,* he will eliminate the possibility of using it for *B.* An extremely important principle in the management of personal finance, and the basis for making a budget.

Forceps. Metal tongs that are used in difficult deliveries to grasp the fetus's head and draw it out of the birth canal.

Foreskin. The loose skin which extends from the shaft of the penis over the glans. In circumcision, this skin is surgically removed.

Frame of reference. The cluster of values, expectations, and factual assumptions which underlies most of a person's perceptions of his roles, his experiences, the feedback he receives and utilizes, and his self-image.

Free feedback. Maximal and unqualified information about the effectiveness of one's behavior.

Frenum. The thin, erotically sensitive tissue on the lower surface of the glans where the foreskin is attached.

Friedman test. Called the *rabbit test,* this test for pregnancy involves the injection of the subject's urine into a female rabbit which has not had its first ovulation. If the gonadotrophic hormone characteristic of pregnancy is present in the subject's urine, detectable changes will occur in the ovarian tissue of the rabbit.

Frigidity. The disinclination or inability in the female to experience orgasm. It is almost always caused by psychological factors.

Frustration. The feeling of depression or anger that occurs when deprivation combines with self-devaluation.

Game. A psychological concept that describes the type of relational power struggle in which the persons almost entirely disregard the goal of resolving conflict and instead covertly emphasize continuing competition and conflict interaction disguised as loving, self-sacrificing, or creatively adjustive behavior. Game playing is probably the most common form of power struggle in marriage; and it is also the most insidious, since it is devious and ostensibly agreeable behavior, and since it easily becomes a patterned behavior in the continuation of an incompatible relation.

Gamete. The germ cell. In the male, it is called the *sperm;* in the female, it is called the *ovum,* or *egg.*

Garnishee. The legal term for attaching the wages of a person who is in arrears in his installment-contract payments.

Genes. The subcellular structures, within the chromosomes in the cell nucleus, which contain the DNA molecules and which determine the traits of the differentiating cells of the organism.

Genitalia. The external reproductive organs.

Genotype. The underlying genetic makeup which, in contrast to the *phenotype,* is not observable.

Germinal disc. The primordial form of the organism within the hollow of the developing zygote during the germinal period of pregnancy.

Germinal period. The first two weeks of pregnancy—from the formation of the zygote in the Fallopian tube to the embedding of the zygote in the uterine wall. During this period, pregnancy is not reliably detectable.

Glans. The smooth, cone-shaped head of the penis, which is covered (before circumcision) with a heavier, retractable foreskin. It is the chief source of erotic response in the male.

Goal. The object, condition, or activity which provides need satisfaction.

Gonadotropic hormone (HCG—human gonadotropic hormone). The hormone that stimulates the ovarian follicles for development of the ovum. Presence of this hormone in large quantities indicates pregnancy; the hormone is built up enough for diagnosis in from ten to forty days after conception.

Gonococcus. The micro-organism causing gonorrhea. It is found in the mucous discharge from membranes affected by the disease. This discharge is highly infectious.

Gonorrhea. Commonly called *"clap"* and caused by a micro-organism called a *gonococcus,* gonorrhea is the most common of the venereal (or sexually related) diseases. Unlike syphilis, which typically involves the entire body, gonorrhea usually remains localized in the genitalia and is self-limiting (although it may persist and cause considerable pain and even sterility).

Group marriage. A rare form of polygamy in which two or more men and two or more women are participants in a single marriage.

Heterogamy. The mutual attraction and compatibility of persons with opposite and complementary personality traits—for example, dominance-submission, nurturance-dependence, achievement-vicarious.

Heterosexual. Pertaining to sexual interest in and interaction with the opposite sex.

"Holder in due course" clause. A legal and widely used device in installment-plan contracts which provides that a dealer may sell his contract with a customer to a finance company, which then becomes the "holder in due course." This new holder of the contract is under no obligation to guarantee the item sold and cannot be legally involved in any dispute between the seller and customer regarding shoddy merchandise, failure to provide service, or misrepresentation of any type.

Homeostasis. The tendency of organisms to maintain their physiological functioning within the optimal limits necessary for survival.

Homogamy. The strongly practical attraction of persons who share similar objective characteristics, such as race, religion, ethnic group, intelligence, education, social class, age, or interests and skills.

Homosexual. Pertaining to sexual interest in and interaction with the same sex.

Hostility—abasement needs. The basis of a complementary relation, wherein one person is generally hostile, aggressive, and destructive and the other is generally deferring, withdrawn, and self-devaluating.

Hymen. The membrane that in most young girls partially closes the entrance to the vagina. Also termed the *maidenhead*, the hymen is ruptured with copulation, with active play, or with the use of tampons.

Hysterectomy. The surgical removal of the uterus.

Identification. Empathizing, or identifying, with the characteristics, personality, and behavior of another person in a primary relation. It is an important experience in the socialization and psychological development of children.

Immunologic pregnancy tests. Recently developed chemical tests for the pregnancy-indicating hormone HCG. These tests are quicker and easier than the biological tests, such as the A-Z and Friedman, since they require only two minutes to two hours (instead of two days) and they can be performed in a physician's office (rather than in a laboratory). The two forms of the test—slide and tube—are often done simultaneously for higher accuracy.

Impotence. The inability of a male to obtain an erection. It is usually psychological and almost always temporary.

Impunitive behavior. Responding to the tension of frustration with a neutral and therapeutic activity, such as walking, reading, or working hard.

Inadequate personality. A person who responds to intellectual, emotional, social, and physical demands with ineptness, poor judgment, and rigidity.

Incest. Copulation between closely blood-tied relatives. The degree of closeness that is considered incestuous depends upon societal attitudes, but all societies proscribe sexual relations between parents and children and between siblings.

Incomplete breech. The birth of a fetus, feet first.

Independency need. The need for autonomy—for thinking and acting for oneself and accepting the responsibility for one's actions.

Individuation. The anatomical, physiological, and psychological variables that combine to make each person unique.

Infancy. The period from the second month after birth to the time when a baby is walking and beginning to talk (usually about 15 months).

Infantile love. Immature, dependent love.

Infatuation. The idealization of a person based chiefly on fantasy and often mistaken for love. There are two categories of infatuation objects: (1) the *distant infatuation object*, whom one knows just slightly or not at all; and (2) the *associative infatuation object*, whom one knows and dates and with whom one may form a deep paired relation.

Infertility. The temporary inability of a male or female to reproduce.

Inflation. An abnormal increase in available currency and credit beyond the proportion of available goods, resulting in a sharp and continuing rise in price levels.

Instinctive behavior. A complex pattern of behavior that is innate·rather than learned and that is characteristic of lower animals. (In contrast, man's behavior patterns are learned.)

Institution. A collective solution to a social or personal need. There are two categories of institutions: *primary* and *secondary.*

Instrumental. Pertaining to manipulation of the environment.

Insurance-plus-investment. A life-insurance policy dividing the premiums into two parts, one of which pays for a life-insurance feature while the other is invested for the policy holder and earns interest and an increasing cash-surrender value. This type of life insurance guarantees the payment of the face value of the policy throughout the lifetime of the insured. Comes in many forms, such as ordinary life, straight life, 20-payment life, 20-year endowment, etc. Attractive on the surface, but in actual practice a very bad buy in comparison to term insurance.

Interaction. Communication and exchange between persons in a relation.

Interdependency. Role interaction in which there is a mutuality of need fulfillment.

Intermarriage. The marriage of persons of different races, ethnic groups, religions, or social classes. Also termed *mixed marriage.*

Internal compromise. The resolution of an external marital conflict through the transformation of the conflict, by one or both of the spouses, into an internal conflict and, thereby, into a decision by either spouse to sacrifice his immediate need satisfaction for what he perceives to be a greater satisfaction—the fulfillment of the other's need.

Internal conflict. A conflict between needs which is felt or perceived by one person.

Intimacy. Spontaneous and complete absorption with the immediacy of a present experience. It is the most rewarding of all interactions, whether with the material world or with another person. In an interpersonal relation, intimate behavior must be non-manipulative and must involve the abandonment of defenses, total self-awareness, and a genuine and unself-conscious involvement and interest in the other person.

Intrapunitive behavior. The directing of frustration reaction inward, upon oneself.

Intrauterine device. A contraceptive device which is inserted into the uterus, where it may remain indefinitely, acting as a harmless irritant that prevents the zygote from lodging in the uterine wall.

Intrinsic marriage. A marriage that is characterized by intimacy, intensity of feeling, and physical and psychological interdependency. Such a relation, although ideal, is relatively rare after the first few years of marriage.

Investing. A long-term savings program in which money is left undisturbed to utilize the "growth on growth" principle of capital funds, doubling and redoubling itself over the years.

Labia majora. The erotically sensitive outer lips of the vulva.

Labia minora. The inner lips of the vulva which are even more erotically sensitive than the labia majora.

Labor. The process by which the fetus is expulsed from the mother's body. It occurs in three stages: (1) the contraction of the uterus and dilation of the cervix; (2) a continuation of the contraction and the forcing of the fetus through the cervix and the vagina; (3) the expulsion of the afterbirth.

Learned behavior. Behavior patterns that are learned through interaction with the environment (as opposed to the instinctive behavior of lower animals).

Legal separation. A legal decree that forbids cohabitation by husband and wife and provides for separate maintenance and support of the wife and children by the husband. A legally separated couple are still bound by their marital contract and may not remarry.

Lesbianism. Female homosexuality.

Lesion. Any localized, abnormal change in bodily tissue, such as a sore, ulcer, pimple, acne, cold sore, wound, hurt, etc.

Life style. The manner in which a person characteristically responds to his environment, and the means that he utilizes to make these responses.

Limited feedback. The reception of incomplete or inconclusive information about the effectiveness of one's behavior.

Love. A learned and positive emotion, usually profound, which arises within a relation with a love object that provides significant need satisfactions to the person who is in love. Particularly in dating, marriage, and child rearing, there are four categories of love: altruistic love, companionate love, sexual love, and romantic love.

Maladjustment. A lack of harmony with self or with environment.

Marital adjustment. The resolution of the inevitable marital conflicts.

Mass society. An industrialized and urbanized society that functions according to mass production, mass consumption, mass manipulation of taste, and highly specialized institutional and individual roles. In a mass society, with its relative decline of primary institutions and intrinsic satisfactions, the person is often disoriented, devalued, and desperately in need of the intrinsic love, nurture, and emotional support that is provided by the paired relation.

Mastery skills. The skills, knowledge, and information necessary for environmental manipulation and control.

Masturbation. The practice of sexual arousal and orgasm through self-manipulation. It is the commonest mode before marriage of sexual expression, and it usually serves adolescents of both sexes as a training ground for the understanding and control of their sexuality.

Mature love. The capacity, characteristic of emotional maturity, for deriving satisfaction primarily through the provision of nurture and need fulfillment (as opposed to the receiving of nurture and need fulfillment).

Meatus. The opening of the urethra at the end of the penis.

Meiosis. The division of parent germ cells into sperm or ova. In meiosis, which is also termed *reduction division,* the 46 chromosomes of the parent cells do not split to become chromatids but instead simply separate, with one chromosome of each pair going to each of the new cells, the sperm or the ova. Because of this process of meiosis, sperm and ova contain only 23 chromosomes; and when the sperm and ovum combine with conception, the new cell, the zygote, contains the characteristic 46 chromosomes, with one of each pair of chromosomes contributed by the sperm and one by the ovum.

Menarche. The beginning of ovulation and the menstrual cycle in the pubescent female.

Menopause. The cessation of ovulation, menstruation, and fertility in the female. It usually occurs between ages 45 and 50.

Menstrual cycle. The 28-day cycle of the postpubescent female in which ovulation, engorgement of the uterine wall with blood and nutrients,

and expulsion of this material through the vagina (when the ovum is not fertilized) occurs. The cycle ceases with menopause. The final stage of this cycle, *menstruation,* lasts for about three or four days.

Mesoderm. The differentiated tissue of the embryo which will become the bone, muscle, and supportive tissue of the fetus.

Metabolism. The chemical processes of the body.

Miscegenation. Interracial marriage.

Mitosis. The division of a cell into two new cells. In mitosis, the 46 chromosomes of a cell split (becoming chromatids), with one half of each chromosome going to each new cell, which then contains 46 chromosomes exactly duplicating the 46 chromosomes of the original cell.

Monogamy. The marriage of two persons.

Mons. The fleshy mound, or pad, just over the vulva of the female. Like the clitoris and the vestibule, the mons is a primary source of erotic arousal.

Morning erection. The phenomenon in males of a penile erection upon waking. It was traditionally ascribed to the pressure of a full bladder after a night's sleep, but its cause is now acknowledged to be unknown.

Morning sickness. The nausea and vomiting that sometimes occurs, particularly in the morning, during the first few months of pregnancy.

Motivation. The conscious and unconscious inner state which is variously described as desire, need, or drive and which stimulates action and directs behavior toward goals.

Natural childbirth. Labor and childbirth with little or no sedation. This method is proposed as the safest and most emotionally gratifying mode of childbirth, because it eliminates the dangers (to mother and neonate) of heavy anesthesia, and because it allows the mother to cooperate in the delivery and to be lucid at the first breath and sound of her child.

Need. A biological or psychological condition which demands gratification if homeostasis is to be maintained or if self-actualization is to be achieved.

Negative reinforcement. Punishment with the purpose of changing behavior.

Neonate. The infant during the first month of extrauterine life. During the neonatal period, the child must make the extremely complex transition from fetal to postnatal ways of living.

Neurosis. A personality disorder which is characterized by anxiety, depression, and inadequacy.

Nocturnal emission. The phenomenon in the male of involuntary ejaculation during sleep. It is also termed a *wet dream.*

Non-profit-making credit. That shadowy region of potential financial difficulty in which a person borrows money or makes a financed credit purchase to satisfy an immediate and non-profitable need, the satisfaction of which he values more than he does the cost of the finance charges. This use of credit requires the greatest exercise of judgment and is highly subjective in value.

Nuclear family. A father, mother, and their offspring, living in a single household and in mutual interdependence.

Nurturance-dependence needs. The basis of a complementary relation in which one person is characteristically nurturant and the other person is characteristically dependent in their relation.

Nurturant need. The need to derive satisfaction by giving physical and emotional support and affection.

Nurture. The provision of physical needs, protection, affection, and emotional support.

Obstetrics. The branch of medicine dealing with childbirth and the care of the mother preceding and following delivery.

Open credit. Credit advanced with no finance charges, usually available with such services as newspaper subscriptions, doctors' and dentists' statements, and businesses willing to provide their services or products in advance of payment. This form of credit is a real bargain and convenience if the account can be settled in full at the end of the billing cycle.

Operation. Any behavior that has a specific purpose or direction.

Operational definition. The definition of a concept in terms of its functions and/or processes.

Oral contraceptive. Hormonal materials (in pill form) which suspend ovulation by creating a false state of pregnancy and which, therefore, prevent conception.

Orgasm. The climactic third phase of sexual response in both male and female; characterized by involuntary muscular spasms, anoxia (shortage of oxygen and gasping), and varying degrees of intense sensory pleasure. There is no difference in the male and female orgasmic experience, except that ejaculation accompanies male orgasm.

Osmosis. Diffusion of solutions through a semi-permeable membrane which tends to equalize the concentrations on either side of the membrane.

Ossification. The hardening of cartilage into bone.

Other-centered. The tendency of the emotionally mature person to direct much of his activity toward the well-being of others.

Other-directed. The tendency of the emotionally immature person to behave as he thinks others expect, rather than to behave in terms of his own innermost needs.

Ovaries. The female gonads—organs to produce the germ cells, or ova.

Overlearning. Modification of behavior through a schedule of repetition; characteristic of motor skills, such as eating, walking, etc.

Overprotection. The tendency of parents to restrain a child to the extent that his experiences are extremely limited. This can result in the child's inability to cope with his environment.

Ovulation. The regular monthly process in the fertile female whereby an ovarian follicle ruptures and releases a mature ovum.

Ovum (egg). The female gamete, or germ cell, produced in the ovaries.

Paired relation. An intimate and relatively enduring primary relation with a significant other.

Parent germ cells. The 46-chromosome cells from which the sperm and ova are split off (meiosis) within the testicles and ovaries.

Passive-congenial marriage. A form of utilitarian marriage which lacks depth in its emotional interaction.

Peers. Persons who are of about the same age and status in society.

Penis. The male sex organ which, in its erect state during copulation, deposits sperm within the vagina of the female. It is the most erotically sensitive area of the male body.

Perception. A single unified awareness derived from sensory processes while a stimulus is present.

Perineum. The erotically sensitive area between the anus and the genitalia.

Peristalsis. The rhythmic, undulating contractions of the muscular structure of such tubal walls as those of the Fallopian tubes and the intestines.

Permissive acceptance. A method of conflict resolution in a relation; consists of one person's voluntarily granting the other dominance in decision making and need satisfaction.

Permissiveness (in child rearing). The practice of setting a minimum of restrictions for a child.

Personal allowance. A budgeted sum that the person may spend freely for whatever he wishes without making an accounting.

Personal finance. Sound money management, consisting simply of allocating available funds in ways that maximize need fulfillment and minimize deprivation.

Personality. The uniquely individual qualities that are manifested by a person in his relations with his environment.

Petting. A mode of sexual behavior involving all deliberate physical and erotically arousing contact between persons except copulation.

Phenotype. An observable genetic trait.

Phylogenetic scale. The arrangement of animals into groups according to their evolutionary relationships.

Physiological needs. The physical requirements (warmth, food, oxygen, sex, etc.) that are essential to the maintenance of homeostasis in a person.

Placenta. The organ, developing from the chorionic villi, that joins the fetus to the uterine tissue. The placenta serves as the medium for the metabolic exchange between the mother and the fetus.

Plateau phase. The second phase of erotic response in which the arousal state of the excitement phase is maintained, with only minor physiological changes.

Play. Activity which lacks specific direction and which is characterized by pleasure, spontaneity, and self-expression. Play is an important mode of parental socialization of a child in our society.

Polyandry. A form of marriage in which one woman has more than one husband.

Polygamy. Marriage with multiple spouses (as opposed to monogamy, one spouse).

Polygyny. A form of marriage in which one man has more than one wife.

Position. The particular function a person fulfills at any moment in a relation.

Positive reinforcement. Anything which tends to perpetuate a response. In child rearing, it involves reward or praise with the purpose of changing or perpetuating a behavior pattern.

Power structure (in marital interaction). The dominance and deference of each person in various aspects of their relation.

Power struggle. The attempts of spouses to gain the dominant position in the relation. This struggle generally ensues from the inability of the husband and wife to resolve their conflicts in a mutually acceptable way and often results in the failure of the marriage.

Pre-ejaculatory fluid. A clear, viscous fluid secreted by the erect penis when the male becomes very aroused prior to orgasm.

Pregnancy. The period of intrauterine development of a new organism—from conception to childbirth.

Prepubertal orgasm. The experience of orgasm before sexual maturity. It·is physiologically identical to mature orgasm in both males and females, except that in prepubertal males semen is not yet being produced and ejaculation does not occur.

Prepuce (clitoral). The loose skin that partially covers the clitoris and is homologous to the male foreskin.

Prenatal. Before birth.

Primary relation. A relation characterized by affection, respect, informality, immediacy, spontaneity, intimacy, and intrinsic satisfaction of needs.

Primate. The order of mammals, including man, the apes, and lemurs, which are characterized by a combination of binocular vision, the ability to grasp with the appendages, and a large and differentiated brain.

Primordial ova. The immature reproductive cells of the female, which are present in the ovarian follicles in the fetus.

Procedure. A type of ritual in which some′ physical object is manipulated in the performance of the procedure.

Profit-making credit. Financed loans or credit purchases that promise a financial return—a sound use of credit if the consumer will eventually profit more from the use of the borrowed money or credit purchase than he will pay in finance charges. Borrowing for an education or purchasing necessary tools for one's job are good examples.

Projection. A defense mechanism whereby the individual attributes his own unacceptable feelings to others.

Propinquity. The proximity of geographic location.

Prostaglandin. A new drug which may prove to be the basis for the long-sought chemical abortifacient which will cause the implanted embryo to be sloughed off with menstruation up to a month after conception.

Prostate. The tube-shaped organ that produces a portion of the seminal fluid.

Psychological needs. The emotional requirements (emotional support, confirmation, tactile nurture, status) that are essential to self-actualization in a person.

Psychosomatic. Pertaining to a physical condition, usually an ailment, that is produced by psychological maladjustment.

Puberty. The period in which a male or female achieves sexual maturity. In the male, it occurs at about age 13, and it is characterized by the production of semen and by ejaculation during orgasm. In the female, it occurs at about age 12, and it is characterized by the beginning of the menstrual cycle (menarche).

Purchasing power. The value of money in terms of what it can buy at a specified time compared to what it could buy at some earlier period established as a base. The current inflationary decline in purchasing power is a little over 5 percent a year.

Quickening. The first fetal movements that the mother can feel, usually at about the seventeenth week of pregnancy.

Rationalization. A defense mechanism in which a person attributes his actions to rational reasons but not to the real reasons.

Reality-oriented. Behavior that is directed toward fulfilling the basic need which initiated the behavior. The reality-oriented person can acknowledge present difficulties and make appropriate efforts to resolve them. He can sacrifice short-term goals in order to achieve long-term ones.

Reality testing. The sampling of another person's responses and the subsequent modification of one's behavior in accordance with the feedback.

Recessive genes. Genes producing hereditary traits that are subordinate to dominant traits and can be cancelled out by the presence of a dominant gene. In other words, the presence of one dominant gene produces a particular trait regardless of the trait encoded in the other, recessive gene. Two recessive genes must be present for the inheritance of recessive traits like blue eyes, normal vision, and, possibly, left-handedness.

Recognition need. The need to receive confirmation, commendation, and status.

Reflex erection. Penile erection caused by tactile stimulation.

Reflexive behavior. The various inborn responses to particular stimuli (the knee jerk, the startle response, the reflex erection).

Refractory period. A characteristic of the resolution phase of male erotic response during which the person is physiologically incapable of responding to erotic stimulation; its duration may be anywhere from a few minutes to several hours, or even a day or more.

Regression. Defense-oriented behavior in which the individual returns to an earlier (and outgrown) form of behavior.

Reinforcement. Reward (positive reinforcement) or punishment (negative reinforcement) which brings about a change in behavior patterns.

Relation. An association and/or interaction.

Relational. Pertaining to relations between persons and implying supportive and nurturant behavior.

Repression. The basis (along with displacement) of all defense-oriented behavior; the individual "forgets," or pushes into his unconscious, unpleasant impulses or experiences.

Resolution phase. The fourth and last phase of erotic response which is characterized by a return to normal functioning after orgasm; includes the refractory period in the male.

Rhythm method. A natural method of contraception in which the couple abstain from copulation during the female's fertile days (3 or 4 days prior to ovulation, and 1 day following).

Ritual. A culturally prescribed format for a brief exchange of recognition and confirmation in a relation, enabling people to relate without inventing new responses for each occasion. It is the simplest interaction of role behavior.

Role. The behavior appropriate to a position in a particular relation, or interaction, between persons.

Role reciprocation. The mutual responses of marital partners in fulfilling one another's needs. If each spouse strives to perceive and then perform the role that is expected of him by the other, they will have a successful marital interaction.

Role taking. A special technique of creative problem solving, in which each person states his own and then the other's point of view, so that the conflict of needs and perceptions can be clarified and resolved.

Role taking (in children's play). The imitation by children of adult roles as a mode of learning and practicing the roles they will one day assume.

Role theory. The theory that a person relates to others chiefly on the basis of learned (socialized) behavior that is appropriate to the position of each person in the relation. Thus, the presentation of the social self occurs chiefly through roles.

Romantic love. Characterized by a preoccupation with love or by the idealizing of love or the love-object.

Rooming in. The practice of placing the neonate in the mother's room a few hours after delivery, so that the mother (and father) can care for and relate to their baby.

Rush of waters. The release from the uterus of the amniotic fluid during the rupture of the amniotic sac in the first stage of labor.

Salpingectomy. A method of permanent contraception in which the Fallopian tubes are surgically cut and tied off.

Saving. The budgeting and accumulation of money for deferred spending and for an emergency reserve.

Scrotum. The external sac containing the testicles.

Secondary relation. A relation that is formal, impersonal, highly structured, positional, and functional, with rewards symbolic and delayed, rather than intrinsic and immediate. In such a relation, each person is important to the other chiefly for the function he performs.

Secondary sex characteristics. Physiological, sex-linked characteristics (body hair, breast development) which have nothing to do with reproduction.

Self. The integrating core of an individual's personality.

Self-acceptance. The acknowledgment of one's personality and adequacy; an indication of emotional maturity.

Self-actualization. The realization of one's potential as a unique human being.

Self-centered. The tendency of the emotionally immature person to characteristically achieve satisfaction at the expense of others (as opposed to other-centered).

Self-devaluation. The depreciation of one's self-acceptance and self-image.

Self-directed. The ability to make decisions and abide by their consequences; characteristic of emotional maturity (as opposed to other-directed, which is characteristic of emotional immaturity).

Self-image. The manner in which a person perceives himself in relation to his environment.

Self-love. Experiencing oneself as a love object.

Semen. The fluid which carries sperm through the urethra and which is ejaculated during orgasm by the mature male.

Seminal vesicles. The glands, located near the rectal wall, that produce part of the semen.

Seminiferous tubules. The long, tightly coiled tubules within the testicles in which sperm are produced.

Sense of autonomy. The sense of independence and competence within the environment. This early form of self-acceptance is an important element in the successful socialization of a child and is based on the child's *sense of trust*, which develops chiefly from the emotional support he receives as an infant.

Sense of trust. The trusting reliance of an infant on the support and nurture of a significant other — usually his mother. The success of a child's socialization is dependent on adequate physical and emotional support.

Serial polygamy. The practice of marrying more than once, by divorcing and remarrying.

Set. A particular determination or value within a person's frame of reference which causes him to respond to subsequent related stimuli in a predictable way.

Sex hormones. Hormones secreted by the gonads and responsible for the development of the secondary sexual characteristics.

Sexologist. One who studies the physiology and psychology of sex.

Sexual disinclination. An antipathy, generally of psychological origins, toward engaging in sexual activity.

Sexual dysfunction. An inability to obtain orgasm or satisfaction from sexual behavior; found by Masters and Johnson to be cheifly based on "sociocultural deprivation and ignorance of sexual physiology rather than on psychiatric or medical illness".

Sexual identification. The learning of appropriate sex roles.

Sexual love. The emotion which a person experiences when the love object is also the sex object.

Sexual perversion. Sexual behavior that is socially taboo or biologically or psychologically harmful. Since social proscriptions vary from society to society, the only objective criteria for determining sexually perverse behavior are biological or psychological harm.

Shaft. The main body of the penis.

Shoulder presentation. The birth of a fetus, shoulder first.

Show. The discharge from the vagina of the cervical plug of mucus spotted with blood, followed by varying amounts of bloody discharge. Because this plug discharges as the cervix expands during early labor, it is a sign of the imminence of childbirth (the heavier the bloody discharge, the closer the birth).

Siblings. Children born of the same parents.

Significant other. The other person in a paired relation upon whom one depends for intimate feedback and confirmation and for nurture, affection, and role reciprocation.

Significant paired relation. A primary relation that includes deep emotional attachment, mutual and significant need fulfillment, and relative permanence.

Smegma. A mucous-like substance which is secreted by Tyson's glands and which may collect under the foreskin of the penis and become a breeding ground for infection.

Social attitude. An attitude held in common with many people.

Social class. A classification into which people of similar income, occupation, residence, membership in organizations, genealogy, etc. are placed. It is used as a basis for correlating behavioral differences among individuals within a society.

Social-class mobility. The movement of persons in a society from one social class into another, generally higher social class.

Socialization. The process of a person's learning—from parents, peers, societal institutions, and other sources—the information, skills, knowledge, and roles necessary for competent and socially acceptable behavior in the society.

Social structure. The institutional composition and the stratification of a society.

Society. An aggregate of persons in an associational group that has some measure of permanence.

Somites. The spinal segments that appear on the fetus two or three weeks after conception and that develop into the vertebrae.

Spectator role. Instead of getting involved and forgetting everything else during sexual behavior, the person mentally sets himself apart, observing his own and his partner's responses. Masters and Johnson propose this behavior as a chief cause of sexual dysfunction.

Sperm. The male gamete, which is produced in the seminiferous tubules of the testicles.

Spermaticides. The chemical substances which destroy or immobilize sperm and are used as contraceptives.

Spermatogenesis. The production of sperm from parent germ cells.

Sperm count. The examination of the ejaculate to try to determine whether the sperm are healthy and numerous enough to reach the ovum in the Fallopian tube.

Spirochete. A spiral-shaped micro-organism that causes syphilis. Transmission of the spirochete from one host to another is invariably from an infectious lesion of a person in the first or second stages of syphilis through mucous membrane or broken skin of the person contracting the disease.

Status. The hierarchical position of an individual in relation to others in the society and to the society in general.

Status congruence. The tendency of a person to have either a cluster of things "actively wanted" according to the values of the society or a cluster of things "actively avoided." For example, the rich tend to be healthy, respected, skilled, and well-informed, while the poor tend to be sickly, scorned, unskilled, and ignorant.

Status needs. The needs related to the achievement of high status within the social group.

Sterility. The permanent inability to reproduce.

Stimulus. A phenomenon that produces a response.

Stratification. The hierarchical ranking of persons in a society ac-

cording to the particular standards and values of the society.

Stress. Heightened, perceived tension, either environmental or internal, which results in behavior that attempts to restore biological and psychological balance.

Sublimation (of sexual energy). The doctrine of sublimation holds that sexual energy may be permanently diverted into other non-sexual activities. This theory has been found to be false. (*Temporary* sublimation, the doctrine that sexual energy may be temporarily diverted, has been neither proven nor disproven, but it is highly suspect.)

Submissive need. The need to be dominated in a relation. A person with a strong submissive need is likely to form a complementary relation with someone who has a strong dominance need.

Substitution. Defense-oriented behavior in which an individual directs hostility toward a safe target rather than toward the object that aroused his hostility.

Symbiosis. The cohabitation of two dissimilar organisms in an intimate and mutually advantageous relationship.

Symbiote. One of the partners of symbiosis.

Syphilis. A venereal disease caused by a micro-organism called a *spirochete*. Syphilis goes through four stages, each with separate and distinct characteristics, and can involve every part of the body. It is transmitted by contact of mucous membrane or broken skin with an infectious syphlitic lesion.

Tactile. Pertaining to the sensation of touch.

Taxonomy. The branch of biological science which names, classifies, and attempts to account for differences among individuals in a species.

Temperament. The aspects of personality pertaining to mood, activity, and energy level.

Term insurance. The least expensive of two basic types of life insurance, term insurance guarantees the payment of the face value of the policy at death for a prescribed period of time (a "term") from the signing of the policy contract. When the insured reaches age 65, the term policy is usually cancelled and non-renewable. Comes in many forms, such as decreasing-term, renewable-term, convertible renewable-term, mortgage insurance, etc.

Testicles. The sperm-producing gonads which are contained in the scrotum. They are external organs because they must be maintained at a temperature lower than that of the body cavity if they are to function.

Togetherness. The uniquely American expectation, especially prevalent in the middle class, that a husband and wife will share all of their interests and activities and will have an almost complete identification with one another. This highly romantic attitude is not only unrealistic but

may be a major factor in the devitalization and disharmony in many marriages in our society.

Trophoblast. The multicellular wall surrounding the zygote and the germinal hollow and disc within it. The trophoblast functions to embed the zygote in the uterine wall, to develop the chorionic villi which nurture the organism and eventually become the placenta, and to form the chorionic sac which protects the organism and eventually fuses with the amnion as the fetus grows larger.

Tyson's glands. The glands which are situated on each side of the frenum and which produce a substance called smegma.

Umbilical cord. The long, rubbery tube which serves as the nurturant connection between the fetus and the uterus. It forms, at about the fifth week, from the body stalk and the yolk sac.

Urethra. A membranous canal for the external discharge of urine from the bladder in the male and female and for the ejaculation of semen in the male.

Uterus. The thick-walled, expandable female organ which contains, protects, and nurtures the developing embryo and fetus and which, at full term, employs regular muscular contractions to force the fetus through the cervix and vagina.

Utilitarian marriage. The most common category of marriage, comprising a *conflict-habituated*, a *devitalized*, or a *passive-congenial* relation.

Vagina. The elastic sex organ of the female which extends from the lips of the erotically sensitive external genitalia to the cervix, the opening to the uterus.

Vaginal lubrication. The sweating of the vaginal walls which is the most important physiological sign of sexual excitement.

Variable, or discretionary, expenses. All those necessities and wants that are not fixed as a specific and unvarying monthly expense—for example, food, clothing, entertainment, savings, etc.

Vas deferens. The tubes that carry the sperm from the testicles into the urethra.

Vasectomy. The surgical severing and tying off of the vas deferens in order to stop the movement of sperm into the urethra and, thus, to prevent conception.

Venereal disease (VD). Those diseases caused by organisms which are usually transmitted from person to person during sexual contact. Gonorrhea and syphilis are the most common venereal diseases.

Vertex presentation. The birth of a fetus, head first—the normal delivery position.

Vestibule. The entrance to the vagina.

Vicarious-achievement need. The need to derive satisfaction from the achievements of another.

Vulva. The external genitalia of the female.

Withdrawal. A contraceptive method in which the penis is withdrawn from the vagina just before ejaculation. Also, the term for a defense mechanism in which the person becomes passive and apathetic in a stressful situation.

Withholding of need fulfillment. A form of power struggle in marriage which involves a covert struggle of attrition.

Womb. The uterus.

X chromosome. The chromosome that determines female traits. All ova and one half of all sperm carry an x chromosome.

Y chromosome. The chromosome that determines male traits. One half of all sperm carry the y chromosome; the ova carry only x chromosomes.

Yolk sac. A large and very nearly vestigial organ which develops from the cluster of cells containing the germinal disc and the amnion. In the embryonic period it gradually grows smaller and eventually integrates into the umbilical cord. It functions briefly as an aid in the manufacture of blood cells.

Zygote. The single-celled organism which occurs with the fusion of the sperm and the ovum in the Fallopian tube. Immediately after fertilization, it begins to proliferate by cell division into the differentiated tissue of the germinal disc, the embryo, the fetus, and, finally, the neonate, whose traits are determined by the genetic materials contributed by both the sperm and the ovum.

Name Index

Subject Index